Programming WCF Services

Other Microsoft Windows resources from O'Reilly

SECOND EDITION

Programming WCF Services

Juval Löwy

O'REILLY®

Beijing · Cambridge · Farnham · Köln · Sebastopol · Taipei · Tokyo

Programming WCF Services, Second Edition
by Juval Löwy

Copyright © 2009 Juval Löwy. All rights reserved.
Printed in the United States of America.

Published by O'Reilly Media, Inc., 1005 Gravenstein Highway North, Sebastopol, CA 95472.

O'Reilly books may be purchased for educational, business, or sales promotional use. Online editions are also available for most titles (*safari.oreilly.com*). For more information, contact our corporate/institutional sales department: (800) 998-9938 or *corporate@oreilly.com*.

Editor: John Osborn	**Indexer:** Lucie Haskins
Production Editor: Rachel Monaghan	**Cover Designer:** Karen Montgomery
Copyeditor: Rachel Head	**Interior Designer:** David Futato
Proofreader: Emily Quill	**Illustrator:** Jessamyn Read

Printing History:

February 2007:	First Edition.
November 2008:	Second Edition.

 This book uses RepKover™, a durable and flexible lay-flat binding.

ISBN: 978-0-596-52130-1

[M]

To my children,
Abigail, Eleanor, and Adam

Table of Contents

Forewords

From the moment that Samuel Morse demonstrated his first telegraph message on May 24, 1844 until now, communications have been changing our world. The information age has revolutionized our planet in ways that were unimaginable to our ancestors, and here in the early years of the 21st century we realize that the revolution in many respects has only begun.

Web services have emerged as the primary way for applications to communicate, and if you are writing applications on the Microsoft .NET platform, Windows Communication Foundation (WCF) is the way you should write them. This rich platform for web services is powerful and broad, capable of supporting many different communication patterns and protocols as well as being extensible in almost any way you can imagine.

As you explore this vast platform for communications, you will need a guide who knows the terrain, and there are few people alive today who know WCF as well as Juval Löwy. The best testament to this is to wander the halls of building 42 in Redmond (where the WCF team works); in many of the offices you will see *Programming WCF Services* on the shelf. I've had the privilege of knowing Juval since 2001 when I reviewed one of his earlier books, and have always been impressed with his grasp of technology and his dogged pursuit of detail in his drive to plumb the depths.

If you choose to learn WCF, you've chosen well. If you choose to learn with the resource and guidance of Juval Löwy, you've done even better. My well-worn copy of the first edition of *Programming WCF Services* sits on the desk next to my computer at this very moment, and I can't tell you how much I'm looking forward to this next edition.

—Ron Jacobs
Senior Technical Evangelist for WCF
Microsoft Corporation

Juval Löwy, the author of this most excellent book, and I share a passion: designing and building distributed systems—or, as they are increasingly called today, connected systems. Both of us have walked a very similar path on the technology trail, even though we've always been working in different companies and on different projects and, for most of our careers, also on different continents.

In the early 1990s when both of us slowly got hooked on the idea of doing something on one computer that would cause something to happen on another computer, the world of distributed systems application platform technologies just began taking shape around us.

As workstations and server hardware became more affordable and increasingly commoditized, building large systems that weren't dependent on a single transaction hub in the middle became an economically attractive proposition. The same was true for wide-area data exchange options. It's difficult to believe these days, but my telephone company insisted back then that more than 1,200 bits per second would never be possible over phone lines. Today they run 6 MBps and more over the same copper. These were exciting times.

With the technology for affordable distributed computing coming together, two large distributed systems technology camps emerged in the early '90s: DCE, led by Digital Equipment Corporation (eventually gobbled up by Compaq, gobbled up by HP) and CORBA, driven by the OMG consortium, with a great dose of IBM backing. In 1996–1997, all of those great engineering efforts came to an effective stop. Here was the Internet and the world started to be obsessed with (a) HTML, (b) HTTP, (c) venture capital, and (d) IPOs.

It took the industry 10 years to recover from the bubble and its bursting. Not only economically, but also from a technology perspective. The good that came from that is that there are no longer two distributed system technology camps, but just one— or several dozen, depending on your perspective.

As of 2007, the industry is still in great disagreement about the "right way" to write code for distributed systems. Someone from Sun Microsystems or BEA will likely tell you that it's got to be Java; my colleagues here at Microsoft (and I) will most certainly tell you that we believe that C# or Visual Basic is the way to go. What neither Sun, nor BEA, nor IBM, nor we here at Microsoft are disagreeing about anymore is how to talk to each other on the wire. Given the DCE versus CORBA wars of the past, the fact that consensus was reached over the specification that is the foundation of this truce—SOAP 1.1—was quite a spectacular sensation.

More than six years have passed since SOAP 1.1 was submitted as a technical note to the W3C. Since then, a great number of SOAP-based specifications, ranging from fundamentals, such as addressing, and a broad range of security options up to enterprise protocols, such as atomic transaction coordination, have been developed and negotiated between many industry partners.

My team here at Microsoft, which still informally calls itself by its product's code name, "Indigo," has been at the heart of these development and negotiation efforts. Without IBM's, Microsoft's, and other partners' strong commitment to creating a common set of standards, even though we are all competing fiercely in the enterprise space, little of this open-standards framework would exist, much less would there be multiple implementations from so many vendors and such a variety of platforms.

Admittedly, it took a year or two longer than it probably should have. Agreement takes time and we would simply not have released our software, the Windows Communication Foundation, without making sure it would interoperate well with our industry partners and competitors. Design also takes time and we would not have released our software without knowing that we have a development experience that feels familiar to our customers who have invested time in learning and adopting our previous distributed systems technology wave, which included ASP.NET Services, the Web Services Enhancements (WSE), .NET Remoting, Messaging/MSMQ, and Enterprise Services/COM+.

The technology list I just cited has five technology names on it, and if you were counting the respective unmanaged code counterparts and underpinnings there would even be more. One of our most important design goals for the Windows Communication Foundation can be summed up in a simple phrase: one way to program. Whether you want to build a queuing application, a transactional N-Tier application, a mesh of P2P clients, an RSS feed server, or your own Enterprise Services Bus, you will no longer have to master a multitude of different technologies that each solve a part of the problem. The Windows Communication Foundation is what you learn and use. One way to program.

Programming WCF Services shows you in great detail what we here at Microsoft have built as a foundation for your applications and services, and the book conveys it with the accuracy, teaching skill, and dedication to architecture that Juval is justly renowned for around the globe.

We from the Connected Framework team at Microsoft are very satisfied with what we've built. We give you an infrastructure that unifies the distributed technology stack, is broadly interoperable, promotes service orientation, is straightforward to learn, and is very productive to build on. Juval Löwy is one of the most prominent distributed systems experts in the world today, and we are very proud that Juval is dedicated to the Windows Communication Foundation. We are quite confident that Juval will help you understand why we, Juval, and our early-adopter community are thrilled about the product and the new opportunities that it creates. Enjoy the book and have fun building your first WCF services.

—Clemens Vasters
Program Manager, Connected Framework Team
Microsoft Corporation

Preface

In August 2001 I first learned the details of a Microsoft effort to rewrite COM+ using managed code. Nothing much happened after that. Then, during a C# 2.0 Strategic Design Review in July 2002, the remoting program manager outlined in broad strokes plans to rework remoting into something that developers should actually use. At the same time, Microsoft was also working on incorporating the new security specs for web services into the ASMX stack and actively working with others on drafting a score of additional web services specs.

In July 2003 I was given access to a new transactional infrastructure that improved on the deficiencies in transactional .NET programming. At the time, there was no cohesive programming model that unified these distinct technologies. Toward the end of 2003 I was privileged to be invited to join a small team of outside industry experts and to participate in the strategic design review of a new development platform code-named *Indigo*. Some of the smartest and nicest people I know were part of that team. Over the next two to three years, Indigo went through some three generations of programming models. The current declarative, endpoint-driven object model debuted in early 2005, was stabilized by August of that year, and was named the Windows Communication Foundation (WCF).

It is difficult to get a consistent answer from different people on what WCF is. To the web service developer, it is the ultimate interoperability solution, an implementation of a long list of industry standards. To the distributed application developer, it is the easiest way of making remote calls and even queued calls. To the system developer, it is the next generation of productivity-oriented features, such as transactions and hosting, that provide off-the-shelf plumbing for applications. To the application developer, it is a declarative programming model for structuring applications. And to the architect, it is how one can finally build service-oriented applications. WCF is in actuality all of those, simply because it was designed that way—to be the unified next generation of Microsoft's disparate technologies.

To me, WCF is the next development platform, which to a large extent subsumes raw .NET programming. All .NET developers should use WCF, regardless of their application types, sizes, or industry domains. WCF is a fundamental technology that provides an easy and clean way to generate services and applications in compliance with what I regard as sound design principles. WCF is engineered from the ground up to simplify application development and deployment, and to lower the overall cost of ownership. WCF services are used to build service-oriented applications, from standalone desktop applications to web-based applications and services to high-end Enterprise applications.

How This Book Is Organized

This book covers the topics and skills you need to design and develop service-oriented WCF-based applications, illustrating how to take advantage of built-in features such as service hosting, instance management, concurrency management, transactions, disconnected queued calls, and security. While the book shows you how to use these features, it focuses on the "why" and on the rationale behind particular design decisions. You'll learn about not only WCF programming and the related system issues, but also relevant design options, tips, best practices, and pitfalls. I approach almost every topic and aspect from a software engineering standpoint, because my objective is to make you not just a WCF expert, but also a better software engineer. Armed with the insights this text provides, you can engineer your applications for maintainability, extensibility, reusability, and productivity.

While the first edition of this book was published in early 2007, it was actually based on material I had that dated back to 2005. This second edition has provided me with an opportunity to publish a further three years' worth of techniques, ideas, and helper classes, and even a few breakthroughs. I believe this new material will make this edition valuable even to readers of the first edition.

Over the past few years I have interacted with WCF developers on all continents apart from Antarctica, both while teaching WCF and designing systems. This has helped me immensely in finding the best ways of presenting various aspects of WCF and in discovering what concepts many developers struggle with and what they take for granted. This accumulated insight is reflected throughout this second edition, both in the old and the new material.

This book avoids many implementation details of WCF and largely confines its coverage to the possibilities and practical aspects of using WCF: how to apply the technology and how to choose among the available design and programming models. It makes the most of what .NET 3.5 Service Pack 1 has to offer, and in some respects is an advanced C# book as well.

In addition, the book contains many useful utilities, tools, and helper classes I have written, collectively known as *ServiceModelEx*. My tools, helper classes, and attributes aim at increasing your productivity and the quality of your WCF services. *ServiceModelEx* is literally a small framework that sits on top of WCF and compensates for some oversights in its design. It also simplifies and automates certain tasks. This book is as much about my tools, ideas, and techniques as it is about native WCF, and my framework also demonstrates how you can extend WCF. Many readers have told me that aside from the explanations in this book, *ServiceModelEx* is the most valuable asset the book offers, and readers have asked me to highlight it more and to provide an explicit catalog. I have done so in this edition, but I have also kept to my guideline that in principle, readers should not have to use all (or any part) of *ServiceModelEx*. In practice, *ServiceModelEx* is your WCF power tools collection. You can also use each helper class, utility, or framework individually, as there are few, if any, interdependencies.

During the past four years I have published a number of WCF articles in *MSDN Magazine*, and I write the WCF section of the Foundations column for the magazine as well. I used these articles to seed the chapters in this book, and I am grateful to the magazine for allowing me to do so. Even if you have read the articles, you should still read the corresponding chapters here. The chapters are much more comprehensive, are wider in scope (offering additional angles, techniques, and samples) and up-to-date, and often tie their subjects into other chapters.

Each chapter addresses a single topic and discusses it in depth. However, the chapters often rely on those that precede them, so you should read the book in order.

Here is a brief summary of the chapters and appendixes in this book:

Chapter 1, *WCF Essentials*
> This first chapter starts by explaining what WCF is, and then describes essential WCF concepts and building blocks (such as addresses, contracts, bindings, endpoints, hosting, and clients) and key concepts such as reliability and transport sessions. The chapter includes a discussion of the WCF architecture, which is really the linchpin of all that follows in the subsequent chapters. This chapter assumes that you understand the basic motivation and benefit of service-orientation. If that is not the case, you should first read Appendix A. Even if you are already familiar with the basic concepts of WCF, I recommend that you give this chapter at least a cursory reading, not only to ensure that you have a solid foundation, but also because some of the helper classes and terms introduced here will be used and extended throughout the book.

Chapter 2, *Service Contracts*
> Chapter 2 is dedicated to the topic of designing and working with service contracts. First, it covers some useful techniques for service contract overloading and inheritance, and some advanced techniques. The chapter next discusses how

to design and factor contracts that cater to reuse, maintainability, and extensibility. It ends by showing you how to interact programmatically at runtime with the metadata of the exposed contracts.

Chapter 3, *Data Contracts*

Chapter 3 deals with how the client and the service can exchange data without ever actually sharing the data type itself or using the same development technology. In this chapter you will see how to deal with some interesting real-life issues, such as data versioning, and how to pass collections of items.

Chapter 4, *Instance Management*

This chapter is dedicated to answering the question of which service instance handles which client's request. WCF supports several service instance management, activation, and lifetime management techniques, and your choices will have drastic implications for scalability, performance, the programming model, and the business workflow. This chapter presents the rationale behind each of the instance management modes, offers guidelines on when and how to best use them, and also addresses some related topics, such as durability and throttling.

Chapter 5, *Operations*

Chapter 5 deals with the types of operations clients can invoke on a service and related design guidelines, such as how to improve on and extend the basic WCF offering to support callback setup and teardown, manage callback ports and channels, and provide for type-safe duplex proxies.

Chapter 6, *Faults*

This chapter discusses the best practices of error handling, enabling you to decouple the client's error handling from the service's. When required, the chapter shows how services can report errors and exceptions back to their clients, since constructs such as exceptions and exception handling are technology-specific and should not transcend the service boundary. This chapter also demonstrates how you can extend and improve on WCF's basic error-handling mechanism.

Chapter 7, *Transactions*

This chapter begins by explaining the motivation for transactions in general, and then discusses the many aspects of transactional services: the transaction management architecture, transaction propagation configuration, the declarative transaction support offered by WCF, and how clients can create transactions. The chapter ends by discussing relevant design guidelines such as transactional service state management and instancing modes.

Chapter 8, *Concurrency Management*

Chapter 8 first describes the powerful yet simple declarative way WCF offers for managing concurrency and synchronization, both for the client and the service. The chapter then presents more advanced aspects of concurrency management, such as callbacks, reentrancy, thread affinity, and synchronization context, best practices and guidelines for avoiding deadlocks, and asynchronous call management.

Chapter 9, *Queued Services*

Chapter 9 shows how clients can queue up calls to services, thus enabling asynchronous, disconnected work. The chapter starts by showing how to set up and configure queued services, and then focuses on aspects such as transactions, instance management, and failures and their impact on both the business model of the service and its implementation. It also presents techniques for streamlining queues, call management, and several original design ideas (such as a queued response service).

Chapter 10, *Security*

This chapter demystifies service-oriented security by breaking down this multi-faceted task into its basic elements, such as message transfer, authentication, and authorization. It also demonstrates how to provide security for key scenarios such as intranet and Internet applications. Finally, it presents my framework for declarative WCF security, designed to automate security setup and to considerably simplify managing security.

Appendix A, *Introduction to Service-Orientation*

This first appendix is designed for readers who want to understand what service-orientation is all about: it presents my take on service-orientation and puts it in a concrete context. The appendix defines service-oriented applications (as opposed to mere architecture) and the services themselves, and examines the benefits of the methodology. It then presents the principles of service-orientation and augments the abstract tenets with a few more practical points required by most applications. In this appendix, I also share my perspective on where SOA and WCF are heading.

Appendix B, *Headers and Contexts*

This appendix introduces two distinct techniques for enabling the client to pass out-of-band parameters to the service, resulting in a custom logical context: you will see how to use either the message headers or the context binding to achieve this goal. This appendix also presents my helper classes, which greatly simplify and encapsulate the required programming. These helper classes and custom contexts are used in several places in the book.

Appendix C, *Publish-Subscribe Service*

Appendix C presents my framework for implementing a publish-subscribe event management solution. The framework lets you develop a publishing and a subscription service in at most one line of code. While this pattern could have been included in Chapter 5, I've instead put it in a dedicated appendix because it utilizes aspects described in other chapters of this book, such as transactions and queued calls.

Appendix D, *Code-Access Security*

Appendix D starts by explaining what code-access security is and discussing the limited programming model WCF supports out of the box, and then presents my breakthrough for restoring full code-access security for WCF. You will see how partially trusted clients can use WCF, how to host services in a partially trusted environment, and how to execute services in partial trust. This appendix uses advanced .NET and WCF programming techniques, yet the resulting programming model is that of plain WCF.

Appendix E, *Generic Interceptor*

This appendix presents a general-purpose extensible framework for intercepting calls to your WCF services. It walks through the technique and thought process behind such an extension and shows two examples of how to utilize this simple yet powerful and useful technique.

Appendix F, *WCF Coding Standard*

Appendix F is basically a consolidated list of all the best practices and dos and don'ts mentioned throughout this book. The standard is all about the "how" and the "what," not the "why." The rationale behind it is found in the rest of the book. The standard also uses the terms and helper classes discussed in this book.

Appendix G, *ServiceModelEx Catalog*

The final appendix presents a catalog of the 100 or so public helper types (excluding internal helper types) of *ServiceModelEx* mentioned in the book, arranged by categories and techniques, with a short description of each.

Some Assumptions About the Reader

I assume that you, the reader, are an experienced developer and that you are comfortable with object-oriented concepts such as encapsulation and inheritance. I will take advantage of your existing understanding of object and component technology and terminology, and port that knowledge to WCF. You should ideally have a fair understanding of .NET and know basic C# 2.0 (including use of generics and anonymous methods) and C# 3.0 (mostly lambda expressions, extension methods, and anonymous properties). Although the book uses C# for the most part, it is just as pertinent to Visual Basic developers.

What You Need to Use This Book

To use this book, you will need .NET 3.5 with Service Pack 1 and Visual Studio 2008. Unless I explicitly mention otherwise, the contents apply to Windows XP SP2, Windows Server 2003 SP1, Windows Vista, and Windows Server 2008 or later. You may also install additional Windows components, such as MSMQ and IIS.

Conventions Used in This Book

The following typographic conventions are used in this book:

Italic

Used for technical terms, URLs, addresses, filenames, and file extensions.

Constant width

Used for code samples, statements, namespaces, classes, assemblies, interface directives, operators, attributes, and reserved words.

Constant width bold

Used for emphasis in code samples.

This icon signifies a tip, suggestion, or general note.

This icon indicates a warning or caution.

Whenever I wish to make a point in a code sample, I do so with the static Assert method of the Debug class:

```
int number = 1+2;
Debug.Assert(number == 3);
```

The Assert method accepts a Boolean statement and throws an exception when the statement is false.

The book follows the recommended naming guidelines and coding style presented in Appendix E of my book *Programming .NET Components,* Second Edition (O'Reilly). Whenever it deviates from that standard, it is likely the result of space or line-length constraints. As for naming conventions, I use "Pascal casing" for public member methods and properties; this means the first letter of each word in the name is capitalized. For local variables and method parameters I use "camel casing," in which the first letter of each word in the name is capitalized, with the exception of the first word. The names of private member variables are prefixed with m_:

```
class SomeClass
{
   int m_Number;

   public int Number
   {get;set};
}
```

I use ellipses between curly braces to indicate the presence of code that is necessary but unspecified:

```
class SomeClass
{...}
```

In the interest of clarity and space, code examples often do not contain all the using statements needed to specify all the namespaces the examples require; instead, such examples include only the new namespaces introduced in the preceding text.

Using Code Examples

This book is here to help you get your job done. In general, you may use the code in this book in your programs and documentation. You do not need to contact us for permission unless you're reproducing a significant portion of the code. For example, writing a program that uses several chunks of code from this book does not require permission. Selling or distributing a CD-ROM of examples from this book *does* require permission. Answering a question by citing this book and quoting example code does not require permission. Incorporating a significant amount of example code from this book into your product's documentation *does* require permission.

We appreciate, but do not require, attribution. An attribution usually includes the title, author, publisher, and ISBN. For example: "*Programming WCF Services,* Second Edition, by Juval Löwy. Copyright 2009 Juval Löwy, 978-0-596-52130-1."

If you feel your use of code examples falls outside fair use or the permission given above, feel free to contact us at *permissions@oreilly.com.*

How to Contact Us

Please address comments and questions concerning this book to the publisher:

> O'Reilly Media, Inc.
> 1005 Gravenstein Highway North
> Sebastopol, CA 95472
> 800-998-9938 (in the United States or Canada)
> 707-829-0515 (international/local)
> 707-829-0104 (fax)

There is a web page for this book, which lists errata, examples, or any additional information. You can access this page at:

> *http://www.oreilly.com/catalog/9780596521301/*

You'll find the code samples under the "Examples" link.

To comment or ask technical questions about this book, send email to:

> *bookquestions@oreilly.com*

You can also contact the author at:

http://www.idesign.net

The author has posted a comprehensive code library on the IDesign website with more than 150 downloads related to WCF essentials, contract design, instance management, operations and calls, faults, transactions, concurrency, queuing, and security. The downloads articulate in a working fashion many of the code snippets in this book. However, because these secondary, accompanying examples do not themselves appear in the book, they are provided separately from the official sources.

Safari® Books Online

When you see a Safari® Books Online icon on the cover of your favorite technology book, that means the book is available online through the O'Reilly Network Safari Bookshelf.

Safari offers a solution that's better than e-books. It's a virtual library that lets you easily search thousands of top tech books, cut and paste code samples, download chapters, and find quick answers when you need the most accurate, current information. Try it for free at *http://safari.oreilly.com*.

Acknowledgments

I would not have been able to come to terms with WCF in its early days without the constant support of and interaction with the WCF (then Indigo) program managers. I am especially grateful to my friend Steve Swartz, one of the WCF architects, not just for his knowledge and insight, but also for his patience with me and those long IM sessions. Thanks go to Yasser Shohoud, Doug Purdy, and Shy Cohen for the fascinating strategic design reviews, and to Krish Srinivasan for his almost philosophical approach to engineering. Working with you guys has been the best part of learning WCF and a privilege in its own right. The following WCF program managers also shared their time and helped clarify WCF: Andy Milligan, Brian McNamara, Eugene Osovetsky, Kenny Wolf, Kirill Gavrylyuk, Max Feingold, Michael Marucheck, Mike Vernal, and Steve Millet. Thanks also to the group manager, Angela Mills.

Outside Microsoft, I am grateful to Nicholas Paldino for his help. Nick's knowledge of the .NET Framework is second to none, and his meticulous attention to details contributed greatly to the quality and cohesiveness of this book. Several times during tech review I was in awe of Nick's original techniques and improvements to the book.

Finally, to my family: my wife, Dana, who keeps encouraging me to write down my ideas and techniques, while knowing all too well that writing a book entails precious time away from her and the kids; and to my parents, who imparted to me the love for engineering. I dedicate this book to my children, nine-year-old Abigail, six-year-old Eleanor, and Adam, our newborn. You all mean the world to me.

CHAPTER 1

WCF Essentials

This chapter describes the essential concepts and building blocks of WCF and its architecture, enabling you to build simple services. You will learn the basic terms regarding addresses, bindings, contracts, and endpoints; see how to host a service; learn how to write a client; come to understand some related topics, such as in-proc hosting, reliability, and transport sessions; and see how to utilize WCF in Visual Studio 2008. Even if you are already familiar with the basic concepts of WCF, I recommend that you give this chapter at least a cursory reading, not only to ensure that you have a solid foundation, but also because some of the helper classes and terms introduced here will be used and extended throughout the book.

What Is WCF?

Windows Communication Foundation (WCF) is a software development kit for developing and deploying services on Windows. WCF provides a runtime environment for your services, enabling you to expose Common Language Runtime (CLR) types as services and to consume other services as CLR types. Although in theory you could build services without WCF, in practice building services is significantly easier with WCF. WCF is Microsoft's implementation of a set of industry standards defining service interactions, type conversions, marshaling, and the management of various protocols. Consequently, WCF provides interoperability between services.

WCF provides developers with the essential off-the-shelf plumbing required by almost any application, and as such, it greatly increases productivity. The first release of WCF (as part of .NET 3.0) provided many useful facilities for developing services, such as hosting, service instance management, asynchronous calls, reliability, transaction management, disconnected queued calls, and security. The second release of WCF (as part of .NET 3.5) provided additional tools and extended the original offering with additional communication options.

WCF also has an elegant extensibility model that you can use to enrich the basic offering. In fact, WCF itself is written using this extensibility model. The rest of the chapters in this book are dedicated to exploring those aspects and features.

WCF is part of .NET 3.5 and requires .NET 2.0, so it can run only on operating systems that support it. Presently, this list consists of Windows XP SP2, Windows Server 2003, Windows Vista, and Windows Server 2008 or later.

Most of the WCF functionality is included in a single assembly called *System.Service-Model.dll*, located in the `System.ServiceModel` namespace.

Services

A *service* is a unit of functionality exposed to the world. In that respect, it is the next evolutionary step in the long journey from functions to objects to components to services. *Service-orientation* (SO) is an abstract set of principles and best practices for building service-oriented applications. If you are unfamiliar with the principles of service-orientation, Appendix A provides a concise overview and outlines the motivation for using this methodology. The rest of this book assumes you are familiar with these principles. A *service-oriented application* aggregates services into a single logical application, similar to the way a component-oriented application aggregates components or an object-oriented application aggregates objects, as shown in Figure 1-1.

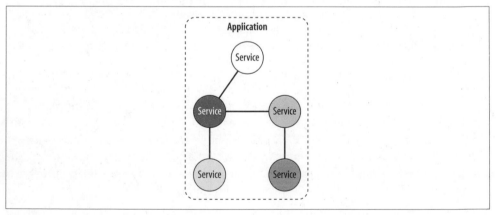

Figure 1-1. A service-oriented application

The services can be local or remote, can be developed by multiple parties using any technologies, can be versioned independently, and can even execute on different timelines. Inside a service, you will find concepts such as languages, technologies, platforms, versions, and frameworks, yet between services, only prescribed communication patterns are allowed.

The *client* of a service is merely the party consuming its functionality. The client can be literally anything—for instance, a Windows Forms class, an ASP.NET page, or another service.

Clients and services interact by sending and receiving *messages*. Messages may be transferred directly from the client to the service, or be sent via an intermediary. With WCF, messages are usually SOAP messages. These messages are independent of transport protocols—unlike web services, WCF services may communicate over a variety of transports (not just HTTP). WCF clients may interoperate with non-WCF services, and WCF services can interact with non-WCF clients. That said, typically if you develop both the client and the service, you can construct the application so that both ends require WCF to utilize WCF-specific advantages.

Because the making of the service is opaque from the outside, a WCF service typically exposes *metadata* describing the available functionality and possible ways of communicating with the service. The metadata is published in a predefined, technology-neutral way, such as using WSDL over HTTP-GET, or an industry standard for metadata exchange. A non-WCF client can import the metadata to its native environment as native types. Similarly, a WCF client can import the metadata of a non-WCF service and consume it as native CLR classes and interfaces.

Service Execution Boundaries

With WCF, the client never interacts with a service directly, even when dealing with a local, in-memory service. Instead, the client always uses a proxy to forward calls to the service. The proxy exposes the same operations as the service, plus some proxy-management methods.

WCF allows the client to communicate with a service across all execution boundaries. On the same machine, the client can consume services in the same app domain, across app domains in the same process, or across processes (see Figure 1-2).

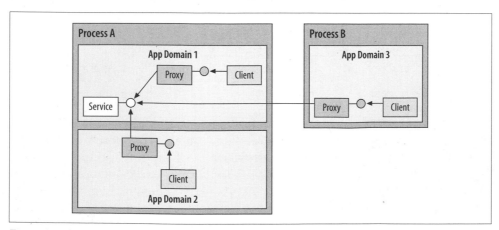

Figure 1-2. Same-machine communication using WCF

Across machine boundaries (Figure 1-3), the client can interact with services in its intranet or across the Internet.

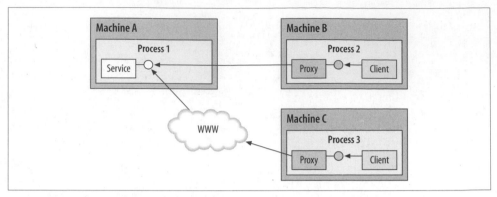

Figure 1-3. Cross-machine communication using WCF

WCF and location transparency

In the past, distributed computing technologies such as DCOM and .NET Remoting aspired to provide the same programming model to the client regardless of whether the object was local or remote. In the case of a local call, the client used a direct reference, and when dealing with a remote object, the client used a proxy. The problem with trying to use the local programming model as the remote programming model was that there is much more to a remote call than an object with a wire. Complex issues such as lifecycle management, reliability, state management, and security raised their heads, making the remote programming model significantly more complex. Numerous problems arose, all because the remote object was trying to be what it is not—a local object.

WCF also strives to provide the client with the same programming model regardless of the location of the service. However, the WCF approach is the exact opposite: it takes the remote programming model of instantiating and using a proxy and uses it even in the most local case. Because all interactions are done via a proxy, requiring the same configuration and hosting, WCF maintains the same programming model for the local and remote cases; thus, it not only enables you to switch locations without affecting the client, but also significantly simplifies the application programming model.

Addresses

In WCF, every service is associated with a unique address. The address provides two important elements: the location of the service, and the transport protocol, or *transport schema*, used to communicate with the service. The location portion of the address indicates the name of the target machine, site, or network; a communication port, pipe, or queue; and an optional specific path, or *URI* (Universal Resource Identifier). A URI can be any unique string, such as the service name or a globally unique identifier (GUID).

WCF supports the following transport schemas:

- HTTP
- TCP
- Peer network
- IPC (Inter-Process Communication)
- MSMQ

Addresses always have the following format:

```
[base address]/[optional URI]
```

The base address is always in this format:

```
[transport]://[machine or domain][:optional port]
```

Here are a few sample addresses:

```
http://localhost:8001
http://localhost:8001/MyService
net.tcp://localhost:8002/MyService
net.pipe://localhost/MyPipe
net.msmq://localhost/private/MyQueue
net.msmq://localhost/MyQueue
```

The way to read an address such as this:

```
http://localhost:8001
```

is like this: "Using HTTP, go to the machine called localhost, where on port 8001 someone is waiting for my calls."

If there is also a URI, as in:

```
http://localhost:8001/MyService
```

the address will read as follows: "Using HTTP, go to the machine called localhost, where on port 8001 someone called MyService is waiting for my calls."

TCP Addresses

TCP addresses use net.tcp for transport and typically include a port number, as in:

```
net.tcp://localhost:8002/MyService
```

When a port number is not specified, the TCP address defaults to port 808:

```
net.tcp://localhost/MyService
```

It is possible for two TCP addresses (from the same host, as discussed later in this chapter) to share a port:

```
net.tcp://localhost:8002/MyService
net.tcp://localhost:8002/MyOtherService
```

TCP-based addresses are used throughout this book.

You can configure TCP-based addresses from different service hosts to share a port.

HTTP Addresses

HTTP addresses use http for transport, and can also use https for secure transport. You typically use HTTP addresses with outward-facing Internet-based services, and you can specify a port as shown here:

```
http://localhost:8001
```

When the port number is unspecified, it defaults to 80 (and port 443 for HTTPS). As with TCP addresses, two HTTP addresses from the same host can share a port, even on the same machine.

HTTP-based addresses are also used throughout this book.

IPC Addresses

IPC addresses use net.pipe for transport, to indicate the use of the Windows named pipe mechanism. In WCF, services that use IPC can only accept calls from the same machine. Consequently, you must specify either the explicit local machine name or localhost for the machine name, followed by a unique string for the pipe name:

```
net.pipe://localhost/MyPipe
```

You can open a named pipe only once per machine, so it is not possible for two named pipe addresses to share a pipe name on the same machine.

IPC-based addresses are used throughout this book.

 The IPC address format is incorrect, indicating the mechanism instead of the protocol. The correct schema format should have been net.ipc instead of net.pipe, much like the TCP address uses net.tcp rather than net.socket.

MSMQ Addresses

MSMQ addresses use net.msmq for transport, to indicate the use of the Microsoft Message Queue (MSMQ). You must specify the queue name. When you're dealing with private queues you must also specify the queue type, but that can be omitted for public queues:

```
net.msmq://localhost/private/MyService
net.msmq://localhost/MyService
```

Chapter 9 is dedicated to making queued calls.

Peer Network Addresses

Peer network addresses use `net.p2p` for transport, to indicate the use of the Windows peer network transport. You must specify the peer network name as well as a unique path and port. Using and configuring peer networks is beyond the scope of this book, and you will see very little mention of peer networks in subsequent chapters. In most cases, a desire to use a peer network actually indicates a need for the publish-subscribe pattern. Appendix C presents my helper framework for this pattern.

Contracts

In WCF, all services expose *contracts*. The contract is a platform-neutral and standard way of describing what the service does. WCF defines four types of contracts:

Service contracts
> Describe which operations the client can perform on the service. Service contracts are the subject of the next chapter, but they are used extensively in every chapter in this book.

Data contracts
> Define which data types are passed to and from the service. WCF defines implicit contracts for built-in types such as `int` and `string`, but you can easily define explicit opt-in data contracts for custom types. Chapter 3 is dedicated to defining and using data contracts, and subsequent chapters make use of data contracts as required.

Fault contracts
> Define which errors are raised by the service, and how the service handles and propagates errors to its clients. Chapter 6 is dedicated to defining and using fault contracts.

Message contracts
> Allow the service to interact directly with messages. Message contracts can be typed or untyped and are useful in interoperability cases when another party has already dictated some explicit (typically proprietary) message format. That, however, is by no means the usual case for common WCF applications, so this book makes no use of message contracts. Unless you are required to leverage the flexibility, power, and extensibility of message contracts, you should avoid them, as they add no value but do add complexity. In many cases, the desire to use message contracts indicates a need for a custom application context, which can be addressed using custom headers (a useful alternative technique used throughout this book). For more on message headers, see Appendix B.

The Service Contract

The ServiceContractAttribute is defined as:

```
[AttributeUsage(AttributeTargets.Interface|AttributeTargets.Class,
                Inherited = false)]
public sealed class ServiceContractAttribute : Attribute
{
   public string Name
   {get;set;}
   public string Namespace
   {get;set;}
   //More members
}
```

This attribute allows you to define a service contract. You can apply the attribute on an interface or a class, as shown in Example 1-1.

Example 1-1. Defining and implementing a service contract

```
[ServiceContract]
interface IMyContract
{
   [OperationContract]
   string MyMethod(string text);

   //Will not be part of the contract
   string MyOtherMethod(string text);
}
class MyService : IMyContract
{
   public string MyMethod(string text)
   {
      return "Hello " + text;
   }
   public string MyOtherMethod(string text)
   {
      return "Cannot call this method over WCF";
   }
}
```

The ServiceContract attribute maps a CLR interface (or inferred interface, as you will see later) to a technology-neutral service contract. The ServiceContract attribute exposes a CLR interface (or a class) as a WCF contract, independently of that type's visibility. The type visibility has no bearing on WCF, because visibility is a CLR concept. Applying the ServiceContract attribute on an internal interface exposes that interface as a public service contract, ready to be consumed across the service boundary. Without the ServiceContract attribute, the interface is not visible to WCF clients, in line with the service-oriented tenet that service boundaries should be explicit. To enforce that tenet, all contracts must explicitly opt in: only interfaces (or classes) decorated with the ServiceContract attribute will be considered as WCF contracts; other types will not.

In addition, none of the members of the type will ever be part of the contract when using the ServiceContract attribute. You must explicitly indicate to WCF which methods to expose as part of the WCF contract using the OperationContractAttribute, defined as:

```
[AttributeUsage(AttributeTargets.Method)]
public sealed class OperationContractAttribute : Attribute
{
   public string Name
   {get;set;}
   //More members
}
```

You can apply the OperationContract attribute only on methods, and not on properties, indexers, or events, which are CLR concepts. WCF only understands *operations*—logical functions—and the OperationContract attribute exposes a contract method as a logical operation to perform as part of the service contract. Other methods on the interface (or class) that do not have the OperationContract attribute will not be part of the contract. This enforces explicit service boundaries and maintains an explicit opt-in model for the operations themselves. In addition, a contract operation cannot use object references as parameters: only primitive types or data contracts are allowed.

Applying the ServiceContract attribute

WCF lets you apply the ServiceContract attribute on an interface or on a class. When you apply it on an interface, some class needs to implement that interface. In general, you use plain C# or VB to implement the interface, and nothing in the service class code pertains to it being a WCF service:

```
[ServiceContract]
interface IMyContract
{
   [OperationContract]
   string MyMethod();
}
class MyService : IMyContract
{
   public string MyMethod()
   {
      return "Hello WCF";
   }
}
```

You can use implicit or explicit interface implementation:

```
class MyService : IMyContract
{
   string IMyContract.MyMethod()
   {
      return "Hello WCF";
   }
}
```

A single class can support multiple contracts by deriving and implementing multiple interfaces decorated with the ServiceContract attribute:

```
[ServiceContract]
interface IMyContract
{
   [OperationContract]
   string MyMethod( );
}
[ServiceContract]
interface IMyOtherContract
{
   [OperationContract]
   void MyOtherMethod( );
}
class MyService : IMyContract,IMyOtherContract
{
   public string MyMethod( )
   {...}
   public void MyOtherMethod( )
   {...}
}
```

There are, however, a few implementation constraints on the service implementation class. You should avoid parameterized constructors, because WCF will only use the default constructor. Also, although the class can use internal properties, indexers, and static members, no WCF client will ever be able to access them.

WCF also lets you apply the ServiceContract attribute directly on the service class, without defining a separate contract first:

```
//Avoid
[ServiceContract]
class MyService
{
   [OperationContract]
   string MyMethod( )
   {
      return "Hello WCF";
   }
}
```

Under the covers, WCF will infer the contract definition. You can apply the OperationContract attribute on any method of the class, be it private or public.

 Avoid using the ServiceContract attribute directly on the service class. Always define a separate contract, so that you can use it in other contexts.

Names and namespaces

You can and should define a namespace for your contract. The contract namespace serves the same purpose in WCF as it does in .NET programming: to scope a type of contract and reduce the overall chance of a collision. You use the Namespace property of the ServiceContract attribute to provide a namespace:

```
[ServiceContract(Namespace = "MyNamespace")]
interface IMyContract
{...}
```

Unspecified, the contract namespace defaults to http://tempuri.org. For outward-facing services you would typically use your company's URL, and for intranet services you can use any meaningful unique name, such as MyApplication.

By default, the exposed name of the contract will be the name of the interface used. However, you can use an alias for a contract to expose a different name to the clients in the metadata, by using the Name property of the ServiceContract attribute:

```
[ServiceContract(Name = "IMyContract")]
interface IMyOtherContract
{...}
```

Similarly, the name of the publicly exposed operation defaults to the method name, but you can use the Name property of the OperationContract attribute to alias it to a different publicly exposed name:

```
[ServiceContract]
interface IMyContract
{
    [OperationContract(Name = "SomeOperation")]
    void MyMethod(string text);
}
```

You will see a use for these properties in the next chapter.

Hosting

The WCF service class cannot exist in a void. Every WCF service must be hosted in a Windows process called the *host process*. A single host process can host multiple services, and the same service type can be hosted in multiple host processes. WCF makes no demand on whether or not the host process is also the client process, although having a separate process obviously promotes fault and security isolation. It is also immaterial who provides the process and what kind of process is involved. The host can be provided by Internet Information Services (IIS), by the Windows Activation Service (WAS) on Windows Vista or Windows Server 2008 or later, or by the developer as part of the application.

In-process (or *in-proc*) hosting, where the service resides in the same process as the client, is a special case. The host for the in-proc case is, by definition, provided by the developer.

IIS 5/6 Hosting

The main advantage of hosting a service in the Microsoft IIS web server is that the host process is launched automatically upon the first client request, and you rely on IIS 5/6 to manage the lifecycle of the host process. The main disadvantage of IIS 5/6 hosting is that you can only use HTTP. With IIS 5, you are further restricted to having all services use the same port number.

Hosting in IIS is very similar to hosting a classic ASMX web service. You need to create a virtual directory under IIS and supply an *.svc* file. The *.svc* file functions similarly to an *.asmx* file and is used to identify the service code behind the file and class. Example 1-2 shows the syntax for the *.svc* file.

Example 1-2. A .svc file

```
<%@ ServiceHost
    Language   = "C#"
    Debug      = "true"
    CodeBehind = "~/App_Code/MyService.cs"
    Service    = "MyService"
%>
```

You can even inject the service code inline in the *.svc* file, but that is not advisable, as is the case with ASMX web services.

When you use IIS 5/6 hosting, the base address used for the service always has to be the same as the address of the *.svc* file.

Using Visual Studio 2008

You can use Visual Studio 2008 to generate a boilerplate IIS-hosted service. From the File menu, select New Web Site, and then select WCF Service from the New Web Site dialog box. This causes Visual Studio 2008 to create a new website, service code, and a matching *.svc* file. You can also use the Add New Item dialog to add another service later.

The Web.Config file

The website config file (*Web.Config*) typically lists the types you want to expose as services. You need to use fully qualified type names, including the assembly name if the service type comes from an unreferenced assembly:

```
<system.serviceModel>
   <services>
      <service name = "MyNamespace.MyService">
         ...
      </service>
   </services>
</system.serviceModel>
```

Self-Hosting

Self-hosting is the name for the technique used when the developer is responsible for providing and managing the lifecycle of the host process. Self-hosting is used both when you want a process (or machine) boundary between the client and the service, and when using the service in-proc—that is, in the same process as the client. The process you need to provide can be any Windows process, such as a Windows Forms application, a Console application, or a Windows NT Service. Note that the process must be running before the client calls the service, which typically means you have to prelaunch it. This is not an issue for NT Services or in-proc hosting. Providing a host can be done with only a few lines of code, and it does offer a few advantage over IIS 5/6 hosting.

As with IIS 5/6 hosting, the hosting application config file (*App.Config*) typically lists the types of the services you wish to host and expose to the world:

```
<system.serviceModel>
   <services>
      <service name = "MyNamespace.MyService">
         ...
      </service>
   </services>
</system.serviceModel>
```

In addition, the host process must explicitly register the service types at runtime and open the host for client calls, which is why the host process must be running before the client calls arrive. Creating the host is typically done in the Main( ) method using the class ServiceHost, defined in Example 1-3.

Example 1-3. The ServiceHost class

```
public interface ICommunicationObject
{
   void Open( );
   void Close( );
   //More members
}
public abstract class CommunicationObject : ICommunicationObject
{...}
public abstract class ServiceHostBase : CommunicationObject,IDisposable,...
{...}
public class ServiceHost : ServiceHostBase,...
{
```

Example 1-3. The ServiceHost class (continued)

```
    public ServiceHost(Type serviceType,params Uri[] baseAddresses);
    //More members
}
```

You need to provide the constructor of ServiceHost with the service type, and optionally with default base addresses. The set of base addresses can be an empty set, and even if you provide base addresses, the service can be configured to use different base addresses. Having a set of base addresses enables the service to accept calls on multiple addresses and protocols, and to use only a relative URI.

Note that each ServiceHost instance is associated with a particular service type, and if the host process needs to host multiple types of services, you will need a matching number of ServiceHost instances. By calling the Open( ) method on the host you allow calls in, and by calling the Close( ) method you gracefully exit the host instance, allowing calls in progress to complete yet refusing future client calls even if the host process is still running. Closing is typically done on host process shutdown. For example, to host this service in a Windows Forms application:

```
[ServiceContract]
interface IMyContract
{...}
class MyService : IMyContract
{...}
```

you would have the following hosting code:

```
public static void Main()
{
    ServiceHost host = new ServiceHost(typeof(MyService));

    host.Open();

    //Can do blocking calls:
    Application.Run(new MyForm());

    host.Close();
}
```

Opening a host loads the WCF runtime and launches worker threads to monitor incoming requests. Incoming calls are dispatched by the monitoring threads to worker threads from the I/O completion thread pool (where there are 1,000 threads by default). Since worker threads are involved, you can perform blocking operations after opening the host.

Because the host is closed gracefully, the amount of time it will take is undetermined. By default, the host will block for 10 seconds waiting for Close( ) to return and will proceed with the shutdown after that timeout has expired. Before opening the host, you can configure a different close timeout with the CloseTimeout property of ServiceHostBase:

```
public abstract class ServiceHostBase : ...
{
   public TimeSpan CloseTimeout
   {get;set;}
   //More members
}
```

For example, you could use programmatic calls to set the close timeout to 20 seconds:

```
ServiceHost host = new ServiceHost(...);
host.CloseTimeout = TimeSpan.FromSeconds(20);
host.Open();
```

You can do the same in a config file by placing the close timeout in the host section of the service:

```
<system.serviceModel>
   <services>
      <service name = "MyNamespace.MyService">
         <host>
            <timeouts
               closeTimeout = "00:00:20"
            />
         </host>
         ...
      </service>
   </services>
</system.serviceModel>
```

Using Visual Studio 2008

Visual Studio 2008 allows you to add a WCF service to any application project by selecting WCF Service from the Add New Item dialog box. A service added this way is, of course, in-proc toward the host process, but out-of-proc clients can also access it.

Self-hosting and base addresses

You can launch a service host without providing any base address by omitting the base addresses altogether:

```
ServiceHost host = new ServiceHost(typeof(MyService));
```

Do not provide a null instead of an empty list, because that will throw an exception:

```
ServiceHost host;
host = new ServiceHost(typeof(MyService),null);
```

You can also register multiple base addresses separated by commas, as in the following snippet, as long as the addresses do not use the same transport schema (note the use of the params qualifier in Example 1-3):

```
Uri tcpBaseAddress  = new Uri("net.tcp://localhost:8001/");
Uri httpBaseAddress = new Uri("http://localhost:8002/");
```

```
ServiceHost host = new ServiceHost(typeof(MyService),
                                   tcpBaseAddress,httpBaseAddress);
```

WCF also lets you list the base addresses in the host config file:

```
<system.serviceModel>
   <services>
      <service name = "MyNamespace.MyService">
         <host>
            <baseAddresses>
               <add baseAddress = "net.tcp://localhost:8001/"/>
               <add baseAddress = "http://localhost:8002/"/>
            </baseAddresses>
         </host>
         ...
      </service>
   </services>
</system.serviceModel>
```

When you create the host, it will use whichever base addresses it finds in the config file, plus any base addresses you provide programmatically. Take extra care to ensure that the configured base addresses and the programmatic ones do not overlap in the schema.

You can even register multiple hosts for the same type, as long as the hosts use different base addresses:

```
Uri baseAddress1  = new Uri("net.tcp://localhost:8001/");
ServiceHost host1 = new ServiceHost(typeof(MyService),baseAddress1);
host1.Open();

Uri baseAddress2  = new Uri("net.tcp://localhost:8002/");
ServiceHost host2 = new ServiceHost(typeof(MyService),baseAddress2);
host2.Open();
```

However, with the exception of some threading issues discussed in Chapter 8, opening multiple hosts this way offers no real advantage. In addition, opening multiple hosts for the same type does not work with base addresses supplied in the config file and requires use of the ServiceHost constructor.

Advanced hosting features

The ICommunicationObject interface supported by ServiceHost offers some advanced features, listed in Example 1-4.

Example 1-4. The ICommunicationObject interface

```
public interface ICommunicationObject
{
   void Open();
   void Close();
   void Abort();

   event EventHandler Closed;
   event EventHandler Closing;
```

Example 1-4. The ICommunicationObject interface (continued)

```
   event EventHandler Faulted;
   event EventHandler Opened;
   event EventHandler Opening;

   IAsyncResult BeginClose(AsyncCallback callback,object state);
   IAsyncResult BeginOpen(AsyncCallback callback,object state);
   void EndClose(IAsyncResult result);
   void EndOpen(IAsyncResult result);

   CommunicationState State
   {get;}
 //More members
}
public enum CommunicationState
{
   Created,
   Opening,
   Opened,
   Closing,
   Closed,
   Faulted
}
```

If opening or closing the host is a lengthy operation, you can do so asynchronously with the BeginOpen( ) and BeginClose( ) methods. You can subscribe to hosting events such as state changes or faults, and you can use the State property to query for the host status. Finally, the ServiceHost class also offers the Abort( ) method. Abort( ) is an ungraceful exit—when called, it immediately aborts all service calls in progress and shuts down the host. Active clients will each get an exception.

The ServiceHost<T> class

You can improve on the WCF-provided ServiceHost class by defining the ServiceHost<T> class, as shown in Example 1-5.

Example 1-5. The ServiceHost<T> class

```
public class ServiceHost<T> : ServiceHost
{
   public ServiceHost( ) : base(typeof(T))
   {}
   public ServiceHost(params string[] baseAddresses) :
                                    base(typeof(T),Convert(baseAddresses))
   {}
   public ServiceHost(params Uri[] baseAddresses) : base(typeof(T),baseAddresses)
   {}
   static Uri[] Convert(string[] baseAddresses)
   {
      Converter<string,Uri> convert = (address)=>
                             {
                                return new Uri(address);
                             };
```

Example 1-5. The ServiceHost<T> class (continued)

```
        return baseAddresses.ConvertAll(convert);
    }
}
```

ServiceHost<T> provides simple constructors that do not require the service type as a construction parameter and that can operate on raw strings instead of the cumbersome Uri. I'll add quite a few extensions, features, and capabilities to ServiceHost<T> in the rest of this book.

WAS Hosting

The Windows Activation Service (WAS) is a system service available with Windows Vista and Windows Server 2008 (or later). WAS is part of IIS7, but it can be installed and configured separately. To use WAS for hosting your WCF service, you need to supply a *.svc* file, just as with IIS 5/6. All the other development aspects, such as support in Visual Studio 2008, remain exactly the same. The main difference between IIS and WAS is that WAS is not limited to HTTP and can be used with any of the available WCF transports, ports, and queues.

WAS offers many advantages over self-hosting, including application pooling, recycling, idle time management, identity management, and isolation, and it is the host process of choice when available—that is, when you can target either a Windows Server 2008 (or later) machine for scalability, or a Windows Vista (or later) client machine for a handful of clients.

That said, self-hosted processes do offer singular advantages, such as in-proc hosting, dealing well with unknown customer environments, and easy programmatic access to the advanced hosting features described previously. In addition, in some instance-management cases (such as lengthy sessions or singleton services) it is better to use self-hosting so that you can avoid WAS autorecycling of the host process and control when to launch the host.

Custom Hosting in IIS/WAS

It is often the case that you need to interact with the host instance. While this is integral to the use of a self-hosting solution, when using IIS 5/6 or WAS, you have no direct access to the host. To overcome this hurdle, WCF provides a hook called a *host factory*. Using the Factory tag in the *.svc* file, you can specify a class you provide that creates the host instance:

```
<%@ ServiceHost
    Language  = "C#"
    Debug     = "true"
    CodeBehind = "~/App_Code/MyService.cs"
    Service   = "MyService"
    Factory   = "MyServiceFactory"
%>
```

Array and Iterator Extensions

It would be nice if the iterator (any collection or array) supported a method that converted it to another collection or an array, such as the ConvertAll( ) call in Example 1-5. Sadly, .NET 3.5 does not provide such a method. However, using C# 3.0 extension methods, you can add methods to existing types to compensate for this oversight:

```
public static class CollectionExtensions
{
    public static IEnumerable<U> ConvertAll<T,U>(
                           this IEnumerable<T> collection,
                           Converter<T,U> converter)
    {
        foreach(T item in collection)
        {
            yield return converter(item);
        }
    }
    //More extensions
}
public static class ArrayExtensions
{
    public static U[] ConvertAll<T,U>(this T[] array,
                                  Converter<T,U> converter)
    {
        IEnumerable<T> enumerable = array;
        return enumerable.ConvertAll(converter).ToArray();
    }
    //More extensions
}
```

CollectionExtensions first extends the IEnumerable<T> interface that all collections and arrays support to include a ConvertAll( ) method using the this keyword. CollectionExtensions.ConvertAll( ) uses C# iterators to convert the collection into another collection by invoking the supplied Converter<T,U> delegate on every item in the collection. When used on an array (that supports IEnumerable<T>), it will convert an array of T into an IEnumerable<U>. To return a proper U[], define the ArrayExtensions class with its own ConvertAll( ) method. ArrayExtensions. ConvertAll( ) calls CollectionExtensions.ConvertAll( ) to convert the array into IEnumerable<U>, followed by a call to the LINQ method ToArray( ) to convert the iterator into an array. These extension methods are part of my *ServiceModelEx* library, which includes many other type extensions for the iterator and the array (such as ForEach( )). In addition, I have provided all of the LINQ functionality that normally returns an IEnumerable<T> interface as array extensions that return a proper array of T.

The host factory class must derive from the ServiceHostFactory class and override the CreateServiceHost( ) virtual method:

```
    public class ServiceHostFactory : ...
    {
        protected virtual ServiceHost CreateServiceHost(Type serviceType,
                                                        Uri[] baseAddresses);
        //More members
    }
```

For example:

```
    class MyServiceFactory : ServiceHostFactory
    {
        protected override ServiceHost CreateServiceHost(Type serviceType,
                                                         Uri[] baseAddresses)
        {
            ServiceHost host = new ServiceHost(serviceType,baseAddresses);

            //Custom steps here

            return host;
        }
    }
```

Bindings

There are multiple aspects of communication with any given service, and there are many possible communication patterns: messages can follow a synchronous request-reply or asynchronous fire-and-forget pattern, messages can be bidirectional, messages can be delivered immediately or queued, and the queues can be durable or volatile. As discussed previously, there are many possible transport protocols for the messages, such as HTTP (or HTTPS), TCP, IPC, and MSMQ. There are also a few possible message encoding options: you can choose plain text to enable interoperability, binary encoding to optimize performance, or the Message Transport Optimization Mechanism (MTOM) for large payloads. Finally, there are multiple options for securing messages: you can choose not to secure them at all, to provide transport-level security only, or to provide message-level privacy and security, and of course there are numerous ways to authenticate and authorize the clients. Message delivery might be unreliable or reliable end-to-end across intermediaries and dropped connections, and the messages might be processed in the order they were sent or in the order they were received. Your service might need to interoperate with other services or clients that are aware of only the basic web service protocol, or with clients and services capable of using the score of WS-* modern protocols, such as WS-Security and WS-Atomic Transactions. Your service may need to be able to interoperate with any client, or you may want to restrict your service to interoperate only with another WCF service or client.

If you were to count all the possible communication and interaction options, you'd probably find that the number of permutations is in the tens of thousands. Some of those choices may be mutually exclusive, and some may mandate other choices.

Clearly, both the client and the service must be aligned on all these options in order to communicate properly. Managing this level of complexity adds no business value to most applications, and yet the productivity and quality implications of making the wrong decisions are severe.

To simplify these choices and make them manageable, WCF groups together sets of such communication aspects in *bindings*. A binding is merely a consistent, canned set of choices regarding the transport protocol, message encoding, communication pattern, reliability, security, transaction propagation, and interoperability. All you need to do is decide on the target scenario for your service, and WCF makes a correct multidimensional decision for you regarding all the aspects of the communication. Ideally, you would extract all these "plumbing" aspects from your service code and allow the service to focus solely on the implementation of the business logic. Bindings enable you to use the same service logic over drastically different plumbing.

You can use the WCF-provided bindings out-of-the-box, you can tweak their properties, or you can write your own custom bindings from scratch. The service publishes its choice of binding in its metadata, enabling clients to query for the type and specific properties of the binding. This is important because the client must use the exact same binding values as the service. A single service can support multiple bindings on separate addresses.

The Common Bindings

WCF defines six frequently used bindings:

Basic binding
> Offered by the BasicHttpBinding class, this is designed to expose a WCF service as a legacy ASMX web service, so that old clients can work with new services. The basic binding makes your service look, on the wire, like a legacy web service that communicates over the basic web service profile. When used by clients, this binding enables new WCF clients to work with old ASMX services.

TCP binding
> Offered by the NetTcpBinding class, this uses TCP for cross-machine communication on the intranet. It supports a variety of features, including reliability, transactions, and security, and is optimized for WCF-to-WCF communication. As a result, it requires both the client and the service to use WCF.

IPC binding
> Offered by the NetNamedPipeBinding class, this uses named pipes as a transport for same-machine communication. It is the most secure binding, since it cannot accept calls from outside the machine. The IPC binding supports a variety of features, similar to the TCP binding. It is also the most performant binding, since IPC is a lighter protocol than TCP.

The `NetNamedPipeBinding` class is named incorrectly, since the binding naming convention is to refer to the protocol, not the communication mechanism (thus, we have `NetTcpBinding` rather than `NetSocketBinding`). The correct name for this binding should have been `NetIpcBinding`. Throughout this book, I will refer to the `NetNamedPipeBinding` as the IPC binding.

Web Service (WS) binding

Offered by the `WSHttpBinding` class, this uses HTTP or HTTPS for transport, and is designed to offer a variety of features (such as reliability, transactions, and security) over the Internet, all using the WS-* standards. This binding is designed to interoperate with any party that supports the WS-* standards.

Dual WS binding

Offered by the `WSDualHttpBinding` class, this is similar to the WS binding except it also supports bidirectional duplex communication from the service to the client, as discussed in Chapter 5. While this binding does use industry standards (it is nothing more than two `WSHttpBinding` bindings wired up against each other to support callbacks), there is no industry standard for setting up the callback, and therefore the `WSDualHttpBinding` is not interoperable.

MSMQ binding

Offered by the `NetMsmqBinding` class, this uses MSMQ for transport and is designed to offer support for disconnected queued calls. Using this binding is the subject of Chapter 9.

Format and encoding

Each of the frequently used bindings uses a different transport schema and encoding, as listed in Table 1-1. Where multiple encodings are possible, the defaults are shown in bold.

Table 1-1. Transport and encoding for common bindings

Name	Transport	Encoding	Interoperable
BasicHttpBinding	HTTP/HTTPS	**Text**, MTOM	Yes
NetTcpBinding	TCP	Binary	No
NetNamedPipeBinding	IPC	Binary	No
WSHttpBinding	HTTP/HTTPS	**Text**, MTOM	Yes
WSDualHttpBinding	HTTP	**Text**, MTOM	No
NetMsmqBinding	MSMQ	Binary	No

Having a text-based encoding typically enables a WCF service (or client) to communicate over HTTP with any other service (or client), regardless of its technology and across firewalls. Binary encoding over TCP, IPC, or MSMQ yields the best performance, but at the expense of interoperability, because it mandates WCF-to-WCF communication.

That said, with the TCP, IPC, and MSMQ bindings, interoperability is often not required. In the case of IPC, since the call can never leave the client machine, the client can rest assured that the target machine is running Windows and has WCF installed on it. In the case of the TCP binding, while your application may need to interoperate with other applications written in other technologies, internally applications themselves do tend to be homogeneous. As such, as long as your application spans only the local intranet, you can typically assume a homogenous Windows environment, without internal firewalls between machines. Finally, the MSMQ binding requires the use of MSMQ server, which of course is Windows-specific.

 This binary encoder used by the TCP, IPC, and MSMQ bindings is proprietary to WCF. Do not attempt to write a custom parser for it on other platforms. Microsoft reserves the right to change its format over time, in order to keep optimizing and evolving it.

Choosing a Binding

When choosing a binding for your service, you should follow the decision diagram shown in Figure 1-4.

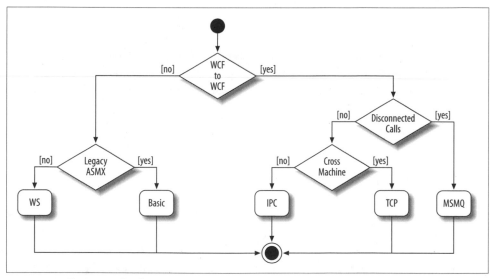

Figure 1-4. Choosing a binding

The first question you should ask yourself is whether your service needs to interact with non-WCF clients. If the answer is yes, and those clients expect the basic web service protocol (ASMX web services), choose the BasicHttpBinding, which exposes your WCF service to the outside world as if it were an ASMX web service (that is, a WSI-basic profile). The downside of this choice is that you cannot take advantage of most of the modern WS-* protocols. If, however, the non-WCF client can understand these standards, you can instead choose one of the WS bindings

(WSHttpBinding or WSDualHttpBinding). If you can assume that the client is a WCF client and yet requires offline or disconnected interaction, choose the NetMsmqBinding, which uses MSMQ for transporting the messages. If the client requires connected communication but could be calling across machine boundaries, choose the NetTcpBinding, which communicates over TCP. If the client is on the same machine as the service, choose the NetNamedPipeBinding, which uses IPC to maximize performance.

> Most bindings work well even outside their target scenarios. For example, you could use the TCP binding for same-machine or even in-proc communication, and you could use the basic binding for intranet WCF-to-WCF communication. However, do try to choose a binding according to Figure 1-4.

Additional Bindings

In addition to the six frequently used bindings described so far, WCF provides three specializations of these bindings: the BasicHttpContextBinding, the WSHttpContextBinding, and the NetTcpContextBinding. The context bindings (described in Appendix B) all derive from their respective regular bindings, adding support for a context protocol. The context protocol allows you to pass out-of-band parameters to the service. The context bindings can also be used for durable services support, as described in Chapter 4.

Finally, WCF defines six infrequently used bindings. These bindings (listed next) are each designed for a specific target scenario and cannot easily be used outside that scenario. This book makes no use of these bindings, due to their somewhat esoteric nature:

Peer network binding
> Offered by the NetPeerTcpBinding class, this uses peer networking as a transport: the peer-network-enabled client and services all subscribe to the same grid and broadcast messages to it. Peer networking is beyond the scope of this book, since it requires an understanding of grid topology and mesh computing strategies.

Federated WS binding
> Offered by the WSFederationHttpBinding class, this is a specialization of the WS binding that offers support for federated security. Federated security is beyond the scope of this book, since by and large, the industry presently lacks good support (both in technology and in business models) for true federated scenarios. I do expect federation to become mainstream as time goes by.

Federated WS 2007 binding
> Offered by the WS2007FederationHttpBinding class, this is an update of WSFederationHttpBinding.

MSMQ integration binding

> Offered by the `MsmqIntegrationBinding` class, this is the analogous queued-world binding to the basic binding. The integration binding converts WCF messages to and from MSMQ messages and is designed to interoperate with legacy MSMQ clients.

Web binding

> Offered by the `WebHttpBinding` class, this binding allows your service to accept simple calls over web protocols such as HTTP-GET using the REST/POX/JSON patterns. This binding could be useful for a web-scripting client such as an AJAX page.

WS 2007 binding

> Offered by the `WS2007HttpBinding` class, this binding derives from the `WSHttpBinding` class; it adds support for the emerging coordination standard, as well as updates for the transaction, security, and reliability standards.

Using a Binding

Each binding offers literally dozens of configurable properties. There are three ways of working with bindings: you can use the built-in bindings as they are, if they fit your requirements; you can tweak and configure some of their properties, such as transaction propagation, reliability, and security; or you can write your own custom bindings. The most common scenario is using an existing binding mostly as it is, and merely configuring two or three of its aspects. Application developers will hardly ever need to write a custom binding, but framework developers may need to.

Endpoints

Every service is associated with an address that defines where the service is, a binding that defines how to communicate with the service, and a contract that defines what the service does. This triumvirate governing the service is easy to remember as the *ABC* of the service. WCF formalizes this relationship in the form of an *endpoint*. The endpoint is the fusion of the address, contract, and binding (see Figure 1-5).

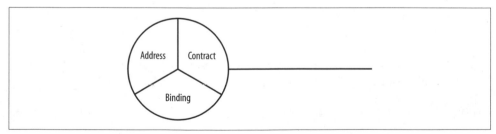

Figure 1-5. The endpoint

Every endpoint must have all three elements, and the host exposes the endpoint. Logically, the endpoint is the service's interface and is analogous to a CLR or COM interface. Note in Figure 1-5 the use of the traditional "lollipop" notation to denote an endpoint.

 Conceptually, even in C# or VB you have endpoints: the address is the memory address of the type's virtual table, the binding is CLR, and the contract is the interface itself. Because in classic .NET programming you never deal with addresses or bindings, you take them for granted, and you've probably gotten used to equating in your mind's eye the interface (which is merely a programming construct) with all that it takes to interface with an object. The WCF endpoint is a true interface, because it contains all the information required to interface with the object. In WCF, the address and the binding are not preordained and need to be configured.

Every service must expose at least one business endpoint, and each endpoint has exactly one contract. All endpoints on a service have unique addresses, and a single service can expose multiple endpoints. These endpoints can use the same or different bindings and can expose the same or different contracts. There is absolutely no relationship between the various endpoints a service provides.

It is important to point out that nothing in the service code pertains to its endpoints, and they are always external to the service code. You can configure endpoints either administratively, using a config file, or programmatically.

Administrative Endpoint Configuration

Configuring an endpoint administratively requires placing the endpoint details in the hosting process's config file. For example, given this service definition:

```
namespace MyNamespace
{
    [ServiceContract]
    interface IMyContract
    {...}
    class MyService : IMyContract
    {...}
}
```

Example 1-6 shows the required entries in the config file. Under each service type, you list its endpoints.

Example 1-6. Administrative endpoint configuration

```
<system.serviceModel>
  <services>
    <service name = "MyNamespace.MyService">
```

Example 1-6. Administrative endpoint configuration (continued)

```
        <endpoint
            address  = "http://localhost:8000/MyService"
            binding  = "wsHttpBinding"
            contract = "MyNamespace.IMyContract"
        />
    </service>
  </services>
</system.serviceModel>
```

When you specify the service and the contract type, you need to use fully qualified type names. I will omit the namespace in the examples throughout the remainder of this book, but you should use a namespace when applicable. Note that if the endpoint provides a base address, that address schema must be consistent with the binding, such as HTTP with WSHttpBinding. A mismatch causes an exception at service load time.

Example 1-7 shows a config file defining a single service that exposes multiple endpoints. You can configure multiple endpoints with the same base address as long as the URI is different.

Example 1-7. Multiple endpoints on the same service

```
<service name = "MyService">
    <endpoint
        address  = "http://localhost:8000/MyService"
        binding  = "wsHttpBinding"
        contract = "IMyContract"
    />
    <endpoint
        address  = "net.tcp://localhost:8001/MyService"
        binding  = "netTcpBinding"
        contract = "IMyContract"
    />
    <endpoint
        address  = "net.tcp://localhost:8002/MyService"
        binding  = "netTcpBinding"
        contract = "IMyOtherContract"
    />
</service>
```

Administrative configuration is the option of choice in the majority of cases because it provides the flexibility to change the service address, binding, and even exposed contracts without rebuilding and redeploying the service.

Using base addresses

In Example 1-7, each endpoint provided its own base address. When you provide an explicit base address, it overrides any base address the host may have provided.

You can also have multiple endpoints use the same base address, as long as the endpoint addresses differ in their URIs:

```
<service name = "MyService">
   <endpoint
      address  = "net.tcp://localhost:8001/MyService"
      binding  = "netTcpBinding"
      contract = "IMyContract"
   />
   <endpoint
      address  = "net.tcp://localhost:8001/MyOtherService"
      binding  = "netTcpBinding"
      contract = "IMyContract"
   />
</service>
```

Alternatively, if the host provides a base address with a matching transport schema, you can leave out the address. In this case, the endpoint address will be the same as the base address of the matching transport:

```
<endpoint
   binding  = "wsHttpBinding"
   contract = "IMyContract"
/>
```

If the host does not provide a matching base address, loading the service host will fail with an exception.

When you configure the endpoint address, you can add just the relative URI under the base address:

```
<endpoint
   address  = "SubAddress"
   binding  = "wsHttpBinding"
   contract = "IMyContract"
/>
```

The endpoint address in this case will be the matching base address plus the URI, and again, the host must provide a matching base address.

Binding configuration

You can use the config file to customize the binding used by the endpoint. To that end, add the bindingConfiguration tag to the endpoint section, and name a customized section in the bindings section of the config file. Example 1-8 demonstrates using this technique to enable transaction propagation. What the transactionFlow tag does is explained in Chapter 7.

Example 1-8. Service-side binding configuration

```
<system.serviceModel>
   <services>
      <service name = "MyService">
         <endpoint
```

Example 1-8. Service-side binding configuration (continued)

```
            address = "net.tcp://localhost:8000/MyService"
            bindingConfiguration = "TransactionalTCP"
            binding = "netTcpBinding"
            contract = "IMyContract"
         />
         <endpoint
            address = "net.tcp://localhost:8001/MyService"
            bindingConfiguration = "TransactionalTCP"
            binding = "netTcpBinding"
            contract = "IMyOtherContract"
         />
      </service>
   </services>
   <bindings>
      <netTcpBinding>
         <binding name = "TransactionalTCP"
            transactionFlow = "true"
         />
      </netTcpBinding>
   </bindings>
</system.serviceModel>
```

As shown in Example 1-8, you can reuse the named binding configuration in multiple endpoints simply by referring to it.

Programmatic Endpoint Configuration

Programmatic endpoint configuration is equivalent to administrative configuration, but instead of resorting to a config file, you rely on programmatic calls to add endpoints to the ServiceHost instance. Again, these calls are always outside the scope of the service code. ServiceHost provides overloaded versions of the AddServiceEndpoint( ) method:

```
public class ServiceHost : ServiceHostBase
{
   public ServiceEndpoint AddServiceEndpoint(Type implementedContract,
                                             Binding binding,
                                             string address);

   //Additional members
}
```

You can provide AddServiceEndpoint( ) methods with either relative or absolute addresses, just as with a config file. Example 1-9 demonstrates programmatic configuration of the same endpoints as in Example 1-7.

Example 1-9. Service-side programmatic endpoint configuration

```
ServiceHost host = new ServiceHost(typeof(MyService));

Binding wsBinding  = new WSHttpBinding( );
Binding tcpBinding = new NetTcpBinding( );
```

```
host.AddServiceEndpoint(typeof(IMyContract),wsBinding,
                        "http://localhost:8000/MyService");
host.AddServiceEndpoint(typeof(IMyContract),tcpBinding,
                        "net.tcp://localhost:8001/MyService");
host.AddServiceEndpoint(typeof(IMyOtherContract),tcpBinding,
                        "net.tcp://localhost:8002/MyService");

host.Open( );
```

When you add an endpoint programmatically, the address is given as a string, the contract as a Type, and the binding as one of the subclasses of the abstract class Binding, as in:

```
public class NetTcpBinding : Binding,...
{...}
```

To rely on the host base address, provide an empty string if you want to use only the base address, or just the URI to use the base address plus that URI:

```
Uri tcpBaseAddress = new Uri("net.tcp://localhost:8000/");

ServiceHost host = new ServiceHost(typeof(MyService),tcpBaseAddress);

Binding tcpBinding = new NetTcpBinding( );

//Use base address as address
host.AddServiceEndpoint(typeof(IMyContract),tcpBinding,"");
//Add relative address
host.AddServiceEndpoint(typeof(IMyContract),tcpBinding,"MyService");
//Ignore base address
host.AddServiceEndpoint(typeof(IMyContract),tcpBinding,
                        "net.tcp://localhost:8001/MyService");
host.Open( );
```

As with administrative configuration using a config file, the host must provide a matching base address; otherwise, an exception occurs. In fact, in terms of capabilities, there is no difference between programmatic and administrative configuration. When you use a config file, all WCF does is parse the file and execute the appropriate programmatic calls in its place.

Binding configuration

You can programmatically set the properties of the binding used. For example, here is the code required to enable transaction propagation (similar to Example 1-8):

```
ServiceHost host = new ServiceHost(typeof(MyService));
NetTcpBinding tcpBinding = new NetTcpBinding( );

tcpBinding.TransactionFlow = true;

host.AddServiceEndpoint(typeof(IMyContract),tcpBinding,
                        "net.tcp://localhost:8000/MyService");
host.Open( );
```

Note that when you're dealing with specific binding properties you typically interact with a concrete binding subclass, such as NetTcpBinding, rather than its abstract base class, Binding (as was done in Example 1-9).

Metadata Exchange

By default, the service will not publish its metadata. However, this does not preclude clients that have obtained the metadata via some other mechanism from invoking operations on the service. A service that does not publish metadata is the WCF analogy to an internal class in .NET.

Publishing your service's metadata involves significant effort, since you have to convert CLR types and binding information into WSDL or some other low-level representation, and all that effort does not add any business value. But fortunately, the host already knows everything there is to know about your service and its endpoints, so it can publish the metadata for you if explicitly instructed to do so.

There are two options for publishing a service's metadata: you can provide the metadata over HTTP-GET, a simple text-based protocol that most platforms support, or you can use a dedicated endpoint (as discussed later).

WCF can provide the metadata for your service over HTTP-GET automatically; all you need to do is enable it by adding an explicit service behavior. Behaviors are described fully in subsequent chapters. For now, all you need to know is that a behavior is a local aspect of the service, such as whether or not it wants to have the host publish its metadata over HTTP-GET. You can add this behavior administratively or programmatically.

Enabling Metadata Exchange Administratively

Example 1-10 shows a host application config file, where both hosted services reference a custom behavior section that enables metadata publishing over HTTP-GET.

Example 1-10. Enabling metadata exchange behavior using a config file

```
<system.serviceModel>
   <services>
      <service name = "MyService" behaviorConfiguration = "MEXGET">
         <host>
            <baseAddresses>
               <add baseAddress = "http://localhost:8000/"/>
            </baseAddresses>
         </host>
         ...
      </service>
      <service name = "MyOtherService" behaviorConfiguration = "MEXGET">
         <host>
            <baseAddresses>
```

```
                <add baseAddress = "http://localhost:8001/"/>
            </baseAddresses>
        </host>
        ...
    </service>
  </services>
  <behaviors>
    <serviceBehaviors>
        <behavior name = "MEXGET">
            <serviceMetadata httpGetEnabled = "true"/>
        </behavior>
    </serviceBehaviors>
  </behaviors>
</system.serviceModel>
```

By default, the address the clients need to use for HTTP-GET is the registered HTTP
base address of the service. If the host is not configured with an HTTP base address,
loading the service will throw an exception. You can also specify a different address
(or just a URI appended to the HTTP base address) at which to publish the metadata by setting the httpGetUrl property of the serviceMetadata tag:

```
<behavior name = "MEXGET">
    <serviceMetadata httpGetEnabled = "true" httpGetUrl = "http://localhost:8002"/>
</behavior>
```

Once you have enabled the metadata exchange over HTTP-GET, you can navigate to
the address you configured (the HTTP base address, by default, or an explicit
address) using a browser. If all is well, you will get a confirmation page like the one
shown in Figure 1-6, letting you know that you have successfully hosted a service.
The confirmation page is unrelated to IIS hosting, and you can use a browser to navigate to the service address even when self-hosting.

Enabling Metadata Exchange Programmatically

To programmatically enable metadata exchange over HTTP-GET, you first need to
add the behavior to the collection of behaviors the host maintains for the service
type. The ServiceHostBase class offers the Description property of the type
ServiceDescription:

```
public abstract class ServiceHostBase : ...
{
    public ServiceDescription Description
    {get;}
    //More members
}
```

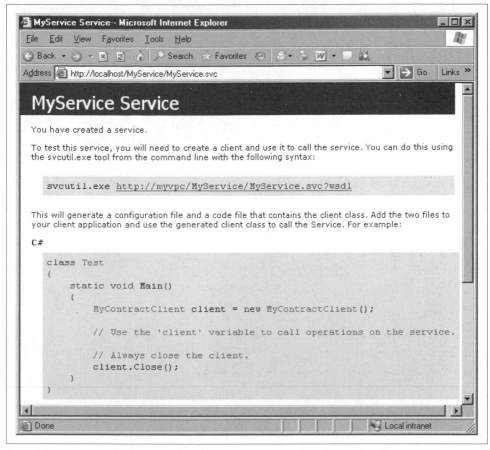

Figure 1-6. A service confirmation page

The service description, as its name implies, is the description of the service with all its aspects and behaviors. ServiceDescription contains a property called Behaviors of the type KeyedByTypeCollection<T>, with IServiceBehavior as the generic type parameter:

```
public class KeyedByTypeCollection<T> : KeyedCollection<Type,T>
{
   public T Find<T>();
   public T Remove<T>();
   //More members
}
public class ServiceDescription
{
   public KeyedByTypeCollection<IServiceBehavior> Behaviors
   {get;}
}
```

IServiceBehavior is the interface that all behavior classes and attributes implement. KeyedByTypeCollection<I> offers the generic method Find<T>( ), which returns the requested behavior if it is in the collection, and null otherwise. A given behavior type can be found in the collection at most once.

Example 1-11 shows how to enable the metadata exchange behavior programmatically.

Example 1-11. Enabling the metadata exchange behavior programmatically

```
ServiceHost host = new ServiceHost(typeof(MyService));

ServiceMetadataBehavior metadataBehavior;
metadataBehavior = host.Description.Behaviors.Find<ServiceMetadataBehavior>( );
if(metadataBehavior == null)
{
   Debug.Assert(BaseAddresses.Any(urn uri.Scheme == "http"));

   metadataBehavior = new ServiceMetadataBehavior( );
   metadataBehavior.HttpGetEnabled = true;
   host.Description.Behaviors.Add(metadataBehavior);
}

host.Open( );
```

Note the defensive manner in which the hosting code first verifies that no metadata behavior was provided in the config file, by calling the Find<T>( ) method of KeyedByTypeCollection<I> and using ServiceMetadataBehavior as the type parameter. ServiceMetadataBehavior is defined in the System.ServiceModel.Description namespace:

```
public class ServiceMetadataBehavior : IServiceBehavior
{
   public bool HttpGetEnabled
   {get;set;}

   public Uri HttpGetUrl
   {get;set;}
   //More members
}
```

If the returned behavior is null, it means the config file contains no metadata behavior. In this case, the hosting code creates a new ServiceMetadataBehavior instance, sets HttpGetEnabled to true, and adds it to the behaviors in the service description. By defensively checking for the presence of the behavior first, the hosting code avoids overriding the config file and always allowing the administrator to tweak the behavior or turn it on or off. Note also that the code asserts the presence of an HTTP base address. The assertion uses the LINQ Any( ) query on an inline lambda predicate that checks whether the base addresses collection contains an HTTP base address.

The Metadata Exchange Endpoint

Publishing metadata over HTTP-GET is merely a WCF feature; there are no guarantees that other platforms you interact with will support it. There is, however, a standard way for publishing metadata over a special endpoint called the *metadata exchange endpoint* (sometimes referred to as the *MEX endpoint*). Figure 1-7 shows a service with business endpoints and a metadata exchange endpoint. However, you typically do not show the metadata exchange endpoint in your design diagrams.

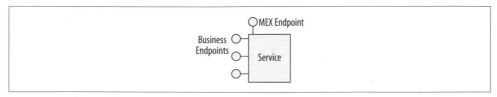

Figure 1-7. The metadata exchange endpoint

The MEX endpoint supports an industry standard for exchanging metadata, represented in WCF by the IMetadataExchange interface:

```
[ServiceContract(...)]
public interface IMetadataExchange
{
   [OperationContract(...)]
   Message Get(Message request);
   //More members
}
```

The details of this interface are inconsequential. Like most of these industry standards, it is difficult to implement, but fortunately WCF can have the service host automatically provide the implementation of IMetadataExchange and expose the metadata exchange endpoint. All you need to do is designate the address and the binding to use, and add the service metadata behavior. For the bindings, WCF provides dedicated binding transport elements for the HTTP, HTTPS, TCP, and IPC protocols. For the address, you can provide a full address or use any of the registered base addresses. There is no need to enable the HTTP-GET option, but there is no harm in doing so. Example 1-12 shows a service that exposes three MEX endpoints, over HTTP, TCP, and IPC. For demonstration purposes, the TCP and IPC MEX endpoints use relative addresses and the HTTP endpoint uses an absolute address.

Example 1-12. Adding MEX endpoints

```
<services>
   <service name = "MyService" behaviorConfiguration = "MEX">
      <host>
         <baseAddresses>
            <add baseAddress = "net.tcp://localhost:8001/"/>
            <add baseAddress = "net.pipe://localhost/"/>
         </baseAddresses>
```

Example 1-12. Adding MEX endpoints (continued)

```
        </host>
        <endpoint
            address  = "MEX"
            binding  = "mexTcpBinding"
            contract = "IMetadataExchange"
        />
        <endpoint
            address  = "MEX"
            binding  = "mexNamedPipeBinding"
            contract = "IMetadataExchange"
        />
        <endpoint
            address  = "http://localhost:8000/MEX"
            binding  = "mexHttpBinding"
            contract = "IMetadataExchange"
        />
    </service>
</services>
<behaviors>
    <serviceBehaviors>
        <behavior name = "MEX">
            <serviceMetadata/>
        </behavior>
    </serviceBehaviors>
</behaviors>
```

Note in Example 1-12 that all you have to do to have the host implement the MEX endpoint for your service is include the serviceMetadata tag in the behavior. If you do not reference the behavior, the host will expect your service to implement IMetadataExchange. While this normally adds no value, it is the only way to provide for custom implementation of IMetadataExchange for advanced interoperability needs.

Adding MEX endpoints programmatically

Like any other endpoint, you can only add a metadata exchange endpoint programmatically before opening the host. WCF does not offer a dedicated binding type for the metadata exchange endpoint. Instead, you need to construct a custom binding that uses the matching transport binding element, and then provide that binding element as a construction parameter to an instance of a custom binding. Finally, call the AddServiceEndpoint( ) method of the host, providing it with the address, the custom binding, and the IMetadataExchange contract type. Example 1-13 shows the code required to add a MEX endpoint over TCP. Note that before adding the endpoint you must verify the presence of the metadata behavior.

Example 1-13. Adding a TCP MEX endpoint programmatically

```
BindingElement bindingElement = new TcpTransportBindingElement();
CustomBinding binding = new CustomBinding(bindingElement);

Uri tcpBaseAddress = new Uri("net.tcp://localhost:9000/");
ServiceHost host = new ServiceHost(typeof(MyService),tcpBaseAddress);

ServiceMetadataBehavior metadataBehavior;
metadataBehavior = host.Description.Behaviors.Find<ServiceMetadataBehavior>();
if(metadataBehavior == null)
{
   metadataBehavior = new ServiceMetadataBehavior();
   host.Description.Behaviors.Add(metadataBehavior);
}
host.AddServiceEndpoint(typeof(IMetadataExchange),binding,"MEX");
host.Open();
```

Streamlining with ServiceHost<T>

You can extend ServiceHost<T> to automate the code in Examples 1-11 and 1-13. ServiceHost<T> offers overloaded versions of the EnableMetadataExchange() method, which you can call to both publish metadata over HTTP-GET and add the MEX endpoints:

```
public class ServiceHost<T> : ServiceHost
{
   public bool EnableMetadataExchange();
   public bool EnableMetadataExchange(bool enableHttpGet);

   public bool HasMexEndpoint
   {get;}
   public void AddAllMexEndPoints();
   //More members
}
```

The parameter-less EnableMetadataExchange() publishes metadata over HTTP-GET, and if no MEX endpoint is available, EnableMetadataExchange() adds a MEX endpoint for each registered base address scheme. Using ServiceHost<T>, Examples 1-11 and 1-13 are reduced to:

```
ServiceHost<MyService> host = new ServiceHost<MyService>();
host.EnableMetadataExchange();
host.Open();
```

EnableMetadataExchange() will not override the behavior in the config file if one is present.

EnableMetadataExchange() can also accept a parameter controlling publishing over HTTP-GET (that is, MEX endpoints only).

ServiceHost<T> offers the HasMexEndpoint Boolean property, which returns true if the service has any MEX endpoint (regardless of transport protocol), and the AddAllMexEndPoints( ) method, which adds a MEX endpoint for each registered base address of the scheme type of HTTP, TCP, or IPC. Example 1-14 shows the implementation of these methods.

Example 1-14. Implementing EnableMetadataExchange and its supporting methods

```
public class ServiceHost<T> : ServiceHost
{
   public void EnableMetadataExchange( )
   {
      EnableMetadataExchange(true);
   }
   public void EnableMetadataExchange(bool enableHttpGet)
   {
      if(State == CommunicationState.Opened)
      {
         throw new InvalidOperationException("Host is already opened");
      }
      ServiceMetadataBehavior metadataBehavior
                     = Description.Behaviors.Find<ServiceMetadataBehavior>( );

      if(metadataBehavior == null)
      {
         metadataBehavior = new ServiceMetadataBehavior( );
         Description.Behaviors.Add(metadataBehavior);

         if(BaseAddresses.Any((uri)=>uri.Scheme == "http"))
         {
            metadataBehavior.HttpGetEnabled = enableHttpGet;
         }
      }
      AddAllMexEndPoints( );
   }
   public bool HasMexEndpoint
   {
      get
      {
         return Description.Endpoints.Any(
                              endpoint=>endpoint.Contract.ContractType ==
                              typeof(IMetadataExchange));
      }
   }
   public void AddAllMexEndPoints( )
   {
      Debug.Assert(HasMexEndpoint == false);

      foreach(Uri baseAddress in BaseAddresses)
      {
         BindingElement bindingElement = null;
```

```
        switch(baseAddress.Scheme)
        {
           case "net.tcp":
           {
              bindingElement = new TcpTransportBindingElement( );
              break;
           }
           case "net.pipe":
           {...}
           case "http":
           {...}
           case "https":
           {...}
        }
        if(bindingElement != null)
        {
           Binding binding = new CustomBinding(bindingElement);
           AddServiceEndpoint(typeof(IMetadataExchange),binding,"MEX");
        }
     }
  }
}
```

EnableMetadataExchange( ) verifies that the host has not been opened yet using the State property of the CommunicationObject base class. The HasMexEndpoint property uses the LINQ Any( ) query on an inline lambda predicate that checks whether a given endpoint's contract is indeed IMetadataExchange. Any( ) invokes the predicate on each endpoint in the collection, returning true if any one of the endpoints in the collection satisfies the predicate (that is, if the invocation of the lambda expression method returned true), and false otherwise. The AddAllMexEndPoints( ) method iterates over the BaseAddresses collection. For each base address found, it creates a matching MEX transport-binding element, creates a custom binding, and uses that (as in Example 1-13) to add the endpoint.

The Metadata Explorer

The metadata exchange endpoint provides metadata that describes not just contracts and operations, but also information about data contracts, security, transactions, reliability, and faults. To visualize the metadata of a running service, I developed the Metadata Explorer tool, which is available along with the rest of the source code of this book. Figure 1-8 shows the Metadata Explorer reflecting the endpoints of Example 1-7. To use the Metadata Explorer, simply provide it with the HTTP-GET address or the metadata exchange endpoint of the running service, and it will reflect the returned metadata.

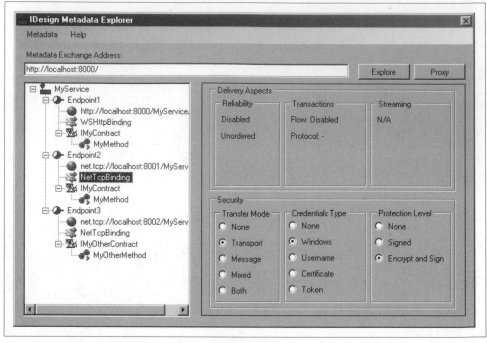

Figure 1-8. The Metadata Explorer

Client-Side Programming

To invoke operations on a service, a client first needs to import the service contract to the client's native representation. If the client uses WCF, the common way of invoking operations is to use a proxy. The proxy is a CLR class that exposes a single CLR interface representing the service contract. Note that if the service supports several contracts (over at least as many endpoints), the client needs one proxy per contract type. The proxy provides the same operations as the service's contract, but also has additional methods for managing the proxy lifecycle and the connection to the service. The proxy completely encapsulates every aspect of the service: its location, its implementation technology and runtime platform, and the communication transport.

Generating the Proxy

You can use Visual Studio 2008 to import the service metadata and generate a proxy. If the service is self-hosted outside the solution, first launch the service and then select Add Service Reference from the client project's context menu. If the service is self-hosted in the same solution, first launch it without the debugger, and then select the Add Service Reference option from the context menu.

The WCF-Provided Host

Visual Studio 2008 ships with a ready-made, general-purpose service host. The executable is called *WcfSvcHost.exe*, and after a normal installation it is found under *C:\ Program Files\Microsoft Visual Studio 9.0\Common7\IDE*. For ease of use, I recommend adding that location to your system's Path variable. WcfSvcHost is a simple command-line utility that accepts two parameters: the filename (and path) reference to a .NET assembly containing the service class or classes, and a filename (and path) reference to the host config file. For example:

```
WcfSvcHost.exe /service:MyService.dll  /config:App.config
```

The specified service assembly can be a class library assembly (DLL) or an application assembly (EXE). WcfSvcHost launches a new process that automatically hosts all the service classes listed in the services section of the specified config file. Note that these service classes and their service contracts and data contracts need not be public types—they can be internal. In addition, the autohosted services need not provide any metadata, but they can publish metadata if they choose to.

WcfSvcHost is a Windows Forms application that resides as a desktop tray icon. If you click on the WcfSvcHost tray icon, it will bring up a dialog listing all the hosted services. The dialog also shows the status of the service and its metadata address, which you can copy to the clipboard (perhaps for use later, when adding a reference to the service). Closing the WcfSvcHost UI merely collapses it back to the tray. To close the host, simply select Exit from the tray icon's context menu. Terminating the host this way is an ungraceful exit; WcfSvcHost will abort all calls currently in progress, and the clients are likely to receive an exception.

WcfSvcHost is designed to negate the need during development for a separate host assembly accompanying your service library. Developing such host projects is a repetitive task, as these hosts typically contain the same lines of code over and over again, and they tend to bloat the solution when you have multiple service libraries. For development and testing purposes, you can integrate WcfSvcHost directly into your Visual Studio 2008 service library projects. In the Debug pane of the project properties, specify *WcfSvcHost.exe* as the external program to start and your class library name and its config file (the one autogenerated and autocopied to the *bin* folder) as arguments.

With that done, when you launch the class library it will automatically be hosted by WcfSvcHost, with the debugger attached to that process. When you stop debugging, Visual Studio 2008 will abort the host ungracefully.

The last feature of WcfSvcHost is its ability to automatically launch a client application and even provide the client with optional parameters specific for that application:

```
WcfSvcHost.exe /service:MyService.dll  /config:App.config
               /client:MyClient.exe    /clientArgs:123,ABC
```

This is useful in automated testing and even simple deployment scenarios to launch both the host and the client.

—continued—

The main advantage of using WcfSvcHost is that during development, you will not need to develop, build, and own a separate host project. Its major drawback is that it is only suitable for simple scenarios, where you do not require programmatic access to the host instance before opening it or programmatic access to its event model once it's been opened. Unlike when hosting with IIS 5/6 or WAS, there is no equivalent service host factory support. Consequently, there is no ability to dynamically add base addresses, configure endpoints, throttle the calls, configure custom behaviors at the host level, and so on. My experience with WCF is that in all but the simplest cases, eventually you will need programmatic access to the host instance. Thus, I do not view WcfSvcHost as a full-fledged production-worthy host, like WAS or a dedicated self host.

If the service is hosted in IIS 5/6 or WAS, there is no need to prelaunch the service; simply select Add Service Reference from the client project's context menu, and Visual Studio will bring up the Add Service Reference dialog, shown in Figure 1-9.

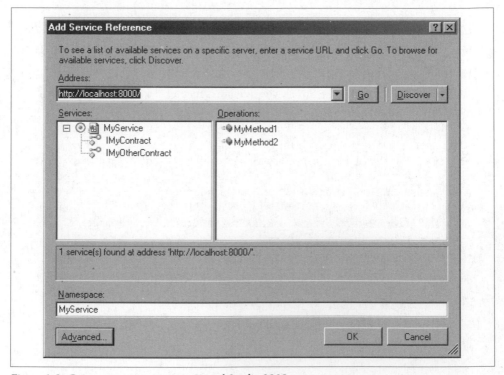

Figure 1-9. Generating a proxy using Visual Studio 2008

  In order for the Add Service Reference option to appear in a project's context menu, the project must be configured to target .NET Framework 3.0 or later.

In the Add Service Reference dialog, specify the service metadata address (not the service URL, as the dialog states) and click Go to view the available service endpoints (not "Services" as labeled). Specify a namespace (such as MyService) to contain the generated proxy, then click OK to generate the proxy and update the config file. The Discover button lets you discover WCF services in your own solution, as long as they are hosted either in a website project or in one of the WCF service library project types. In the case of a website project, Visual Studio 2008 will either retrieve the metadata from IIS or launch the ASP.NET filesystem-based development server. In the case of a WCF service library, WCF will automatically launch its host (WcfSvcHost, described in the sidebar "The WCF-Provided Host") to get the metadata.

The Advanced button brings up the settings dialog, where you can tweak the proxy generation options (see Figure 1-10).

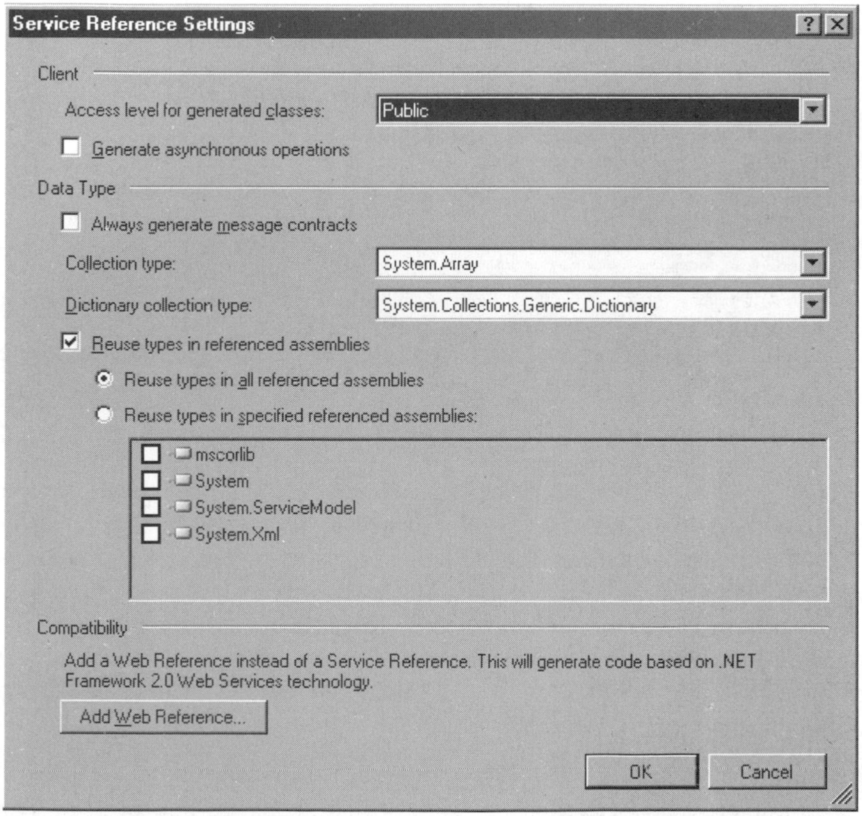

Figure 1-10. Advanced options for the service reference

The more intuitive options let you configure the visibility of the generated proxy and contracts (public or internal), and you can generate message contracts for your data types for advanced interoperability scenarios, where you have to comply with an existing (typically custom) message format. You can also click the Add Web Reference button to convert the reference to an old ASMX web service reference, as long as the service is using the basic binding.

Once you've added a reference, your project will have a new folder called *Service References*. In it, you'll find a service reference item for each referenced service (see Figure 1-11).

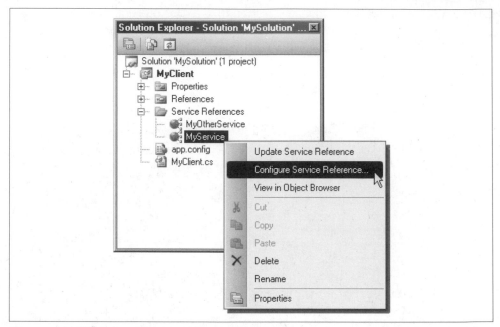

Figure 1-11. The Service References folder

At any point, you can right-click on a reference and select Update Service Reference to regenerate the proxy. This is possible because each service reference item also contains a file that records the original metadata address used. You can also select Configure Service Reference to bring up a dialog similar to the advanced settings dialog used when adding a reference. The Configure Service Reference dialog lets you change the service metadata address, as well as the rest of the advanced proxy settings.

Generating the proxy using SvcUtil

As an alternative to Visual Studio 2008, you can use the *SvcUtil.exe* command-line utility to import the service metadata and generate a proxy. You need to provide SvcUtil with the metadata exchange address and, optionally, with a proxy filename. The default proxy filename is *output.cs*, but you can use the /out switch to indicate a different name.

For example, if you're hosting the service MyService in IIS 5/6 or WAS and have enabled metadata publishing over HTTP-GET, you can simply run this command line:

```
SvcUtil http://localhost/MyService/MyService.svc /out:Proxy.cs
```

With self-hosting, suppose that the self-hosted service has enabled metadata publishing over HTTP-GET on this base address:

```
http://localhost:8000/
```

and has exposed MEX endpoints using these addresses:

```
http://localhost:8000/MEX
http://localhost:8001/MEX
net.tcp://localhost:8002/MEX
net.pipe://localhost/MyPipe/MEX
```

After launching the host, you'll be able to use the following commands to generate the proxy:

```
SvcUtil http://localhost:8000          /out:Proxy.cs
SvcUtil http://localhost:8000/MEX      /out:Proxy.cs
SvcUtil http://localhost:8001/MEX      /out:Proxy.cs
SvcUtil net.tcp://localhost:8002/MEX   /out:Proxy.cs
SvcUtil net.pipe://localhost/MyPipe/MEX /out:Proxy.cs
```

 The main advantage of using SvcUtil over Visual Studio 2008 is that you can include the command line for generating the proxy as a pre-build event.

SvcUtil offers numerous command-line switches that correspond to the options in the Visual Studio advanced settings dialog shown in Figure 1-10.

Regardless of whether you use Visual Studio 2008 or SvcUtil to generate the proxy, Example 1-15 shows the imported contract and generated proxy for this service definition:

```
[ServiceContract(Namespace = "MyNamespace")]
interface IMyContract
{
   [OperationContract]
   void MyMethod( );
}
class MyService : IMyContract
{
   public void MyMethod( )
   {...}
}
```

You can safely remove many of the gunk attributes the tools generate, which merely state the defaults, so that you end up with the cleaned-up proxy shown in Example 1-15.

Example 1-15. Client proxy file

```
[ServiceContract(Namespace = "MyNamespace")]
interface IMyContract
{
   [OperationContract]
   void MyMethod( );
}

partial class MyContractClient : ClientBase<IMyContract>,IMyContract
{
   public MyContractClient( )
   {}
   public MyContractClient(string endpointName) : base(endpointName)
   {}
   public MyContractClient(Binding binding,EndpointAddress remoteAddress) :
                                          base(binding,remoteAddress)

   {}

   /* Additional constructors */

   public void MyMethod( )
   {
      Channel.MyMethod( );
   }
}
```

The most glaring aspect of the proxy class is that it has no reference to the service-implementing class, only to the contract exposed by the service. You can use the proxy in conjunction with a client-side config file that provides the address and the binding, or you can use it without a config file. Note that each proxy instance points at exactly one endpoint. The endpoint to interact with is provided to the proxy at construction time. As I mentioned previously, if the service-side contract does not provide a namespace, it will default to the http://tempuri.org namespace.

Administrative Client Configuration

The client needs to know where the service is located, use the same binding as the service, and, of course, import the service contract definition. In essence, this is exactly the same information captured in the service's endpoint. To reflect that, the client config file can contain information about the target endpoints and even uses the same endpoint configuration schema as the host.

Example 1-16 shows the client configuration file required to interact with a service whose host is configured according to Example 1-6.

Example 1-16. Client config file

```
<system.serviceModel>
   <client>
      <endpoint name = "MyEndpoint"
```

Example 1-16. Client config file (continued)

```
        address  = "http://localhost:8000/MyService"
        binding  = "wsHttpBinding"
        contract = "IMyContract"
    />
  </client>
</system.serviceModel>
```

The client config file may list as many endpoints as the services it deals with support, and the client may use any one of them. Example 1-17 shows the client config file matching the host config file of Example 1-7. There is no relationship between the various endpoints in the client's config file: they could all be pointing at the same endpoint on the service, at different endpoints on the service, at different endpoints on different services, or any mix and match in between. Note also that on the client side you typically name endpoints with unique names (you will see why shortly). Naming the endpoints on the client side is optional, just as it is optional on the service side, yet on the service side you typically do not name the endpoints, while on the client side you typically do.

Example 1-17. Client config file with multiple target endpoints

```
<system.serviceModel>
  <client>
    <endpoint name = "FirstEndpoint"
        address  = "http://localhost:8000/MyService"
        binding  = "wsHttpBinding"
        contract = "IMyContract"
    />
    <endpoint name = "SecondEndpoint"
        address  = "net.tcp://localhost:8001/MyService"
        binding  = "netTcpBinding"
        contract = "IMyContract"
    />
    <endpoint name = "ThirdEndpoint"
        address  = "net.tcp://localhost:8002/MyService"
        binding  = "netTcpBinding"
        contract = "IMyOtherContract"
    />
  </client>
</system.serviceModel>
```

Binding configuration

You can customize the client-side bindings to match the service binding in a manner identical to the service configuration, as shown in Example 1-18.

Example 1-18. Client-side binding configuration

```
<system.serviceModel>
  <client>
    <endpoint name = "MyEndpoint"
```

Example 1-18. Client-side binding configuration (continued)

```
         address  = "net.tcp://localhost:8000/MyService"
         bindingConfiguration = "TransactionalTCP"
         binding  = "netTcpBinding"
         contract = "IMyContract"
      />
   </client>
   <bindings>
      <netTcpBinding>
         <binding name = "TransactionalTCP"
            transactionFlow = "true"
         />
      </netTcpBinding>
   </bindings>
</system.serviceModel>
```

Generating the client config file

When you add a service reference in Visual Studio 2008, it will also try to automatically edit the client's config file and insert in it the required client section describing the service's endpoints. However, in most cases Visual Studio 2008 is not smart enough to infer the cleanest binding values, and it will therefore butcher the config file by stating all the default values for the bindings, which effectively renders the file unreadable. (This issue will be addressed in a future release of Visual Studio.) Visual Studio 2008 similarly butchers the config file when updating a service reference. If you care about maintaining the client's config file, before adding (or updating) a reference you should open the file, add (or update) the reference, and then perform a single Undo (Ctrl-Z) and manually add the config file entries in the client section.

Like Visual Studio 2008, SvcUtil also autogenerates a client-side config file called *output.config*. You can specify a different config filename using the /config switch:

```
SvcUtil http://localhost:8002/MyService/  /out:Proxy.cs /config:App.Config
```

The config files SvcUtil produces are also unreadable, as it's no better at inferring binding values. However, unlike with Visual Studio, with SvcUtil you can suppress generating the config file by using the /noconfig switch:

```
SvcUtil http://localhost:8002/MyService/  /out:Proxy.cs /noconfig
```

I recommend never letting SvcUtil or Visual Studio 2008 control the config file.

In-proc configuration

With in-proc hosting the client config file is also the service host config file, and the same file contains both service and client entries, as shown in Example 1-19.

Example 1-19. In-proc hosting config file

```
<system.serviceModel>
   <services>
      <service name = "MyService">
```

Example 1-19. In-proc hosting config file (continued)

```
      <endpoint
         address = "net.pipe://localhost/MyPipe"
         binding = "netNamedPipeBinding"
         contract = "IMyContract"
      />
   </service>
 </services>
 <client>
   <endpoint name = "MyEndpoint"
      address = "net.pipe://localhost/MyPipe"
      binding = "netNamedPipeBinding"
      contract = "IMyContract"
   />
 </client>
</system.serviceModel>
```

Note the use of the named pipe binding for in-proc hosting.

The SvcConfigEditor

WCF provides a config file editor called *SvcConfigEditor.exe* that can edit both host and client configuration files (see Figure 1-12). You can launch the editor from within Visual Studio by right-clicking on the configuration file (for either the client or the host) and selecting Edit WCF Configuration.

> Due to a bug in Visual Studio 2008, you may have to launch the editor first from the Tools menu.

I have mixed feelings about SvcConfigEditor. On the one hand, it edits the config files nicely, and it saves developers the need to learn the configuration schema. But on the other hand, it does not shield developers from needing to thoroughly understand WCF configuration, and it's often faster to do the light editing that's typically required in a config file by hand than it is using Visual Studio 2008.

Working with the proxy

The proxy class derives from the class ClientBase<T>, defined as:

```
public abstract class ClientBase<T> : ICommunicationObject,IDisposable
{
   protected ClientBase(string endpointName);
   protected ClientBase(Binding binding,EndpointAddress remoteAddress);
   public void Open();
   public void Close();
   protected T Channel
   {get;}
   //Additional members
}
```

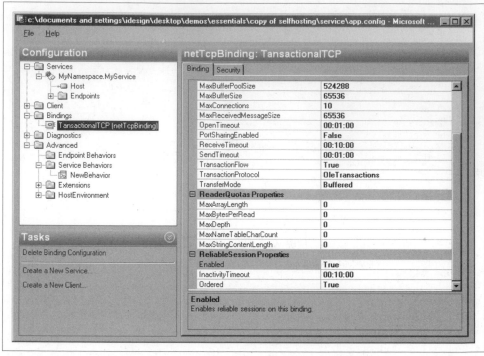

Figure 1-12. SvcConfigEditor is used to edit both host and client config files

ClientBase<T> accepts a single generic type parameter identifying the service contract that this proxy encapsulates. The Channel property of ClientBase<T> is of that type parameter. As shown in Example 1-15, the generated subclass of ClientBase<T> simply delegates the method call to Channel. Calling the method on the Channel property sends the appropriate WCF message to the service.

To use the proxy, the client first needs to instantiate a proxy object and to provide the constructor with endpoint information: either the endpoint section name from the config file, or the endpoint address and binding objects if you're not using a config file. The client can then use the proxy methods to call the service, and when it is done, the client needs to close the proxy instance. For example, given the same definitions as in Examples 1-15 and 1-16, the client constructs the proxy, identifying the endpoint to use from the config file, and then invokes the method and closes the proxy:

```
MyContractClient proxy = new MyContractClient("MyEndpoint");
proxy.MyMethod();
proxy.Close();
```

When specifying the endpoint name to the proxy, its constructor also verifies that the contract configured for that endpoint matches the proxy's type parameter. Because of this verification ability, if exactly one endpoint is defined in the client config file for the type of contract the proxy is using, the client can omit the endpoint name from the proxy's constructor:

```
MyContractClient proxy = new MyContractClient();
proxy.MyMethod();
proxy.Close();
```

The proxy will simply look up that endpoint (named or not in the config file) and use it. However, if you use this technique when multiple (or zero) endpoints are available for the same contract type, the proxy will throw an exception.

Closing the proxy

It is a recommended best practice to always close the proxy when the client is done using it. Closing the proxy releases the connection held toward the service, which is particularly important to do in the presence of a transport session (as discussed later in this chapter). It also helps ensure that the threshold for the maximum number of connections on the client's machine is not reached. Furthermore, as you will see in Chapter 4, closing the proxy terminates the session with the service instance.

Instead of closing the proxy, you can use its Dispose( ) method. Internally, Dispose( ) just calls Close( ). The advantage of the Dispose( ) method is that you can use the using statement to call it even in the face of exceptions:

```
using(MyContractClient proxy = new MyContractClient())
{
    //Any exception here automatically closes the proxy;
}
```

If the client is declaring the contract directly instead of the concrete proxy class, the client can either query for the presence of IDisposable:

```
IMyContract proxy = new MyContractClient();
proxy.MyMethod();
IDisposable disposable = proxy as IDisposable;
if(disposable != null)
{
    disposable.Dispose();
}
```

or collapse the query inside the using statement:

```
IMyContract proxy = new MyContractClient();
using(proxy as IDisposable)
{
    proxy.MyMethod();
}
```

Call timeout

Each call made by a WCF client must complete within a configurable timeout. If for whatever reason the call duration exceeds the timeout, the call is aborted and the client gets a TimeoutException. This behavior is very handy, since it offers an elegant way to deal with deadlocks on the service side or just poor availability. In traditional .NET, the client would have to spin a worker thread and have the worker thread call the class (and potentially hang), and the client would then monitor some timed-out event that the worker thread would have to signal when done. This is obviously a complicated programming model. The advantage of using a proxy for every call is that the proxy can do all this for you. The exact value of the timeout is a property of the binding, and the default timeout is one minute. To provide a different timeout, set the SendTimeout property of the abstract Binding base class:

```
public abstract class Binding : ...
{
    public TimeSpan SendTimeout
    {get;set;}
    //More members
}
```

For example, here's how to configure the WSHttpBinding with a five-minute call timeout:

```
<client>
    <endpoint
        ...
        binding = "wsHttpBinding"
        bindingConfiguration = "LongTimeout"
        ...
    />
</client>
<bindings>
    <wsHttpBinding>
        <binding name = "LongTimeout" sendTimeout = "00:05:00"/>
    </wsHttpBinding>
</bindings>
```

Programmatic Client Configuration

Instead of relying on a config file, the client can programmatically construct address and binding objects matching the service endpoint and provide them to the proxy constructor. There is no need to provide the contract, since that was provided in the form of the generic type parameter of the proxy. To represent the address, the client needs to instantiate an EndpointAddress class, defined as:

```
public class EndpointAddress
{
    public EndpointAddress(string uri);
    //More members
}
```

Example 1-20 demonstrates this technique, showing the code equivalent of Example 1-16 targeting the service in Example 1-9.

Example 1-20. Programmatic client configuration

```
Binding wsBinding = new WSHttpBinding( );
EndpointAddress endpointAddress = new EndpointAddress("http://localhost:8000/MyService");

MyContractClient proxy = new MyContractClient(wsBinding,endpointAddress);
```

Example 1-20. Programmatic client configuration (continued)

```
proxy.MyMethod( );
proxy.Close( );
```

Similar to using a binding section in a config file, the client can programmatically configure the binding properties:

```
WSHttpBinding wsBinding = new WSHttpBinding( );
wsBinding.SendTimeout = TimeSpan.FromMinutes(5);
wsBinding.TransactionFlow = true;

EndpointAddress endpointAddress =
        new EndpointAddress("http://localhost:8000/MyService");

MyContractClient proxy = new MyContractClient(wsBinding,endpointAddress);
proxy.MyMethod( );
proxy.Close( );
```

Again, note the use of the concrete subclass of Binding in order to access binding-specific properties such as the transaction flow.

The WCF-Provided Test Client

Visual Studio 2008 ships with a simple general-purpose test client for rudimentary testing that you can use to invoke operations on most services. The test client is called *WcfTestClient.exe*, and after a normal installation it is found under *C:\Program Files\Microsoft Visual Studio 9.0\Common7\IDE*. You can provide WcfTestClient with a single command-line argument containing the metadata address of the service to test:

```
WcfTestClient.exe http://localhost:9000/
```

You can specify any metadata address (be it an HTTP-GET address, or a metadata exchange endpoint over HTTP, TCP, or IPC). You can also specify multiple metadata addresses:

```
WcfTestClient.exe http://localhost:8000/ net.tcp://localhost:9000/MEX
```

You can also launch the test client without a command-line parameter. Once it's running, you can add a new service by selecting Add Service from the File menu and then specify the metadata address in the Add Service dialog. You can also remove a service by right-clicking on it in the services tree.

WcfTestClient is a Windows Forms 3.5 application. The tree control in the left pane contains the tested services and their endpoints. You can drill into an endpoint's contract and select an operation to display a dedicated tab for that invocation in the pane on the right. For example, for this simple contract and implementation:

```
[ServiceContract]
interface IMyContract
{
    [OperationContract]
```

```
      string MyMethod(int someNumber,string someText);
   }
   class MyService : IMyContract
   {
      public string MyMethod(int someNumber,string someText)
      {
         return "Hello";
      }
   }
```

the method tab will let you provide an integer and a string as operation parameters in the Request section, as shown in Figure 1-13.

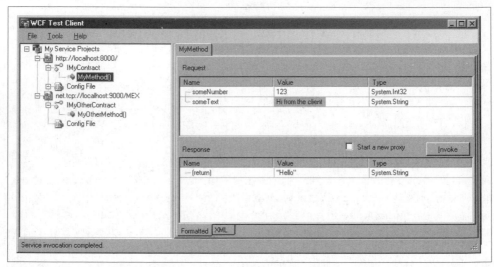

Figure 1-13. Using WcfTestClient

When you click the Invoke button, WcfTestClient will dispatch the call to the service and display the returned value or out-parameters in the Response section. In case of an exception, WcfTestClient will display the exception information in a message box and allow you to issue additional calls. All calls are made on new proxy instances. In addition, all calls are made asynchronously, so that the UI is kept responsive. However, while the calls are asynchronous, WcfTestClient will let you dispatch only one call at a time.

The way WcfTestClient functions is by silently creating an assembly from a proxy file, complete with a config file, and then loading it for use from a temporary location. If you click on the Config File item in the tree on the left, you can actually grab that config file (the same config file generated when adding a service reference) and display the config file in its own tab. You can even edit the config file using SvcConfigEditor.

WcfTestClient allows you to invoke operations with enumerations, composite parameters such as classes or structures (each of which is a composite of other classes or structures), and even collections and arrays of parameters. Simply expand the items in the Request section, set their values from the drop-down lists (e.g., enum values), and invoke the call. If the operation accepts a collection or an array, you will also need to set the length. Again, the Response pane will contain any composite returned value or out-parameters.

As with WcfSvcHost (see the earlier sidebar "The WCF-Provided Host"), you can integrate WcfTestClient directly into your Visual Studio 2008 solution. First, add a class library project to the solution, and delete from it all references, folders, and source files, since you have no need for those. Next, set *WcfTestClient.exe* as the external start program, and provide the metadata address (or addresses) of the tested service (or services). This may be the *.svc* address of an IIS 5/6- or WAS-hosted project, or, for that matter, any other metadata address of a host project, whether inside or outside your solution.

Of course, you can combine the use of WcfTestClient and WcfSvcHost in a single step to automatically host a service in a service library and test it:

```
WcfSvcHost.exe /service:MyService.dll    /config:App.config
               /client:WcfTestClient.exe /clientArgs:http://localhost:9000/
```

However, with WcfSvcHost, specifying the metadata arguments is optional. By default, WcfSvcHost will pipe into the specified client application any metadata addresses it finds in the service config file. You should specify a service's metadata address explicitly only if the service (or services) does not provide its own metadata, or if you would like the test client to use different addresses. If the service config file contains multiple metadata endpoints for a given service, they will be provided in this precedence order: HTTP, TCP, IPC, HTTP-GET.

You can incorporate these steps into Visual Studio 2008 for a seamless hosting and testing experience. To do this, specify *WcfSvcHost.exe* as the startup program along with the config file, and specify *WcfTestClient.exe* as the client. When you invoke WcfTestClient using /client, closing the test client also terminates the host.

Programmatic Versus Administrative Configuration

The two techniques shown so far for configuring both the client and the service complement each other. Administrative configuration gives you the option to change major aspects of the service and the client post-deployment, without the need to rebuild or redeploy. The major downside of administrative configuration is that it is not type-safe, and configuration errors will be discovered only at runtime.

Programmatic configuration is useful when the configuration decision is either completely dynamic—i.e., when it is taken at runtime based on the current input or conditions—or is static and never changes, in which case you might as well hardcode it. For example, if you are interested in hosting in-proc calls only, you can hardcode the use of the NetNamedPipeBinding and its configuration. However, by and large, most clients and services resort to using a config file.

WCF Architecture

So far in this chapter, I've covered all that is required to set up and consume simple WCF services. However, as you'll see in the rest of the book, WCF offers immensely valuable support for reliability, transactions, concurrency management, security, and instance activation, all of which rely on the WCF interception-based architecture. Having the client interact with a proxy means that WCF is always present between the service and the client, intercepting the call and performing pre- and post-call processing. The interception starts when the proxy serializes the call stack frame to a message and sends the message down a chain of *channels*. The channel is merely an interceptor, whose purpose is to perform a specific task. Each client-side channel does pre-call processing of the message. The exact structure and composition of the chain depends mostly on the binding. For example, one of the channels may be responsible for encoding the message (binary, text, or MTOM), another for passing the security call context, another for propagating the client transaction, another for managing the reliable session, another for encrypting the message body (if so configured), and so on. The last channel on the client side is the transport channel, which sends the message over the configured transport to the host.

On the host side the message goes through another chain of channels, which perform host-side pre-call processing of the message. The first channel on the host side is the transport channel, which receives the message from the transport. Subsequent channels perform various tasks, such as decryption of the message body, decoding of the message, joining the propagated transaction, setting the security principal, managing the session, and activating the service instance. The last channel on the host side passes the message to the dispatcher. The dispatcher converts the message to a stack frame and calls the service instance. This sequence is depicted in Figure 1-14.

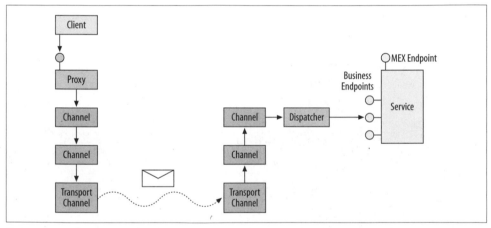

Figure 1-14. The WCF architecture

The service has no way of knowing that it was not called by a local client. In fact, it *was* called by a local client—the dispatcher. The interception both on the client and the service sides ensures that the client and the service get the runtime environments they require to operate properly.

The service instance executes the call and returns control to the dispatcher, which then converts the returned values and error information (if any) into a return message. The process is now reversed: the dispatcher passes the message through the host-side channels to perform post-call processing, such as managing the transaction, deactivating the instance, encoding the reply, encrypting it, and so on. The returned message then goes to the transport channel, which sends it to the client-side channels for client-side post-call processing. This process in turn consists of tasks such as decryption, decoding, committing or aborting the transaction, and so on.

The last channel passes the message to the proxy, which converts the returned message to a stack frame and returns control to the client.

Most noteworthy is that almost all the points in the architecture provide hooks for extensibility—you can provide custom channels for proprietary interaction, custom behaviors for instance management, custom security behavior, and so on. In fact, the standard facilities that WCF offers are all implemented using the same extensibility model. You will see many examples and uses of extensibility throughout this book.

Host Architecture

It is also important to explore how the transition is made from a technology-neutral, service-oriented interaction to CLR interfaces and classes. The bridging is done via the host. Each .NET host process can have many app domains, and each app domain can have zero or more service host instances. Each service host instance is dedicated to a particular service type. Thus, when you create a host instance, you are in effect registering that service host instance with all the endpoints for that type on the host machine that correspond to its base addresses. Each service host instance has zero or more *contexts*. The context is the innermost execution scope of the service instance. A context is associated with zero or one service instance, meaning it could also be empty (i.e., not associated with any service instance). This architecture is shown in Figure 1-15.

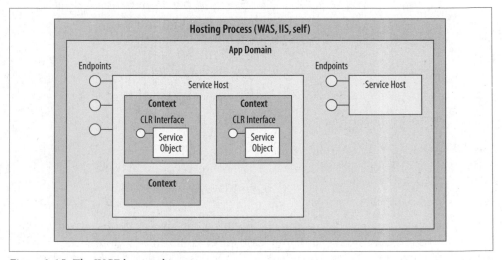

Figure 1-15. The WCF host architecture

 The WCF context is conceptually similar to the Enterprise Services context or the .NET context-bound object context.

It is the combined work of the service host and the context that exposes a native CLR type as a service. After the message is passed through the channels, the host maps that message to a new or existing context (and the object instance inside) and lets it process the call.

Working with Channels

You can use channels directly to invoke operations on a service, without ever resorting to using a proxy class. The ChannelFactory<T> class (and its supporting types), shown in Example 1-21, enables you to create a proxy on the fly.

Example 1-21. TheChannelFactory<T> class

```
public class ContractDescription
{
   public Type ContractType
   {get;set;}
   //More members
}

public class ServiceEndpoint
{
   public ServiceEndpoint(ContractDescription contract,Binding binding,
                          EndpointAddress address);
   public EndpointAddress Address
   {get;set;}
   public Binding Binding
   {get;set;}
   public ContractDescription Contract
   {get;}
   //More members
}

public abstract class ChannelFactory : ...
{
   public ServiceEndpoint Endpoint
   {get;}
   //More members
}
public class ChannelFactory<T> : ChannelFactory,...
{
   public ChannelFactory(ServiceEndpoint endpoint);
   public ChannelFactory(string configurationName);
   public ChannelFactory(Binding binding,EndpointAddress endpointAddress);
   public static T CreateChannel(Binding binding,EndpointAddress endpointAddress);
   public T CreateChannel();
   //More members
}
```

You need to provide the constructor of ChannelFactory<T> with the endpoint. This can be either the endpoint name from the client config file, or the binding and address objects, or a ServiceEndpoint object. Next, use the CreateChannel() method to obtain a reference to the proxy and use its methods. Finally, close the proxy by either casting it to IDisposable and calling the Dispose() method or casting it to ICommunicationObject and calling the Close() method:

```
ChannelFactory<IMyContract> factory = new ChannelFactory<IMyContract>();

IMyContract proxy1 = factory.CreateChannel();
using(proxy1 as IDisposable)
{
    proxy1.MyMethod();
}

IMyContract proxy2 = factory.CreateChannel();
proxy2.MyMethod();
ICommunicationObject channel = proxy2 as ICommunicationObject;
Debug.Assert(channel != null);
channel.Close();
```

You can also use the shorthand static CreateChannel() method to create a proxy given a binding and an address, without directly constructing an instance of ChannelFactory<T>:

```
Binding binding = new NetTcpBinding();
EndpointAddress address = new EndpointAddress("net.tcp://localhost:8000");

IMyContract proxy = ChannelFactory<IMyContract>.CreateChannel(binding,address);
using(proxy as IDisposable)
{
    proxy.MyMethod();
}
```

The InProcFactory Class

To demonstrate the power of ChannelFactory<T>, consider my static helper class InProcFactory, defined as:

```
public static class InProcFactory
{
    public static I CreateInstance<S,I>() where I : class
                                          where S : I;
    public static void CloseProxy<I>(I instance) where I : class;
    //More members
}
```

InProcFactory is designed to streamline and automate in-proc hosting. The CreateInstance() method takes two generic type parameters: the type of the service S and the type of the supported contract I. CreateInstance() constrains S to derive from I. Using InProcFactory is straightforward:

```
IMyContract proxy = InProcFactory.CreateInstance<MyService,IMyContract>( );

proxy.MyMethod( );

InProcFactory.CloseProxy(proxy);
```

It literally takes a service class and hoists it up as a WCF service. This is as close as you can get in WCF to the C# new operator, as these two lines are equivalent in their coupling to the service type:

```
IMyContract proxy = InProcFactory.CreateInstance<MyService,IMyContract>( );
IMyContract obj = new MyService( );
```

In the case of C#, the compiler verifies that the type supports the requested interface and then, in effect, casts the interface into the variable. In the absence of compiler support, InProcFactory requires the interface type so it will know which interface type to return.

Implementing InProcFactory<T>

All in-proc calls should use named pipes and should flow all transactions. You can use programmatic configuration to automate the configurations of both the client and the service, and use ChannelFactory<T> to avoid the need for a proxy. Example 1-22 shows the implementation of InProcFactory, with some of the code removed for brevity.

Example 1-22. The InProcFactory class

```
public static class InProcFactory
{
   struct HostRecord
   {
      public HostRecord(ServiceHost host,string address)
      {
         Host = host;
         Address = new EndpointAddress(address);
      }
      public readonly ServiceHost Host;
      public readonly EndpointAddress Address;
   }
   static readonly Uri BaseAddress = new Uri("net.pipe://localhost/" +
                                     Guid.NewGuid( ).ToString( ));
   static readonly Binding Binding;
   static Dictionary<Type,HostRecord> m_Hosts = new Dictionary<Type,HostRecord>( );

   static InProcFactory( )
   {
      NetNamedPipeBinding binding = new NetNamedPipeBinding( );
      binding.TransactionFlow = true;
      Binding = binding;
```

Example 1-22. The InProcFactory class (continued)

```csharp
        AppDomain.CurrentDomain.ProcessExit += delegate
                                              {
                                                 foreach(HostRecord hostRecord in
                                                         m_Hosts.Values)
                                                 {
                                                    hostRecord.Host.Close( );
                                                 }
                                              };
      }
   public static I CreateInstance<S,I>( ) where I : class
                                          where S : I
   {
      HostRecord hostRecord = GetHostRecord<S,I>( );
      return ChannelFactory<I>.CreateChannel(Binding,hostRecord.Address);
   }
   static HostRecord GetHostRecord<S,I>( ) where I : class
                                           where S : I
   {
      HostRecord hostRecord;
      if(m_Hosts.ContainsKey(typeof(S)))
      {
         hostRecord = m_Hosts[typeof(S)];
      }
      else
      {
         ServiceHost host = new ServiceHost(typeof(S),BaseAddress);
         string address = BaseAddress.ToString() + Guid.NewGuid( ).ToString( );
         hostRecord = new HostRecord(host,address);
         m_Hosts.Add(typeof(S),hostRecord);
         host.AddServiceEndpoint(typeof(I),Binding,address);
         host.Open( );
      }
      return hostRecord;
   }
   public static void CloseProxy<I>(I instance) where I : class
   {
      ICommunicationObject proxy = instance as ICommunicationObject;
      Debug.Assert(proxy != null);
      proxy.Close( );
   }
}
```

InProcFactory's static constructor is called once per app domain, allocating in each case a new unique base address using a GUID. This enables InProcFactory to be used multiple times on the same machine, across app domains and processes.

The main challenge facing InProcFactory is that CreateInstance( ) can be called to instantiate services of every type. For every service type, there should be a single matching host (an instance of ServiceHost). Allocating a host instance for each call is not a good idea. The problem is what CreateInstance( ) should do when it is asked to instantiate a second object of the same type, like so:

```
IMyContract proxy1 = InProcFactory.CreateInstance<MyService,IMyContract>();
IMyContract proxy2 = InProcFactory.CreateInstance<MyService,IMyContract>();
```

The solution is for InProcFactory to internally manage a dictionary that maps service types to a particular host instance. When CreateInstance() is called to create an instance of a particular type, it looks in the dictionary, using a helper method called GetHostRecord(). If the dictionary does not already contain the service type, this helper method creates a host instance for it. If it needs to create a host, GetHostRecord() programmatically adds an endpoint to that host, using a new GUID as the unique pipe name. CreateInstance() then grabs the address of the endpoint from the host record and uses ChannelFactory<T> to create the proxy. In its static constructor, which is called upon the first use of the class, InProcFactory subscribes to the process exit event, using an anonymous method to close all hosts when the process shuts down. Finally, to help the clients close the proxy, InProcFactory provides the CloseProxy() method, which queries the proxy to ICommunicationObject and closes it.

Transport-Level Sessions

In traditional programming, an object is indirectly associated with a client by virtue of the call stack. That is, each object is tied to a particular client. But in WCF, since the client sends a message to the service and never invokes the instance directly, such an association is not possible. The analogous concept in WCF is the *transport session*, which ensures that all messages coming from a particular client are sent to the same transport channel on the host. It is as if the client and the channel maintain a logical session at the transport level (hence the name). As in traditional programming, with a transport session the calls (or rather, the messages) are strictly processed in the order in which they were received. The transport session is unrelated to any application-level session the client may or may not have with the instance itself. Note that using a transport session is optional and is largely an aspect of the binding configuration, so the client and the service may or may not have a transport session. The transport session is one of the key fundamental concepts of WCF, affecting reliability, instance management, error management, synchronization, transactions, and security.

A transport session relies on WCF's ability to identify the client and correlate all its messages to a particular channel. Thus, there has to be something in the transport or in the message that identifies the client.

Transport Session and Binding

Both the TCP and the IPC bindings are connection-full. That is, all calls from the client come on the same connection or pipe, enabling WCF to easily identify the client.

However, HTTP is by definition a connectionless protocol, and every message from the client comes on a new connection. Consequently, when using the basic binding, there is never a transport session; or, more precisely, there is a transport session, but it lasts for only one call, and after the call returns the channel is destroyed along with the connection. The next call will come on a new connection and will be routed to a new channel. The WS binding can improve on this situation by emulating a transport session. If configured to do so, it will insert in each message a unique ID identifying the client and will keep sending this ID for every call from that client. You will see more about that ID in Chapter 4.

Transport Session Termination

Typically, the transport session will end once the client closes the proxy. However, in case the client terminates ungracefully or in case of a communication problem, each transport session also has an idle-time timeout that defaults to 10 minutes. The transport session will automatically terminate after 10 minutes of inactivity from the client, even if the client still intends to use the proxy. If the client tries to use its proxy after the transport session has been terminated due to the idle timeout, it will get a CommunicationObjectFaultedException. Both the client and the service can configure a different timeout by setting a different value in the binding. The bindings that support a transport-level session provide the ReliableSession property, which can be of the type ReliableSession or OptionalReliableSession. The ReliableSession class offers the InactivityTimeout property, which you can use to configure a new idle-time timeout:

```
public class ReliableSession
{
   public TimeSpan InactivityTimeout
   {get;set;}
   //More members
}
public class OptionalReliableSession : ReliableSession
{...}
public class NetTcpBinding : Binding,...
{
   public OptionalReliableSession ReliableSession
   {get;}
   //More members
}
public abstract class WSHttpBindingBase : ...
{
   public OptionalReliableSession ReliableSession
   {get;}
   //More members
}
public class WSHttpBinding : WSHttpBindingBase,...
{...}
```

```
public class WSDualHttpBinding : Binding,...
{
    public ReliableSession ReliableSession
    {get;}
    //More members
}
```

For example, here is the code required to programmatically configure an idle time-out of 25 minutes for the TCP binding:

```
NetTcpBinding tcpSessionBinding = new NetTcpBinding();
tcpSessionBinding.ReliableSession.InactivityTimeout = TimeSpan.FromMinutes(25);
```

Here is the equivalent configuration setting using a config file:

```
<netTcpBinding>
    <binding name = "TCPSession">
        <reliableSession inactivityTimeout = "00:25:00"/>
    </binding>
</netTcpBinding>
```

If both the client and the service configure a timeout, the shorter timeout prevails.

 There is another esoteric service-side configuration for session termination: the ServiceBehavior attribute offers an advanced option for managing session shutdown via the AutomaticSessionShutdown property. This property is intended for optimizing certain callback scenarios, and it can safely be ignored in most cases. In a nutshell, AutomaticSessionShutdown defaults to true so that when the client closes the proxy, the session is terminated. Setting it to false causes the session to continue until the service explicitly closes its sending channel. When this attribute is set to false, the client of a duplex session (discussed in Chapter 5) must manually close the output session on the duplex client channel; otherwise, the client will hang waiting for the session to terminate.

Reliability

WCF and other service-oriented technologies make a distinction between transport reliability and message reliability. *Transport reliability* (such as that offered by TCP/IP) offers point-to-point guaranteed delivery at the network packet level, and also guarantees in-order delivery of the packets. Transport reliability is not resilient to dropped network connections and a variety of other communication problems.

Message reliability, as the name implies, deals with reliability at the message level, independent of how many packets are required to deliver the message. Message reliability provides for end-to-end guaranteed delivery and order of messages, regardless of how many intermediaries are involved and how many network hops are required to deliver the message from the client to the service. Message reliability is based on an industry standard for reliable message-based communication that maintains a session at the transport level and supports retries in case of transport failures such as dropping a wireless connection. It automatically deals with congestion, message buffering, and flow control and can adjust the flow of messages accordingly. Message reliability also deals with connection management, verifying connections and cleaning them up when they are no longer needed.

 Message reliability does not guarantee message delivery. All it provides is a guarantee that if the message does not reach its destination, the sender will know about it.

Bindings, Reliability, and Ordered Messages

In WCF, reliability is controlled and configured in the binding. A particular binding can support or not support reliable messaging, and if it's supported, it can be enabled or disabled. Whether a binding supports reliability is driven by the target scenario for that particular binding. Table 1-2 summarizes the relationship between binding, reliability, and ordered delivery for the six commonly used bindings and lists the respective default values.

Table 1-2. Reliability and ordered delivery

Binding name	Supports reliability	Default reliability	Supports ordered delivery	Default ordered delivery
BasicHttpBinding	No	N/A	No	N/A
NetTcpBinding	Yes	Off	Yes	On
NetNamedPipeBinding	No	N/A (On)	Yes	N/A (On)
WSHttpBinding	Yes	Off	Yes	On
WSDualHttpBinding	Yes	On	Yes	On
NetMsmqBinding	No	N/A	No	N/A

Reliability is not supported by the BasicHttpBinding or the NetMsmqBinding: the BasicHttpBinding is oriented toward the legacy ASMX web services world, which does not support reliability, while the NetMsmqBinding is for disconnected calls and has its own notion of reliability (discussed in Chapter 9).

Reliability is always enabled in the WSDualHttpBinding, to keep the callback channel to the client alive even over HTTP.

Reliability is disabled by default but can be enabled in the NetTcpBinding and the WSHttpBinding. Finally, the NetNamedPipeBinding is considered inherently reliable because it always has exactly one hop from the client to the service.

Message reliability also provides ordered delivery assurance, allowing messages to be executed in the order in which they were sent, not the order in which they were delivered. In addition, it guarantees that each message is delivered exactly once.

WCF lets you enable reliability but not ordered delivery, in which case messages are instead executed in the order in which they were received. The default for all bindings that support reliability is that when reliability is enabled, ordered delivery is enabled as well. Ordered delivery requires reliability. Thus, if ordered delivery is turned on but reliability is turned off, the calls will be delivered unordered.

Configuring Reliability

You can configure reliability (and ordered delivery) both programmatically and administratively. When you enable reliability, you must do so on both the client and the service host sides, or the client will not be able to communicate with the service. You can only configure reliability for the bindings that support it. Example 1-23 shows a service-side config file that uses a binding configuration section to enable reliability when using the TCP binding.

Example 1-23. Enabling reliability with the TCP binding

```
<system.serviceModel>
   <services>
      <service name = "MyService">
         <endpoint
            address  = "net.tcp://localhost:8000/MyService"
            binding  = "netTcpBinding"
            bindingConfiguration = "ReliableTCP"
            contract = "IMyContract"
         />
      </service>
   </services>
   <bindings>
      <netTcpBinding>
         <binding name = "ReliableTCP">
            <reliableSession enabled = "true"/>
         </binding>
      </netTcpBinding>
   </bindings>
</system.serviceModel>
```

When it comes to programmatic configuration, the TCP and WS bindings both offer a construction parameter and a property for configuring reliability. For example, the NetTcpBinding binding accepts a Boolean construction parameter for enabling reliability:

```
public class NetTcpBinding : Binding,...
{
   public NetTcpBinding(...,bool reliableSessionEnabled);
   //More members
}
```

You can also enable reliability post-construction by accessing the ReliableSession property:

```
    public class ReliableSession
    {
        public bool Ordered
        {get;set;}
        //More members
    }
    public class OptionalReliableSession : ReliableSession
    {
        public bool Enabled
        {get;set;}
        //More members
    }
    public class NetTcpBinding : Binding,...
    {
        public OptionalReliableSession ReliableSession
        {get;}
        //More members
    }
```

Requiring Ordered Delivery

In theory, the service code and the contract definition should be independent of the binding used and of its properties. The service should not care about the binding, and nothing in service code pertains to the binding used. The service should be able to work with any aspect of the configured binding. In practice, however, the service implementation or the contract itself may depend on ordered delivery of the messages. To enable the contract or service developer to constrain the allowed bindings, WCF defines the DeliveryRequirementsAttribute:

```
[AttributeUsage(AttributeTargets.Class|AttributeTargets.Interface
                AllowMultiple = true)]
public sealed class DeliveryRequirementsAttribute : Attribute,...
{
    public Type TargetContract
    {get;set;}
    public bool RequireOrderedDelivery
    {get;set;}

    //More members
}
```

The DeliveryRequirements attribute can be applied at the service level, affecting all endpoints of the service, or only at those endpoints that expose a particular contract. When applied at the service level, it means that requiring ordered delivery is an implementation decision. For example, to demand that all endpoints of the service, regardless of contracts, have ordered delivery enabled, apply the attribute directly on the service class:

```
[DeliveryRequirements(RequireOrderedDelivery = true)]
class MyService : IMyContract,IMyOtherContract
{...}
```

By setting the TargetContract property, you can demand that only endpoints of the service that support the specified contract be constrained to have reliable ordered delivery:

```
[DeliveryRequirements(TargetContract = typeof(IMyContract),
                      RequireOrderedDelivery = true)]
class MyService : IMyContract,IMyOtherContract
{...}
```

The attribute can also be used at the contract level, affecting all services that support that contract. When applied at the contract level, it means that requiring ordered delivery is a design decision. Enforcing the constraint is done at service load time. If an endpoint has a binding that does not support reliability, supports reliability but has it disabled, or has reliability enabled but ordered delivery disabled, loading the service will fail with an InvalidOperationException.

By applying the DeliveryRequirements attribute on the contract interface, you place the constraint on all services that support it:

```
[ServiceContract]
[DeliveryRequirements(RequireOrderedDelivery = true)]
interface IMyContract
{...}

class MyService : IMyContract
{...}

class MyOtherService : IMyContract
{...}
```

The default value of RequireOrderedDelivery is false, so merely applying the attribute has no effect. For example, these statements are equivalent:

```
[ServiceContract]
interface IMyContract
{...}

[ServiceContract]
[DeliveryRequirements]
interface IMyContract
{...}

[ServiceContract]
[DeliveryRequirements(RequireOrderedDelivery = false)]
interface IMyContract
{...}
```

The IPC binding satisfies the ordered delivery constraint.

CHAPTER 2

Service Contracts

The ServiceContract attribute presented in the previous chapter exposes an interface (or a class) as a service-oriented contract, allowing you to program in languages such as C#, using constructs such as interfaces, while exposing those constructs as WCF contracts and services. This chapter starts by discussing how to better bridge the gap between the two programming models by enabling operation overloading and contract inheritance. Next, it presents a few simple yet powerful service contract design and factoring guidelines and techniques. The chapter ends by showing you how to interact programmatically at runtime with the metadata of the exposed contracts.

Operation Overloading

Programming languages such as C++ and C# support *method overloading*; that is, defining two methods with the same name but with different parameters. For example, this is a valid C# interface definition:

```
interface ICalculator
{
    int Add(int arg1,int arg2);
    double Add(double arg1,double arg2);
}
```

However, operation overloading is invalid in the world of WSDL-based operations, since all operations must have unique names (they are identified by name in the messages). Consequently, while the following contract definition compiles, it will throw an InvalidOperationException at the service host load time:

```
//Invalid contract definition:
[ServiceContract]
interface ICalculator
{
    [OperationContract]
    int Add(int arg1,int arg2);

    [OperationContract]
    double Add(double arg1,double arg2);
}
```

However, you can manually enable operation overloading. The trick is using the Name property of the OperationContract attribute to alias the operation:

```
[AttributeUsage(AttributeTargets.Method)]
public sealed class OperationContractAttribute : Attribute
{
   public string Name
   {get;set;}
   //More members
}
```

You need to alias the operation both on the service and on the client side. On the service side, provide a unique name for each overloaded operation, as shown in Example 2-1.

Example 2-1. Service-side operation overloading

```
[ServiceContract]
interface ICalculator
{
   [OperationContract(Name = "AddInt")]
   int Add(int arg1,int arg2);

   [OperationContract(Name = "AddDouble")]
   double Add(double arg1,double arg2);
}
```

When the client imports the contract and generates the proxy, the imported operations will have the aliased names:

```
[ServiceContract]
interface ICalculator
{
   [OperationContract]
   int AddInt(int arg1,int arg2);

   [OperationContract]
   double AddDouble(double arg1,double arg2);
}
class CalculatorClient : ClientBase<ICalculator>,ICalculator
{
   public int AddInt(int arg1,int arg2)
   {
      return Channel.AddInt(arg1,arg2);
   }
   public double AddDouble(double arg1,double arg2)
   {
      return Channel.AddDouble(arg1,arg2);
   }
   //Rest of the proxy
}
```

The client can use the generated proxy and contract as they are, but you can also rework them to provide overloading on the client side. Rename the methods on the imported contract and the proxy to the overloaded names, and make sure the proxy class makes calls on the internal proxy using the overloaded methods, as in:

```
public int Add(int arg1,int arg2)
{
   return Channel.Add(arg1,arg2);
}
```

Finally, use the Name property on the imported contract on the client side to alias and overload the methods, matching the imported operation names, as shown in Example 2-2.

Example 2-2. Client-side operation overloading

```
[ServiceContract]
interface ICalculator
{
   [OperationContract(Name = "AddInt")]
   int Add(int arg1,int arg2);

   [OperationContract(Name = "AddDouble")]
   double Add(double arg1,double arg2);
}

class CalculatorClient : ClientBase<ICalculator>,ICalculator
{
   public int Add(int arg1,int arg2)
   {
      return Channel.Add(arg1,arg2);
   }
   public double Add(double arg1,double arg2)
   {
      return Channel.Add(arg1,arg2);
   }
   //Rest of the proxy
}
```

Now the client can benefit from the readable and smooth programming model offered by overloaded operations:

```
CalculatorClient proxy = new CalculatorClient();

int result1 = proxy.Add(1,2);
double result2 = proxy.Add(1.0,2.0);

proxy.Close();
```

Contract Inheritance

Service contract interfaces can derive from each other, enabling you to define a hierarchy of contracts. However, the ServiceContract attribute is not inheritable:

```
[AttributeUsage(Inherited = false,...)]
public sealed class ServiceContractAttribute : Attribute
{...}
```

Consequently, every level in the interface hierarchy must explicitly have the ServiceContract attribute, as shown in Example 2-3.

Example 2-3. Service-side contract hierarchy

```
[ServiceContract]
interface ISimpleCalculator
{
   [OperationContract]
   int Add(int arg1,int arg2);
}
[ServiceContract]
interface IScientificCalculator : ISimpleCalculator
{
   [OperationContract]
   int Multiply(int arg1,int arg2);
}
```

When it comes to implementing a contract hierarchy, a single service class can implement the entire hierarchy, just as with classic C# programming:

```
class MyCalculator : IScientificCalculator
{
   public int Add(int arg1,int arg2)
   {
      return arg1 + arg2;
   }
   public int Multiply(int arg1,int arg2)
   {
      return arg1 * arg2;
   }
}
```

The host can expose a single endpoint for the bottommost interface in the hierarchy:

```
<service name = "MyCalculator">
   <endpoint
      address  = "http://localhost:8001/MyCalculator/"
      binding  = "basicHttpBinding"
      contract = "IScientificCalculator"
   />
</service>
```

Client-Side Contract Hierarchy

When a client imports the metadata of a service endpoint whose contract is part of an interface hierarchy, the resulting contract on the client side will not maintain the original hierarchy. Instead, it will include a flattened hierarchy in the form of a single contract named after the endpoint's contract. The single contract will have a union of all the operations from all the interfaces leading down to it in the hierarchy, including itself. However, the imported interface definition will maintain, in the `Action` and `ResponseAction` properties of the `OperationContract` attribute, the name of the original contract that defined each operation:

```
[AttributeUsage(AttributeTargets.Method)]
public sealed class OperationContractAttribute : Attribute
{
    public string Action
    {get;set;}
    public string ReplyAction
    {get;set;}
    //More members
}
```

Finally, a single proxy class will implement all methods in the imported contract. Given the definitions in Example 2-3, Example 2-4 shows the imported contract and the generated proxy class.

Example 2-4. Client-side flattened hierarchy

```
[ServiceContract]
interface IScientificCalculator
{
    [OperationContract(Action = ".../ISimpleCalculator/Add",
                       ReplyAction = ".../ISimpleCalculator/AddResponse")]
    int Add(int arg1,int arg2);

    [OperationContract(Action = ".../IScientificCalculator/Multiply",
                       ReplyAction = ".../IScientificCalculator/MultiplyResponse")]
    int Multiply(int arg1,int arg2);
}

class ScientificCalculatorClient :
                    ClientBase<IScientificCalculator>,IScientificCalculator
{
    public int Add(int arg1,int arg2)
    {...}
    public int Multiply(int arg1,int arg2)
    {...}
    //Rest of the proxy
}
```

Restoring the hierarchy on the client

The client can manually rework the proxy and the imported contract definitions to restore the contract hierarchy, as shown in Example 2-5.

Example 2-5. Client-side contract hierarchy

```
[ServiceContract]
interface ISimpleCalculator
{
   [OperationContract]
   int Add(int arg1,int arg2);
}
class SimpleCalculatorClient : ClientBase<ISimpleCalculator>,ISimpleCalculator
{
   public int Add(int arg1,int arg2)
   {
      return Channel.Add(arg1,arg2);
   }
   //Rest of the proxy
}

[ServiceContract]
interface IScientificCalculator : ISimpleCalculator
{
   [OperationContract]
   int Multiply(int arg1,int arg2);
}
class ScientificCalculatorClient :
                          ClientBase<IScientificCalculator>,IScientificCalculator
{
   public int Add(int arg1,int arg2)
   {
      return Channel.Add(arg1,arg2);
   }
   public int Multiply(int arg1,int arg2)
   {
      return Channel.Multiply(arg1,arg2);
   }
   //Rest of the proxy
}
```

Using the value of the Action property in the various operations, the client can factor out the definitions of the comprising contracts in the service contract hierarchy and provide interface and proxy definitions (for example, ISimpleCalculator and SimpleCalculatorClient in Example 2-5). There is no need to set the Action and ResponseAction properties, and you can safely remove them all. Next, manually add the interface to the inheritance chain as required:

```
[ServiceContract]
interface IScientificCalculator : ISimpleCalculator
{...}
```

Even though the service may have exposed just a single endpoint for the bottom-most interface in the hierarchy, the client can view it as different endpoints with the same address, where each endpoint corresponds to a different level in the contract hierarchy:

```
<client>
   <endpoint name = "SimpleEndpoint"
      address  = "http://localhost:8001/MyCalculator/"
      binding  = "basicHttpBinding"
      contract = "ISimpleCalculator"
   />
   <endpoint name = "ScientificEndpoint"
      address  = "http://localhost:8001/MyCalculator/"
      binding  = "basicHttpBinding"
      contract = "IScientificCalculator"
   />
</client>
```

The client can now write the following code, taking full advantage of the contract hierarchy:

```
SimpleCalculatorClient proxy1 = new SimpleCalculatorClient();
proxy1.Add(1,2);
proxy1.Close();

ScientificCalculatorClient proxy2 = new ScientificCalculatorClient();
proxy2.Add(3,4);
proxy2.Multiply(5,6);
proxy2.Close();
```

The advantage of the proxy refactoring in Example 2-5 is that each level in the contract is kept separately and decoupled from the levels underneath it. Anyone on the client side that expects a reference to ISimpleCalculator can now be given a reference to IScientificCalculator:

```
void UseCalculator(ISimpleCalculator calculator)
{...}

ISimpleCalculator proxy1 = new SimpleCalculatorClient();
ISimpleCalculator proxy2 = new ScientificCalculatorClient();
IScientificCalculator  proxy3 = new ScientificCalculatorClient();
SimpleCalculatorClient  proxy4 = new SimpleCalculatorClient();
ScientificCalculatorClient proxy5 = new ScientificCalculatorClient();

UseCalculator(proxy1);
UseCalculator(proxy2);
UseCalculator(proxy3);
UseCalculator(proxy4);
UseCalculator(proxy5);
```

However, there is no Is-A relationship between the proxies. The IScientificCalculator interface derives from ISimpleCalculator, but a ScientificCalculatorClient is not a SimpleCalculatorClient. In addition, you have to repeat the implementation of the base contract in the proxy for the subcontract. You can rectify that by using a technique I call *proxy chaining*, illustrated in Example 2-6.

Example 2-6. Proxy chaining

```
class SimpleCalculatorClient :
                    ClientBase<IScientificCalculator>,ISimpleCalculator
{
   public int Add(int arg1,int arg2)
   {
      return Channel.Add(arg1,arg2);
   }
   //Rest of the proxy
}

class ScientificCalculatorClient :
                    SimpleCalculatorClient,IScientificCalculator
{
   public int Multiply(int arg1,int arg2)
   {
      return Channel.Multiply(arg1,arg2);
   }
   //Rest of the proxy
}
```

Only the proxy that implements the topmost base contract derives directly from ClientBase<T>, providing it as a type parameter with the bottommost subinterface. All the other proxies derive from the proxy immediately above them and the respective contract.

Proxy chaining gives you an Is-A relationship between the proxies, as well as enabling code reuse. Anyone on the client side that expects a reference to SimpleCalculatorClient can now be given a reference to ScientificCalculatorClient:

```
void UseCalculator(SimpleCalculatorClient calculator)
{...}

SimpleCalculatorClient proxy1 = new SimpleCalculatorClient();
SimpleCalculatorClient proxy2 = new ScientificCalculatorClient();
ScientificCalculatorClient proxy3 = new ScientificCalculatorClient();

UseCalculator(proxy1);
UseCalculator(proxy2);
UseCalculator(proxy3);
```

Service Contract Factoring and Design

Syntax aside, how do you go about designing service contracts? How do you know which operations to allocate to which service contract? How many operations should each contract have? Answering these questions has little to do with WCF and a lot to do with abstract service-oriented analysis and design. An in-depth discussion of how to decompose a system into services and how to discover contract methods is beyond the scope of this book. Nonetheless, this section offers a few pieces of advice to guide you in your service contracts design effort.

Contract Factoring

A service contract is a grouping of logically related operations. What constitutes "logically related" is usually domain-specific. You can think of service contracts as different facets of some entity. Once you have identified (after requirements analysis) all the operations the entity supports, you need to allocate those operations to contracts. This is called *service contract factoring*. When you factor a service contract, always think in terms of reusable elements. In a service-oriented application, the basic unit of reuse is the service contract. Ask yourself, will this particular contract factoring yield contracts that other entities in the system can reuse? What facets of the entity can logically be factored out and used by other entities?

As a concrete yet simple example, suppose you wish to model a dog service. The requirements are that the dog should be able to bark and fetch, that it should have a veterinary clinic registration number, and that you should be able to vaccinate it. You could define the IDog service contract and have different kinds of services, such as the PoodleService and the GermanShepherdService, implement the IDog contract:

```
[ServiceContract]
interface IDog
{
   [OperationContract]
   void Fetch();

   [OperationContract]
   void Bark();

   [OperationContract]
   long GetVetClinicNumber();

   [OperationContract]
   void Vaccinate();
}
class PoodleService : IDog
{...}
class GermanShepherdService : IDog
{...}
```

However, this composition of the IDog service contract is not well factored. Even though all the operations are things a dog should support, Fetch() and Bark() are more logically related to each other than to GetVetClinicNumber() and Vaccinate(): Fetch() and Bark() involve one facet of the dog, as a living, active canine entity, while GetVetClinicNumber() and Vaccinate() involve a different facet, one that relates it as a record of a pet in a veterinary clinic. A better approach is to factor out the GetVetClinicNumber( ) and Vaccinate( ) operations to a separate contract called IPet:

```
[ServiceContract]
interface IPet
{
   [OperationContract]
   long GetVetClinicNumber( );

   [OperationContract]
   void Vaccinate( );
}

[ServiceContract]
interface IDog
{
   [OperationContract]
   void Fetch( );

   [OperationContract]
   void Bark( );
}
```

Because the pet facet is independent of the canine facet, other entities (such as cats) can reuse the IPet service contract and support it:

```
[ServiceContract]
interface ICat
{
   [OperationContract]
   void Purr( );

   [OperationContract]
   void CatchMouse( );
}

class PoodleService : IDog,IPet
{...}

class SiameseService : ICat,IPet
{...}
```

This factoring, in turn, allows you to decouple the clinic-management aspect of the application from the actual service (be it dogs or cats). Factoring operations into separate interfaces is usually done when there is a weak logical relation between the operations. However, identical operations are sometimes found in several unrelated contracts, and these operations are logically related to their respective contracts. For example, both cats and dogs need to shed fur and nurse their offspring. Logically, shedding is just as much a dog operation as barking, and just as much a cat operation as purring.

In such cases, you can factor the service contracts into a hierarchy of contracts instead of separate contracts:

```
[ServiceContract]
interface IMammal
{
   [OperationContract]
   void Shed( );

   [OperationContract]
   void Lactate( );
}
[ServiceContract]
interface IDog : IMammal
{...}

[ServiceContract]
interface ICat : IMammal
{...}
```

Factoring Metrics

As you can see, proper contract factoring results in more specialized, loosely coupled, fine-tuned, and reusable contracts, and subsequently, those benefits apply to the system as well. In general, contract factoring results in contracts with fewer operations.

When you design a service-based system, however, you need to balance two countering forces (see Figure 2-1). One is the cost of implementing the service contracts, and the other is the cost of putting them together or integrating them into a cohesive application.

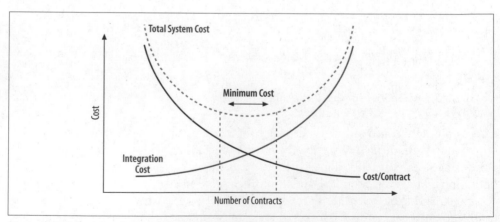

Figure 2-1. Balancing the number of services and their size

If you have too many granular service contracts, it will be easy to implement each contract, but the overall cost of integrating all those service contracts will be prohibitive. On the other hand, if you have only a few complex, large service contracts, the cost of implementing those contracts will be a prohibitive factor, even though the cost of integrating them might be low.

The relationship between size of a service contract and cost of implementation is not linear, because complexity is not linear to size—something that's twice as big may be four or six times as complex. Similarly, the relationship between integration cost and the number of service contracts to integrate is not linear, because the number of possible connections is not linear to the number of participating services.

In any given system, the total effort involved in designing and maintaining the services that implement the contracts is the sum of those two factors (cost of implementation and cost of integration). As you can see from Figure 2-1, there is an area of minimum cost or effort in relation to the size and number of service contracts. A well-designed system has not too many but not too few services, and those services are not too big but not too small.

Because these contract-factoring issues are independent of the service technology used, I can extrapolate from my own and others' experiences of factoring and architecting large-scale applications and share a few rules of thumb and metrics I have collected about service-contract factoring.

Service contracts with just one operation are possible, but you should avoid them. A service contract is a facet of an entity, and that facet must be pretty dull if you can express it with just one operation. Examine that single operation, and ask yourself some questions about it. Is it using too many parameters? Is it too coarse, and therefore should it be factored into several operations? Should you factor this operation into an already existing service contract?

The optimal number of service contract members (in my opinion and experience) is between three and five. If you design a service contract with more operations—say, six to nine—you are still doing relatively well. However, look at the operations and try to determine whether any can be collapsed into each other, since it's quite possible to over-factor operations. If you have a service contract with 12 or more operations, you should definitely look for ways to factor the operations into either separate service contracts or a hierarchy of contracts. Your coding standard should set some upper limit never to be exceeded, regardless of the circumstances (say, 20).

Another rule involves the use of property-like operations, such as this:

```
[OperationContract]
long GetVetClinicNumber();
```

You should avoid such operations. Service contracts allow clients to invoke abstract operations, without caring about actual implementation details. Properties in general are better than public member variables, but methods are better than properties. I say that properties provide *just-enough encapsulation*, and this is why WCF (unlike C#) does not support properties directly—although you can easily circumvent that by defining property-like operations. Such property-like operations would encapsulate the business logic of setting and reading the variables' values on the service side.

Ideally, however, you shouldn't bother clients with properties at all. That is, clients should be able to simply invoke operations and let the service worry about how to manage its state. The interaction should be in terms of *DoSomething( )*, like Vaccinate( ). How the service goes about doing that and whether or not a vet clinic number is involved should be of no concern to the client.

 A word of caution about factoring metrics: rules of thumb and generic metrics are only tools to help you evaluate your particular design. There is no substitute for domain expertise and experience. Always be practical, apply judgment, and question what you do in light of these guidelines.

Contract Queries

Sometimes the client needs to programmatically verify whether a particular endpoint (identified by its address) supports a particular contract. For example, imagine an application where the end user specifies or configures the application during setup (or even at runtime) to consume and interact with a service. If the service does not support the required contracts, the application should alert the user that an invalid address was specified, and ask for an alternative or a correct address. For example, the Credentials Manager application used in Chapter 10 has just such a feature: the user needs to provide it with the address of the security credentials service that manages account membership and roles. Credentials Manager only allows the user to select a valid address, after verifying that the address supports the required service contracts.

Programmatic Metadata Processing

In order to support such functionality, the application needs to retrieve the service's metadata and see if at least one of the endpoints supports the requested contract. As explained in Chapter 1, the metadata may be available either in special metadata exchange endpoints (if the service supports them), or over the HTTP-GET protocol. When you use HTTP-GET, the address of the metadata exchange is the HTTP-GET address (usually just the HTTP base address of the service, suffixed by ?wsdl). To ease the task of parsing the returned metadata WCF offers a few helper classes, available in the System.ServiceModel.Description namespaces, as shown in Example 2-7.

Example 2-7. Metadata processing supporting types

```
public enum MetadataExchangeClientMode
{
   MetadataExchange,
   HttpGet
}
public class MetadataSet : ...
{...}
```

Example 2-7. Metadata processing supporting types (continued)

```
public class ServiceEndpointCollection : Collection<ServiceEndpoint>
{...}

public class MetadataExchangeClient
{
   public MetadataExchangeClient();
   public MetadataExchangeClient(Binding mexBinding);
   public MetadataSet GetMetadata(Uri address,MetadataExchangeClientMode mode);
   //More members
}
public abstract class MetadataImporter
{
   public abstract ServiceEndpointCollection ImportAllEndpoints();
   //More members
}
public class WsdlImporter : MetadataImporter
{
   public WsdlImporter(MetadataSet metadata);
   //More members
}
public class ServiceEndpoint
{
   public EndpointAddress Address
   {get;set;}
   public Binding Binding
   {get;set;}
   public ContractDescription Contract
   {get;}
   //More members
}
public class ContractDescription
{
   public string Name
   {get;set;}
   public string Namespace
   {get;set;}
   //More members
}
```

MetadataExchangeClient can use the binding associated with metadata exchange in the application config file. You can also provide the MetadataExchangeClient constructor with an already initialized binding instance that has some custom values, such as a capacity for larger messages if the metadata returned exceeds the default received message size. The GetMetadata() method of MetadataExchangeClient accepts an endpoint address instance wrapping the metadata exchange address, as well as an enum specifying the access method. It returns the metadata in an instance of MetadataSet, but you should not work with that type directly. Instead, instantiate a subclass of MetadataImporter, such as WsdlImporter, and provide the raw metadata as a construction parameter; then call the ImportAllEndpoints() method to obtain a collection of all endpoints found in the metadata. The endpoints are represented by the ServiceEndpoint class.

ServiceEndpoint provides the Contract property of the type ContractDescription. ContractDescription provides the name and namespace of the contract.

Using HTTP-GET, to find out if a specified base address supports a particular contract, follow the steps just described. This will yield the collection of endpoints. Then, find out if any of the endpoints in the collection support the contract by comparing the Name and Namespace properties in the ContractDescription with the requested contract, as shown in Example 2-8.

Example 2-8. Querying an address for a contract

```
bool contractSupported = false;

string mexAddress = "...?WSDL";

MetadataExchangeClient MEXClient = new MetadataExchangeClient(new Uri(mexAddress),
                                        MetadataExchangeClientMode.HttpGet);
MetadataSet metadata =  MEXClient.GetMetadata();
MetadataImporter importer = new WsdlImporter(metadata);
ServiceEndpointCollection endpoints = importer.ImportAllEndpoints();
bool contractSupported = endpoints.Any(endpoint =>
                                endpoint.Contract.Namespace == "MyNamespace" &&
                                endpoint.Contract.Name == "IMyContract");
```

 The Metadata Explorer tool presented in Chapter 1 follows steps similar to those in Example 2-8 to retrieve the service endpoints. When given an HTTP-based address, the tool tries both HTTP-GET and an HTTP-based metadata exchange endpoint. The Metadata Explorer can also retrieve the metadata using a TCP- or IPC-based metadata exchange endpoint. The bulk of the implementation of the tool was in processing the metadata and rendering it because the difficult task of retrieving and parsing the metadata is done by the WCF-provided classes.

The MetadataResolver class

Example 2-8 queries the metadata in two phases: MetadataExchangeClient is used to obtain the metadata, and MetadataImporter is used to parse it and extract the endpoints. WCF combines these two steps for you with the MetadataResolver static class:

```
public static class MetadataResolver
{
    public static ServiceEndpointCollection Resolve(Type contract,
                                        EndpointAddress address);
    public static ServiceEndpointCollection Resolve(Type contract,Uri address,
                                        MetadataExchangeClientMode mode);

    //Additional members
}
```

Here is the same querying logic as that in Example 2-8, using the `MetadataResolver`:

```
bool contractSupported = false;

Uri mexAddress = new Uri("...?WSDL");

ServiceEndpointCollection endpoints =
                            MetadataResolver.Resolve(typeof(ISimpleCalculator),
                                mexAddress,MetadataExchangeClientMode.HttpGet);
if(endpoints.Count > 0)
{
   contractSupported = true;
}
```

The MetadataHelper Class

While the WCF-provided `MetadataResolver` is a step in the right direction, I wanted to streamline obtaining metadata further and encapsulate advanced steps such as setting the metadata message size. To this end, I created a general-purpose static utility class called `MetadataHelper`, which offers methods such as `QueryContract()`:

```
public static class MetadataHelper
{
   public static bool QueryContract(string mexAddress,Type contractType);
   //More members
}
```

You can provide `MetadataHelper` with either the `Type` of the contract you wish to query for, or the name and namespace of the contract:

```
string address = "...";
bool contractSupported = MetadataHelper.QueryContract(address,typeof(IMyContract));
```

For a metadata exchange address, you can provide `MetadataHelper` with an HTTP-GET address, or a MEX endpoint address over HTTP, HTTPS, TCP, or IPC. Example 2-9 shows the implementation of `MetadataHelper.QueryContract()`, with some of the error-handling code removed.

Example 2-9. Implementing MetadataHelper.QueryContract()

```
public static class MetadataHelper
{
  const int MessageMultiplier = 5;

  static ServiceEndpointCollection QueryMexEndpoint(string mexAddress,
                                         BindingElement bindingElement)
  {
     CustomBinding binding = new CustomBinding(bindingElement);

     MetadataExchangeClient MEXClient = new MetadataExchangeClient(binding);
     MetadataSet metadata = MEXClient.GetMetadata(new EndpointAddress(mexAddress));
     MetadataImporter importer = new WsdlImporter(metadata);
     return importer.ImportAllEndpoints();
  }
```

Example 2-9. Implementing MetadataHelper.QueryContract( ) (continued)

```
public static ServiceEndpoint[] GetEndpoints(string mexAddress)
{
    /* Some error handling */
    Uri address = new Uri(mexAddress);
    ServiceEndpointCollection endpoints = null;

    if(address.Scheme == "net.tcp")
    {
        TcpTransportBindingElement tcpBindingElement =
                                        new TcpTransportBindingElement( );
        tcpBindingElement.MaxReceivedMessageSize *= MessageMultiplier;
        endpoints = QueryMexEndpoint(mexAddress,tcpBindingElement);
    }
    if(address.Scheme == "net.pipe")
    {...}
    if(address.Scheme == "http")  //Checks for HTTP-GET as well
    {...}
    if(address.Scheme == "https") //Checks for HTTPS-GET as well
    {...}

    return endpoints.ToArray( );
}
public static bool QueryContract(string mexAddress,Type contractType)
{
    if(contractType.IsInterface == false)
    {
        Debug.Assert(false,contractType + " is not an interface");
        return false;
    }
    object[] attributes = contractType.GetCustomAttributes(
                                    typeof(ServiceContractAttribute),false);
    if(attributes.Length == 0)
    {
        Debug.Assert(false,"Interface " + contractType +
                    " does not have the ServiceContractAttribute");
        return false;
    }
    ServiceContractAttribute attribute = attributes[0] as
                                            ServiceContractAttribute;
    if(attribute.Name == null)
    {
        attribute.Name = contractType.ToString( );
    }
    if(attribute.Namespace == null)
    {
        attribute.Namespace = "http://tempuri.org/";
    }
    return QueryContract(mexAddress,attribute.Namespace,attribute.Name);
}
public static bool QueryContract(string mexAddress,string contractNamespace,
                                string contractName)
{
```

Example 2-9. Implementing MetadataHelper.QueryContract() (continued)

```
    if(String.IsNullOrEmpty(contractNamespace))
    {
       Debug.Assert(false,"Empty namespace");
       return false;
    }
    if(String.IsNullOrEmpty(contractName))
    {
       Debug.Assert(false,"Empty name");
       return false;
    }
    try
    {
       ServiceEndpoint[] endpoints = GetEndpoints(mexAddress);

       return endpoints.Any(endpoint =>
                            endpoint.Contract.Namespace == contractNamespace &&
                            endpoint.Contract.Name == contractName);
    }
    catch
    {}
    return false;
  }
}
```

In Example 2-9, the GetEndpoints( ) method parses out the schema of the metadata exchange address. According to the transport schema found (e.g., TCP), GetEndpoints( ) constructs a binding element to use so that it can set its MaxReceivedMessageSize property:

```
public abstract class TransportBindingElement : BindingElement
{
   public virtual long MaxReceivedMessageSize
   {get;set;}
}
public abstract class ConnectionOrientedTransportBindingElement :
                                             TransportBindingElement,...
{...}
public class TcpTransportBindingElement : ConnectionOrientedTransportBindingElement
{...}
```

MaxReceivedMessageSize defaults to 64K. While this is adequate for simple services, services that have many endpoints that use complex types will generate larger messages, causing the call to MetadataExchangeClient.GetMetadata( ) to fail. My experimentations indicate that 5 is an adequate fudge factor for most cases.

GetEndpoints( ) then uses the QueryMexEndpoint( ) private method to actually retrieve the metadata. QueryMexEndpoint( ) accepts the metadata exchange endpoint address and the binding element to use. It uses the binding element to construct a custom binding and provide it to an instance of MetadataExchangeClient, which retrieves the metadata and returns the endpoint collection. Instead of returning a ServiceEndpointCollection, GetEndpoints( ) uses LINQ to return an array of endpoints.

The QueryContract( ) method that accepts a Type first verifies that the type is an interface and that it is decorated with the ServiceContract attribute. Because the ServiceContract attribute can be used to alias both the name and namespace of the requested type of contract, QueryContract( ) uses those for looking up the contract. If no aliasing is used, QueryContract( ) uses the name of the type and the default http://tempuri.org for the namespace, and calls the QueryContract( ) method that operates on the name and namespace. That version of QueryContract( ) calls GetEndpoints( ) to obtain the array of endpoints, and returns true if it finds at least one endpoint that supports the contract. Any errors make QueryContract( ) return false.

Example 2-10 shows additional metadata querying methods offered by MetadataHelper.

Example 2-10. The MetadataHelper class

```
public static class MetadataHelper
{
   public static ServiceEndpoint[] GetEndpoints(string mexAddress);
   public static string[] GetAddresses(Type bindingType,string mexAddress,
                                       Type contractType);
   public static string[] GetAddresses(string mexAddress,Type contractType);
   public static string[] GetAddresses(Type bindingType,string mexAddress,
                                       string contractNamespace,
                                       string contractName);
   public static string[] GetAddresses(string mexAddress,string contractNamespace,
                                       string contractName);
   public static string[] GetContracts(Type bindingType,string mexAddress);
   public static string[] GetContracts(string mexAddress);
   public static string[] GetOperations(string mexAddress,Type contractType);
   public static string[] GetOperations(string mexAddress,
                                        string contractNamespace,
                                        string contractName);
   public static bool QueryContract(string mexAddress,Type contractType);
   public static bool QueryContract(string mexAddress,
                                    string contractNamespace,string contractName);
   //More members
}
```

These powerful and useful features are often required during setup or in administration applications and tools, and yet their implementation is all based on processing the array of endpoints returned from the GetEndpoints( ) method.

The GetAddresses( ) methods return either all the endpoint addresses that support a particular contract, or only the addresses of those endpoints that also use a particular binding. Similarly, GetContracts( ) returns all the contracts supported across all endpoints, or the contracts supported across all endpoints that use a particular binding. Finally, GetOperations( ) returns all the operations on a particular contract.

 Chapter 10 uses the MetadataHelper class in the Credentials Manager application, and Appendix C uses it for administering persistent subscribers.

CHAPTER 3

Data Contracts

WCF provides the ability to host and expose native CLR types (interfaces and classes) as services, and the ability to consume services as native CLR interfaces and classes. WCF service operations accept and return CLR types such as integers and strings, and the WCF clients pass in and process returned CLR types. However, such CLR types are specific to .NET. This poses a problem, because one of the core tenets of service-orientation is that services do not betray their implementation technologies across the service boundary. As a result, any client, regardless of its own technology, can interact with any service. This, of course, means that WCF cannot allow you to expose the CLR data types across the service boundary. What you need is a way of converting CLR types to and from a standard neutral representation. That representation is a simple XML-based schema, also known as an *infoset*. In addition, the service needs a formal way of declaring how the conversion is to take place. This formal specification is called a *data contract*, and it is the subject of this chapter. The first part of the chapter shows how data contracts enable type marshaling and conversions, and how the infrastructure deals with class hierarchies and data contract versioning. The second part shows how to use various .NET types, such as enumerations, delegates, data tables, and collections, as data contracts.

Serialization

The data contract is part of the contractual obligation the service supports, just like the service operations are part of that contract. The data contract is published in the service's metadata, allowing clients to convert the neutral, technology-agnostic representation of the data types to their native representations. Because objects and local references are CLR concepts, you cannot pass CLR objects and references to and from a WCF service operation. Allowing you to do so not only would violate the core service-oriented principle discussed previously, but also would be impractical, since an object is comprised of both its state and the code manipulating it. There is no way of sending the code or the logic as part of a C# or Visual Basic method invocation, let alone marshaling it to another platform and technology. In fact, when passing an object (or a value type) as an operation parameter, all you really need to send is the state of that object, and you let the receiving side convert it back to its own native representation. Such an approach for passing state around is called *marshaling by value*. The easiest way to perform marshaling by value is to rely on the built-in support most platforms (.NET included) offer for serialization. The approach is simple enough, as shown in Figure 3-1.

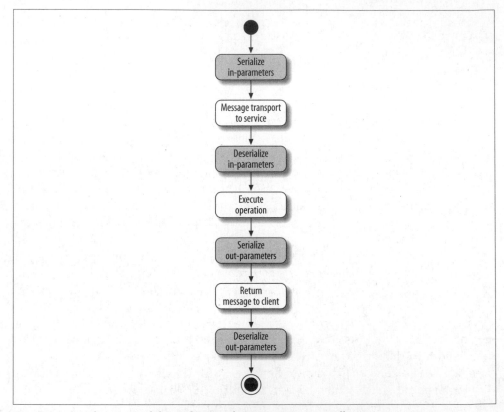

Figure 3-1. Serialization and deserialization during an operation call

On the client side, WCF will serialize the in-parameters from the CLR native representation to an XML infoset and bundle them in the outgoing message to the client. Once the message is received on the service side, WCF will deserialize it and convert the neutral XML infoset to the corresponding CLR representation before dispatching the call to the service. The service will then process the native CLR parameters. Once the service has finished executing the operation, WCF will serialize the out-parameters and the returned values into a neutral XML infoset, package them in the returned message, and post the returned message to the client. Finally, on the client side, WCF will deserialize the returned values into native CLR types and return them to the client.

The double dose of serialization and deserialization in every call is the real bottleneck of WCF, performance-wise. The cost of running a message through the interceptors on the client and service sides is minuscule compared with the overhead of serialization.

.NET Serialization

WCF could make use of .NET's ready-made support for serialization. .NET automatically serializes and deserializes objects using reflection. .NET captures the value of each of the object's fields and serializes it to memory, to a file, or to a network connection. For deserializing, .NET creates a new object of the matching type, reads its persisted field values, and sets the values of its fields using reflection. Because reflection can access private fields, including base-class fields, .NET takes a complete snapshot of the state of an object during serialization and perfectly reconstructs that state during deserialization. .NET serializes the object state into a *stream*, which is a logical sequence of bytes, independent of a particular medium such as a file, memory, a communication port, or any other resource.

The Serializable attribute

By default, user-defined types (classes and structs) are not serializable. The reason is that .NET has no way of knowing whether a reflection-based dump of the object state to a stream makes sense. Perhaps the object members have some transient value or state (such as an open database connection or communication port). If .NET simply serialized the state of such an object, after constructing a new object by deserializing it from the stream, you would end up with a defective object. Consequently, serialization has to be performed by consent of the class's developer.

To indicate to .NET that instances of your class are serializable, you add the SerializableAttribute to your class or struct definition:

```
[AttributeUsage(AttributeTargets.Delegate|
                AttributeTargets.Enum    |
                AttributeTargets.Struct  |
                AttributeTargets.Class,
                Inherited = false)]
public sealed class SerializableAttribute : Attribute
{}
```

For example:

```
[Serializable]
class MyClass
{...}
```

The NonSerialized attribute

When a class is serializable, .NET insists that all its member variables be serializable as well, and if it discovers a nonserializable member, it throws an exception. However, what if the class or a struct that you want to serialize has a member that cannot be serialized? That type will not have the Serializable attribute and will preclude the containing type from being serialized. Commonly, that nonserializable member is a reference type requiring some special initialization. The solution to this problem requires marking such a member as nonserializable and taking a custom step to initialize it during deserialization.

To allow a serializable type to contain a nonserializable type as a member variable, you need to mark the member with the NonSerialized field attribute. For example:

```
class MyOtherClass
{...}

[Serializable]
class MyClass
{
   [NonSerialized]
   MyOtherClass m_OtherClass;
   /* Methods and properties */
}
```

When .NET serializes a member variable, it first reflects it to see whether it has the NonSerialized attribute. If so, .NET ignores that variable and simply skips over it.

You can even use this technique to exclude from serialization normally serializable types, such as string:

```
[Serializable]
class MyClass
{
   [NonSerialized]
   string m_Name;
}
```

The .NET formatters

.NET offers two formatters used for serializing and deserializing types. The BinaryFormatter serializes into a compact binary format, enabling fast serialization and deserialization. The SoapFormatter uses a .NET-specific SOAP XML format.

Both formatters support the IFormatter interface, defined as:

```
public interface IFormatter
{
   object Deserialize(Stream serializationStream);
   void Serialize(Stream serializationStream,object graph);
   // More members
}
```

```
public sealed class BinaryFormatter : IFormatter,...
{...}
public sealed class SoapFormatter : IFormatter,...
{...}
```

In addition to the state of the object, both formatters persist the type's assembly and versioning information to the stream, so that they can deserialize it back to the correct type. This renders them inadequate for service-oriented interaction, however, because it requires the other party not only to have the type assembly, but also to be using .NET. The use of the Stream is also an imposition, because it requires the client and the service to somehow share the stream.

The WCF Formatters

Due to the deficiencies of the classic .NET formatters, WCF has to provide its own service-oriented formatter. The formatter, DataContractSerializer, is capable of sharing just the data contract, not the underlying type information. DataContractSerializer is defined in the System.Runtime.Serialization namespace and is partially listed in Example 3-1.

Example 3-1. The DataContractSerializer formatter

```
public abstract class XmlObjectSerializer
{
    public virtual object ReadObject(Stream stream);
    public virtual object ReadObject(XmlReader reader);
    public virtual void WriteObject(XmlWriter writer,object graph);
    public void WriteObject(Stream stream,object graph);
    //More members
}
public sealed class DataContractSerializer : XmlObjectSerializer
{
    public DataContractSerializer(Type type);
    //More members
}
```

DataContractSerializer only captures the state of the object according to the serialization or data contract schema. Note also that DataContractSerializer does not support IFormatter.

WCF automatically uses DataContractSerializer under the covers, and developers never need to interact with it directly. However, you can use DataContractSerializer to serialize types to and from a .NET stream, similar to using the legacy formatters. Unlike when using the binary or SOAP formatters, however, you need to supply the DataContractSerializer constructor with the type to operate on, because no type information will be present in the stream:

```
MyClass obj1 = new MyClass();
DataContractSerializer formatter = new DataContractSerializer(typeof(MyClass));

using(Stream stream = new MemoryStream())
{
   formatter.WriteObject(stream,obj1);
   stream.Seek(0,SeekOrigin.Begin);
   MyClass obj2 = (MyClass)formatter.ReadObject(stream);
}
```

While you can use DataContractSerializer with .NET streams, you can also use it in conjunction with XML readers and writers, when the only form of input is the raw XML itself, as opposed to some medium such as a file or memory.

Note the use of the amorphous object in the definition of DataContractSerializer in Example 3-1. This means that there will be no compile-time type safety, because the constructor can accept one type, the WriteObject() method can accept a second type, and the ReadObject() method can cast to yet a third type.

To compensate for that, you can define your own generic wrapper around DataContractSerializer, as shown in Example 3-2.

Example 3-2. The generic DataContractSerializer<T>

```
public class DataContractSerializer<T> : XmlObjectSerializer
{
   DataContractSerializer m_DataContractSerializer;

   public DataContractSerializer()
   {
      m_DataContractSerializer = new DataContractSerializer(typeof(T));
   }
   public new T ReadObject(Stream stream)
   {
      return (T)m_DataContractSerializer.ReadObject(stream);
   }
   public new T ReadObject(XmlReader reader)
   {
      return (T)m_DataContractSerializer.ReadObject(reader);
   }
   public void WriteObject(Stream stream,T graph)
   {
      m_DataContractSerializer.WriteObject(stream,graph);
   }
   public void WriteObject(XmlWriter writer,T graph)
   {
      m_DataContractSerializer.WriteObject(writer,graph);
   }
   //More members
}
```

The generic class DataContractSerializer<T> is much safer to use than the object-based DataContractSerializer:

```
MyClass obj1 = new MyClass();
DataContractSerializer<MyClass> formatter = new DataContractSerializer<MyClass>();

using(Stream stream = new MemoryStream())
{
   formatter.WriteObject(stream,obj1);
   stream.Seek(0,SeekOrigin.Begin);
   MyClass obj2 = formatter.ReadObject(stream);
}
```

WCF also offers the NetDataContractSerializer formatter, which is polymorphic with IFormatter:

```
public sealed class NetDataContractSerializer : IFormatter,...
{...}
```

As its name implies, similar to the legacy .NET formatters, the NetDataContractSerializer formatter captures the type information in addition to the state of the object. It is used just like the legacy formatters:

```
MyClass obj1 = new MyClass();
IFormatter formatter = new NetDataContractSerializer();

using(Stream stream = new MemoryStream())
{
   formatter.Serialize(stream,obj1);
   stream.Seek(0,SeekOrigin.Begin);
   MyClass obj2 = (MyClass)formatter.Deserialize(stream);
}
```

NetDataContractSerializer is designed to complement DataContractSerializer. You can serialize a type using NetDataContractSerializer and deserialize it using DataContractSerializer:

```
MyClass obj1 = new MyClass();
Stream stream = new MemoryStream();

IFormatter formatter1 = new NetDataContractSerializer();
formatter1.Serialize(stream,obj1);

stream.Seek(0,SeekOrigin.Begin);

DataContractSerializer formatter2 = new DataContractSerializer(typeof(MyClass));
MyClass obj2 = (MyClass)formatter2.ReadObject(stream);
stream.Close();
```

This ability opens the way for versioning tolerance and for migrating legacy code that shares type information into a more service-oriented approach where only the data schema is maintained.

Data Contract via Serialization

When a service operation accepts or returns any type or parameter, WCF uses DataContractSerializer to serialize and deserialize that parameter. This means that you can pass any serializable type as a parameter or returned value from a contract operation, as long as the other party has the definition of the data schema or the data contract. All the .NET built-in primitive types are serializable. For example, here are the definitions of the int and string types:

```
[Serializable]
public struct Int32 : ...
{...}

[Serializable]
public sealed class String : ...
{...}
```

This is the only reason why any of the service contracts shown in the previous chapters actually worked: WCF offers *implicit data contracts* for the primitive types because there is an industry standard for the schemas of those types.

To be able to use a custom type as an operation parameter, there are two requirements: first, the type must be serializable, and second, both the client and the service need to have a local definition of that type that results in the same data schema.

Consider the IContactManager service contract used to manage a contacts list:

```
[Serializable]
struct Contact
{
    public string FirstName;
    public string LastName;
}

[ServiceContract]
interface IContactManager
{
    [OperationContract]
    void AddContact(Contact contact);

    [OperationContract]
    Contact[] GetContacts();
}
```

If the client uses an equivalent definition of the Contact structure, it will be able to pass a contact to the service. An equivalent definition might be anything that results in the same data schema for serialization. For example, the client might use this definition instead:

```
[Serializable]
struct Contact
{
    public string FirstName;
    public string LastName;

    [NonSerialized]
    public string Address;
}
```

Data Contract Attributes

While using the `Serializable` attribute is workable, it is not ideal for service-oriented interaction between clients and services. Rather than denoting all members in a type as serializable and therefore part of the data schema for that type, it would be preferable to have an opt-in approach, where only members the contract developer wants to explicitly include in the data contract are included. The `Serializable` attribute forces the data type to be serializable in order to be used as a parameter in a contract operation, and it does not offer clean separation between the ability to use the type as a WCF operation parameter (the "serviceness" aspect of the type) and the ability to serialize it. The attribute offers no support for aliasing type names or members, or for mapping a new type to a predefined data contract. The attribute operates directly on member fields and completely bypasses any logical properties used to access those fields. It would be better to allow those properties to add their values when accessing the fields. Finally, there is no direct support for versioning, because the formatter supposedly captures any versioning information. Consequently, it is difficult to deal with versioning over time.

Yet again, the WCF solution is to come up with new service-oriented opt-in attributes. The first of these attributes is the `DataContractAttribute`, defined in the `System.Runtime.Serialization` namespace:

```
[AttributeUsage(AttributeTargets.Enum |
                AttributeTargets.Struct|
                AttributeTargets.Class,
                Inherited = false,
                AllowMultiple = false)]
public sealed class DataContractAttribute : Attribute
{
    public string Name
    {get;set;}
    public string Namespace
    {get;set;}
}
```

Applying the `DataContract` attribute on a class or struct does not cause WCF to serialize any of its members:

```
[DataContract]
struct Contact
{
    //Will not be part of the data contract
    public string FirstName;
    public string LastName;
}
```

All the `DataContract` attribute does is opt-in the type, indicating that the type is willing to be marshaled by value. To serialize any of its members, you must apply the `DataMemberAttribute`, defined as:

```
[AttributeUsage(AttributeTargets.Field|AttributeTargets.Property,
                Inherited = false,AllowMultiple = false)]
public sealed class DataMemberAttribute : Attribute
{
   public bool IsRequired
   {get;set;}
   public string Name
   {get;set;}
   public int Order
   {get;set;}
}
```

You can apply the DataMember attribute on the fields directly:

```
[DataContract]
struct Contact
{
   [DataMember]
   public string FirstName;

   [DataMember]
   public string LastName;
}
```

Or you can apply it on properties (either explicit properties, where you provide the property implementation, or automatic properties, where the compiler generates the underlying member and access implementation):

```
[DataContract]
struct Contact
{
   string m_FirstName;

   [DataMember]
   public string FirstName
   {
      get
      {
         return m_FirstName;
      }
      set
      {
         m_FirstName =  value;
      }
   }

   [DataMember]
   public string LastName
   {get;set;}
}
```

As with service contracts, the visibility of the data members and the data contract itself is of no consequence to WCF. Thus, you can include internal types with private data members in the data contract:

```
[DataContract]
struct Contact
{
    [DataMember]
    string m_FirstName;

    [DataMember]
    string m_LastName;
}
```

Some of the code in this chapter applies the DataMember attribute directly on public data members, for brevity's sake. In real code, you should of course use properties instead of public members.

 Data contracts are case-sensitive, both at the type and the member level.

Importing a Data Contract

When a data contract is used in a contract operation, it is published in the service metadata. When the client uses a tool such as Visual Studio 2008 to import the definition of the data contract, the client will end up with an equivalent definition, but not necessarily an identical one. The difference is a function of the tool, not the published metadata. With Visual Studio 2008, the imported definition will maintain the original type designation of a class or a structure as well as the original type namespace, but with SvcUtil, only the data contract will maintain the namespace. For example, given this service-side definition:

```
namespace MyNamespace
{
    [DataContract]
    struct Contact
    {...}

    [ServiceContract]
    interface IContactManager
    {
        [OperationContract]
        void AddContact(Contact contact);

        [OperationContract]
        Contact[] GetContacts();
    }
}
```

the imported definition will be:

```
namespace MyNamespace
{
    [DataContract]
    struct Contact
    {...}
}
[ServiceContract]
interface IContactManager
{
    [OperationContract]
    void AddContact(Contact contact);

    [OperationContract]
    Contact[] GetContacts();
}
```

To override this default and provide an alternative namespace for the data contract, you can assign a value to the Namespace property of the DataContract attribute. The tools treat the provided namespace differently. Given this service-side definition:

```
namespace MyNamespace
{
    [DataContract(Namespace = "MyOtherNamespace")]
    struct Contact
    {...}
}
```

Visual Studio 2008 imports it exactly as defined, while SvcUtil imports it as published:

```
namespace MyOtherNamespace
{
    [DataContract]
    struct Contact
    {...}
}
```

When using Visual Studio 2008, the imported definition will always have properties decorated with the DataMember attribute, even if the original type on the service side did not define any properties. If the original service-side definition applied the DataMember attribute on fields directly, the imported type definition will have properties accessing fields whose names will be the names of the data members, suffixed with Field. For example, for this service-side definition:

```
[DataContract]
struct Contact
{
    [DataMember]
    public string FirstName;

    [DataMember]
    public string LastName;
}
```

the imported client-side definition will be:

```
[DataContract]
public partial struct Contact
{
   string FirstNameField;
   string LastNameField;

   [DataMember]
   public string FirstName
   {
      get
      {
         return FirstNameField;
      }
      set
      {
         FirstNameField = value;
      }
   }

   [DataMember]
   public string LastName
   {
      get
      {
         return LastNameField;
      }
      set
      {
         LastNameField = value;
      }
   }
}
```

The client can, of course, manually rework any imported definition to be just like a
service-side definition.

 Even if the DataMember attribute on the service side is applied on a private field or property, as shown here:

```
[DataContract]
struct Contact
{
   [DataMember]
   string FirstName
   {get;set;}

   [DataMember]
   string LastName;
}
```

the imported definition will have a public property instead.

If the DataMember attribute is applied on a property as part of the service-side data contract, the imported definition will have an identical set of properties. The client-side properties will wrap a field named after the property, suffixed by Field. For example, given this service-side data contract:

```
[DataContract]
public partial struct Contact
{
    string m_FirstName;
    string m_LastName;

    [DataMember]
    public string FirstName
    {
        get
        {
            return m_FirstName;
        }
        set
        {
            m_FirstName = value;
        }
    }

    [DataMember]
    public string LastName
    {get;set;}
}
```

the imported definition will be:

```
[DataContract]
public partial struct Contact
{
    string FirstNameField;
    string LastNameField;

    [DataMember]
    public string FirstName
    {
        get
        {
            return FirstNameField;
        }
        set
        {
            FirstNameField = value;
        }
    }

    [DataMember]
    public string LastName
    {
        get
```

```
    {
        return LastNameField;
    }
    set
    {
        LastNameField = value;
    }
    }
}
```

When the `DataMember` attribute is applied on a property (either on the service or the client side), that property must have get and set accessors. Without them, you will get an `InvalidDataContractException` at call time. The reason is that when the property itself is the data member, WCF uses the property during serialization and deserialization, letting you apply any custom logic in the property.

 Do not apply the `DataMember` attribute both on a property and on its underlying field—this will result in duplication of the members on the importing side.

It is important to realize that the method just described for utilizing the `DataMember` attribute applies to both the service and the client side. When the client uses the `DataMember` attribute (and its related attributes, described elsewhere in this chapter), it affects the data contract it is using to either serialize and send parameters to the service or deserialize and use the values returned from the service. It is quite possible for the two parties to use equivalent yet not identical data contracts, and, as you will see later, even to use nonequivalent data contracts. The client controls and configures its data contract independently of the service.

Data Contracts and the Serializable Attribute

The service can still use a type that is only marked with the `Serializable` attribute:

```
[Serializable]
struct Contact
{
    string m_FirstName;
    public string LastName;
}
```

When importing the metadata of such a type, the imported definition will use the `DataContract` attribute. In addition, since the `Serializable` attribute affects only fields, it will be as if every serializable member (whether public or private) is a data member, resulting in a set of wrapping properties named exactly like the original fields:

```
[DataContract]
public partial struct Contact
{
    string LastNameField;
    string m_FirstNameField;

    [DataMember(...)]
    public string LastName
    {
        ... //Accesses LastNameField
    }
    [DataMember(...)]
    public string m_FirstName
    {
        ... //Accesses m_FirstNameField
    }
}
```

The client can also use the Serializable attribute on its data contract to have it marshaled in much the same way.

> A type marked only with the DataContract attribute cannot be serialized using the legacy formatters. If you want to serialize such a type, you must apply both the DataContract attribute and the Serializable attribute on it. In the resulting data contract for the type, the effect will be the same as if only the DataContract attribute had been applied, and you will still need to use the DataMember attribute on the members you want to serialize.

Data Contracts and XML Serialization

.NET offers yet another serialization mechanism: raw XML serialization, using a dedicated set of attributes. When you're dealing with a data type that requires explicit control over XML serialization, you can use the XmlSerializerFormatAttribute on individual operations in the contract definition to instruct WCF to use XML serialization at runtime. If all the operations in the contract require this form of serialization, you can use the /serializer:XmlSerializer switch of SvcUtil (described in Chapter 1) to instruct it to automatically apply the XmlSerializerFormat attribute on all operations in all imported contracts. Use that switch with caution, though, because it will affect all data contracts, including those that do not require explicit control over XML serialization.

Inferred Data Contracts

Service Pack 1 for .NET 3.5 introduced support for *inferred data contracts*. If the marshaled type is a public type and it is not decorated with the DataContract attribute, WCF will automatically infer such an attribute and apply the DataMember attribute to all public members (fields or properties) of the type.

For example, given this service contract definition:

```
public struct Contact
{
    public string FirstName
    {get;set;}

    public string LastName;

    internal string PhoneNumber;

    string Address;
}
[ServiceContract]
interface IContactManager
{
    [OperationContract]
    void AddContact(Contact contact);
    ...
}
```

WCF will infer a data contract, as if the service contract developer had defined it as:

```
[DataContract]
public class Contact
{
    [DataMember]
    public string FirstName
    {get;set;}

    [DataMember]
    public string LastName;
}
```

The inferred data contract will be published in the service metadata.

If the type already contains DataMember attributes (but not a DataContract attribute), these data member contracts will be ignored, as if they were not present. If the type does contain a DataContract attribute, no data contract is inferred. Likewise, if the type is internal, no data contract is inferred. Furthermore, all subclasses of a class that utilizes an inferred data contract must themselves be inferable; that is, they must be public classes, and have no DataContract attribute.

 Inferred data contracts are sometimes called POCO, or Plain Old CLR Object.

In my opinion, relying on inferred data contracts is a sloppy hack that goes against the grain of most everything else in WCF. Much as WCF does not infer a service contract from a mere interface definition, or enable transactions or reliability by default, it should not infer a data contract. Service-orientation (with the exception of security) is heavily biased toward opting out by default, as it should be, to maximize encapsulation and decoupling. Do use the `DataContract` attribute, and be explicit about your data contracts. This will enable you to tap into data contract features such as versioning. The rest of this book does not use or rely on inferred data contracts.

Composite Data Contracts

When you define a data contract, you can apply the `DataMember` attribute on members that are themselves data contracts, as shown in Example 3-3.

Example 3-3. A composite data contract

```
[DataContract]
class Address
{
   [DataMember]
   public string Street;

   [DataMember]
   public string City;

   [DataMember]
   public string State;

   [DataMember]
   public string Zip;
}
[DataContract]
struct Contact
{
   [DataMember]
   public string FirstName;

   [DataMember]
   public string LastName;

   [DataMember]
   public Address Address;
}
```

Being able to aggregate other data contracts in this way illustrates the fact that data contracts are actually recursive in nature. When you serialize a composite data contract, the `DataContractSerializer` will chase all applicable references in the object graph and capture their state as well. When you publish a composite data contract, all its comprising data contracts will be published as well. For example, using the same definitions as those in Example 3-3, the metadata for this service contract:

```
[ServiceContract]
interface IContactManager
{
   [OperationContract]
   void AddContact(Contact contact);
```

```
    [OperationContract]
    Contact[] GetContacts( );
}
```

will include the definition of the Address structure as well.

Data Contract Events

.NET 2.0 introduced support for serialization events for serializable types, and WCF provides the same support for data contracts. WCF calls designated methods on your data contract when serialization and deserialization take place. Four serialization and deserialization events are defined. The *serializing event* is raised just before serialization takes place, and the *serialized event* is raised just after serialization. Similarly, the *deserializing event* is raised just before deserialization, and the *deserialized event* is raised after deserialization. You designate methods as serialization event handlers using method attributes, as shown in Example 3-4.

Example 3-4. Applying the serialization event attributes
```
[DataContract]
class MyDataContract
{
   [OnSerializing]
   void OnSerializing(StreamingContext context)
   {...}

   [OnSerialized]
   void OnSerialized(StreamingContext context)
   {...}

   [OnDeserializing]
   void OnDeserializing(StreamingContext context)
   {...}

   [OnDeserialized]
   void OnDeserialized(StreamingContext context)
   {...}
   //Data members
}
```

Each serialization event-handling method must have the following signature:
```
    void <Method Name>(StreamingContext context);
```

This is required because internally WCF still uses reflection and delegates to subscribe to and invoke the event-handling methods. If the serialization event attributes (defined in the System.Runtime.Serialization namespace) are applied on methods with incompatible signatures, WCF will throw an exception.

StreamingContext is a structure that is used to inform the type of why it is being serialized, but it can be ignored for WCF data contracts.

As their names imply, the OnSerializing attribute designates a method to handle the serializing event, and the OnSerialized attribute designates a method to handle the serialized event. Similarly, the OnDeserializing attribute designates a method to handle the deserializing event, and the OnDeserialized attribute designates a method to handle the deserialized event.

Figure 3-2 is an activity diagram depicting the order in which events are raised during serialization.

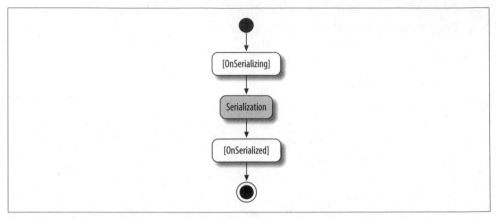

Figure 3-2. Events raised during serialization

WCF first raises the serializing event, thus invoking the corresponding event handler. Next, WCF serializes the object, and finally the serialized event is raised and its event handler is invoked.

Figure 3-3 is an activity diagram depicting the order in which deserialization events are raised. WCF first raises the deserializing event, thus invoking the corresponding event handler. Next, WCF deserializes the object, and finally the deserialized event is raised and its event handler is invoked.

Note that in order to call the deserializing event-handling method, WCF has to first construct an object—however, it does so without ever calling your data contract class's default constructor.

 WCF does not allow you to apply the same serialization event attribute on multiple methods of the data contract type. This is somewhat regrettable because it precludes support for partial types, where each part deals with its own serialization events.

Using the deserializing event

Since no constructor calls are ever made during deserialization, the deserializing event-handling method is logically your deserialization constructor. It is intended for performing some custom pre-deserialization steps—typically, initialization of class

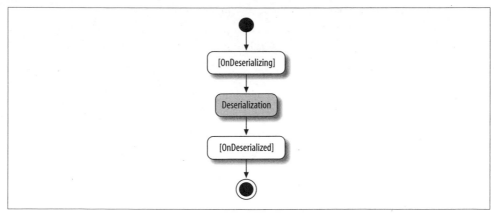

Figure 3-3. Events raised during deserialization

members not marked as data members. Any value settings on members marked as data members will be in vain, because WCF will set those members again during deserialization, using values from the message. Other steps you can take in the deserializing event-handling method are setting specific environment variables (such as thread local storage), performing diagnostics, or signaling some global synchronization events. I would even go as far as to say that if you do provide such a deserializing event-handling method, you should have both the default constructor and the event handler call the same helper method, so that anyone instantiating the type using regular .NET will perform exactly the same steps that you do and you will have a single place to maintain that code:

```
[DataContract]
class MyClass
{
   public MyClass()
   {
      OnDeserializing();
   }
   [OnDeserializing]
   void OnDeserializing(StreamingContext context)
   {
      OnDeserializing();
   }
   void OnDeserializing()
   {...}
}
```

Using the deserialized event

The deserialized event lets your data contract initialize or reclaim non-data members, while utilizing already deserialized values. Example 3-5 demonstrates this point, using the deserialized event to initialize a database connection. Without the event, the data contract will not be able to function properly—since the constructor is never called, it will have a `null` for the connection object.

Example 3-5. Initializing nonserializable resources using the deserialized event

```
[DataContract]
class MyDataContract
{
   IDbConnection m_Connection;

   [OnDeserialized]
   void OnDeserialized(StreamingContext context)
   {
      m_Connection = new SqlConnection(...);
   }
   /* Data members */
}
```

Shared Data Contracts

When adding a service reference in Visual Studio 2008, you must provide a unique new namespace for each service reference. The imported types will be defined in that new namespace. This presents a problem when adding references for two different services that share the same data contract, since you will get two distinct types, in two different namespaces, representing the same data contract.

By default, however, if any of the assemblies referenced by the client has a data contract type that matches a data contract type already exposed in the metadata of the referenced service, Visual Studio 2008 will not import that type again. It is worth emphasizing again that the existing data contract reference must be in another referenced assembly, not in the client project itself. This limitation may be addressed in a future release of Visual Studio, but for now, the workaround and best practice is obvious: factor all of your shared data contracts to a designated class library, and have all clients reference that assembly. You can then control and configure which referenced assemblies (if any) to consult regarding those shared data contracts via the advanced settings dialog for the service reference (shown in Figure 1-10). The "Reuse types in referenced assemblies" checkbox is checked by default, but you can turn off this feature if you so desire. Despite its name, it will share only data contracts, not service contracts. Using the radio buttons underneath it, you can also instruct Visual Studio 2008 to reuse data contracts across all referenced assemblies, or restrict the sharing to specific assemblies by selecting them in the list.

Data Contract Hierarchy

Your data contract class may be a subclass of another data contract class. WCF requires that every level in the class hierarchy explicitly opt in for a given data contract, because the DataContract attribute is not inheritable:

```
[DataContract]
class Contact
{
   [DataMember]
   public string FirstName;

   [DataMember]
   public string LastName;
}
[DataContract]
class Customer : Contact
{
   [DataMember]
   public int OrderNumber;
}
```

Failing to designate every level in the class hierarchy as serializable or as a data contract will result in an InvalidDataContractException at the service load time. WCF lets you mix the Serializable and DataContract attributes in the class hierarchy:

```
[Serializable]
class Contact
{...}

[DataContract]
class Customer : Contact
{...}
```

However, the Serializable attribute will typically be at the root of the class hierarchy, if it appears at all, because new classes should use the DataContract attribute. When you export a data contract hierarchy, the metadata maintains the hierarchy, and all levels of the class hierarchy are exported when you make use of the subclass in a service contract:

```
[ServiceContract]
interface IContactManager
{
   [OperationContract]
   void AddCustomer(Customer customer); //Contact is exported as well
   ...
}
```

Known Types

In traditional object-oriented programming, a reference to a subclass is also a reference to its base class, so the subclass maintains an Is-A relationship with its base class. Any method that expects a reference to a base class can also accept a reference to its subclass. This is a direct result of the way the compiler spans the state of the subclass in memory, by appending it right after the base class section.

While languages such as C# let you substitute a subclass for a base class in this manner, this is not the case with WCF operations. By default, you cannot use a subclass of a data contract class instead of its base class. Consider this service contract:

```
[ServiceContract]
interface IContactManager
{
   //Cannot accept Customer object here:
   [OperationContract]
   void AddContact(Contact contact);

   //Cannot return Customer objects here:
   [OperationContract]
   Contact[] GetContacts();
}
```

Suppose the client defined the Customer class as well:

```
[DataContract]
class Customer : Contact
{
   [DataMember]
   public int OrderNumber;
}
```

While the following code compiles successfully, it will fail at runtime:

```
Contact contact = new Customer()
                         {
                            ...
                         };

ContactManagerClient proxy = new ContactManagerClient();
//Service call will fail:
proxy.AddContact(contact);
proxy.Close();
```

The reason is that you are not actually passing an object reference; you are instead passing the object's state. When you pass in a Customer instead of a Contact, as in the previous example, the service does not know it should deserialize the Customer portion of the state.

Likewise, when a Customer is returned instead of a Contact the client does not know how to deserialize it, because all it knows about are Contacts, not Customers:

```
///////////////////////// Service Side /////////////////////////////
[DataContract]
class Customer : Contact
{
   [DataMember]
   public int OrderNumber;
}
class CustomerManager : IContactManager
{
   List<Customer> m_Customers = new List<Customer>();

   public Contact[] GetContacts()
   {
      return m_Customers.ToArray();
   }
}
```

```
    //Rest of the implementation
}
///////////////////////// Client Side /////////////////////////////
ContactManagerClient proxy = new ContactManagerClient();
//Call will fail:
Contact[] contacts = proxy.GetContacts();
proxy.Close();
```

The solution is to explicitly tell WCF about the Customer class using the KnownTypeAttribute, defined as:

```
[AttributeUsage(AttributeTargets.Struct|AttributeTargets.Class,
                AllowMultiple = true)]
public sealed class KnownTypeAttribute : Attribute
{
    public KnownTypeAttribute(Type type);
    //More members
}
```

The KnownType attribute allows you to designate acceptable subclasses for the data contract:

```
[DataContract]
[KnownType(typeof(Customer))]
class Contact
{...}

[DataContract]
class Customer : Contact
{...}
```

On the host side, the KnownType attribute affects all contracts and operations using the base class, across all services and endpoints, allowing it to accept subclasses instead of base classes. In addition, it includes the subclass in the metadata, so that the client will have its own definition of the subclass and will be able to pass the subclass instead of the base class. If the client also applies the KnownType attribute on its copy of the base class, it can in turn receive the known subclass back from the service.

Service Known Types

The downside of using the KnownType attribute is that it may be too broad in scope. WCF also provides the ServiceKnownTypeAttribute, defined as:

```
[AttributeUsage(AttributeTargets.Interface|
                AttributeTargets.Method   |
                AttributeTargets.Class,
                AllowMultiple = true)]
public sealed class ServiceKnownTypeAttribute : Attribute
{
    public ServiceKnownTypeAttribute(Type type);
    //More members
}
```

Instead of using the KnownType attribute on the base data contract, you can apply the ServiceKnownType attribute on a specific operation on the service side. Then, only that operation (across all supporting services) can accept the known subclass:

```
[DataContract]
class Contact
{...}

[DataContract]
class Customer : Contact
{...}

[ServiceContract]
interface IContactManager
{
    [OperationContract]
    [ServiceKnownType(typeof(Customer))]
    void AddContact(Contact contact);

    [OperationContract]
    Contact[] GetContacts();
}
```

Other operations cannot accept the subclass.

When the ServiceKnownType attribute is applied at the contract level, all the operations in that contract can accept the known subclass, across all implementing services:

```
[ServiceContract]
[ServiceKnownType(typeof(Customer))]
interface IContactManager
{
    [OperationContract]
    void AddContact(Contact contact);

    [OperationContract]
    Contact[] GetContacts();
}
```

 Do not apply the ServiceKnownType attribute on the service class itself. Although the code will compile, this will have an effect only when you don't define the service contract as an interface (something I strongly discourage in any case). If you apply the ServiceKnownType attribute on the service class while there is a separate contract definition, it will have no effect.

Whether you apply the ServiceKnownType attribute at the operation or the contract level, the exported metadata and the generated proxy will have no trace of it and will include the KnownType attribute on the base class only. For example, given this service-side definition:

```
[ServiceContract]
[ServiceKnownType(typeof(Customer))]
interface IContactManager
{...}
```

The imported definition will be:

```
[DataContract]
[KnownType(typeof(Customer))]
class Contact
{...}
[DataContract]
class Customer : Contact
{...}
[ServiceContract]
interface IContactManager
{...}
```

You can manually rework the client-side proxy class to correctly reflect the service-side semantic by removing the KnownType attribute from the base class and applying the ServiceKnownType attribute to the appropriate level in the contract.

Multiple Known Types

You can apply the KnownType and ServiceKnownType attributes multiple times to inform WCF about as many known types as required:

```
[DataContract]
class Contact
{...}

[DataContract]
class Customer : Contact
{...}

[DataContract]
class Person : Contact
{...}

[ServiceContract]
[ServiceKnownType(typeof(Customer))]
[ServiceKnownType(typeof(Person))]
interface IContactManager
{...}
```

The WCF formatter uses reflection to collect all the known types of the data contracts, and then examines the provided parameter to see if it is of any of the known types.

Note that you must explicitly add all levels in the data contract class hierarchy. Adding a subclass does not add its base class(es):

```
[DataContract]
class Contact
{...}
```

```
[DataContract]
class Customer : Contact
{...}

[DataContract]
class Person : Customer
{...}

[ServiceContract]
[ServiceKnownType(typeof(Customer))]
[ServiceKnownType(typeof(Person))]
interface IContactManager
{...}
```

Configuring Known Types

The main downside of the known types attributes is that they require the service or the client to know in advance about all possible subclasses the other party may want to use. Adding a new subclass necessitates changing the code, recompiling, and redeploying. To alleviate this, WCF lets you configure the known types in the service's or client's config file, as shown in Example 3-6. You need to provide not just the type names, but also the names of their containing assemblies.

Example 3-6. Known types in config file

```
<system.runtime.serialization>
   <dataContractSerializer>
      <declaredTypes>
         <add type = "Contact,Host,Version = 1.0.0.0,Culture = neutral,
                      PublicKeyToken = null">
            <knownType type = "Customer,MyClassLibrary,Version = 1.0.0.0,
                               Culture = neutral,PublicKeyToken = null"/>
         </add>
      </declaredTypes>
   </dataContractSerializer>
</system.runtime.serialization>
```

When not relying on string name or assembly version resolution, you can just use the assembly-friendly name:

```
<add type = "Contact,Host">
   <knownType type = "Customer,MyClassLibrary"/>
</add>
```

Including the known types in the config file has the same effect as applying the KnownType attribute on the data contract, and the published metadata will include the known types definition.

Interestingly enough, using a config file to declare a known type is the only way to add a known type that is internal to another assembly.

Objects and Interfaces

The base type of a data contract class or a struct can be an interface:

```
interface IContact
{
    string FirstName
    {get;set;}
    string LastName
    {get;set;}
}
[DataContract]
class Contact : IContact
{...}
```

You can use such a base interface in your service contract, or as a data member in a data contract, as long as you use the ServiceKnownType attribute to designate the actual data type:

```
[ServiceContract]
[ServiceKnownType(typeof(Contact))]
interface IContactManager
{
    [OperationContract]
    void AddContact(IContact contact);

    [OperationContract]
    IContact[] GetContacts();
}
```

You cannot apply the KnownType attribute on the base interface, because the interface itself will not be included in the exported metadata. Instead, the imported service contract will be object-based, and it will include the data contract subclass or struct without the derivation:

```
//Imported definitions:
[DataContract]
class Contact
{...}

[ServiceContract]
interface IContactManager
{
    [OperationContract]
    [ServiceKnownType(typeof(Contact))]
    [ServiceKnownType(typeof(object[]))]
    void AddContact(object contact);

    [OperationContract]
    [ServiceKnownType(typeof(Contact))]
    [ServiceKnownType(typeof(object[]))]
    object[] GetContacts();
}
```

The imported definition will always have the ServiceKnownType attribute applied at the operation level, even if it was originally defined at the scope of the contract. In addition, every operation will include a union of all the ServiceKnownType attributes required by all the operations, including a redundant service known type attribute for the array. These are relics from a time when these definitions were required in a pre-released version of WCF.

You can manually rework the imported definition to have only the required ServiceKnownType attributes:

```
[DataContract]
class Contact
{...}

[ServiceContract]
interface IContactManager
{
    [OperationContract]
    [ServiceKnownType(typeof(Contact))]
    void AddContact(object contact);

    [OperationContract]
    [ServiceKnownType(typeof(Contact))]
    object[] GetContacts();
}
```

Or better yet, if you have the definition of the base interface on the client side, or if you refactor that definition, you can use that instead of object. This gives you an added degree of type safety, as long as you add a derivation from the interface to the data contract:

```
[DataContract]
class Contact : IContact
{...}

[ServiceContract]
interface IContactManager
{
    [OperationContract]
    [ServiceKnownType(typeof(Contact))]
    void AddContact(IContact contact);

    [OperationContract]
    [ServiceKnownType(typeof(Contact))]
    IContact[] GetContacts();
}
```

However, you cannot replace the object in the imported contract with the concrete data contract type, because it is no longer compatible:

```
//Invalid client-side contract
[ServiceContract]
interface IContactManager
```

```
{
    [OperationContract]
    void AddContact(Contact contact);

    [OperationContract]
    Contact[] GetContacts();
}
```

Data Contract Equivalence

Two data contracts are considered *equivalent* if they have the same wire representation—that is, if they have the same infoset schema. This can be the case if they define the same type (but not necessarily the same version of the type), or if the two data contracts refer to two different types with the same data contract and data member names. Equivalent data contracts are interchangeable: WCF will let any service that was defined with one data contract operate with an equivalent data contract.

The most common way of defining an equivalent data contract is to use the DataContract and DataMember attributes' Name properties to map one data contract to another. In the case of the DataContract attribute, the Name property defaults to the type's name, so these two definitions are identical:

```
[DataContract]
struct Contact
{...}

[DataContract(Name = "Contact")]
struct Contact
{...}
```

In fact, the full name of the data contract always includes its namespace as well, but as you have seen, you can assign a different namespace.

In the case of the DataMember attribute, the Name property defaults to the member name, so these two definitions are identical:

```
[DataMember]
string FirstName;

[DataMember(Name = "FirstName")]
string FirstName;
```

By assigning different names to the data contract and data members, you can generate an equivalent data contract from a different type. For example, these two data contracts are equivalent:

```
[DataContract]
struct Contact
{
    [DataMember]
    public string FirstName;
```

```
   [DataMember]
   public string LastName;
}
[DataContract(Name = "Contact")]
struct Person
{
   [DataMember(Name = "FirstName")]
   public string Name;

   [DataMember(Name = "LastName")]
   public string Surname;
}
```

In addition to having identical names, the types of the data members have to match.

 A class and a structure that support the same data contract are interchangeable.

Serialization Order

In classic .NET, a subclass can define a member of the same name and type as a private member of its base class, and in turn, its own subclass can do the same:

```
class A
{
   string Name;
}
class B : A
{
   string Name;
}
class C : B
{
   string Name;
}
```

If the class hierarchy is also a data contract, this presents a problem when serializing into a message an instance of the subclass, since the message will contain multiple copies of a data member with the same name and type. To distinguish between them, WCF places the data members in the message in a particular order.

The default serialization order inside a type is simply alphabetical, and across a class hierarchy the order is top-down. In case of a mismatch in the serialization order, the members will be initialized to their default values. For example, when serializing a Customer instance, defined as:

```
[DataContract]
class Contact
{
   [DataMember]
   public string FirstName;
```

```
    [DataMember]
    public string LastName;
}
[DataContract]
class Customer : Contact
{
    [DataMember]
    public int CustomerNumber;
}
```

the members will be serialized in the following order: FirstName, LastName, CustomerNumber.

Of course, equivalent data contracts must serialize and deserialize their members in the same order. The problem now is that combining a data contract hierarchy with aliasing contracts and members might break the serialization order. For example, the following data contract is not equivalent to the Customer data contract:

```
[DataContract(Name = "Customer")]
public class Person
{
    [DataMember(Name = "FirstName")]
    public string Name;

    [DataMember(Name = "LastName")]
    public string Surname;

    [DataMember]
    public int CustomerNumber;
}
```

because the serialization order is CustomerNumber, FirstName, LastName. To resolve this conflict, you need to provide WCF with the order of serialization by setting the Order property of the DataMember attribute. The value of the Order property defaults to -1, meaning the default WCF ordering, but you can assign to it values indicating the required order:

```
[DataContract(Name = "Customer")]
public class Person
{
    [DataMember(Name = "FirstName",Order = 1)]
    public string Name;

    [DataMember(Name = "LastName",Order = 2)]
    public string Surname;

    [DataMember(Order = 3)]
    public int CustomerNumber;
}
```

When renaming data members, you must take care to manually change their order. Even without renaming, with a large number of data members, the sorting can quickly get out of hand. Fortunately, if another member has the same value for its

Order property, WCF will order them alphabetically. You can take advantage of this behavior by assigning the same number to all members coming from the same level in the original class hierarchy, or, better yet, simply assign them their levels in that hierarchy:

```
[DataContract(Name = "Customer")]
public class Person
{
   [DataMember(Name = "FirstName",Order = 1)]
   public string Name;

   [DataMember(Name = "LastName",Order = 1)]
   public string Surname;

   [DataMember(Order = 2)]
   public int CustomerNumber;
}
```

Versioning

Services should be decoupled from their clients as much as possible, especially when it comes to versioning and technologies. Any version of the client should be able to consume any version of the service, and should do so without resorting to version numbers (such as those in assemblies), because those are .NET-specific. When a service and a client share a data contract, an important objective is allowing the service and client to evolve their versions of the data contract separately. To allow such decoupling, WCF needs to enable both backward and forward compatibility, without even sharing types or version information. There are three main versioning scenarios:

- New members
- Missing members
- Round-tripping, where a new data contract version is passed to and from a client or service with an older version, requiring both backward and forward compatibility

By default, data contracts are version tolerant and will silently ignore incompatibilities.

New Members

The most common change made to a data contract is adding new members on one side and sending the new contract to an old client or service. When deserializing the type, DataContractSerializer will simply ignore the new members. As a result, both the service and the client can accept data with new members that were not part of the original contract. For example, the service may be built against this data contract:

```
[DataContract]
struct Contact
{
```

```
        [DataMember]
        public string FirstName;

        [DataMember]
        public string LastName;
    }
```

yet the client may send it this data contract instead:

```
    [DataContract]
    struct Contact
    {
        [DataMember]
        public string FirstName;

        [DataMember]
        public string LastName;

        [DataMember]
        public string Address;
    }
```

Note that adding new members and having them ignored in this way breaks the data contract schema compatibility, because a service (or a client) that is compatible with one schema is all of a sudden compatible with a new schema.

Missing Members

By default, WCF lets either party remove members from the data contract. That is, you can serialize a type without certain members, and send it to another party that expects the missing members. Although normally you probably won't intentionally remove members, the more likely scenario is when a client that is written against an old definition of the data contract interacts with a service written against a newer definition of that contract that expects new members. When, on the receiving side, DataContractSerializer does not find in the message the information required to deserialize those members, it will silently deserialize them to their default values; that is, null for reference types and a zero whitewash for value types. In effect, it will be as if the sending party never initialized those members. This default policy enables a service to accept data with missing members, or return data with missing members to the client. Example 3-7 demonstrates this point.

Example 3-7. Missing members are initialized to their default values

```
/////////////////////////// Service Side ///////////////////////////////
[DataContract]
struct Contact
{
    [DataMember]
    public string FirstName;
```

```
   [DataMember]
   public string LastName;

   [DataMember]
   public string Address;
}

[ServiceContract]
interface IContactManager
{
   [OperationContract]
   void AddContact(Contact contact);
   ...
}

class ContactManager : IContactManager
{
   public void AddContact(Contact contact)
   {
      Trace.WriteLine("First name = " + contact.FirstName);
      Trace.WriteLine("Last name = " + contact.LastName);
      Trace.WriteLine("Address = " + (contact.Address ?? "Missing"));
      ...
   }
   ...
}
/////////////////////////// Client Side ///////////////////////////////
[DataContract]
struct Contact
{
   [DataMember]
   public string FirstName;

   [DataMember]
   public string LastName;
}

Contact contact = new Contact()
                  {
                     FirstName = "Juval",
                     LastName  = "Lowy"
                  };

ContactManagerClient proxy = new ContactManagerClient();
proxy.AddContact(contact);

proxy.Close();
```

The output of Example 3-7 will be:

```
   First name = Juval
   Last name = Lowy
   Address = Missing
```

because the service received `null` for the `Address` data member and coalesced the trace to `Missing`. The problem with Example 3-7 is that you will have to manually compensate this way at every place the service (or any other service or client) uses this data contract.

Using the OnDeserializing event

When you do want to share your compensation logic across all parties using the data contract, it's better to use the `OnDeserializing` event to initialize potentially missing data members based on some local heuristic. If the message contains values for those members, they will override your settings in the `OnDeserializing` event. If it doesn't, the event handling method provides some nondefault values. Using the technique shown here:

```
[DataContract]
struct Contact
{
   [DataMember]
   public string FirstName;

   [DataMember]
   public string LastName;

   [DataMember]
   public string Address;

   [OnDeserializing]
   void OnDeserializing(StreamingContext context)
   {
      Address = "Some default address";
   }
}
```

the output of Example 3-7 will be:

```
First name = Juval
Last name = Lowy
Address = Some default address
```

Required members

Unlike ignoring new members, which for the most part is benign, the default handling of missing members may very likely cause the receiving side to fail further down the call chain, because the missing members may be essential for correct operation. This may have disastrous results. You can instruct WCF to avoid invoking the operation and to fail the call if a data member is missing by setting the `IsRequired` property of the `DataMember` attribute to true:

```
[DataContract]
struct Contact
{
   [DataMember]
   public string FirstName;
```

```
    [DataMember]
    public string LastName;

    [DataMember(IsRequired = true)]
    public string Address;
}
```

The default value of IsRequired is false; that is, to ignore the missing member. When, on the receiving side, DataContractSerializer does not find the information required to deserialize a member marked as required in the message, it will abort the call, resulting in a NetDispatcherFaultException on the sending side. For instance, if the data contract on the service side in Example 3-7 were to mark the Address member as required, the call would not reach the service. The fact that a particular member is required is published in the service metadata, and when it is imported to the client, the generated proxy definition will also have that member as required.

Both the client and the service can mark some or all of the data members in their data contracts as required, completely independently of each other. The more members that are marked as required, the safer the interaction with a service or a client will be, but at the expense of flexibility and versioning tolerance.

When a data contract that has a required new member is sent to a receiving party that is not even aware of that member, such a call is actually valid and will be allowed to go through. In other words, if Version 2 (V2) of a data contract has a new member for which IsRequired is set to true, you can send V2 to a party expecting Version 1 (V1) that does not even have the member in the contract, and the new member will simply be ignored. IsRequired has an effect only when the V2-aware party is missing the member. Assuming that V1 does not know about a new member added by V2, Table 3-1 lists the possible permutations of allowed or disallowed interactions as a product of the versions involved and the value of the IsRequired property.

Table 3-1. Versioning tolerance with required members

IsRequired	V1 to V2	V2 to V1
False	Yes	Yes
True	No	Yes

An interesting situation relying on required members has to do with serializable types. Since serializable types have no tolerance toward missing members by default, when they are exported the resulting data contract will have all data members as required. For example, this Contact definition:

```
[Serializable]
struct Contact
{
```

```
      public string FirstName;
      public string LastName;
   }
```

will have the metadata representation of:

```
[DataContract]
struct Contact
{
   [DataMember(IsRequired = true)]
   public string FirstName
   {get;set;}

   [DataMember(IsRequired = true)]
   public string LastName
   {get;set;}
}
```

To set the same versioning tolerance regarding missing members as the DataContract attribute, apply the OptionalField attribute on the optional member. For example, this Contact definition:

```
[Serializable]
struct Contact
{
   public string FirstName;

   [OptionalField]
   public string LastName;
}
```

will have the metadata representation of:

```
[DataContract]
struct Contact
{
   [DataMember(IsRequired = true)]
   public string FirstName
   {get;set;}

   [DataMember]
   public string LastName
   {get;set;}
}
```

Versioning Round-Trip

The versioning tolerance techniques discussed so far for ignoring new members and defaulting missing ones are suboptimal: they enable a point-to-point client-to-service call but have no support for a wider-scope pass-through scenario. Consider the two interactions shown in Figure 3-4.

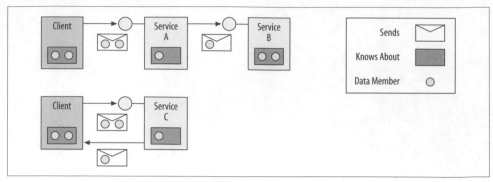

Figure 3-4. Versioning round-trip may degrade overall interaction

In the first interaction, a client that is built against a new data contract with new members passes that data contract to Service A, which does not know about the new members. Service A then passes the data to Service B, which is aware of the new data contract. However, the data passed from Service A to Service B does not contain the new members—they were silently dropped during deserialization from the client because they were not part of the data contract for Service A. A similar situation occurs in the second interaction, where a client that is aware of the new data contract with new members passes the data to Service C, which is aware only of the old contract that does not have the new members. The data Service C returns to the client will not have the new members.

This situation of new-old-new interaction is called a *versioning round-trip*. WCF supports handling of versioning round-trips by allowing a service (or client) with knowledge of only the old contract to simply pass through the state of the members defined in the new contract, without dropping them. The problem is how to enable services/clients that are not aware of the new members to serialize and deserialize those unknown members without their schemas, and where to store them between calls. WCF's solution is to have the data contract type implement the IExtensibleDataObject interface, defined as:

```
public interface IExtensibleDataObject
{
    ExtensionDataObject ExtensionData
    {get;set;}
}
```

IExtensibleDataObject defines a single property of the type ExtensionDataObject. The exact definition of ExtensionDataObject is irrelevant, since developers never have to interact with it directly. ExtensionDataObject has an internal linked list of object references and type information, and that is where the unknown data members are stored. In other words, if the data contract type supports IExtensibleDataObject, when unrecognized new members are available in the message, they are deserialized and stored in that list. When the service (or client) calls out—passing the old data contract type, which now includes the unknown data members inside ExtensionDataObject—the unknown members are serialized out into the message in order. If the receiving side knows about the new data contract, it will get a valid new data contract without any missing members. Example 3-8 demonstrates implementing and relying on IExtensibleDataObject. As you can see, the implementation is straightforward: just add an ExtensionDataObject automatic property with explicit interface implementation.

Example 3-8. Implementing IExtensibleDataObject

```
[DataContract]
class Contact : IExtensibleDataObject
{
   ExtensionDataObject IExtensibleDataObject.ExtensionData
   {get;set;}

   [DataMember]
   public string FirstName;

   [DataMember]
   public string LastName;
}
```

Schema compatibility

While implementing IExtensibleDataObject enables round-tripping, it has the downside of enabling a service that is compatible with one data contract schema to interact successfully with another service that expects another data contract schema. In some esoteric cases, the service may decide to disallow round-tripping and enforce its own version of the data contract on downstream services. Using the ServiceBehavior attribute (discussed at length in the next chapter), services can instruct WCF to override the handling of unknown members by IExtensibleDataObject and ignore them even if the data contract supports IExtensibleDataObject. The ServiceBehavior attribute offers the Boolean property IgnoreExtensionDataObject, defined as:

```
[AttributeUsage(AttributeTargets.Class)]
public sealed class ServiceBehaviorAttribute : Attribute,...
{
   public bool IgnoreExtensionDataObject
   {get;set;}
   //More members
}
```

The default value of IgnoreExtensionDataObject is false. Setting it to true ensures that all unknown data members across all data contracts used by the service will always be ignored:

```
[ServiceBehavior(IgnoreExtensionDataObject = true)]
class ContactManager : IContactManager
{...}
```

When you import a data contract using Visual Studio 2008, the generated data contract type always supports IExtensibleDataObject, even if the original data contract did not. I believe that the best practice is to always have your data contracts implement IExtensibleDataObject and to avoid setting IgnoreExtensionDataObject to true. IExtensibleDataObject decouples the service from its downstream services, allowing them to evolve separately.

 There is no need to implement IExtensibleDataObject when dealing with known types, because the subclass is always deserialized without a loss.

Enumerations

Enumerations are always serializable by definition. When you define a new enum, there is no need to apply the DataContract attribute on it, and you can freely use it in a data contract, as shown in Example 3-9. All the values in the enum will implicitly be included in the data contract.

Example 3-9. Using an enum in a data contract

```
enum ContactType
{
   Customer,
   Vendor,
   Partner
}

[DataContract]
struct Contact
{
   [DataMember]
   public ContactType ContactType;

   [DataMember]
   public string FirstName;

   [DataMember]
   public string LastName;
}
```

If you want to exclude certain enum values from the data contract, you need to first decorate the enum with the DataContract attribute, and then explicitly apply the EnumMemberAttribute to all enum values you want to include in the enum data contract. The EnumMember attribute is defined as:

```
[AttributeUsage(AttributeTargets.Field,Inherited = false)]
public sealed class EnumMemberAttribute : Attribute
{
   public string Value
   {get;set;}
}
```

Any enum value not decorated with the `EnumMember` attribute will not be part of the data contract for that enum. For example, this enum:

```
[DataContract]
enum ContactType
{
    [EnumMember]
    Customer,

    [EnumMember]
    Vendor,

    //Will not be part of data contract
    Partner
}
```

will result in this wire representation:

```
enum ContactType
{
    Customer,
    Vendor
}
```

The other use for the `EnumMember` attribute is to alias certain enum values to an already existing enum data contract, using the `Value` property. For example, this enum:

```
[DataContract]
enum ContactType
{
    [EnumMember(Value = "MyCustomer")]
    Customer,

    [EnumMember]
    Vendor,

    [EnumMember]
    Partner
}
```

will result with this wire representation:

```
enum ContactType
{
    MyCustomer,
    Vendor,
    Partner
}
```

The effect the `EnumMember` attribute has is local to the party using it. When publishing the metadata (or when defining it on the client side), the resulting data contract has no trace of it, and only the final product is used.

Delegates and Data Contracts

All delegate definitions are compiled into serializable classes, so in theory your data contract types could contain delegates as member variables:

```
[DataContract]
class MyDataContract
{
    [DataMember]
    public EventHandler MyEvent;
}
```

or even as events (note the use of the field qualifier):

```
[DataContract]
class MyDataContract
{
    [field:DataMember]
    public event EventHandler MyEvent;
}
```

In practice, however, when the data contract refers to a custom delegate, the imported data contract will contain an invalid delegate definition. While you could manually fix that definition, the bigger problem is that when you serialize an object that has a delegate member variable, the internal invocation list of the delegates is serialized too. In most cases this is not the desired effect with services and clients, because the exact structure of the list is local to the client or the service and should not be shared across the service boundary. In addition, there are no guarantees that the target objects in the internal list are serializable or are valid data contracts. Consequently, sometimes the serialization will work, and sometimes it will fail.

The simplest way to avoid this pitfall is not to apply the DataMember attribute on delegates. If the data contract is a serializable type, you need to explicitly exclude the delegate from the data contract:

```
[Serializable]
public class MyClass
{
    [NonSerialized]
    public EventHandler MyEvent;
}
```

Data Sets and Tables

One of the most common types of data contract exchanged between clients and services involves data that originates in or is destined for a database. In .NET, a common way of interacting with databases is via ADO.NET's data set and data table types. Applications can use the raw DataSet and DataTable types, or use the data access management tools in Visual Studio 2008 to generate type-safe derivatives.

The raw DataSet and DataTable types are serializable (i.e., marked with the Serializable attribute):

```
[Serializable]
public class DataSet : ...
{...}

[Serializable]
public class DataTable : ...
{...}
```

This means that you can define valid service contracts that accept or return data tables or data sets:

```
[DataContract]
struct Contact
{...}

[ServiceContract]
interface IContactManager
{
   [OperationContract]
   void AddContact(Contact contact);

   [OperationContract]
   void AddContacts(DataTable contacts);

   [OperationContract]
   DataTable GetContacts();
}
```

You can also use the type-safe subclasses of DataSet and DataTable in your contracts. For example, suppose in your database you have a table called Contacts that contains your contacts, with columns such as FirstName and LastName. You can use Visual Studio 2008 to generate a type-safe data set called MyDataSet that has a nested class called ContactsDataTable, as well as a type-safe row and type-safe data adapter, as shown in Example 3-10.

Example 3-10. Type-safe data set and data table

```
[Serializable]
public partial class MyDataSet : DataSet
{
   public ContactsDataTable Contacts
   {get;}

   [Serializable]
   public partial class ContactsDataTable : ...
   {
      public void AddContactsRow(ContactsRow row);
      public ContactsRow AddContactsRow(string FirstName,string LastName);
      //More members
   }
```

Example 3-10. Type-safe data set and data table (continued)

```
public partial class ContactsRow : DataRow
{
   public string FirstName
   {get;set;}

   public string LastName
   {get;set;}
   //More members
}
//More members
}
public partial class ContactsTableAdapter : Component
{
   public virtual MyDataSet.ContactsDataTable GetData();
   //More members
}
```

You can then use the type-safe data table in your service contract:

```
[DataContract]
struct Contact
{...}

[ServiceContract]
interface IContactManager
{
   [OperationContract]
   void AddContact(Contact contact);

   [OperationContract]
   void AddContacts(MyDataSet.ContactsDataTable contacts);

   [OperationContract]
   MyDataSet.ContactsDataTable GetContacts();
}
```

 The data row itself is not serializable, so you cannot use it (or its type-safe subclass) in operations, like this:

```
//Invalid definition
[OperationContract]
void AddContact(MyDataSet.ContactsRow contact);
```

The type-safe data table will be part of the published metadata of the service. When importing it to the client, Visual Studio 2008 is smart enough to regenerate the type-safe data table, and the proxy file will include not just the data contract, but the code itself. If the client already has a local definition of the type-safe table, you can remove the definition from the proxy file.

Using Arrays Instead of Tables

ADO.NET and the Visual Studio tools make it trivial for both WCF clients and services to use `DataSet` and `DataTable` and their type-safe derivatives. However, these data access types are specific to .NET. While they are serializable, their resulting data contract schema is so complex that trying to interact with it on other platforms is impractical. There are additional drawbacks to using a table or a data set in a service contract: you may be exposing your internal data structure to the world, and the clients are unlikely to care about internal data storage artifacts such as IDs, keys, and foreign key relationships. The client may also care about only a subset of the information in the table. Furthermore, future changes to the database schema will break your clients, so any service that defines a service contract in terms of its underlying data table must hold that table schema as immutable (something you will find difficult to do). Unless you are designing a data access service, in general it is better to expose operations on the data as opposed to the data itself. In short, sending the data table across the service boundary is rarely a good idea.

If you do need to pass around the data itself, it is best to do so using a neutral data structure such as an array, and transform the individual rows into some data contract that encapsulates the original schema.

Converting legacy data tables

All versions of Visual Studio up until Visual Studio 2008 generated a type-safe data table that derived from the `DataTable` class, without a type-safe way of enumerating over the table or converting it to an array:

```
[Serializable]
public partial class ContactsDataTable : DataTable,IEnumerable
{...}
```

To streamline the task of converting a data table to an array, you can use my `DataTableHelper` class, defined as:

```
public static class DataTableHelper
{
    public static T[] ToArray<R,T>(this DataTable table,Func<R,T> converter)
                                                     where R : DataRow;
}
```

`DataTableHelper` defines the `DataTable` extension method `ToArray( )`.

All `DataTableHelper` requires is a converter from a data row in the table to the data contract. `DataTableHelper` also adds some compile-time and runtime type-safety verification. Example 3-11 demonstrates using `DataTableHelper`.

Example 3-11. Using DataTableHelper

```
[DataContract]
struct Contact
{
   [DataMember]
   public string FirstName;

   [DataMember]
   public string LastName;
}
[ServiceContract]
interface IContactManager
{
   [OperationContract]
   Contact[] GetContacts();
   ...
}
class ContactManager : IContactManager
{
   public Contact[] GetContacts()
   {
      ContactsTableAdapter adapter = new ContactsTableAdapter();
      MyDataSet.ContactsDataTable contactsTable = adapter.GetData();

      Func<MyDataSet.ContactsRow,Contact> converter = (row)=>
                                                {
                                                   return new Contact()
                                                         {
                                                  FirstName = row.FirstName,
                                                  LastName = row.LastName
                                                         };
                                                };
      return contactsTable.ToArray(converter);
   }
   //Rest of the implementation
}
```

In Example 3-11, the GetContacts() method uses the type-safe table adapter
ContactsTableAdapter (listed in Example 3-10) to get the records from the database
in the form of the type-safe table MyDataSet.ContactsDataTable. GetContacts() then
defines a lambda expression that converts an instance of the type-safe data row
MyDataSet.ContactsRow to a Contact instance. Finally, GetContacts() calls the
ToArray() extension, providing it with the table and the converter.

Example 3-12 shows the implementation of DataTableHelper.ToArray().

Example 3-12. The DataTableHelper class

```
public static class DataTableHelper
{
   public static T[] ToArray<R,T>(this DataTable table,Func<R,T> converter)
                                                where R : DataRow
```

Example 3-12. The DataTableHelper class (continued)

```
{
   //Verify [DataContract] or [Serializable] on T
   Debug.Assert(IsDataContract(typeof(T)) || typeof(T).IsSerializable);

   if(table.Rows.Count == 0)
   {
      return new T[]{};
   }

   //Verify table contains correct rows
   Debug.Assert(MatchingTableRow<R>(table));

   return table.Rows.Cast<R>().Select(converter).ToArray();
}
static bool IsDataContract(Type type)
{
   object[] attributes =
                type.GetCustomAttributes(typeof(DataContractAttribute),false);
   return attributes.Length == 1;
}
static bool MatchingTableRow<R>(DataTable table)
{
   if(table.Rows.Count == 0)
   {
      return true;
   }
   return table.Rows[0] is R;
}
}
}
```

DataTableHelper.ToArray() first uses the Cast() LINQ extension method to convert
each row (which is an object) into an R, then it uses a Select() query to convert that
collection of rows to a collection of Ts, and finally converts that collection into an
array.

DataTableHelper adds some type safety. At compile time, it constrains the type parameter R to be a data row. At runtime, DataTableHelper verifies that the type parameter T is decorated either with the DataContract attribute or the Serializable attribute.
Verifying the presence of the DataContract attribute is done via the helper method
IsDataContract(), which uses reflection to look up the attribute. Verifying the
Serializable attribute is done by checking whether the IsSerializable bit is set on
the type. The method returns an empty array if the table is empty. Finally, ToArray()
verifies that the provided table has the rows specified with the type parameter R. This
is done via the MatchingTableRow() helper method, which gets the first row and verifies its type.

Converting new data tables

Visual Studio 2008 introduced support for strongly typed queries and LINQ. When using Visual Studio 2008 to generate a table, the table derives from TypedTableBase<T>:

```
[Serializable]
public partial class ContactsDataTable : TypedTableBase<ContactsRow>
{...}
```

This makes it easier to use LINQ to convert the table directly into an array. Using the same definitions as Example 3-11, you can now write:

```
public Contact[] GetContacts()
{
   Func<CustomersDataSet.ContactsRow,Contact> converter = (row)=>
                                                 {
                                                    return new Contact()
                                                            {
                                                    FirstName = row.FirstName,
                                                    LastName = row.LastName
                                                            };
                                                  };
   return contactsTable.Select(converter).ToArray();
}
```

Or even:

```
public Contact[] GetContacts()
{
   return contactsTable.Select(row => new Contact(){
               FirstName = row.FirstName,LastName = row.LastName}).ToArray();
}
```

Using LINQ to SQL

Instead of using tables, you can use LINQ to SQL and Visual Studio 2008 to generate the code for a strongly typed data context. However, the strongly-typed object collection on the context is not decorated with either the Serializable or the DataContract attribute, forcing you to rely on the inferred data contract, as shown in Example 3-13.

Example 3-13. Using LINQ to SQL with inferred data contract

```
public partial class ContactsDataContext : DataContext
{
   public Table<Contact> Contacts
   {get;}
   //More members
}

public partial class Contact
{
```

Example 3-13. Using LINQ to SQL with inferred data contract (continued)

```
   public string FirstName
   {get;set;}

   public string LastName
   {get;set;}
}

[ServiceContract]
interface IContactManager
{
   [OperationContract]
   Contact[] GetContacts( );
   ...
}
class ContactManager : IContactManager
{
   public Contact[] GetContacts( )
   {
      using(ContactsDataContext context = new ContactsDataContext( ))
      {
         return context.Contacts.ToArray( );
      }
   }
}
```

Instead of an inferred data contract (or changing the machine-generated code), you can convert the strongly typed machine-generated type into a data contract you manage, as shown in Example 3-14, using the same definitions as in Example 3-13.

Example 3-14. Using LINQ to SQL without inferred data contract

```
[DataContract(Name = "Contact")]
class MyContact
{
   [DataMember]
   public string FirstName
   {get;set;}

   [DataMember]
    public string LastName
   {get;set;}
}

[ServiceContract]
interface IContactManager
{
   [OperationContract]
   MyContact[] GetContacts( );
   ...
}
```

```
class ContactManager : IContactManager
{
   public MyContact[] GetContacts()
   {
      using(ContactsDataContext context = new ContactsDataContext())
      {
         return context.Contacts.Select(row => new MyContact(){
                  FirstName = row.FirstName,LastName = row.LastName}).ToArray();
      }
   }
}
```

Generics

You cannot define WCF contracts that rely on generic type parameters. Generics are specific to .NET, and using them would violate the service-oriented nature of WCF. However, you can use bounded generic types in your data contracts, as long as you specify the type parameters in the service contract and as long as the specified type parameters have valid data contracts, as shown in Example 3-15.

Example 3-15. Using bounded generic types

```
[DataContract]
class MyClass<T>
{
   [DataMember]
   public T MyMember;
}

[ServiceContract]
interface IMyContract
{
   [OperationContract]
   void MyMethod(MyClass<int> obj);
}
```

When you import the metadata of a data contract such as the one in Example 3-15, the imported types have all type parameters replaced with specific types, and the data contract itself is renamed to this format:

```
<Original name>Of<Type parameter names><hash>
```

Using the same definitions as in Example 3-15, the imported data contract and service contract will look like this:

```
[DataContract]
class MyClassOfint
{
   int MyMemberField;

   [DataMember]
   public int MyMember
```

```
    {
        get
        {
            return MyMemberField;
        }
        set
        {
            MyMemberField = value;
        }
    }
}

[ServiceContract]
interface IMyContract
{
    [OperationContract]
    void MyMethod(MyClassOfint obj);
}
```

If, however, the service contract were to use a custom type such as SomeClass instead of int:

```
[DataContract]
class SomeClass
{...}

[DataContract]
class MyClass<T>
{...}

[OperationContract]
void MyMethod(MyClass<SomeClass> obj);
```

the exported data contract might look like this:

```
[DataContract]
class SomeClass
{...}

[DataContract]
class MyClassOfSomeClassMTRdqN6P
{...}

[OperationContract(...)]
void MyMethod(MyClassOfSomeClassMTRdqN6P obj);
```

where MTRdqN6P is some quasi-unique hash of the generic type parameter and the containing namespace. Different data contracts and namespaces will generate different hashes. The hash is in place to reduce the overall potential for a conflict with another data contract that might use another type parameter with the same name. No hash is created for the implicit data contracts of the primitives when they are used as generic type parameters, since the type int is a reserved word and the definition of MyClassOfint is unique.

In most cases, the hash is a cumbersome over-precaution. You can specify a different name for the exported data contract by simply assigning it to the data contract's Name property. For example, given this service-side data contract:

```
[DataContract]
class SomeClass
{...}

[DataContract(Name = "MyClass")]
class MyClass<T>
{...}

[OperationContract]
void MyMethod(MyClass<SomeClass> obj);
```

the exported data contract will be:

```
[DataContract]
class SomeClass
{...}

[DataContract]
class MyClass
{...}

[OperationContract]
void MyMethod(MyClass obj);
```

However, by doing this you run the risk of some ambiguity, since two different custom generic types will result in the same type name.

If you would still like to combine the name of the generic type parameter with that of the data contract, use the {<number>} directive, where the number is the ordinal number of the type parameter. For example, given this service-side definition:

```
[DataContract]
class SomeClass
{...}

[DataContract(Name = "MyClassOf{0}{1}")]
class MyClass<T,U>
{...}

[OperationContract]
void MyMethod(MyClass<SomeClass,int> obj);
```

the exported definition will be:

```
[DataContract]
class SomeClass
{...}

[DataContract]
class MyClassOfSomeClassint
{...}
```

```
[OperationContract(...)]
void MyMethod(MyClassOfSomeClassint obj);
```

 The number of type parameters specified is not verified at compile time. Any mismatch will yield a runtime exception.

Finally, you can append # after the number to generate the unique hash. For example, given this data contract definition:

```
[DataContract]
class SomeClass
{...}

[DataContract(Name = "MyClassOf{0}{#}")]
class MyClass<T>
{...}

[OperationContract]
void MyMethod(MyClass<SomeClass> obj);
```

the exported definition will be:

```
[DataContract]
class SomeClass
{...}

[DataContract]
class MyClassOfSomeClassMTRdqN6P
{...}

[OperationContract]
void MyMethod(MyClassOfSomeClassMTRdqN6P obj);
```

Collections

In .NET, a *collection* is any type that supports the IEnumerable or IEnumerable<T> interface. All of the built-in collections in .NET, such as the array, the list, and the stack, support these interfaces. A data contract can include a collection as a data member, and a service contract can define operations that interact with a collection directly. Because .NET collections are .NET-specific, WCF cannot expose them in the service metadata, yet because they are so useful, WCF offers dedicated marshaling rules for collections.

Whenever you define a service operation that uses the collection interfaces IEnumerable<T>, IList<T>, or ICollection<T>, the resulting metadata always uses an array. For example, this service contract definition and implementation:

```
[ServiceContract]
interface IContactManager
{
    [OperationContract]
    IEnumerable<Contact> GetContacts();
    ...
}
class ContactManager : IContactManager
{
    List<Contact> m_Contacts = new List<Contact>();

    public IEnumerable<Contact> GetContacts()
    {
        return m_Contacts;
    }
    ...
}
```

will be exported as:

```
[ServiceContract]
interface IContactManager
{
    [OperationContract]
    Contact[] GetContacts();
}
```

Concrete Collections

If the collection in the contract is a concrete collection (not an interface) and is a serializable collection—that is, it is marked with the Serializable attribute but not with
the DataContract attribute—WCF can normalize the collection automatically to an
array of the collection's type, provided the collection contains an Add( ) method with
either one of these signatures:

```
public void Add(object obj); //Collection uses IEnumerable
public void Add(T item);     //Collection uses IEnumerable<T>
```

For example, consider this contract definition:

```
[ServiceContract]
interface IContactManager
{
    [OperationContract]
    void AddContact(Contact contact);

    [OperationContract]
    List<Contact> GetContacts();
}
```

The list class is defined as:

```
public interface ICollection<T> : IEnumerable<T>
{...}
public interface IList<T> : ICollection<T>
{...}
```

```
[Serializable]
public class List<T> : IList<T>
{
   public void Add(T item);
   //More members
}
```

Because it is a valid collection and it has an Add( ) method, the resulting representation of the contract will be:

```
[ServiceContract]
interface IContactManager
{
   [OperationContract]
   void AddContact(Contact contact);

   [OperationContract]
   Contact[] GetContacts( );
}
```

That is, a List<Contact> is marshaled as a Contact[]. The service may still return a List<Contact>, and yet the client will interact with an array, as shown in Example 3-16.

Example 3-16. Marshaling a list as an array

```
///////////////////////////// Service Side /////////////////////////////////
[ServiceContract]
interface IContactManager
{
   [OperationContract]
   void AddContact(Contact contact);

   [OperationContract]
   List<Contact> GetContacts( );
}
//Service implementation
class ContactManager : IContactManager
{
   List<Contact> m_Contacts = new List<Contact>( );

   public void AddContact(Contact contact)
   {
      m_Contacts.Add(contact);
   }

   public List<Contact> GetContacts( )
   {
      return m_Contacts;
   }
}
///////////////////////////// Client Side /////////////////////////////////
[ServiceContract]
interface IContactManager
{
```

Example 3-16. Marshaling a list as an array (continued)

```
   [OperationContract]
   void AddContact(Contact contact);

   [OperationContract]
   Contact[] GetContacts();
}
class ContactManagerClient : ClientBase<IContactManager>,IContactManager
{
   public Contact[] GetContacts()
   {
      return Channel.GetContacts();
   }
   //More members
}
//Client code
ContactManagerClient proxy = new ContactManagerClient();
Contact[] contacts = proxy.GetContacts();
proxy.Close();
```

Note that while the collection must have the Add( ) method for it to be marshaled as an array, the collection need not implement the Add( ) method at all.

Custom Collections

It's not just the built-in collections that can be automatically marshaled as arrays—any custom collection can abide by the same prerequisites and be marshaled as an array, as shown in Example 3-17. In this example, the collection MyCollection<string> is marshaled as a string[].

Example 3-17. Marshaling a custom collection as an array

```
///////////////////////// Service Side /////////////////////////////
[Serializable]
public class MyCollection<T> : IEnumerable<T>
{
   public void Add(T item)
   {}

   IEnumerator<T> IEnumerable<T>.GetEnumerator()
   {...}
   //Rest of the implementation
}
[ServiceContract]
interface IMyContract
{
   [OperationContract]
   MyCollection<string> GetCollection();
}

///////////////////////// Client Side /////////////////////////////
```

Example 3-17. Marshaling a custom collection as an array (continued)

```
[ServiceContract]
interface IMyContract
{
   [OperationContract]
   string[] GetCollection();
}
```

The CollectionDataContract Attribute

The mechanism shown so far for marshaling a concrete collection is suboptimal. For one thing, it requires the collection to be serializable and does not work with the service-oriented DataContract attribute. Also, while one party is dealing with a collection, the other is dealing with an array, and the two are not semantically equivalent: the collection is likely to offer some advantages, or it would not have been chosen in the first place. Furthermore, there is no compile-time or runtime verification of the presence of the Add() method or the IEnumerable and IEnumerable<T> interfaces, resulting in an unworkable data contract if they are missing. WCF's solution is yet another dedicated attribute called CollectionDataContractAttribute, defined as:

```
[AttributeUsage(AttributeTargets.Struct|AttributeTargets.Class,Inherited = false)]
public sealed class CollectionDataContractAttribute : Attribute
{
   public string Name
   {get;set;}
   public string Namespace
   {get;set;}
   //More members
}
```

The CollectionDataContract attribute is analogous to the DataContract attribute, and similarly, it does not make the collection serializable. When applied on a collection, the CollectionDataContract attribute exposes the collection to the client as a generic linked list. While the linked list may have nothing to do with the original collection, it does offer a more collection-like interface than an array.

For example, given this collection definition:

```
[CollectionDataContract(Name = "MyCollectionOf{0}")]
public class MyCollection<T> : IEnumerable<T>
{
   public void Add(T item)
   {}

   IEnumerator<T>  IEnumerable<T>.GetEnumerator()
   {...}
   //Rest of the implementation
}
```

and this service-side contract definition:

```
[ServiceContract]
interface IContactManager
{
    [OperationContract]
    void AddContact(Contact contact);

    [OperationContract]
    MyCollection<Contact> GetContacts();
}
```

the definitions the client ends up with after importing the metadata will be:

```
[CollectionDataContract]
public class MyCollectionOfContact : List<Contact>
{}

[ServiceContract]
interface IContactManager
{
    [OperationContract]
    void AddContact(Contact contact);

    [OperationContract]
    MyCollectionOfContact GetContacts();
}
```

In addition, at service load time the CollectionDataContract attribute verifies the presence of the Add( ) method as well as either IEnumerable or IEnumerable<T>. Failing to have these on the collection will result in an InvalidDataContractException.

Note that you cannot apply both the DataContract attribute and the CollectionDataContract attribute on a collection. Again, this is verified at service load time.

Referencing a Collection

WCF can even let you preserve the same collection on the client side as on the service side. The advanced settings dialog for the service reference (see Figure 1-10) contains a "Collection type" combo box that lets you specify how to represent to the client certain kinds of collections and arrays found in the service metadata. For example, if the service operation returns one of the collections IEnumerable<T>, IList<T>, or ICollection<T>, by default the proxy will present it as an array (the default item in the combo box). However, you can request Visual Studio 2008 to use another collection, such as BindingList for data binding, a List<T>, Collection, or LinkedList<T>, and so on. If a conversion is possible, the proxy will use the requested collection type instead of an array. For example:

```
[OperationContract]
List<int> GetNumbers();
```

When the collection is then defined in another assembly referenced by the client's project, as we've discussed, that collection will be imported as-is. This feature is very useful when interacting with one of the built-in .NET collections, such as the Stack<T> collection defined in the *System.dll*, which is referenced by practically all .NET projects.

Dictionaries

A *dictionary* is a special type of collection that maps one data instance to another. As such, dictionaries do not marshal well either as arrays or as lists. Not surprisingly, dictionaries get their own representation in WCF.

If the dictionary is a serializable collection that supports the IDictionary interface, it will be exposed as a Dictionary<object,object>. For example, this service contract definition:

```
[Serializable]
public class MyDictionary : IDictionary
{...}

[ServiceContract]
interface IContactManager
{
    ...
    [OperationContract]
    MyDictionary GetContacts();
}
```

will be exposed as this definition:

```
[ServiceContract]
interface IContactManager
{
    ...
    [OperationContract]
    Dictionary<object,object> GetContacts();
}
```

This, by the way, includes using the HashTable collection.

If the serializable collection supports the IDictionary<K,T> interface, as in:

```
[Serializable]
public class MyDictionary<K,T> : IDictionary<K,T>
{...}

[ServiceContract]
interface IContactManager
{
    ...
    [OperationContract]
    MyDictionary<int,Contact> GetContacts();
}
```

the exported representation will be as a Dictionary<K,T>:

```
[ServiceContract]
interface IContactManager
{
    ...
    [OperationContract]
    Dictionary<int,Contact> GetContacts();
}
```

This includes making direct use of Dictionary<K,T> in the original definition, instead of MyDictionary<K,T>.

If instead of merely being a serializable collection the dictionary is decorated with the CollectionDataContract attribute, it will be marshaled as a subclass of the respective representation. For example, this service contract definition:

```
[CollectionDataContract]
public class MyDictionary : IDictionary
{...}

[ServiceContract]
interface IContactManager
{
    ...
    [OperationContract]
    MyDictionary GetContacts();
}
```

will have this representation:

```
[CollectionDataContract]
public class MyDictionary : Dictionary<object,object>
{}

[ServiceContract]
interface IContactManager
{
    ...
    [OperationContract]
    MyDictionary GetContacts();
}
```

while this generic collection:

```
[CollectionDataContract(Name = "MyDictionary")]
public class MyDictionary<K,T> : IDictionary<K,T>
{...}

[ServiceContract]
interface IContactManager
{
    ...
    [OperationContract]
    MyDictionary<int,Contact> GetContacts();
}
```

will be published in the metadata as:

```
[CollectionDataContract]
public class MyDictionary : Dictionary<int,Contact>
{}

[ServiceContract]
interface IContactManager
{
   ...
   [OperationContract]
   MyDictionary GetContacts();
}
```

As for a collection, in the advanced settings dialog for a service reference (see Figure 1-10) you can request other dictionary types, such as the SortedDictionary<T,K>, HashTable, or ListDictionary type, and the proxy will use that dictionary instead if possible.

CHAPTER 4

Instance Management

Instance management is my name for the set of techniques WCF uses to bind client requests to service instances, governing which service instance handles which client request, and when. Instance management is necessary because of the extent to which applications differ in their needs for scalability, performance, throughput, durability, transactions, and queued calls—there simply isn't a one-size-fits-all solution. However, there are a few canonical instance management techniques that are applicable across the range of applications, thus enabling a wide variety of scenarios and programming models. These techniques are the subject of this chapter, and understanding them is essential to developing scalable and consistent applications. WCF supports three types of instance activation: *per-call services* allocate (and destroy) a new service instance for each client request; *sessionful services* allocate a service instance for each client connection; and *singleton services* share the same service instance for all clients, across all connections and activations. This chapter provides the rationale for each of these instance management modes, and offers guidelines on when and how to best use them. It also addresses some related topics, such as behaviors, contexts, demarcating operations, instance deactivation, durable services, and throttling.[*]

Behaviors

By and large, the service instance mode is strictly a service-side implementation detail that should not manifest itself on the client side in any way. To support that and a few other local service-side aspects, WCF defines the notion of *behaviors*. A behavior is a local attribute of a service that does not affect its communication patterns. Clients should be unaware of behaviors, and behaviors do not manifest themselves in the service's binding or published metadata. WCF defines two types of service-side

---

[*] This chapter contains excerpts from my articles "WCF Essentials: Discover Mighty Instance Management Techniques for Developing WCF Apps" (*MSDN Magazine*, June 2006) and "Managing State with Durable Services" (*MSDN Magazine*, October 2008).

behaviors, governed by two corresponding attributes. The ServiceBehaviorAttribute is used to configure *service behaviors*; that is, behaviors that affect all endpoints (all contracts and operations) of the service. The ServiceBehavior attribute is applied directly on the service implementation class. You have already seen two behaviors in the previous chapters: Chapter 1 used the service metadata behavior to instruct the host to publish the service's metadata, and Chapter 3 used the service behavior to ignore the data object extension. No client could ever tell simply by examining the communication and the exchanged messages if the service is ignoring the data object extension or who was publishing its metadata.

The OperationBehaviorAttribute is used to configure *operation behaviors*; that is, behaviors that affect only the implementation of a particular operation. The OperationBehavior attribute can be applied only on a method that implements a contract operation, never on the operation definition in the contract itself. You will see the use of OperationBehavior later in this chapter, and in subsequent chapters as well.

In the context of this chapter, the ServiceBehavior attribute is used to configure the service instance mode. As shown in Example 4-1, the attribute defines the InstanceContextMode property of the enum type InstanceContextMode. The value of the InstanceContextMode enum controls which instance mode is used for the service.

Example 4-1. ServiceBehaviorAttribute used to configure the instance context mode

```
public enum InstanceContextMode
{
   PerCall,
   PerSession,
   Single
}
[AttributeUsage(AttributeTargets.Class)]
public sealed class ServiceBehaviorAttribute : Attribute,...
{
   public InstanceContextMode InstanceContextMode
   {get;set;}
   //More members
}
```

The enum is correctly called InstanceContextMode rather than InstanceMode because it actually controls the instantiation mode of the context hosting the instance, rather than that of the instance itself (recall from Chapter 1 that the instance context is the innermost execution scope of the service). By default, however, the instance and its context are treated as a single unit, so the enum does control the life of the instance as well. You will see later in this chapter and subsequent chapters how (and when) you can disengage the two, and for what purposes.

Per-Call Services

When the service type is configured for *per-call activation*, a service instance (the CLR object) exists only while a client call is in progress. Every client request (that is, a method call on the WCF contract) gets a new dedicated service instance. The following list details how per-call activation works, and the steps are illustrated in Figure 4-1:

1. The client calls the proxy and the proxy forwards the call to the service.
2. WCF creates a service instance and calls the method on it.
3. When the method call returns, if the object implements IDisposable, WCF calls IDisposable.Dispose( ) on it.
4. The client calls the proxy and the proxy forwards the call to the service.
5. WCF creates an object and calls the method on it.

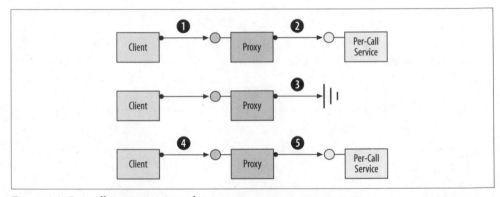

Figure 4-1. Per-call instantiation mode

Disposing of the service instance is an interesting point. As I just mentioned, if the service supports the IDisposable interface, WCF will automatically call the Dispose( ) method, allowing the service to perform any required cleanup. Note that Dispose( ) is called on the same thread that dispatched the original method call, and that Dispose( ) has an operation context (presented later). Once Dispose( ) is called, WCF disconnects the instance from the rest of the WCF infrastructure, making it a candidate for garbage collection.

Benefits of Per-Call Services

In the classic client/server programming model, using languages such as C++ or C#, every client gets its own dedicated server object. The fundamental problem with this approach is that it doesn't scale well. Imagine an application that has to serve many clients. Typically, these clients create the objects they need when the client application starts and dispose of them when the client application shuts down.

What impedes scalability with the client/server model is that the client applications can hold onto objects for long periods of time, while actually using them for only a fraction of that time. Those objects may hold expensive or scarce resources, such as database connections, communication ports, or files. If you allocate an object for each client, you will tie up such crucial and/or limited resources for long periods, and you will eventually run out of resources.

A better activation model is to allocate an object for a client only while a call is in progress from the client to the service. That way, you have to create and maintain in memory only as many objects as there are concurrent calls, not as many objects as there are outstanding clients. My personal experience indicates that in a typical Enterprise system, especially one that involves users, only 1 percent of all clients make concurrent calls (in a high-load Enterprise system, that figure rises to 3 percent). Thus, if your system can concurrently sustain 100 expensive service instances, it can still typically serve as many as 10,000 outstanding clients. This is precisely the benefit the per-call instance activation mode offers. In between calls, the client holds a reference on a proxy that doesn't have an actual object at the end of the wire. This means that you can dispose of the expensive resources the service instance occupies long before the client closes the proxy. By that same token, acquiring the resources is postponed until they are actually needed by a client.

Keep in mind that creating and destroying a service instance repeatedly on the service side without tearing down the connection to the client (with its client-side proxy) is a lot cheaper than repeatedly creating an instance and a connection. The second benefit is that forcing the service instance to reallocate or connect to its resources on every call caters very well to transactional resources and transactional programming (discussed in Chapter 7), because it eases the task of enforcing consistency with the instance state. The third benefit of per-call services is that they can be used in conjunction with queued disconnected calls (described in Chapter 9), because they allow easy mapping of service instances to discrete queued messages.

Configuring Per-Call Services

To configure a service type as a per-call service, you apply the ServiceBehavior attribute with the InstanceContextMode property set to InstanceContextMode.PerCall:

```
[ServiceContract]
interface IMyContract
{...}

[ServiceBehavior(InstanceContextMode = InstanceContextMode.PerCall)]
class MyService : IMyContract
{...}
```

Example 4-2 lists a simple per-call service and its client. As you can see from the program output, for each client method call a new service instance is constructed.

Example 4-2. Per-call service and client

```
//////////////////////// Service Code ////////////////////////
[ServiceContract]
interface IMyContract
{
   [OperationContract]
   void MyMethod();
}
[ServiceBehavior(InstanceContextMode = InstanceContextMode.PerCall)]
class MyService : IMyContract,IDisposable
{
   int m_Counter = 0;

   MyService()
   {
      Trace.WriteLine("MyService.MyService()");
   }
   public void MyMethod()
   {
      m_Counter++;
      Trace.WriteLine("Counter = " + m_Counter);
   }
   public void Dispose()
   {
      Trace.WriteLine("MyService.Dispose()");
   }
}
//////////////////////// Client Code ////////////////////////
MyContractClient proxy = new MyContractClient();

proxy.MyMethod();
proxy.MyMethod();

proxy.Close();

//Possible output
MyService.MyService()
Counter = 1
MyService.Dispose()
MyService.MyService()
Counter = 1
MyService.Dispose()
```

Per-Call Services and Transport Sessions

The use of a per-call service is independent from the presence of a transport session (described in Chapter 1). A transport session correlates all messages from a particular client to a particular channel. If the service is configured for per-call instantiation, there can still be a transport session, but for every call WCF will create a new context used just for that call. If transport-level sessions are not used, as you will see later, the service always behaves as a per-call service, regardless of its configuration.

If the per-call service has a transport session, communication from the client is subjected to the inactivity timeout of the transport session (which defaults to 10 minutes). Once the timeout has expired, the client can no longer use the proxy to invoke operations on the per-call service, since the transport session has ended.

The biggest effect transport sessions have on per-call services is that when the service is configured for single-threaded access (the WCF default, explained in Chapter 8), the transport session enforces a lock-step execution, where calls to the per-call service from the same proxy are serialized. That is, even if the client issues the calls concurrently, they are executed against different instances, one at a time, in order. This has particular implications for disposing of the instance. WCF does not block the client while it disposes of the service instance. However, if during the call to Dispose( ) the client has issued a second call, that call will be allowed to access a new instance only after Dispose( ) has returned. For example, the output at the end of Example 4-2 represents a case where there is a transport session, since the second call can only execute once Dispose( ) has returned. If Example 4-2 had no transport session, you might end up with the same output but also an out-of-order invocation where Dispose( ) is nonblocking, such as:

```
MyService.MyService( )
Counter = 1
MyService.MyService( )
Counter = 1
MyService.Dispose( )
MyService.Dispose( )
```

Designing Per-Call Services

Although in theory you can use the per-call instance activation mode on any service type, in practice you need to design the service and its contracts to support this mode from the ground up. The main problem is that the client doesn't know it's getting a new instance each time it makes a call. Per-call services must be *state-aware*; that is, they must proactively manage their state, giving the client the illusion of a continuous session. A state-aware service isn't the same as a stateless service. In fact, if the per-call service were truly stateless, there would be no need for per-call activation in the first place. It is precisely because it has state, and an expensive state at that, that you need the per-call mode. An instance of a per-call service is created just before every method call and is destroyed immediately after each call. Therefore, at the beginning of each call, the object should initialize its state from values saved in some storage, and at the end of the call it should return its state to the storage. Such storage is typically either a database or the filesystem, but volatile storage (e.g., static variables) may be used instead.

Not all of the object's state can be saved as-is, however. For example, if the state contains a database connection, the object must reacquire the connection at construction or at the beginning of every call and dispose of the connection at the end of the call or in its implementation of IDisposable.Dispose( ).

Using the per-call instance mode has one important implication for operation design: every operation must include a parameter to identify the service instance whose state needs to be retrieved. The instance uses that parameter to get *its* state from the storage, and not the state of another instance of the same type. Consequently, state storage is typically keyed (for example, as a static dictionary in memory or a database table). Examples of such state parameters are the account number for a bank account service, the order number for an order-processing service, and so on.

Example 4-3 shows a template for implementing a per-call service.

Example 4-3. Implementing a per-call service

```
[DataContract]
class Param
{...}

[ServiceContract]
interface IMyContract
{
   [OperationContract]
   void MyMethod(Param stateIdentifier);
}
[ServiceBehavior(InstanceContextMode = InstanceContextMode.PerCall)]
class MyPerCallService : IMyContract,IDisposable
{
   public void MyMethod(Param stateIdentifier)
   {
      GetState(stateIdentifier);
      DoWork();
      SaveState(stateIdentifier);
   }
   void GetState(Param stateIdentifier)
   {...}
   void DoWork()
   {...}
   void SaveState(Param stateIdentifier)
   {...}
   public void Dispose()
   {...}
}
```

The class implements the MyMethod( ) operation, which accepts a parameter of type Param (a pseudotype invented for this example) that identifies the instance:

```
   public void MyMethod(Param stateIdentifier);
```

The instance then uses the identifier to retrieve its state and to save the state back at the end of the method call. Any piece of state that is common to all clients can be allocated at the constructor and disposed of in Dispose( ).

The per-call activation mode works best when the amount of work to be done in each method call is finite, and there are no more activities to complete in the background once a method returns. Because the object will be discarded once the method returns, you should not spin off background threads or dispatch asynchronous calls back into the instance.

Since the per-call service retrieves its state from some storage in every method call, per-call services work very well in conjunction with a load-balancing machine, as long as the state repository is some global resource accessible to all machines. The load balancer can redirect calls to different machines at will, knowing that each per-call service can execute the call after retrieving its state.

Per-call services and performance

Per-call services clearly offer a trade-off between performance (the overhead of retrieving and saving the instance state on each method call) and scalability (holding onto the state and the resources it ties in). There are no hard-and-fast rules as to when and to what extent you should trade some performance for a lot of scalability. You may need to profile your system and ultimately design some services to use per-call activation and others not to use it.

Cleanup operations

Whether or not the service type supports IDisposable is an implementation detail and is of no relevance to the client. In fact, the client has no way of calling the Dispose( ) method anyway. When you design a contract for a per-call service, avoid defining operations that are dedicated for state or resource cleanup, like this:

```
//Avoid
[ServiceContract]
interface IMyContract
{
   void DoSomething( );
   void Cleanup( );
}
[ServiceBehavior(InstanceContextMode = InstanceContextMode.PerCall)]
class MyPerCallService : IMyContract,IDisposable
{
   public void DoSomething( )
   {...}
   public void Cleanup( )
   {...}
   public void Dispose( )
   {
      Cleanup( );
   }
}
```

The folly of such a design is obvious: if the client does call the cleanup method, it has the detrimental effect of creating an object just so the client can call Cleanup( ) on it, followed by a call to IDisposable.Dispose( ) (if present) by WCF to do the cleanup again.

Choosing Per-Call Services

While the programming model of per-call services may look somewhat alien to client/server developers, per-call services are actually the preferred instance management mode for many WCF services. This is simply because per-call services scale better, or at least are scale-invariant. When designing a service, my golden rule for scalability is *10X*. That is, every service should be designed to handle a load at least an order of magnitude greater than what its requirements call for. In every other engineering discipline, engineers never design a system to handle its exact nominal specified load. You would not want to enter a building whose beams can support only the exact load they were required to handle, ride in an elevator whose cable can handle only the exact number of passengers it's rated for, and so on. Software systems are no different—why design a system for the specific current load while every other person in the company is working to increase business and the implied load? You should design software systems to last years and to sustain current and future loads. As a result, when using the 10X golden rule, you very quickly end up needing the scalability of the per-call service.

Per-Session Services

WCF can maintain a logical session between a client and a particular service instance. When the client creates a new proxy to a service configured as a *sessionful service*, the client gets a new dedicated service instance that is independent of all other instances of the same service. That instance will typically remain in service until the client no longer needs it. This activation mode (sometimes also referred to as the *private-session mode*) is very much like the classic client/server model: each private session uniquely binds a proxy and its set of client- and service-side channels to a particular service instance, or, more specifically, to its channel. It follows that a transport session is required for the private-session instantiation mode, as discussed later in this section.

Because the service instance remains in memory throughout the session, it can maintain state in memory, and the programming model is very much like that of the classic client/server model. Consequently, it suffers from the same scalability and transaction issues as the classic client/server model. A service configured for private sessions cannot typically support more than a few dozen (or perhaps up to one or two hundred) outstanding clients, due to the cost associated with each such dedicated service instance.

The client session is per service endpoint per proxy. If the client creates another proxy to the same or a different endpoint, that second proxy will be associated with a new instance and session.

Configuring Private Sessions

There are three elements to supporting a session: behavior, binding, and contract. The behavior part is required so that WCF will keep the service instance context alive throughout the session, and to direct the client messages to it. This local behavior facet is achieved by setting the InstanceContextMode property of the ServiceBehavior attribute to InstanceContextMode.PerSession:

```
[ServiceBehavior(InstanceContextMode = InstanceContextMode.PerSession)]
class MyService : IMyContract
{...}
```

Since InstanceContextMode.PerSession is the default value of the InstanceContextMode property, these definitions are equivalent:

```
class MyService : IMyContract
{...}

[ServiceBehavior]
class MyService : IMyContract
{...}

[ServiceBehavior(InstanceContextMode = InstanceContextMode.PerSession)]
class MyService : IMyContract
{...}
```

The session typically terminates when the client closes the proxy, which causes the proxy to notify the service that the session has ended. If the service supports IDisposable, the Dispose( ) method will be called asynchronously to the client. However, Disposed( ) will be called on a worker thread without an operation context.

In order to correlate all messages from a particular client to a particular instance, WCF needs to be able to identify the client. As explained in Chapter 1, this is exactly what the transport session achieves. If your service is designed to be used as a sessionful service, there has to be some contract-level way for you to express that expectation. The contractual element is required across the service boundary, because the client-side WCF runtime needs to know it should use a session. To that end, the ServiceContract attribute offers the property SessionMode, of the enum type SessionMode:

```
public enum SessionMode
{
   Allowed,
   Required,
   NotAllowed
}
[AttributeUsage(AttributeTargets.Interface|AttributeTargets.Class,
                Inherited=false)]
public sealed class ServiceContractAttribute : Attribute
{
```

```
        public SessionMode SessionMode
        {get;set;}
        //More members
    }
```

SessionMode defaults to SessionMode.Allowed. The configured SessionMode value is included in the service metadata and is reflected correctly when the client imports the contract metadata. The enum value of SessionMode has nothing to do with the service session; in fact, its proper name should have been TransportSessionMode since it pertains to the transport session, not to the logical session maintained between the client and the instance.

SessionMode.Allowed

SessionMode.Allowed is the default value of the SessionMode property, so these definitions are equivalent:

```
[ServiceContract]
interface IMyContract
{...}

[ServiceContract(SessionMode = SessionMode.Allowed)]
interface IMyContract
{...}
```

All bindings support configuring the contract on the endpoint with SessionMode. Allowed. When the SessionMode property is configured with this value, transport sessions are allowed, but not enforced. The exact resulting behavior is a product of the service configuration and the binding used. If the service is configured for per-call activation, it still behaves as per-call service, as is the case in Example 4-2. When the service is configured for per-session activation, it will behave as a per-session service only if the binding used maintains a transport-level session. For example, the BasicHttpBinding can never have a transport-level session, due to the connectionless nature of the HTTP protocol. The WSHttpBinding without security and without reliable messaging will also not maintain a transport-level session. In both of these cases, even though the service is configured with InstanceContextMode.PerSession and the contract with SessionMode.Allowed, the service will behave as a per-call service.

However, if you use the WSHttpBinding with security (its default configuration) or with reliable messaging, or if you use the NetTcpBinding or the NetNamedPipeBinding, the service will behave as a per-session service. For example, assuming use of the NetTcpBinding, this service behaves as sessionful:

```
[ServiceContract]
interface IMyContract
{...}

class MyService : IMyContract
{...}
```

Note that the previous code snippet simply takes the default of both the `SessionMode` and the `InstanceContextMode` properties.

SessionMode.Required

The `SessionMode.Required` value mandates the use of a transport-level session, but not necessarily an application-level session. You cannot have a contract configured with `SessionMode.Required` with a service endpoint whose binding does not maintain a transport-level session, and this constraint is verified at the service load time. However, you can still configure the service to be a per-call service, and the service instance will be created and destroyed on each client call. Only if the service is configured as a sessionful service will the service instance persist throughout the client's session:

```
[ServiceContract(SessionMode = SessionMode.Required)]
interface IMyContract
{...}

class MyService : IMyContract
{...}
```

When designing a sessionful contract, I recommend explicitly using `SessionMode.Required` and not relying on the default of `SessionMode.Allowed`. The rest of the code samples in this book actively apply `SessionMode.Required` when sessionful interaction is by design.

Example 4-4 lists the same service and client as in Example 4-2, except the contract and service are configured to require a private session. As you can see from the output, the client got a dedicated instance.

Example 4-4. Per-session service and client

```
///////////////////////// Service Code /////////////////////////
[ServiceContract(SessionMode = SessionMode.Required)]
interface IMyContract
{
   [OperationContract]
   void MyMethod( );
}
class MyService : IMyContract,IDisposable
{
   int m_Counter = 0;

   MyService( )
   {
      Trace.WriteLine("MyService.MyService( )");
   }
   public void MyMethod( )
   {
```

Example 4-4. Per-session service and client (continued)

```
        m_Counter++;
        Trace.WriteLine("Counter = " + m_Counter);
    }
    public void Dispose()
    {
        Trace.WriteLine("MyService.Dispose()");
    }
}
/////////////////////////// Client Code ///////////////////////
MyContractClient proxy = new MyContractClient();

proxy.MyMethod();
proxy.MyMethod();

proxy.Close();

//Output
MyService.MyService()
Counter = 1
Counter = 2
MyService.Dispose()
```

SessionMode.NotAllowed

SessionMode.NotAllowed disallows the use of a transport-level session, which precludes an application-level session. Regardless of the service configuration, when this value is used the service will always behave as a per-call service.

Since both the TCP and IPC protocols maintain a session at the transport level, you cannot configure a service endpoint that uses the NetTcpBinding or the NetNamedPipeBinding to expose a contract marked with SessionMode.NotAllowed, and this is verified at the service load time. However, the use of the WSHttpBinding with an emulated transport session is still allowed. In the interest of readability, I recommend that when selecting SessionMode.NotAllowed, you always also configure the service as per-call:

```
[ServiceContract(SessionMode = SessionMode.NotAllowed)]
interface IMyContract
{...}

[ServiceBehavior(InstanceContextMode = InstanceContextMode.PerCall)]
class MyService : IMyContract
{...}
```

Since the BasicHttpBinding cannot have a transport-level session, endpoints that use it behave as if the contract is always configured with SessionMode.NotAllowed. I view SessionMode.NotAllowed as a setting available for the sake of completeness more than anything else, and I would not explicitly choose it.

Bindings, contracts, and service behavior

Table 4-1 summarizes the resulting instance mode as a product of the binding being used, the session mode in the contract, and the configured instance context mode in the service behavior. The table does not list invalid configurations, such as `SessionMode.Required` with the `BasicHttpBinding`.

Table 4-1. Instance mode as a product of the binding, contract configuration, and service behavior

Binding	Session mode	Context mode	Instance mode
Basic	Allowed/NotAllowed	PerCall/PerSession	PerCall
TCP, IPC	Allowed/Required	PerCall	PerCall
TCP, IPC	Allowed/Required	PerSession	PerSession
WS (no security, no reliability)	NotAllowed/Allowed	PerCall/PerSession	PerCall
WS (with security or reliability)	Allowed/Required	PerSession	PerSession
WS (with security or reliability)	NotAllowed	PerCall/PerSession	PerCall

Consistent configuration

I strongly recommend that if one contract the service implements is a sessionful contract, then all contracts should be sessionful, and that you should avoid mixing per-call and sessionful contracts on the same per-session service type (even though WCF allows it):

```
[ServiceContract(SessionMode = SessionMode.Required)]
interface IMyContract
{...}

[ServiceContract(SessionMode = SessionMode.NotAllowed)]
interface IMyOtherContract
{...}

//Avoid
class MyService : IMyContract,IMyOtherContract
{...}
```

The reason is obvious: per-call services need to proactively manage their state, while per-session services do not. While the two contracts will be exposed on two different endpoints and can be consumed independently by two different clients, this duality requires cumbersome implementation for the underlying service class.

Sessions and Reliability

The session between the client and the service instance is only as reliable as the underlying transport session. Consequently, a service that implements a sessionful contract should have all of its endpoints that expose that contract use bindings that enable reliable transport sessions. Make sure to always use a binding that supports reliability and to explicitly enable it at both the client and the service, either programmatically or administratively, as shown in Example 4-5.

Example 4-5. Enabling reliability for per-session services

```
<!--Host configuration:-->
<system.serviceModel>
   <services>
      <service name = "MyPerSessionService">
         <endpoint
            address  = "net.tcp://localhost:8000/MyPerSessionService"
            binding  = "netTcpBinding"
            bindingConfiguration = "TCPSession"
            contract = "IMyContract"
         />
      </service>
   </services>
   <bindings>
      <netTcpBinding>
         <binding name = "TCPSession">
            <reliableSession enabled = "true"/>
         </binding>
      </netTcpBinding>
   </bindings>
</system.serviceModel>

<!--Client configuration:-->
<system.serviceModel>
   <client>
      <endpoint
         address  = "net.tcp://localhost:8000/MyPerSessionService/"
         binding  = "netTcpBinding"
         bindingConfiguration = "TCPSession"
         contract = "IMyContract"
      />
   </client>
   <bindings>
      <netTcpBinding>
         <binding name = "TCPSession">
            <reliableSession enabled = "true"/>
         </binding>
      </netTcpBinding>
   </bindings>
</system.serviceModel>
```

The one exception to this rule is the IPC binding. This binding has no need for the reliable messaging protocol (all calls will be on the same machine anyway), and it is considered an inherently reliable transport.

Just as a reliable transport session is optional, so is ordered delivery of messages, and WCF will provide for a session even when ordered delivery is disabled. However, by the very nature of an application session, a client that interacts with a sessionful service expects all messages to be delivered in the order they are sent. Luckily, ordered delivery is enabled by default when reliable transport sessions are enabled, so no additional setting is required.

The Session ID

Every session has a unique ID that both the client and the service can obtain. The session ID is largely in the form of a GUID, and it can be used for logging and diagnostics. The service can access the session ID via the *operation call context*, which is a set of properties (including the session ID) that are used for callbacks, message headers, transaction management, security, host access, and access to the object representing the execution context itself. Every service operation has an operation call context, accessible via the OperationContext class. A service can obtain a reference to the operation context of the current method via the Current static method of the OperationContext class:

```
public sealed class OperationContext : ...
{
   public static OperationContext Current
   {get;set;}
   public string SessionId
   {get;}
}
```

To access the session ID, the service needs to read the value of the SessionId property, which returns (almost) a GUID in the form of a string, followed by the ordinal number of the session from that host:

```
string sessionID = OperationContext.Current.SessionId;
Trace.WriteLine(sessionID);
//Traces:
//uuid:8a0480da-7ac0-423e-9f3e-b2131bcbad8d;id=1
```

If a per-call service without a transport session accesses the SessionId property, the session ID will be null, since there is no session and therefore no ID.

The client can access the session ID via the proxy. As introduced in Chapter 1, the class ClientBase<T> is the base class of the proxy. ClientBase<T> provides the read-only property InnerChannel of the type IClientChannel. IClientChannel derives from the interface IContextChannel, which provides a SessionId property that returns the session ID in the form of a string:

```
public interface IContextChannel : ...
{
   string SessionId
   {get;}
   //More members
}
```

```
public interface IClientChannel : IContextChannel,...
{...}
public abstract class ClientBase<T> : ...
{
    public IClientChannel InnerChannel
    {get;}
    //More members
}
```

Given the definitions in Example 4-4, the client might obtain the session ID like this:

```
MyContractClient proxy = new MyContractClient();
proxy.MyMethod();

string sessionID = proxy.InnerChannel.SessionId;
Trace.WriteLine(sessionID);
//Traces:
//urn:uuid:c8141f66-51a6-4c66-9e03-927d5ca97153
```

However, the degree to which the client-side session ID matches that of the service (and even when the client is allowed to access the SessionId property) is a product of the binding used and its configuration. What correlates the client-side and service-side session IDs is the reliable session at the transport level. If the TCP binding is used, when a reliable session is enabled (as it should be) the client can obtain a valid session ID only after issuing the first method call to the service to establish the session, or after explicitly opening the proxy. In this case, the session ID obtained by the client will match that of the service. (If the client accesses the session ID before the first call, the SessionId property will be set to null.) If the TCP binding is used but reliable sessions are disabled, the client can access the session ID before making the first call, but the ID obtained will be different from that obtained by the service. With either of the WS bindings, if reliable messaging is enabled the session ID will be null until after the first call (or after the client opens the proxy), but after that the client and the service will always have the same session ID. Without reliable messaging, the client must first use the proxy (or just open it) before accessing the session ID, or risk an InvalidOperationException. After opening the proxy, the client and the service will have a correlated session ID. With the IPC binding, the client can access the SessionId property before making the first call, but the client will always get a session ID different from that of the service. When using this binding, it is therefore better to ignore the session ID altogether.

Session Termination

Typically, the session will end once the client closes the proxy. However, in case the client neglects to close the proxy, or when the client terminates ungracefully or there is a communication problem, the session will also terminate once the inactivity time-out of the transport session is exceeded.

Singleton Service

The *singleton service* is the ultimate sharable service. When a service is configured as a singleton, all clients are independently connected to the same single well-known instance, regardless of which endpoint of the service they connect to. The singleton is created exactly once, when the host is created, and lives forever: it is disposed of only when the host shuts down.

 A singleton hosted in the WAS is created when the host process is launched (typically only when the first request to any service in that process is made).

Using a singleton does not require clients to maintain a logical session with the singleton instance, or to use a binding that supports a transport-level session. If the contract the client consumes has a session, during the call the singleton will have the same session ID as the client (binding permitting), but closing the client proxy will terminate only the transport session, not the singleton instance. If the singleton service supports contracts without a session, those contracts will not be per-call: they too will be connected to the same instance. By its very nature, the singleton is shared, and each client should simply create its own proxy or proxies to it.

You configure a singleton service by setting the `InstanceContextMode` property to `InstanceContextMode.Single`:

```
[ServiceBehavior(InstanceContextMode = InstanceContextMode.Single)]
class MySingleton : ...
{...}
```

Example 4-6 demonstrates a singleton service with two contracts, one that requires a session and one that does not. As you can see from the client call, the calls on the two endpoints were routed to the same instance, and closing the proxies did not terminate the singleton.

Example 4-6. A singleton service and client

```
///////////////////////// Service Code /////////////////////
[ServiceContract(SessionMode = SessionMode.Required)]
interface IMyContract
{
   [OperationContract]
   void MyMethod( );
}
[ServiceContract(SessionMode = SessionMode.NotAllowed)]
interface IMyOtherContract
{
   [OperationContract]
   void MyOtherMethod( );
}
```

Example 4-6. A singleton service and client (continued)

```
[ServiceBehavior(InstanceContextMode=InstanceContextMode.Single)]
class MySingleton : IMyContract,IMyOtherContract,IDisposable
{
   int m_Counter = 0;

   public MySingleton()
   {
      Trace.WriteLine("MySingleton.MySingleton()");
   }
   public void MyMethod()
   {
      m_Counter++;
      Trace.WriteLine("Counter = " + m_Counter);
   }
   public void MyOtherMethod()
   {
      m_Counter++;
      Trace.WriteLine("Counter = " + m_Counter);
   }
   public void Dispose()
   {
      Trace.WriteLine("Singleton.Dispose()");
   }
}
/////////////////////////// Client Code ////////////////////////
MyContractClient proxy1 = new MyContractClient();
proxy1.MyMethod();
proxy1.Close();

MyOtherContractClient proxy2 = new MyOtherContractClient();
proxy2.MyOtherMethod();
proxy2.Close();

//Output
MySingleton.MySingleton()
Counter = 1
Counter = 2
```

Initializing a Singleton

Sometimes, you may not want to create and initialize the singleton using just the default constructor. Perhaps initializing the state requires some custom steps or specific knowledge that the clients should not be bothered with, or that is not available to the clients. Whatever the reason, you may want to create the singleton using some other mechanism besides the WCF service host. To support such scenarios, WCF allows you to directly create the singleton instance beforehand using normal CLR instantiation, initialize it, and then open the host with that instance in mind as the singleton service. The ServiceHost class offers a dedicated constructor that accepts an object:

```
public class ServiceHost : ServiceHostBase,...
{
   public ServiceHost(object singletonInstance,params Uri[] baseAddresses);
   public object SingletonInstance
   {get;}
   //More members
}
```

Note that the object must be configured as a singleton. For instance, consider the code in Example 4-7. The class MySingleton will be first initialized and then hosted as a singleton.

Example 4-7. Initializing and hosting a singleton

```
//Service code
[ServiceContract]
interface IMyContract
{
   [OperationContract]
   void MyMethod();
}
[ServiceBehavior(InstanceContextMode = InstanceContextMode.Single)]
class MySingleton : IMyContract
{
   public int Counter
   {get;set;}

   public void MyMethod()
   {
      Counter++;
      Trace.WriteLine("Counter = " + Counter);
   }
}
//Host code
MySingleton singleton = new MySingleton();
singleton.Counter = 287;

ServiceHost host = new ServiceHost(singleton);
host.Open();
//Do some blocking calls then
host.Close();

//Client code
MyContractClient proxy = new MyContractClient();
proxy.MyMethod();
proxy.Close();

//Output:
Counter = 288
```

If you do initialize and host a singleton this way, you may also want to be able to access it directly on the host side. WCF enables downstream objects to reach back into the singleton directly using the SingletonInstance property of ServiceHost.

Any party on the call chain leading down from an operation call on the singleton can always access the host via the operation context's read-only Host property:

```
public sealed class OperationContext : ...
{
   public ServiceHostBase Host
   {get;}
   //More members
}
```

Once you have the singleton reference, you can interact with it directly:

```
ServiceHost host = OperationContext.Current.Host as ServiceHost;
Debug.Assert(host != null);
MySingleton singleton = host.SingletonInstance as MySingleton;
Debug.Assert(singleton != null);
singleton.Counter = 388;
```

If no singleton instance was provided to the host, SingletonInstance returns null.

Streamlining with ServiceHost<T>

The ServiceHost<T> class presented in Chapter 1 can be extended to offer type-safe singleton initialization and access:

```
public class ServiceHost<T> : ServiceHost
{
   public ServiceHost(T singleton,params Uri[] baseAddresses) :
                                            base(singleton,baseAddresses)
   {}
   public virtual T Singleton
   {
      get
      {
         if(SingletonInstance == null)
         {
            return default(T);
         }
         return (T)SingletonInstance;
      }
   }
   //More members
}
```

The type parameter provides type-safe binding for the object used for construction:

```
MySingleton singleton = new MySingleton();
singleton.Counter = 287;

ServiceHost<MySingleton> host = new ServiceHost<MySingleton>(singleton);
host.Open();
```

and the object returned from the Singleton property:

```
ServiceHost<MySingleton> host = OperationContext.Current.Host
                                            as ServiceHost<MySingleton>;

Debug.Assert(host != null);
host.Singleton.Counter = 287;
```

The InProcFactory<T> (presented in Chapter 1) is similarly extended to
initialize a singleton instance.

Choosing a Singleton

The singleton service is the sworn enemy of scalability. The reason has to do with
singleton state synchronization, rather than the cost of that single instance. Having a
singleton implies that the singleton has some valuable state that you wish to share
across multiple clients. The problem is that when multiple clients connect to the singleton, they may all do so concurrently, and the incoming client calls will be on multiple worker threads. The singleton must therefore synchronize access to its state to
avoid state corruption. This in turn means that only one client at a time can access
the singleton. This constraint may degrade throughput, responsiveness, and availability to the point that the singleton is unusable in a decent-sized system. For example, if an operation on a singleton takes one-tenth of a second, the singleton can
service only 10 clients per second. If there are many more clients (say 20 or 100), the
system's performance will be inadequate.

In general, you should use a singleton only if it maps well to a natural singleton in
the application domain. A *natural singleton* is a resource that is, by its very nature,
single and unique. Examples of natural singletons are a global logbook to which all
services should log their activities, a single communication port, or a single mechanical motor. Avoid using a singleton if there is even the slightest chance that the business logic will allow more than one such service in the future (for example, adding
another motor or a second communication port). The reason is clear: if your clients
all depend on implicitly being connected to the well-known instance, and more than
one service instance is available, the clients will suddenly need to have a way to bind
to the correct instance. This can have severe implications for the application's programming model. Because of these limitations, I recommend that you avoid singletons in the general case and find ways to share the state of the singleton instead of
the singleton instance itself. That said, there are cases when using a singleton is
acceptable, as mentioned above.

Demarcating Operations

Sometimes, a sessionful contract has an implied order of operation invocations.
Some operations cannot be called first, while other operations must be called last.
For example, consider this contract, used to manage customer orders:

```
[ServiceContract(SessionMode = SessionMode.Required)]
interface IOrderManager
{
   [OperationContract]
   void SetCustomerId(int customerId);

   [OperationContract]
   void AddItem(int itemId);

   [OperationContract]
   decimal GetTotal();

   [OperationContract]
   bool ProcessOrders();
}
```

The contract has the following constraints: the client must provide the customer ID as the first operation in the session, or else no other operations can take place; items may be added, and the total calculated, and as often as the client wishes; processing the order terminates the session, and therefore must come last. In classic .NET, such requirements often forced the developers to support some state machine or state flags and to verify the state on every operation.

WCF, however, allows contract designers to designate contract operations as operations that can or cannot start or terminate the session, using the IsInitiating and IsTerminating properties of the OperationContract attribute:

```
[AttributeUsage(AttributeTargets.Method)]
public sealed class OperationContractAttribute : Attribute
{
   public bool IsInitiating
   {get;set;}
   public bool IsTerminating
   {get;set;}
   //More members
}
```

These properties can be used to demarcate the boundary of the session; hence, I call this technique *demarcating operations*. At service load time (or during the proxy use time on the client side), if these properties are set to their nondefault values, WCF verifies that the demarcating operations are part of a contract that mandates sessions (i.e., that SessionMode is set to SessionMode.Required) and throws an InvalidOperationException otherwise. Both a sessionful service and a singleton can implement contracts that use demarcating operations to manage their client sessions.

The default values of these properties are true for IsInitiating and false for IsTerminating. Consequently, these two definitions are equivalent:

```
[OperationContract]
void MyMethod();

[OperationContract(IsInitiating = true,IsTerminating = false)]
void MyMethod();
```

As you can see, you can set both properties on the same method. In addition, operations do not demarcate the session boundary by default—operations can be called first, last, or in between any other operations in the session. Using nondefault values enables you to dictate that a method is not called first, or that it is called last, or both:

```
[ServiceContract(SessionMode = SessionMode.Required)]
interface IMyContract
{
    [OperationContract]
    void StartSession( );

    [OperationContract(IsInitiating = false)]
    void CannotStart( );

    [OperationContract(IsTerminating = true)]
    void EndSession( );

    [OperationContract(IsInitiating = false,IsTerminating = true)]
    void CannotStartCanEndSession( );
}
```

Going back to the order-management contract, you can use demarcating operations to enforce the interaction constraints:

```
[ServiceContract(SessionMode = SessionMode.Required)]
interface IOrderManager
{
    [OperationContract]
    void SetCustomerId(int customerId);

    [OperationContract(IsInitiating = false)]
    void AddItem(int itemId);

    [OperationContract(IsInitiating = false)]
    decimal GetTotal( );

    [OperationContract(IsInitiating = false,IsTerminating = true)]
    bool ProcessOrders( );
}
//Client code
OrderManagerClient proxy = new OrderManagerClient( );

proxy.SetCustomerId(123);
proxy.AddItem(4);
proxy.AddItem(5);
proxy.AddItem(6);
proxy.ProcessOrders( );

proxy.Close( );
```

When IsInitiating is set to true (its default), it means the operation will start a new session if it is the first method the client calls but will be part of the ongoing session if another operation is called first. When IsInitiating is set to false, it means that a client can never call that operation as the first operation in a new session, and that the method can only be part of an ongoing session.

When `IsTerminating` is set to `false` (its default), it means the session continues after the operation returns. When `IsTerminating` is set to `true`, it means the session terminates once the method returns, and WCF disposes of the service instance asynchronously. The client will not be able to issue additional calls on the proxy. Note that the client should still close the proxy.

> When you generate a proxy to a service that uses demarcating operations, the imported contract definition contains the property settings. In addition, WCF enforces the demarcation separately on the client and service sides, so you could actually employ them independently.

Instance Deactivation

The sessionful service instance management technique as described so far connects a client (or clients) to a service instance. Yet, the real picture is more complex. Recall from Chapter 1 that each service instance is hosted in a context, as shown in Figure 4-2.

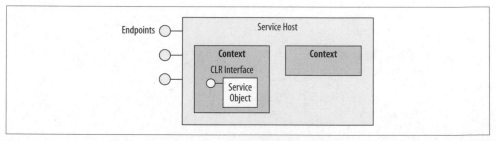

Figure 4-2. Contexts and instances

What sessions actually do is correlate the client messages not to the instance, but to the context that hosts it. When the session starts, the host creates a new context. When the session ends, the context is terminated. By default, the lifetime of the context is the same as that of the instance it hosts. However, for optimization and extensibility purposes, WCF provides the service designer with the option of separating the two lifetimes and deactivating the instance separately from its context. In fact, WCF also allows a context to exist without an associated instance at all, as shown in Figure 4-2. I call this instance management technique *context deactivation*. The common way of controlling context deactivation is via the `ReleaseInstanceMode` property of the `OperationBehavior` attribute:

```
public enum ReleaseInstanceMode
{
    None,
    BeforeCall,
```

```
        AfterCall,
        BeforeAndAfterCall,
    }
    [AttributeUsage(AttributeTargets.Method)]
    public sealed class OperationBehaviorAttribute : Attribute,...
    {
        public ReleaseInstanceMode ReleaseInstanceMode
        {get;set;}
        //More members
    }
```

ReleaseInstanceMode is of the enum type ReleaseInstanceMode. The various values of ReleaseInstanceMode control when to release the instance in relation to the method call: before, after, before and after, or not at all. When releasing the instance, if the service supports IDisposable, the Dispose( ) method is called and Dispose( ) has an operation context.

You typically apply instance deactivation on some but not all service methods, or with different values on different methods:

```
    [ServiceContract(SessionMode = SessionMode.Required)]
    interface IMyContract
    {
        [OperationContract]
        void MyMethod( );

        [OperationContract]
        void MyOtherMethod( );
    }
    class MyService : IMyContract,IDisposable
    {
        [OperationBehavior(ReleaseInstanceMode = ReleaseInstanceMode.AfterCall)]
        public void MyMethod( )
        {...}
        public void MyOtherMethod( )
        {...}
        public void Dispose( )
        {...}
    }
```

The reason you typically apply it sporadically is that if you were to apply it uniformly you would end up with a per-call-like service, in which case you might as well have configured the service as per-call.

If relying on instance deactivation assumes a certain call order, you can try to enforce that order using demarcating operations.

Configuring with ReleaseInstanceMode.None

The default value for the ReleaseInstanceMode property is ReleaseInstanceMode.None, so these two definitions are equivalent:

```
[OperationBehavior(ReleaseInstanceMode = ReleaseInstanceMode.None)]
public void MyMethod( )
{...}

public void MyMethod( )
{...}
```

ReleaseInstanceMode.None means that the instance lifetime is not affected by the call, as shown in Figure 4-3.

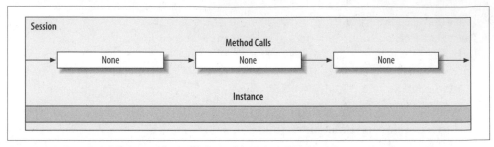

Figure 4-3. Instance lifetime with methods configured with ReleaseInstanceMode.None

Configuring with ReleaseInstanceMode.BeforeCall

When a method is configured with ReleaseInstanceMode.BeforeCall, if there is already an instance in the session, before forwarding the call WCF will deactivate it, create a new instance in its place, and let that new instance service the call, as shown in Figure 4-4.

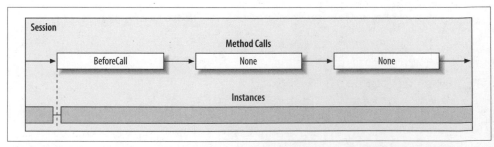

Figure 4-4. Instance lifetime with methods configured with ReleaseInstanceMode.BeforeCall

WCF deactivates the instance and calls Dispose( ) before the call is done on the incoming call thread, while the client blocks. This ensures that the deactivation is indeed done before the call, not concurrently with it. ReleaseInstanceMode.BeforeCall is designed to optimize methods such as Create( ) that acquire some valuable resources, yet wish to release the previously allocated resources. Instead of acquiring the resources when the session starts, you wait until the call to the Create( ) method and then both release the previously allocated resources and allocate new ones. After Create( ) is called, you are ready to start calling other methods on the instance, which are typically configured with ReleaseInstanceMode.None.

Configuring with ReleaseInstanceMode.AfterCall

When a method is configured with `ReleaseInstanceMode.AfterCall`, WCF deactivates the instance after the call, as shown in Figure 4-5.

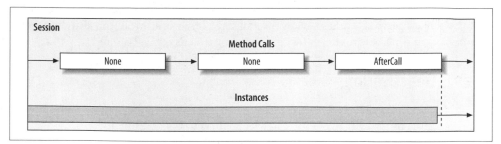

Figure 4-5. Instance lifetime with methods configured with ReleaseInstanceMode.AfterCall

This is designed to optimize a method such as `Cleanup()` that cleans up valuable resources held by the instance, without waiting for the session to terminate. `ReleaseInstanceMode.AfterCall` is typically applied on methods called after methods configured with `ReleaseInstanceMode.None`.

Configuring with ReleaseInstanceMode.BeforeAndAfterCall

As its name implies, configuring a method with `ReleaseInstanceMode.BeforeAndAfterCall` has the combined effect of using `ReleaseInstanceMode.BeforeCall` and `ReleaseInstanceMode.AfterCall`. If the context has an instance before the call is made, just before the call WCF deactivates that instance and creates a new instance to service the call. It then deactivates the new instance after the call, as shown in Figure 4-6.

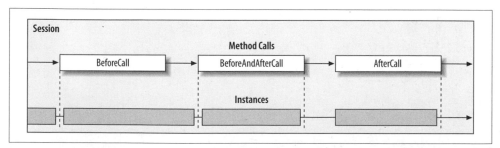

Figure 4-6. Instance lifetime with methods configured with ReleaseInstanceMode.
BeforeAndAfterCall

`ReleaseInstanceMode.BeforeAndAfterCall` may look superfluous at first glance, but it actually complements the other values. It is designed to be applied on methods called after methods marked with `ReleaseInstanceMode.BeforeCall` or `None`, or before methods marked with `ReleaseInstanceMode.AfterCall` or `None`. Consider a situation where the sessionful service wants to benefit from state-aware behavior (like a per-call service), while holding onto resources only when needed to optimize resource allocation and security lookup. If ReleaseInstanceMode.BeforeCall were the only available option, there would be a period of time after the call when the resources would still be allocated to the object, but would not be in use. A similar situation would occur if ReleaseInstanceMode.AfterCall were the only available option, because there would be a period of time before the call when the resources would be wasted.

Explicit Deactivation

Instead of making a design-time decision on which methods to use to deactivate an instance, you can make a runtime decision to deactivate the instance after the method returns. You do that by calling the ReleaseServiceInstance() method on the instance context. You obtain the instance context via the InstanceContext property of the operation context:

```
public sealed class InstanceContext : ...
{
   public void ReleaseServiceInstance();
   //More members
}
public sealed class OperationContext : ...
{
   public InstanceContext InstanceContext
   {get;}
   //More members
}
```

Example 4-8 demonstrates this technique.

Example 4-8. Using ReleaseServiceInstance()

```
[ServiceContract(SessionMode = SessionMode.Required)]
interface IMyContract
{
   [OperationContract]
   void MyMethod();
}
class MyService : IMyContract,IDisposable
{
   public void MyMethod()
   {
      //Do some work then
      OperationContext.Current.InstanceContext.ReleaseServiceInstance();
   }
   public void Dispose()
   {...}
}
```

Calling ReleaseServiceInstance() has a similar effect to using ReleaseInstanceMode. AfterCall. When used in a method decorated with ReleaseInstanceMode.BeforeCall, it has a similar effect to using ReleaseInstanceMode.BeforeAndAfterCall.

Instance deactivation affects a singleton as well, although combining the two makes little sense—by its very definition, it is permissible and even desirable to never deactivate the singleton.

Using Instance Deactivation

Instance deactivation is an optimization technique, and like all optimization techniques, you should avoid it in the general case. Consider using instance deactivation only after failing to meet both your performance and scalability goals and when careful examination and profiling has proven beyond a doubt that using instance deactivation will improve the situation. If scalability and throughput are your concerns, you should take advantage of the simplicity of the per-call instancing mode and avoid instance deactivation. The main reason I share this technique with you is that WCF itself makes extensive use of instance deactivation; thus, knowledge of it is instrumental in demystifying other aspects of WCF, such as durable services and transactions.

Durable Services

Consider the case of a long-running business process or workflow, comprised of multiple execution sequences, that lasts many days or even weeks.

I use the term *workflow* to denote a business workflow in general, not one that is necessarily supported by or related to the Windows Workflow Foundation.

Such long-running processes may involve clients (or even end users) that connect to the application, perform a finite amount of work, transition the workflow to a new state, and then disconnect for an indeterminate amount of time before connecting again and continuing to execute the workflow. The clients may at any point also decide to terminate the workflow and start a new one, or the backend service supporting the workflow may end it. Obviously, there is little point in keeping proxies and services in memory waiting for the clients to call. Such an approach will not robustly withstand the test of time; at the very least, timeout issues will inevitably terminate the connection, and there is no easy way to allow machines on both sides to reboot or log off. The need to allow the clients and the services to have independent lifecycles is an important one in a long-running business process, because without it there is no way to enable the clients to connect, perform some work against the workflow, and disconnect. On the host side, over time you may even want to redirect calls between machines.

The solution for long-running services is to avoid keeping the service state in memory, and to handle each call on a new instance with its own temporary in-memory state.

For every operation, the service should retrieve its state from some durable storage (such as a file or a database), perform the requested unit of work for that operation, and then save the state back to the durable storage at the end of the call. Services that follow this model are called *durable services*. Since the durable storage can be shared across machines, using durable services also gives you the ability to route calls to different machines at different times, be it for scalability, redundancy, or maintenance purposes.

Durable Services and Instance Management Modes

This approach to state management for durable services is very much like the one proposed previously for per-call services, which proactively manage their state. Using per-call services makes additional sense because there is no point in keeping the instance around between calls if its state is coming from durable storage. The only distinguishing aspect of a durable service compared with a classic per-call service is that the state repository needs to be durable.

While in theory nothing prevents you from basing a durable service on a sessionful or even a singleton service and having that service manage its state in and out of the durable storage, in practice this would be counterproductive. In the case of a sessionful service, you would have to keep the proxy open on the client side for long periods of time, thus excluding clients that terminate their connections and then reconnect. In the case of a singleton service, the very notion of a singleton suggests an infinite lifetime with clients that come and go, so there is no need for durability. Consequently, the per-call instantiation mode offers the best choice all around. Note that with durable per-call services, because the primary concern is long-running workflows rather than scalability or resource management, supporting IDisposable is optional. It is also worth pointing out that the presence of a transport session is optional for a durable service, since there is no need to maintain a logical session between the client and the service. The transport session will be a facet of the transport channel used and will not be used to dictate the lifetime of the instance.

Initiating and terminating

When the long-running workflow starts, the service must first write its state to the durable storage, so that subsequent operations will find the state in the storage. When the workflow ends, the service must remove its state from the storage; otherwise, over time, the storage will become bloated with instance state not required by anyone.

Instance IDs and Durable Storage

Since a new service instance is created for every operation, an instance must have a way of looking up and loading its state from the durable storage. The client must therefore provide some state identifier for the instance. That identifier is called the *instance ID*.

To support clients that connect to the service only occasionally, and client applications or even machines that recycle between calls, as long as the workflow is in progress the client will typically save the instance ID in some durable storage on the client side (such as a file) and provide that ID for every call. When the workflow ends, the client can discard that ID. For an instance ID, it is important to select a type that is serializable and equatable. Having a serializable ID is important because the service will need to save the ID along with its state into the durable storage. Having an equatable ID is required in order to allow the service to obtain the state from the storage. All the .NET primitives (such as int, string, and Guid) qualify as instance IDs.

The durable storage is usually some kind of dictionary that pairs the instance ID with the instance state. The service typically will use a single ID to represent all its state, although more complex relationships involving multiple keys and even hierarchies of keys are possible. For simplicity's sake, I will limit the discussion here to a single ID. In addition, the service often uses a dedicated helper class or a structure to aggregate all its member variables, and stores that type in and retrieves it from the durable storage. Finally, access to the durable storage itself must be thread-safe and synchronized. This is required because multiple instances may try to access and modify the store concurrently.

To help you implement and support simple durable services, I wrote the FileInstanceStore<ID,T> class:

```
public interface IInstanceStore<ID,T> where ID : IEquatable<ID>
{
   void RemoveInstance(ID instanceId);
   bool ContainsInstance(ID instanceId);
   T this[ID instanceId]
   {get;set;}
}

public class FileInstanceStore<ID,T> : IInstanceStore<ID,T> where ID :
                                                    IEquatable<ID>
{
   protected readonly string Filename;

   public FileInstanceStore(string fileName);

   //Rest of the implementation
}
```

FileInstanceStore<ID,T> is a general-purpose file-based instance store. FileInstanceStore<ID,T> takes two type parameters: the ID type parameter is constrained to be an equatable type, and the T type parameter represents the instance state. FileInstanceStore<ID,T> verifies at runtime in a static constructor that both T and ID are serializable types.

`FileInstanceStore<ID,T>` provides a simple indexer allowing you to read and write the instance state to the file. You can also remove an instance state from the file, and check whether the file contains the instance state. These operations are defined in the `IInstanceStore<ID,T>` interface. The implementation of `FileInstanceStore<ID,T>` encapsulates a dictionary, and on every access it serializes and deserializes the dictionary to and from the file. When `FileInstanceStore<ID,T>` is used for the first time, if the file is empty `FileInstanceStore<ID,T>` will initialize it with an empty dictionary.

Explicit Instance IDs

The simplest way a client can provide the instance ID to the service is as an explicit parameter for every operation designed to access the state. Example 4-9 demonstrates such a client and service, along with the supporting type definitions.

Example 4-9. Passing explicit instance IDs

```
[DataContract]
class SomeKey : IEquatable<SomeKey>
{...}

[ServiceContract]
interface IMyContract
{
   [OperationContract]
   void MyMethod(SomeKey instanceId);
}

//Helper type used by the service to capture its state
[Serializable]
struct MyState
{...}

[ServiceBehavior(InstanceContextMode = InstanceContextMode.PerCall)]
class MyService : IMyContract
{
   public void MyMethod(SomeKey instanceId)
   {
      GetState(instanceId);
      DoWork();
      SaveState(instanceId);
   }
   void DoWork()
   {...}

   //Get and set MyState from durable storage
   void GetState(SomeKey instanceId)
   {...}

   void SaveState(SomeKey instanceId)
   {...}
}
```

To make Example 4-9 more concrete, consider Example 4-10, which supports a pocket calculator with durable memory stored in a file.

Example 4-10. Calculator with explicit instance ID

```
[ServiceContract]
interface ICalculator
{
   [OperationContract]
   double Add(double number1,double number2);

   /* More arithmetic operations */

   //Memory management operations

   [OperationContract]
   void MemoryStore(string instanceId,double number);

   [OperationContract]
   void MemoryClear(string instanceId);
}

[ServiceBehavior(InstanceContextMode = InstanceContextMode.PerCall)]
class MyCalculator : ICalculator
{
   static IInstanceStore<string,double> Memory =
            new FileInstanceStore<string,double>(Settings.Default.MemoryFileName);

   public double Add(double number1,double number2)
   {
      return number1 + number2;
   }
   public void MemoryStore(string instanceId,double number)
   {
      lock(typeof(MyCalculator))
      {
         Memory[instanceId] = number;
      }
   }
   public void MemoryClear(string instanceId)
   {
      lock(typeof(MyCalculator))
      {
         Memory.RemoveInstance(instanceId);
      }
   }
   //Rest of the implementation
}
```

In Example 4-10, the filename is available in the properties of the project in the Settings class. All instances of the calculator use the same static memory, in the form of a FileInstanceStore<string,double>. The calculator synchronizes access to the memory in every operation across all instances by locking on the service type.

Clearing the memory signals to the calculator the end of the workflow, so it purges its state from the storage.

Instance IDs in Headers

Instead of explicitly passing the instance ID, the client can provide the instance ID in the message headers. Using message headers as a technique for passing out-of-band parameters used for custom contexts is described in detail in Appendix B. In this case, the client can use my HeaderClientBase<T,H> proxy class, and the service can read the ID in the relevant operations using my GenericContext<H> helper class. The service can use GenericContext<H> as-is or wrap it in a dedicated context.

The general pattern for this technique is shown in Example 4-11.

Example 4-11. Passing instance IDs in message headers

```
[ServiceContract]
interface IMyContract
{
   [OperationContract]
   void MyMethod();
}
//Client-side
class MyContractClient : HeaderClientBase<IMyContract,SomeKey>,IMyContract
{
   public MyContractClient(SomeKey instanceId)
   {}
   public MyContractClient(SomeKey instanceId,string endpointName) :
                                           base(instanceId,endpointName)
   {}

   //More constructors

   public void MyMethod()
   {
      Channel.MyMethod();
   }
}
//Service-side
[ServiceBehavior(InstanceContextMode = InstanceContextMode.PerCall)]
class MyService : IMyContract
{
   public void MyMethod()
   {
      SomeKey instanceId = GenericContext<SomeKey>.Current.Value;
      ...
   }
   //Rest same as Example 4-9
}
```

Again, to make Example 4-11 less abstract, Example 4-12 shows the calculator using the message headers technique.

Example 4-12. Calculator with instance ID in headers

```
[ServiceContract]
interface ICalculator
{
   [OperationContract]
   double Add(double number1,double number2);

   /* More arithmetic operations */

   //Memory management operations

   [OperationContract]
   void MemoryStore(double number);

   [OperationContract]
   void MemoryClear();
}
//Client-side
class MyCalculatorClient : HeaderClientBase<ICalculator,string>,ICalculator
{
   public MyCalculatorClient(string instanceId)
   {}

   public MyCalculatorClient(string instanceId,string endpointName) :
                                            base(instanceId,endpointName)

   {}

   //More constructors

   public double Add(double number1,double number2)
   {
      return Channel.Add(number1,number2);
   }

   public void MemoryStore(double number)
   {
      Channel.MemoryStore(number);
   }

   //Rest of the implementation
}
//Service-side
//If using GenericContext<T> is too raw, can encapsulate:
class CalculatorContext
{
   public static string Id
   {
```

Example 4-12. Calculator with instance ID in headers (continued)

```
      get
      {
          return GenericContext<string>.Current.Value ?? String.Empty;
      }
   }
}

[ServiceBehavior(InstanceContextMode = InstanceContextMode.PerCall)]
class MyCalculator : ICalculator
{
   static IInstanceStore<string,double> Memory =
              new FileInstanceStore<string,double>(Settings.Default.MemoryFileName);

   public double Add(double number1,double number2)
   {
      return number1 + number2;
   }
   public void MemoryStore(double number)
   {
      lock(typeof(MyCalculator))
      {
          Memory[CalculatorContext.Id] = number;
      }
   }
   public void MemoryClear()
   {
      lock(typeof(MyCalculator))
      {
          Memory.RemoveInstance(CalculatorContext.Id);
      }
   }
   //Rest of the implementation
}
```

Context Bindings for Instance IDs

WCF provides dedicated bindings for passing custom context parameters. These bindings, called *context bindings*, are also explained in Appendix B. Clients can use my ContextClientBase<T> class to pass the instance ID over the context binding protocol. Since the context bindings require a key and a value for every contextual parameter, the clients will need to provide both to the proxy. Using the same IMyContract as in Example 4-11, such a proxy will look like this:

```
   class MyContractClient : ContextClientBase<IMyContract>,IMyContract
   {
      public MyContractClient(string key,string instanceId) : base(key,instanceId)
      {}
      public MyContractClient(string key,string instanceId,string endpointName) :
                                              base(key,instanceId,endpointName)

      {}
```

```
        //More constructors

        public void MyMethod( )
        {
            Channel.MyMethod( );
        }
    }
```

Note that the context protocol only supports strings for keys and values. Because the value of the key must be known to the service in advance, the client might as well hardcode the same key in the proxy itself. The service can then retrieve the instance ID using my ContextManager helper class (described in Appendix B). As with message headers, the service can also encapsulate the interaction with ContextManager in a dedicated context class.

Example 4-13 shows the general pattern for passing an instance ID over the context bindings. Note that the proxy hardcodes the key for the instance ID, and that the same ID is known to the service.

Example 4-13. Passing the instance ID over a context binding

```
//Client-side
class MyContractClient : ContextClientBase<IMyContract>,IMyContract
{
    public MyContractClient(string instanceId) : base("MyKey",instanceId)
    {}

    public MyContractClient(string instanceId,string endpointName) :
                                        base("MyKey",instanceId,endpointName)
    {}

    //More constructors

    public void MyMethod( )
    {
        Channel.MyMethod( );
    }
}
//Service-side
[ServiceBehavior(InstanceContextMode = InstanceContextMode.PerCall)]
class MyService : IMyContract
{
    public void MyMethod( )
    {
        string instanceId = ContextManager.GetContext("MyKey");

        GetState(instanceId);
        DoWork( );
        SaveState(instanceId);
    }
    void DoWork( )
    {...}
```

Example 4-13. Passing the instance ID over a context binding (continued)

```
   //Get and set state from durable storage
   void GetState(string instanceId)
   {...}

   void SaveState(string instanceId)
   {...}
}
```

Example 4-14 shows the matching concrete calculator example.

Example 4-14. Calculator with instance ID over context binding

```
//Client-side
class MyCalculatorClient : ContextClientBase<ICalculator>,ICalculator
{
   public MyCalculatorClient(string instanceId) : base("CalculatorId",instanceId)
   {}
   public MyCalculatorClient(string instanceId,string endpointName) :
                                    base("CalculatorId",instanceId,endpointName)

   {}

   //More constructors

   public double Add(double number1,double number2)
   {
      return Channel.Add(number1,number2);
   }
   public void MemoryStore(double number)
   {
      Channel.MemoryStore(number);
   }

   //Rest of the implementation
}
//Service-side
class CalculatorContext
{
   public static string Id
   {
      get
      {
         return ContextManager.GetContext("CalculatorId") ?? String.Empty;
      }
   }
}

[ServiceBehavior(InstanceContextMode = InstanceContextMode.PerCall)]
class MyCalculator : ICalculator
{
   //Same as Example 4-12
}
```

Using the standard ID for context binding

The need to hardcode and know in advance the key used for the instance ID is a liability. The context bindings were designed with durable services in mind, so every context binding always contains an autogenerated instance ID in the form of a Guid (in string format), accessible via the reserved key of instanceId. The client and the service will see the same value for the instance ID. The value is initialized once the first call on the proxy returns, after the binding has had the chance to correlate it between the client and the service. Like any other parameter passed over a context binding, the value of the instance ID is immutable throughout the life of the proxy.

To streamline interacting with the standard instance ID, I extended ContextManager with ID management methods, properties, and proxy extension methods, as shown in Example 4-15.

Example 4-15. Standard instance ID management with ContextManager

```
public static class ContextManager
{
   public const string InstanceIdKey = "instanceId";

   public static Guid InstanceId
   {
      get
      {
         string id = GetContext(InstanceIdKey) ?? Guid.Empty.ToString();
         return new Guid(id);
      }
   }
   public static Guid GetInstanceId(IClientChannel innerChannel)
   {
      try
      {
         string instanceId =
            innerChannel.GetProperty<IContextManager>().GetContext()[InstanceIdKey];
         return new Guid(instanceId);
      }
      catch(KeyNotFoundException)
      {
         return Guid.Empty;
      }
   }
   public static void SetInstanceId(IClientChannel innerChannel,Guid instanceId)
   {
      SetContext(innerChannel,InstanceIdKey,instanceId.ToString());
   }
   public static void SaveInstanceId(Guid instanceId,string fileName)
   {
      using(Stream stream =
                  new FileStream(fileName,FileMode.OpenOrCreate,FileAccess.Write))
```

```
        {
            IFormatter formatter = new BinaryFormatter();
            formatter.Serialize(stream,instanceId);
        }
    }

    public static Guid LoadInstanceId(string fileName)
    {
        try
        {
            using(Stream stream = new FileStream(fileName,FileMode.Open,
                                                 FileAccess.Read))
            {
                IFormatter formatter = new BinaryFormatter();
                return (Guid)formatter.Deserialize(stream);
            }
        }
        catch
        {
            return Guid.Empty;
        }
    }
    //More members
}
```

ContextManager offers the GetInstanceId( ) and SetInstanceId( ) methods to enable the client to read an instance ID from and write it to the context. The service uses the InstanceId read-only property to obtain the ID. ContextManager adds type safety by treating the instance ID as a Guid and not as a string. It also adds error handling.

Finally, ContextManager provides the LoadInstanceId( ) and SaveInstanceId( ) methods to read the instance ID from and write it to a file. These methods are handy on the client side to store the ID between client application sessions against the service.

While the client can use ContextClientBase<T> (as in Example 4-13) to pass the standard ID, it is better to tighten it and provide built-in support for the standard instance ID, as shown in Example 4-16.

Example 4-16. Extending ContextClientBase<T> to support standard IDs

```
public abstract class ContextClientBase<T> : ClientBase<T> where T : class
{
    public Guid InstanceId
    {
        get
        {
            return ContextManager.GetInstanceId(InnerChannel);
        }
    }
    public ContextClientBase(Guid instanceId) :
                        this(ContextManager.InstanceIdKey,instanceId.ToString())
    {}
```

```
   public ContextClientBase(Guid instanceId,string endpointName) :
            this(ContextManager.InstanceIdKey,instanceId.ToString( ),endpointName)
   {}

   //More constructors
}
```

Example 4-17 shows the calculator client and service using the standard ID.

Example 4-17. Calculator using standard ID

```
//Client-side
class MyCalculatorClient : ContextClientBase<ICalculator>,ICalculator
{
   public MyCalculatorClient( )
   {}
   public MyCalculatorClient(Guid instanceId) : base(instanceId)
   {}
   public MyCalculatorClient(Guid instanceId,string endpointName) :
                                           base(instanceId,endpointName)
   {}

   //Rest same as Example 4-14
}
//Service-side
[ServiceBehavior(InstanceContextMode = InstanceContextMode.PerCall)]
class MyCalculator : ICalculator
{
   static IInstanceStore<Guid,double> Memory =
             new FileInstanceStore<Guid,double>(Settings.Default.MemoryFileName);

   public double Add(double number1,double number2)
   {
      return number1 + number2;
   }
   public void MemoryStore(double number)
   {
      lock(typeof(MyCalculator))
      {
         Memory[ContextManager.InstanceId] = number;
      }
   }
   public void MemoryClear( )
   {
      lock(typeof(MyCalculator))
      {
         Memory.RemoveInstance(ContextManager.InstanceId);
      }
   }
   //Rest of the implementation
}
```

Automatic Durable Behavior

All the techniques shown so far for durable services require a nontrivial amount of work by the service—in particular, providing a durable state storage and explicitly managing the instance state against it in every operation. Given the repetitive nature of this work, WCF can automate it for you, and serialize and deserialize the service state on every operation from an indicated state store, using the standard instance ID.

When you let WCF manage your instance state, it follows these rules:

- If the client does not provide an ID, WCF will create a new service instance by exercising its constructor. After the call, WCF will serialize the instance to the state store.

- If the client provides an ID to the proxy and the store already contains state matching that ID, WCF will not call the instance constructor. Instead, the call will be serviced on a new instance deserialized out of the state store.

- When the client provides a valid ID, for every operation WCF will deserialize an instance out of the store, call the operation, and serialize the new state modified by the operation back to the store.

- If the client provides an ID not found in the state store, WCF will throw an exception.

The durable service behavior attribute

To enable this automatic durable behavior, WCF provides the `DurableService` behavior attribute, defined as:

```
public sealed class DurableServiceAttribute : Attribute,IServiceBehavior,...
{...}
```

You apply this attribute directly on the service class. Most importantly, the service class must be marked either as serializable or as a data contract with the `DataMember` attribute on all members requiring durable state management:

```
[Serializable]
[DurableService]
class MyService : IMyContract
{
   /* Serializable member variables only  */

   public void MyMethod( )
   {
      //Do work
   }
}
```

The instance can now manage its state in member variables, just as if it were a regular instance, trusting WCF to manage those members for it. If the service is not marked as serializable (or a data contract), the first call to it will fail once WCF tries to serialize it to the store. Any service relying on automatic durable state management must be configured as per-session, yet it will always behave as a per-call service (WCF uses context deactivation after every call). In addition, the service must use one of the context bindings with every endpoint to enable the standard instance ID, and the contract must allow or require a transport session, but cannot disallow it. These two constraints are verified at service load time.

The durable operation behavior attribute

A service can optionally use the DurableOperation behavior attribute to instruct WCF to purge its state from the store at the end of the workflow:

```
[AttributeUsage(AttributeTargets.Method)]
public sealed class DurableOperationAttribute : Attribute,...
{
   public bool CanCreateInstance
   {get;set;}

   public bool CompletesInstance
   {get;set;}
}
```

Setting the CompletesInstance property to true instructs WCF to remove the instance ID from the store once the operation call returns. The default value of the CompletesInstance property is false. In case the client does not provide an instance ID, you can also prevent an operation from creating a new instance by setting the CanCreateInstance property to false. Example 4-18 demonstrates the use of the CompletesInstance property on the MemoryClear( ) operation of the calculator.

Example 4-18. Using CompletesInstance to remove the state

```
[Serializable]
[DurableService]
class MyCalculator : ICalculator
{
   double Memory
   {get;set;}

   public double Add(double number1,double number2)
   {
      return number1 + number2;
   }
   public void MemoryStore(double number)
   {
      Memory = number;
   }
   [DurableOperation(CompletesInstance = true)]
   public void MemoryClear( )
   {
      Memory = 0;
   }
   //Rest of the implementation
}
```

The problem with relying on CompletesInstance is that the context ID is immutable. This means that if the client tries to make additional calls on the proxy after calling an operation for which CompletesInstance is set to true, all of those calls will fail, since the store will no longer contain the instance ID. The client must be aware, therefore, that it cannot continue to use the same proxy: if the client wants to make further calls against the service, it must do so on a new proxy that does not have an instance ID yet, and by doing so, the client will start a new workflow. One way of enforcing this is to simply close the client program after completing the workflow (or create a new proxy reference). Using the proxy definition of Example 4-17, Example 4-19 shows how to manage the calculator proxy after clearing the memory while seamlessly continuing to use the proxy.

Example 4-19. Resetting the proxy after completing a workflow

```
class CalculatorProgram
{
   MyCalculatorClient m_Proxy;

   public CalculatorProgram( )
   {
      Guid calculatorId =
            ContextManager.LoadInstanceId(Settings.Default.CalculatorIdFileName);

      m_Proxy = new MyCalculatorClient(calculatorId);
   }
   public void Add( )
   {
      m_Proxy.Add(2,3);
   }
   public void MemoryClear( )
   {
      m_Proxy.MemoryClear( );

      ResetDurableSession(ref m_Proxy);
   }
   public void Close( )
   {
      ContextManager.SaveInstanceId(m_Proxy.InstanceId,
                              Settings.Default.CalculatorIdFileName);
      m_Proxy.Close( );
   }
   void ResetDurableSession(ref MyCalculatorClient proxy)
   {
      ContextManager.SaveInstanceId(Guid.Empty,
                              Settings.Default.CalculatorIdFileName);
      Binding binding = proxy.Endpoint.Binding;
      EndpointAddress address = proxy.Endpoint.Address;

      proxy.Close( );

      proxy = new MyCalculatorClient(binding,address);
   }
}
```

Example 4-19 uses my `ContextManager` helper class to load an instance ID and save it to a file. The constructor of the client program creates a new proxy using the ID found in the file. As shown in Example 4-15, if the file does not contain an instance ID, `LoadInstanceId( )` returns `Guid.Empty`. My `ContextClientBase<T>` is designed to expect an empty GUID for the context ID: if an empty GUID is provided, `ContextClientBase<T>` constructs itself without an instance ID, thus ensuring a new workflow. After clearing the memory of the calculator, the client calls the `ResetDurableSession( )` helper method. `ResetDurableSession( )` first saves an empty GUID to the file, and then duplicates the existing proxy. It copies the old proxy's address and binding, closes the old proxy, and sets the proxy reference to a new proxy constructed using the same address and binding as the old one and with an implicit empty GUID for the instance ID.

Programmatic instance management

WCF offers a simple helper class for durable services called `DurableOperationContext`:

```
public static class DurableOperationContext
{
   public static void AbortInstance( );
   public static void CompleteInstance( );
   public static Guid InstanceId
   {get;}
}
```

The `CompleteInstance( )` method lets the service programmatically (instead of declaratively via the `DurableOperation` attribute) complete the instance and remove the state from the store once the call returns. `AbortInstance( )`, on the other hand, cancels any changes made to the store during the call, as if the operation was never called. The `InstanceId` property is similar to `ContextManager.InstanceId`.

Persistence providers

While the `DurableService` attribute instructs WCF when to serialize and deserialize the instance, it does not say anything about where to do so, or, for that matter, provide any information about the state storage. WCF actually uses a bridge pattern in the form of a provider model, which lets you specify the state store separately from the attribute. The attribute is thus decoupled from the store, allowing you to rely on the automatic durable behavior for any compatible storage.

If a service is configured with the `DurableService` attribute, you must configure its host with a persistence provider factory. The factory derives from the abstract class `PersistenceProviderFactory`, and it creates a subclass of the abstract class `PersistenceProvider`:

```
public abstract class PersistenceProviderFactory : CommunicationObject
{
   protected PersistenceProviderFactory( );
   public abstract PersistenceProvider CreateProvider(Guid id);
}
```

```
public abstract class PersistenceProvider : CommunicationObject
{
   protected PersistenceProvider(Guid id);

   public Guid Id
   {get;}

   public abstract object Create(object instance,TimeSpan timeout);
   public abstract void   Delete(object instance,TimeSpan timeout);
   public abstract object Load(TimeSpan timeout);
   public abstract object Update(object instance,TimeSpan timeout);

   //Additional members
}
```

The most common way of specifying the persistence provider factory is to include it in the host config file as a service behavior, and to reference that behavior in the service definition:

```
<behaviors>
   <serviceBehaviors>
      <behavior name = "DurableService">
         <persistenceProvider
            type = "...type...,...assembly ..."
            <!-- Provider-specific parameters  -->
         />
      </behavior>
   </serviceBehaviors>
</behaviors>
```

Once the host is configured with the persistence provider factory, WCF uses the created PersistenceProvider for every call to serialize and deserialize the instance. If no persistence provider factory is specified, WCF aborts creating the service host.

Custom persistence providers

A nice way to demonstrate how to write a simple custom persistence provider is my FilePersistenceProviderFactory, defined as:

```
public class FilePersistenceProviderFactory : PersistenceProviderFactory
{
   public FilePersistenceProviderFactory( );
   public FilePersistenceProviderFactory(string fileName);
   public FilePersistenceProviderFactory(NameValueCollection parameters);
}
public class FilePersistenceProvider : PersistenceProvider
{
   public FilePersistenceProvider(Guid id,string fileName);
}
```

FilePersistenceProvider wraps my FileInstanceStore<ID,T> class. The constructor of FilePersistenceProviderFactory requires you to specify the desired filename. If no filename is specified, FilePersistenceProviderFactory defaults the filename to *Instances.bin*.

The key for using a custom persistence factory in a config file is to define a constructor that takes a `NameValueCollection` of parameters. These parameters are simple text-formatted pairs of the keys and values specified in the provider factory behavior section in the config file. Virtually any free-formed keys and values will work. For example, here's how to specify the filename:

```
<behaviors>
   <serviceBehaviors>
      <behavior name = "Durable">
         <persistenceProvider
            type = "FilePersistenceProviderFactory,ServiceModelEx"
            fileName = "MyService.bin"
         />
      </behavior>
   </serviceBehaviors>
</behaviors>
```

The constructor can then use the `parameters` collection to access these parameters:

```
string fileName = parameters["fileName"];
```

The SQL Server persistence provider

WCF ships with a persistence provider, which stores the instance state in a dedicated SQL Server table. After a default installation, the installation scripts for the database are found under *C:\Windows\Microsoft.NET\Framework\v3.5\SQL\EN*. Note that with the WCF-provided SQL persistence provider you can only use SQL Server 2005 or SQL Server 2008 for state storage. The SQL provider comes in the form of `SqlPersistenceProviderFactory` and `SqlPersistenceProvider`, found in the `System.WorkflowServices` assembly under the `System.ServiceModel.Persistence` namespace.

All you need to do is specify the SQL provider factory and the connection string name:

```
<connectionStrings>
   <add name = "DurableServices"
      connectionString = "..."
      providerName = "System.Data.SqlClient"
   />
</connectionStrings>

<behaviors>
   <serviceBehaviors>
      <behavior name = "Durable">
         <persistenceProvider
            type = "System.ServiceModel.Persistence.SqlPersistenceProviderFactory,
                    System.WorkflowServices,Version=3.5.0.0,Culture=neutral,
                    PublicKeyToken=31bf3856ad364e35"
            connectionStringName = "DurableServices"
         />
      </behavior>
   </serviceBehaviors>
</behaviors>
```

You can also instruct WCF to serialize the instances as text (instead of the default binary serialization), perhaps for diagnostics or analysis purposes:

```
<persistenceProvider
    type = "System.ServiceModel.Persistence.SqlPersistenceProviderFactory,
            System.WorkflowServices,Version=3.5.0.0,Culture=neutral,
            PublicKeyToken=31bf3856ad364e35"
    connectionStringName = "DurableServices"
    serializeAsText = "true"
/>
```

Throttling

While it is not a direct instance management technique, *throttling* enables you to restrain client connections and the load they place on your service. You need throttling because software systems are not elastic, as shown in Figure 4-7.

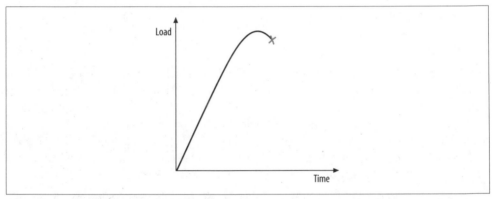

Figure 4-7. The inelastic nature of all software systems

That is, you cannot keep increasing the load on the system and expect an infinite, gradual decline in its performance, as if stretching chewing gum. Most systems will initially handle the increase in load well, but then begin to yield and abruptly snap and break. All software systems behave this way, for reasons that are beyond the scope of this book and are related to queuing theory and the overhead inherent in managing resources. This snapping, inelastic behavior is of particular concern when there are spikes in load, as shown in Figure 4-8.

Even if a system is handling a nominal load well (the horizontal line in Figure 4-8), a spike may push it beyond its design limit, causing it to snap and resulting in the clients experiencing a significant degradation in their level of service. Spikes can also pose a challenge in terms of the rate at which the load grows, even if the absolute level reached would not otherwise cause the system problems.

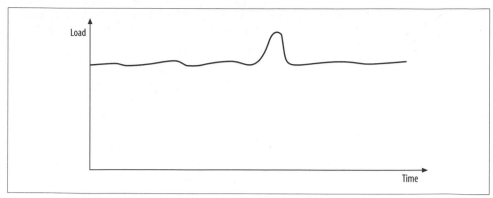

Figure 4-8. A spike in load may push the system beyond its design limit

Throttling enables you to avoid maxing out your service and the underlying resources it allocates and uses. When throttling is engaged, if the settings you configure are exceeded, WCF will automatically place the pending callers in a queue and serve them out of the queue in order. If a client's call timeout expires while its call is pending in the queue, the client will get a `TimeoutException`. Throttling is inherently an unfair technique, because those clients whose requests are buffered will see a degradation in their level of service. However, in this case, it is better to be smart than just: if all the callers in the spike are allowed in, that will be fair, but all callers will then see a significant drop in the level of service as the system snaps. Throttling therefore makes sense when the area under the spike is relatively small compared with the area under the entire load graph, implying that the probability of the same caller being queued successively is very low. Every once in a while, in response to a spike, some callers will get buffered, but the system as a whole will still function well. Throttling does *not* work well when the load increases to a new level and remains constant at that level for a long time (as shown in Figure 4-9). In that case, all it does is defer the problems a bit, eventually causing all callers to time out. Such a system should be designed from the ground up to handle the higher level of load.

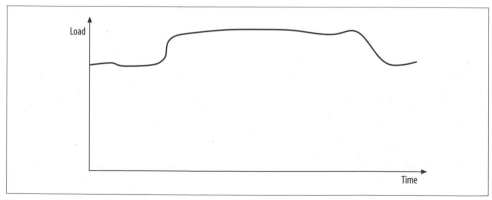

Figure 4-9. Inadequate justification for throttling

Throttling is done per service type; that is, it affects all instances of the service and all its endpoints. This is done by associating the throttle with every channel dispatcher the service uses.

WCF lets you control some or all of the following service consumption parameters:

Maximum number of concurrent sessions

Indicates the overall number of outstanding clients that can have a transport session with the service. In plain terms, this represents the maximum overall number of outstanding clients using TCP, IPC, or either of the WS bindings (with reliability, security, or both). Because the connectionless nature of a basic HTTP connection implies a very short transport session that exists only for the duration of the call, this number usually has no effect on clients using the basic binding or a WS binding without a transport session; such clients are instead limited by the maximum allowed number of concurrent calls. The default value is 10.

Maximum number of concurrent calls

Limits the total number of calls that can currently be in progress across all service instances. This number should usually be kept at 1 to 3 percent of the maximum number of concurrent sessions. The default value is 16.

Maximum number of concurrent instances

Controls the total number of concurrently alive contexts. The default value is unlimited. How instances map to contexts is a product of the instance context management mode, as well as context and instance deactivation. With a per-session service, the maximum number of instances is both the total number of concurrently active instances and the total number of concurrent sessions. When instance deactivation is employed, there may be far fewer instances than contexts, and yet clients will be blocked if the number of contexts has reached the maximum number of concurrent instances. With a per-call service, the number of instances is actually the same as the number of concurrent calls. Consequently, the maximum number of instances with a per-call service is the lesser of the configured maximum concurrent instances and maximum concurrent calls. The value of this parameter is ignored with a singleton service, since it can only have a single instance anyway.

 Throttling is an aspect of hosting and deployment. When you design a service, you should make no assumptions about throttling configuration—always assume your service will bear the full brunt of the client's load. This is why, although it is fairly easy to write a throttling behavior attribute, WCF does not offer one.

Configuring Throttling

Administrators typically configure throttling in the config file. This enables you to throttle the same service code differently over time or across deployment sites. The host can also programmatically configure throttling based on some runtime decisions.

Administrative throttling

Example 4-20 shows how to configure throttling in the host config file. Using the `behaviorConfiguration` tag, you add to your service a custom behavior that sets throttled values.

Example 4-20. Administrative throttling

```
<system.serviceModel>
   <services>
      <service name = "MyService" behaviorConfiguration = "ThrottledBehavior">
         ...
      </service>
   </services>
   <behaviors>
      <serviceBehaviors>
         <behavior name = "ThrottledBehavior">
            <serviceThrottling
               maxConcurrentCalls     = "500"
               maxConcurrentSessions  = "10000"
               maxConcurrentInstances = "100"
            />
         </behavior>
      </serviceBehaviors>
   </behaviors>
</system.serviceModel>
```

Programmatic throttling

The host process can programmatically throttle the service based on some runtime parameters. You can only configure the throttle programmatically before the host is opened. Although the host can override the throttling behavior found in the config file by removing it and adding its own, you typically should provide a programmatic throttling behavior only when there is no throttling behavior in the config file.

The `ServiceHostBase` class offers the `Description` property of the type `ServiceDescription`:

```
public abstract class ServiceHostBase : ...
{
   public ServiceDescription Description
   {get;}
   //More members
}
```

The service description, as its name implies, is a description of the service, with all its aspects and behaviors. ServiceDescription contains a property called Behaviors of the type KeyedByTypeCollection<I>, with IServiceBehavior as the generic parameter.

Example 4-21 shows how to set the throttled behavior programmatically.

Example 4-21. Programmatic throttling

```
ServiceHost host = new ServiceHost(typeof(MyService));

ServiceThrottlingBehavior throttle;
throttle = host.Description.Behaviors.Find<ServiceThrottlingBehavior>();
if(throttle == null)
{
   throttle = new ServiceThrottlingBehavior();
   throttle.MaxConcurrentCalls     = 12;
   throttle.MaxConcurrentSessions  = 34;
   throttle.MaxConcurrentInstances = 56;
   host.Description.Behaviors.Add(throttle);
}

host.Open();
```

First, the hosting code verifies that no service throttling behavior was provided in the config file. This is done by calling the Find<T>() method of KeyedByTypeCollection<I>, using ServiceThrottlingBehavior as the type parameter.

ServiceThrottlingBehavior is defined in the System.ServiceModel.Design namespace:

```
public class ServiceThrottlingBehavior : IServiceBehavior
{
   public int MaxConcurrentCalls
   {get;set;}
   public int MaxConcurrentSessions
   {get;set;}
   public int MaxConcurrentInstances
   {get;set;}
   //More members
}
```

If the returned throttle is null, then the hosting code creates a new ServiceThrottlingBehavior, sets its values, and adds it to the behaviors in the service description.

Streamlining with ServiceHost<T>

Using C# 3.0 extensions, you can extend ServiceHost (or any subclass of it, such as ServiceHost<T>) to automate the code in Example 4-21, as shown in Example 4-22.

Example 4-22. Extending ServiceHost to handle throttling

```
public static class ServiceThrottleHelper
{
   public static void SetThrottle(this ServiceHost host,
                                  int maxCalls,int maxSessions,int maxInstances)
   {
      ServiceThrottlingBehavior throttle = new ServiceThrottlingBehavior( );
      throttle.MaxConcurrentCalls = maxCalls;
      throttle.MaxConcurrentSessions = maxSessions;
      throttle.MaxConcurrentInstances = maxInstances;
      host.SetThrottle(throttle);
   }
   public static void SetThrottle(this ServiceHost host,
                                  ServiceThrottlingBehavior serviceThrottle,
                                  bool overrideConfig)
   {
      if(host.State == CommunicationState.Opened)
      {
         throw new InvalidOperationException("Host is already opened");
      }
      ServiceThrottlingBehavior throttle =
                  host.Description.Behaviors.Find<ServiceThrottlingBehavior>( );
      if(throttle == null)
      {
         host.Description.Behaviors.Add(serviceThrottle);
         return;
      }
      if(overrideConfig == false)
      {
         return;
      }
      host.Description.Behaviors.Remove(throttle);
      host.Description.Behaviors.Add(serviceThrottle);
   }
   public static void SetThrottle(this ServiceHost host,
                                  ServiceThrottlingBehavior serviceThrottle)
   {
      host.SetThrottle(serviceThrottle,false);
   }
}
```

ServiceThrottleHelper offers the SetThrottle( ) method, which accepts the throttle to use, and a Boolean flag indicating whether or not to override the configured values, if present. The default value (using an overloaded version of SetThrottle( )) is false. SetThrottle( ) verifies that the host hasn't been opened yet using the State property of the CommunicationObject base class. If it is required to override the configured throttle, SetThrottle( ) removes it from the description. The rest of Example 4-22 is similar to Example 4-21. Here is how to use ServiceHost<T> to set a throttle programmatically:

```
ServiceHost<MyService> host = new ServiceHost<MyService>( );
host.SetThrottle(12,34,56);
host.Open( );
```

The InProcFactory<T> class presented in Chapter 1 was similarly extended to streamline throttling.

Reading throttle values

Service developers can read the throttle values at runtime, for diagnostic and analytical purposes. For a service instance to access its throttle properties from its dispatcher at runtime, it must first obtain a reference to the host from the operation context.

The host base class ServiceHostBase offers the read-only ChannelDispatchers property:

```
public abstract class ServiceHostBase : CommunicationObject,...
{
    public ChannelDispatcherCollection ChannelDispatchers
    {get;}
    //More members
}
```

ChannelDispatchers is a strongly typed collection of ChannelDispatcherBase objects:

```
public class ChannelDispatcherCollection :
                                SynchronizedCollection<ChannelDispatcherBase>
{...}
```

Each item in the collection is of the type ChannelDispatcher. ChannelDispatcher offers the property ServiceThrottle:

```
public class ChannelDispatcher : ChannelDispatcherBase
{
    public ServiceThrottle ServiceThrottle
    {get;set;}
    //More members
}
public sealed class ServiceThrottle
{
    public int MaxConcurrentCalls
    {get;set;}
    public int MaxConcurrentSessions
    {get;set;}
    public int MaxConcurrentInstances
    {get;set;}
}
```

ServiceThrottle contains the configured throttle values:

```
class MyService : ...
{
    public void MyMethod( ) //Contract operation
    {
        ChannelDispatcher dispatcher = OperationContext.Current.
                            Host.ChannelDispatchers[0] as ChannelDispatcher;

        ServiceThrottle serviceThrottle = dispatcher.ServiceThrottle;
```

```
            Trace.WriteLine("Max Calls = " + serviceThrottle.MaxConcurrentCalls);
            Trace.WriteLine("Max Sessions = " + serviceThrottle.MaxConcurrentSessions);
            Trace.WriteLine("Max Instances = " + serviceThrottle.MaxConcurrentInstances);
      }
   }
```

Note that the service can only read the throttle values and has no way of affecting them. If the service tries to set the throttle values, it will get an InvalidOperationException.

Again, you can streamline the throttle lookup via ServiceHost<T>. First, add a ServiceThrottle property:

```
public class ServiceHost<T> : ServiceHost
{
   public ServiceThrottle Throttle
   {
      get
      {
         if(State == CommunicationState.Created)
         {
            throw new InvalidOperationException("Host is not opened");
         }

         ChannelDispatcher dispatcher = OperationContext.Current.
                              Host.ChannelDispatchers[0] as ChannelDispatcher;
         return dispatcher.ServiceThrottle;
      }
   }
   //More members
}
```

Then, use ServiceHost<T> to host the service and use the ServiceThrottle property to access the configured throttle:

```
//Hosting code
ServiceHost<MyService> host = new ServiceHost<MyService>( );
host.Open( );

class MyService : ...
{
   public void MyMethod( )
   {
      ServiceHost<MyService> host = OperationContext.Current.
                                          Host as ServiceHost<MyService>;

      ServiceThrottle serviceThrottle = host.Throttle;
      ...
   }
}
```

 You can only access the Throttle property of ServiceHost<T> after the host is opened, because the dispatcher collection is initialized only after that point.

Throttled Connections in the Binding

When you use the TCP and IPC bindings, you can also configure the maximum number of connections for a particular endpoint in the binding itself. Both the NetTcpBinding and the NetNamedPipeBinding offer the MaxConnections property:

```
public class NetTcpBinding : Binding,...
{
   public int MaxConnections
   {get;set;}
}
public class NetNamedPipeBinding : Binding,...
{
   public int MaxConnections
   {get;set;}
}
```

On the host side, you can set that property either programmatically or using a config file:

```
<bindings>
   <netTcpBinding>
      <binding name = "TCPThrottle" maxConnections = "25"/>
   </netTcpBinding>
</bindings>
```

The maximum number of connections defaults to 10. When both a binding-level throttle and a service-behavior throttle set the value, WCF chooses the lesser of the two.

CHAPTER 5

Operations

The classic object- or component-oriented programming models offered only a single way for clients to call a method: the client would issue a call, block while the call was in progress, and continue executing once the method returned. Any other calling model had to be handcrafted, often incurring productivity and quality penalties. While WCF supports this classic invocation model, it also provides built-in support for additional operation types: one-way calls for fire-and-forget operations, duplex callbacks for allowing the service to call back to the client, and streaming to allow the client or the service to handle large payloads. In general, the type of operation used is part of the service contract and is an intrinsic part of the service design. The operation type may even place some constraints on the allowed bindings. Consequently, clients and services should be designed from the ground up with the operation type in mind, and you will not be able to switch easily between the various operation types. This chapter is dedicated to the various ways of invoking WCF operations and the related design guidelines.* Two other ways of invoking operations—asynchronously and queued—are addressed in subsequent chapters.

Request-Reply Operations

All the samples in the previous chapters included contracts whose operations were of the type known as *request-reply*. As the name implies, in these operations the client issues a request in the form of a message and blocks until it gets the reply message. If the service does not respond within a default timeout of one minute, the client will get a TimeoutException. Request-reply is the default operation mode. Programming against request-reply operations is simple enough and resembles programming using the classic client/server model. The returned response message containing the results or returned values is converted to normal method return values. In addition, the proxy will throw an exception on the client side if there are any communication or

---

* This chapter contains excerpts from my article "WCF Essentials: What You Need to Know About One-Way Calls, Callbacks, and Events" (*MSDN Magazine*, October 2006).

service-side exceptions. Apart from the `NetPeerTcpBinding` and the `NetMsmqBinding`, all bindings support request-reply operations.

One-Way Operations

There are cases when an operation has no return value, and the client does not care about the success or failure of the invocation. To support this sort of fire-and-forget invocation, WCF offers *one-way* operations: once the client issues the call, WCF generates a request message, but no correlated reply message will ever return to the client. As a result, one-way operations cannot return values, and any exceptions thrown on the service side will not make their way to the client.

Ideally, when the client calls a one-way method, it should be blocked only for the briefest moment required to dispatch the call. However, in reality, one-way calls do not equate to asynchronous calls. When one-way calls reach the service, they may not be dispatched all at once but may instead be queued up on the service side to be dispatched one at a time, according to the service's configured concurrency mode behavior. (Chapter 8 will discuss concurrency management and one-way calls in depth.) How many messages the service is willing to queue up (be they one-way or request-reply operations) is a product of the configured channel and reliability mode. If the number of queued messages has exceeded the queue's capacity, the client will be blocked even if it's issued a one-way call. However, once the call is queued, the client will be unblocked and can continue executing, while the service processes the operation in the background.

It's also wrong to equate one-way calls with concurrent calls. If the client uses the same proxy yet utilizes multiple threads to invoke one-way calls, the calls may or may not execute concurrently on the service, and the exact nature of the interaction will be determined by the service concurrency management mode and the transport session (see Chapter 8 for more on this subject).

All of the WCF bindings support one-way operations.

Configuring One-Way Operations

The `OperationContract` attribute offers the Boolean `IsOneWay` property:

```
[AttributeUsage(AttributeTargets.Method)]
public sealed class OperationContractAttribute : Attribute
{
    public bool IsOneWay
    {get;set;}
    //More members
}
```

`IsOneWay` defaults to `false`, which means a request-reply operation (hence the WCF default). However, setting `IsOneWay` to `true` configures the method as a one-way operation:

```
[ServiceContract]
interface IMyContract
{
   [OperationContract(IsOneWay = true)]
   void MyMethod( );
}
```

The client doesn't have to do anything special or different when invoking a one-way operation. The value of the IsOneWay property is reflected in the service metadata. Note that both the service contract definition and the definition imported by the client must have the same value for IsOneWay.

Because there is no reply associated with a one-way operation, there is no point in having any returned values or results. For example, here is an invalid definition of a one-way operation that returns a value:

```
//Invalid contract
[ServiceContract]
interface IMyContract
{
   [OperationContract(IsOneWay = true)]
   int MyMethod( );
}
```

In fact, WCF enforces this by verifying the method signature when loading the host or opening the proxy and throwing an InvalidOperationException in the case of a mismatch.

One-Way Operations and Reliability

The fact that the client does not care about the result of the invocation does not mean that the client does not care whether the invocation took place at all. In general, you should turn on reliability for your services, even for one-way calls. This will ensure delivery of the requests to the service. However, the client may or may not care about the invocation order of the one-way operations. This is one of the main reasons why WCF allows you to separate enabling reliable delivery from enabling ordered delivery and execution of messages. Obviously, both the client and the service have to agree beforehand on these details, or the binding configuration will not match.

One-Way Operations and Sessionful Services

WCF will let you design a sessionful contract with one-way operations:

```
[ServiceContract(SessionMode = SessionMode.Required)]
interface IMyContract
{
   [OperationContract(IsOneWay = true)]
   void MyMethod( );
}
```

With this configuration, if the client issues a one-way call and then closes the proxy while the method executes, the client will still be blocked until the operation completes.

While technically possible, I believe that in general one-way operations in a sessionful contract (and per-session instantiation) indicate bad design. The reason is that having a session usually implies that the service manages state on behalf of the client. Any exception that may happen will be likely to fault that state, and yet the client may be unaware of it. In addition, typically the client (or the service) will choose a sessionful interaction because the contract used requires some lock-step execution advancing through some state machine. One-way calls do not fit this model very well. Consequently, I recommend that one-way operations should be applied on per-call or singleton services only.

If you do employ one-way operations on a sessionful contract, strive to make only the last operation terminating the session a one-way operation (and make sure it complies with one-way rules, such as having a void return type). You can use demarcating operations to enforce that:

```
[ServiceContract(SessionMode = SessionMode.Required)]
interface IOrderManager
{
   [OperationContract]
   void SetCustomerId(int customerId);

   [OperationContract(IsInitiating = false)]
   void AddItem(int itemId);

   [OperationContract(IsInitiating = false)]
   decimal GetTotal();

   [OperationContract(IsOneWay = true,IsInitiating = false,
                                      IsTerminating = true)]
   void ProcessOrders();
}
```

One-Way Operations and Exceptions

Although one-way operations do not return values or exceptions from the service itself, it's wrong to perceive them as a one-way street or a "black hole" from which nothing can come out. The client should still expect exceptions from a one-way call, and can even deduce that the call failed on the service. When dispatching a one-way operation, any error because of communication problems (such as a wrong address or the host being unavailable) will throw an exception on the side of the client trying to invoke the operation. Furthermore, depending on the service instance mode and the binding used, the client may be affected by service-side exceptions. (The following discussion assumes that the service does not throw a FaultException or a derived exception, as discussed in Chapter 6.)

When there is no transport session (for example, when using the BasicHttpBinding or the WSHttpBinding without reliable messaging and security), if an exception takes place during the invocation of a one-way operation, the client is unaffected and can continue to issue calls on the same proxy instance:

```
[ServiceContract]
interface IMyContract
{
   [OperationContract(IsOneWay = true)]
   void MethodWithError();

   [OperationContract]
   void MethodWithoutError();
}
class MyService : IMyContract
{
   public void MethodWithError()
   {
      throw new Exception();
   }
   public void MethodWithoutError()
   {}
}
//Client side without transport session:
MyContractClient proxy = new MyContractClient();
proxy.MethodWithError();
proxy.MethodWithoutError();
proxy.Close();
```

However, in the presence of a transport session, a service-side exception—including one thrown by a one-way operation—will fault the channel, and the client will not be able to issue any new calls using the same proxy instance:

```
[ServiceContract]
interface IMyContract
{
   [OperationContract(IsOneWay = true)]
   void MethodWithError();

   [OperationContract]
   void MethodWithoutError();
}

class MyService : IMyContract
{
   public void MethodWithError()
   {
      throw new Exception();
   }
   public void MethodWithoutError()
   {}
}
//Client side with transport session
```

```
MyContractClient proxy = new MyContractClient();
proxy.MethodWithError();
try
{
   proxy.MethodWithoutError(); //Will throw because channel faulted
   proxy.Close();
}
catch
{}
```

The client will not even be able to safely close the proxy.

I find these inconsistencies disturbing, to say the least, first because the choice of a binding should not affect the client code, but also because it is a violation of the semantics of true one-way operations, enabling the caller to discover that something went wrong on the service during a one-way invocation.

Callback Operations

WCF supports allowing a service to call back to its clients. During a callback, in many respects the tables are turned: the service is the client, and the client becomes the service (see Figure 5-1). Callback operations can be used in a variety of scenarios and applications, but they are especially useful when it comes to events, or notifying the client(s) that some event has happened on the service side.

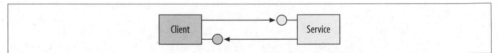

Figure 5-1. A callback allows the service to call back to the client

Callbacks are also commonly referred to as *duplex operations*. There are two immediate challenges to supporting duplex communication. First, how does the service know where the callback endpoint is? Second, how does the client facilitate hosting the callback object?

Not all bindings support callback operations. Only bidirectional-capable bindings support callback operations. For example, because of its connectionless nature, HTTP cannot be used for callbacks, and therefore you cannot use callbacks over the BasicHttpBinding or the WSHttpBinding. To support callbacks over HTTP, WCF offers the WSDualHttpBinding, which actually sets up two WS channels: one for the calls from the client to the service and one for the calls from the service to the client. WCF also offers callback support for the NetTcpBinding and the NetNamedPipeBinding, because by their very nature, the TCP and the IPC protocols support duplex communication.

Duplex callbacks are nonstandard, as there is no industry standard that states how the client endpoint reference is passed to the service, or how the service publishes the callback contract in the first place. Duplex callbacks (including those over the WS dual binding) are a pure Microsoft feature.

The Callback Contract

Callback operations are part of the service contract, and it is up to the service contract to define its own callback contract. A service contract can have at most one callback contract. Once defined, the clients are required to support the callback and provide the callback endpoint to the service in every call. To define a callback contract, the ServiceContract attribute offers the CallbackContract property of the type Type:

```
[AttributeUsage(AttributeTargets.Interface|AttributeTargets.Class)]
public sealed class ServiceContractAttribute : Attribute
{
    public Type CallbackContract
    {get;set;}
    //More members
}
```

When you define a service contract with a callback contract, you need to provide the ServiceContract attribute with the type of the callback contract and the definition of the callback contract, as shown in Example 5-1.

Example 5-1. Defining and configuring a callback contract

```
interface ISomeCallbackContract
{
    [OperationContract]
    void OnCallback();
}

[ServiceContract(CallbackContract = typeof(ISomeCallbackContract))]
interface IMyContract
{
    [OperationContract]
    void DoSomething();
}
```

Note that the callback contract need not be marked with the ServiceContract attribute—the ServiceContract attribute is implied because it is defined as a callback contract and will be included in the service metadata. Of course, you still need to mark all the callback interface methods with the OperationContract attribute.

When the client imports the metadata of the callback contract, the imported callback interface will not have the same name on the client as in the original service-side definition. The name on the client will be the name of the service contract interface, suffixed with the word Callback. For example, a client that imports the definitions of Example 5-1 will end up with these definitions instead:

```
interface IMyContractCallback
{
    [OperationContract]
    void OnCallback();
}
```

```
[ServiceContract(CallbackContract = typeof(IMyContractCallback))]
interface IMyContract
{
   [OperationContract]
   void DoSomething( );
}
```

 For simplicity's sake, I recommend using this naming convention also on the service side (i.e., naming the callback contract with the service contract interface name suffixed by Callback).

Client Callback Setup

It is up to the client to host the callback object and expose a callback endpoint. Recall from Chapter 1 that the innermost execution scope of the service instance is the instance context. The InstanceContext class provides a constructor that takes the service instance to the host:

```
public sealed class InstanceContext : CommunicationObject,...
{
   public InstanceContext(object implementation);
   public object GetServiceInstance( );
   //More members
}
```

All the client needs to do to host a callback object is instantiate the callback object and construct a context around it:

```
class MyCallback : IMyContractCallback
{
   public void OnCallback( )
   {...}
}
IMyContractCallback callback = new MyCallback( );
InstanceContext context = new InstanceContext(callback);
```

It is also worth mentioning that although the callback methods are on the client side, they are WCF operations in every respect and therefore have an operation call context, accessible via OperationContext.Current.

Duplex proxies

Whenever a client is interacting with a service endpoint whose contract defines a callback contract, the client must use a proxy that will set up the bidirectional communication and pass the callback endpoint reference to the service. To that end, the proxy the client uses must derive from the specialized proxy class DuplexClientBase<T>, shown in Example 5-2.

Example 5-2. The DuplexClientBase<T> class

```
public interface IDuplexContextChannel : IContextChannel
{
   InstanceContext CallbackInstance
   {get;set;}
   //More members
}
public abstract class DuplexClientBase<T> : ClientBase<T> where T : class
{
   protected DuplexClientBase(InstanceContext callbackContext);
   protected DuplexClientBase(InstanceContext callbackContext,string endpointName);
   protected DuplexClientBase(InstanceContext callbackContext,Binding binding,
                             EndpointAddress remoteAddress);
   protected DuplexClientBase(object callbackInstance);
   protected DuplexClientBase(object callbackInstance,string endpointName);
   protected DuplexClientBase(object callbackInstance,Binding binding,
                             EndpointAddress remoteAddress);

   public IDuplexContextChannel InnerDuplexChannel
   {get;}
   //More members
}
```

The client needs to provide the constructor of DuplexClientBase<T> with the instance context hosting the callback object (as well as the service endpoint information, as with a regular proxy). The proxy will construct an endpoint around the callback context, while inferring the details of the callback endpoint from the service endpoint configuration: the callback endpoint contract is the one defined by the service contract callback type. The callback endpoint will use the same binding (and transport) as the outgoing call. For the address, WCF will use the client's machine name, and it will even select a port when using HTTP. Simply passing the instance context to the duplex proxy and using the proxy to call the service will expose that client-side callback endpoint. To streamline the process, DuplexClientBase<T> also offers constructors that accept the callback object directly and wrap it internally with a context. If for any reason the client needs to access that context, DuplexClientBase<T> additionally offers the InnerDuplexChannel property of the type IDuplexContextChannel, which provides access to the context via the CallbackInstance property.

When you use Visual Studio 2008 to generate a proxy class targeting a service with a callback contract, the tool will generate a class that derives from DuplexClientBase<T>, as shown in Example 5-3.

Example 5-3. VS 2008-generated duplex proxy

```
class MyContractClient : DuplexClientBase<IMyContract>,IMyContract
{
   public MyContractClient(InstanceContext callbackContext) : base(callbackContext)
   {}
```

Example 5-3. VS 2008-generated duplex proxy (continued)

```
    public MyContractClient(InstanceContext callbackContext,string endpointName) :
                                        base(callbackContext,endpointName)
    {}
    public MyContractClient(InstanceContext callbackContext,Binding binding,
                    EndpointAddress remoteAddress) :
                                        base(callbackContext,binding,remoteAddress)
    {}
    //More constructors

    public void DoSomething()
    {
        Channel.DoSomething();
    }
}
```

Using that derived proxy class, the client can construct a callback instance, host it in a context, create a proxy, and call the service, thus passing the callback endpoint reference:

```
    class MyCallback : IMyContractCallback
    {
        public void OnCallback()
        {...}
    }
    IMyContractCallback callback = new MyCallback();
    InstanceContext context = new InstanceContext(callback);

    MyContractClient proxy = new MyContractClient(context);
    proxy.DoSomething();
```

Note that as long as the client is expecting callbacks, the client cannot close the proxy. Doing so will close the callback endpoint and cause an error on the service side when the service tries to call back.

It is often the case that the client itself implements the callback contract, in which case the client will typically use a member variable for the proxy and close it when the client is disposed of, as shown in Example 5-4.

Example 5-4. Client implementing the callback contract

```
class MyClient : IMyContractCallback,IDisposable
{
    MyContractClient m_Proxy;

    public void CallService()
    {
        InstanceContext context = new InstanceContext(this);
        m_Proxy = new MyContractClient(context);
        m_Proxy.DoSomething();
    }
    public void OnCallback()
    {...}
```

Example 5-4. Client implementing the callback contract (continued)

```
   public void Dispose( )
   {
      m_Proxy.Close( );
   }
}
```

The generated proxy does not take advantage of the streamlined constructors of DuplexClientBase<T> that accept the callback object directly, but you can rework the proxy manually to add that support, as shown in Example 5-5.

Example 5-5. Using a reworked object-based proxy

```
class MyContractClient : DuplexClientBase<IMyContract>,IMyContract
{
   public MyContractClient(object callbackInstance) : base(callbackInstance)
   {}
   //More constructors
   public void DoSomething( )
   {
      Channel.DoSomething( );
   }
}
class MyClient : IMyContractCallback,IDisposable
{
   MyContractClient m_Proxy;

   public void CallService( )
   {
      m_Proxy = new MyContractClient(this);
      m_Proxy.DoSomething( );
   }
   public void OnCallback( )
   {...}
   public void Dispose( )
   {
      m_Proxy.Close( );
   }
}
```

Service-Side Callback Invocation

The client-side callback endpoint reference is passed along with every call the client makes to the service, and it is part of the incoming message. The OperationContext class provides the service with easy access to the callback reference via the generic method GetCallbackChannel<T>( ):

```
   public sealed class OperationContext : ...
   {
      public T GetCallbackChannel<T>( );
      //More members
   }
```

Exactly what the service does with the callback reference and when it decides to use it is completely at the discretion of the service. The service can extract the callback reference from the operation context and store it for later use, or it can use it during the service operation to call back to the client. Example 5-6 demonstrates the first option.

Example 5-6. Storing the callback references for later use

```
[ServiceBehavior(InstanceContextMode = InstanceContextMode.PerCall)]
class MyService : IMyContract
{
    static List<IMyContractCallback> m_Callbacks = new List<IMyContractCallback>();
    public void DoSomething()
    {
        IMyContractCallback callback = OperationContext.Current.
                                       GetCallbackChannel<IMyContractCallback>();

        if(m_Callbacks.Contains(callback) == false)
        {
            m_Callbacks.Add(callback);
        }
    }
    public static void CallClients()
    {
        Action<IMyContractCallback> invoke = (callback)=>
                                             {
                                                 callback.OnCallback();
                                             };
        m_Callbacks.ForEach(invoke);
    }
}
```

The service uses a static, generic linked list to store references to interfaces of the type IMyContractCallback. Because the service is not aware of which client is calling it and whether or not the client has called it already, in every call the service checks to see whether the list already contains the passed-in callback reference. If the list does not contain the reference, the service adds the callback to the list.

The service class also offers the static method CallClients( ), which any party on the host side can use to call back to the clients:

```
MyService.CallClients();
```

Here, the invoking party is using some host-side thread for the callback invocation. That thread is unrelated to any thread executing the incoming service call.

 Example 5-6 (and similar examples in this chapter) does not synchronize access to the callback list. Obviously, real application code will need to do that. Concurrency management (and, in particular, synchronizing access to shared resources) is discussed in Chapter 8.

Callback reentrancy

The service may also want to invoke the callback reference that's passed in (or a saved copy of it) during the execution of a contract operation. However, such invocations are disallowed by default. The reason is the default service concurrency management. By default, the service class is configured for single-threaded access: the service instance context is associated with a lock, and only one thread at a time can own the lock and access the service instance inside that context. Calling out to the client during an operation call requires blocking the service thread and invoking the callback. The problem is that processing the reply message from the client on the same channel once the callback returns requires reentering the same context and negotiating ownership of the same lock, which will result in a deadlock. Note that the service may still invoke callbacks to other clients or call other services; it is the callback to its calling client that will cause the deadlock.

To prevent such a deadlock, if the single-threaded service instance tries to call back to its client, WCF will throw an InvalidOperationException. There are three possible solutions. The first is to configure the service for multithreaded access. Callbacks to the calling client will then be allowed because the service instance will not be associated with a lock; however, this will increase the burden on the service developer, because of the need to provide synchronization for the service. The second solution is to configure the service for reentrancy. When configured for reentrancy, the service instance context is still associated with a lock, and only single-threaded access is allowed. However, if the service is calling back to its client, WCF will silently release the lock first. Chapter 8 is dedicated to the synchronization modes and their implications on the programming model. For now, all you need to know is that if your service needs to call back to its clients, you can set its concurrency behavior to either multithreaded or reentrant using the ConcurrencyMode property of the ServiceBehavior attribute:

```
public enum ConcurrencyMode
{
   Single, //Default
   Reentrant,
   Multiple
}

[AttributeUsage(AttributeTargets.Class)]
public sealed class ServiceBehaviorAttribute : ...
{
   public ConcurrencyMode ConcurrencyMode
   {get;set;}
   //More members
}
```

Example 5-7 demonstrates a service configured for reentrancy. During the operation execution, the service accesses the operation context, grabs the callback reference, and invokes it. Control will only return to the service once the callback returns, and the service's own thread will need to reacquire the lock.

Example 5-7. Configuring for reentrancy to allow callbacks

```
[ServiceContract(CallbackContract = typeof(IMyContractCallback))]
interface IMyContract
{
   [OperationContract]
   void DoSomething( );
}
interface IMyContractCallback
{
   [OperationContract]
   void OnCallback( );
}
[ServiceBehavior(ConcurrencyMode = ConcurrencyMode.Reentrant)]
class MyService : IMyContract
{
   public void DoSomething( )
   {
      IMyContractCallback callback = OperationContext.Current.
                              GetCallbackChannel<IMyContractCallback>( );
      callback.OnCallback( );
   }
}
```

The third solution that allows the service to safely call back to the client is to configure the callback contract operations as one-way operations. Doing so will enable the
service to call back even when the concurrency mode is set to single-threaded,
because there will not be any reply message to contend for the lock. Example 5-8
demonstrates this configuration. Note that the service defaults to single-threaded
concurrency mode.

Example 5-8. One-way callbacks are allowed by default

```
[ServiceContract(CallbackContract = typeof(IMyContractCallback))]
interface IMyContract
{
   [OperationContract]
   void DoSomething( );
}
interface IMyContractCallback
{
   [OperationContract(IsOneWay = true)]
   void OnCallback( );
}
class MyService : IMyContract
{
   public void DoSomething( )
   {
      IMyContractCallback callback = OperationContext.Current.
                              GetCallbackChannel<IMyContractCallback>( );
      callback.OnCallback( );
   }
}
```

Callback Connection Management

The callback mechanism supplies nothing like a higher-level protocol for managing the connection between the service and the callback endpoint. It is up to the developer to come up with some application-level protocol or a consistent pattern for managing the lifecycle of the connection. As mentioned previously, the service can only call back to the client if the client-side channel is still open, which is typically achieved by not closing the proxy. Keeping the proxy open will also prevent the callback object from being garbage-collected. If the service maintains a reference on a callback endpoint and the client-side proxy is closed or the client application itself is gone, when the service invokes the callback it will get an ObjectDisposedException from the service channel. It is therefore preferable for the client to inform the service when it no longer wishes to receive callbacks or when the client application is shutting down. To that end, you can add an explicit Disconnect() method to the service contract. Since every method call carries the callback reference with it, in the Disconnect() method the service can remove the callback reference from its internal store.

In addition, for symmetry's sake, I recommend adding an explicit Connect() method. Having a Connect() method will enable the client to connect or disconnect multiple times, as well as provide a clearly delineated point in time as to when to expect a callback (only after a call to Connect()). Example 5-9 demonstrates this technique. In both the Connect() and Disconnect() methods, the service needs to obtain the callback reference. In Connect(), the service verifies that the callback list does not already contain the callback reference before adding it to the list (this makes multiple calls to Connect() benign). In Disconnect(), the service verifies that the list contains the callback reference, and it throws an exception otherwise.

Example 5-9. Explicit callback connection management

```
[ServiceContract(CallbackContract = typeof(IMyContractCallback))]
interface IMyContract
{
   [OperationContract]
   void DoSomething();

   [OperationContract]
   void Connect();

   [OperationContract]
   void Disconnect();
}
interface IMyContractCallback
{
   [OperationContract]
   void OnCallback();
}
```

Example 5-9. Explicit callback connection management (continued)

```
[ServiceBehavior(InstanceContextMode = InstanceContextMode.PerCall)]
class MyService : IMyContract
{
   static List<IMyContractCallback> m_Callbacks = new List<IMyContractCallback>();

   public void Connect()
   {
      IMyContractCallback callback = OperationContext.Current.
                                  GetCallbackChannel<IMyContractCallback>();
      if(m_Callbacks.Contains(callback) == false)
      {
         m_Callbacks.Add(callback);
      }
   }
   public void Disconnect()
   {
      IMyContractCallback callback = OperationContext.Current.
                                  GetCallbackChannel<IMyContractCallback>();
      if(m_Callbacks.Contains(callback) == true)
      {
         m_Callbacks.Remove(callback);
      }
      else
      {
         throw new InvalidOperationException("Cannot find callback");
      }
   }
   public static void CallClients()
   {
      Action<IMyContractCallback> invoke = (callback)=>
                                       {
                                          callback.OnCallback();
                                       };
      m_Callbacks.ForEach(invoke);
   }
   public void DoSomething()
   {...}
}
```

Connection management and instance mode

A per-call service can use a callback reference during the operation call itself, or store it in some kind of a global repository such as a static variable, as you have seen in the examples so far. The per-call service must use some static variable to store the reference, since any instance state the service may use to store the reference will be gone when the operation returns. Using a Disconnect()-like method is therefore especially required for per-call services, as without it, the shared store will become bloated over time with dead callback references. A similar need exists with a singleton service. The singleton lifetime has no end, so it will accumulate an unlimited number of callback references, and as time goes by most of them will become stale because the callback clients will no longer be running. Having a Disconnect() method will keep the singleton connected only to the relevant alive clients.

Interestingly enough, a per-session service may get by without a Disconnect() method, as long as it maintains the callback reference in some instance member variable. The reason is that the service instance will automatically be disposed of when the session ends (when the client closes the proxy or times out), and there is no danger in keeping the reference throughout the session, as it is guaranteed to always be valid. However, if the sessionful service stores its callback reference in some global repository for the use of other host-side parties or across sessions, adding a Disconnect() method is required in order to remove the callback reference explicitly, because the callback reference is not available during the call to Dispose().

You may also want to add the Connect() and Disconnect() pair on a sessionful service simply as a feature, because it enables the client to decide when to start or stop receiving callbacks during the session.

The Duplex Proxy and Type Safety

The WCF-provided DuplexClientBase<T> is not strongly typed to the callback interface used. The compiler will let you pass in any object, including an invalid callback interface. The compiler will even let you use for T a service contract type that has no callback contract defined at all. At runtime, you can successfully instantiate the proxy. The incompatibility will be discovered only when you try to use the proxy, yielding an InvalidOperationException. Much the same way, InstanceContext is object-based and is not verified at compile time to actually have a valid callback contract instance. When it's passed as a constructor parameter to the duplex proxy, there is no compile-time check to correlate the InstanceContext with the callback instance the duplex proxy expects, and the error will be discovered only when you try to use the proxy. You can use generics to compensate to some degree for these oversights and discover the error at runtime, as soon as you declare the proxy.

First, define the type-safe, generic InstanceContext<T> class, shown in Example 5-10.

Example 5-10. The InstanceContext<T> class

```
public class InstanceContext<T>
{
   public InstanceContext Context
   {get;private set;}

   public InstanceContext(T callbackInstance)
   {
      Context = new InstanceContext(callbackInstance);
   }
   public void ReleaseServiceInstance()
   {
      Context.ReleaseServiceInstance();
   }
}
```

Example 5-10. The InstanceContext<T> class (continued)

```
   public T ServiceInstance
   {
      get
      {
         return (T)Context.GetServiceInstance();
      }
   }
}
```

By using generics, you also provide type-safe access to the hosted callback object and capture the desired callback type.

Next, define a new type-safe, generic subclass of `DuplexClientBase<T>`, as shown in Example 5-11.

Example 5-11. The DuplexClientBase<T,C>class

```
//T is the service contract and C is the callback contract
public abstract class DuplexClientBase<T,C> : DuplexClientBase<T> where T : class
{
   protected DuplexClientBase(InstanceContext<C> context) : base(context.Context)
   {}
   protected DuplexClientBase(InstanceContext<C> context,string endpointName) :
                                          base(context.Context,endpointName)
   {}
   protected DuplexClientBase(InstanceContext<C> context,Binding binding,
                        EndpointAddress remoteAddress) :
                                    base(context.Context,binding,remoteAddress)
   {}
   protected DuplexClientBase(C callback) : base(callback)
   {}
   protected DuplexClientBase(C callback,string endpointName) :
                                             base(callback,endpointName)
   {}
   protected DuplexClientBase(C callback,Binding binding,
                        EndpointAddress remoteAddress) :
                                       base(callback,binding,remoteAddress)
   {}

   /* More constructors */

   static DuplexClientBase()
   {
      VerifyCallback();
   }
   internal static void VerifyCallback()
   {
      Type contractType = typeof(T);
      Type callbackType = typeof(C);

      object[] attributes = contractType.GetCustomAttributes(
                                    typeof(ServiceContractAttribute),false);
```

Example 5-11. The DuplexClientBase<T,C>class (continued)

```
     if(attributes.Length != 1)
     {
         throw new InvalidOperationException("Type of " + contractType +
                                         " is not a service contract");
     }
     ServiceContractAttribute serviceContractAttribute;
     serviceContractAttribute = attributes[0] as ServiceContractAttribute;
     if(callbackType != serviceContractAttribute.CallbackContract)
     {
         throw new InvalidOperationException("Type of " + callbackType +
                 " is not configured as callback contract for " + contractType);
     }
   }
}
```

The DuplexClientBase<T,C> class uses two type parameters: T is used for the service contract type parameter and C is used for the callback contract type parameter. The constructors of DuplexClientBase<T,C> can accept either a raw C instance or an instance of InstanceContext<C> wrapping a C instance. These enable the compiler to ensure that only compatible contexts are used. However, C# 3.0 does not support a way to constrain a declarative relationship between T and C. The workaround is to perform a single runtime check before any use of DuplexClientBase<T,C>, and abort the use of the wrong type immediately, before any damage can be done. The trick is to place the runtime verification in the C# static constructor. The static constructor of DuplexClientBase<T,C> calls the static helper method VerifyCallback( ). VerifyCallback( ) uses reflection to first verify that T is decorated with the ServiceContract attribute. Then it verifies that it has a type set for the callback contract that is the type parameter C. If not, an exception will be thrown in the static constructor, enabling you to discover the error as soon as possible at runtime.

Performing the callback contract verification in the static constructor is a technique applicable to any constraint that you cannot enforce at compile time, yet you have some programmatic way of determining and enforcing it at runtime.

Next, you need to rework the tool-generated proxy class on the client side to derive from the type-safe DuplexClientBase<T,C> class:

```
class MyContractClient : DuplexClientBase<IMyContract,IMyContractCallback>,
                                                            IMyContract
{
    public MyContractClient(InstanceContext<IMyContractCallback> context) :
                                                            base(context)
    {}
    public MyContractClient(IMyContractCallback callback) : base(callback)
    {}

    /* Rest of the constructors */
```

```
    public void DoSomething( )
    {
        Channel.DoSomething( );
    }
}
```

You can provide the reworked proxy either with a type-safe instance context, or with the callback instance directly:

```
//Client code
class MyCallback : IMyContractCallback
{...}

IMyContractCallback callback = new MyCallback( );
MyContractClient proxy1 = new MyContractClient(callback);

InstanceContext<IMyContractCallback> context =
                            new InstanceContext<IMyContractCallback>(callback);
MyContractClient proxy2 = new MyContractClient(context);
```

Either way, the compiler will verify that the type parameters provided to the proxy match the context type parameter or the callback instance, and the static constructor will verify the relationship between the service contract and the callback instance upon instantiation.

The Duplex Factory

Similar to the ChannelFactory<T> class, WCF also offers DuplexChannelFactory<T>, which can be used for setting up duplex proxies programmatically:

```
public class DuplexChannelFactory<T> : ChannelFactory<T>
{
    public DuplexChannelFactory(object callback);
    public DuplexChannelFactory(object callback,string endpointName);
    public DuplexChannelFactory(InstanceContext context,string endpointName);

    public T CreateChannel(InstanceContext context);
    public static T CreateChannel(object callback,string endpointName);
    public static T CreateChannel(InstanceContext context,string endpointName);
    public static T CreateChannel(object callback,Binding binding,
                              EndpointAddress endpointAddress);
    public static T CreateChannel(InstanceContext context,Binding binding,
                              EndpointAddress endpointAddress);

    //More members
}
```

DuplexChannelFactory<T> is used just like its base class, ChannelFactory<T>, except its constructors expect either a callback instance or a callback context. Note again the use of object for the callback instance and the lack of type safety. Example 5-12 shows the reworked DuplexChannelFactory<T,C> class, which provides both compile-time and runtime type safety (similar to the fixed-up DuplexClientBase<T> class presented in Example 5-11).

Example 5-12. The DuplexChannelFactory<T,C> class

```
public class DuplexChannelFactory<T,C> : DuplexChannelFactory<T> where T : class
{
   static DuplexChannelFactory( )
   {
      DuplexClientBase<T,C>.VerifyCallback( );
   }

   public static T CreateChannel(C callback,string endpointName)
   {
      return DuplexChannelFactory<T>.CreateChannel(callback,endpointName);
   }
   public static T CreateChannel(InstanceContext<C> context,string endpointName)
   {
      return DuplexChannelFactory<T>.CreateChannel(context.Context,endpointName);
   }
   public static T CreateChannel(C callback,Binding binding,
                                 EndpointAddress endpointAddress)
   {
      return DuplexChannelFactory<T>.CreateChannel(callback,binding,
                                                   endpointAddress);
   }
   public static T CreateChannel(InstanceContext<C> context,Binding binding,
                                 EndpointAddress endpointAddress)
   {
      return DuplexChannelFactory<T>.CreateChannel(context,binding,
                                                   endpointAddress);
   }
   public DuplexChannelFactory(C callback) : base(callback)
   {}
   public DuplexChannelFactory(C callback,string endpointName) :
                                                 base(callback,endpointName)
   {}
   public DuplexChannelFactory(InstanceContext<C> context,string endpointName) :
                                       base(context.Context,endpointName)
   {}
   //More constructors
}
```

As an example of utilizing the duplex channel factory, consider Example 5-13, which adds callback ability to the InProcFactory static helper class presented in Chapter 1.

Example 5-13. Adding duplex support to InProcFactory

```
public static class InProcFactory
{
   public static I CreateInstance<S,I,C>(C callback) where I : class
                                                     where S : class,I
   {
      InstanceContext<C> context = new InstanceContext<C>(callback);
      return CreateInstance<S,I,C>(context);
   }
```

Example 5-13. Adding duplex support to InProcFactory (continued)

```
    public static I CreateInstance<S,I,C>(InstanceContext<C> context)
                                                    where I : class
                                                    where S : class,I
    {
        HostRecord hostRecord = GetHostRecord<S,I>();
        return DuplexChannelFactory<I,C>.CreateChannel(context,Binding,
                                            hostRecord.Address);
    }
    //More members
}
//Sample client
IMyContractCallback callback = new MyCallback();

IMyContract proxy = InProcFactory.CreateInstance<MyService,IMyContract,
                                        IMyContractCallback>(callback);
proxy.DoSomething();
InProcFactory.CloseProxy(proxy);
```

Callback Contract Hierarchy

An interesting constraint on the design of callback contracts is that a service contract can designate a callback contract only if that contract is a subinterface of all callback contracts defined by the contract's own base contracts. For example, here is an invalid callback contract definition:

```
    interface ICallbackContract1
    {...}

    interface ICallbackContract2
    {...}

    [ServiceContract(CallbackContract = typeof(ICallbackContract1))]
    interface IMyBaseContract
    {...}

    //Invalid
    [ServiceContract(CallbackContract = typeof(ICallbackContract2))]
    interface IMySubContract : IMyBaseContract
    {...}
```

IMySubContract cannot designate ICallbackContract2 as a callback contract because ICallbackContract2 is not a subinterface of ICallbackContract1, which IMyBaseContract (the base of IMySubContract) defines as its own callback contract.

The reason for this constraint is obvious: if a client passes an endpoint reference to a service implementation of IMySubContract, that callback reference must satisfy the callback type expected by IMyBaseContract. WCF verifies the callback contract hierarchy at service load time and throws an InvalidOperationException in the case of a violation.

The straightforward way to satisfy the constraint is to reflect the service contract hierarchy in the callback contract hierarchy:

```
interface ICallbackContract1
{...}

interface ICallbackContract2 : ICallbackContract1
{...}

[ServiceContract(CallbackContract = typeof(ICallbackContract1))]
interface IMyBaseContract
{...}

[ServiceContract(CallbackContract = typeof(ICallbackContract2))]
interface IMySubContract : IMyBaseContract
{...}
```

However, you can also use multiple interface inheritance by a single callback contract and avoid mimicking the service contract hierarchy:

```
interface ICallbackContract1
{...}
interface ICallbackContract2
{...}
interface ICallbackContract3 : ICallbackContract2,ICallbackContract1
{...}

[ServiceContract(CallbackContract = typeof(ICallbackContract1))]
interface IMyBaseContract1
{...}
[ServiceContract(CallbackContract = typeof(ICallbackContract2))]
interface IMyBaseContract2
{...}
[ServiceContract(CallbackContract = typeof(ICallbackContract3))]
interface IMySubContract : IMyBaseContract1,IMyBaseContract2
{...}
```

Note, also, that a service can implement its own callback contract:

```
[ServiceContract(CallbackContract = typeof(IMyContractCallback))]
interface IMyContract
{...}
[ServiceContract]
interface IMyContractCallback
{...}
class MyService : IMyContract,IMyContractCallback
{...}
```

The service can even store a reference to itself in some callback store (if it wishes to be called back as if it were a client).

Callbacks, Ports, and Channels

When you use either the TCP or the IPC binding, the callbacks enter the client on the outgoing channel the binding maintains to the service. There is no need to open a new port or a pipe for the callbacks. When you use the WSDualHttpBinding, WCF maintains a separate, dedicated HTTP channel for the callbacks, because HTTP itself is a unidirectional protocol. WCF selects port 80 by default for that callback channel, and it passes the service a callback address that uses HTTP, the client machine name, and port 80.

While using port 80 makes sense for Internet-based services, it is of little value to intranet-based services. In addition, if the client machine happens to also have IIS 5 or 6 running, port 80 will already be reserved, and the client will not be able to host the callback endpoint. (IIS7, by default, will allow sharing the port.) While the likelihood of an intranet application being forced to use the WSDualHttpBinding is somewhat low, it is quite common for developers who develop Internet-based applications to have IIS installed on their machines and have the callback port therefore conflict with IIS during testing and debugging.

Assigning a callback address

Fortunately, the WSDualHttpBinding offers the ClientBaseAddress property, which you can use to configure a different callback address on the client:

```
public class WSDualHttpBinding : Binding,...
{
    public Uri ClientBaseAddress
    {get;set;}
    //More members
}
```

For example, here is how to configure a base address in the client's config file:

```
<system.serviceModel>
   <client>
      <endpoint
         address = "http://localhost:8008/MyService"
         binding = "wsDualHttpBinding"
         bindingConfiguration = "ClientCallback"
         contract = "IMyContract"
      />
   </client>
   <bindings>
      <wsDualHttpBinding>
         <binding name = "ClientCallback"
            clientBaseAddress = "http://localhost:8009/"
         />
      </wsDualHttpBinding>
   </bindings>
</system.serviceModel>
```

The problem with using a config file to set the callback base address is that it precludes running multiple instances of the client on the same machine, which is something you are likely to do in any decent testing scenario. However, since the callback port need not be known to the service in advance, in actuality any available port will do. It is therefore better to set the client base address programmatically to any available port. You can automate this using the extension method SetClientBaseAddress( ) of my WsDualProxyHelper static helper class, shown in Example 5-14.

Example 5-14. The WsDualProxyHelper class

```
public static class WsDualProxyHelper
{
   public static void SetClientBaseAddress<T>(this DuplexClientBase<T> proxy,
                                              int port) where T : class
   {
      WSDualHttpBinding binding = proxy.Endpoint.Binding as WSDualHttpBinding;
      Debug.Assert(binding != null);
      binding.ClientBaseAddress = new Uri("http://localhost:"+ port + "/");
   }
   public static void SetClientBaseAddress<T>(this DuplexClientBase<T> proxy)
                                                          where T : class
   {
      lock(typeof(WsDualProxyHelper))
      {
         int portNumber = FindPort( );
         SetClientBaseAddress(proxy,portNumber);
         proxy.Open( );
      }
   }
   internal static int FindPort( )
   {
      IPEndPoint endPoint = new IPEndPoint(IPAddress.Any,0);
      using(Socket socket = new Socket(AddressFamily.InterNetwork,
                                       SocketType.Stream,
                                       ProtocolType.Tcp))
      {
         socket.Bind(endPoint);
         IPEndPoint local = (IPEndPoint)socket.LocalEndPoint;
         return local.Port;
      }
   }
}
```

WsDualProxyHelper offers two overloaded versions of the SetClientBaseAddress( ) extension method to the DuplexClientBase<T> class. The first simply takes a proxy instance and a port number: it verifies that the proxy is using the WSDualHttpBinding, and then it sets the client base address using the provided port. The second version of SetClientBaseAddress( ) automatically selects an available port and calls the first with the available port. To avoid a race condition with other concurrent invocations of SetClientBaseAddress( ) in the same app domain, it locks on the type itself during the sequence of looking up the available port and setting the base address, and then it opens the proxy to lock in the port. Note that a race condition is still possible with other processes or app domains on the same machine.

Using WsDualProxyHelper is straightforward:

```
//Sample client code:
class MyClient : IMyContractCallback
{...}

IMyContractCallback callback = new MyClient();
InstanceContext context = new InstanceContext(callback);

MyContractClient proxy = new MyContractClient(context);
proxy.SetClientBaseAddress();
```

Assigning the callback address declaratively

You can even automate the process further and assign the callback port declaratively, using a custom attribute. My CallbackBaseAddressBehaviorAttribute is a contract behavior attribute that affects only callback endpoints that use the WSDualHttpBinding. The CallbackBaseAddressBehavior attribute offers a single integer property called CallbackPort:

```
[AttributeUsage(AttributeTargets.Class)]
public class CallbackBaseAddressBehaviorAttribute : Attribute,IEndpointBehavior
{
    public int CallbackPort
    {get;set;}
}
```

CallbackPort defaults to 80. If you leave it unset, applying the CallbackBaseAddressBehavior attribute will result in the default behavior for the WSDualHttpBinding, so these two definitions are equivalent:

```
class MyClient : IMyContractCallback
{...}

[CallbackBaseAddressBehavior]
class MyClient : IMyContractCallback
{...}
```

You can explicitly specify a callback port as follows:

```
[CallbackBaseAddressBehavior(CallbackPort = 8009)]
class MyClient : IMyContractCallback
{...}
```

However, if you set CallbackPort to 0, the CallbackBaseAddressBehavior attribute will automatically select any available port for the callback:

```
[CallbackBaseAddressBehavior(CallbackPort = 0)]
class MyClient : IMyContractCallback
{...}
```

Example 5-15 lists the code implementing the CallbackBaseAddressBehavior attribute.

Example 5-15. The CallbackBaseAddressBehavior attribute

```
[AttributeUsage(AttributeTargets.Class)]
public class CallbackBaseAddressBehaviorAttribute : Attribute,IEndpointBehavior
{
   int m_CallbackPort = 80;

   public int CallbackPort //Accesses m_CallbackPort
   {get;set;}
   void IEndpointBehavior.AddBindingParameters(ServiceEndpoint endpoint,
                                    BindingParameterCollection bindingParameters)
   {
      if(CallbackPort == 80)
      {
         return;
      }
      lock(typeof(WsDualProxyHelper))
      {
         if(CallbackPort == 0)
         {
            CallbackPort = WsDualProxyHelper.FindPort();
         }
         WSDualHttpBinding binding = endpoint.Binding as WSDualHttpBinding;
         if(binding != null)
         {
            binding.ClientBaseAddress = new Uri(
                                 "http://localhost:" + CallbackPort + "/");
         }
      }
   }
   //Do-nothing methods of IEndpointBehavior
}
```

The `CallbackBaseAddressBehavior` attribute is an endpoint behavior attribute that allows you to intercept (either on the client or the service side) the configuration of the endpoint. The attribute supports the `IEndpointBehavior` interface:

```
public interface IEndpointBehavior
{
   void AddBindingParameters(ServiceEndpoint endpoint,
                           BindingParameterCollection bindingParameters);
   //More members
}
```

WCF calls the `AddBindingParameters()` method on the client side just before using the proxy to the service for the first time, allowing the attribute to configure the binding used for the callback. `AddBindingParameters()` checks the value of `CallbackPort`. If it is 80, it does nothing. If it is 0, `AddBindingParameters()` finds an available port and assigns it to `CallbackPort`. Then, `AddBindingParameters()` looks up the binding used to call the service. If the call is `WSDualHttpBinding`, `AddBindingParameters()` sets the client base address using the callback port.

With the `CallbackBaseAddressBehavior` attribute, a race condition is possible with another callback object grabbing the same port, even in the same app domain.

Events

The basic WCF callback mechanism does not indicate anything about the nature of the interaction between the client and the service. They may be equal peers in a commutative interaction, each calling and receiving calls from the other. However, the canonical use for duplex callbacks is with *events*. Events allow the client or clients to be notified about something that has occurred on the service side. An event may result from a direct client call, or it may be the result of something the service monitors. The service firing the event is called the *publisher*, and the client receiving the event is called the *subscriber*. Events are a required feature in almost any type of application, as shown in Figure 5-2.

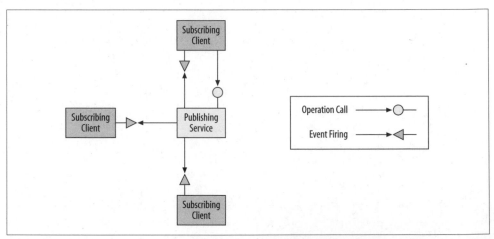

Figure 5-2. A publishing service can fire events at multiple subscribing clients

While events in WCF are nothing more than callback operations, by their very nature events usually imply a looser relationship between the publisher and the subscriber than the typical relationship between a client and a service. When dealing with events, the service typically publishes the same event to multiple subscribing clients. The publisher often does not care about the order of invocation of the subscribers, or any errors the subscribers might have while processing the events. All the publisher knows is that it should deliver the event to the subscribers. If they have a problem with the event, there is nothing the service can do about it anyway. In addition, the service does not care about returned results from the subscribers.

Consequently, event-handling operations should have a void return type, should not have any outgoing parameters, and should be marked as one-way. I also recommend factoring the events to a separate callback contract, and not mixing events with regular callbacks in the same contract:

```
interface IMyEvents
{
    [OperationContract(IsOneWay = true)]
    void OnEvent1( );

    [OperationContract(IsOneWay = true)]
    void OnEvent2(int number);

    [OperationContract(IsOneWay = true)]
    void OnEvent3(int number,string text);
}
```

On the subscriber side, even when using one-way callback operations, the implementation of the event-handling methods should be of short duration. There are two reasons for this. First, if there is a large volume of events to publish, the publisher may get blocked if a subscriber has maxed out its ability to queue up callbacks because it is still processing the previous events. Blocking the publisher may prevent the event from reaching other subscribers in a timely manner. Second, if there are a large number of subscribers to the event, the accumulated processing time of each subscriber could exceed the publisher's timeout.

The publisher may add dedicated operations to its contract, allowing clients to explicitly subscribe to or unsubscribe from the events. If the publisher supports multiple event types, it may want to allow the subscribers to choose exactly which event(s) they want to subscribe to or unsubscribe from.

How the service internally goes about managing the list of subscribers and their preferences is a completely service-side implementation detail that should not affect the clients. The publisher can even use .NET delegates to manage the list of subscribers and the publishing act itself. Example 5-16 demonstrates this technique, as well as the other design considerations discussed so far.

Example 5-16. Events management using delegates

```
enum EventType
{
    Event1 = 1,
    Event2 = 2,
    Event3 = 4,
    AllEvents = Event1|Event2|Event3
}
```

Example 5-16. Events management using delegates (continued)

```csharp
[ServiceContract(CallbackContract = typeof(IMyEvents))]
interface IMyContract
{
   [OperationContract]
   void DoSomething( );

   [OperationContract]
   void Subscribe(EventType mask);

   [OperationContract]
   void Unsubscribe(EventType mask);
}
[ServiceBehavior(InstanceContextMode = InstanceContextMode.PerCall)]
class MyPublisher : IMyContract
{
   static Action m_Event1           = delegate{};
   static Action <int> m_Event2     = delegate{};
   static Action <int,string> m_Event3 = delegate{};

   public void Subscribe(EventType mask)
   {
      IMyEvents subscriber =  OperationContext.Current.
                                        GetCallbackChannel<IMyEvents>( );

      if((mask & EventType.Event1) == EventType.Event1)
      {
         m_Event1 += subscriber.OnEvent1;
      }
      if((mask & EventType.Event2) == EventType.Event2)
      {
         m_Event2 += subscriber.OnEvent2;
      }
      if((mask & EventType.Event3) == EventType.Event3)
      {
         m_Event3 += subscriber.OnEvent3;
      }
   }
   public void Unsubscribe(EventType mask)
   {
      //Similar to Subscribe( ) but uses -=
   }
   public static void FireEvent(EventType eventType)
   {
      switch(eventType)
      {
         case EventType.Event1:
         {
            m_Event1( );
            return;
         }
```

Example 5-16. Events management using delegates (continued)

```
            case EventType.Event2:
            {
                m_Event2(42);
                return;
            }
            case EventType.Event3:
            {
                m_Event3(42,"Hello");
                return;
            }
            default:
            {
                throw new InvalidOperationException("Unknown event type");
            }
        }
    }
    public void DoSomething()
    {...}
}
```

The service contract IMyContract defines the Subscribe( ) and Unsubscribe( ) methods. These methods each take an enum of the type EventType, whose individual fields are set to integer powers of 2. This enables the subscribing client to combine the values into a mask indicating the types of events it wants to subscribe to or unsubscribe from. For example, to subscribe to Event1 and Event3 but not Event2, the subscriber would call Subscribe( ) like this:

```
class MySubscriber : IMyEvents
{
    void OnEvent1( )
    {...}
    void OnEvent2(int number)
    {...}
    void OnEvent2(int number,string text)
    {...}
}
IMyEvents subscriber = new MySubscriber( );
InstanceContext context = new InstanceContext(subscriber);
MyContractClient proxy = new MyContractClient(context);
proxy.Subscribe(EventType.Event1|EventType.Event3);
```

Internally, MyPublisher maintains three static delegates, each corresponding to an event type.

Both the Subscribe( ) and Unsubscribe( ) methods check the supplied EventType value and either add the subscriber's callback to or remove it from the corresponding delegate. To fire an event, MyPublisher offers the static FireEvent( ) method. FireEvent( ) accepts the event to fire and invokes the corresponding delegate.

Again, the fact that the MyPublisher service uses delegates is purely an implementation detail simplifying event lookup. The service could have used a linked list, although that would require more complex code.

Appendix C presents a framework for supporting a better design approach for events, called the publish-subscribe pattern.

Streaming

By default, when the client and the service exchange messages, these messages are buffered on the receiving end and delivered only once the entire message has been received. This is true whether it is the client sending a message to the service or the service returning a message to the client. As a result, when the client calls the service, the service is invoked only after the client's message has been received in its entirety; likewise, the client is unblocked only once the returned message with the results of the invocation has been received in its entirety.

For sufficiently small messages, this exchange pattern provides for a simple programming model because the latency caused by receiving the message is usually negligible compared with the message processing itself. However, when it comes to much larger messages—such as ones involving multimedia content, large files, or batches of data—blocking until the entire message has been received may be impractical. To handle such cases, WCF enables the receiving side (be it the client or the service) to start processing the data in the message while the message is still being received by the channel. This type of processing is known as *streaming transfer mode*. With large payloads, streaming provides improved throughput and responsiveness because neither the receiving nor the sending side is blocked while the message is being sent or received.

I/O Streams

For message streaming, WCF requires the use of the .NET `Stream` class. In fact, the contract operations used for streaming look just like conventional I/O methods. The `Stream` class is the base class of all the I/O streams in .NET (such as the `FileStream`, `NetworkStream`, and `MemoryStream` classes), allowing you to stream content from any of these I/O sources. All you need to do is return or receive a `Stream` as an operation parameter, as shown in Example 5-17.

Example 5-17. Streaming operations

```
[ServiceContract]
interface IMyContract
{
   [OperationContract]
   Stream StreamReply1();

   [OperationContract]
   void StreamReply2(out Stream stream);

   [OperationContract]
   void StreamRequest(Stream stream);
```

Example 5-17. Streaming operations (continued)

```
   [OperationContract(IsOneWay = true)]
   void OneWayStream(Stream stream);
}
```

Note that you can only define as an operation parameter the abstract class Stream or a specific serializable subclass such as MemoryStream. Subclasses such as FileStream are not serializable; you will have to use the base Stream instead.

WCF lets services stream the reply, the request, or both the request and the reply.

Streaming and Binding

Only the TCP, IPC, and basic HTTP bindings support streaming. With all of these bindings streaming is disabled by default, and the binding will buffer the message in its entirety even when a Stream is used. You have to enable streaming by setting the TransferMode property according to the desired streaming mode. For example, when using the BasicHttpBinding:

```
   public enum TransferMode
   {
       Buffered, //Default
       Streamed,
       StreamedRequest,
       StreamedResponse
   }
   public class BasicHttpBinding : Binding,...
   {
       public TransferMode TransferMode
       {get;set;}
       //More members
   }
```

TransferMode.Streamed supports all streaming modes, and this is the only transfer mode that can support all the operations in Example 5-17. However, if the contract contains only a specific type of streaming, such as streamed reply:

```
   [ServiceContract]
   interface IMyContract
   {
       //Stream reply
       [OperationContract]
       Stream GetStream1();

       [OperationContract]
       int MyMethod();
   }
```

you can have a buffered request and streamed reply by selecting TransferMode. StreamedResponse.

You will need to configure the binding on the client or service side (or both) per the required stream mode:

```
<configuration>
    <system.serviceModel>
        <client>
            <endpoint
                binding = "basicHttpBinding"
                bindingConfiguration = "StreamedHTTP"
                ...
            />
        </client>
        <bindings>
            <basicHttpBinding>
                <binding name = "StreamedHTTP"
                    transferMode = "Streamed"
                />
            </basicHttpBinding>
        </bindings>
    </system.serviceModel>
</configuration>
```

Streaming and Transport

It is important to realize that WCF streaming is merely a programming model nicety. The underlying transport itself is not streamed, and the default maximum message size is set to 64K. This may be a problem with the sort of data you are likely to use streaming with, because streamed messages tend to be very large (hence the motivation for streaming in the first place). If the default limit proves insufficient, you can increase the maximum message size on the receiving side by setting the MaxReceivedMessageSize property to the expected maximum message size:

```
public class BasicHttpBinding : Binding,...
{
    public long MaxReceivedMessageSize
    {get;set;}
    //More memebrs
}
```

You can even use trial-and-error at runtime to find out what the streamed message size is and set the binding accordingly.

Typically, though, you would place that piece of configuration in the config file and avoid doing it programmatically, as message size tends to be deployment-specific:

```
<bindings>
    <basicHttpBinding>
        <binding name = "StreamedHTTP"
            transferMode = "Streamed"
            maxReceivedMessageSize = "120000"
        />
    </basicHttpBinding>
</bindings>
```

Stream Management

When a client passes a request stream to a service, the service may read from the stream long after the client is gone. The client has no way of knowing when the service is done using the stream, and consequently should not close the stream itself. WCF will automatically close the client-side stream once the service is done using it.

A similar problem exists when a client interacts with a response stream: the stream is produced on the service side, but the service should not close it because it has no way of knowing when the client is done using the stream. In this case, WCF can't help, because it has no idea what the client is doing with the stream. The client is therefore always responsible for closing reply streams.

When you use streaming, you cannot use message-level transfer security. This is the main reason why only the TCP, IPC, and basic bindings (and their subclasses) support streaming: with these bindings, you typically do not (and, in the case of IPC, cannot) use message security. When streaming with the TCP binding, you also cannot enable reliable messaging.

You'll see more on security in Chapter 10.

Using streamed messages has a few additional implications. First, you need to synchronize access to the streamed content; for example, by opening the file stream in a read-only mode to allow other parties to access the file, or opening the stream in an exclusive mode to prevent others from accessing it if so required. In addition, you cannot use streaming when the contract is configured with SessionMode.Required.

CHAPTER 6
Faults

Any service operation can, at any moment, encounter an unexpected error. The question is how (if at all) that error should be reported back to the client. Concepts such as exceptions and exception handling are technology-specific and should not transcend the service boundary. In addition, attempts by clients to handle errors invariably lead to increased coupling. Typically, error handling is a local implementation detail that should not affect the client, partly because the client may not care about the details of the errors (other than the fact that something went wrong), but mostly because in a well-designed application, the service is encapsulated so that the client does not have to do anything meaningful about the error anyway. A well-designed service should be as autonomous as possible, and should not depend on its clients to handle and recover errors. Anything beyond a blank error notification should in fact be part of the contractual interaction between the client and the service. This chapter describes just how the service and the client should handle these declared faults, and how you can extend and improve on the basic mechanism.

Error Isolation and Decoupling

In traditional .NET programming, any unhandled exception (except `ThreadAbortException`) immediately terminated the process in which it occurred. While this is a very conservative behavior, it does not provide for proper fault isolation, which would enable the client to keep functioning even after the object blew up. Much the same way, after any unhandled error on the client side, the object would go down with the ship. Developers that did not like this had to provide for process isolation between the client and the object, which greatly complicated the programming model. That is not the WCF behavior, however. If a service call on behalf of one client causes an exception, it must not be allowed to take down the hosting process. Other clients accessing the service, or other services hosted by the same process, should not be affected. As a result, when an unhandled exception leaves the service scope, the dispatcher silently catches and handles it by serializing it in the returned message to the client. When the returned message reaches the proxy, the proxy throws an exception on the client side. This behavior provides every WCF service with process-level isolation. The client and service can share a process, and yet be completely isolated as far as errors. The only exceptions that will take down the host process are critical errors that blow up .NET itself, such as stack overflows. Fault isolation, however, is only one of three key error-decoupling features of WCF. The second is error masking, and the third is faulting the channel.

Error Masking

The client can actually encounter three types of errors when trying to invoke a service. The first type of error is a communication error, which may occur because of network unavailability, an incorrect address, the host process not running, and so on. Communication exceptions are manifested on the client side by a CommunicationException or a CommunicationException-derived class such as EndpointNotFoundException.

The second type of error the client might encounter is related to the state of the proxy and the channels. There are many such possible exceptions. For example, these errors may occur when the client is trying to access an already closed proxy, resulting in an ObjectDisposedException; when there is a mismatch between the contract and the binding security protection level resulting in an InvalidOperationException; when the client's credentials are denied by the service resulting in a SecurityNegotiationException in case of authentication failure, or SecurityAccessDeniedException in case of authorization failure; or when the transport session times out, resulting in a TimeoutException.

The third type of error is an error that originates in the execution of the service call itself, as a result of either the service throwing an exception, or the service calling another object or resource and having that internal call throw an exception.

As stated at the beginning of this chapter, it is a common illusion that clients care about errors or have anything meaningful to do when they occur. Any attempt to bake such capabilities into the client creates an inordinate degree of coupling between the client and the object, raising serious design questions. How could the client possibly know more about the error than the service, unless it is tightly coupled to it? What if the error originated several layers below the service—should the client be coupled to those low-level layers? Should the client try the call again? How often and how frequently? Should the client inform the user of the error? Is there a user?

All that the client cares about is that something went wrong. The best practice for most clients is to simply let the exception go up the call chain. The topmost client typically will catch the exception, not in order to handle it, but simply to prevent the application from shutting down abruptly. A well-designed client should never care about the actual error; WCF enforces this. In the interest of encapsulation and decoupling, by default all exceptions thrown on the service side always reach the client as FaultExceptions:

```
public class FaultException : CommunicationException
{...}
```

By having all service exceptions be indistinguishable from each other, WCF decouples the client from the service. The less the client knows about what happened on the service side, the more decoupled the interaction will be.

Channel Faulting

In traditional .NET programming, the client can catch the exception and keep calling the object. Consider this definition of a class and an interface:

```
interface IMyContract
{
    void MyMethod();
}
class MyClass : IMyContract
{...}
```

If the client snuffs out the exception thrown by the object, it can call it again:

```
IMyContract obj = new MyClass();
try
{
    obj.MyMethod();
}
catch
{}
obj.MyMethod();
```

This is a fundamental flaw of .NET as a platform. Exceptions, by their very nature, are for exceptional cases. Here, something totally unexpected and horrible has happened. How could the client possibly pretend otherwise? The object is hopelessly broken, and yet the client keeps using it. In classic .NET, developers that did not approve of this behavior had to maintain a flag in each object, set the flag before throwing an exception (or after catching any downstream exceptions), and check the flag inside any public method, refusing to use the object if it was called after an exception had been thrown. This, of course, is cumbersome and tedious. WCF automates this best practice. If the service has a transport session, any unhandled exceptions (save those derived from FaultException, as described next) fault the channel (the proxy's state is changed to CommunicationState.Faulted), thus preventing the client from using the proxy, and the object behind it, after an exception. In other words, for this service and proxy definition:

```
[ServiceContract]
interface IMyContract
{
    [OperationContract]
    void MyMethod();
}
class MyClass : IMyContract
{...}

class MyContractClient : ClientBase<IMyContract>,IMyContract
{...}
```

the following client code results in a CommunicationObjectFaultedException:

```
IMyContract proxy = new MyContractClient();
try
{
    proxy.MyMethod();
}
catch
{}

//Throws CommunicationObjectFaultedException
proxy.MyMethod();
```

The obvious conclusion is that the client should never try to use a WCF proxy after an exception. If there was a transport session, the client cannot even close the proxy.

 If there is no transport-level session, the client can technically keep using the proxy after an exception, except again, it should not.

The only thing a client might safely do after an exception is to abort the proxy, perhaps to trigger tracing, or raise events for state changes in the proxy, or to prevent others from using the proxy (even if there was no transport session):

```
MyContractClient proxy = new MyContractClient();
try
{
    proxy.MyMethod();
}
catch
{
    proxy.Abort();
}
```

Closing the proxy and the using statement

I recommend against relying on the using statement to close the proxy. The reason is that in the presence of a transport session, any service-side exception will fault the channel. Trying to dispose of the proxy when the channel is faulted throws a CommunicationObjectFaultedException, so code after the using statement will never get called, even if you catch all exceptions inside the using statement:

```
using(MyContractClient proxy = new MyContractClient())
{
    try
    {
        proxy.MyMethod();
    }
    catch
    {}
}
Trace.WriteLine("This trace may never get called");
```

This reduces the readability of the code and may introduce defects, since the code will behave differently than most developers will expect. The only remedy is to encase the using statement itself in a try/catch statement:

```
try
{
   using(MyContractClient proxy = new MyContractClient())
   {
      try
      {
         proxy.MyMethod();
      }
      catch
      {}
   }
}
catch
{}
Trace.WriteLine("This trace always gets called");
```

It is therefore far better to call Close( ). In the case of an exception, the exception will skip over the call to Close( ):

```
MyContractClient proxy = new MyContractClient();
proxy.MyMethod();
proxy.Close();
```

You can, of course, catch the exception, but now the code is readable:

```
try
{
   MyContractClient proxy = new MyContractClient();
   proxy.MyMethod();
   proxy.Close();
}
catch
{
   proxy.Abort();
}
Trace.WriteLine("This trace always gets called");
```

Exceptions and instance management

When the service is configured as per-call or as sessionful (which mandates the use of a transport session), the client can never access the same instance after an exception occurs. With a per-call service this is, of course, always true, but with a sessionful service this is the result of faulting the channel and terminating the transport session. The one exception to the rule here is a singleton. When the client calls a singleton service and encounters an exception, the singleton instance is not terminated and continues running. If there was no transport session (or if the exception was a FaultException-derived class, as described next), the client can keep using the proxy to connect to the singleton object. Even if the channel is faulted, the client can create a new proxy instance and reconnect to the singleton.

In the case of a durable service, the DurableService attribute offers the UnknownExceptionAction property, defined as:

```
public enum UnknownExceptionAction
{
    TerminateInstance,
    AbortInstance
}

[AttributeUsage(AttributeTargets.Class)]
public sealed class DurableServiceAttribute : ...
{
    public UnknownExceptionAction UnknownExceptionAction
    {get;set;}
    //More members
}
```

UnknownExceptionAction defaults to UnknownExceptionAction.TerminateInstance, meaning that any unhandled exception will not only fault the channel but also remove the instance state from the store, thus terminating the workflow. This behavior is analogous to simply faulting the channel with a regular service, preventing future use of the object. The value UnknownExceptionAction.AbortInstance, on the other hand, terminates the channel to the client but keeps the state in the store. While any changes made to the instance are not persisted, this value is analogous to not faulting the channel in the case of a regular service.

Fault Propagation

While the default error-masking policy of WCF is a best practice, there are times when you are refrained from relying on it. This is typically the case when there is an existing application (or communication pattern) in place, and the service is required to throw particular exceptions as it processes inputs, reaches certain states, or encounters errors. The client is required to respond to these exceptions in a prescribed way. Obviously, controlling the flow of the application using expectations is hardly a good idea, as it leads to nonstructured programming and couples the client to the service. And yet, the underlying requirements remain: the service is required to report specific errors to the client, and the default masking of the errors by WCF precludes that. Another fundamental problem pertaining to propagating the error to the client is that exceptions are technology-specific, and as such should not be shared across the service boundary. For seamless interoperability, you need a way to map technology-specific exceptions to some neutral error information. This representation is called a *SOAP fault*. SOAP faults are based on an industry standard that is independent of any technology-specific exceptions, such as CLR, Java, or C++ exceptions. To return a SOAP fault (or just a fault, for short), the service cannot throw a raw CLR exception. Instead, the service must throw an instance of the FaultException<T> class, defined in Example 6-1.

Example 6-1. The FaultException<T> class

```
[Serializable] //More attributes
public class FaultException : CommunicationException
{
   public FaultException();
   public FaultException(string reason);
   public FaultException(FaultReason reason);
   public virtual MessageFault CreateMessageFault();
   //More members
}

[Serializable]
public class FaultException<T> : FaultException
{
   public FaultException(T detail);
   public FaultException(T detail,string reason);
   public FaultException(T detail,FaultReason reason);
   //More members
}
```

FaultException<T> is a specialization of FaultException, so any client that programs against FaultException will be able to handle FaultException<T> as well.

The type parameter T for FaultException<T> conveys the error details. The detailing type can be any type, and doesn't necessarily have to be an Exception-derived class. The only constraint is that the type must be marked as serializable or a data contract.

Example 6-2 demonstrates a simple calculator service that throws a FaultException<DivideByZeroException> in its implementation of the Divide() operation when asked to divide by zero.

Example 6-2. Throwing a FaultException<T>

```
[ServiceContract]
interface ICalculator
{
   [OperationContract]
   double Divide(double number1,double number2);
   //More methods
}

class Calculator : ICalculator
{
   public double Divide(double number1,double number2)
   {
      if(number2 == 0)
      {
         DivideByZeroException exception = new DivideByZeroException();
         throw new FaultException<DivideByZeroException>(exception);
      }
      return number1 / number2;
   }
   //Rest of the implementation
}
```

Instead of FaultException<DivideByZeroException>, the service could also have thrown a non-Exception-derived class:

```
throw new FaultException<double>(number2);
```

However, I find that using an Exception-derived detailing type is more in line with conventional .NET programming practices and results in more readable code. In addition, it allows for exception promotion, discussed later in this chapter.

The reason parameter passed to the constructor of FaultException<T> is used as the exception message. You can pass a string for the reason:

```
DivideByZeroException exception = new DivideByZeroException( );
throw new FaultException<DivideByZeroException>(exception,"number2 is 0");
```

or you can pass a FaultReason, which is useful when localization is required.

Fault Contracts

By default, any exception thrown by a service reaches the client as a FaultException. This is the case even if the service throws a FaultException<T>. The reason is that anything beyond communication errors that the service wishes to share with the client must be part of the service contract in order for the service to inform WCF that it wishes to pierce the error mask. To that end, WCF provides *fault contracts*, which are a way for the service to list the types of errors it can throw. The idea is that these types of errors should be the same as the type parameters used with FaultException<T>, and by listing them in fault contracts, the service enables its WCF clients to distinguish between contracted faults and other errors.

The service defines its fault contracts using the FaultContractAttribute:

```
[AttributeUsage(AttributeTargets.Method,AllowMultiple = true,Inherited = false)]
public sealed class FaultContractAttribute : Attribute
{
   public FaultContractAttribute(Type detailType);
   //More members
}
```

You apply the FaultContract attribute directly on a contract operation, specifying the error detailing type, as shown in Example 6-3.

Example 6-3. Defining a fault contract

```
[ServiceContract]
interface ICalculator
{
   [OperationContract]
   double Add(double number1,double number2);

   [OperationContract]
   [FaultContract(typeof(DivideByZeroException))]
   double Divide(double number1,double number2);
   //More methods
}
```

The effect of the FaultContract attribute is limited to the method it decorates. That is, only that method can throw that fault and have it propagated to the client.

In addition, if the operation throws an exception that is not in the contract, it will reach the client as a plain FaultException. To propagate the exception, the service must throw exactly the same detailing type listed in the fault contract. For example, to satisfy this fault contract definition:

```
[FaultContract(typeof(DivideByZeroException))]
```

The service must throw a FaultException<DivideByZeroException>. The service cannot even throw a subclass of the fault contract's detailing type and have it satisfy the contract:

```
[ServiceContract]
interface IMyContract
{
    [OperationContract]
    [FaultContract(typeof(Exception))]
    void MyMethod( );
}

class MyService : IMyContract
{
    public void MyMethod( )
    {
        //Will not satisfy contract
        throw new FaultException<DivideByZeroException>(new DivideByZeroException( ));
    }
}
```

The FaultContract attribute is configured to allow multiple usages, so you can list multiple fault contracts in a single operation:

```
[ServiceContract]
interface ICalculator
{
    [OperationContract]
    [FaultContract(typeof(InvalidOperationException))]
    [FaultContract(typeof(string))]
    double Add(double number1,double number2);

    [OperationContract]
    [FaultContract(typeof(DivideByZeroException))]
    double Divide(double number1,double number2);
    //More methods
}
```

This enables the service to throw any of the exceptions in the contracts and have them propagate to the client.

You cannot provide a fault contract on a one-way operation, because in theory nothing should be returned from a one-way operation:

```
//Invalid definition
[ServiceContract]
interface IMyContract
{
    [OperationContract(IsOneWay = true)]
    [FaultContract(...)]
    void MyMethod( );
}
```

Trying to do so will result in an InvalidOperationException at service load time (or when the proxy is created).

Fault handling

The fault contracts are published along with the rest of the service metadata. When a WCF client imports that metadata, the contract definitions contain the fault contracts as well as the fault detailing type definition, including the relevant data contracts. This last point is important if the detailing type is some custom exception type with various dedicated fields.

The client can expect to catch and handle the imported fault types. For example, when you write a client against the contract shown in Example 6-3, the client can catch FaultException<DivideByZeroException>:

```
CalculatorClient proxy = new CalculatorClient( );
try
{
    proxy.Divide(2,0);
    proxy.Close( );
}

catch(FaultException<DivideByZeroException> exception)
{...}

catch(FaultException exception)
{...}

catch(CommunicationException exception)
{...}

catch(TimeoutException exception)
{...}

catch(Exception exception)
{...}
```

Note that the client can still encounter communication exceptions, or any other exception thrown by the service.

The client can choose to treat all non-communication service-side exceptions uniformly by simply handling only the FaultException base exception:

```
CalculatorClient proxy = new CalculatorClient();
try
{
   proxy.Divide(2,0);
   proxy.Close();
}

catch(FaultException exception)
{...}

catch(CommunicationException exception)
{...}
```

 A somewhat esoteric case is when the client's developer manually changes the definition of the imported contract by removing the fault contract on the client side. In that case, even when the service throws an exception listed in a service-side fault contract, the exception will manifest itself on the client as a plain FaultException, not as the contracted fault.

Faults and channels

Listing an expected error in a fault contract hardly makes it an exceptional unexpected case. As a result, when the service throws an exception listed in a service-side fault contract, the exception will not fault the communication channel. The client can catch that exception and continue using the proxy, or safely close the proxy. This enables the service class to treat the errors listed in the fault contracts differently from regular exceptions, knowing that they will not fault the channel. This ability is not limited to the service class, though. If any downstream .NET class the service invokes throws such an error, it will not fault the channel to the client. The problem is, how can downstream classes know about the fault contracts of the upstream services that call them? Clearly, having this knowledge present downstream introduces undesirable coupling into the system.

To support the ability of a downstream class to throw an exception without faulting the channel, WCF treats any FaultException (or FaultException-derived class) as a special case that does not fault the channel. In fact, WCF does not actually treat FaultException<T> itself as a special case at all—the reason a fault listed in the contract does not fault the channel is because it is derived from FaultException, not because it is listed in the contract.

Even without any fault contracts, the service (or any downstream object it uses) can throw an instance of FaultException directly:

```
throw new FaultException("Some Reason");
```

The Message property of the exception object on the client side will be set to the reason construction parameter of FaultException. I call this throwing an *unknown fault* that will not fault the communication channel, so the client can keep using the proxy as if the exception was part of a fault contract. Throwing an unknown fault also allows the client to handle the exception separately from any other communication error.

 Any FaultException<T> thrown by the service will reach the client as either a FaultException<T> or a FaultException. If no fault contract is in place (or if T is not in the contract), both a FaultException and a FaultException<T> thrown by the service will reach the client as FaultException.

Fault Debugging

A deployed service should be decoupled as much as possible from its clients, declaring in the service fault contracts only the absolute bare minimum and providing as little information as possible about any errors that occur. However, during testing and debugging, it is very useful to include all exceptions in the information sent back to the client. In fact, for a test client, it is instrumental to know exactly which error was thrown as a result of a particular input or use case, to see if the test cases break the service as they should. In such a case, dealing with the all-encompassing yet opaque FaultException is simply inadequate. For that purpose, you should use the ExceptionDetail class, defined as:

```
[DataContract]
public class ExceptionDetail
{
    public ExceptionDetail(Exception exception);

    [DataMember]
    public string HelpLink
    {get;private set;}

    [DataMember]
    public ExceptionDetail InnerException
    {get;private set;}

    [DataMember]
    public string Message
    {get;private set;}

    [DataMember]
    public string StackTrace
    {get;private set;}

    [DataMember]
    public string Type
    {get;private set;}
}
```

You need to create an instance of ExceptionDetail and initialize it with the exception you want to propagate to the client. Next, instead of throwing the intended exception, throw a FaultException<ExceptionDetail> with the instance of ExceptionDetail as a construction parameter, and also provide the original exception's message as the fault reason. This sequence is shown in Example 6-4.

Example 6-4. Including the service exception in the fault message

```
[ServiceContract]
interface IMyContract
{
   [OperationContract]
   void MethodWithError();
}
class MyService : IMyContract
{
   public void MethodWithError()
   {
      InvalidOperationException exception =
                              new InvalidOperationException("Some error");
      ExceptionDetail detail = new ExceptionDetail(exception);
      throw new FaultException<ExceptionDetail>(detail,exception.Message);
   }
}
```

Doing so will enable the client to discover the original exception type and message. The client-side fault object will have a Detail.Type property containing the name of the original service exception, and the Message property will contain the original exception message. Example 6-5 shows the client code processing the exception thrown in Example 6-4.

Example 6-5. Processing the included exception

```
MyContractClient proxy = new MyContractClient();
try
{
   proxy.MethodWithError();
}
catch(FaultException<ExceptionDetail> exception)
{
   Debug.Assert(exception.Detail.Type ==
                              typeof(InvalidOperationException).ToString());
   Debug.Assert(exception.Message == "Some error");
}
```

Since FaultException<ExceptionDetail> derives from FaultException, throwing it will not fault the channel. I do not consider this the desired behavior.

Including exceptions declaratively

The ServiceBehavior attribute offers IncludeExceptionDetailInFaults, a Boolean property defined as:

```
[AttributeUsage(AttributeTargets.Class)]
public sealed class ServiceBehaviorAttribute : Attribute, ...
{
   public bool IncludeExceptionDetailInFaults
   {get;set;}
   //More members
}
```

IncludeExceptionDetailInFaults defaults to false. Setting it to true, as in this snippet:

```
[ServiceBehavior(IncludeExceptionDetailInFaults = true)]
class MyService : IMyContract
{...}
```

has a similar effect as the code in Example 6-4, only automated. All noncontractual faults and exceptions thrown by the service or any of its downstream objects are propagated to the client and included in the returned fault message for the client program to process them, as in Example 6-5:

```
[ServiceBehavior(IncludeExceptionDetailInFaults = true)]
class MyService : IMyContract
{
   public void MethodWithError()
   {
      throw new InvalidOperationException("Some error");
   }
}
```

Any fault thrown by the service (or its downstream objects) that is listed in the fault contracts is unaffected and is propagated as-is to the client.

Another important difference between using the declarative support for including the fault details compared with manually throwing FaultException<ExceptionDetail> is that it will correctly fault the channel, preventing the client from reusing the proxy (if a transport session was present).

While including all exceptions is beneficial for debugging, great care should be taken to avoid shipping and deploying the service with IncludeExceptionDetailInFaults set to true. To avoid this potential pitfall automatically you can use conditional compilation, as shown in Example 6-6.

Example 6-6. Setting IncludeExceptionDetailInFaults to true in debug only

```
public static class DebugHelper
{
   public const bool IncludeExceptionDetailInFaults =
#if DEBUG
      true;
#else
      false;
#endif
}
```

Example 6-6. Setting IncludeExceptionDetailInFaults to true in debug only (continued)

```
[ServiceBehavior(IncludeExceptionDetailInFaults =
                DebugHelper.IncludeExceptionDetailInFaults)]
class MyService : IMyContract
{...}
```

Host and exception diagnostics

Obviously, including all exceptions in the fault message contributes greatly in debugging, but it's also useful when you're trying to analyze a problem in an already deployed service. Fortunately, you can set IncludeExceptionDetailInFaults to true both programmatically and administratively in the host config file. To set this behavior programmatically, before opening the host you need to find the service behavior in the service description and set the IncludeExceptionDetailInFaults property:

```
ServiceHost host = new ServiceHost(typeof(MyService));

ServiceBehaviorAttribute debuggingBehavior =
                        host.Description.Behaviors.Find<ServiceBehaviorAttribute>();

debuggingBehavior.IncludeExceptionDetailInFaults = true;

host.Open();
```

You can streamline this procedure by encapsulating it in ServiceHost<T>, as shown in Example 6-7.

Example 6-7. ServiceHost<T> and returning unknown exceptions

```
public class ServiceHost<T> : ServiceHost
{
   public bool IncludeExceptionDetailInFaults
   {
      set
      {
         if(State == CommunicationState.Opened)
         {
            throw new InvalidOperationException("Host is already opened");
         }
         ServiceBehaviorAttribute debuggingBehavior =
                           Description.Behaviors.Find<ServiceBehaviorAttribute>();
         debuggingBehavior.IncludeExceptionDetailInFaults = value;
      }
      get
      {
         ServiceBehaviorAttribute debuggingBehavior =
                           Description.Behaviors.Find<ServiceBehaviorAttribute>();
         return debuggingBehavior.IncludeExceptionDetailInFaults;
      }
   }
   //More members
}
```

Using ServiceHost<T> is trivial and readable:

```
ServiceHost<MyService> host = new ServiceHost<MyService>( );
host.IncludeExceptionDetailInFaults = true;
host.Open( );
```

To apply this behavior administratively, add a custom behavior section in the host config file and reference it in the service definition, as shown in Example 6-8.

Example 6-8. Administratively including exceptions in the fault message

```
<system.serviceModel>
   <services>
     <service name = "MyService" behaviorConfiguration = "Debugging">
        ...
     </service>
   </services>
   <behaviors>
      <serviceBehaviors>
         <behavior name = "Debugging">
            <serviceDebug includeExceptionDetailInFaults = "true"/>
         </behavior>
      </serviceBehaviors>
   </behaviors>
</system.serviceModel>
```

The advantage of administrative configuration in this case is the ability to toggle the behavior in production post-deployment without affecting the service code.

Exception extraction

While including the exception details in the fault is a useful diagnostic technique, it is a cumbersome programming model: the client has to take extra steps to extract the error information out of the ExceptionDetail object. More deterring is the fact that the client must use a single massive catch statement (that catches a single FaultException<ExceptionDetail>) to catch all possible exceptions, and sort them all inside the catch statement. In the world of .NET, this is akin to always catching a mere Exception, and avoiding cascading catch statements.

In addition, when writing a test client, you want to know as much as possible about the original exception that happened on the service side, since your test cases are predicated on producing specific errors. The test client could extract the original exception from the ExceptionDetail object and recursively build the inner exception chain. However, that would be tedious and redundant, and it would require repeated code on every use of the service by the test client. It is therefore better to encapsulate these steps in the proxy using C# 3.0 extensions. To that end, I wrote the ExtractException( ) extension method to FaultException<ExceptionDetail>, defined as:

```
public static class DebugHelper
{
   public static Exception ExtractException(
                                 this FaultException<ExceptionDetail> fault);
   //More members
}
```

The implementation of FaultException<ExceptionDetail> has nothing to do with WCF, so I won't show it here (but it is available with *ServiceModelEx*). The best way of using the extension is to encapsulate it within the proxy, as shown in Example 6-9.

Example 6-9. Automatically extracting the exception

```
[ServiceContract]
interface IMyContract
{
   [OperationContract]
   void MethodWithError( );
}
class MyContractClient : ClientBase<IMyContract>,IMyContract
{
   public MyContractClient( )
   {}
   /* More constructors */

   public void MethodWithError( )
   {
      try
      {
         Channel.MethodWithError( );
      }
      catch(FaultException<ExceptionDetail> exception)
      {
         Abort( );
         throw exception.ExtractException( );
      }
   }
}
```

In Example 6-9, in the case of a FaultException<ExceptionDetail>, the proxy aborts itself (to prevent the proxy from being used again) regardless of whether a transport session is present or how exactly the service threw the exception. The proxy uses the extension method to throw the extracted exception, allowing the client to catch the raw CLR exception. For example, for this service definition in debug mode:

```
[ServiceContract]
interface IMyContract
{
   [OperationContract]
   void MyMethod( );
}

[ServiceBehavior(IncludeExceptionDetailInFaults =
               DebugHelper.IncludeExceptionDetailInFaults)]
class MyService : IMyContract
{
```

```
    public void MyMethod()
    {
        throw new InvalidOperationException();
    }
}
```

when using the proxy from Example 6-9, the client can expect to catch an InvalidOperationException:

```
MyContractClient proxy = new MyContractClient();
try
{
    proxy.MyMethod();
}
catch(InvalidOperationException exception)
{...}
```

 Exception extraction should be used judiciously, only in specific diagnostic and testing cases, since it negates the core benefit of fault masking and decoupling from the nature of the error and the technology.

Faults and Callbacks

Callbacks to the client can, of course, fail due to communication exceptions, or because the callback itself threw an exception. Similar to service contract operations, callback contract operations can define fault contracts, as shown in Example 6-10.

Example 6-10. Callback contract with fault contract

```
[ServiceContract(CallbackContract = typeof(IMyContractCallback))]
interface IMyContract
{
    [OperationContract]
    void DoSomething();
}
interface IMyContractCallback
{
    [OperationContract]
    [FaultContract(typeof(InvalidOperationException))]
    void OnCallBack();
}
```

 Callbacks in WCF are usually configured as one-way calls, and as such cannot define their own fault contracts.

However, unlike with a normal service invocation, what is propagated to the service and how the error manifests itself also depend upon the following:

- When the callback is being invoked (i.e., whether the callback is invoked during a service call to its calling client or is invoked out-of-band by some other party on the host side)
- The binding used
- The type of the exception thrown

If the callback is invoked out-of-band—that is, by some party other than the service during a service operation—the callback behaves like a normal WCF operation invocation. Example 6-11 demonstrates out-of-band invocation of the callback contract defined in Example 6-10.

Example 6-11. Fault handling in out-of-band invocation

```
[ServiceBehavior(InstanceContextMode = InstanceContextMode.PerCall)]
class MyService : IMyContract
{
    static List<IMyContractCallback> m_Callbacks = new List<IMyContractCallback>();
    public void DoSomething()
    {
        IMyContractCallback callback =
                    OperationContext.Current.GetCallbackChannel<IMyContractCallback>();

        if(m_Callbacks.Contains(callback) == false)
        {
            m_Callbacks.Add(callback);
        }
    }
    public static void CallClients()
    {
        Action<IMyContractCallback> invoke = (callback)=>
                                        {
                                            try
                                            {
                                                callback.OnCallBack();
                                            }
                                            catch(FaultException<...> exception)
                                            {...}
                                            catch(FaultException exception)
                                            {...}
                                           catch(CommunicationException exception)
                                            {...}
                                        };
        m_Callbacks.ForEach(invoke);
    }
}
```

As you can see, it is valid to expect to handle the callback fault contract, because faults are propagated to the host side according to it. If the client callback throws an exception listed in the callback fault contract, or if the callback throws a FaultException or any of its subclasses, it will not fault the callback channel, and you can catch the exception and continue using the callback channel. However, as with service calls, after an exception that is not part of the fault contract occurs, you should avoid using the callback channel.

Likewise, when the service calls back to its calling client, if the callback throws a FaultException or any of its subclasses it will not fault the callback channel, and the service can catch the exception and continue using the callback channel (just as with the out-of-band invocation):

```
[ServiceBehavior(ConcurrencyMode = ConcurrencyMode.Reentrant)]
class MyService : IMyContract
{
    public void DoSomething( )
    {
        IMyContractCallback callback =
                OperationContext.Current.GetCallbackChannel<IMyContractCallback>( );
        try
        {
            callback.OnCallBack( );
        }
        catch(FaultException exception)
        {...}
    }
}
```

Note that the service must be configured for reentrancy to avoid a deadlock, as explained in Chapter 5.

The scenario gets considerably more complex when the service invokes the callback during a service operation, calling back to its calling client, and the exception is not FaultException and does not derive from FaultException. Recall that all bindings capable of duplex communication maintain a transport-level session. The exception during the callback terminates the transport session from the client to the service, as well as from the service to the client (in the case of the WS dual binding). How that exception reflects itself to the client and the service is a product of the binding.

Since both the TCP and IPC bindings use the same transport for calls from the client to the service and callbacks from the service to the client, when the callback throws such an exception the client that called the service in the first place immediately receives a CommunicationException, even if the service catches the exception. This is a direct result of reusing the same transport for both directions, and having faulted the callback transport (which is tantamount to faulting the client-to-service transport as well). The service can catch and handle the exception, but the client still gets its exception:

```
[ServiceBehavior(ConcurrencyMode = ConcurrencyMode.Reentrant)]
class MyService : IMyContract
{
    public void DoSomething( )
    {
        IMyContractCallback callback =
                OperationContext.Current.GetCallbackChannel<IMyContractCallback>( );
        try
```

```
    {
        callback.OnCallBack( );
    }
    catch(FaultException exception) //Client still gets CommunicationException
    {...}
    }
}
```

If the service uses the WS dual binding, when the callback throws such an exception it has to fault both transports used. The client that called the service in the first place immediately receives a CommunicationException, even if the service catches the exception. Meanwhile, the service is blocked, and it will eventually be unblocked with a TimeoutException:

```
[ServiceBehavior(ConcurrencyMode = ConcurrencyMode.Reentrant)]
class MyService : IMyContract
{
    public void DoSomething( )
    {
        IMyContractCallback callback =
                OperationContext.Current.GetCallbackChannel<IMyContractCallback>( );
        try
        {
            callback.OnCallBack( );
        }
        catch(TimeoutException exception)
        {...}
    }
}
```

 The large degree of discrepancy in callback behaviors just described is a design deficiency of WCF; that is, it is a direct result of the channels architecture. It may be partially addressed in future releases.

Callback debugging

While the callback can use the same technique shown in Example 6-4 to manually include the exception in the fault message, the CallbackBehavior attribute provides the Boolean property IncludeExceptionDetailInFaults, which can be used to include all non-contract exceptions in the message:

```
[AttributeUsage(AttributeTargets.Class)]
public sealed class CallbackBehaviorAttribute : Attribute,...
{
    public bool IncludeExceptionDetailInFaults
    {get;set;}
    //More members
}
```

As for the service, including the exceptions is instrumental in debugging:

```
[CallbackBehavior(IncludeExceptionDetailInFaults =
                    DebugHelper.IncludeExceptionDetailInFaults)]
class MyClient : IMyContractCallback
{
    public void OnCallBack( )
    {
        ...
        throw new InvalidOperationException( );
    }
}
```

You can also configure this behavior administratively in the client config file:

```
<client>
    <endpoint ... behaviorConfiguration = "Debug"
    ...
    />
</client>
<behaviors>
    <endpointBehaviors>
        <behavior name = "Debug">
            <callbackDebug includeExceptionDetailInFaults = "true"/>
        </behavior>
    </endpointBehaviors>
</behaviors>
```

Note the use of the endpointBehaviors tag to affect the client's callback endpoint.

Error-Handling Extensions

WCF enables developers to customize the default exception reporting and propagation behavior, and even to provide for a hook for custom logging. This extensibility is applied per channel dispatcher (that is, per endpoint), although you are most likely to simply utilize it across all dispatchers.

To install your own error-handling extension, you need to provide the dispatchers with an implementation of the IErrorHandler interface, defined as:

```
public interface IErrorHandler
{
    bool HandleError(Exception error);
    void ProvideFault(Exception error,MessageVersion version,ref Message fault);
}
```

Any party can provide this implementation, but typically it will be provided either by the service itself or by the host. In fact, you can have multiple error-handling extensions chained together. You will see how to install the extensions later in this section.

Providing a Fault

The ProvideFault( ) method of the extension object is called immediately after any unhandled exception is thrown by the service or any object on the call chain downstream from a service operation. WCF calls ProvideFault( ) before returning control to the client, and before terminating the session (if present) and disposing of the service instance (if required). Because ProvideFault( ) is called on the incoming call thread while the client is still blocked waiting for the operation to complete, you should avoid lengthy execution inside ProvideFault( ).

Using ProvideFault( )

ProvideFault( ) is called regardless of the type of exception thrown, be it a regular CLR exception, an unlisted fault, or a fault listed in the fault contract. The error parameter is a reference to the exception just thrown. If ProvideFault( ) does nothing, the exception the client gets will be determined by the fault contract (if any) and the exception type being thrown, as discussed previously in this chapter:

```
class MyErrorHandler : IErrorHandler
{
   public bool HandleError(Exception error)
   {...}

   public void ProvideFault(Exception error,MessageVersion version,
                          ref Message fault)
   {
      //Nothing here - exception will go up as usual
   }
}
```

However, ProvideFault( ) can examine the error parameter and either return it to the client as-is, or provide an alternative fault. This alternative behavior will affect even exceptions that are in the fault contracts. To provide an alternative fault, you need to use the CreateMessageFault( ) method of FaultException to create an alternative fault message. If you are providing a new fault contract message, you must create a new detailing object, and you cannot reuse the original error reference. You then provide the created fault message to the static CreateMessage( ) method of the Message class:

```
public abstract class Message : ...
{
   public static Message CreateMessage(MessageVersion version,
                                    MessageFault fault,string action);
   //More members
}
```

Note that you need to provide CreateMessage( ) with the action of the fault message used. This intricate sequence is demonstrated in Example 6-12.

Example 6-12. Creating an alternative fault

```
class MyErrorHandler : IErrorHandler
{
   public bool HandleError(Exception error)
   {...}
   public void ProvideFault(Exception error,MessageVersion version,
                            ref Message fault)
   {
      FaultException<int> faultException = new FaultException<int>(3);
      MessageFault messageFault = faultException.CreateMessageFault();
      fault = Message.CreateMessage(version,messageFault,faultException.Action);
   }
}
```

In Example 6-12, the ProvideFault( ) method provides FaultException<int> with a value of 3 as the fault thrown by the service, irrespective of the actual exception that was thrown.

The implementation of ProvideFault( ) can also set the fault parameter to null:

```
class MyErrorHandler : IErrorHandler
{
    public bool HandleError(Exception error)
    {...}
    public void ProvideFault(Exception error,MessageVersion version,
                             ref Message fault)
    {
        fault = null; //Suppress any faults in contract
    }
}
```

Doing so will result in all exceptions being propagated to the client as FaultExceptions, even if the exceptions were listed in the fault contracts. Setting fault to null is therefore an effective way of suppressing any fault contracts that may be in place.

Exception promotion

One possible use for ProvideFault( ) is a technique I call *exception promotion*. A service may use downstream objects, which could be called by a variety of services. In the interest of decoupling, these objects may very well be unaware of the particular fault contracts of the service calling them. In case of errors, the objects simply throw regular CLR exceptions. If a downstream object throws an exception of type T, where FaultException<T> is part of the operation fault contract, by default the service will report that exception to the client as an opaque FaultException. What the service could do instead is use an error-handling extension to examine the exception thrown. If that exception is of the type T, where FaultException<T> is part of the operation fault contract, the service could then promote that exception to a full-fledged FaultException<T>. For example, given this service contract:

```
[ServiceContract]
interface IMyContract
{
   [OperationContract]
   [FaultContract(typeof(InvalidOperationException))]
   void MyMethod( );
}
```

if the downstream object throws an InvalidOperationException, ProvideFault( ) will promote it to FaultException<InvalidOperationException>, as shown in Example 6-13.

Example 6-13. Exception promotion

```
class MyErrorHandler : IErrorHandler
{
   public bool HandleError(Exception error)
   {...}
   public void ProvideFault(Exception error,MessageVersion version,
                            ref Message fault)
   {
      if(error is InvalidOperationException)
      {
         FaultException<InvalidOperationException> faultException =
                              new FaultException<InvalidOperationException>(
                              new InvalidOperationException(error.Message));
         MessageFault messageFault = faultException.CreateMessageFault( );
         fault = Message.CreateMessage(version,messageFault,faultException.Action);
      }
   }
}
```

The problem with Example 6-13 is that the code is coupled to a specific fault contract, and implementing it across all services requires a lot of tedious work—not to mention that any change to the fault contract will necessitate a change to the error extension.

Fortunately, you can automate exception promotion using my ErrorHandlerHelper static class:

```
public static class ErrorHandlerHelper
{
   public static void PromoteException(Type serviceType,
                                       Exception error,
                                       MessageVersion version,
                                       ref Message fault);
   //More members
}
```

The ErrorHandlerHelper.PromoteException( ) method requires the service type as a parameter. It uses reflection to examine all the interfaces and operations on that service type, looking for fault contracts for the particular operation (it gets the faulted operation by parsing the error object). PromoteException( ) lets exceptions in the contract go up the call stack unaffected, but it will promote a CLR exception to a contracted fault if the exception type matches any one of the detailing types defined in the fault contracts for that operation.

Using `ErrorHandlerHelper`, Example 6-13 can be reduced to one or two lines of code:

```
class MyErrorHandler : IErrorHandler
{
    public bool HandleError(Exception error)
    {...}
    public void ProvideFault(Exception error,MessageVersion version,
                             ref Message fault)
    {
        Type serviceType = ...;
        ErrorHandlerHelper.PromoteException(serviceType,error,version,ref fault);
    }
}
```

The implementation of `PromoteException()` has little to do with WCF, so it is not listed in this chapter. However, you can examine it as part of the source code available with *ServiceModelEx*. The implementation makes use of some advanced C# programming techniques, such as generics and reflection, and generics late binding.

Handling a Fault

The `HandleError()` method of `IErrorHandler` is defined as:

```
bool HandleError(Exception error);
```

`HandleError()` is called by WCF after control returns to the client. `HandleError()` is strictly for service-side use, and nothing it does affects the client in any way. Calling in the background enables you to perform lengthy processing, such as logging to a database without impeding the client.

Because you can have multiple error-handling extensions installed in a list, WCF also enables you to control whether extensions down the list should be used. If `HandleError()` returns false, WCF will continue to call `HandleError()` on the rest of the installed extensions. If `HandleError()` returns true, WCF stops invoking the error-handling extensions. Obviously, most extensions should return false.

The error parameter of `HandleError()` is the original exception thrown. The classic use for `HandleError()` is for logging and tracing, as shown in Example 6-14.

Example 6-14. Logging the error log to a logbook service

```
class MyErrorHandler : IErrorHandler
{
    public bool HandleError(Exception error)
    {
        try
        {
            LogbookServiceClient proxy = new LogbookServiceClient();
            proxy.Log(...);
            proxy.Close();
        }
```

Example 6-14. Logging the error log to a logbook service (continued)

```
      catch
      {}
      finally
      {
         return false;
      }
   }
   public void ProvideFault(Exception error,MessageVersion version,
                            ref Message fault)

   {...}
}
```

The logbook service

The source code available with this book in *ServiceModelEx* contains a standalone service called `LogbookManager` that is dedicated to error logging. `LogbookManager` logs the errors into a SQL Server database. The service contract also provides operations for retrieving the entries in the logbook and clearing the logbook. *ServiceModelEx* also contains a simple logbook viewer and management tool. In addition to error logging, `LogbookManager` allows you to log entries explicitly into the logbook, independently of exceptions. The architecture of this framework is depicted in Figure 6-1.

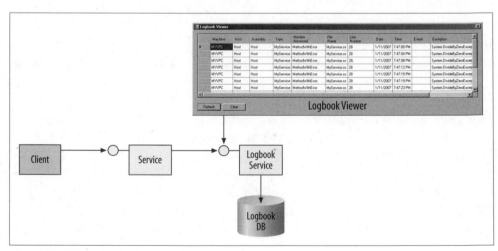

Figure 6-1. The logbook service and viewer

You can automate error logging to `LogbookManager` using the `LogError( )` method of my `ErrorHandlerHelper` static class:

```
   public static class ErrorHandlerHelper
   {
      public static void LogError(Exception error);
      //More members
   }
```

The error parameter is simply the exception you wish to log. LogError( ) encapsulates the call to LogbookManager. For example, instead of the code in Example 6-14, you can simply write a single line:

```
class MyErrorHandler : IErrorHandler
{
    public bool HandleError(Exception error)
    {
        ErrorHandlerHelper.LogError(error);
        return false;
    }
    public void ProvideFault(Exception error,MessageVersion version,
                                    ref Message fault)
    {...}
}
```

In addition to capturing the raw exception information, LogError( ) performs extensive parsing of the exception and other environment variables for a comprehensive record of the error and its related information.

Specifically, LogError( ) captures the following information:

- Where the exception occurred (machine name and host process name)
- The code where the exception took place (the assembly name, the filename, and the line number if debug symbols are provided)
- The type where the exception took place and the member being accessed
- The date and time when the exception occurred
- The exception name and message

Implementing LogError( ) has little to do with WCF, so this method is not shown in this chapter. The code, however, makes extensive use of interesting .NET programming techniques such as string and exception parsing, along with obtaining the environment information. The error information is passed to LogbookManager in a dedicated data contract.

Installing Error-Handling Extensions

Every channel dispatcher in WCF offers a collection of error extensions:

```
public class ChannelDispatcher : ChannelDispatcherBase
{
    public Collection<IErrorHandler> ErrorHandlers
    {get;}
    //More members
}
```

Installing your own custom implementation of IErrorHandler requires merely adding it to the desired dispatcher (usually all of them).

You must add the error extensions before the first call arrives to the service, but after the host constructs the collection of dispatchers. This narrow window of opportunity exists after the host is initialized, but before it is opened. To act in that window, the best solution is to treat error extensions as custom service behaviors, because the behaviors are given the opportunity to interact with the dispatchers at just the right time. As mentioned in Chapter 4, all service behaviors implement the IServiceBehavior interface, defined as:

```
public interface IServiceBehavior
{
    void AddBindingParameters(ServiceDescription description,
                              ServiceHostBase host,
                              Collection<ServiceEndpoint> endpoints,
                              BindingParameterCollection bindingParameters);

    void ApplyDispatchBehavior(ServiceDescription description,
                               ServiceHostBase host);

    void Validate(ServiceDescription description,ServiceHostBase host);
}
```

The ApplyDispatchBehavior( ) method is your cue to add the error extensions to the dispatchers. You can safely ignore all other methods of IServiceBehavior and provide empty implementations for them.

In ApplyDispatchBehavior( ), you need to access the collection of dispatchers available in the ChannelDispatchers property of ServiceHostBase:

```
public class ChannelDispatcherCollection :
                                    SynchronizedCollection<ChannelDispatcherBase>
{}
public abstract class ServiceHostBase : ...
{
    public ChannelDispatcherCollection ChannelDispatchers
    {get;}
    //More members
}
```

Each item in ChannelDispatchers is of the type ChannelDispatcher. You can add the implementation of IErrorHandler to all dispatchers, or just add it to specific dispatchers associated with a particular binding. Example 6-15 demonstrates adding an implementation of IErrorHandler to all of a service's dispatchers.

Example 6-15. Adding an error extension object

```
class MyErrorHandler : IErrorHandler
{...}

class MyService : IMyContract,IServiceBehavior
{
   public void ApplyDispatchBehavior(ServiceDescription description,
                                      ServiceHostBase host)
```

Example 6-15. Adding an error extension object (continued)

```
   {
      IErrorHandler handler = new MyErrorHandler( );
      foreach(ChannelDispatcher dispatcher in host.ChannelDispatchers)
      {
         dispatcher.ErrorHandlers.Add(handler);
      }
   }
   public void Validate(...)
   {}
   public void AddBindingParameters(...)
   {}
   //More members
}
```

In Example 6-15, the service itself implements IServiceBehavior. In ApplyDispatchBehavior( ), the service obtains the dispatchers collection and adds an instance of the MyErrorHandler class to each dispatcher.

Instead of relying on an external class to implement IErrorHandler, the service class itself can support IErrorHandler directly, as shown in Example 6-16.

Example 6-16. Service class supporting IErrorHandler

```
class MyService : IMyContract,IServiceBehavior,IErrorHandler
{
   public void ApplyDispatchBehavior(ServiceDescription description,
                                     ServiceHostBase host)
   {
      foreach(ChannelDispatcher dispatcher in host.ChannelDispatchers)
      {
         dispatcher.ErrorHandlers.Add(this);
      }
   }
   public bool HandleError(Exception error)
   {...}

   public void ProvideFault(Exception error,MessageVersion version,
                            ref Message fault)
   {...}
   //More members
}
```

The ErrorHandlerBehavior attribute

The problem with Examples 6-15 and 6-16 is that they pollute the service class code with WCF plumbing; instead of focusing exclusively on the business logic, the service also has to wire up error extensions. Fortunately, you can provide the same plumbing declaratively using my ErrorHandlerBehaviorAttribute, defined as:

```
   public class ErrorHandlerBehaviorAttribute : Attribute,IErrorHandler,
                                                IServiceBehavior
```

```
{
    protected Type ServiceType
    {get;set;}
}
```

Applying the ErrorHandlerBehavior attribute is straightforward:

```
[ErrorHandlerBehavior]
class MyService : IMyContract
{...}
```

The attribute installs itself as an error-handling extension. Its implementation uses ErrorHandlerHelper both to automatically promote exceptions to fault contracts, if required, and to automatically log the exceptions to LogbookManager. Example 6-17 lists the implementation of the ErrorHandlerBehavior attribute.

Example 6-17. The ErrorHandlerBehavior attribute

```
[AttributeUsage(AttributeTargets.Class)]
public class ErrorHandlerBehaviorAttribute : Attribute,IServiceBehavior,
                                                             IErrorHandler
{
    protected Type ServiceType
    {get;set;}

    void IServiceBehavior.ApplyDispatchBehavior(ServiceDescription description,
                                        ServiceHostBase host)
    {
        ServiceType = description.ServiceType;
        foreach(ChannelDispatcher dispatcher in host.ChannelDispatchers)
        {
            dispatcher.ErrorHandlers.Add(this);
        }
    }
    bool IErrorHandler.HandleError(Exception error)
    {
        ErrorHandlerHelper.LogError(error);
        return false;
    }
    void IErrorHandler.ProvideFault(Exception error,MessageVersion version,
                                ref Message fault)
    {
        ErrorHandlerHelper.PromoteException(ServiceType,error,version,ref fault);
    }
    void IServiceBehavior.Validate(...)
    {}
    void IServiceBehavior.AddBindingParameters(...)
    {}
}
```

Note in Example 6-17 that ApplyDispatchBehavior( ) saves the service type in a protected property. The reason is that the call to ErrorHandlerHelper.PromoteException( ) in ProvideFault( ) requires the service type.

The Host and Error Extensions

While the ErrorHandlerBehavior attribute greatly simplifies the act of installing an error extension, the attribute does require the service developer to apply the attribute. It would be nice if the host could add error extensions independently of whether or not the service provides any. However, due to the narrow timing window available for installing extensions, having the host add such an extension requires multiple steps. First, you need to provide an error-handling extension type that supports both IServiceBehavior and IErrorHandler. The implementation of IServiceBehavior will add the error extension to the dispatchers, as shown previously. Next, you must derive a custom host class from ServiceHost and override the OnOpening() method defined by the CommunicationObject base class:

```
public abstract class CommunicationObject : ICommunicationObject
{
   protected virtual void OnOpening();
   //More members
}
public abstract class ServiceHostBase : CommunicationObject ,...
{...}
public class ServiceHost : ServiceHostBase,...
{...}
```

In OnOpening(), you need to add the custom error-handling type to the collection of service behaviors in the service description. That behaviors collection was described in Chapters 1 and 4:

```
public class Collection<T> : IList<T>,...
{
   public void Add(T item);
   //More members
}
public abstract class KeyedCollection<K,T> : Collection<T>
{...}
public class KeyedByTypeCollection<I> : KeyedCollection<Type,I>
{...}
public class ServiceDescription
{
   public KeyedByTypeCollection<IServiceBehavior> Behaviors
   {get;}
}
public abstract class ServiceHostBase : ...
{
   public ServiceDescription Description
   {get;}
   //More members
}
```

This sequence of steps is already encapsulated and automated in ServiceHost<T>:

```
        public class ServiceHost<T> : ServiceHost
        {
            public void AddErrorHandler(IErrorHandler errorHandler);
            public void AddErrorHandler( );
            //More members
        }
```

ServiceHost<T> offers two overloaded versions of the AddErrorHandler( ) method.
The one that takes an IErrorHandler object will internally associate it with a behavior, so you can provide it with any class that supports just IErrorHandler, not
IServiceBehavior:

```
        class MyService : IMyContract
        {...}

        class MyErrorHandler : IErrorHandler
        {...}

        ServiceHost<MyService> host = new ServiceHost<MyService>( );
        host.AddErrorHandler(new MyErrorHandler( ));
        host.Open( );
```

The AddErrorHandler( ) method that takes no parameters will install an error-handling
extension that uses ErrorHandlerHelper, just as if the service class was decorated with
the ErrorHandlerBehavior attribute:

```
        class MyService : IMyContract
        {...}

        ServiceHost<MyService> host = new ServiceHost<MyService>( );
        host.AddErrorHandler( );
        host.Open( );
```

Actually, for this last example, ServiceHost<T> does internally use an instance of the
ErrorHandlerBehavior attribute.

Example 6-18 shows the implementation of the AddErrorHandler( ) method.

Example 6-18. Implementing AddErrorHandler()

```
public class ServiceHost<T> : ServiceHost
{
   class ErrorHandlerBehavior : IServiceBehavior,IErrorHandler
   {
      IErrorHandler m_ErrorHandler;

      public ErrorHandlerBehavior(IErrorHandler errorHandler)
      {
         m_ErrorHandler = errorHandler;
      }
      void IServiceBehavior.ApplyDispatchBehavior(ServiceDescription description,
                                                 ServiceHostBase host)
      {
```

Example 6-18. Implementing AddErrorHandler() (continued)

```
        foreach(ChannelDispatcher dispatcher in host.ChannelDispatchers)
        {
            dispatcher.ErrorHandlers.Add(this);
        }
    }
    bool IErrorHandler.HandleError(Exception error)
    {
        return m_ErrorHandler.HandleError(error);
    }
    void IErrorHandler.ProvideFault(Exception error,MessageVersion version,
                                    ref Message fault)
    {
        m_ErrorHandler.ProvideFault(error,version,ref fault);
    }
    //Rest of the implementation
}

List<IServiceBehavior> m_ErrorHandlers = new List<IServiceBehavior>();

public void AddErrorHandler(IErrorHandler errorHandler)
{
    if(State == CommunicationState.Opened)
    {
        throw new InvalidOperationException("Host is already opened");
    }
    IServiceBehavior errorHandlerBehavior =
                                  new ErrorHandlerBehavior(errorHandler);
    m_ErrorHandlers.Add(errorHandlerBehavior);
}
public void AddErrorHandler()
{
    AddErrorHandler(new ErrorHandlerBehaviorAttribute());
}
protected override void OnOpening()
{
    foreach(IServiceBehavior behavior in m_ErrorHandlers)
    {
        Description.Behaviors.Add(behavior);
    }
    base.OnOpening();
}
//Rest of the implementation
}
```

To avoid forcing the provided IErrorHandler reference to also support IServiceBehavior, ServiceHost<T> defines a private nested class called ErrorHandlerBehavior. ErrorHandlerBehavior implements both IErrorHandler and IServiceBehavior. To construct ErrorHandlerBehavior, you need to provide it with an implementation of IErrorHandler. That implementation is saved for later use.

The implementation of `IServiceBehavior` adds the instance itself to the error-handler collection of all dispatchers. The implementation of `IErrorHandler` simply delegates to the saved construction parameter. `ServiceHost<T>` defines a list of `IServiceBehavior` references in the `m_ErrorHandlers` member variable. The `AddErrorHandler( )` method that accepts an `IErrorHandler` reference uses it to construct an instance of `ErrorHandlerBehavior` and then adds it to `m_ErrorHandlers`. The `AddErrorHandler( )` method that takes no parameter uses an instance of the `ErrorHandlerBehavior` attribute, because the attribute is merely a class that supports `IErrorHandler`. Finally, the `OnOpening( )` method iterates over `m_ErrorHandlers`, adding each behavior to the behaviors collection.

Callbacks and Error Extensions

The client-side callback object can also provide an implementation of `IErrorHandler` for error handling. Compared with the service-error extensions, the main difference is that to install the callback extension you need to use the `IEndpointBehavior` interface, defined as:

```
public interface IEndpointBehavior
{
   void AddBindingParameters(ServiceEndpoint endpoint,
                             BindingParameterCollection bindingParameters);
   void ApplyClientBehavior(ServiceEndpoint endpoint,
                            ClientRuntime clientRuntime);
   void ApplyDispatchBehavior(ServiceEndpoint endpoint,
                              EndpointDispatcher endpointDispatcher);
   void Validate(ServiceEndpoint endpoint);
}
```

`IEndpointBehavior` is the interface all callback behaviors support. The only relevant method for the purpose of installing an error extension is the `ApplyClientBehavior( )` method, which lets you associate the error extension with the single dispatcher of the callback endpoint. The `clientRuntime` parameter is of the type `ClientRuntime`, which offers the `CallbackDispatchRuntime` property of the type `DispatchRuntime`. The `DispatchRuntime` class offers the `ChannelDispatcher` property, with its collection of error handlers:

```
public sealed class ClientRuntime
{
   public DispatchRuntime CallbackDispatchRuntime
   {get;}
   //More members
}
public sealed class DispatchRuntime
{
   public ChannelDispatcher ChannelDispatcher
   {get;}
   //More members
}
```

As with a service-side error-handling extension, you need to add to that collection your custom error-handling implementation of IErrorHandler.

The callback object itself can implement IEndpointBehavior, as shown in Example 6-19.

Example 6-19. Implementing IEndpointBehavior

```
class MyErrorHandler : IErrorHandler
{...}

class MyClient : IMyContractCallback,IEndpointBehavior
{
   public void OnCallBack()
   {...}

   void IEndpointBehavior.ApplyClientBehavior(ServiceEndpoint serviceEndpoint,
                                            ClientRuntime clientRuntime)
   {
      IErrorHandler handler = new MyErrorHandler();

      clientRuntime.CallbackDispatchRuntime.ChannelDispatcher.ErrorHandlers.
                                                            Add(handler);
   }

   void IEndpointBehavior.AddBindingParameters(...)
   {}
   void IEndpointBehavior.ApplyDispatchBehavior(...)
   {}
   void IEndpointBehavior.Validate(...)
   {}
   //More members
}
```

Instead of using an external class for implementing IErrorHandler, the callback class itself can implement IErrorHandler directly:

```
class MyClient : IMyContractCallback,IEndpointBehavior,IErrorHandler
{
   public void OnCallBack()
   {...}

   void IEndpointBehavior.ApplyClientBehavior(ServiceEndpoint serviceEndpoint,
                                            ClientRuntime clientRuntime)
   {
      clientRuntime.CallbackDispatchRuntime.ChannelDispatcher.ErrorHandlers.Add(this);
   }
   public bool HandleError(Exception error)
   {...}
   public void ProvideFault(Exception error,MessageVersion version,
                         ref Message fault)
   {...}
   //More members
}
```

The CallbackErrorHandlerBehavior attribute

Code such as that shown in Example 6-19 can be automated with the CallbackErrorHandlerBehaviorAttribute, defined as:

```
public class CallbackErrorHandlerBehaviorAttribute : ErrorHandlerBehaviorAttribute,
                                                     IEndpointBehavior
{
   public CallbackErrorHandlerBehaviorAttribute(Type clientType);
}
```

The CallbackErrorHandlerBehavior attribute derives from the service-side ErrorHandlerBehavior attribute and adds explicit implementation of IEndpointBehavior. The attribute uses ErrorHandlerHelper to promote and log the exception.

In addition, the attribute requires as a construction parameter the type of the callback on which it is applied:

```
[CallbackErrorHandlerBehavior(typeof(MyClient))]
class MyClient : IMyContractCallback
{
   public void OnCallBack()
   {...}
}
```

The type is required because there is no other way to get hold of the callback type, which is required by ErrorHandlerHelper.PromoteException( ).

The implementation of the CallbackErrorHandlerBehavior attribute is shown in Example 6-20.

Example 6-20. Implementing the CallbackErrorHandlerBehavior attribute

```
public class CallbackErrorHandlerBehaviorAttribute : ErrorHandlerBehaviorAttribute,
                                                     IEndpointBehavior
{
   public CallbackErrorHandlerBehaviorAttribute(Type clientType)
   {
      ServiceType = clientType;
   }
   void IEndpointBehavior.ApplyClientBehavior(ServiceEndpoint serviceEndpoint,
                                              ClientRuntime clientRuntime)
   {
      clientRuntime.CallbackDispatchRuntime.ChannelDispatcher.ErrorHandlers.Add(this);
   }
   void IEndpointBehavior.AddBindingParameters(...)
   {}
   void IEndpointBehavior.ApplyDispatchBehavior(...)
   {}
   void IEndpointBehavior.Validate(...)
   {}
}
```

Note in Example 6-20 how the provided callback client type is stored in the ServiceType property, defined as protected in Example 6-17.

CHAPTER 7

Transactions

Transactions are the key to building robust, high-quality applications. WCF provides simple, declarative transaction support for service developers, enabling you to configure parameters such as enlistment and voting, all outside the scope of your service. In addition, WCF allows client applications to create transactions and to propagate transactions across service boundaries. This chapter starts by introducing the problem space transactions address and the basic transactions terminology, and then discusses the support for transactions and transaction management offered by WCF. The rest of the chapter is dedicated to transactional programming models, both for services and clients, and to how transactions relate to other aspects of WCF, such as instance management and callbacks.

The Recovery Challenge

Proper error handling and recovery is the Achilles' heel of many applications. When an application fails to perform a particular operation, you should recover from it and restore the system—that is, the collection of interacting services and clients—to a consistent state (usually, the state the system was at before the operation that caused the error took place). Operations that can fail typically consist of multiple potentially concurrent smaller steps. Some of those steps can fail while others succeed. The problem with recovery is the sheer number of partial success and partial failure permutations that you have to code against. For example, an operation comprising 10 smaller concurrent steps has some three million recovery scenarios, because for the recovery logic, the order in which the suboperations fail matters as well, and the factorial of 10 is roughly three million.

Trying to handcraft recovery code in a decent-sized application is often a futile attempt, resulting in fragile code that is very susceptible to any changes in the application execution or the business use case, incurring both productivity and performance penalties. The productivity penalty results from all the effort required for handcrafting the recovery logic. The performance penalty is inherited with such an approach because you need to execute huge amounts of code after every operation to verify that all is well. In reality, developers tend to deal only with the easy recovery cases; that is, the cases that they are both aware of and know how to handle. More insidious error scenarios, such as intermediate network failures or disk crashes, go unaddressed. In addition, because recovery is all about restoring the system to a consistent state (typically the state before the operations), the real problem has to do with the steps that succeeded, rather than those that failed. The failed steps failed to affect the system; the challenge is actually the need to undo successful steps, such as deleting a row from a table, or a node from a linked list, or a call to a remote service. The scenarios involved could be very complex, and your manual recovery logic is almost certain to miss a few successful suboperations.

The more complex the recovery logic becomes, the more error-prone the recovery itself becomes. If you have an error in the recovery, how would you recover the recovery? How do developers go about designing, testing, and debugging complex recovery logic? How do they simulate the endless number of errors and failures that are possible? Not only that, but what if before the operation failed, as it was progressing along executing its suboperations successfully, some other party accessed your application and acted upon the state of the system—the state that you are going to roll back during the recovery? That other party is now acting on inconsistent information and, by definition, is in error too. Moreover, your operation may be just one step in some other, much wider operation that spans multiple services from multiple vendors on multiple machines. How would you recover the system as a whole in such a case? Even if you have a miraculous way of recovering your service, how would that recovery logic plug into the cross-service recovery? As you can see, it is practically impossible to write error-recovery code by hand.

Transactions

The best (and perhaps only) way of maintaining system consistency and dealing properly with the error-recovery challenge is to use *transactions*. A transaction is a set of potentially complex operations, in which the failure of any single operation causes the entire set to fail, as one atomic operation. As illustrated in Figure 7-1, while the transaction is in progress the system is allowed to be in a temporary inconsistent state, but once the transaction is complete it is guaranteed to be in a consistent state. That state may be either a new consistent state (B), or the original consistent state the system was in before the transaction started (A).

A transaction that executes successfully and manages to transfer the system from the consistent state A to the consistent state B is called a *committed transaction*. If the transaction encounters an error during its execution and rolls back all the intermediate steps that have already succeeded, it is called an *aborted transaction*. If the transaction failed to either commit or abort, it is called an *in-doubt transaction*. In-doubt transactions usually require administrator or user assistance to resolve and are beyond the scope of this book.

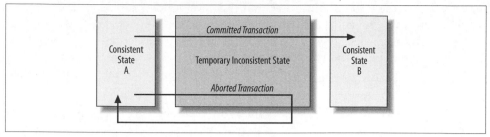

Figure 7-1. A transaction transfers the system between consistent states

Transactional Resources

Transactional programming requires working with a resource (such as a database or a message queue) that is capable of participating in a transaction, and being able to commit or roll back the changes made during the transaction. Such resources have been around in one form or another for decades. Traditionally, you had to inform a resource that you would like to perform transactional work against it. This act is called *enlisting* the resource in the transaction. Some resources support *auto-enlistment*; that is, they can detect that they are being accessed by a transaction and automatically enlist in it. Once enlisted, you can then perform work against the resource. If no error occurs, the resource is asked to commit the changes made to its state; if any error is encountered, the resource is asked to roll back the changes. During a transaction, it is vital that you do not access any nontransactional resources (such as the filesystem on Windows XP), because changes made to those resources will not roll back if the transaction is aborted.

Transaction Properties

When you make use of transactions in your service-oriented applications, you must abide by four core properties, known as *ACID* (atomic, consistent, isolated, and durable). When you design transactional services, you must adhere to the ACID requirements—they are not optional. As you will see throughout this chapter, WCF enforces them rigorously.

The atomic property

In order for it to be *atomic,*[*] when a transaction completes, all the individual changes it has made to the resource state must be made as if they were all one atomic, indivisible operation. The changes made to the resource are made as if everything else in the

---

[*] The word "atom" comes from the Greek word "atomos," meaning *indivisible*. The ancient Greeks thought that if you started dividing matter, and continued dividing it, eventually you would get to indivisible pieces, which they called "atomos." The ancient Greeks were, of course, wrong, as atoms can be divided into sub-atomic particles such as electrons, protons, and neutrons. Transactions, however, are truly atomic.

universe stops, the changes are made, and then everything resumes. It must not be possible for a party outside the transaction to observe the resources involved with only some of the changes made, but not all of them. A transaction should not leave anything to be done in the background once it is done, as those operations would violate atomicity. Every operation resulting from the transaction must be included in the transaction itself.

Atomic transactions make client applications a lot easier to develop. The client does not have to manage partial failures of its requests, or have complex recovery logic. The client knows that the transaction will either succeed or fail as a whole. In the case of failure, the client can choose to issue a new request (start a new transaction), or do something else, such as alerting the user. The important thing is that the client does not have to recover the system.

The consistent property

Consistent means the transaction must leave the system in a consistent state. Note that consistency is different from atomicity. Even if all the changes are committed as one atomic operation, the transaction is required to guarantee that all those changes are consistent (i.e., that they "make sense"). Usually, it is up to the developer to ensure that the semantics of the operations are consistent. All the transaction is required to do is to transfer the system from one consistent state to another.

The isolated property

Isolated means no other entity (transactional or not) is able to see the intermediate state of the resources during the transaction, because that state may be inconsistent. In fact, even if it is consistent, the transaction could still abort, and the changes could be rolled back. Isolation is crucial to overall system consistency. Suppose transaction A allows transaction B access to its intermediate state, and then transaction A aborts while transaction B decides to commit. The problem is that transaction B based its execution on system state that was rolled back, and therefore transaction B is left unknowingly inconsistent.

Managing isolation is not trivial. The resources participating in a transaction must lock the data accessed by the transaction from all other parties, and must unlock access to that data when the transaction commits or aborts.

The durable property

Traditionally, transactional support by a resource implies not just a transaction-aware resource, but also a *durable* one. This is because at any moment the application could crash, and the memory it was using could be erased. If the changes to the system's state were in-memory changes, they would be lost, and the system would be left in an inconsistent state. However, durability is really a range of options.

How resilient to such catastrophes the resource should be is an open question that depends on the nature and sensitivity of the data, your budget, available time and available system administration staff, and so on.

If durability is a range that actually means various degrees of persistence, then you can also consider the far end of the spectrum: volatile, in-memory resources. The advantage of volatile resources is that they offer better performance than durable resources, and, more importantly, they allow you to approximate much better conventional programming models while using transaction support for error recovery. You will see later in this chapter how and when your services can benefit from volatile resource managers (VRMs).

Transaction Management

WCF services can work directly against a transactional resource and manage the transaction explicitly using a programming model such as that offered by ADO.NET. As shown in Example 7-1, using this model you are responsible for explicitly starting and managing the transaction.

Example 7-1. Explicit transaction management

```
[ServiceContract]
interface IMyContract
{
   [OperationContract]
   void MyMethod( );
}

class MyService : IMyContract
{
   public void MyMethod( )
   {
      //Avoid this programming model:

      string connectionString = "...";
      IDbConnection connection = new SqlConnection(connectionString);
      connection.Open( );
      IDbCommand command = new SqlCommand( );
      command.Connection = connection;
      IDbTransaction transaction = connection.BeginTransaction( ); //Enlisting
      command.Transaction = transaction;

      using(connection)
      using(command)
      using(transaction)
      {
         try
         {
            /* Interact with database here, then commit the transaction */
            transaction.Commit( );
```

Example 7-1. Explicit transaction management (continued)

```
        }
        catch
        {
            transaction.Rollback( ); //Abort transaction
        }
    }
  }
}
```

You obtain an object representing the underlying database transaction by calling BeginTransaction( ) on the connection object. BeginTransaction( ) returns an implementation of the interface IDbTransaction, used to manage the transaction. When the database is enlisted, it does not really execute any of the requests that are made. Instead, it merely logs the requests against the transaction. If at the end all updates and other changes made to the database are consistent and no error has taken place, you simply call Commit( ) on the transaction object. This instructs the database to commit the changes as one atomic operation. If any exception occurred, the call to Commit( ) is skipped over, and the catch statement aborts the transaction by calling Rollback( ). Aborting the transaction instructs the database to discard all the changes logged so far.

The transaction management challenge

While the explicit programming model is straightforward, requiring nothing of the service performing the transaction, it is most suitable for a client calling a single service interacting with a single database (or a single transactional resource), where the service starts and manages the transaction, as shown in Figure 7-2.

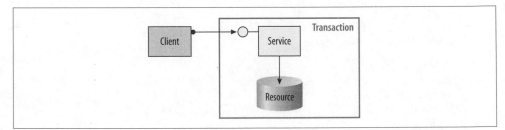

Figure 7-2. Single service/single resource transaction

This is due to the transaction coordination problem. Consider, for example, a service-oriented application where the client interacts with multiple services that in turn interact with each other and with multiple resources, as shown in Figure 7-3.

The question now is, which one of the participating services is responsible for beginning the transaction and enlisting each resource? If all of them will do that, you will end up with multiple transactions. Putting the enlistment logic in the service code

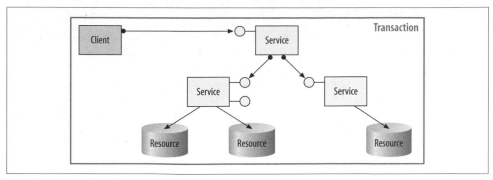

Figure 7-3. Distributed transactional service-oriented application

will create a great deal of coupling between the services and the resources. Furthermore, which one of the services is responsible for committing or rolling back the transaction? How would one service know what the rest of the services feel about the transaction? How would the service managing the transaction inform the other services about the transaction's ultimate outcome? Trying to pass the transaction object or some identifier as an operation parameter is not service-oriented, because the clients and the services could all be using different implementation platforms and technologies. The services could also be deployed in different processes or even across different machines or sites. In this case, issues such as network failures or machine crashes introduce additional complexity for managing the transaction, because one service might crash while others continue processing the transaction.

One possible solution is to couple the clients and the services by adding logic for coordinating the transaction, but such an approach is very fragile and would not withstand even minor changes to the business flow or the number of participating services. In addition, if different vendors developed the services, this will preclude any such coordination. And even if you find a way of solving the coordination problem at the service level, when multiple resources are involved you have multiple independent points of failure, because each of the resources could fail independently of the services.

Distributed transactions

The type of transaction just described is called a *distributed transaction*. A distributed transaction contains two or more independent services (often in different execution contexts), or even just a single service with two or more transactional resources. It is impractical to try to explicitly manage the potential error cases of a distributed transaction. For a distributed transaction, you need to rely on the two-phase commit protocol, and a dedicated transaction manager. A *transaction manager* is a third party that will manage the transaction for you, because the last thing you want is to place the transaction management logic in your service code.

The two-phase commit protocol

To overcome the complexity of a distributed transaction, the transaction manager uses a transaction management protocol called the *two-phase commit* protocol to decide on the outcome of the transaction as well as to commit or roll back the changes to the system state. The two-phase commit protocol is what enforces atomicity and consistency in a distributed system. The protocol enables WCF to support transactions that involve multiple clients, services, and resources. You will see later in this chapter just how transactions start and how they flow across service boundaries. For now, the important thing to note is that while a transaction is in progress, the transaction manager stays largely out of the way. New services may join the transaction, and every resource accessed is enlisted with that transaction. The services execute business logic, and the resources record the changes made under the scope of the transaction. During the transaction, all the services (and the clients participating in the transaction) must *vote* on whether they want to commit the changes they've performed or abort the transaction for whatever reason.

When the transaction ends (you will see when transactions end later in this chapter), the transaction manager checks the combined vote of the participating services. If any service or client voted to abort, the transaction is doomed: all the participating resources are instructed to discard the changes made during the transaction. If, however, all the services in the transaction voted to commit, the two-phase commit protocol starts. In the first phase, the transaction manager asks all the resources that took part in the transaction if they have any reservations about committing the changes recorded during the transaction. That is, if they were asked to commit, would they? Note that the transaction manager is not instructing the resources to commit the changes at this point; it is merely asking for their votes on the matter. At the end of the first phase, the transaction manager has the combined vote of the resources. The second phase of the protocol is acting upon that combined vote. If all the resources voted to commit the transaction in the first phase, the transaction manager instructs all of them to commit the changes. But if even one of the resources said in phase one that it would not commit the changes, then in phase two the transaction manager instructs all the resources to roll back the changes made, thus aborting the transaction and restoring the system to its pre-transaction state.

It is important to emphasize that a resource voting that it would commit if asked to constitutes an unbreakable promise. If a resource votes to commit a transaction, it means that it cannot fail if subsequently, in the second phase, it is instructed to commit. The resource should verify before voting to commit that all the changes are consistent and legitimate. A resource can never go back on its vote. This is the basis for enabling distributed transactions, and the various resource vendors have gone to great lengths to implement this behavior exactly.

WCF Resource Managers

A *WCF resource manager* (RM) is any resource that supports both automatic enlistment and the two-phase commit protocol managed by one of WCF's transaction managers. The resource must be able to detect that it is being accessed by a transaction and automatically enlist in it exactly once. The RM can be either a durable resource or a volatile resource, such as a transactional integer, string, or collection. While the RM must support the two-phase commit protocol, it can optionally also implement an optimized protocol used when it is the only RM in the transaction. That optimized protocol is called the *single-phase commit* protocol, when the RM is the one informing the transaction manager in one step about the success or failure of an attempt to commit.

Transaction Propagation

WCF can propagate transactions across the service boundary. This enables a service to participate in a client's transaction, and the client to include operations on multiple services in the same transaction. The client itself may or may not be a WCF service. Both the binding and the operation contract configuration control the decision as to whether or not the client's transaction is propagated to the service. I call any binding that is capable of propagating the client's transaction to the service if configured to do so a *transaction-aware* binding. Only the TCP, IPC, and WS bindings are transaction-aware.

Transaction Flow and Bindings

By default, transaction-aware bindings do not propagate transactions. The reason is that, like most everything else in WCF, it is an opt-in setting: the service host or administrator has to explicitly give its consent to accepting incoming transactions, potentially from across the organization or the business boundaries. To propagate a transaction, you must explicitly enable it in the binding on both the service host and client sides. All transaction-aware bindings offer the Boolean property TransactionFlow, such as:

```
public class NetTcpBinding : Binding,...
{
   public bool TransactionFlow
   {get;set;}
   //More members
}
```

TransactionFlow defaults to false. To enable propagation, simply set this property to true, either programmatically or in the host config file. For example, in the case of the TCP binding:

```
NetTcpBinding tcpBinding = new NetTcpBinding( );
tcpBinding.TransactionFlow = true;
```

or when using a config file:

```
<bindings>
   <netTcpBinding>
      <binding name = "TransactionalTCP"
         transactionFlow = "true"
      />
   </netTcpBinding>
</bindings>
```

Transactions and Reliability

Strictly speaking, transactions do not require reliable messaging. The reason is that when reliability is disabled, if WCF messages are dropped or the client or service becomes disconnected, the transaction will abort. Because the client is guaranteed complete success or complete failure of the transactional operation, transactions are reliable in their own way. However, enabling reliability will decrease the likelihood of aborted transactions, because it will make the communication reliable; this means the transaction will be less likely to abort due to communication problems. I therefore recommend as a best practice also enabling reliability when enabling transactions with the NetTcpBinding and WSHttpBinding:

```
<netTcpBinding>
   <binding name = "TransactionalTCP"
           transactionFlow = "true">
      <reliableSession enabled = "true"/>
   </binding>
</netTcpBinding>
```

There is no need to enable reliability for the NetNamedPipeBinding and the WSDualHttpBinding because, as discussed in Chapter 1, these two bindings are always reliable.

Transaction Flow and the Operation Contract

Using a transaction-aware binding and even enabling transaction flow does not mean that the service wants to use the client's transaction in every operation, or that the client necessarily has a transaction to propagate in the first place. Such service-level decisions should be part of the contractual agreement between the client and the service. To that end, WCF provides the TransactionFlowAttribute method attribute, which controls if and when the client's transaction flows into the service:

```
public enum TransactionFlowOption
{
    Allowed,
    NotAllowed,
    Mandatory
}

[AttributeUsage(AttributeTargets.Method)]
public sealed class TransactionFlowAttribute : Attribute,IOperationBehavior
{
    public TransactionFlowAttribute(TransactionFlowOption flowOption);
}
```

Note that the `TransactionFlow` attribute is a method-level attribute because WCF insists that the decision on transaction flow be made on a per-operation level, not at the service level:

```
[ServiceContract]
interface IMyContract
{
    [OperationContract]
    [TransactionFlow(TransactionFlowOption.Allowed)]
    void MyMethod( );
}
```

This is deliberate, to enable the granularity of having some methods that use the client's transaction and some that do not.

The value of the `TransactionFlow` attribute is included in the published metadata of the service, so when you import a contract definition, the imported definition will contain the configured value. WCF will also let you apply the `TransactionFlow` attribute directly on the service class implementing the operation:

```
[ServiceContract]
interface IMyContract
{
    [OperationContract]
    void MyMethod( );
}
class MyService : IMyContract
{
    [TransactionFlow(TransactionFlowOption.Allowed)]
    public void MyMethod( )
    {...}
}
```

However, such use is discouraged because it splits the definition of the logical service contract that will be published.

TransactionFlowOption.NotAllowed

When the operation is configured to disallow transaction flow, the client cannot propagate its transaction to the service. Even if transaction flow is enabled at the binding and the client has a transaction, it will be silently ignored and will not propagate to the service. As a result, the service will never use the client's transaction, and the service and the client can select any binding with any configuration. TransactionFlowOption.NotAllowed is the default value of the TransactionFlowOption attribute, so these two definitions are equivalent:

```
[ServiceContract]
interface IMyContract
{
    [OperationContract]
    void MyMethod( );
}

[ServiceContract]
interface IMyContract
{
    [OperationContract]
    [TransactionFlow(TransactionFlowOption.NotAllowed)]
    void MyMethod( );
}
```

TransactionFlowOption.Allowed

When the operation is configured to allow transaction flow, if the client has a transaction, the service will allow the client's transaction to flow across the service boundary. However, just because the client propagates its transaction doesn't mean the service will necessarily use it. When you choose TransactionFlowOption.Allowed, the service can be configured to use any binding, be it transaction-aware or not, but the client and the service must be compatible in their binding configuration. In the context of transaction flow, "compatible" means that when the service operation allows transaction flow but the binding disallows it, the client should also disallow it in the binding on its side: trying to flow the client's transaction will cause an error, because the service will not understand the transaction information in the message. However, when the service-side binding configuration is set to allow transaction flow, the client may or may not want to enable propagation on its side, so it may elect to set TransactionFlow to false in the binding even if the service has it set to true.

TransactionFlowOption.Mandatory

When the operation is configured with TransactionFlowOption.Mandatory, the service and the client must use a transaction-aware binding with transaction flow enabled. WCF verifies this requirement at the service load time and throws an InvalidOperationException if the service has at least one incompatible endpoint. TransactionFlowOption.Mandatory means the client must have a transaction to propagate to the service. Trying to call a service operation without a transaction results in a FaultException on the client side stating that the service requires a transaction. With mandatory flow, the client's transaction always propagates to the service, but again, the service may or may not use the client's transaction.

The test client *WcfTestClient.exe* discussed in Chapter 1 does not support mandatory transaction flow. It does not create a transaction on the client side, and therefore will fail all calls to an operation that mandates transaction flow.

One-Way Calls

Propagating the client's transaction to the service requires, by its very nature, allowing the service to abort the client's transaction if so desired. This implies that you cannot flow the client's transaction to a service over a one-way operation, because that call does not have a reply message. WCF validates this at the service load time and will throw an exception when a one-way operation is configured with anything but TransactionFlowOption.NotAllowed:

```
//Invalid definition:
[ServiceContract]
interface IMyContract
{
    [OperationContract(IsOneWay = true)]
    [TransactionFlow(TransactionFlowOption.Allowed)]
    void MyMethod();
}
```

Transaction Protocols and Managers

By and large, WCF developers need never concern themselves with transaction protocols and transaction managers. You should rely on WCF to select the correct protocol and transaction manager, and focus instead on implementing your logic. However, I have found that developers typically care a great deal about this issue, so I've chosen to include a discussion of transaction protocols and managers (mostly to demonstrate that there is no practical reason to actually deal with them in the first place).

The transaction management protocol WCF chooses depends on the execution scope of the participating parties in the transaction. The word protocol may be misleading here, because in the abstract the protocol being used is the two-phase commit protocol. The differences between the transaction management protocols have to do with the type of remote calls and communication protocol used, and the kind of boundaries it can cross. The options are:

The lightweight protocol
> This protocol is used to manage transactions in a local context only, inside the same app domain. It cannot propagate the transaction across the app domain boundary (let alone the process or machine boundary), nor can it flow the transaction across any service boundary (that is, from a client to a service). The lightweight protocol is used only inside a service or between two parties in the same app domain, never between services. The lightweight protocol yields the best performance compared with the other protocols.

The OleTx protocol

This protocol is used to propagate transactions across app domain, process, and machine boundaries, and to manage the two-phase commit protocol. The protocol uses RPC calls, and the exact binary format of the calls is Windows-specific. As a result of the use of both the RPC and the Windows-specific format, it cannot be used across firewalls or to interoperate with non-Windows parties. This is usually not a problem, because the primary use for the OleTx protocol is for managing transactions in an intranet, in a homogenous Windows environment, and when a single transaction manager is involved.

The WS-Atomic Transaction (WSAT) protocol

This protocol is similar to the OleTx protocol in that it too can propagate transactions across app domain, process, and machine boundaries and can be used to manage the two-phase commit protocol. However, unlike the OleTx protocol, the WSAT protocol is based on an industry standard and can typically be used across firewalls. Although you can use the WSAT protocol in an intranet in a heterogeneous environment, its primary use is for transaction management across the Internet, where multiple transaction managers are involved.

Protocols and Bindings

No binding supports the lightweight protocol, because the protocol cannot propagate transactions across the service boundary anyway. However, the various transaction-aware bindings differ in their support for the two other transaction-management protocols. The TCP and IPC bindings can be configured to work with both the OleTx and WSAT protocols, or with just one of them. Both bindings default to the OleTx protocol and will switch to the WSAT protocol if required. In addition, these two intranet bindings let you configure the protocol either in a config file or programmatically, like any other binding property.

WCF provides the `TransactionProtocol` abstract class, defined as:

```
public abstract class TransactionProtocol
{
   public static TransactionProtocol Default
   {get;}
   public static TransactionProtocol OleTransactions
   {get;}
   public static TransactionProtocol WSAtomicTransactionOctober2004
   {get;}
   public static TransactionProtocol WSAtomicTransaction11
   {get;}
}
```

Both the TCP and IPC bindings offer the `TransactionProtocol` property of the matching type. For example:

```
public class NetTcpBinding : Binding,...
{
   TransactionProtocol TransactionProtocol
   {get;set;}
   //More members
}
```

To set the protocol programmatically, first construct the specific binding type, then set the property using one of the static methods:

```
NetTcpBinding tcpBinding = new NetTcpBinding();
//Protocol only matters with propagation
tcpBinding.TransactionFlow = true;
tcpBinding.TransactionProtocol =
                    TransactionProtocol.WSAtomicTransactionOctober2004;
```

Note that the transaction protocol configuration is meaningful only when transaction propagation is enabled as well.

To configure the protocol in a config file, define a binding section as usual:

```
<bindings>
   <netTcpBinding>
      <binding name = "TransactionalTCP"
         transactionFlow = "true"
         transactionProtocol = "WSAtomicTransactionOctober2004"
      />
   </netTcpBinding>
</bindings>
```

When you configure a protocol for the TCP or IPC binding, the service and the client must use the same protocol.

Since the TCP and IPC bindings can be used only in an intranet, there is really no practical value to configuring them for the WSAT protocol, and this ability is available largely for the sake of completeness.

The WS bindings (WSHttpBinding, WS2007HttpBinding, WSDualHttpBinding, WSFederationHttpBinding, and WS2007FederationHttpBinding) are designed for use across the Internet, when multiple transaction managers are involved, using the WSAT protocol. However, in an Internet scenario where only a single transaction manager is involved, these bindings will default to the OleTx protocol. There is no need or ability to configure a particular protocol.

Transaction Managers

Recall from the discussion at the beginning of this chapter that the last thing you should do is manage a transaction yourself. The best solution is to have a third party, called the transaction manager, manage the two-phase commit protocol for your clients and services. WCF can work with not one but three different transaction managers in a provider model, as shown in Figure 7-4.

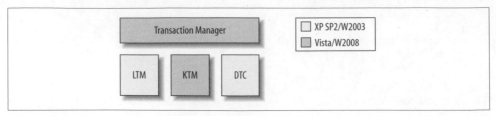

Figure 7-4. WCF transaction managers

The three transaction managers are the *Lightweight Transaction Manager* (LTM), the *Kernel Transaction Manager* (KTM), and the *Distributed Transaction Coordinator* (DTC). As a function of the platform used, what the application does, the services it calls, and the resources it consumes, WCF will assign the appropriate transaction manager. By automatically assigning the transaction manager, WCF decouples the transaction management from the service code and from the transaction protocol used. Again, developers need never bother themselves with the transaction managers, and the following discussion is intended only to alleviate some common concerns regarding performance and efficiency.

The LTM

The LTM can manage only a local transaction; that is, a transaction inside a single app domain. The LTM uses the lightweight transaction protocol to manage the two-phase commit protocol. It can only manage a transaction that involves at most a single durable resource manager. The LTM can also manage as many volatile resource managers as are present. If only a single resource manager is present, and that resource supports single-phase commit, the LTM will use that optimized protocol. Most importantly, the LTM can only manage a transaction inside a single service, and only when that service does not flow the transaction to other services. The LTM is the most performant transaction manager, on a par performance-wise with performing direct transactions against the resource.

The KTM

The KTM can be used to manage transactional kernel resource managers (KRMs) on Windows Vista and Windows Server 2008 or later—specifically, the transactional files system (TxF) and the transactional registry (TxR). The KTM uses the lightweight transaction protocol over both direct memory and kernel calls. The KTM can only manage the transaction if it involves at most a single durable KRM, but the transaction can have as many volatile resource managers as desired. As with the LTM, the transaction can involve at most one service, as long as that service does not propagate the transaction to other services.

The DTC

The DTC is capable of managing transactions across any execution boundary, from the most local (i.e., a transaction within the same app domain) scope to the most remote (e.g., a transaction that crosses process, machine, or site boundaries). The DTC can use either the OleTx or the WSAT protocol. The DTC is the transaction manager used when transactions flow across the service boundary. The DTC can easily manage a transaction that involves any number of services and resource managers.

The DTC is a system service available by default on every machine running WCF, and WCF is tightly integrated with the DTC. The DTC creates new transactions, collects the votes of the resource managers, and instructs the resource managers to abort or commit the transaction. For example, consider the application shown in Figure 7-5, where a nontransactional client calls to a service on Machine A. The service on Machine A is configured to use a transaction. That service becomes the *root* of the transaction, and it will get the opportunity not just to start the transaction but also to indicate when the transaction is done.

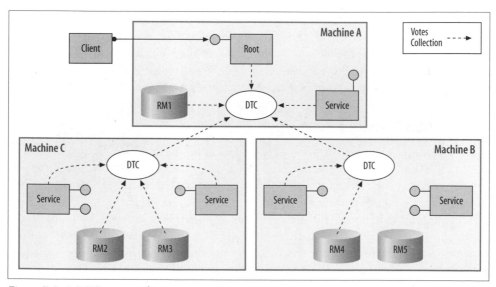

Figure 7-5. A DTC-managed transaction

 Every transaction in WCF has at most one root service, because a non-service client can also be the root of the transaction.

When a service that is part of a transaction on Machine A tries to access another service or a resource on Machine B, it actually has a proxy to the remote service or resource. That proxy propagates the transaction ID to Machine B. The call interception on Machine B contacts the local DTC on Machine B, passing it the transaction ID and informing it to start managing that transaction on Machine B. Because the transaction ID gets propagated to Machine B, resource managers on Machine B can now auto-enlist in it. Similarly, the transaction ID is propagated to Machine C.

When the transaction is done, if the combined services' vote was to try to commit the transaction, it is time to start the two-phase commit protocol. The DTC on the root machine collects the resource managers' votes on that machine and contacts the DTC on every other machine that took part in the transaction, instructing them to conduct the first phase on their machines. The DTCs on the remote machines collect the resource managers' votes on their machines and forward the results back to the DTC on the root machine. After the DTC on the root machine receives the results from all the remote DTCs, it has the combined resource managers' vote. If all of them vote to commit, the DTC on the root machine again contacts all the DTCs on the remote machines, instructing them to conduct phase two on their respective machines and to commit the transaction. If even one resource manager voted to abort the transaction, however, the DTC on the root machine informs all the DTCs on the remote machines to conduct phase two on their respective machines and to abort the transaction. Note that only the DTC on the root machine has the combined vote of phase one, and only it can instruct the final abort or commit.

Transaction Manager Promotion

WCF dynamically assigns the appropriate transaction manager for the transaction. If one transaction manager is inadequate, WCF will *promote* the transaction; that is, ask the next-level-up transaction manager to handle the transaction. A single transaction can be promoted multiple times. Once promoted, the transaction stays elevated and cannot be demoted. The previous transaction manager used to manage the transaction is relegated to a pass-through mode. Because of this dynamic promotion, developers are precluded from interacting with the transaction managers directly (doing so would bypass promotion). Promotion is yet another reason why you should not write code such as that in Example 7-1: it eliminates any chance of promotion.

LTM promotion

Every transaction in WCF always starts out as a transaction managed by the LTM. As long as the transaction interacts with a single durable resource and as long as there is no attempt to flow the transaction to a WCF service, the LTM can manage the transaction and yield the best throughput and performance. The LTM can manage as many volatile resource managers as required. However, if the transaction tries to enlist a second durable resource or the transaction is propagated to a service,

WCF will promote the transaction from the LTM to the DTC. Another type of promotion takes place if the first durable resource accessed is a KTM resource, in which case WCF will promote the transaction from the LTM to the KTM.

KTM promotion

The KTM can manage a transaction as long as it interacts with a single KRM and as long as the transaction is local. The KTM can manage as many volatile resource managers as required. The KTM transaction is promoted to the DTC when the transaction flows to another service or if a second durable resource (kernel or regular) is enlisted.

Resources and promotion

At the time of this writing, the only resources that can participate in an LTM transaction and promote from it are volatile resource managers, and the various flavors of SQL Server 2005 and 2008. Legacy resource managers such as SQL Server 2000, Oracle, DB2, and MSMQ can only participate in DTC transactions. Consequently, when a legacy resource is accessed by an LTM transaction, even if it is the single resource in the transaction, the transaction is automatically promoted to the DTC.

The relationship between resources and transaction managers is summarized in Table 7-1.

Table 7-1. Resources and transaction managers

Resource	LTM	KTM	DTC
Volatile	Yes	Yes	Yes
SQL Server 2005/2008	Yes	No	Yes
Kernel	No	Yes	Yes
Any other RM	No	No	Yes

 With an Oracle database, ODP.NET Release 10.2.0.3 can support a local LTM transaction only or a distributed DTC transaction only, but cannot promote from the LTM to the DTC. An LTM transaction encountering a promotion event is not promoted to the DTC, but rather aborts with an exception. A transaction can also be configured to always start as a DTC transaction.

The Transaction Class

The Transaction class from the System.Transactions namespace, introduced in .NET 2.0, represents the transaction that all WCF transaction managers work with:

```
[Serializable]
public class Transaction : IDisposable,ISerializable
{
    public static Transaction Current
    {get;set;}

    public void Rollback(); //Abort the transaction
    public void Dispose();

    //More members
}
```

Developers rarely need to interact with the Transaction class directly. The main use of the Transaction class is to manually abort a transaction by calling the Rollback() method. Additional features of the Transaction class include enlisting resource managers, setting the isolation level, subscribing to transaction events, cloning the transaction for concurrent threads, and obtaining the transaction status and other information.

The Ambient Transaction

.NET 2.0 defined a concept called the *ambient transaction*, which is the transaction in which your code executes. To obtain a reference to the ambient transaction, call the static Current property of Transaction:

```
Transaction ambientTransaction = Transaction.Current;
```

If there is no ambient transaction, Current will return null. Every piece of code, be it client or service, can always reach out for its ambient transaction. The ambient transaction object is stored in the thread local storage (TLS). As a result, when the thread winds its way across multiple objects and methods on the same call chain, all objects and methods can access their ambient transactions.

In the context of WCF, the ambient transaction is paramount. When present, any WCF resource manager will automatically enlist in the ambient transaction. When a client calls a WCF service, if the client has an ambient transaction and the binding and the contract are configured to allow transaction flow, the ambient transaction will propagate to the service.

 The client cannot propagate an already aborted transaction to the service. Doing so will yield an exception.

Local Versus Distributed Transactions

The Transaction class is used both for local and distributed transactions. Each transaction object has two identifiers used to identify the local and the distributed transaction. You obtain the transaction identifiers by accessing the TransactionInformation property of the Transaction class:

```
[Serializable]
public class Transaction : IDisposable,ISerializable
{
   public TransactionInformation TransactionInformation
   {get;}
   //More members
}
```

The `TransactionInformation` property is of the type `TransactionInformation`, defined as:

```
public class TransactionInformation
{
   public Guid DistributedIdentifier
   {get;}
   public string LocalIdentifier
   {get;}
   //More members
}
```

`TransactionInformation` offers access to the two identifiers. The main use of these identifiers is for logging, tracing, and analysis. In this chapter, I will use the identifiers as a convenient way to demonstrate transaction flow in code as a result of configuration.

The local transaction identifier

The *local transaction identifier* (local ID) contains both an identifier for the LTM in the current app domain as well as an ordinal number enumerating the transaction. You access the local ID via the `LocalIdentifier` property of `TransactionInformation`. The local ID is always available with the ambient transaction, and as such is never null: as long as there is an ambient transaction, it will have a valid local ID.

The value of the local ID has two parts: a constant GUID that is unique for each app domain and represents the assigned LTM for that app domain, and an incremented integer enumerating the transactions managed so far by that LTM.

For example, if a service traces three consecutive transactions, starting with the first call, it will get something like this:

```
8947aec9-1fac-42bb-8de7-60df836e00d6:1
8947aec9-1fac-42bb-8de7-60df836e00d6:2
8947aec9-1fac-42bb-8de7-60df836e00d6:3
```

The GUID is constant per app domain. If the service is hosted in the same app domain as the client, they will have the same GUID. If the client makes a cross-app domain call, the client will have its own unique GUID identifying its own local LTM.

The distributed transaction identifier

The *distributed transaction identifier* (distributed ID) is generated automatically whenever an LTM- or KTM-managed transaction is promoted to a DTC-managed transaction (for example, when the ambient transaction flows to another service). You access the distributed ID via the `DistributedIdentifier` property of `TransactionInformation`. The distributed ID is unique per transaction, and no two transactions will ever have the same distributed ID. Most importantly, the distributed ID will be uniform across the service boundaries and across the entire call chain, from the topmost client through every service and object down the call chain. As such, it is useful in logging and tracing. Note that for a transaction that has not yet been promoted, the value of the distributed ID will be `Guid.Empty`. The distributed ID is usually `Guid.Empty` on the client side when the client is the root of the transaction and it has not yet called a service, and on the service side it will be empty if the service does not use the client's transaction and instead starts its own local transaction.

Transactional Service Programming

For services, WCF offers a simple and elegant declarative programming model. This model is, however, unavailable for non-service code called by services and for non-service WCF clients.

Setting the Ambient Transaction

By default, the service class and all its operations have no ambient transaction. This is the case even when the client's transaction is propagated to the service. Consider the following service:

```
[ServiceContract]
interface IMyContract
{
   [OperationContract]
   [TransactionFlow(TransactionFlowOption.Mandatory)]
   void MyMethod();
}
class MyService : IMyContract
{
   public void MyMethod()
   {
      Transaction transaction = Transaction.Current;
      Debug.Assert(transaction == null);
   }
}
```

The ambient transaction of the service will be `null`, even though the mandatory transaction flow guarantees the client's transaction propagation. To have an ambient transaction, for each contract method the service must indicate that it wants WCF to scope the body of the method with a transaction. For that purpose, WCF provides the `TransactionScopeRequired` property of the `OperationBehaviorAttribute`:

```
[AttributeUsage(AttributeTargets.Method)]
public sealed class OperationBehaviorAttribute : Attribute,...
```

```
{
    public bool TransactionScopeRequired
    {get;set;}
    //More members
}
```

The default value of `TransactionScopeRequired` is `false`, which is why by default the service has no ambient transaction. Setting `TransactionScopeRequired` to `true` provides the operation with an ambient transaction:

```
class MyService : IMyContract
{
    [OperationBehavior(TransactionScopeRequired = true)]
    public void MyMethod()
    {
        Transaction transaction = Transaction.Current;
        Debug.Assert(transaction != null);
    }
}
```

If the client's transaction is propagated to the service, WCF will set the client's transaction as the operation's ambient transaction. If not, WCF will create a new transaction for that operation and set the new transaction as the ambient transaction.

 The service class constructor does not have a transaction: it can never participate in the client's transaction, and you cannot ask WCF to scope it with a transaction. Unless you manually create a new ambient transaction (as shown later), do not perform transactional work in the service constructor and never expect to participate in the transaction of the client that created the instance inside the constructor.

Figure 7-6 demonstrates which transaction a WCF service uses as a product of the binding configuration, the contract operation, and the local operation behavior attribute.

In the figure, a nontransactional client calls Service 1. The operation contract is configured with `TransactionFlowOption.Allowed`. Even though transaction flow is enabled in the binding, since the client has no transaction, no transaction is propagated. The operation behavior on Service 1 is configured to require a transaction scope. As a result, WCF creates a new transaction for Service 1 (Transaction A in Figure 7-6). Service 1 then calls three other services, each configured differently. The binding used for Service 2 has transaction flow enabled, and the operation contract mandates the flow of the client transaction. Since the operation behavior is configured to require transaction scope, WCF sets Transaction A as the ambient transaction for Service 2. The call to Service 3 has the binding and the operation contract disallow transaction flow. However, since Service 3 has its operation behavior require a transaction scope, WCF creates a new transaction for Service 3 (Transaction B) and sets it as the ambient transaction for Service 3. Similar to Service 3, the call to Service 4 has the binding and the operation contract disallow transaction flow. But since Service 4 does not require a transaction scope, it has no ambient transaction.

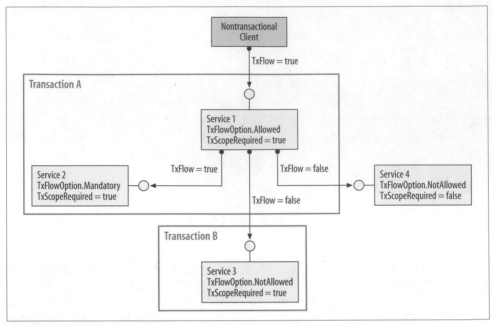

Figure 7-6. Transaction propagation as the product of contract, binding, and operation behavior

Transaction Propagation Modes

Which transaction the service uses is determined by the flow property of the binding (two values), the flow option in the operation contract (three values), and the value of the transaction scope property in the operation behavior (two values). There are therefore 12 possible configuration settings. Out of these 12, 4 are inconsistent and are precluded by WCF (such as flow disabled in the binding, yet mandatory flow in the operation contract) or are just plain impractical or inconsistent. Table 7-2 lists the remaining eight permutations.[*]

Table 7-2. Transaction modes as the product of binding, contract, and behavior

Binding transaction flow	TransactionFlowOption	TransactionScopeRequired	Transaction mode
False	Allowed	False	None
False	Allowed	True	Service
False	NotAllowed	False	None
False	NotAllowed	True	Service
True	Allowed	False	None
True	Allowed	True	Client/Service

[*] I first presented my designation of transaction propagation modes in the article "WCF Transaction Propagation" (*MSDN Magazine*, May 2007).

Binding transaction flow	TransactionFlowOption	TransactionScopeRequired	Transaction mode
True	Mandatory	False	None
True	Mandatory	True	Client

Those eight permutations actually result in only four transaction propagation modes. I call these four modes *Client/Service*, *Client*, *Service*, and *None*. Table 7-2 also shows in bold font the recommended way to configure each mode. Each of these modes has its place in designing your application, and understanding how to select the correct mode is not only a key to sound design, but also greatly simplifies thinking about and configuring transaction support.

Client/Service transaction mode

The Client/Service mode, as its name implies, ensures the service uses the client's transaction if possible, or a service-side transaction when the client does not have a transaction. To configure this mode:

1. Select a transactional binding and enable transaction flow by setting `TransactionFlow` to true.

2. Set the transaction flow option in the operation contract to `TransactionFlowOption.Allowed`.

3. Set the `TransactionScopeRequired` property of the operation behavior to true.

The Client/Service mode is the most decoupled configuration, because in this mode the service minimizes its assumptions about what the client is doing. The service will join the client's transaction if the client has a transaction to flow, which is always good for overall system consistency: if the service has a transaction separate from that of the client, one of those transactions could commit while the other aborts, leaving the system in an inconsistent state. However, if the service joins the client's transaction, all the work done by the client and the service (and potentially other services the client calls) will be committed or aborted as one atomic operation. If the client does not have a transaction, the service still requires the protection of a transaction, so this mode provides a contingent transaction to the service by making it the root of a new transaction.

Example 7-2 shows a service configured for the Client/Service transaction mode.

Example 7-2. Configuring for the Client/Service transaction mode

```
[ServiceContract]
interface IMyContract
{
   [OperationContract]
   [TransactionFlow(TransactionFlowOption.Allowed)]
   void MyMethod();
}
```

Example 7-2. Configuring for the Client/Service transaction mode (continued)

```
class MyService : IMyContract
{
   [OperationBehavior(TransactionScopeRequired = true)]
   public void MyMethod( )
   {
      Transaction transaction = Transaction.Current;
      Debug.Assert(transaction != null);
   }
}
```

Note in Example 7-2 that the service can assert that it always has a transaction, but it cannot assume or assert whether it is the client's transaction or a locally created one. The Client/Service mode is applicable when the service can be used standalone or as part of a bigger transaction. When you select this mode, you should be mindful of potential deadlocks—if the resulting transaction is a service-side transaction, it may deadlock with other transactions trying to access the same resources, because the resources will isolate access per transaction and the service-side transaction will be a new transaction. When you use the Client/Service mode, the service may or may not be the root of the transaction, and the service must not behave differently when it is the root and when it is joining the client's transaction.

Requiring transaction flow

The Client/Service mode requires the use of a transaction-aware binding with transaction flow enabled, but this is not enforced by WCF at service load time. To tighten this loose screw, you can use my BindingRequirementAttribute:

```
[AttributeUsage(AttributeTargets.Class)]
public class BindingRequirementAttribute : Attribute,IServiceBehavior
{
   public bool TransactionFlowEnabled //Default is false
   {get;set;}
   //More members
}
```

You apply the attribute directly on the service class. The default of TransactionFlowEnabled is false. However, when you set it to true, per endpoint, if the contract of the endpoint has at least one operation with the TransactionFlow attribute configured with TransactionFlowOption.Allowed, the BindingRequirement attribute will enforce that the endpoint uses a transaction-aware binding with the TransactionFlowEnabled property set to true:

```
[ServiceContract]
interface IMyContract
{
   [OperationContract]
   [TransactionFlow(TransactionFlowOption.Allowed)]
   void MyMethod( );
}
```

```
[BindingRequirement(TransactionFlowEnabled = true)]
class MyService : IMyContract
{...}
```

To enforce the binding requirement, in the case of a mismatch an InvalidOperationException is thrown when the host is launched. Example 7-3 shows a somewhat simplified implementation of the BindingRequirement attribute.

Example 7-3. BindingRequirement attribute implementation

```
[AttributeUsage(AttributeTargets.Class)]
public class BindingRequirementAttribute : Attribute,IServiceBehavior
{
   public bool TransactionFlowEnabled
   {get;set;}

   void IServiceBehavior.Validate(ServiceDescription description,
                                  ServiceHostBase host)
   {
      if(TransactionFlowEnabled == false)
      {
         return;
      }
      foreach(ServiceEndpoint endpoint in description.Endpoints)
      {
         foreach(OperationDescription operation in endpoint.Contract.Operations)
         {
           TransactionFlowAttribute attribute =
                           operation.Behaviors.Find<TransactionFlowAttribute>();
            if(attribute != null)
            {
               if(attribute.Transactions == TransactionFlowOption.Allowed)
               {
                  if(endpoint.Binding is NetTcpBinding)
                  {
                     NetTcpBinding tcpBinding = endpoint.Binding as NetTcpBinding;
                     if(tcpBinding.TransactionFlow == false)
                     {
                        throw new InvalidOperationException(...);
                     }
                     continue;
                  }
                  ... //Similar checks for the rest of the transaction-aware
                      //bindings

                  throw new InvalidOperationException(...);
               }
            }
         }
      }
   }
   void IServiceBehavior.AddBindingParameters(...)
   {}
```

Example 7-3. BindingRequirement attribute implementation (continued)

```
    void IServiceBehavior.ApplyDispatchBehavior(...)
    {}
}
```

The `BindingRequirementAttribute` class is a service behavior, so it supports the `IServiceBehavior` interface introduced in Chapter 6. The `Validate()` method of `IServiceBehavior` is called during the host launch time, enabling you to abort the service load sequence. The first thing `Validate()` does is to check whether the `TransactionFlowEnabled` property is set to `false`. If so, `Validate()` does nothing and returns. If `TransactionFlowEnabled` is true, `Validate()` iterates over the collection of service endpoints available in the service description. For each endpoint, it obtains the collection of operations, and for each operation, it accesses its collection of operation behaviors. All operation behaviors implement the `IOperationBehavior` interface, including the `TransactionFlowAttribute`. If the `TransactionFlowAttribute` behavior is found, `Validate()` checks whether the attribute is configured with `TransactionFlowOption.Allowed`. If so, `Validate()` checks the binding. For each transaction-aware binding, it verifies that the `TransactionFlow` property is set to `true`, and if not, it throws an `InvalidOperationException`. `Validate()` also throws an `InvalidOperationException` if a nontransactional binding is used for the endpoint.

 The technique shown in Example 7-3 for implementing the `BindingRequirement` attribute is a general-purpose technique you can use to enforce any binding requirement or custom validation rule. For example, the `BindingRequirement` attribute has another property, called `WCFOnly`, that enforces the use of WCF-to-WCF bindings only, and a `ReliabilityRequired` property that insists on the use of a reliable binding with reliability enabled:

```
[AttributeUsage(AttributeTargets.Class)]
public class BindingRequirementAttribute :
                            Attribute,IServiceBehavior
{
    public bool ReliabilityRequired
    {get;set;}
    public bool TransactionFlowEnabled
    {get;set;}
    public bool WCFOnly
    {get;set;}
}
```

Client transaction mode

The Client mode ensures the service uses only the client's transaction. To configure this mode:

---

1. Select a transactional binding and enable transaction flow by setting TransactionFlow to true.
2. Set the transaction flow option in the operation contract to TransactionFlowOption.Mandatory.
3. Set the TransactionScopeRequired property of the operation behavior to true.

You should select the Client transaction mode when the service must use its client's transactions and can never be used standalone, by design. The main motivation for this is to maximize overall system consistency, since the work of the client and the service is always treated as one atomic operation. Another motivation is that by having the service share the client's transaction you reduce the potential for a deadlock, because all resources accessed will enlist in the same transaction. This means no other transactions will compete for access to the same resources and underlying locks.

Example 7-4 shows a service configured for the Client transaction mode.

Example 7-4. Configuring for the Client transaction mode

```
[ServiceContract]
interface IMyContract
{
   [OperationContract]
   [TransactionFlow(TransactionFlowOption.Mandatory)]
   void MyMethod();
}
class MyService : IMyContract
{
   [OperationBehavior(TransactionScopeRequired = true)]
   public void MyMethod()
   {
      Transaction transaction = Transaction.Current;
      Debug.Assert(transaction.TransactionInformation.
                  DistributedIdentifier != Guid.Empty);
   }
}
```

Note in Example 7-4 that MyMethod() asserts the fact that the ambient transaction is a distributed one, meaning it originated with the client.

Service transaction mode

The Service mode ensures that the service always has a transaction, separate from any transaction its clients may or may not have. The service will always be the root of a new transaction. To configure this mode:

1. You can select any binding. If you select a transaction-aware binding, leave its default value for the `TransactionFlow` property, or explicitly set it to `false`.

2. Do not apply the `TransactionFlow` attribute, or configure it with `TransactionFlowOption.NotAllowed`.

3. Set the `TransactionScopeRequired` property of the operation behavior to `true`.

You should select the Service transaction mode when the service needs to perform transactional work outside the scope of the client's transaction (e.g., when you want to perform some logging or audit operations, or when you want to publish events to subscribers regardless of whether the client's transaction commits or aborts). As an example, consider a logbook service that performs error logging into a database. When an error occurs on the client side, the client will use the logbook service to log it or some other entries. But after it's logged, the error on the client side aborts the client's transaction. If the service were to use the client's transaction, once the client's transaction aborts, the logged error would be discarded from the database, and you would have no trace of it (defeating the purpose of the logging in the first place). Configuring the service to have its own transaction, on the other hand, ensures that the log of the error is committed even when the client's transaction aborts.

The downside, of course, is the potential for jeopardizing the consistency of the system, because the service's transaction could abort while the client's commits. To avoid this pitfall, if the service-side transaction aborts, WCF throws an exception on the calling client side, even if the client was not using transactions or if the binding did not propagate any transaction. I therefore recommend that you only choose the Service mode if you have a supporting heuristic. The heuristic must be that the service's transaction is much more likely to succeed and commit than the client's transaction. In the example of the logging service, this is often the case, because once deterministic logging is in place it will usually work (unlike business transactions, which may fail for a variety of reasons).

In general, you should be extremely careful when using the Service transaction mode, and verify that the two transactions (the client's and the service's) do not jeopardize consistency if one aborts and the other commits. Logging and auditing services are the classic candidates for this mode.

Example 7-5 shows a service configured for the Service transaction mode.

Example 7-5. Configuring for the Service transaction mode

```
[ServiceContract]
interface IMyContract
{
   [OperationContract]
   void MyMethod( );
}
class MyService : IMyContract
{
   [OperationBehavior(TransactionScopeRequired = true)]
   public void MyMethod( )
```

Example 7-5. Configuring for the Service transaction mode (continued)

```
   {
      Transaction transaction = Transaction.Current;
      Debug.Assert(transaction.TransactionInformation.
                   DistributedIdentifier == Guid.Empty);
   }
}
```

Note in Example 7-5 that the service can assert that it actually has a local transaction.

None transaction mode

If the None transaction mode is configured, the service never has a transaction. To configure this mode:

1. You can select any binding. If you select a transaction-aware binding, leave its default value for the TransactionFlow property, or explicitly set it to false.

2. Do not apply the TransactionFlow attribute, or configure it with TransactionFlowOption.NotAllowed.

3. You do not need to set the TransactionScopeRequired property of the operation behavior, but if you do, you should set it to false.

The None transaction mode is useful when the operations performed by the service are nice to have but not essential, and should not abort the client's transaction if they fail. For example, a service that prints a receipt for a money transfer should not be able to abort the client transaction if it fails because the printer is out of paper. Another example where the None mode is useful is when you want to provide some custom behavior, and you need to perform your own programmatic transaction support or manually enlist resources (for example, when calling legacy code, as in Example 7-1). Obviously, there is danger when using the None mode because it can jeopardize the system's consistency. Say the calling client has a transaction and it calls a service configured for the None transaction mode. If the client aborts its transaction, changes made to the system state by the service will not roll back. Another pitfall of this mode is that if a service configured for the None mode calls another service configured for the Client mode, the call will fail because the calling service has no transaction to propagate.

Example 7-6 shows a service configured for the None transaction mode.

Example 7-6. Configuring for the None transaction mode

```
[ServiceContract]
interface IMyContract
{
   [OperationContract]
   void MyMethod( );
}
class MyService : IMyContract
{
```

Example 7-6. Configuring for the None transaction mode (continued)

```
    public void MyMethod( )
    {
        Transaction transaction = Transaction.Current;
        Debug.Assert(transaction == null);
    }
}
```

Note that the service in Example 7-6 can assert that it has no ambient transaction.

The None mode allows you to have a nontransactional service be called by a transactional client. As stated previously, the None mode is typically used for services that perform nice-to-have operations. The problem with this usage is that any exception thrown by the None service will abort the calling client's transaction, which should be avoided for mere nice-to-have operations. The solution is to have the client catch all exceptions from the None service to avoid contaminating the client's transaction. For example, here's how a client could call the service from Example 7-6:

```
    MyContractClient proxy = new MyContractClient( );
    try
    {
        proxy.MyMethod( );
        proxy.Close( );
    }
    catch
    {}
```

You need to encase the call to the None service in a catch statement even when configuring that service's operations as one-way operations, because one-way operations can still throw delivery exceptions.

Choosing a service transaction mode

The Service and None transaction modes are somewhat esoteric. They are useful in the context of the particular scenarios I've mentioned, but in other scenarios they harbor the danger of jeopardizing the system's consistency. You should typically use the Client/Service or Client transaction mode. Choose between these two based on the ability of the service to be used standalone (that is, based on the consistency consequences of using the service in its own transaction, and the potential for a deadlock). Avoid the Service and None modes.

Voting and Completion

Although WCF is responsible for every aspect of transaction propagation and the overall management of the two-phase commit protocol across the resource managers, it does not itself know whether a transaction should commit or abort. WCF simply has no way of knowing whether the changes made to the system state are consistent (that is, if they make sense). Every participating service must vote on the outcome of the transaction and voice an opinion about whether the transaction should commit or abort. In addition, WCF does not know when to start the two-phase commit protocol; that is, when the transaction ends and when all the services are done with their work. That too is something the services (actually, just the root service) need to indicate to WCF. WCF offers two programming models for services to vote on the outcome of the transaction: a declarative model and an explicit model. As you will see, voting is strongly related to completing and ending the transaction.

Declarative voting

WCF can automatically vote on behalf of a service to commit or abort the transaction. Automatic voting is controlled via the Boolean TransactionAutoComplete property of the OperationBehavior attribute:

```
[AttributeUsage(AttributeTargets.Method)]
public sealed class OperationBehaviorAttribute : Attribute,...
{
   public bool TransactionAutoComplete
   {get;set;}
   //More members
}
```

The TransactionAutoComplete property defaults to true, so these two definitions are equivalent:

```
[OperationBehavior(TransactionScopeRequired = true,TransactionAutoComplete = true)]
public void MyMethod( )
{...}

[OperationBehavior (TransactionScopeRequired = true)]
public void MyMethod( )
{...}
```

When this property is set to true, if there were no unhandled exceptions in the operation, WCF will automatically vote to commit the transaction. If there was an unhandled exception, WCF will vote to abort the transaction. Note that even though WCF has to catch the exception in order to abort the transaction, it then rethrows it, allowing it to go up the call chain.

To rely on automatic voting, the service method must have TransactionScopeRequired set to true, because automatic voting only works when it was WCF that set the ambient transaction for the service.

It is very important when TransactionScopeRequired is set to true to avoid catching and handling exceptions and explicitly voiding to abort:

```
//Avoid
[OperationBehavior(TransactionScopeRequired = true)]
public void MyMethod( )
{
   try
   {
      ...
   }
   catch
   {
      Transaction.Current.Rollback( );
   }
}
```

Even though your service catches the exception, the operation will still result in an exception since WCF will throw an exception such as TransactionAbortedException on the client side. WCF does that because your service could be part of a much larger transaction that spans multiple services, machines, and sites. All other parties involved in this transaction are working hard, consuming system resources and locking out other parties, yet it is all in vain because your service has voted to abort, and nobody knows about it. By returning an exception to the client WCF ensures that the exception will abort all objects in its path, eventually reaching the root service or client and terminating the transaction. This will improve throughput and performance. If you want to catch the exception for some local handling such as logging, make sure to rethrow it:

```
[OperationBehavior(TransactionScopeRequired = true)]
public void MyMethod( )
{
   try
   {
      ...
   }
   catch
   {
      /* Some local handling here */
      throw;
   }
}
```

Explicit voting

Explicit voting is required when TransactionAutoComplete is set to false. You can only set TransactionAutoComplete to false when TransactionScopeRequired is set to true.

When declarative voting is disabled, WCF will vote to abort all transactions by default, regardless of exceptions or a lack thereof. You must explicitly vote to commit using the SetTransactionComplete( ) method of the operation context:

```
public sealed class OperationContext : ...
{
   public void SetTransactionComplete( );
   //More members
}
```

Make sure you do not perform any work, especially transactional work, after the call to SetTransactionComplete( ). Calling SetTransactionComplete( ) should be the last line of code in the operation just before it returns:

```
[OperationBehavior(TransactionScopeRequired = true,
                   TransactionAutoComplete = false)]
public void MyMethod( )
{
   /* Do transactional work here, then: */
   OperationContext.Current.SetTransactionComplete( );
}
```

If you try to perform any transactional work (including accessing Transaction. Current) after the call to SetTransactionComplete( ), WCF will throw an InvalidOperationException and abort the transaction.

Not performing any work after SetTransactionComplete( ) ensures that any exception raised before the call to SetTransactionComplete( ) will cause SetTransactionComplete( ) to be skipped, so WCF will default to aborting the transaction. As a result, there is no need to catch the exception, unless you want to do some local handling. As with declarative voting, since the method aborts, WCF will return a TransactionAbortedException to the client. In the interest of readability, if you do catch the exception, make sure to rethrow it:

```
[OperationBehavior(TransactionScopeRequired = true,
                   TransactionAutoComplete = false)]
public void MyMethod( )
{
   try
   {
      /* Do transactional work here, then: */
      OperationContext.Current.SetTransactionComplete( );
   }
   catch
   {
      /* Do some error handling then */
      throw;
   }
}
```

Explicit voting is designed for the case when the vote depends on other information obtained throughout the transaction (besides exceptions and errors). However, for the vast majority of applications and services, you should prefer the simplicity of declarative voting.

 Setting TransactionAutoComplete to false should not be done lightly. In fact, it is only allowed for per-session services with required session mode, because it has drastic effects on the service instance's affinity to a transaction. (In order to obtain information for the vote throughout a transaction, it must be the same transaction and the same instance.) You will see later why, when, and how you can set TransactionAutoComplete to false.

Terminating a transaction

When the transaction ends is determined by who starts it. Consider a client that either does not have a transaction or just does not propagate its transaction to the service. If that client calls a service operation configured with TransactionScopeRequired set to true, that service operation becomes the root of the transaction. The root service can call other services and propagate the transaction to them. The transaction will end once the root operation completes the transaction, which it can do either declaratively by setting TransactionAutoComplete to true, or explicitly by setting it to false and calling SetTransactionComplete( ). This is partly why both TransactionAutoComplete and SetTransactionComplete( ) are named the way they are; they are used for more than just voting; they complete and terminate the transaction for a root service. Note, however, that any of the downstream services called by the root operation can only use them to vote on the transaction, not to complete it. Only the root both votes on and completes the transaction.

When a non-service client starts the transaction, the transaction ends when the client disposes of the transaction object. You will see more on that in the section on explicit transaction programming.

Transaction Isolation

In general, the more isolated transactions are, the more consistent their results will be. The highest degree of isolation is called Serializable. At this level, the results obtained from a set of concurrent transactions are identical to the results that would be obtained by running each transaction serially. To achieve this goal, all the resources a transaction touches must be locked from any other transaction. If other transactions try to access those resources, they are blocked and cannot continue executing until the original transaction commits or aborts.

The isolation level is defined using the IsolationLevel enumeration, found in the System.Transactions namespace:

```
public enum IsolationLevel
{
    Serializable,
    RepeatableRead,
    ReadCommitted,
    ReadUncommitted,
    Snapshot, //Special form of ReadCommitted supported by SQL 2005/2008
    Chaos,    //No isolation whatsoever
    Unspecified
}
```

The difference between the four isolation levels (ReadUncommitted, ReadCommitted, RepeatableRead, and Serializable) is in the way the different levels use read and write locks. A lock can be held only while the transaction is accessing the data in the resource manager, or it can be held until the transaction is committed or aborted: the former is better for throughput; the latter for consistency. The two kinds of locks and the two kinds of operations (read/write) give four basic isolation levels. However, not all resource managers support all levels of isolation, and they may elect to take part in the transaction at a higher level than the one configured for it. Every isolation level apart from Serializable is susceptible to some sort of inconsistency resulting from more than one transaction accessing the same information.

Selecting an isolation level other than Serializable is commonly used for read-intensive systems, and it requires a solid understanding of transaction processing theory and of the semantics of the transaction itself, the concurrency issues involved, and the consequences for system consistency. The reason other isolation levels are available is that a high degree of isolation comes at the expense of overall system throughput, because the resource managers involved have to hold on to both read and write locks for as long as a transaction is in progress, and all other transactions are blocked. However, there are some situations where you may be willing to trade system consistency for throughput by lowering the isolation level. Imagine, for example, a banking system where one of the requirements is to retrieve the total amount of money in all customer accounts combined. Although it would be possible to execute that transaction with the Serializable isolation level, if the bank has hundreds of thousands of accounts, it might take quite a while to complete. The transaction might also time out and abort, because some accounts could be accessed by other transactions at the same time. However, the number of accounts may be a blessing in disguise. On average (statistically speaking), if the transaction is allowed to run at a lower transaction level, it may get the wrong balance for some accounts, but those incorrect balances will tend to cancel each other out. The actual resulting error may be acceptable for the bank's needs.

In WCF, the isolation level is a service behavior, so all service operations use the same configured isolation level. Isolation is configured via the TransactionIsolationLevel property of the ServiceBehavior attribute:

```
[AttributeUsage(AttributeTargets.Class)]
public sealed class ServiceBehaviorAttribute : Attribute,...
{
    public IsolationLevel TransactionIsolationLevel
    {get;set;}
    //More members
}
```

You can only set the TransactionIsolationLevel property if the service has at least one operation configured with TransactionScopeRequired set to true. There is no way to configure the isolation level in the host configuration file.

Isolation and transaction flow

The default value of `TransactionIsolationLevel` is `IsolationLevel.Unspecified`, so these two statements are equivalent:

```
class MyService : IMyContract
{...}

[ServiceBehavior(TransactionIsolationLevel = IsolationLevel.Unspecified)]
class MyService : IMyContract
{...}
```

When a service configured with `IsolationLevel.Unspecified` joins the client transaction, the service will use the client's isolation level. However, if the service specifies an isolation level other than `IsolationLevel.Unspecified`, the client must match that level, and a mismatch will throw an exception.

When the service is the root of the transaction and the service is configured with `IsolationLevel.Unspecified`, WCF will set the isolation level to `IsolationLevel.Serializable`. If the root service provides a level other than `IsolationLevel.Unspecified`, WCF will use that specified level.

Transaction Timeout

The introduction of isolation locks raises the possibility of a deadlock when one transaction tries to access a resource manager owned by another. If a transaction takes a long time to complete, it may be indicative of a transactional deadlock. To address that possibility, the transaction will automatically abort if it takes longer than a predetermined timeout (60 seconds, by default) to complete, even if no exceptions took place. Once it's aborted, any attempt to flow that transaction to a service will result in an exception. The timeout is a service behavior property, and all operations across all endpoints of the service use the same timeout. You configure the timeout by setting the `TransactionTimeout` time-span `string` property of `ServiceBehaviorAttribute`:

```
[AttributeUsage(AttributeTargets.Class)]
public sealed class ServiceBehaviorAttribute : Attribute,...
{
   public string TransactionTimeout
   {get;set;}
   //More members
}
```

For example, you would use the following to configure a 30-second timeout:

```
[ServiceBehavior(TransactionTimeout = "00:00:30")]
class MyService : ...
{...}
```

You can also configure the transaction timeout in the host config file by creating a custom behavior section and referencing it in the service section:

```
<services>
   <service name = "MyService" behaviorConfiguration = "ShortTransactionBehavior">
      ...
   </service>
</services>
<behaviors>
   <serviceBehaviors>
      <behavior name = "ShortTransactionBehavior"
         transactionTimeout = "00:00:30"
      />
   </serviceBehaviors>
</behaviors>
```

The maximum allowed transaction timeout is 10 minutes, and this value will be used even when a larger value is specified. If you want to override the default maximum timeout of 10 minutes and specify, say, 40 minutes, add (or modify) the following in *machine.config*:

```
<configuration>
   <system.transactions>
      <machineSettings maxTimeout = "00:40:00"/>
   </system.transactions>
</configuration>
```

> Setting any value in *machine.config* will affect all applications on the machine.

Configuring such a long timeout is useful mostly for debugging, when you want to try to isolate a problem in your business logic by stepping through your code and you do not want the transaction you're debugging to time out while you figure out the problem. Be extremely careful with using a long timeout in all other cases, because it means there are no safeguards against transaction deadlocks.

You may also want to set the timeout to a value less than the default 60 seconds. You typically do this in two cases. The first is during development, when you want to test the way your application handles aborted transactions. By setting the timeout to a small value (such as one millisecond), you can cause your transactions to fail so you can observe your error-handling code.

The second case where it can be useful to set the transaction timeout to less than the default value is when you have reason to believe that a service is involved in more than its fair share of resource contention, resulting in deadlocks. If you are unable to redesign and redeploy the service, you want to abort the transaction as soon as possible and not wait for the default timeout to expire.

Transaction flow and timeout

When a transaction flows into a service that is configured with a shorter timeout than that of the incoming transaction, the transaction adopts the service's timeout and the service gets to enforce the shorter timeout. This behavior is designed to support resolving deadlocks in problematic services, as just discussed. When a transaction flows into a service that is configured with a longer timeout than the incoming transaction, the service configuration has no effect.

Explicit Transaction Programming

The transactional programming model described so far can only be used declaratively by transactional services. Non-service clients, nontransactional services, and plain .NET objects called downstream by a service cannot take advantage of it. For all these cases, WCF relies on the transactional infrastructure available with .NET 2.0 in the System.Transactions namespace. You may also rely on System.Transactions even in transactional services, when exploiting some advanced features such as transaction events, cloning, asynchronous commits, and manual transactions. I described the capabilities of System.Transactions in my MSDN whitepaper "Introducing System.Transactions in the .NET Framework 2.0" (published April 2005; updated December 2005). The following sections contain excerpts from that article describing how to use the core aspects of System.Transactions in the context of WCF. Please refer to the whitepaper for detailed discussions of the rest of the features.

The TransactionScope Class

The most common way of using transactions explicitly is via the TransactionScope class:

```
public sealed class TransactionScope : IDisposable
{
   public TransactionScope();
   //Additional constructors

   public void Complete();
   public void Dispose();
}
```

As its name implies, the TransactionScope class is used to scope a code section with a transaction, as demonstrated in Example 7-7.

Example 7-7. Using TransactionScope

```
using(TransactionScope scope = new TransactionScope())
{
   /* Perform transactional work here */

   //No errors - commit transaction
   scope.Complete();
}
```

The scope constructor can create a new LTM transaction and make it the ambient transaction by setting Transaction.Current, or can join an existing ambient transaction. TransactionScope is a disposable object—if the scope creates a new transaction, the transaction will end once the Dispose( ) method is called (this is done at the end of the using statement in Example 7-7). The Dispose( ) method also restores the original ambient transaction (null, in the case of Example 7-7).

Finally, if the TransactionScope object is not used inside a using statement, it will become garbage once the transaction timeout has expired and the transaction is aborted.

TransactionScope voting

The TransactionScope object has no way of knowing whether the transaction should commit or abort. To address this, every TransactionScope object has a consistency bit, which by default is set to false. You can set the consistency bit to true by calling the Complete( ) method. Note that you can only call Complete( ) once; subsequent calls to Complete( ) will raise an InvalidOperationException. This is deliberate, to encourage developers to have no transactional code after the call to Complete( ).

If the transaction ends (due to calling Dispose( ) or garbage collection) and the consistency bit is set to false, the transaction will abort. For example, the following scope object will abort its transaction, because the consistency bit is never changed from its default value:

```
using(TransactionScope scope = new TransactionScope( ))
{}
```

By having the call to Complete( ) as the last action in the scope, you have an automated way for voting to abort in the case of an error: any exception thrown inside the scope will skip over the call to Complete( ), the finally statement in the using statement will dispose of the TransactionScope object, and the transaction will abort. On the other hand, if you do call Complete( ) and the transaction ends with the consistency bit set to true, as in Example 7-7, the transaction will try to commit. Note that after calling Complete( ), you cannot access the ambient transaction, and an attempt to do so will result in an InvalidOperationException. You can access the ambient transaction again (via Transaction.Current) once the scope object has been disposed of.

The fact that the code in the scope called Complete( ) does not guarantee that the transaction will be committed. Even if you call Complete( ) and the scope is disposed of, all that will do is try to commit the transaction. The ultimate success or failure of that attempt depends upon the outcome of the two-phase commit protocol, which may involve multiple resources and services of which your code is unaware. As a result, Dispose( ) will throw a TransactionAbortedException if it fails to commit the transaction. You can catch and handle that exception, perhaps by alerting the user, as shown in Example 7-8.

Example 7-8. TransactionScope and error handling

```
try
{
   using(TransactionScope scope = new TransactionScope())
   {
      /* Perform transactional work here */
      //No errors - commit transaction
      scope.Complete();
   }
}
catch(TransactionAbortedException exception)
{
   Trace.WriteLine(exception.Message);
}
catch //Any other exception took place
{
   Trace.WriteLine("Cannot complete transaction");
   throw;
}
```

Transaction Flow Management

Transaction scopes can nest both directly and indirectly. In Example 7-9, scope2 simply nests directly inside scope1.

Example 7-9. Direct scope nesting

```
using(TransactionScope scope1 = new TransactionScope())
{
   using(TransactionScope scope2 = new TransactionScope())
   {
      scope2.Complete();
   }
   scope1.Complete();
}
```

The scope can also nest indirectly. This happens when you call a method that uses TransactionScope from within a method that uses its own scope, as is the case with the RootMethod() in Example 7-10.

Example 7-10. Indirect scope nesting

```
void RootMethod()
{
   using(TransactionScope scope = new TransactionScope())
   {
      /* Perform transactional work here */
      SomeMethod();
      scope.Complete();
   }
}
```

Example 7-10. Indirect scope nesting (continued)

```
void SomeMethod( )
{
   using(TransactionScope scope = new TransactionScope( ))
   {
      /* Perform transactional work here */
      scope.Complete( );
   }
}
```

A transaction scope can also nest in a service method, as in Example 7-11. The service method may or may not be transactional.

Example 7-11. Scope nesting inside a service method

```
class MyService : IMyContract
{
   [OperationBehavior(TransactionScopeRequired = true)]
   public void MyMethod( )
   {
      using(TransactionScope scope = new TransactionScope( ))
      {
         scope.Complete();
      }
   }
}
```

If the scope creates a new transaction for its use, it is called the *root scope*. Whether or not a scope becomes a root scope depends on the scope configuration and the presence of an ambient transaction. Once a root scope is established, there is an implicit relationship between it and all its nested scopes and any downstream services called.

The TransactionScope class provides several overloaded constructors that accept an enum of the type TransactionScopeOption:

```
public enum TransactionScopeOption
{
   Required,
   RequiresNew,
   Suppress
}
public sealed class TransactionScope : IDisposable
{
   public TransactionScope(TransactionScopeOption scopeOption);
   public TransactionScope(TransactionScopeOption scopeOption,
                           TransactionOptions transactionOptions);
   public TransactionScope(TransactionScopeOption scopeOption,
                           TimeSpan scopeTimeout);
   //Additional constructors and members
}
```

The value of TransactionScopeOption lets you control whether the scope takes part in a transaction and, if so, whether it will join the ambient transaction or will be the root scope of a new transaction.

For example, here is how you specify the value of TransactionScopeOption in the scope's constructor:

```
using(TransactionScope scope = new
                              TransactionScope(TransactionScopeOption.Required))
{...}
```

The default value for the scope option is TransactionScopeOption.Required, meaning this is the value used when you call one of the constructors that does not accept a TransactionScopeOption parameter. So, these two definitions are equivalent:

```
using(TransactionScope scope = new TransactionScope())
{...}

using(TransactionScope scope =
                       new TransactionScope(TransactionScopeOption.Required))
{...}
```

The TransactionScope object determines which transaction to belong to when it is constructed. Once that's been determined, the scope will always belong to that transaction. TransactionScope bases its decision on two factors: whether an ambient transaction is present, and the value of the TransactionScopeOption parameter.

A TransactionScope object has three options:

- Join the ambient transaction
- Be a new scope root (that is, start a new transaction and have that transaction be the new ambient transaction inside its own scope)
- Not take part in a transaction at all

If the scope is configured with TransactionScopeOption.Required and an ambient transaction is present, the scope will join that transaction. If, on the other hand, there is no ambient transaction, the scope will create a new transaction and become the root scope.

If the scope is configured with TransactionScopeOption.RequiresNew, it will always be a root scope. It will start a new transaction, and its transaction will be the new ambient transaction inside the scope.

If the scope is configured with TransactionScopeOption.Suppress, it will never be part of a transaction, regardless of whether an ambient transaction is present. A scope configured with TransactionScopeOption.Suppress will always have null as its ambient transaction.

Voting inside a nested scope

It is important to realize that although a nested scope can join the ambient transaction of its parent scope, the two scope objects will have two distinct consistency bits. Calling Complete( ) in the nested scope has no effect on the parent scope:

```
using(TransactionScope scope1 = new TransactionScope())
{
   using(TransactionScope scope2 = new TransactionScope())
   {
      scope2.Complete();
   }
   //scope1's consistency bit is still false
}
```

Only if all the scopes, from the root scope down to the last nested scope, vote to commit the transaction will the transaction commit. In addition, only the root scope dictates the life span of the transaction. When a TransactionScope object joins an ambient transaction, disposing of that scope does not end the transaction. The transaction ends only when the root scope is disposed of, or when the service method that started the transaction returns.

TransactionScopeOption.Required

TransactionScopeOption.Required is not just the most commonly used value; it is also the most decoupled value. If your scope has an ambient transaction, the scope will join that ambient transaction to improve consistency. If there is no ambient transaction to join, the scope will provide the code with a new ambient transaction. When TransactionScopeOption.Required is used, the code inside the TransactionScope must not behave differently when it is the root and when it is just joining the ambient transaction. It should operate identically in both cases. On the service side, the most common use for TransactionScopeOption.Required is by non-service downstream classes called by the service, as shown in Example 7-12.

Example 7-12. Using TransactionScopeOption.Required in a downstream class

```
class MyService : IMyContract
{
   [OperationBehavior(TransactionScopeRequired = true)]
   public void MyMethod()
   {
      MyClass obj = new MyClass();
      obj.SomeMethod();
   }
}
class MyClass
{
   public void SomeMethod()
   {
```

```
    using(TransactionScope scope = new TransactionScope())
    {
        //Do some work then
        scope.Complete();
    }
  }
}
```

While the service itself can use `TransactionScopeOption.Required` directly, such a practice adds no value:

```
class MyService : IMyContract
{
    [OperationBehavior(TransactionScopeRequired = true)]
    public void MyMethod()
    {
        //One transaction only
        using(TransactionScope scope = new TransactionScope())
        {
            //Do some work then
            scope.Complete();
        }
    }
}
```

The reason is obvious: the service can simply ask WCF to scope the operation with a transaction scope by setting `TransactionScopeRequired` to true (this is also the origin of that property's name). Note that even though the service may use declarative voting, any downstream (or directly nested) scope must still explicitly call `Complete()` in order for the transaction to commit. The same is true when the service method uses explicit voting:

```
[OperationBehavior(TransactionScopeRequired = true,
                   TransactionAutoComplete = false)]
public void MyMethod()
{
    using(TransactionScope scope = new TransactionScope())
    {
        //Do some work then
        scope.Complete();
    }
    /* Do transactional work here, then: */
    OperationContext.Current.SetTransactionComplete();
}
```

In short, voting to abort in a scope with `TransactionScopeRequired` nested in a service call will abort the service's transaction regardless of exceptions or the use of declarative voting (via `TransactionAutoComplete`) or explicit voting by the service (via `SetTransactionComplete()`).

TransactionScopeOption.RequiresNew

Configuring the scope with TransactionScopeOption.RequiresNew is useful when you want to perform transactional work outside the scope of the ambient transaction (for example, when you want to perform some logging or audit operations, or when you want to publish events to subscribers, regardless of whether your ambient transaction commits or aborts):

```
class MyService : IMyContract
{
    [OperationBehavior(TransactionScopeRequired = true)]
    public void MyMethod( )
    {
        //Two distinct transactions
        using(TransactionScope scope =
                        new TransactionScope(TransactionScopeOption.RequiresNew))
        {
            //Do some work then
            scope.Complete( );
        }
    }
}
```

Note that you must complete the scope in order for the new transaction to commit. You may also want to consider encasing a scope that uses TransactionScopeOption.RequiresNew in a try and catch statement to isolate it from the service's ambient transaction.

You should be extremely careful when using TransactionScopeOption.RequiresNew, and verify that the two transactions (the ambient transaction and the one created for your scope) do not jeopardize consistency if one aborts and the other commits.

TransactionScopeOption.Suppress

TransactionScopeOption.Suppress is useful for both the client and the service when the operations performed by the code section are nice to have but should not cause the ambient transaction to abort in the event that they fail. TransactionScopeOption.Suppress allows you to have a nontransactional code section inside a transactional scope or service operation, as shown in Example 7-13.

Example 7-13. Using TransactionScopeOption.Suppress

```
[OperationBehavior(TransactionScopeRequired = true)]
public void MyMethod( )
{
    try
    {
        //Start of nontransactional section
        using(TransactionScope scope =
                        new TransactionScope(TransactionScopeOption.Suppress))
        {
```

Example 7-13. Using TransactionScopeOption.Suppress (continued)

```
            //Do nontransactional work here
        } //Restores ambient transaction here
    }
    catch
    {}
}
```

Note in Example 7-13 that there is no need to call Complete( ) on the suppressed scope. Another example where TransactionScopeOption.Suppress is useful is when you want to provide some custom behavior and you need to perform your own programmatic transaction support or manually enlist resources.

That said, you should be careful when mixing transactional scopes or service methods with nontransactional scopes. That can jeopardize isolation and consistency, because changes made to the system state inside the suppressed scope will not roll back along with the containing ambient transaction. In addition, the nontransactional scope may have errors, but those errors should not affect the outcome of the ambient transaction. This is why, in Example 7-13, the suppressed scope is encased in a try and catch statement that also suppresses any exception coming out of it.

 Do not call a service configured for the Client transaction mode (basically, with mandatory transaction flow) inside a suppressed scope, because that call is guaranteed to fail.

TransactionScope timeout

If the code inside the transactional scope takes a long time to complete, it may be indicative of a transactional deadlock. To address that possibility, the transaction will automatically abort if it takes longer than a predetermined timeout to complete (60 seconds, by default). You can configure the default timeout in the application config file. For example, to configure a default timeout of 30 seconds, add this to the config file:

```
<system.transactions>
    <defaultSettings timeout = "00:00:30"/>
</system.transactions>
```

Placing the new default in the application config file affects all scopes used by all clients and services in that application. You can also configure a timeout for a specific transaction scope. A few of the overloaded constructors of TransactionScope accept a value of type TimeSpan, used to control the timeout of the transaction. For example:

```
public TransactionScope(TransactionScopeOption scopeOption,
                        TimeSpan scopeTimeout);
```

To specify a timeout different from the default of 60 seconds, simply pass in the desired value:

```
TimeSpan timeout = TimeSpan.FromSeconds(30);
using(TransactionScope scope =
                new TransactionScope(TransactionScopeOption.Required,timeout))
{...}
```

When a TransactionScope joins the ambient transaction, if it specifies a shorter time-out than the one the ambient transaction is set to, it has the effect of enforcing the new, shorter timeout on the ambient transaction; the transaction must end within the nested time specified, or it is automatically aborted. If the scope's timeout is greater than that of the ambient transaction, it has no effect.

TransactionScope isolation level

If the scope is a root scope, by default the transaction will execute with the isolation level set to Serializable. Some of the overloaded constructors of TransactionScope accept a structure of the type TransactionOptions, defined as:

```
public struct TransactionOptions
{
   public IsolationLevel IsolationLevel
   {get;set;}
   public TimeSpan Timeout
   {get;set;}
   //Other members
}
```

Although you can use the TransactionOptions Timeout property to specify a timeout, the main use for TransactionOptions is for specifying the isolation level. You can assign into the TransactionOptions IsolationLevel property a value of the enum type IsolationLevel presented earlier:

```
TransactionOptions options = new TransactionOptions();
options.IsolationLevel = IsolationLevel.ReadCommitted;
options.Timeout = TransactionManager.DefaultTimeout;

using(TransactionScope scope =
                new TransactionScope(TransactionScopeOption.Required,options))
{...}
```

When a scope joins an ambient transaction, it must be configured to use exactly the same isolation level as the ambient transaction; otherwise, an ArgumentException is thrown.

Non-Service Clients

Although services can take advantage of TransactionScope, by far its primary use is by non-service clients. Using a transaction scope is practically the only way a non-service client can group multiple service calls into single transaction, as shown in Figure 7-7.

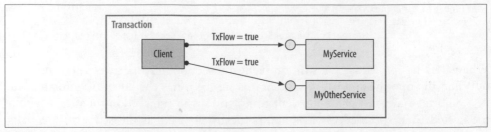

Figure 7-7. A non-service client using a single transaction to call multiple services

Having the option to create a root transaction scope enables the client to flow its transaction to services and to manage and commit the transaction based on the aggregated result of the services, as shown in Example 7-14.

Example 7-14. Using TransactionScope to call services in a single transaction

```
///////////////////////// Service Side /////////////////////////
[ServiceContract]
interface IMyContract
{
   [OperationContract]
   [TransactionFlow(TransactionFlowOption.Allowed)]
   void MyMethod( );
}
[ServiceContract]
interface IMyOtherContract
{
   [OperationContract]
   [TransactionFlow(TransactionFlowOption.Mandatory)]
   void MyOtherMethod( );
}
class MyService : IMyContract
{
   [OperationBehavior(TransactionScopeRequired = true)]
   public void MyMethod( )
   {...}
}
class MyOtherService : IMyOtherContract
{
   [OperationBehavior(TransactionScopeRequired = true)]
   public void MyOtherMethod( )
   {...}
}
///////////////////////// Client Side /////////////////////////
using(TransactionScope scope = new TransactionScope( ))
{
   MyContractClient proxy1 = new MyContractClient( );
   proxy1.MyMethod( );
   proxy1.Close( );
```

```
    MyOtherContractClient proxy2 = new MyOtherContractClient( );
    proxy2.MyOtherMethod( );
    proxy2.Close( );

    scope.Complete( );
}

//Can combine in single using block:
using(MyContractClient proxy3 = new MyContractClient( ))
using(MyOtherContractClient proxy4 = new MyOtherContractClient( ))
using(TransactionScope scope = new TransactionScope( ))
{
    proxy3.MyMethod( );
    proxy4.MyOtherMethod( );
    scope.Complete( );
}
```

Service State Management

The sole purpose of transactional programming is to address the recovery challenge by always leaving the system in a consistent state. The state of the system consists of all the resources that were involved in the transaction, plus the in-memory clients and service instances. Besides benefits such as auto-enlistment and participation in the two-phase commit protocol, the basic and obvious advantage of using a resource manager is that any change made to its state during a transaction will automatically roll back if the transaction aborts. This, however, is not true when it comes to the in-memory instance members and static members of the participating services, which means that if the transaction aborts the system will not be left in a consistent state. The problem is compounded by the fact that any transaction a service participates in may span multiple services, machines, and sites. Even if that service instance encounters no errors and votes to commit the transaction, other parties across the service boundary may eventually abort the transaction. If the service were to simply store its state in memory, how would it know about the outcome of the transaction so that it would somehow manually roll back the changes it had made to its state?

The solution to this instance state management problem is to develop the service as a state-aware service and proactively manage its state. As explained in Chapter 4, a state-aware service is not the same as a stateless service. If the service were truly stateless, there would not be any problem with instance state rollback. As long as a transaction is in progress, the service instance is allowed to maintain state in memory. Between transactions, the service should store its state in a resource manager. That state resource manager may be unrelated to any other business-logic-specific resource accessed during the transaction, or it may be one and the same. At the beginning of the transaction, the service should retrieve its state from the resource and, by doing so, enlist the resource in the transaction. At the end of the transaction, the service should save its state back to the resource manager.

The elegant thing about this technique is that it provides for state autorecovery. Any changes made to the instance state will commit or roll back as part of the transaction. If the transaction commits, the next time the service gets its state it will have the new state. If the transaction aborts, the next time it will have its pre-transaction state. Either way, the service will have a consistent state ready to be accessed by a new transaction. To force the service instance to purge all its in-memory state this way, by default, once the transaction completes WCF destroys the service instance, ensuring there are no leftovers in memory that might jeopardize consistency.

The Transaction Boundary

There are two remaining problems when writing transactional state-aware services. The first is how a service can know when transactions start and end, so that it can get and save its state. The service may be part of a much larger transaction that spans multiple services and machines. At any moment between service calls, the transaction might end. Who will call the service, letting it know to save its state? The second problem has to do with isolation. Different clients might call the service concurrently, on different transactions. How can the service isolate changes made to its state by one transaction from another? The service cannot allow cross-transactional calls, because doing so would jeopardize isolation. If the other transaction were to access its state and operate based on its values, that transaction would be contaminated with foul state if the original transaction aborted and the changes rolled back.

The solution to both problems is for the service to equate method boundaries with transaction boundaries. At the beginning of every method call, the service should read its state, and at the end of each method call the service should save its state to the resource manager. Doing so ensures that if a transaction ends between method calls, the service's state will either persist or roll back with it. Because the service equates method boundaries with transaction boundaries, the service instance must also vote on the transaction's outcome at the end of every method call. From the service perspective, the transaction completes once the method returns. This is really why the `TransactionAutoComplete` property is named that instead of something like `TransactionAutoVote`: the service states that, as far as it is concerned, the transaction is complete. If the service is also the root of the transaction, completing it will indeed terminate the transaction.

In addition, reading and storing the state in the resource manager in each method call addresses the isolation challenge, because the service simply lets the resource manager isolate access to the state between concurrent transactions.

Instance Management and Transactions

As hinted previously, the transactional configuration of the service is intimately related to the service instance lifecycle, and it drastically changes the programming model. All transactional services must store their state in a resource manager or managers.

Those resource managers could be volatile or durable, shared between the instances or per instance, and could support multiple services, all according to your design of both the service and its resources.

Volatile Resource Managers

In the article "Volatile Resource Managers in .NET Bring Transactions to the Common Type" (*MSDN Magazine*, May 2005), I presented my technique for implementing a general-purpose volatile resource manager called Transactional<T>:

```
public class Transactional<T> : ...
{
   public Transactional(T value);
   public Transactional();
   public T Value
   {get;set;}
   /* Conversion operators to and from T */
}
```

By specifying any serializable type parameter (such as an int or a string) to Transactional<T>, you turn that type into a full-blown volatile resource manager that auto-enlists in the ambient transaction, participates in the two-phase commit protocol, and isolates the current changes from all other transactions using my original transaction-based lock.

For example, in the following code snippet, the scope is not completed. As a result the transaction aborts, and the values of number and city revert to their pre-transaction state:

```
Transactional<int> number = new Transactional<int>(3);
Transactional<string> city =
                    new Transactional<string>("New York");

using(TransactionScope scope = new TransactionScope())
{
   city.Value = "London";
   number.Value = 4;
   number.Value++;
   Debug.Assert(number.Value == 5);
   Debug.Assert(number == 5);
}
Debug.Assert(number == 3);
Debug.Assert(city == "New York");
```

In addition to Transactional<T>, I have provided a transactional array called TransactionalArray<T>, and transactional versions for all of the collections in System. Collections.Generic, such as TransactionalDictionary<K,T> and TransactionalList<T>. The volatile resource managers (or VRMs, for short) are available with *ServiceModelEx*. Their implementation has nothing to do with WCF, so I chose not to include it in this book. That implementation, however, makes intensive use of some of the more advanced features of C# 2.0, System.Transactions, and .NET system programming, so you may find it of interest on its own merit.

Per-Call Transactional Services

With a per-call service, once the call returns, the instance is destroyed. Therefore, the resource manager used to store the state between calls must be outside the scope of the instance. Because there could be many instances of the same service type accessing the same resource manager, every operation must contain some parameters that allow the service instance to find its state in the resource manager and bind against it. The best approach is to have each operation contain some key as a parameter identifying the state. I call that parameter the *state identifier*. The client must provide the state identifier with every call to the per-call service. Typical state identifiers are account numbers, order numbers, and so on. For example, the client creates a new transactional order-processing object, and on every method call the client must provide the order number as a parameter, in addition to other parameters.

Example 7-15 shows a template for implementing a transactional per-call service.

Example 7-15. Implementing a transactional service

```
[DataContract]
class Param
{...}

[ServiceContract]
interface IMyContract
{
   [OperationContract]
   [TransactionFlow(...)]
   void MyMethod(Param stateIdentifier);
}
[ServiceBehavior(InstanceContextMode = InstanceContextMode.PerCall)]
class MyService : IMyContract,IDisposable
{
   [OperationBehavior(TransactionScopeRequired = true)]
   public void MyMethod(Param stateIdentifier)
   {
      GetState(stateIdentifier);
      DoWork();
      SaveState(stateIdentifier);
   }
   void GetState(Param stateIdentifier)
   {...}
   void DoWork()
   {...}
   void SaveState(Param stateIdentifier)
   {...}
   public void Dispose()
   {...}
}
```

The MyMethod() signature contains a state identifier parameter of the type Param (a pseudotype invented for this example), used to get the state from a resource manager

---

with the GetState( ) helper method. The service instance then performs its work using the DoWork( ) helper method and saves its state back to the resource manager using the SaveState( ) method, specifying its identifier.

Note that not all of the service instance's state can be saved by value to the resource manager. If the state contains references to other objects, GetState( ) should create those objects, and SaveState( ) (or Dispose( )) should dispose of them.

Because the service instance goes through the trouble of retrieving its state and saving it on every method call, transactional programming is natural for per-call services. The behavioral requirements for a state-aware transactional object and a per-call object are the same: both retrieve and save their state at the method boundaries. Compare Example 7-15 with Example 4-3. The only difference is that the state store used by the service in Example 7-15 should be transactional.

A far as a per-call service call is concerned, transactional programming is almost incidental. Every call on the service gets a new instance, and that call may or may not be in the same transaction as the previous call (see Figure 7-8).

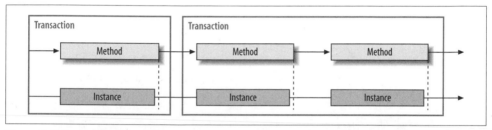

Figure 7-8. Per-call service and transactions

Regardless of transactions, in every call the service gets its state from a resource manager and then saves it back, so the methods are always guaranteed to operate either on consistent state from the previous transaction or on the temporary yet well-isolated state of the current transaction in progress. A per-call service must vote and complete its transaction in every method call. In fact, a per-call service must always use auto-completion (i.e., have TransactionAutoComplete set to its default value, true).

From the client's perspective, the same service proxy can participate in multiple transactions or in the same transaction. For example, in the following code snippet, every call will be in a different transaction:

```
MyContractClient proxy = new MyContractClient();

using(TransactionScope scope = new TransactionScope())
{
   proxy.MyMethod(...);
   scope.Complete();
}
```

```
using(TransactionScope scope = new TransactionScope())
{
   proxy.MyMethod(...);
   scope.Complete();
}

proxy.Close();
```

Or, the client can use the same proxy multiple times in the same transaction, and even close the proxy independently of any transactions:

```
MyContractClient proxy = new MyContractClient();
using(TransactionScope scope = new TransactionScope())
{
   proxy.MyMethod(...);
   proxy.MyMethod(...);
   scope.Complete();
}
proxy.Close();
```

 The call to Dispose() on a per-call service has no ambient transaction.

With a per-call service, any resource manager can be used to store the service state. For example, you might use a database, or you might use volatile resource managers accessed as static member variables, as shown in Example 7-16.

Example 7-16. Per-call service using a VRM

```
[ServiceContract]
interface ICounterManager
{
   [OperationContract]
   [TransactionFlow(...)]
   void Increment(string stateIdentifier);
}
[ServiceBehavior(InstanceContextMode = InstanceContextMode.PerCall)]
class MyService : ICounterManager
{
   static TransactionalDictionary<string,int> m_StateStore =
                                  new TransactionalDictionary<string,int>();

   [OperationBehavior(TransactionScopeRequired = true)]
   public void Increment(string stateIdentifier)
   {
      if(m_StateStore.ContainsKey(stateIdentifier) == false)
      {
         m_StateStore[stateIdentifier] = 0;
      }
      m_StateStore[stateIdentifier]++;
   }
}
```

The transaction lifecycle

When the per-call service is the root of a transaction (that is, when it is configured for the Client/Service transaction mode and there is no client transaction, or when it is configured for the Service transaction mode), the transaction ends once the service instance is deactivated. WCF completes and ends the transaction as soon as the method returns, even before `Dispose()` is called. When the client is the root of the transaction (or whenever the client's transaction flows to the service and the service joins it), the transaction ends when the client's transaction ends.

Per-Session Transactional Services

While it is possible to develop transactional sessionful services with great ease using my volatile resource managers, WCF was designed without them in mind, simply because these technologies evolved more or less concurrently. Consequently, the WCF architects did not trust developers to properly manage the state of their sessionful service in the face of transactions—something that is rather cumbersome and difficult, as you will see, if all you have at your disposal is raw .NET and WCF. The WCF architects made the extremely conservative decision to treat a sessionful transactional service as a per-call service by default in order to enforce a proper state-aware programming model. In fact, the default transaction configuration of WCF will turn any service, regardless of its instancing mode, into a per-call service. This, of course, negates the very need for a per-session service in the first place. That said, WCF does allow you to maintain the session semantic with a transactional service, using several distinct programming models. A per-session transactional service instance can be accessed by multiple transactions, or the instance can establish an affinity to a particular transaction, in which case, until it completes, only that transaction is allowed to access it. However, as you will see, unless you use volatile resource managers this support harbors a disproportional cost in programming model complexity and constraints.

Releasing the service instance

The lifecycle of any transactional service is controlled by the `ServiceBehavior` attribute's Boolean property, `ReleaseServiceInstanceOnTransactionComplete`:

```
[AttributeUsage(AttributeTargets.Class)]
public sealed class ServiceBehaviorAttribute : Attribute,...
{
   public bool ReleaseServiceInstanceOnTransactionComplete
   {get;set;}
   //More members
}
```

When `ReleaseServiceInstanceOnTransactionComplete` is set to true (the default value), it disposes of the service instance once the instance completes the transaction.

WCF uses context deactivation (discussed in Chapter 4) to terminate the sessionful service instance and its in-memory state, while maintaining the transport session and the instance context.

Note that the release takes place once the instance completes the transaction, not necessarily when the transaction really completes (which could be much later). When ReleaseServiceInstanceOnTransactionComplete is true, the instance has two ways of completing the transaction and being released: at the method boundary if the method has TransactionAutoComplete set to true, or when any method that has TransactionAutoComplete set to false calls SetTransactionComplete( ).

ReleaseServiceInstanceOnTransactionComplete has two interesting interactions with other service and operation behavior properties. First, it cannot be set (to either true or false) unless at least one operation on the service has TransactionScopeRequired set to true. This is validated at the service load time by the set accessor of the ReleaseServiceInstanceOnTransactionComplete property.

For example, this is a valid configuration:

```
[ServiceBehavior(ReleaseServiceInstanceOnTransactionComplete = true)]
class MyService : IMyContract
{
    [OperationBehavior(TransactionScopeRequired = true)]
    public void MyMethod( )
    {...}

    [OperationBehavior(...)]
    public void MyOtherMethod( )
    {...}
}
```

What this constraint means is that even though the default of ReleaseServiceInstanceOnTransactionComplete is true, the following two definitions are not semantically equivalent, because the second one will throw an exception at the service load time:

```
class MyService : IMyContract
{
    public void MyMethod( )
    {...}
}

//Invalid definition:
[ServiceBehavior(ReleaseServiceInstanceOnTransactionComplete = true)]
class MyService : IMyContract
{
    public void MyMethod( )
    {...}
}
```

The second constraint involved in using ReleaseServiceInstanceOnTransactionComplete relates to concurrent multithreaded access to the service instance.

Concurrency management is the subject of the next chapter. For now, all you need to know is that the ConcurrencyMode property of the ServiceBehavior attribute controls concurrent access to the service instance:

```
public enum ConcurrencyMode
{
   Single,
   Reentrant,
   Multiple
}

[AttributeUsage(AttributeTargets.Class)]
public sealed class ServiceBehaviorAttribute : ...
{
   public ConcurrencyMode ConcurrencyMode
   {get;set;}
   //More members
}
```

The default value of ConcurrencyMode is ConcurrencyMode.Single.

At the service load time, WCF will verify that, if TransactionScopeRequired is set to true for at least one operation on the service when ReleaseServiceInstanceOnTransactionComplete is true (by default or explicitly), the service concurrency mode is ConcurrencyMode.Single.

For example, given this contract:

```
[ServiceContract]
interface IMyContract
{
   [OperationContract]
   [TransactionFlow(...)]
   void MyMethod();

   [OperationContract]
   [TransactionFlow(...)]
   void MyOtherMethod();
}
```

the following two definitions are equivalent and valid:

```
class MyService : IMyContract
{
   [OperationBehavior(TransactionScopeRequired = true)]
   public void MyMethod()
   {...}

   public void MyOtherMethod()
   {...}
}

[ServiceBehavior(ConcurrencyMode = ConcurrencyMode.Single,
                 ReleaseServiceInstanceOnTransactionComplete = true)]
class MyService : IMyContract
```

```
{
   [OperationBehavior(TransactionScopeRequired = true)]
   public void MyMethod( )
   {...}

   public void MyOtherMethod( )
   {...}
}
```

The following definition is also valid, since no method requires a transaction scope
even though ReleaseServiceInstanceOnTransactionComplete is true:

```
[ServiceBehavior(ConcurrencyMode = ConcurrencyMode.Multiple)]
class MyService : IMyContract
{
   public void MyMethod( )
   {...}

   public void MyOtherMethod( )
   {...}
}
```

In contrast, the following definition is invalid, because at least one method requires a
transaction scope, ReleaseServiceInstanceOnTransactionComplete is true, and yet the
concurrency mode is not ConcurrencyMode.Single:

```
//Invalid configuration:
[ServiceBehavior(ConcurrencyMode = ConcurrencyMode.Multiple)]
class MyService : IMyContract
{
   [OperationBehavior(TransactionScopeRequired = true)]
   public void MyMethod( )
   {...}

   public void MyOtherMethod( )
   {...}
}
```

 The concurrency constraint applies to all instancing modes.

The ReleaseServiceInstanceOnTransactionComplete property can enable a transactional session interaction between the client and the service. With its default value of
true, once the service instance completes the transaction (either declaratively or
explicitly), the return of the method will deactivate the service instance as if it were a
per-call service.

For example, the service in Example 7-17 behaves just like a per-call service.

Example 7-17. Per-session yet per-call transactional service

```
[ServiceContract(SessionMode = SessionMode.Required)]
interface IMyContract
{
   [OperationContract]
   [TransactionFlow(...)]
   void MyMethod( );
}
class MyService : IMyContract
{
   [OperationBehavior(TransactionScopeRequired = true)]
   public void MyMethod( )
   {...}
}
```

Every time the client calls MyMethod( ), the client will get a new service instance. The new client call may come in on a new transaction as well, and the service instance has no affinity to any transaction. The relationship between the service instances and the transactions is just as in Figure 7-8. The service needs to proactively manage its state just as it did in Example 7-15, as demonstrated in Example 7-18.

Example 7-18. Proactive state management by default with a per-session transactional service

```
[DataContract]
class Param
{...}

[ServiceContract(SessionMode = SessionMode.Required)]
interface IMyContract
{
   [OperationContract]
   [TransactionFlow(...)]
   void MyMethod(Param stateIdentifier);
}
class MyService : IMyContract
{
   [OperationBehavior(TransactionScopeRequired = true)]
   public void MyMethod(Param stateIdentifier)
   {
      GetState(stateIdentifier);
      DoWork( );
      SaveState(stateIdentifier);
   }
   void GetState(Param stateIdentifier)
   {...}
   void DoWork( )
   {...}
   void SaveState(Param stateIdentifier)
   {...}
}
```

The transactional per-session service can also, of course, use VRMs, as was done in Example 7-16.

Disabling releasing the service instance

Obviously, a configuration such as that in Examples 7-17 or 7-18 adds no value to configuring the service as sessionful. The client must still pass a state identifier, and the service is de facto a per-class service. To behave as a per-session service, the service can set ReleaseServiceInstanceOnTransactionComplete to false, as in Example 7-19.

Example 7-19. Per-session transactional service

```
[ServiceContract(SessionMode = SessionMode.Required)]
interface IMyContract
{
   [OperationContract]
   [TransactionFlow(...)]
   void MyMethod();
}
[ServiceBehavior(ReleaseServiceInstanceOnTransactionComplete = false)]
class MyService : IMyContract
{
   [OperationBehavior(TransactionScopeRequired = true)]
   public void MyMethod()
   {...}
}
```

When ReleaseServiceInstanceOnTransactionComplete is false, the instance will not be disposed of when transactions complete, as shown in Figure 7-9.

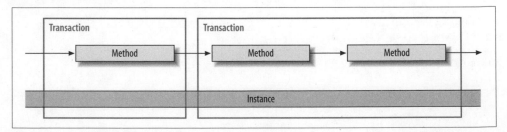

Figure 7-9. Sessionful transactional instance and transactions

The interaction in Figure 7-9 might, for example, be the result of the following client code, where all calls went to the same service instance:

```
MyContractClient proxy = new MyContractClient();
using(TransactionScope scope = new TransactionScope())
{
   proxy.MyMethod();
   scope.Complete();
}
```

```
using(TransactionScope scope = new TransactionScope())
{
   proxy.MyMethod();
   proxy.MyMethod();
   scope.Complete();
}
proxy.Close();
```

State-aware per-session services

When `ReleaseServiceInstanceOnTransactionComplete` is false, WCF will stay out of the way and will let the service developer worry about managing the state of the service instance in the face of transactions. Obviously, you have to somehow monitor transactions and roll back any changes made to the state of the instance if a transaction aborts. The per-session service still must equate method boundaries with transaction boundaries, because every method may be in a different transaction, and a transaction may end between method calls in the same session. There are two possible programming models. The first is to be state-aware, but use the session ID as a state identifier. With this model, at the beginning of every method the service gets its state from a resource manager using the session ID as a key, and at the end of every method the service instance saves the state back to the resource manager, as shown in Example 7-20.

Example 7-20. State-aware, transactional per-session service

```
[ServiceBehavior(ReleaseServiceInstanceOnTransactionComplete = false)]
class MyService : IMyContract,IDisposable
{
   readonly string m_StateIdentifier;

   public MyService()
   {
      InitializeState();
      m_StateIdentifier = OperationContext.Current.SessionId;
      SaveState();
   }
   [OperationBehavior(TransactionScopeRequired = true)]
   public void MyMethod()
   {
      GetState();
      DoWork();
      SaveState();
   }
   public void Dispose()
   {
      RemoveState();
   }

   //Helper methods
```

Example 7-20. State-aware, transactional per-session service (continued)

```
    void InitializeState()
    {...}
    void GetState()
    {
        //Use m_StateIdentifier to get state
        ...
    }
    void DoWork()
    {...}
    void SaveState()
    {
        //Use m_StateIdentifier to save state
        ...
    }
    void RemoveState()
    {
        //Use m_StateIdentifier to remove the state from the RM
        ...
    }
}
```

In Example 7-20, the constructor first initializes the state of the object and then saves the state to a resource manager, so that any method can retrieve it. Note that the per-session object maintains the illusion of a stateful, sessionful interaction with its client. The client does not need to pass an explicit state identifier, but the service must be disciplined and retrieve and save the state in every operation call. When the session ends, the service purges its state from the resource manager in the Dispose() method.

Stateful per-session services

The second, more modern programming model is to use volatile resource managers for the service members, as shown in Example 7-21.

Example 7-21. Using volatile resource managers to achieve a stateful per-session transactional service

```
[ServiceBehavior(ReleaseServiceInstanceOnTransactionComplete = false)]
class MyService : IMyContract
{
    Transactional<string> m_Text = new Transactional<string>("Some initial value");

    TransactionalArray<int> m_Numbers = new TransactionalArray<int>(3);

    [OperationBehavior(TransactionScopeRequired = true)]
    public void MyMethod()
    {
        m_Text.Value = "This value will roll back if the transaction aborts";

        //These will roll back if the transaction aborts
```

```
      m_Numbers[0] = 11;
      m_Numbers[1] = 22;
      m_Numbers[2] = 33;
   }
}
```

Example 7-21 uses my `Transactional<T>` and `TransactionalArray<T>` volatile resource managers. The per-session service can safely set `ReleaseServiceInstanceOnTransactionComplete` to false and yet freely access its members. The use of the volatile resource managers enables a stateful programming model, and the service instance simply accesses its state as if no transactions were involved. The volatile resource managers auto-enlist in the transaction and isolate that transaction from all other transactions. Any changes made to the state will commit or roll back with the transaction.

Transaction lifecycle

When the per-session service is the root of the transaction, the transaction ends once the service completes the transaction, which is when the method returns. When the client is the root of the transaction (or when a transaction flows to the service), the transaction ends when the client's transaction ends. If the per-session service provides an `IDisposable` implementation, the `Dispose()` method will not have any transaction, regardless of the root.

Concurrent transactions

Because a per-session service can engage the same service instance in multiple client calls, it can also sustain multiple concurrent transactions. Given the service definition of Example 7-19, Example 7-22 shows some client code that launches concurrent transactions on the same instance. scope2 will use a new transaction separate from that of scope1, and yet access the same service instance in the same session.

Example 7-22. Launching concurrent transactions

```
using(TransactionScope scope1 = new TransactionScope())
{
   MyContractClient proxy = new MyContractClient();
   proxy.MyMethod();

   using(TransactionScope scope2 =
                     new TransactionScope(TransactionScopeOption.RequiresNew))
   {
      proxy.MyMethod();
      scope2.Complete();
   }
   proxy.MyMethod();
```

Example 7-22. Launching concurrent transactions (continued)

```
    proxy.Close( );
    scope1.Complete( );
}
```

The resulting transactions of Example 7-22 are depicted in Figure 7-10.

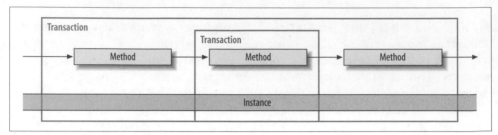

Figure 7-10. Concurrent transactions

 Code such as that in Example 7-22 will almost certainly result in a transactional deadlock over the underlying resources the service accesses. The first transaction will obtain the resource lock, and the second transaction will wait to own that lock while the first transaction waits for the second to complete.

Completing on session end

WCF offers yet another programming model for transactional per-session services, which is completely independent of ReleaseServiceInstanceOnTransactionComplete. This model is available for the case when the entire session fits into a single transaction, and the service equates session boundaries with transaction boundaries. The idea is that the service should not complete the transaction inside the session, because that is what causes WCF to release the service instance. To avoid completing the transaction, a per-session service can set TransactionAutoComplete to false, as shown in Example 7-23.

Example 7-23. Setting TransactionAutoComplete to false

```
[ServiceContract(SessionMode = SessionMode.Required)]
interface IMyContract
{
   [OperationContract]
   [TransactionFlow(...)]
   void MyMethod1( );

   [OperationContract]
   [TransactionFlow(...)]
   void MyMethod2( );
```

Example 7-23. Setting TransactionAutoComplete to false (continued)

```
   [OperationContract]
   [TransactionFlow(...)]
   void MyMethod3( );
}
class MyService : IMyContract
{
   [OperationBehavior(TransactionScopeRequired = true,
                      TransactionAutoComplete = false)]
   public void MyMethod1( )
   {...}

   [OperationBehavior(TransactionScopeRequired = true,
                      TransactionAutoComplete = false)]
   public void MyMethod2( )
   {...}

   [OperationBehavior(TransactionScopeRequired = true,
                      TransactionAutoComplete = false)]
   public void MyMethod3( )
   {...}
}
```

Note that only a per-session service with a contract set to SessionMode.Required can set TransactionAutoComplete to false, and that is verified at the service load time. The problem with Example 7-23 is that the transaction the service participates in will always abort because the service does not vote to commit it by completing it. If the service equates sessions with transactions, the service should vote once the session ends. For that purpose, the ServiceBehavior attribute provides the Boolean property TransactionAutoCompleteOnSessionClose, defined as:

```
   [AttributeUsage(AttributeTargets.Class)]
   public sealed class ServiceBehaviorAttribute : Attribute,...
   {
      public bool TransactionAutoCompleteOnSessionClose
      {get;set;}
      //More members
   }
```

The default of TransactionAutoCompleteOnSessionClose is false. However, when set to true, it will auto-complete all uncompleted methods in the session. If no exceptions occurred during the session, when TransactionAutoCompleteOnSessionClose is true the service will vote to commit. For example, here is how to retrofit Example 7-23:

```
   [ServiceBehavior(TransactionAutoCompleteOnSessionClose = true)]
   class MyService : IMyContract
   {...}
```

Figure 7-11 shows the resulting instance and its session.

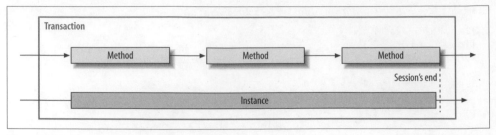

Figure 7-11. Setting TransactionAutoCompleteOnSessionClose to true

During the session, the instance can maintain and access its state in normal member variables, and there is no need for state awareness or volatile resource managers.

 When joining the client's transaction and relying on auto-completion on session close, the service must avoid lengthy processing in Dispose( ) or, in practical terms, avoid implementing IDisposable altogether. The reason is the race condition described here. Recall from Chapter 4 that Dispose( ) is called asynchronously at the end of the session. Auto-completion at session end takes place once the instance has been disposed of. If the client has control before the instance is disposed, the transaction will abort because the service has not yet completed it.

Note that using TransactionAutoCompleteOnSessionClose is risky, because it is always subjected to the transaction timeout. Sessions are by their very nature long-lived entities, while well-designed transactions are short-lived. This programming model is available for the case when the vote decision requires information that will be obtained by future calls throughout the session.

Because having TransactionAutoCompleteOnSessionClose set to true equates the session's end with the transaction's end, it is required that when the client's transaction is used, the client terminates the session within that transaction:

```
using(TransactionScope scope = new TransactionScope( ))
{
    MyContractClient proxy = new MyContractClient( );
    proxy.MyMethod( );
    proxy.MyMethod( );
    proxy.Close( );

    scope.Complete( );
}
```

Failing to do so will abort the transaction. As a side effect, the client cannot easily stack the using statements of the transaction scope and the proxy, because that may cause the proxy to be disposed of after the transaction:

```
//This always aborts:
using(MyContractClient proxy = new MyContractClient( ))
using(TransactionScope scope = new TransactionScope( ))
```

```
    {
        proxy.MyMethod( );
        proxy.MyMethod( );

        scope.Complete( );
    }
```

In addition, because the proxy is basically good for only one-time use, there is little point in storing the proxy in member variables.

Transactional affinity

Setting `TransactionAutoComplete` to `false` has a unique effect that nothing else in WCF provides: it creates an affinity between the service instance context and the transaction, so that only that single transaction can ever access that service instance context. Unless context deactivation is used, this affinity is therefore to the instance as well. The affinity is established once the first transaction accesses the service instance, and once established it is fixed for the life of the instance (until the session ends). Transactional affinity is available only for per-session services, because only a per-session service can set `TransactionAutoComplete` to `false`. Affinity is crucial because the service is not state-aware—it uses normal members, and it must isolate access to them from any other transaction, in case the transaction to which it has an affinity aborts. Affinity thus offers a crude form of transaction-based locking. With transaction affinity, code such as that in Example 7-22 is guaranteed to deadlock (and eventually abort due to timing out) because the second transaction is blocked (independently of any resources the service accesses) waiting for the first transaction to finish, while the first transaction is blocked waiting for the second.

Hybrid state management

WCF also supports a hybrid of two of the sessionful programming models discussed earlier, combining both a state-aware and a regular sessionful transactional per-session service. The hybrid mode is designed to allow the service instance to maintain state in memory until it can complete the transaction, and then recycle that state using `ReleaseServiceInstanceOnTransactionComplete` as soon as possible, instead of delaying completing the transaction until the end of the session. Consider the service in Example 7-24, which implements the contract from Example 7-23.

Example 7-24. Hybrid per-session service

```
[ServiceBehavior(TransactionAutoCompleteOnSessionClose = true)]
class MyService : IMyContract
{
    [OperationBehavior(TransactionScopeRequired = true,
                       TransactionAutoComplete = false)]
    public void MyMethod1( )
    {...}
```

Example 7-24. Hybrid per-session service (continued)

```
    [OperationBehavior(TransactionScopeRequired = true,
                       TransactionAutoComplete = false)]
    public void MyMethod2( )
    {...}
    [OperationBehavior(TransactionScopeRequired = true)]
    public void MyMethod3( )
    {...}
}
```

The service uses the default of ReleaseServiceInstanceOnTransactionComplete (true), yet it has two methods (MyMethod1( ) and MyMethod2( )) that do not complete the transaction with TransactionAutoComplete set to false, resulting in an affinity to a particular transaction. The affinity isolates its members from any other transaction. The problem now is that the transaction will always abort, because the service does not complete it. To compensate for that, the service offers MyMethod3( ), which does complete the transaction. Because the service uses the default of ReleaseServiceInstanceOnTransactionComplete (true), after MyMethod3( ) is called, the transaction is completed and the instance is disposed of, as shown in Figure 7-12. Note that MyMethod3( ) could have instead used explicit voting via SetTransactionComplete( ). The important thing is that it completes the transaction. If the client does not call MyMethod3( ), purely as a contingency, the service in Example 7-24 relies on TransactionAutoCompleteOnSessionClose being set to true to complete and commit the transaction.

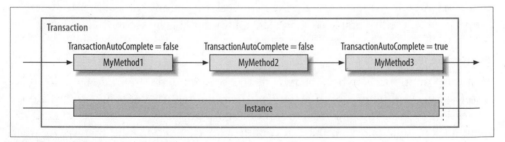

Figure 7-12. Hybrid state management

The hybrid mode is inherently a brittle proposition. The first problem is that the service instance must complete the transaction before it times out, but since there is no telling when the client will call the completing method, you risk timing out before that. In addition, the service holds onto any locks on resource managers it may access for the duration of the session, and the longer the locks are held, the higher the likelihood is of other transactions timing out or deadlocking with this service's transaction. Finally, the service is at the mercy of the client, because the client must call the completing method to end the session. You can and should clearly document the need to call that operation at the end of the transaction:

```
[ServiceContract(SessionMode = SessionMode.Required)]
interface IMyContract
{
   [OperationContract]
   [TransactionFlow(...)]
   void MyMethod1();

   [OperationContract]
   [TransactionFlow(...)]
   void MyMethod2();

   [OperationContract]
   [TransactionFlow(...)]
   void CompleteTransaction();
}
```

Both equating sessions with transactions (while relying solely on TransactionAutoCompleteOnSessionClose) and using the hybrid mode are potential solutions for situations when the transaction execution and subsequent voting decision require information obtained throughout the session. Consider, for example, the following contract used for order processing:

```
[ServiceContract(SessionMode = SessionMode.Required)]
interface IOrderManager
{
   [OperationContract]
   [TransactionFlow(...)]
   void SetCustomerId(int customerId);

   [OperationContract]
   [TransactionFlow(...)]
   void AddItem(int itemId);

   [OperationContract]
   [TransactionFlow(...)]
   bool ProcessOrders();
}
```

The implementing service can only process the order once it has the customer ID and all of the ordered items. However, relying on transactional sessions in this way usually indicates poor design, because of the inferior throughput and scalability implications. Good transactions are inherently short while sessions are inherently long (up to 10 minutes by default), so they are inherently incompatible. The disproportional complexity of prolonging a single transaction across a session outweighs the perceived benefit of using a session. It is usually better to factor the contract so that it provides every operation with all the information it needs to complete and vote:

```
[ServiceContract(SessionMode = ...)]
interface IOrderManager
{
   [OperationContract]
   [TransactionFlow(...)]
   bool ProcessOrders(int customerId,int[] itemIds);
}
```

Done this way, you can either implement the service as per-call or maintain a sessionful programming model, avoid placing operation order constraints on the client, and use any VRMs as member variables and access other transactional resources. You clearly separate the contract from its implementation, both on the client and the service side.

Transactional Durable Services

Recall from Chapter 4 that a durable service retrieves its state from the configured store and then saves its state back into that store on every operation. The state store may or may not be a transactional resource manager. If the service is transactional, it should of course use only a transactional durable storage and enlist it in each operation's transaction. That way, if a transaction aborts, the state store will be rolled back to its pre-transaction state. However, WCF does not know whether a service is designed to propagate its transactions to the state store, and by default it will not enlist the storage in the transaction even if the storage is a transactional resource manager, such as SQL Server 2005/2008. To instruct WCF to propagate the transaction and enlist the underlying storage, set the SaveStateInOperationTransaction property of the DurableService attribute to true:

```
public sealed class DurableServiceAttribute : ...
{
   public bool SaveStateInOperationTransaction
   {get;set;}
}
```

SaveStateInOperationTransaction defaults to false, which means the state storage will not participate in the transaction. It is therefore important to always set SaveStateInOperationTransaction to true to ensure consistent state management in the presence of transactions. Since only a transactional service could benefit from having SaveStateInOperationTransaction set to true, if it is true then WCF will insist that all operations on the service either have TransactionScopeRequired set to true or have mandatory transaction flow. If the operation is configured with TransactionScopeRequired set to true, the ambient transaction of the operation will be the one used to enlist the storage. If the operation is configured for mandatory transaction flow, the client's transaction will be used to enlist the storage (regardless of whether the operation does or does not have an ambient transaction).

Instance ID management

As explained in Chapter 4, the DurableService behavior attribute enforces strict management of the instance ID passed over the context binding. The first operation to start the workflow will have no instance ID, in which case, WCF will create a new instance ID, use it to save the newly created instance state to the storage, and then send the instance ID back to the client. From that point on, until the end of the workflow, the client must pass the same instance ID to the service. If the client provides an instance ID that is not present in the storage, WCF will throw an exception. This presents a potential pitfall with transactional durable services: suppose the client starts a workflow and propagates its transaction to the service. The first operation creates the instance ID, executes successfully, and stores the state in the storage. However, what would happen if the transaction were then to abort, due to some other party (such as the client or another service involved in the transaction) voting to abort? The state storage would roll back the changes made to it, including the newly created instance state and the corresponding ID. The next call coming from the client will present the same ID created by the first call, except now the state storage will not have any record of that ID, so WCF will reject the call, throw an exception, and prevent any other call to the service with that ID from ever executing.

To avoid this pitfall, you need to add to the service contract an explicit first operation whose sole purpose is to guarantee that the first call successfully commits the instance ID to the state storage. For example, in the case of a calculator service, this would be your PowerOn( ) operation. You should explicitly block the client's transaction (by using the default value of TransactionFlowOption.NotAllowed), and avoid placing any code in that method body, thus precluding anything that could go wrong from aborting the transaction. You can enforce having the client call the initiating operation first using demarcating operations (discussed in Chapter 4).

A similar pitfall exists at the end of the workflow. By setting the CompletesInstance property of the DurableOperation attribute to true, you indicate to WCF that the workflow has ended and that WCF should purge the instance state from the storage. However, if the client's transaction aborts after the last operation in the service has executed successfully, the storage will roll back and keep the orphaned state indefinitely. To avoid bloating the state storage with zombie instances (the product of aborted transactions of the completing instance operations), you need to add to the service contract an explicit operation whose sole purpose is to complete the instance and to commit successfully, irrespective of whether the client's transaction commits. For example, in the case of a calculator service, this would be your PowerOff( ) operation. Again, block any client transaction from propagating to the service, and avoid placing any code in the completing method.

Example 7-25 shows a template for defining and implementing a transactional durable service, adhering to these guidelines.

Example 7-25. Transactional durable service

```
[ServiceContract]
interface IMyContract
{
   [OperationContract]
   void SaveState( );

   [OperationContract(IsInitiating = false)]
   void ClearState( );
```

Example 7-25. Transactional durable service (continued)

```
    [OperationContract(IsInitiating = false)]
    [TransactionFlow(...)]
    void MyMethod1();

    [OperationContract(IsInitiating = false)]
    [TransactionFlow(...)]
    void MyMethod2();
}

[Serializable]
[DurableService(SaveStateInOperationTransaction = true)]
class MyService: IMyContract
{
    [OperationBehavior(TransactionScopeRequired = true)]
    public void SaveState()
    {}

    [DurableOperation(CompletesInstance = true)]
    [OperationBehavior(TransactionScopeRequired = true)]
    public void ClearState()
    {}

    [OperationBehavior(TransactionScopeRequired = true)]
    public void MyMethod1()
    {...}
    [OperationBehavior(TransactionScopeRequired = true)]
    public void MyMethod2()
    {...}
}
```

Transactional Behavior*

As far as the DurableService attribute is concerned, the word Durable in its name is a misnomer, since it does not necessarily indicate a durable behavior. All it means is that WCF will automatically deserialize the service state from a configured storage and then serialize it back again on every operation. Similarly, the persistence provider behavior (see Chapter 4) does not necessarily mean persistence, since any provider that derives from the prescribed abstract provider class will comply with WCF's expectation of the behavior.

The fact that the WCF durable service infrastructure is, in reality, a serialization infrastructure enabled me to leverage it into yet another technique for managing service state in the face of transactions, while relying underneath on a volatile resource manager, without having the service instance do anything about it. This further streamlines the transactional programming model of WCF and yields the benefit of the superior programming model of transactions for mere objects.

---

* I presented my approach for transactional behavior in the January 2009 issue of *MSDN Magazine*.

The first step was to define two transactional in-memory provider factories:

```
public abstract class MemoryProviderFactory : PersistenceProviderFactory
{...}

public class TransactionalMemoryProviderFactory : MemoryProviderFactory
{...}
public class TransactionalInstanceProviderFactory : MemoryProviderFactory
{...}
```

The `TransactionalMemoryProviderFactory` uses my `TransactionalDictionary<ID,T>` to store the service instances.

> Unrelated to this section and transactions, you can configure the service to use the `TransactionalMemoryProviderFactory` with or without transactions by simply listing it in the persistence providers section of the service behaviors:
>
> ```
> <behavior name = "TransactionalMemory">
>    <persistenceProvider
>       type = "ServiceModelEx.
>                  TransactionalMemoryProviderFactory,
>             ServiceModelEx"
>    />
> </behavior>
> ```
>
> This will enable you to store the instances in memory, instead of in a file or SQL Server database. This is useful for quick testing and for stress testing, since it avoids the inherent I/O latency of a durable persistent storage.

The in-memory dictionary is shared among all clients and transport sessions, and as long as the host is running, `TransactionalMemoryProviderFactory` allows clients to connect and disconnect from the service. When using `TransactionalMemoryProviderFactory` you should designate a completing operation that removes the instance state from the store as discussed in Chapter 4, using the `CompletesInstance` property of the `DurableOperation` attribute.

`TransactionalInstanceProviderFactory`, on the other hand, matches each transport session with a dedicated instance of `Transactional<T>`. There is no need to call any completing operation since the service state will be cleaned up with garbage collection after the session is closed.

Next, I defined the `TransactionalBehaviorAttribute`, shown in Example 7-26.

Example 7-26. The TransactionalBehavior attribute

```
[AttributeUsage(AttributeTargets.Class)]
public class TransactionalBehaviorAttribute : Attribute,IServiceBehavior
{
   public bool TransactionRequiredAllOperations
   {get;set;}
```

Example 7-26. The TransactionalBehavior attribute (continued)

```
public bool AutoCompleteInstance
{get;set;}

public TransactionalBehaviorAttribute()
{
   TransactionRequiredAllOperations = true;
   AutoCompleteInstance = true;
}
void IServiceBehavior.Validate(ServiceDescription description,
                              ServiceHostBase host)
{
   DurableServiceAttribute durable = new DurableServiceAttribute();
   durable.SaveStateInOperationTransaction = true;
   description.Behaviors.Add(durable);

   PersistenceProviderFactory factory;
   if(AutoCompleteInstance)
   {
      factory = new TransactionalInstanceProviderFactory();
   }
   else
   {
      factory = new TransactionalMemoryProviderFactory();
   }

   PersistenceProviderBehavior persistenceBehavior =
                                 new PersistenceProviderBehavior(factory);
   description.Behaviors.Add(persistenceBehavior);

   if(TransactionRequiredAllOperations)
   {
      foreach(ServiceEndpoint endpoint in description.Endpoints)
      {
         foreach(OperationDescription operation in endpoint.Contract.Operations)
         {
            OperationBehaviorAttribute operationBehavior =
                    operation.Behaviors.Find<OperationBehaviorAttribute>();
            operationBehavior.TransactionScopeRequired = true;
         }
      }
   }
}
void IServiceBehavior.AddBindingParameters(...)
{}
void IServiceBehavior.ApplyDispatchBehavior(...)
{}
}
```

TransactionalBehavior is a service behavior attribute. It always performs these configurations for the service. First, it injects into the service description a DurableService

attribute with SaveStateInOperationTransaction set to true. Second, it adds the use of either TransactionalMemoryProviderFactory or TransactionalInstanceProviderFactory for the persistent behavior according to the value of the AutoCompleteInstance property. If AutoCompleteInstance is set to true (the default) then TransactionalBehavior will use TransactionalInstanceProviderFactory. Finally, TransactionalBehavior provides the TransactionRequiredAllOperations property. When the property is set to true (the default) TransactionalBehavior will set TransactionScopeRequired to true on all the service operation behaviors, thus providing all operations with an ambient transaction. When it is explicitly set to false, the service developer can choose which operations will be transactional.

As a result, using the attribute like so:

```
[Serializable]
[TransactionalBehavior]
class MyService : IMyContract
{
    public void MyMethod( )
    {...}
}
```

is equivalent to this service declaration and configuration:

```
[Serializable]
[DurableService(SaveStateInOperationTransaction = true)]
class MyService : IMyContract
{
    [OperationBehavior(TransactionScopeRequired = true)]
    public void MyMethod( )
    {...}
}

<services>
    <service name = "MyService" behaviorConfiguration = "TransactionalBehavior">
        ...
    </service>
</services>
<behaviors>
    <serviceBehaviors>
        <behavior name = "TransactionalBehavior">
            <persistenceProvider
                type = "ServiceModelEx.TransactionalInstanceProviderFactory,
                        ServiceModelEx"
            />
        </behavior>
    </serviceBehaviors>
</behaviors>
```

When using the TransactionalBehavior attribute with the default values, the client need not manage or interact in any way with the instance ID as shown in Chapter 4. All the client needs to do is use the proxy over one of the context bindings, and let the binding manage the instance ID. For example, for this service definition:

```
[ServiceContract]
interface IMyContract
{
   [OperationContract]
   [TransactionFlow(TransactionFlowOption.Allowed)]
   void IncrementCounter();
}

[Serializable]
[TransactionalBehavior]
class MyService : IMyContract
{
   int m_Counter = 0;

   public void IncrementCounter()
   {
      m_Counter++;
      Trace.WriteLine("Counter = " + m_Counter);
   }
}
```

the following client code:

```
MyContractClient proxy = new MyContractClient();

using(TransactionScope scope = new TransactionScope())
{
   proxy.IncrementCounter();
   scope.Complete();
}

//This transaction will abort since the scope is not completed
using(TransactionScope scope = new TransactionScope())
{
   proxy.IncrementCounter();
}

using(TransactionScope scope = new TransactionScope())
{
   proxy.IncrementCounter();
   scope.Complete();
}

proxy.Close();
```

yields this output:

```
Counter = 1
Counter = 2
Counter = 2
```

Note that the service was interacting with a normal integer as its member variable.

In-proc transactions

The `TransactionalBehavior` attribute substantially simplifies transactional programming and is a fundamental step toward the future, where memory itself will be transactional and it will be possible for every object to be transactional (for more on my vision for the future of the platform, please see Appendix A). `TransactionalBehavior` maintains the programming model of conventional, plain .NET, yet it provides the full benefits of transactions.

To allow the efficient use of `TransactionalBehavior` even in the most intimate execution scopes, *ServiceModelEx* contains the `NetNamedPipeContextBinding` class. As the binding's name implies, it is the IPC binding plus the context protocol (required by the `DurableService` attribute). Appendix B walks through implementing the `NetNamedPipeContextBinding` class.

 Supporting `TransactionalBehavior` over IPC was my main motivation for developing the `NetNamedPipeContextBinding`.

To make the programming model of `TransactionalBehavior` even more accessible, the `InProcFactory` class from Chapter 1 actually uses `NetNamedPipeContextBinding` instead of the built-in `NetNamedPipeBinding`. `InProcFactory` also flows transactions over the binding. This enables the programming model of Example 7-27, without ever resorting to host management or client or service config files.

Example 7-27. Combining TransactionalBehavior with the InProcFactory

```
[ServiceContract]
interface IMyContract
{
   [OperationContract]
   [TransactionFlow(TransactionFlowOption.Allowed)]
   void IncrementCounter();
}

[Serializable]
[TransactionalBehavior]
class MyService : IMyContract
{
   int m_Counter = 0;

   public void IncrementCounter()
   {
      m_Counter++;
      Trace.WriteLine("Counter = " + m_Counter);
   }
}
```

Example 7-27. Combining TransactionalBehavior with the InProcFactory (continued)

```
//Client-code

IMyContract proxy = InProcFactory.CreateInstance<MyService,IMyContract>( );

using(TransactionScope scope = new TransactionScope( ))
{
   proxy.IncrementCounter( );
   scope.Complete( );
}

//This transaction will abort since the scope is not completed
using(TransactionScope scope = new TransactionScope( ))
{
   proxy.IncrementCounter( );
}

using(TransactionScope scope = new TransactionScope( ))
{
   proxy.IncrementCounter( );
   scope.Complete( );
}

InProcFactory.CloseProxy(proxy);

//Traces:
Counter = 1
Counter = 2
Counter = 2
```

Transactional Singleton Service

By default, a transactional singleton behaves like a per-call service. The reason is that by default ReleaseServiceInstanceOnTransactionComplete is set to true, so after the singleton auto-completes a transaction, WCF disposes of the singleton, in the interest of state management and consistency. This, in turn, implies that the singleton must be state-aware and must proactively manage its state in every method call, in and out of a resource manager. The big difference compared to a per-call service is that WCF will enforce the semantic of the single instance, so at any point in time there will be at most a single instance running. WCF uses concurrency management and instance deactivation to enforce this rule. Recall that when ReleaseServiceInstanceOnTransactionComplete is true, the concurrency mode must be ConcurrencyMode.Single to disallow concurrent calls. WCF keeps the singleton context and merely deactivates the instance hosted in the context, as discussed in Chapter 4. What this means is that even though the singleton needs to be state-aware, it does not need the client to provide an explicit state identifier in every call. The singleton can use any type-level constant to identify its state in the state resource manager, as shown in Example 7-28.

Example 7-28. State-aware singleton

```
[ServiceBehavior(InstanceContextMode = InstanceContextMode.Single)]
class MySingleton : IMyContract
{
   readonly static string m_StateIdentifier = typeof(MySingleton).GUID.ToString();

   [OperationBehavior(TransactionScopeRequired = true)]
   public void MyMethod()
   {
      GetState();
      DoWork();
      SaveState();
   }

   //Helper methods
   void GetState()
   {
      //Use m_StateIdentifier to get state
   }
   void DoWork()
   {}
   public void SaveState()
   {
      //Use m_StateIdentifier to save state
   }
   public void RemoveState()
   {
      //Use m_StateIdentifier to remove the state from the resource manager
   }
}
//Hosting code
MySingleton singleton  = new MySingleton();
singleton.SaveState(); //Create the initial state in the resource manager

ServiceHost host = new ServiceHost(singleton);
host.Open();

/* Some blocking calls */

host.Close();
singleton.RemoveState();
```

In this example, the singleton uses the unique GUID associated with every type as a state identifier. At the beginning of every method call the singleton reads its state, and at the end of each method call it saves the state back to the resource manager. However, the first call on the first instance must also be able to bind to the state, so you must prime the resource manager with the state before the first call ever arrives. To that end, before launching the host, you need to create the singleton, save its state to the resource manager, and then provide the singleton instance to ServiceHost (as explained in Chapter 4). After the host shuts down, make sure to remove the singleton state from the resource manager, as shown in Example 7-28. Note that you cannot create the initial state in the singleton constructor, because the constructor will be called for each operation on the singleton and will override the previous saved state.

While a state-aware singleton is certainly possible (as demonstrated in Example 7-28), the overall complexity involved makes it a technique to avoid. It is better to use a stateful transactional singleton, as presented next.

Stateful singleton service

By setting ReleaseServiceInstanceOnTransactionComplete to false, you regain the singleton semantic. The singleton will be created just once, when the host is launched, and the same single instance will be shared across all clients and transactions. The problem is, of course, how to manage the state of the singleton. The singleton has to have state; otherwise, there is no point in using a singleton in the first place. The best solution (as before, with the stateful per-session service) is to use volatile resource managers as member variables, as shown in Example 7-29.

Example 7-29. Achieving a stateful singleton transactional service

```
///////////////////// Service Side ////////////////////////////////////////////
[ServiceBehavior(InstanceContextMode = InstanceContextMode.Single,
                 ReleaseServiceInstanceOnTransactionComplete = false)]
class MySingleton : IMyContract
{
   Transactional<int> m_Counter = new Transactional<int>();

   [OperationBehavior(TransactionScopeRequired = true)]
   public void MyMethod()
   {
      m_Counter.Value++;
      Trace.WriteLine("Counter: " + m_Counter.Value);
   }
}
///////////////////// Client Side ////////////////////////////////////////////
using(TransactionScope scope1 = new TransactionScope())
{
   MyContractClient proxy = new MyContractClient();
   proxy.MyMethod();
   proxy.Close();
   scope1.Complete();
}
using(TransactionScope scope2 = new TransactionScope())
{
   MyContractClient proxy = new MyContractClient();
   proxy.MyMethod();
   proxy.Close();
}
using(TransactionScope scope3 = new TransactionScope())
{
   MyContractClient proxy = new MyContractClient();
   proxy.MyMethod();
```

Example 7-29. Achieving a stateful singleton transactional service (continued)

```
   proxy.Close( );
   scope3.Complete( );
}
/////////////////// Output /////////////////////////////////////////
Counter: 1
Counter: 2
Counter: 2
```

In Example 7-29, a client creates three transactional scopes, each with its own new proxy to the singleton. In each call, the singleton increments a counter it maintains as a `Transactional<int>` volatile resource manager. `scope1` completes the transaction and commits the new value of the counter (1). In `scope2`, the client calls the singleton and temporarily increments the counter to 2. However, `scope2` does not complete its transaction. The volatile resource manager therefore rejects the increment and reverts to its previous value of 1. The call in `scope3` then increments the counter again from 1 to 2, as shown in the trace output.

Note that when setting `ReleaseServiceInstanceOnTransactionComplete`, the singleton must have at least one method with `TransactionScopeRequired` set to `true`.

In addition, the singleton must have `TransactionAutoComplete` set to `true` on every method, which of course precludes any transactional affinity and allows concurrent transactions. All calls and all transactions are routed to the same instance. For example, the following client code will result in the transaction diagram shown in Figure 7-13:

```
using (MyContractClient proxy = new MyContractClient( ))
using(TransactionScope scope = new TransactionScope( ))
{
   proxy.MyMethod( );
   scope.Complete( );
}

using(MyContractClient proxy = new MyContractClient( ))
using(TransactionScope scope = new TransactionScope( ))
{
   proxy.MyMethod( );
   proxy.MyMethod( );
   scope.Complete( );
}
```

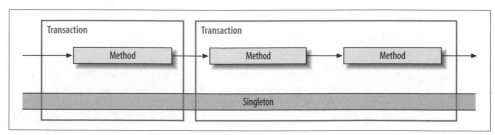

Figure 7-13. Stateful transactional singleton

Instancing Modes and Transactions

To summarize the topic of instance management modes and transactions, Table 7-3 lists the possible configurations discussed so far and their resulting effects. Other combinations may technically be allowed, but I've omitted them because they are either nonsensical or plainly disallowed by WCF.

Table 7-3. Possible instancing modes, configurations, and transactions

Configured instancing mode	Auto-complete	Release on complete	Complete on session close	Resulting instancing mode	State mgmt.	Trans. affinity
Per-call	True	True/False	True/False	Per-call	State-aware	Call
Session	True	True	True/False	Per-call	State-aware	Call
Session	True	False	True/False	Session	VRM members	Call
Session	False	True/False	True	Session	Stateful	Instance context
Session	Hybrid	True	True/False	Hybrid	Hybrid	Instance context
Durable service	True	True/False	True/False	Per-call	Stateful	Call
Singleton	True	True	True/False	Per-call	State-aware	Call
Singleton	True	False	True/False	Singleton	VRM members	Call

With so many options, which mode should you choose? I find that the complexity of an explicit state-aware programming model with sessionful and singleton services outweighs any potential benefits, and this is certainly the case with the hybrid mode as well. Equating sessions with transactions is often impractical and indicates a bad design. For both sessionful and singleton services, I prefer the simplicity and elegance of volatile resource managers as member variables. You can also use a durable service on top of a transactional durable storage or the `TransactionalBehavior` attribute.

Table 7-4 lists these recommended configurations. None of the recommended options relies on transactional affinity or auto-completion on session close, but they all use auto-completion.

Table 7-4. Recommended instancing modes, configurations, and transactions

Configured instancing mode	Release on complete	Resulting instancing mode	State management
Per-call	True/False	Per-call	State-aware
Session	False	Session	VRM members
Durable service	True/False	Per-call	Stateful
Singleton	False	Singleton	VRM members

Callbacks

Callback contracts, just like service contracts, can propagate the service transaction to the callback client. To enable this you apply the `TransactionFlow` attribute, as with a service contract. For example:

```
interface IMyContractCallback
{
   [OperationContract]
   [TransactionFlow(TransactionFlowOption.Allowed)]
   void OnCallback();
}
[ServiceContract(CallbackContract = typeof(IMyContractCallback))]
interface IMyContract
{...}
```

The callback method implementation can use the `OperationBehavior` attribute (just like a service operation) and specify whether to require a transaction scope and auto-completion:

```
class MyClient : IMyContractCallback
{
   [OperationBehavior(TransactionScopeRequired = true)]
   public void OnCallback()
   {
      Transaction transaction = Transaction.Current;
      Debug.Assert(transaction != null);
   }
}
```

Callback Transaction Modes

The callback client can have four modes of configuration: Service, Service/Callback, Callback, and None. These are analogous to the service transaction modes, except the service now plays the client role and the callback plays the service role. For example, to configure the callback for the Service transaction mode (that is, to always use the service's transaction), follow these steps:

1. Use a transaction-aware duplex binding with transaction flow enabled.

2. Set transaction flow to mandatory on the callback operation.

3. Configure the callback operation to require a transaction scope.

Example 7-30 shows a callback client configured for the Service transaction mode.

Example 7-30. Configuring the callback for the Service transaction mode

```
interface IMyContractCallback
{
   [OperationContract]
   [TransactionFlow(TransactionFlowOption.Mandatory)]
   void OnCallback();
}
```

Example 7-30. Configuring the callback for the Service transaction mode (continued)

```
class MyClient : IMyContractCallback
{
   [OperationBehavior(TransactionScopeRequired = true)]
   public void OnCallback( )
   {
      Transaction transaction = Transaction.Current;
      Debug.Assert(transaction.TransactionInformation.
                  DistributedIdentifier != Guid.Empty);
   }
}
```

When the callback operation is configured for mandatory transaction flow, WCF will enforce the use of a transaction-aware binding with transaction flow enabled.

When you configure the callback for the Service/Callback transaction propagation mode, WCF does not enforce enabling of transaction flow in the binding. You can use my BindingRequirement attribute to enforce this:

```
interface IMyContractCallback
{
   [OperationContract]
   [TransactionFlow(TransactionFlowOption.Allowed)]
   void OnCallback( );
}
[BindingRequirement(TransactionFlowEnabled = true)]
class MyClient : IMyContractCallback
{
   [OperationBehavior(TransactionScopeRequired = true)]
   public void OnCallback( )
   {...}
}
```

I extended my BindingRequirement attribute to verify the callback binding by implementing the IEndpointBehavior interface:

```
public interface IEndpointBehavior
{
   void AddBindingParameters(ServiceEndpoint endpoint,
                        BindingParameterCollection bindingParameters);
   void ApplyClientBehavior(ServiceEndpoint endpoint,
                        ClientRuntime clientRuntime);
   void ApplyDispatchBehavior(ServiceEndpoint endpoint,
                        EndpointDispatcher endpointDispatcher);
   void Validate(ServiceEndpoint serviceEndpoint);
}
```

As explained in Chapter 6, the IEndpointBehavior interface lets you configure the client-side endpoint used for the callback by the service. In the case of the BindingRequirement attribute, it uses the IEndpointBehavior.Validate( ) method, and the implementation is almost identical to that of Example 7-3.

Isolation and timeouts

As with a service, the `CallbackBehavior` attribute enables a callback type to control its transaction's timeout and isolation level:

```
[AttributeUsage(AttributeTargets.Class)]
public sealed class CallbackBehaviorAttribute: Attribute,IEndpointBehavior
{
    public IsolationLevel TransactionIsolationLevel
    {get;set;}
    public string TransactionTimeout
    {get;set;}
    //More members
}
```

These properties accept the same values as in the service case, and the same reasoning can be used to choose a particular value.

Callback Voting

By default, WCF will use automatic voting for the callback operation, just as with a service operation. Any exception in the callback will result in a vote to abort the transaction, and without an error WCF will vote to commit the transaction, as is the case in Example 7-30. However, unlike with a service instance, the callback instance lifecycle is managed by the client, and it has no instancing mode. Any callback instance can be configured for explicit voting by setting `TransactionAutoComplete` to false. Voting can then be done explicitly using `SetTransactionComplete()`:

```
class MyClient : IMyContractCallback
{
    [OperationBehavior(TransactionScopeRequired = true,
                       TransactionAutoComplete = false)]
    public void OnCallback()
    {
        /* Do some transactional work then */

        OperationContext.Current.SetTransactionComplete();
    }
}
```

As with a per-session service, explicit voting is for the case when the vote depends on other things besides exceptions. Do not perform any work—especially transactional work—after the call to `SetTransactionComplete()`. Calling `SetTransactionComplete()` should be the last line of code in the callback operation, just before returning. If you try to perform any transactional work (including accessing `Transaction.Current`) after the call to `SetTransactionComplete()`, WCF will throw an `InvalidOperationException` and abort the transaction.

Using Transactional Callbacks

While WCF provides the infrastructure for propagating the service's transaction to the callback, in reality callbacks and service transactions do not mix well. First, callbacks are usually one-way operations, and as such cannot propagate transactions. Second, to be able to invoke the callback to its calling client, the service cannot be configured with ConcurrencyMode.Single; otherwise, WCF will abort the call to avoid a deadlock. Typically, services are configured for either the Client/Service or the Client transaction propagation mode. Ideally, a service should be able to propagate its original calling client's transaction to all callbacks it invokes, even if the callback is to the calling client. Yet, for the service to use the client's transaction, TransactionScopeRequired must be set to true. Since ReleaseServiceInstanceOnTransactionComplete is true by default, it requires ConcurrencyMode.Single, thus precluding the callback to the calling client.

Out-of-band transactional callbacks

There are two types of transactional callbacks. The first is out-of-band callbacks made by non-service parties on the host side using callback references stored by the service. Such parties can easily propagate their transactions to the callback (usually in a TransactionScope) because there is no risk of a deadlock, as shown in Example 7-31.

Example 7-31. Out-of-band callbacks

```
[ServiceBehavior(InstanceContextMode = InstanceContextMode.PerCall)]
class MyService : IMyContract
{
   static List<IMyContractCallback> m_Callbacks = new List<IMyContractCallback>();

   public void MyMethod()
   {
      IMyContractCallback callback = OperationContext.Current.
                                  GetCallbackChannel<IMyContractCallback>();

      if(m_Callbacks.Contains(callback) == false)
      {
         m_Callbacks.Add(callback);
      }
   }
   public static void CallClients()
   {
      Action<IMyContractCallback> invoke = (callback)=>
                                {
                                   using(TransactionScope scope =
                                             new TransactionScope())
                                   {
                                      callback.OnCallback();
                                      scope.Complete();
```

Example 7-31. Out-of-band callbacks (continued)

```
                                                    }
                                       };
      m_Callbacks.ForEach(invoke);
   }
}
//Out-of-band callbacks:
MyService.CallClients();
```

Service transactional callbacks

The second option is to carefully configure the transactional service so that it is able to call back to its calling client. To that end, configure the service with ConcurrencyMode.Reentrant, set ReleaseServiceInstanceOnTransactionComplete to false, and make sure at least one operation has TransactionScopeRequired set to true, as shown in Example 7-32.

Example 7-32. Configuring for transactional callbacks

```
[ServiceContract(CallbackContract = typeof(IMyContractCallback))]
interface IMyContract
{
   [OperationContract]
   [TransactionFlow(TransactionFlowOption.Allowed)]
   void MyMethod();
}
interface IMyContractCallback
{
   [OperationContract]
   [TransactionFlow(TransactionFlowOption.Allowed)]
   void OnCallback();
}
[ServiceBehavior(InstanceContextMode = InstanceContextMode.PerCall,
                 ConcurrencyMode = ConcurrencyMode.Reentrant,
                 ReleaseServiceInstanceOnTransactionComplete = false)]
class MyService : IMyContract
{
   [OperationBehavior(TransactionScopeRequired = true)]
   public void MyMethod()
   {
      Trace.WriteLine("Service ID:     " +
                  Transaction.Current.TransactionInformation.DistributedIdentifier);

      IMyContractCallback callback =
                  OperationContext.Current.GetCallbackChannel<IMyContractCallback>();
      callback.OnCallback();
   }
}
```

The rationale behind this constraint is explained in the next chapter.

Given the definitions of Example 7-32, if transaction flow is enabled in the binding, the following client code:

```
class MyCallback : IMyContractCallback
{
    [OperationBehavior(TransactionScopeRequired = true)]
    public void OnCallback()
    {
        Trace.WriteLine("OnCallback ID: " +
                Transaction.Current.TransactionInformation.DistributedIdentifier);
    }
}
MyCallback callback = new MyCallback();
InstanceContext context = new InstanceContext(callback);
MyContractClient proxy = new MyContractClient(context);

using(TransactionScope scope = new TransactionScope())
{
    proxy.MyMethod();

    Trace.WriteLine("Client ID:      " +
                Transaction.Current.TransactionInformation.DistributedIdentifier);
    scope.Complete();
}
proxy.Close();
```

yields output similar to this:

```
Service ID:      23627e82-507a-45d5-933c-05e5e5a1ae78
OnCallback ID: 23627e82-507a-45d5-933c-05e5e5a1ae78
Client ID:      23627e82-507a-45d5-933c-05e5e5a1ae78
```

indicating that the client's transaction was propagated to the service and into the callback.

CHAPTER 8

Concurrency Management

Incoming client calls are dispatched to the service on threads from the Windows I/O completion thread pool (the pool has 1,000 threads by default). Multiple clients can make multiple concurrent calls, and the service itself can sustain those calls on multiple threads. If the calls are dispatched to the same service instance, you must provide thread-safe access to the service's in-memory state or risk state corruption and errors. The same is true for the client's in-memory state during callbacks, since callbacks too are dispatched on threads from the I/O completion thread pool. In addition to synchronizing access to the instance state when applicable, all services also need to synchronize access to resources shared between instances, such as static variables. Another dimension altogether for concurrency management is ensuring that, if required, the service (or the resources it accesses) executes on particular threads.

WCF offers two modes for synchronization. *Automatic synchronization* instructs WCF to synchronize access to the service instance. Automatic synchronization is simple to use, but it is available only for service and callback classes. *Manual synchronization*, on the other hand, puts the full burden of synchronization on the developer and requires application-specific integration. The developer needs to employ .NET synchronization locks, which is by far an expert discipline. The advantages of manual synchronization are that it is available for service and non-service classes alike, and it allows developers to optimize throughput and scalability. This chapter starts by describing the basic concurrency modes available and then presents more advanced aspects of concurrency management, such as dealing with resource safety and synchronization, thread affinity and custom synchronization contexts, callbacks, and asynchronous calls. Throughout, the chapter shares best practices, concurrency management design guidelines, and custom techniques.

Instance Management and Concurrency

Service-instance thread safety is closely related to the service instancing mode. A per-call service instance is thread-safe by definition, because each call gets its own dedicated instance. That instance is accessible only by its assigned worker thread, and because no other threads will be accessing it, it has no need for synchronization. However, a per-call service is typically state-aware. The state store can be an in-memory resource such as static dictionary, and it can be subject to multithreaded access because the service can sustain concurrent calls, whether from the same client or from multiple clients. Consequently, you must synchronize access to the state store.

A per-session service always requires concurrency management and synchronization, because the client may use the same proxy and yet dispatch calls to the service on multiple client-side threads. A singleton service is even more susceptible to concurrent access, and must support synchronized access. The singleton has some in-memory state that all clients implicitly share. On top of the possibility of the client dispatching calls on multiple threads, as with a per-session service, a singleton may simply have multiple clients in different execution contexts, each using its own thread to call the service. All of these calls will enter the singleton on different threads from the I/O completion thread pool—hence the need for synchronization.

Service Concurrency Modes

Concurrent access to the service instance is governed by the ConcurrencyMode property of the ServiceBehavior attribute:

```
public enum ConcurrencyMode
{
   Single,
   Reentrant,
   Multiple
}

[AttributeUsage(AttributeTargets.Class)]
public sealed class ServiceBehaviorAttribute : ...
{
   public ConcurrencyMode ConcurrencyMode
   {get;set;}
   //More members
}
```

The value of the ConcurrencyMode enum controls if and when concurrent calls are allowed. The name ConcurrencyMode is actually incorrect; the proper name for this property would have been ConcurrencyContextMode, since it synchronizes access not to the instance, but rather to the context containing the instance (much the same way InstanceContextMode controls the instantiation of the context, not the instance). The significance of this distinction—i.e., that the synchronization is related to the context and not to the instance—will become evident later.

ConcurrencyMode.Single

When the service is configured with ConcurrencyMode.Single, WCF will provide automatic synchronization to the service context and disallow concurrent calls by associating the context containing the service instance with a synchronization lock. Every call coming into the service must first try to acquire the lock. If the lock is unowned, the caller will be allowed in. Once the operation returns, WCF will unlock the lock, thus allowing in another caller.

The important thing is that only one caller at a time is ever allowed. If there are multiple concurrent callers while the lock is locked, the callers are all placed in a queue and are served out of the queue in order. If a call times out while blocked, WCF will remove the caller from the queue and the client will get a TimeoutException. ConcurrencyMode.Single is the WCF default setting, so these definitions are equivalent:

```
class MyService : IMyContract
{...}

[ServiceBehavior(ConcurrencyMode = ConcurrencyMode.Single)]
class MyService : IMyContract
{...}
```

Because the default concurrency mode is synchronized access, the susceptible instancing modes of per-session and singleton are also synchronized by default. Note that even calls to a per-call service instance are synchronized by default.

Synchronized access and transactions

As explained in Chapter 7, WCF will verify at service load time whether at least one operation on the service has TransactionScopeRequired set to true and that ReleaseServiceInstanceOnTransactionComplete is true. In this case, the service concurrency mode must be ConcurrencyMode.Single. This is done deliberately to ensure that the service instance can be recycled at the end of the transaction without any danger of there being another thread accessing the disposed instance.

ConcurrencyMode.Multiple

When the service is configured with ConcurrencyMode.Multiple, WCF will stay out of the way and will not synchronize access to the service instance in any way. ConcurrencyMode.Multiple simply means that the service instance is not associated with any synchronization lock, so concurrent calls are allowed on the service instance. Put differently, when a service instance is configured with ConcurrencyMode.Multiple, WCF will not queue up the client messages and dispatch them to the service instance as soon as they arrive.

A large number of concurrent client calls will not result in a matching number of concurrently executing calls on the service. The maximum number of concurrent calls dispatched to the service is determined by the configured maximum concurrent calls throttle value. As mentioned in Chapter 4, the default value is 16.

Obviously, this is of great concern to sessionful and singleton services, which must manually synchronize access to their instance state. The common way of doing that is to use .NET locks such as `Monitor` or a `WaitHandle`-derived class. Manual synchronization, which is covered in great depth in Chapter 8 of my book *Programming .NET Components*, Second Edition (O'Reilly), is not for the faint of heart, but it does enable the service developer to optimize the throughput of client calls on the service instance: you can lock the service instance just when and where synchronization is required, thus allowing other client calls on the same service instance in between the synchronized sections. Example 8-1 shows a manually synchronized sessionful service whose client performs concurrent calls.

Example 8-1. Manual synchronization using fragmented locking

```
[ServiceContract(SessionMode = SessionMode.Required)]
interface IMyContract
{
   void MyMethod( );
}

[ServiceBehavior(ConcurrencyMode = ConcurrencyMode.Multiple)]
class MyService : IMyContract
{
   int[] m_Numbers;
   List<string> m_Names;

   public void MyMethod( )
   {
      lock(m_Numbers)
      {
         ...
      }

      /* Don't access members here */

      lock(m_Names)
      {
         ...
      }
   }
}
```

The service in Example 8-1 is configured for concurrent access. Since the critical sections of the operations that require synchronization are any member variable accesses, the service uses a Monitor (encapsulated in the lock statement) to lock the member variable before accessing it. I call this synchronization technique *fragmented locking,* since it locks only when needed and only what is being accessed. Local variables require no synchronization, because they are visible only to the thread that created them on its own call stack.

There are two problems with fragmented locking. The first is that it is error- and deadlock-prone. Fragmented locking only provides for thread-safe access if every other operation on the service is as disciplined about always locking the members before accessing them. But even if all operations lock all members, you still risk deadlocks: if one operation on thread A locks member M1 while trying to access member M2 while another operation executing concurrently on thread B locks member M2 while trying to access member M1, you will end up with a deadlock.

 WCF resolves service call deadlocks by eventually timing out the call and throwing a TimeoutException. Avoid using a long send timeout, as it decreases WCF's ability to resolve deadlocks in a timely manner.

It is better to reduce the fragmentation by locking the entire service instance instead:

```
public void MyMethod( )
{
   lock(this)
   {
      ...
   }


   /* Don't access members here */

   lock(this)
   {
      ...
   }
}
```

This approach, however, is still fragmented and thus error-prone—if at some point in the future someone adds a method call in the unsynchronized code section that does access the members, it will not be a synchronized access. It is better still to lock the entire body of the method:

```
public void MyMethod( )
{
   lock(this)
   {
      ...
   }
}
```

The problem with this approach is that in the future someone maintaining this code may err and place some code before or after the lock statement. Your best option therefore is to instruct the compiler to automate injecting the call to lock the instance using the `MethodImpl` attribute with the `MethodImplOptions.Synchronized` flag:

```
[ServiceBehavior(ConcurrencyMode = ConcurrencyMode.Multiple)]
class MyService : IMyContract
{
   int[] m_Numbers;
   List<string> m_Names;

   [MethodImpl(MethodImplOptions.Synchronized)]
   public void MyMethod( )
   {
      ...
   }
}
```

You will need to repeat the assignment of the `MethodImpl` attribute on all the service operation implementations.

While this code is thread-safe, you actually gain little from the use of `ConcurrencyMode.Multiple`: the net effect in terms of synchronization is similar to using `ConcurrencyMode.Single`, yet you have increased the overall code complexity and reliance on developers' discipline. In general, you should avoid `ConcurrencyMode.Multiple`. However, there are cases where `ConcurrencyMode.Multiple` is useful, as you will see later in this chapter.

Unsynchronized access and transactions

When the service is configured for `ConcurrencyMode.Multiple`, if at least one operation has `TransactionScopeRequired` set to `true`, then `ReleaseServiceInstanceOnTransactionComplete` must be set to `false`. For example, this is a valid definition, even though `ReleaseServiceInstanceOnTransactionComplete` defaults to true, because no method has `TransactionScopeRequired` set to true:

```
[ServiceBehavior(ConcurrencyMode = ConcurrencyMode.Multiple)]
class MyService : IMyContract
{
   public void MyMethod( )
   {...}
   public void MyOtherMethod( )
   {...}
}
```

The following, on the other hand, is an invalid definition because at least one method has `TransactionScopeRequired` set to true:

```
//Invalid configuration:
[ServiceBehavior(ConcurrencyMode = ConcurrencyMode.Multiple)]
class MyService : IMyContract
{
   [OperationBehavior(TransactionScopeRequired = true)]
   public void MyMethod( )
   {...}
```

```
    public void MyOtherMethod( )
    {...}
}
```

A transactional unsynchronized service must explicitly set ReleaseServiceInstanceOnTransactionComplete to false:

```
[ServiceBehavior(ConcurrencyMode = ConcurrencyMode.Multiple,
                ReleaseServiceInstanceOnTransactionComplete = false)]
class MyService : IMyContract
{
   [OperationBehavior(TransactionScopeRequired = true)]
   public void MyMethod( )
   {...}
   public void MyOtherMethod( )
   {...}
}
```

The rationale behind this constraint is that only a sessionful or a singleton service could possibly benefit from unsynchronized access, so in the case of transactional access, WCF wants to enforce the semantic of the configured instancing mode. In addition, this will avoid having one caller access the instance, complete the transaction, and release the instance, all while another caller is using the instance.

ConcurrencyMode.Reentrant

The ConcurrencyMode.Reentrant value is a refinement of ConcurrencyMode.Single. Similar to ConcurrencyMode.Single, ConcurrencyMode.Reentrant associates the service context with a synchronization lock, so concurrent calls on the same instance are never allowed. However, if the reentrant service calls out to another service or a callback, and that call chain (or *causality*) somehow winds its way back to the service instance, as shown in Figure 8-1, that call is allowed to reenter the service instance.

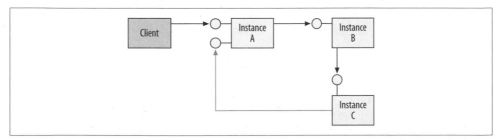

Figure 8-1. Call reentrancy

The implementation of ConcurrencyMode.Reentrant is very simple—when the reentrant service calls out over WCF, WCF silently releases the synchronization lock associated with the instance context. ConcurrencyMode.Reentrant is designed to avoid the potential deadlock of reentrancy, although it will release the lock in case of a callout.

If the service were to maintain the lock while calling out, if the causality tried to enter the same context, a deadlock would occur.

Reentrancy support is instrumental in a number of cases:

- A singleton service calling out risks a deadlock if any of the downstream services it calls tries to call back into the singleton.

- In the same app domain, if the client stores a proxy reference in some globally available variable, then some of the downstream objects called by the service use the proxy reference to call back to the original service.

- Callbacks on non-one-way operations must be allowed to reenter the calling service.

- If the callout the service performs is of long duration, even without reentrancy, you may want to optimize throughput by allowing other clients to use the same service instance while the callout is in progress.

 A service configured with ConcurrencyMode.Multiple is by definition also reentrant, because no lock is held during the callout. However, unlike a reentrant service, which is inherently thread-safe, a service configured with ConcurrencyMode.Multiple must provide for its own synchronization (for example, by locking the instance during every call, as explained previously). It is up to the developer of such a service to decide if it should release the lock before calling out to avoid a reentrancy deadlock.

Designing for reentrancy

It is very important to recognize the liability associated with reentrancy. When a reentrant service calls out, it must leave the service in a workable, consistent state, because others could be allowed into the service instance while the service is calling out. A consistent state means that the reentrant service must have no more interactions with its own members or any other local object or static variable, and that when the callout returns, the reentrant service should simply be able to return control to its client. For example, suppose the reentrant service modifies the state of some linked list and leaves it in an inconsistent state—say, missing a head node—because it needs to get the value of the new head from another service. If the reentrant service then calls out to the other service, it leaves other clients vulnerable, because if they call into the reentrant service and access the linked list they will encounter an error.

Moreover, when the reentrant service returns from its callout, it must refresh all local method state. For example, if the service has a local variable that contains a copy of the state of a member variable, that local variable may now have the wrong value, because during the callout another party could have entered the reentrant service and modified the member variable.

Reentrancy and transactions

A reentrant service faces exactly the same design constraints regarding transactions as a service configured with ConcurrencyMode.Multiple; namely, if at least one operation has TransactionScopeRequired set to true, then ReleaseServiceInstanceOnTransactionComplete must be set to false. This is done to maintain the instance context mode semantics.

Callbacks and reentrancy

Consider now the case of a service designed for single-threaded access with ConcurrencyMode.Single and with duplex callbacks. When a call from the client enters the context, it acquires the synchronization lock. If that service obtains the callback reference and calls back to the calling client, that call out will block the thread used to issue the call from the client while still maintaining the lock on the context. The callback will reach the client, execute there, and return with a reply message from the client. Unfortunately, when the reply message is sent to the same service instance context, it will first try to acquire the lock—the same lock already owned by the original call from the client, which is still blocked waiting for the callback to return—and a deadlock will ensue. To avoid this deadlock, during the operation execution, WCF disallows callbacks from the service to its calling client as long as the service is configured for single-threaded access.

There are three ways of safely allowing the callback. The first is to configure the service for reentrancy. When the service invokes the proxy to the callback object, WCF will silently release the lock, thus allowing the reply message from the callback to acquire the lock when it returns, as shown in Example 8-2.

Example 8-2. Configure for reentrancy to allow callbacks

```
interface IMyContractCallback
{
   [OperationContract]
   void OnCallback();
}
[ServiceContract(CallbackContract = typeof(IMyContractCallback))]
interface IMyContract
{
   [OperationContract]
   void MyMethod();
}

[ServiceBehavior(ConcurrencyMode = ConcurrencyMode.Reentrant)]
class MyService : IMyContract
{
   public void MyMethod()
   {
      IMyContractCallback callback = OperationContext.Current.
                               GetCallbackChannel<IMyContractCallback>();
```

Example 8-2. Configure for reentrancy to allow callbacks (continued)

```
        callback.OnCallback( );
    }
}
```

Control will only return to the service once the callback returns, and the service's own thread will need to reacquire the lock. Configuring for reentrancy is required even of a per-call service, which otherwise has no need for anything but ConcurrencyMode.Single. Note that the service may still invoke callbacks to other clients or call other services; it is the callback to the calling client that is disallowed.

You can, of course, configure the service for concurrent access with ConcurrencyMode.Multiple to avoid having any lock.

The third option (as mentioned in Chapter 5), and the only case where a service configured with ConcurrencyMode.Single can call back to its clients, is when the callback contract operation is configured as one-way because there will not be any reply message to contend for the lock.

Instances and Concurrent Access

Using the same proxy, a single client can issue multiple concurrent calls to a service. The client can use multiple threads to invoke calls on the service, or it can issue one-way calls in rapid succession on the same thread. In both of these cases, whether the calls from the same client are processed concurrently is the product of the service's configured instancing mode, the service's concurrency mode, and the configured delivery mode (that is, the transport session). The following discussion applies equally to request-reply and one-way calls.

Per-Call Services

In the case of a per-call service, if there is no transport-level session, concurrent processing of calls is allowed. Calls are dispatched as they arrive, each to a new instance, and execute concurrently. This is the case regardless of the service concurrency mode. I consider this to be the correct behavior.

If the per-call service has a transport-level session, whether concurrent processing of calls is allowed is a product of the service concurrency mode. If the service is configured with ConcurrencyMode.Single, concurrent processing of the pending calls is not allowed, and the calls are dispatched one at a time. The reason is that with ConcurrencyMode.Single WCF tries to maintain the guarantee of the transport session that messages are processed strictly in the order in which they were received in that session by having exactly one outstanding instance per channel. You should avoid lengthy processing of calls, because it may risk call timeouts.

While this is a direct result of the channel's architecture, I consider this to be a flawed design. If the service is configured with ConcurrencyMode.Multiple, concurrent processing is allowed. Calls are dispatched as they arrive, each to a new instance, and execute concurrently. An interesting observation here is that in the interest of throughput, it is a good idea to configure a per-call service with ConcurrencyMode.Multiple— the instance itself will still be thread-safe (so you will not incur the synchronization liability), yet you will allow concurrent calls from the same client.

> Two clients using two different proxies will have two distinct channels and will have no issue with concurrent calls. It is only concurrent calls on the same transport session that are serialized one at a time to the per-call service.

When the service is configured with ConcurrencyMode.Reentrant, if the service does not call out, it behaves similarly to a service configured with ConcurrencyMode.Single. If the service does call out, the next call is allowed in, and the returning call has to negotiate the lock like all other pending calls.

Sessionful and Singleton Services

In the case of a sessionful or a singleton service, the configured concurrency mode alone governs the concurrent execution of pending calls. If the service is configured with ConcurrencyMode.Single, calls will be dispatched to the service instance one at a time, and pending calls will be placed in a queue. You should avoid lengthy processing of calls, because it may risk call timeouts.

If the service instance is configured with ConcurrencyMode.Multiple, concurrent processing of calls from the same client is allowed. Calls will be executed by the service instance as fast as they come off the channel (up to the throttle limit). Of course, as is always the case with a stateful unsynchronized service instance, you must synchronize access to the service instance or risk state corruption.

If the service instance is configured with ConcurrencyMode.Reentrant, it behaves just as it would with ConcurrencyMode.Single. However, if the service calls out, the next call is allowed to execute. You must follow the guidelines discussed previously regarding programming in a reentrant environment.

> For a per-session service configured with ConcurrencyMode.Multiple to experience concurrent calls, the client must use multiple worker threads to access the same proxy instance. However, if the client threads rely on the auto-open feature of the proxy (that is, just invoking a method and having that call open the proxy if the proxy is not yet open) and call the proxy concurrently, then the calls will actually be serialized until the proxy is opened, and will be concurrent after that. If you want to dispatch concurrent calls regardless of the state of the proxy, the client needs to explicitly open the proxy (by calling the Open( ) method) before issuing any calls on the worker threads.

Resources and Services

Synchronizing access to the service instance using ConcurrencyMode.Single or an explicit synchronization lock only manages concurrent access to the service instance state itself. It does not provide safe access to the underlying resources the service may be using. These resources must also be thread-safe. For example, consider the application shown in Figure 8-2.

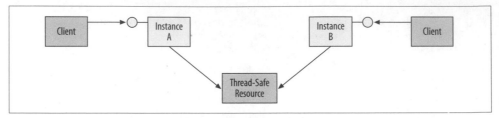

Figure 8-2. Applications must synchronize access to resources

Even though the service instances are thread-safe, the two instances try to concurrently access the same resource (such as a static variable, a helper static class, or a file), and therefore the resource itself must have synchronized access. This is true regardless of the service instancing mode. Even a per-call service could run into the situation shown in Figure 8-2.

Deadlocked Access

The naive solution to providing thread-safe access to resources is to provide each resource with its own lock, potentially encapsulating that lock in the resource itself, and ask the resource to lock the lock when it's accessed and unlock the lock when the service is done with the resource. The problem with this approach is that it is deadlock-prone. Consider the situation depicted in Figure 8-3.

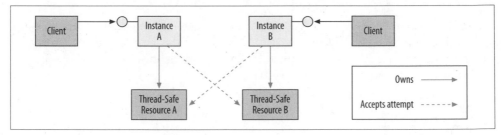

Figure 8-3. Deadlock over resources access

If the figure, Instance A of the service accesses the thread-safe Resource A. Resource A has its own synchronization lock, and Instance A acquires that lock. Similarly, Instance B accesses Resource B and acquires its lock. A deadlock then occurs when

Instance A tries to access Resource B while Instance B tries to access Resource A, since each instance will be waiting for the other to release its lock.

The concurrency and instancing modes of the service are almost irrelevant to avoiding this deadlock. The only case that avoids it is if the service is configured both with InstanceContextMode.Single and ConcurrencyMode.Single, because a synchronized singleton by definition can only have one client at a time and there will be no other instance to deadlock with over access to resources. All other combinations are still susceptible to this kind of deadlock. For example, a per-session synchronized service may have two separate thread-safe instances associated with two different clients, yet the two instances can deadlock when accessing the resources.

Deadlock Avoidance

There are a few possible ways to avoid the deadlock. If all instances of the service meticulously access all resources in the same order (e.g., always trying to acquire the lock of Resource A first, and then the lock of Resource B), there will be no deadlock. The problem with this approach is that it is difficult to enforce, and over time, during code maintenance, someone may deviate from this strict guideline (even inadvertently, by calling methods on helper classes) and trigger the deadlock.

Another solution is to have all resources use the same shared lock. In order to minimize the chances of a deadlock, you'll also want to minimize the number of locks in the system and have the service itself use the same lock. To that end, you can configure the service with ConcurrencyMode.Multiple (even with a per-call service) to avoid using the WCF-provided lock. The first service instance to acquire the shared lock will lock out all other instances and own all underlying resources. A simple technique for using such a shared lock is locking on the service type, as shown in Example 8-3.

Example 8-3. Using the service type as a shared lock

```
[ServiceBehavior(InstanceContextMode = InstanceContextMode.PerCall,
                 ConcurrencyMode = ConcurrencyMode.Multiple)]
class MyService : IMyContract
{
   public void MyMethod( )
   {
      lock(typeof(MyService))
      {
         ...
         MyResource.DoWork( );
         ...
      }
   }
}
```

Example 8-3. Using the service type as a shared lock (continued)

```
static class MyResource
{
   public static void DoWork( )
   {
      lock(typeof(MyService))
      {
         ...
      }
   }
}
```

The resources themselves must also lock on the service type (or some other shared type agreed upon in advance). There are two problems with the approach of using a shared lock. First, it introduces coupling between the resources and the service, because the resource developer has to know about the type of the service or the type used for synchronization. While you could get around that by providing the type as a resource construction parameter, it will likely not be applicable with third-party-provided resources. The second problem is that while your service instance is executing, all other instances (and their respective clients) will be blocked. Therefore, in the interest of throughput and responsiveness, you should avoid lengthy operations when using a shared lock.

If you think the situation in Example 8-3, where the two instances are of the same service, is problematic, imagine what happens if the two instances are of different services. The observation to make here is that services should never share resources. Regardless of concurrency management, resources are local implementation details and therefore should not be shared across services. Most importantly, sharing resources across the service boundary is also deadlock-prone. Such shared resources have no easy way to share locks across technologies and organizations, and the services need to somehow coordinate the locking order. This necessitates a high degree of coupling between the services, violating the best practices and tenets of service-orientation.

Resource Synchronization Context

Incoming service calls execute on worker threads from the I/O completion thread pool and are unrelated to any service or resource threads. This means that by default the service cannot rely on any kind of *thread affinity* (that is, always being accessed by the same thread). Much the same way, the service cannot by default rely on executing on any host-side custom threads created by the host or service developers. The problem with this situation is that some resources may rely on thread affinity. For example, user interface resources updated by the service must execute and be accessed only by the user interface (UI) thread. Other examples are a resource (or a service) that makes use of the thread local storage (TLS) to store out-of-band information shared globally by all parties on the same thread (using the TLS mandates use of the same thread), or accessing components developed using legacy Visual Basic or Visual FoxPro, which also require thread affinity (due to their own use of the TLS). In addition, for scalability and throughput purposes, some resources or frameworks may require access by their own pool of threads.

Whenever an affinity to a particular thread or threads is expected, the service cannot simply execute the call on the incoming WCF worker thread. Instead, the service must marshal the call to the correct thread(s) required by the resource it accesses.

.NET Synchronization Contexts

.NET 2.0 introduced the concept of a *synchronization context*. The idea is that any party can provide an execution context and have other parties marshal calls to that context. The synchronization context can be a single thread or any number of designated threads, although typically it will be just a single, yet particular thread. All the synchronization context does is assure that the call executes on the correct thread or threads.

Note that the word *context* is overloaded. Synchronization contexts have absolutely nothing to do with the service instance context or the operation context described so far in this book. They are simply the synchronizational context of the call.

While conceptually synchronization contexts are a simple enough design pattern to use, implementing a synchronization context is a complex programming task that is not normally intended for developers to attempt.

The SynchronizationContext class

The SynchronizationContext class from the System.Threading namespace represents a synchronization context:

```
public delegate void SendOrPostCallback(object state);

public class SynchronizationContext
{
   public virtual void Post(SendOrPostCallback callback,object state);
   public virtual void Send(SendOrPostCallback callback,object state);
   public static void SetSynchronizationContext(SynchronizationContext context);
   public static SynchronizationContext Current
   {get;}
   //More members
}
```

Every thread in .NET may have a synchronization context associated with it. You can obtain a thread's synchronization context by accessing the static Current property of SynchronizationContext. If the thread does not have a synchronization context, Current will return null. You can also pass the reference to the synchronization context between threads, so that one thread can marshal a call to another thread.

To represent the call to invoke in the synchronization context, you wrap a method with a delegate of the type SendOrPostCallback. Note that the signature of the delegate uses an object. If you want to pass multiple parameters, pack those in a structure and pass the structure as an object.

 Synchronization contexts use an amorphous object. Exercise caution when using synchronization contexts, due to the lack of compile-time type safety.

Working with the synchronization context

There are two ways of marshaling a call to the synchronization context: synchronously and asynchronously, by sending or posting a work item, respectively. The Send( ) method will block the caller until the call has completed in the other synchronization context, while Post( ) will merely dispatch it to the synchronization context and then return control to its caller.

For example, to synchronously marshal a call to a particular synchronization context, you first somehow obtain a reference to that synchronization context, and then use the Send( ) method:

```
//Obtain synchronization context
SynchronizationContext context = ...

SendOrPostCallback doWork = (arg)=>
                            {
                                //The code here is guaranteed to
                                //execute on the correct thread(s)
                            };
context.Send(doWork,"Some argument");
```

Example 8-4 shows a less abstract example.

Example 8-4. Calling a resource on the correct synchronization context

```
class MyResource
{
   public int DoWork( )
   {...}
   public SynchronizationContext MySynchronizationContext
   {get;}
}
class MyService : IMyContract
{
   MyResource GetResource( )
   {...}

   public void MyMethod( )
   {
      MyResource resource = GetResource( );
      SynchronizationContext context = resource.MySynchronizationContext;
```

```
      int result = 0;
      SendOrPostCallback doWork = delegate
                                  {
                                      result = resource.DoWork( );
                                  };
      context.Send(doWork,null);
   }
}
```

In Example 8-4, the service `MyService` needs to interact with the resource `MyResource` and have it perform some work by executing the `DoWork( )` method and returning a result. However, `MyResource` requires that all calls to it execute on its particular synchronization context. `MyResource` makes that execution context available via the `MySynchronizationContext` property. The service operation `MyMethod( )` executes on a WCF worker thread. `MyMethod( )` first obtains the resource and its synchronization context, then defines an anonymous method that wraps the call to `DoWork( )` and assigns that anonymous method to the `doWork` delegate of the type `SendOrPostCallback`. Finally, `MyMethod( )` calls `Send( )` and passes `null` for the argument, since the `DoWork( )` method on the resource requires no parameters. Note the technique used in Example 8-4 to retrieve a returned value from the invocation. Since `Send( )` returns void, the anonymous method assigns the returned value of `DoWork( )` into an outer variable. Without anonymous methods, this task would have required the complicated use of a synchronized member variable.

The problem with Example 8-4 is the excessive degree of coupling between the service and the resource. The service needs to know that the resource is sensitive to its synchronization context, obtain the context, and manage the execution. You must also duplicate such code in any service using the resource. It is much better to encapsulate the need in the resource itself, as shown in Example 8-5.

Example 8-5. Encapsulating the synchronization context

```
class MyResource
{
   public int DoWork( )
   {
      int result = 0;
      SendOrPostCallback doWork = delegate
                                  {
                                      result = DoWorkInternal( );
                                  };
      MySynchronizationContext.Send(doWork,null);
      return result;
   }
   SynchronizationContext MySynchronizationContext
   {get;}
   int DoWorkInternal( )
   {...}
}
```

Example 8-5. Encapsulating the synchronization context (continued)

```
class MyService :   IMyContract
{
    MyResource GetResource()
    {...}
    public void MyMethod()
    {
        MyResource resource = GetResource();
        int result = resource.DoWork();
    }
}
```

Compare Example 8-5 to Example 8-4. All the service in Example 8-5 has to do is access the resource: it is up to the service internally to marshal the call to its synchronization context.

The UI Synchronization Context

The canonical case for utilizing synchronization contexts is with Windows user interface frameworks such as Windows Forms or the Windows Presentation Foundation (WPF). For simplicity's sake, the rest of the discussion in this chapter will refer only to Windows Forms, although it applies equally to WPF. A Windows UI application relies on the underlying Windows messages and a message-processing loop (the *message pump*) to process them. The message loop must have thread affinity, because messages to a window are delivered only to the thread that created it. In general, you must always marshal to the UI thread any attempt to access a Windows control or form, or risk errors and failures. This becomes an issue if your services need to update some user interface as a result of client calls or some other event. Fortunately, Windows Forms supports the synchronization context pattern. Every thread that pumps Windows messages has a synchronization context. That synchronization context is the WindowsFormsSynchronizationContext class:

```
public sealed class WindowsFormsSynchronizationContext : SynchronizationContext,...
{...}
```

Whenever you create any Windows Forms control or form, that control or form ultimately derives from the class Control. The constructor of Control checks whether the current thread that creates it already has a synchronization context, and if it dos not, Control installs WindowsFormsSynchronizationContext as the current thread's synchronization context.

WindowsFormsSynchronizationContext converts the call to Send() or Post() to a custom Windows message and posts that Windows message to the UI thread's message queue. Every Windows Forms UI class that derives from Control has a dedicated method that handles this custom message by invoking the supplied SendOrPostCallback delegate. At some point, the UI thread processes the custom Windows message and the delegate is invoked.

Because the window or control can also be called already in the correct synchronization context, to avoid a deadlock when calling Send( ), the implementation of the Windows Forms synchronization context verifies that marshaling the call is indeed required. If marshaling is not required, it uses direct invocation on the calling thread.

UI access and updates

When a service needs to update a user interface, it must have some proprietary mechanisms to find the window to update in the first place. And once the service has the correct window, it must somehow get hold of that window's synchronization context and marshal the call to it. Such a possible interaction is shown in Example 8-6.

Example 8-6. Using the form synchronization context

```
partial class MyForm : Form
{
   Label m_CounterLabel;
   public SynchronizationContext MySynchronizationContext
   {get;set;}

   public MyForm()
   {
      InitializeComponent();
      MySynchronizationContext = SynchronizationContext.Current;
   }
   void InitializeComponent()
   {
      ...
      m_CounterLabel = new Label();
      ...
   }

   public int Counter
   {
      get
      {
         return Convert.ToInt32(m_CounterLabel.Text);
      }
      set
      {
         m_CounterLabel.Text = value.ToString();
      }
   }
}
[ServiceContract]
interface IFormManager
{
   [OperationContract]
   void IncrementLabel();
}
```

Example 8-6. Using the form synchronization context (continued)

```
class MyService : IFormManager
{
    public void IncrementLabel( )
    {
        MyForm form = Application.OpenForms[0] as MyForm;
        Debug.Assert(form != null);

        SendOrPostCallback callback = delegate
                                    {
                                          form.Counter++;
                                    };
        form.MySynchronizationContext.Send(callback,null);
    }
}
static class Program
{
    static void Main( )
    {
        ServiceHost host = new ServiceHost(typeof(MyService));
        host.Open( );

        Application.Run(new MyForm( ));

        host.Close( );
    }
}
```

Example 8-6 shows the form MyForm, which provides the MySynchronizationContext property that allows its clients to obtain its synchronization context. MyForm initializes MySynchronizationContext in its constructor by obtaining the synchronization context of the current thread. The thread has a synchronization context because the constructor of MyForm is called after the constructor of its topmost base class, Control, was called, and Control has already attached the Windows Forms synchronization context to the thread in its constructor.

MyForm also offers a Counter property that updates the value of a counting Windows Forms label. Only the thread that owns the form can access that label. MyService implements the IncrementLabel( ) operation. In that operation, the service obtains a reference to the form via the static OpenForms collection of the Application class:

```
public class FormCollection : ReadOnlyCollectionBase
{
    public virtual Form this[int index]
    {get;}
    public virtual Form this[string name]
    {get;}
}

public sealed class Application
{
```

```
            public static FormCollection OpenForms
            {get;}
            //Rest of the members
      }
```

Once IncrementLabel( ) has the form to update, it accesses the synchronization context
via the MySynchronizationContext property and calls the Send( ) method. Send( ) is provided with an anonymous method that accesses the Counter property. Example 8-6 is a
concrete example of the programming model shown in Example 8-4, and it suffers from
the same deficiency: namely, tight coupling between all service operations and the form.
If the service needs to update multiple controls, that also results in a cumbersome programming model. Any change to the user interface layout, the controls on the forms,
and the required behavior is likely to cause major changes to the service code.

Safe controls

A better approach is to encapsulate the interaction with the Windows Forms synchronization context in safe controls or safe methods on the form, to decouple them
from the service and to simplify the overall programming model. Example 8-7 lists
the code for SafeLabel, a Label-derived class that provides thread-safe access to its
Text property. Because SafeLabel derives from Label, you still have full design-time
visual experience and integration with Visual Studio, yet you can surgically affect just
the property that requires the safe access.

Example 8-7. Encapsulating the synchronization context

```
public class SafeLabel : Label
{
    SynchronizationContext m_SynchronizationContext =
                                        SynchronizationContext.Current;
    override public string Text
    {
        set
        {
            SendOrPostCallback setText = (text)=>
                                        {
                                            base.Text = text as string;
                                        };
            m_SynchronizationContext.Send(setText,value);
        }
        get
        {
            string text = String.Empty;
            SendOrPostCallback getText = delegate
                                        {
                                            text = base.Text;
                                        };
            m_SynchronizationContext.Send(getText,null);
            return text;
        }
    }
}
```

Upon construction, SafeLabel caches its synchronization context. SafeLabel overrides its base class's Text property and uses an anonymous method in the get and set accessors to send the call to the correct UI thread. Note in the get accessor the use of an outer variable to return a value from Send(), as discussed previously. Using SafeLabel, the code in Example 8-6 is reduced to the code shown in Example 8-8.

Example 8-8. Using a safe control

```csharp
class MyForm : Form
{
    Label m_CounterLabel;

    public MyForm()
    {
        InitializeComponent();
    }
    void InitializeComponent()
    {
        ...
        m_CounterLabel = new SafeLabel();
        ...
    }
    public int Counter
    {
        get
        {
            return Convert.ToInt32(m_CounterLabel.Text);
        }
        set
        {
            m_CounterLabel.Text = value.ToString();
        }
    }
}
class MyService : IFormManager
{
    public void IncrementLabel()
    {
        MyForm form = Application.OpenForms[0] as MyForm;
        Debug.Assert(form != null);

        form.Counter++;
    }
}
```

Note in Example 8-8 that the service simply accesses the form directly:

```csharp
form.Counter++;
```

and that the form is written as a normal form. Example 8-8 is a concrete example of the programming model shown in Example 8-5.

ServiceModelEx contains not only SafeLabel but also other controls you are likely to update at runtime such as SafeButton, SafeListBox, SafeProgressBar, SafeStatusBar, SafeTrackBar, and SafeTextBox.

Service Synchronization Context

The programming techniques shown so far put the onus of accessing the resource on the correct thread squarely on the service or resource developer. It would be preferable if the service had a way of associating itself with a particular synchronization context, and could have WCF detect that context and automatically marshal the call from the worker thread to the associated service synchronization context. In fact, WCF lets you do just that. You can instruct WCF to maintain an affinity between all service instances from a particular host and a specific synchronization context. The ServiceBehavior attribute offers the UseSynchronizationContext Boolean property, defined as:

```
[AttributeUsage(AttributeTargets.Class)]
public sealed class ServiceBehaviorAttribute : ...
{
    public bool UseSynchronizationContext
    {get;set;}
    //More members
}
```

The affinity between the service type, its host, and a synchronization context is locked in when the host is opened. If the thread opening the host has a synchronization context and UseSynchronizationContext is true, WCF will establish an affinity between that synchronization context and all instances of the service hosted by that host. WCF will automatically marshal all incoming calls to the service's synchronization context. All the thread-specific information stored in the TLS, such as the client's transaction or the security information (discussed in Chapter 10), will be marshaled correctly to the synchronization context.

If UseSynchronizationContext is false, regardless of any synchronization context the opening thread might have, the service will have no affinity to any synchronization context. Likewise, even if UseSynchronizationContext is true, if the opening thread has no synchronization context the service will not have one either.

The default value of UseSynchronizationContext is true, so these definitions are equivalent:

```
[ServiceContract]
interface IMyContract
{...}

class MyService : IMyContract
{...}
```

```
[ServiceBehavior(UseSynchronizationContext = true)]
class MyService : IMyContract
{...}
```

Hosting on the UI Thread

The classic use for UseSynchronizationContext is to enable the service to update user interface controls and windows directly, without resorting to techniques such as those illustrated in Examples 8-6 and 8-7. WCF greatly simplifies UI updates by providing an affinity between all service instances from a particular host and a specific UI thread. To achieve that end, host the service on the UI thread that also creates the windows or controls with which the service needs to interact. Since the Windows Forms synchronization context is established during the instantiation of the base window, you need to open the host before that. For example, this sequence from Example 8-6:

```
ServiceHost host = new ServiceHost(typeof(MyService));
host.Open();

Application.Run(new MyForm());
```

will not have the host associate itself with the form synchronization context, since the host is opened before the form is created.

However, this minute change in the order of the lines of instantiation will achieve the desired effect:

```
Form form = new MyForm();

ServiceHost host = new ServiceHost(typeof(MyService));
host.Open();

Application.Run(form);
```

Although this change has no apparent effect in classic .NET, it is actually monumental for WCF, since now the thread that opened the host does have a synchronization context, and the host will use it for all calls to the service. The problem with this approach is that it is fragile—most developers maintaining your code will not be aware that simply rearranging the same independent lines of code will have this effect. It is also wrong to design the form and the service that needs to update it so that they are both at the mercy of the Main() method and the hosting code to such a degree.

The simple solution is to have the window or form that the service needs to interact with be the one that opens the host before loading the form, as shown in Example 8-9.

Example 8-9. The form hosting the service

```
class MyService : IMyContract
{...}

partial class HostForm : Form
{
   ServiceHost m_Host;
   Label m_CounterLabel;

   public HostForm( )
   {
      InitializeComponent( );

      m_Host = new ServiceHost(typeof(MyService));

      m_Host.Open( );
   }
   void OnFormClosed(object sender,EventArgs e)
   {
      m_Host.Close( );
   }

   public int Counter
   {
      get
      {
         return Convert.ToInt32(m_CounterLabel.Text);
      }
      set
      {
         m_CounterLabel.Text = value.ToString( );
      }
   }
}
static class Program
{
   static void Main( )
   {
      Application.Run(new HostForm( ));
   }
}
```

The service in Example 8-9 defaults to using whichever synchronization context its host encounters. The form HostForm stores the service host in a member variable so that the form can close the service when the form is closed. The constructor of HostForm already has a synchronization context, so when it opens the host, an affinity to that synchronization context is established.

Accessing the form

Even though the form hosts the service in Example 8-9, the service instances must have some proprietary application-specific mechanism to reach into the form. If a service instance needs to update multiple forms, you can use the `Application.OpenForms` collections (as in Example 8-6) to find the correct form. Once the service has the form, it can freely access it directly, as opposed to the code in Example 8-6, which required marshaling:

```
class MyService : IFormManager
{
   public void IncrementLabel()
   {
      HostForm form = Application.OpenForms[0] as HostForm;
      Debug.Assert(form != null);
      form.Counter++;
   }
}
```

You could also store references to the forms to use in static variables, but the problem with such global variables is that if multiple UI threads are used to pump messages to different instances of the same form type, you cannot use a single static variable for each form type—you need a static variable for each thread used, which complicates things significantly.

Instead, the form (or forms) can store a reference to itself in the TLS, and have the service instance access that store and obtain the reference. However, using the TLS is a cumbersome and non-type-safe programming model. An improvement on this approach is to use thread-relative static variables. By default, static variables are visible to all threads in an app domain. With thread-relative static variables, each thread in the app domain gets its own copy of the static variable. You use the `ThreadStaticAttribute` to mark a static variable as thread-relative. Thread-relative static variables are always thread-safe because they can be accessed only by a single thread and because each thread gets its own copy of the static variable. Thread-relative static variables are stored in the TLS, yet they provide a type-safe, simplified programming model. Example 8-10 demonstrates this technique.

Example 8-10. Storing form reference in a thread-relative static variable

```
partial class HostForm : Form
{
   Label m_CounterLabel;
   ServiceHost m_Host;

   [ThreadStatic]
   static HostForm m_CurrentForm;

   public static HostForm CurrentForm
   {
      get
      {
```

```
            return m_CurrentForm;
        }
        set
        {
            m_CurrentForm = value;
        }
    }
    public int Counter
    {
        get
        {
            return Convert.ToInt32(m_CounterLabel.Text);
        }
        set
        {
            m_CounterLabel.Text = value.ToString( );
        }
    }
    public HostForm( )
    {
        InitializeComponent( );

        CurrentForm = this;

        m_Host = new ServiceHost(typeof(MyService));
        m_Host.Open( );
    }
    void OnFormClosed(object sender,EventArgs e)
    {
        m_Host.Close( );
    }
}
[ServiceContract]
interface IFormManager
{
    [OperationContract]
    void IncrementLabel( );
}
class MyService : IFormManager
{
    public void IncrementLabel( )
    {
        HostForm form = HostForm.CurrentForm;
        form.Counter++;
    }
}
static class Program
{
    static void Main( )
    {
        Application.Run(new HostForm( ));
    }
}
```

The form HostForm stores a reference to itself in a thread-relative static variable called m_CurrentForm. The service accesses the static property CurrentForm and obtains a reference to the instance of HostForm on that UI thread.

Multiple UI threads

Your service host process can actually have multiple UI threads, each pumping messages to its own set of windows. Such a setup is usually required with UI-intensive applications that want to avoid having multiple windows sharing a single UI thread and hosting the services, because while the UI thread is processing a service call (or a complicated UI update), not all of the windows will be responsive. Since the service synchronization context is established per host, if you have multiple UI threads you will need to open a service host instance for the same service type on each UI thread. Each service host will therefore have a different synchronization context for its service instances. As mentioned in Chapter 1, in order to have multiple hosts for the same service type, you must provide each host with a different base address. The easiest way of doing that is to provide the form constructor with the base address to use as a construction parameter. I also recommend in such a case to use base address-relative addresses for the service endpoints. The clients will still invoke calls on the various service endpoints, yet each endpoint will now correspond to a different host, according to the base address schema and the binding used. Example 8-11 demonstrates this configuration.

Example 8-11. Hosting on multiple UI threads

```
partial class HostForm : Form
{
   public HostForm(string baseAddress)
   {
      InitializeComponent();

      CurrentForm = this;

      m_Host = new ServiceHost(typeof(MyService),new Uri(baseAddress));
      m_Host.Open();
   }
   //Rest same as Example 8-10
}
static class Program
{
   static void Main()
   {
      ParameterizedThreadStart threadMethod = (baseAddress)=>
                                    {
                                    string address = baseAddress as string;
                                    Application.Run(new HostForm(address));
                                    };
```

Example 8-11. Hosting on multiple UI threads (continued)

```
      Thread thread1 = new Thread(threadMethod);
      thread1.Start("http://localhost:8001/");

      Thread thread2 = new Thread(threadMethod);
      thread2.Start("http://localhost:8002/");
   }
}
/* MyService same as Example 8-10 */

/////////////////////////////// Host Config File //////////////////////////////
<services>
   <service name = "MyService">
      <endpoint
         address  = "MyService"
         binding  = "basicHttpBinding"
         contract = "IFormManager"
      />
   </service>
</services>
/////////////////////////////// Client Config File /////////////////////////////
<client>
   <endpoint name = "Form A"
      address  = "http://localhost:8001/MyService/"
      binding  = "basicHttpBinding"
      contract = "IFormManager"
   />
   <endpoint name = "Form B"
      Address  = "http://localhost:8002/MyService/"
      binding  = "basicHttpBinding"
      contract = "IFormManager"
   />
</client>
```

In Example 8-11, the Main( ) method launches two UI threads, each with its own instance of HostForm. Each form instance accepts as a construction parameter a base address that it in turn provides for its own host instance. Once the host is opened, it establishes an affinity to that UI thread's synchronization context. Calls from the client to the corresponding base address are now routed to the respective UI thread.

A Form As a Service

The main motivation for hosting a WCF service on a UI thread is when the service needs to update the UI or the form. The problem is, how does the service reach out and obtain a reference to the form? While the techniques and ideas shown in the examples so far certainly work, the separation between the service and the form is artificial. It would be simpler if the form were the service and hosted itself. For this to work, the form (or any window) must be a singleton service. The reason is that singleton is the only instancing mode that enables you to provide WCF with a live instance to host. In addition, it wouldn't be desirable to use a per-call form that exists only during a client call (which is usually very brief), or a sessionful form that only a single client can establish a session with and update. When a form is also a service, having that form as a singleton is the best instancing mode all around. Example 8-12 lists just such a service.

Example 8-12. Form as a singleton service

```
[ServiceContract]
interface IFormManager
{
   [OperationContract]
   void IncrementLabel();
}
[ServiceBehavior(InstanceContextMode = InstanceContextMode.Single)]
partial class MyForm : Form,IFormManager
{
   Label m_CounterLabel;
   ServiceHost m_Host;

   public MyForm()
   {
      InitializeComponent();
      m_Host = new ServiceHost(this);
      m_Host.Open();
   }
   void OnFormClosed(object sender,EventArgs args)
   {
      m_Host.Close();
   }
   public void IncrementLabel()
   {
      Counter++;
   }
   public int Counter
   {
      get
      {
         return Convert.ToInt32(m_CounterLabel.Text);
      }
      set
      {
         m_CounterLabel.Text = value.ToString();
      }
   }
}
```

MyForm implements the IFormManager contract and is configured as a WCF singleton service. MyForm has a ServiceHost as a member variable, as before. When MyForm constructs the host, it uses the host constructor that accepts an object reference, as shown in Chapter 4. MyForm passes itself as the object. MyForm opens the host when the form is created and closes the host when the form is closed. Updating the form's controls as a result of client calls is done by accessing them directly, because the form, of course, runs in its own synchronization context.

The FormHost<F> class

You can streamline and automate the code in Example 8-12 using my FormHost<F> class, defined as:

```
[ServiceBehavior(InstanceContextMode = InstanceContextMode.Single)]
public abstract class FormHost<F> : Form where F : Form
{
    public FormHost(params string[] baseAddresses);

    protected ServiceHost<F> Host
    {get;}
}
```

Using FormHost<F>, Example 8-12 is reduced to:

```
partial class MyForm : FormHost<MyForm>,IFormManager
{
    Label m_CounterLabel;

    public MyForm()
    {
        InitializeComponent();
    }
    public void IncrementLabel()
    {
        Counter++;
    }
    public int Counter
    {
        get
        {
            return Convert.ToInt32(m_CounterLabel.Text);
        }
        set
        {
            m_CounterLabel.Text = value.ToString();
        }
    }
}
```

The Windows Forms designer is incapable of rendering a form that has an abstract base class, let alone one that uses generics. You will have to change the base class to Form for visual editing, then revert to FormHost<F> for debugging. To compensate, copy the Debug configuration into a new solution configuration called Design, then add the DESIGN symbol to the Design configuration. Finally, define the form to render properly in design mode and to execute properly in debug and release modes:

```
#if DESIGN
public partial class MyForm : Form,IFormManager
#else
public partial class MyForm :
                    FormHost<MyForm>,IFormManager
#endif
{...}
```

Example 8-13 shows the implementation of FormHost<F>.

Example 8-13. Implementing FormHost<F>

```
[ServiceBehavior(InstanceContextMode = InstanceContextMode.Single)]
public abstract class FormHost<F> : Form where F : Form
{
   protected ServiceHost<F> Host
   {get;private set;}

   public FormHost(params string[] baseAddresses)
   {
      Host = new ServiceHost<F>(this as F,baseAddresses);

      Load += delegate
            {
                if(Host.State == CommunicationState.Created)
                {
                    Host.Open();
                }
            };
      FormClosed += delegate
                {
                    if(Host.State == CommunicationState.Opened)
                    {
                        Host.Close();
                    }
                };
   }
}
```

FormHost<F> is an abstract generic class configured as a singleton service. It takes a single type parameter, F, which is constrained to be a Windows Forms Form class. FormHost<F> uses my ServiceHost<T> as a member variable, specifying F for the type parameter for the host. FormHost<F> offers the host access to the derived forms, mostly for advanced configuration, so the Host property is marked as protected.

The constructor of FormHost<F> creates the host, but does not open it. The reason is that the subform may want to perform some host initialization, such as configuring a throttle, and this initialization can only be done before opening the host. The subclass should place that initialization in its own constructor:

```
public MyForm()
{
   InitializeComponent();
   Host.SetThrottle(10,20,1);
}
```

To allow for this, the constructor uses an anonymous method to subscribe to the form's Load event, where it first verifies that the subform has not yet opened the host and then opens it. In a similar manner, the constructor subscribes to the form's FormClosed event, where it closes the host.

The UI Thread and Concurrency Management

Whenever you use hosting on the UI thread (or in any other case of a single-thread affinity synchronization context), deadlocks are possible. For example, the following setup is guaranteed to result with a deadlock: a Windows Forms application is hosting a service with UseSynchronizationContext set to true, and UI thread affinity is established; the Windows Forms application then calls the service in-proc over one of its endpoints. The call to the service blocks the UI thread, while WCF posts a message to the UI thread to invoke the service. That message is never processed due to the blocking UI thread—hence the deadlock.

Another possible case for a deadlock occurs when a Windows Forms application is hosting a service with UseSynchronizationContext set to true and UI thread affinity established. The service receives a call from a remote client, which is marshaled to the UI thread and eventually executed on that thread. If the service is allowed to call out to another service, that may result in a deadlock if the callout causality tries somehow to update the UI or call back to the service's endpoint, since all service instances associated with any endpoint (regardless of the service instancing mode) share the same UI thread. Similarly, you risk a deadlock if the service is configured for reentrancy and it calls back to its client: a deadlock will occur if the callback causality tries to update the UI or enter the service, since that reentrance must be marshaled to the blocked UI thread.

UI responsiveness

Every client call to a service hosted on the UI thread is converted to a Windows message and is eventually executed on the UI thread—the same thread that is responsible for updating the UI and for continuing to respond to user input, as well as updating the user about the state of the application. While the UI thread is processing the service call, it does not process UI messages. Consequently, you should avoid lengthy processing in the service operation, because that can severely degrade the

UI's responsiveness. You can alleviate this somewhat by pumping Windows messages in the service operation, either by explicitly calling the static method `Application.DoEvents()` to process all the queued-up Windows messages or by using a method such as `MessageBox.Show()` that pumps some but not all of the queued messages. The downside of trying to refresh the UI this way is that it may dispatch queued client calls to the service instance and may cause unwanted reentrancy or a deadlock.

To make things even worse, what if clients dispatch a number of calls to the service all at once? Depending on the service concurrency mode (discussed next) even if those service calls are of short duration, the calls will all be queued back-to-back in the Windows message queue, and processing them in order might take time—and all the while, the UI will not be updated.

Whenever you're hosting on a UI thread, carefully examine the calls' duration and frequency to see whether the resulting degradation in UI responsiveness is acceptable. What is acceptable may be application-specific, but as a rule of thumb, most users will not mind a UI latency of less than half a second, will notice a delay of more than three quarters of a second, and will be annoyed if the delay is more than a second. If that is the case, consider hosting parts of the UI (and the associated services) on multiple UI threads, as explained previously. By having multiple UI threads you maximize responsiveness, because while one thread is busy servicing a client call, the rest can still update their windows and controls. If using multiple UI threads is impossible in your application and processing service calls introduces unacceptable UI responsiveness, examine what the service operations do and what is causing the latency. Typically, the latency would be caused not by the UI updates but rather by performing lengthy operations, such as calling other services, or computational-intensive operations, such as image processing. Because the service is hosted on the UI thread, WCF performs all of that work on the UI thread, not just the critical part that interacts with the UI directly. If that is indeed your situation, disallow the affinity to the UI thread altogether by setting `UseSynchronizationContext` to `false`:

```
[ServiceBehavior(UseSynchronizationContext = false)]
class MyService : IMyContract
{
   public void MyMethod()
   {
      Debug.Assert(Application.MessageLoop == false);
      //Rest of the implementation
   }
}
```

(You can even assert that the thread executing the service call does not have a message loop.) Perform the lengthy operations on the incoming worker thread, and use safe controls (such as `SafeLabel`) to marshal the calls to the UI thread only when required, as opposed to all the time. The downside of this approach is that it is an expert programming model: the service cannot be the window or form itself (by relying on the simplicity of FormHost<F>), so you need a way of binding to the form, and the service developer has to work together with the UI developers to ensure they use the safe controls or provide access to the form's synchronization context.

The UI thread and concurrency modes

A service with a UI thread affinity is inherently thread-safe because only that UI thread can ever call its instances. Since only a single thread (and the same thread, at that) can ever access an instance, that instance is by definition thread-safe. Since the service is single-threaded anyway, configuring the service with ConcurrencyMode. Single adds no safety. When you configure with ConcurrencyMode.Single, concurrent client calls are first queued up by the instance lock and then dispatched to the service's message loop one at a time, in order. These client calls are therefore given the opportunity of being interleaved with other UI Windows messages. ConcurrencyMode.Single thus yields the best responsiveness, because the UI thread will alternate between processing client calls and user interactions. When you configure the service with ConcurrencyMode.Multiple, client calls are dispatched to the service message loop as soon as they arrive off the channel and are invoked in order. The problem is that this mode allows the possibility of a batch of client calls arriving either back-to-back or in close proximity to each other in the Windows message queue, and while the UI thread processes that batch, the UI will be unresponsive. Consequently, ConcurrencyMode.Multiple is the worst option for UI responsiveness. When configured with ConcurrencyMode.Reentrant, the service is not reentrant at all, and deadlocks are still possible, as explained at the beginning of this section. Clearly, the best practice with UI thread affinity is to configure the service with ConcurrencyMode.Single. Avoid ConcurrencyMode.Multiple due to its detrimental effect on responsiveness and ConcurrencyMode.Reentrant due to its unfulfilled ability.

Custom Service Synchronization Contexts

While a synchronization context is a general-purpose pattern, out of the box, .NET only implements a single useful one: the Windows Forms synchronization context (there is also the default implementation that uses the .NET thread pool). As it turns out, the ability to automatically marshal calls to a custom synchronization context is one of the most powerful extensibility mechanisms in WCF.

The Thread Pool Synchronizer

There are two aspects to developing a custom service synchronization context: the first is implementing a custom synchronization context, and the second is installing it or even applying it declaratively on the service. *ServiceModelEx* contains my ThreadPoolSynchronizer class, defined as:

```
public class ThreadPoolSynchronizer : SynchronizationContext,IDisposable
{
   public ThreadPoolSynchronizer(uint poolSize);
   public ThreadPoolSynchronizer(uint poolSize,string poolName);

   public void Dispose();
   public void Close();
   public void Abort();

   protected Semaphore CallQueued
   {get;}
}
```

Implementing a custom synchronization context has nothing to do with WCF and is therefore not discussed in this book, although the implementation code is available with *ServiceModelEx*.

ThreadPoolSynchronizer marshals all calls to a custom thread pool, where the calls are first queued up, then multiplexed on the available threads. The size of the pool is provided as a construction parameter. If the pool is maxed out, any calls that come in will remain pending in the queue until a thread is available.

You can also provide a pool name (which will be the prefix of the name of each of the threads in the pool). Disposing of or closing the ThreadPoolSynchronizer kills all threads in the pool gracefully; that is, the ThreadPoolSynchronizer waits for the engaged threads to complete their tasks. The Abort() method is an ungraceful shutdown, as it terminates all threads abruptly.

The classic use for a custom thread pool is with a server application (such as a web server or an email server) that needs to maximize its throughput by controlling the underlying worker threads and their assignment. However, such usage is rare, since most application developers do not write servers anymore. The real use of ThreadPoolSynchronizer is as a stepping-stone to implement other synchronization contexts, which are useful in their own right.

To associate your service with the custom thread pool, you can manually attach ThreadPoolSynchronizer to the thread opening the host using the static SetSynchronizationContext() method of SynchronizationContext, as shown in Example 8-14.

Example 8-14. Using ThreadPoolSynchronizer

```
SynchronizationContext syncContext = new ThreadPoolSynchronizer(3);

SynchronizationContext.SetSynchronizationContext(syncContext);

using(syncContext as IDisposable)
{
   ServiceHost host = new ServiceHost(typeof(MyService));
   host.Open();
```

Example 8-14. Using ThreadPoolSynchronizer (continued)

```
    /* Some blocking operations */

    host.Close( );
}
```

In Example 8-14, the thread pool will have three threads. The service MyService will have an affinity to those three threads, and all calls to the service will be channeled to them, regardless of the service concurrency mode or instancing mode, and across all endpoints and contracts supported by the service. After closing the host, the example disposes of ThreadPoolSynchronizer to shut down the threads in the pool.

Note that a service executing in a custom thread pool is not thread-safe (unless the pool size is 1), so the preceding discussion of concurrency management still applies. The only difference is that now you control the threads.

Declaratively attaching a custom synchronization context

The problem with Example 8-14 is that the service is at the mercy of the hosting code. If by design the service is required to execute in the pool, it would be better to apply the thread pool declaratively, as part of the service definition.

To that end, I wrote the ThreadPoolBehaviorAttribute:

```
[AttributeUsage(AttributeTargets.Class)]
public class ThreadPoolBehaviorAttribute : Attribute,
                                          IContractBehavior,IServiceBehavior
{
    public ThreadPoolBehaviorAttribute(uint poolSize,Type serviceType);
    public ThreadPoolBehaviorAttribute(uint poolSize,Type serviceType,
                                       string poolName);
}
```

You apply this attribute directly on the service, while providing the service type as a constructor parameter:

```
[ThreadPoolBehavior(3,typeof(MyService))]
class MyService : IMyContract
{...}
```

The attribute provides an instance of ThreadPoolSynchronizer to the dispatchers of the service's endpoints. The key in implementing the ThreadPoolBehavior attribute is knowing how and when to hook up the dispatchers with the synchronization context. The ThreadPoolBehavior attribute supports the special WCF extensibility interface IContractBehavior, introduced in Chapter 5:

```
public interface IContractBehavior
{
    void ApplyDispatchBehavior(ContractDescription description,
                               ServiceEndpoint endpoint,
                               DispatchRuntime dispatchRuntime);
    //More members
}
```

When a service is decorated with an attribute that supports IContractBehavior, after opening the host (but before forwarding calls to the service), for each service endpoint WCF calls the ApplyDispatchBehavior( ) method and provides it with the DispatchRuntime parameter, allowing you to affect an individual endpoint dispatcher's runtime and set its synchronization context. Each endpoint has its own dispatcher, and each dispatcher has its own synchronization context, so the attribute is instantiated and ApplyDispatchBehavior( ) is called for each endpoint.

Example 8-15 lists most of the implementation of ThreadPoolBehaviorAttribute.

Example 8-15. Implementing ThreadPoolBehaviorAttribute

```
[AttributeUsage(AttributeTargets.Class)]
public class ThreadPoolBehaviorAttribute : Attribute,IContractBehavior,
                                                          IServiceBehavior
{
   protected string PoolName
   {get;set;}
   protected uint PoolSize
   {get;set;}
   protected Type ServiceType
   {get;set;}

  public ThreadPoolBehaviorAttribute(uint poolSize,Type serviceType) :
                                          this(poolSize,serviceType,null)
   {}
   public ThreadPoolBehaviorAttribute(uint poolSize,Type serviceType,
                                 string poolName)
   {
      PoolName    = poolName;
      ServiceType = serviceType;
      PoolSize    = poolSize;
   }
   protected virtual ThreadPoolSynchronizer ProvideSynchronizer( )
   {
      if(ThreadPoolHelper.HasSynchronizer(ServiceType) == false)
      {
         return new ThreadPoolSynchronizer(PoolSize,PoolName);
      }
      else
      {
         return ThreadPoolHelper.GetSynchronizer(ServiceType);
      }
   }

   void IContractBehavior.ApplyDispatchBehavior(ContractDescription description,
                                        ServiceEndpoint endpoint,
                                        DispatchRuntime dispatchRuntime)
   {
      PoolName = PoolName ?? "Pool executing endpoints of " + ServiceType;

      lock(typeof(ThreadPoolHelper))
      {
```

Example 8-15. Implementing ThreadPoolBehaviorAttribute (continued)

```
            ThreadPoolHelper.ApplyDispatchBehavior(ProvideSynchronizer( ),
                                    PoolSize,ServiceType,PoolName,dispatchRuntime);
        }
    }
    void IServiceBehavior.Validate(ServiceDescription description,
                                   ServiceHostBase serviceHostBase)
    {
        serviceHostBase.Closed += delegate
                                  {
                                      ThreadPoolHelper.CloseThreads(ServiceType);
                                  };
    }
    //Rest of the implementation
}
public static class ThreadPoolHelper
{
    static Dictionary<Type,ThreadPoolSynchronizer> m_Synchronizers =
                             new Dictionary<Type,ThreadPoolSynchronizer>( );

    [MethodImpl(MethodImplOptions.Synchronized)]
    internal static bool HasSynchronizer(Type type)
    {
        return m_Synchronizers.ContainsKey(type);
    }

    [MethodImpl(MethodImplOptions.Synchronized)]
    internal static ThreadPoolSynchronizer GetSynchronizer(Type type)
    {
        return m_Synchronizers[type];
    }
    [MethodImpl(MethodImplOptions.Synchronized)]
    internal static void ApplyDispatchBehavior(ThreadPoolSynchronizer synchronizer,
                                          uint poolSize,Type type,
                                          string poolName,
                                          DispatchRuntime dispatchRuntime)
    {
        if(HasSynchronizer(type) == false)
        {
            m_Synchronizers[type] = synchronizer;
        }
        dispatchRuntime.SynchronizationContext = m_Synchronizers[type];
    }
    [MethodImpl(MethodImplOptions.Synchronized)]
    public static void CloseThreads(Type type)
    {
        if(HasSynchronizer(type))
        {
            m_Synchronizers[type].Dispose( );
            m_Synchronizers.Remove(type);
        }
    }
}
```

The constructors of the ThreadPoolBehavior attribute save the provided service type and pool name. The name is simply passed to the constructor of ThreadPoolSynchronizer.

 The ApplyDispatchBehavior( ) method in Example 8-15 uses the ?? null-coalescing operator (introduced in C# 2.0) to assign a pool name if required. This expression:

```
PoolName = PoolName ??
        "Pool executing endpoints of " + ServiceType;
```
is shorthand for:
```
if(PoolName == null)
{
    PoolName = " Pool executing endpoints of " +
                                    ServiceType;
}
```

It is a best practice to separate the implementation of a WCF custom behavior attribute from the actual behavior: let the attribute merely decide on the sequence of events, and have a helper class provide the actual behavior. Doing so enables the behavior to be used separately (for example, by a custom host). This is why the ThreadPoolBehavior attribute does not do much. It delegates most of its work to a static helper class called ThreadPoolHelper. ThreadPoolHelper provides the HasSynchronizer( ) method, which indicates whether the specified service type already has a synchronization context, and the GetSynchronizer( ) method, which returns the synchronization context associated with the type. The ThreadPoolBehavior attribute uses these two methods in the virtual ProvideSynchronizer( ) method to ensure that it creates the pool exactly once per service type. This check is required because ApplyDispatchBehavior( ) may be called multiple times (once per endpoint). The ThreadPoolBehavior attribute is also a custom service behavior, because it implements IServiceBehavior. The Validate( ) method of IServiceBehavior provides the service host instance the ThreadPoolBehavior attribute uses to subscribe to the host's Closed event, where it asks ThreadPoolHelper to terminate all the threads in the pool by calling ThreadPoolHelper.CloseThreads( ).

ThreadPoolHelper associates all dispatchers of all endpoints of that service type with the same instance of ThreadPoolSynchronizer. This ensures that all calls are routed to the same pool. ThreadPoolHelper has to be able to map a service type to a particular ThreadPoolSynchronizer, so it declares a static dictionary called m_Synchronizers that uses service types as keys and ThreadPoolSynchronizer instances as values.

In ApplyDispatchBehavior( ), ThreadPoolHelper checks to see whether m_Synchronizers already contains the provided service type. If the type is not found, ThreadPoolHelper adds the provided ThreadPoolSynchronizer to m_Synchronizers, associating it with the service type.

The DispatchRuntime class provides the SynchronizationContext property ThreadPoolHelper uses to assign a synchronization context for the dispatcher:

```
public sealed class DispatchRuntime
{
   public SynchronizationContext SynchronizationContext
   {get;set;}
   //More members
}
```

Before making the assignment, ThreadPoolHelper verifies that the dispatcher has no other synchronization context, since that would indicate some unresolved conflict. After that, it simply assigns the ThreadPoolSynchronizer instance to the dispatcher:

```
dispatchRuntime.SynchronizationContext = m_Synchronizers[type];
```

This single line is all that is required to have WCF use the custom synchronization context from now on. In the CloseThreads() method, ThreadPoolHelper looks up the ThreadPoolSynchronizer instance in the dictionary and disposes of it (thus gracefully terminating all the worker threads in the pool). ThreadPoolHelper also verifies that the provided pool size value does not exceed the maximum concurrent calls value of the dispatcher's throttle (this is not shown in Example 8-15).

Thread Affinity

A pool size of 1 will in effect create an affinity between a particular thread and all service calls, regardless of the service's concurrency and instancing modes. This is particularly useful if the service is required not merely to update some UI but to also create a UI (for example, creating a pop-up window and then periodically showing, hiding, and updating it). Having created the window, the service must ensure that the creating thread is used to access and update it. Thread affinity is also required for a service that accesses or creates resources that use the TLS. To formalize such requirements I created the specialized AffinitySynchronizer class, implemented as:

```
public class AffinitySynchronizer : ThreadPoolSynchronizer
{
   public AffinitySynchronizer() : this("AffinitySynchronizer Worker Thread")
   {}
   public AffinitySynchronizer(string threadName): base(1,threadName)
   {}
}
```

While you can install AffinitySynchronizer, as shown in Example 8-14, if by design the service is required to always execute on the same thread it is better not to be at the mercy of the host and the thread that happens to open it. Instead, use my ThreadAffinityBehaviorAttribute:

```
[ThreadAffinityBehavior(typeof(MyService))]
class MyService : IMyContract
{...}
```

ThreadAffinityBehaviorAttribute is a specialization of ThreadPoolBehaviorAttribute that hardcodes the pool size as 1, as shown in Example 8-16.

Example 8-16. Implementing ThreadAffinityBehaviorAttribute

```
[AttributeUsage(AttributeTargets.Class)]
public class ThreadAffinityBehaviorAttribute : ThreadPoolBehaviorAttribute
{
   public ThreadAffinityBehaviorAttribute(Type serviceType) :
                                      this(serviceType,"Affinity Worker Thread")
   {}

   public ThreadAffinityBehaviorAttribute(Type serviceType,string threadName) :
                                      base(1,serviceType,threadName)
   {}
}
```

When relying on thread affinity all service instances are always thread-safe, since only a single thread (and the same thread, at that) can access them.

When the service is configured with ConcurrencyMode.Single, it gains no additional thread safety because the service instance is single-threaded anyway. You do get double queuing of concurrent calls, though: all concurrent calls to the service are first queued in the lock's queue and then dispatched to the single thread in the pool one at a time. With ConcurrencyMode.Multiple, calls are dispatched to the single thread as fast as they arrive and are then queued up to be invoked later, in order and never concurrently. Finally, with ConcurrencyMode.Reentrant, the service is, of course, not reentrant, because the incoming reentering call will be queued up and a deadlock will occur while the single thread is blocked on the callout. It is therefore best to use the default of ConcurrencyMode.Single when relying on thread affinity.

The host-installed synchronization context

If the affinity to a particular synchronization context is a host decision, you can streamline the code in Example 8-14 by encapsulating the installation of the synchronization context with extension methods. For example, the use of thread affinity is such a socialized case, you could define the following extension methods:

```
public static class HostThreadAffinity
{
   public static void SetThreadAffinity(this ServiceHost host,string threadName);
   public static void SetThreadAffinity(this ServiceHost host);
}
```

SetThreadAffinity( ) works equally well on ServiceHost and my ServiceHost<T>:

```
ServiceHost<MyService> host = new ServiceHost<MyService>();
host.SetThreadAffinity();

host.Open();
```

Example 8-17 lists the implementation of the SetThreadAffinity( ) methods.

Example 8-17. Adding thread affinity to the host

```
public static class HostThreadAffinity
{
   public static void SetThreadAffinity(this ServiceHost host,string threadName)
   {
      if(host.State == CommunicationState.Opened)
      {
         throw new InvalidOperationException("Host is already opened");
      }

      AffinitySynchronizer affinitySynchronizer =
                                      new AffinitySynchronizer(threadName);

      SynchronizationContext.SetSynchronizationContext(affinitySynchronizer);

      host.Closing += delegate
                      {
                         using(affinitySynchronizer);
                      };
   }
   public static void SetThreadAffinity(this ServiceHost host)
   {
      SetThreadAffinity(host,"Executing all endpoints of " +
                                       host.Description.ServiceType);
   }
}
```

HostThreadAffinity offers two versions of SetThreadAffinity( ): the parameterized version takes the thread name to provide for AffinitySynchronizer's worker thread, while the parameterless version calls the other SetThreadAffinity( ) method, specifying a thread name inferred from the hosted service type (such as "Executing all endpoints of MyService"). SetThreadAffinity( ) first checks that the host has not yet been opened, because you can only attach a synchronization context before the host is opened. If the host has not been opened, SetThreadAffinity( ) constructs a new AffinitySynchronizer, providing it with the thread name to use, and attaches it to the current thread. Finally, SetThreadAffinity( ) subscribes to the host's Closing event in order to call Dispose( ) on the AffinitySynchronizer, to shut down its worker thread. Since the AffinitySynchronizer member can be null if no one calls SetThreadAffinity( ), OnClosing( ) uses the using statement, which internally checks for null assignment before calling Dispose( ).

Priority Processing*

By default, all calls to your WCF service will be processed in the order in which they arrive. This is true both if you use the I/O completion thread pool or a custom thread pool. Normally, this is exactly what you want. But what if some calls have higher priority and you want to process them as soon as they arrive, rather than in order? Even worse, when such calls arrive, what if the load on your service is such that the underlying service resources are exhausted? What if the throttle is maxed out? In these cases, your higher-priority calls will be queued just like all the other calls, waiting for the service or its resources to become available. Synchronization contexts offer an elegant solution to this problem: you can assign a priority to each call and have the synchronization context sort the calls as they arrive before dispatching them to the thread pool for execution. This is exactly what my PrioritySynchronizer class does:

```
public enum CallPriority
{
   Low,
   Normal,
   High
}
public class PrioritySynchronizer : ThreadPoolSynchronizer
{
   public PrioritySynchronizer(uint poolSize);
   public PrioritySynchronizer(uint poolSize,string poolName);

   public static CallPriority Priority
   {get;set;}
}
```

PrioritySynchronizer derives from ThreadPoolSynchronizer and adds the sorting just mentioned. Since the Send( ) and Post( ) methods of SynchronizationContext do not take a priority parameter, the client of PrioritySynchronizer has two ways of passing the priority of the call: via the Priority property, which stores the priority (a value of the enum type CallPriority) in the TLS of the calling thread, or via the message headers. If unspecified, Priority defaults to CallPriority.Normal.

In addition to the PrioritySynchronizer class, I also provide the matching PriorityCallsBehaviorAttribute, shown in Example 8-18.

Example 8-18. Implementing PriorityCallsBehaviorAttribute

```
[AttributeUsage(AttributeTargets.Class)]
public class PriorityCallsBehaviorAttribute : ThreadPoolBehaviorAttribute
{
   public PriorityCallsBehaviorAttribute(uint poolSize,Type serviceType) :
                                           this(poolSize,serviceType,null)

   {}
```

---

* I first presented my technique for priority processing of WCF calls in my article "Synchronization Contexts in WCF" (*MSDN Magazine*, November 2007).

Example 8-18. Implementing PriorityCallsBehaviorAttribute (continued)

```
   public PriorityCallsBehaviorAttribute(uint poolSize,Type serviceType,
                             string poolName) : base(poolSize,serviceType,poolName)
   {}
   protected override ThreadPoolSynchronizer ProvideSynchronizer()
   {
      if(ThreadPoolHelper.HasSynchronizer(ServiceType) == false)
      {
         return new PrioritySynchronizer(PoolSize,PoolName);
      }
      else
      {
         return ThreadPoolHelper.GetSynchronizer(ServiceType);
      }
   }
}
```

Using the `PriorityCallsBehavior` attribute is straightforward:

```
   [PriorityCallsBehavior(3,typeof(MyService))]
   class MyService : IMyContract
   {...}
```

`PriorityCallsBehaviorAttribute` overrides `ProvideSynchronizer()` and provides an instance of `PrioritySynchronizer` instead of `ThreadPoolSynchronizer`. Because `PrioritySynchronizer` derives from `ThreadPoolSynchronizer`, this is transparent as far as `ThreadPoolHelper` is concerned.

The real challenge in implementing and supporting priority processing is providing the call priority from the client to the service, and ultimately to `PrioritySynchronizer`. Using the `Priority` property of `PrioritySynchronizer` is useful only for non-WCF clients that interact directly with the synchronization context; it is of no use for a WCF client, whose thread is never used to access the service. While you could provide the priority as an explicit parameter in every method, I wanted a generic mechanism that can be applied on any contract and service. To achieve that goal you have to pass the priority of the call out-of-band, via the message headers, using the techniques described in Appendix B. Appendix B explains in detail the use of the incoming and outgoing headers, including augmenting WCF with general-purpose management of extraneous information sent from the client to the service. In effect, I provide a generic yet type-safe and application-specific custom context via my `GenericContext<T>` class, available in *ServiceModelEx*:

```
   [DataContract]
   public class GenericContext<T>
   {
      [DataMember]
      public readonly T Value;

      public GenericContext();
      public GenericContext(T value);
```

```
      public static GenericContext<T> Current
      {get;set;}
   }
```

Literally any data contract (or serializable) type can be used for the type parameter in the custom context, including of course the CallPriority enum.

On the service side, any party can read the value out of the custom headers:

```
    CallPriority priority = GenericContext<CallPriority>.Current.Value;
```

This is exactly what PrioritySynchronizer does when looking for the call priority. It expects the client to provide the priority either in the TLS (via the Priority property) or in the form of a custom context that stores the priority in the message headers.

The client can use my HeaderClientBase<T,H> proxy class (also discussed in Appendix B) to pass the priority to the service in the message headers, or, even better, define a general-purpose priority-enabled proxy class, PriorityClientBase<T>, shown in Example 8-19.

Example 8-19. Defining PriorityClientBase<T>

```
public abstract partial class PriorityClientBase<T> :
                            HeaderClientBase<T,CallPriority> where T : class
{
   public PriorityClientBase( ) : this(PrioritySynchronizer.Priority)
   {}

   public PriorityClientBase(string endpointName) :
                            this(PrioritySynchronizer.Priority,endpointName)
   {}

   public PriorityClientBase(Binding binding,EndpointAddress remoteAddress) :
                        this(PrioritySynchronizer.Priority,binding,remoteAddress)
   {}

   public PriorityClientBase(CallPriority priority) : base(priority)
   {}

   public PriorityClientBase(CallPriority priority,string endpointName) :
                                    base(priority,endpointConfigurationName)
   {}

   public PriorityClientBase(CallPriority priority,Binding binding,
          EndpointAddress remoteAddress) : base(priority,binding,remoteAddress)
   {}
   /* More constructors */
}
```

PriorityClientBase<T> hardcodes the use of CallPriority for the type parameter H. PriorityClientBase<T> defaults to reading the priority from the TLS (yielding CallPriority.Normal when no priority is found), so it can be used like any other proxy class. With very minor changes to your existing proxy classes, you can now add priority-processing support:

```
class MyContractClient : PriorityClientBase<IMyContract>,IMyContract
{
   //Reads priority from TLS
   public MyContractClient( )
   {}

   public MyContractClient(CallPriority priority) : base(priority)
   {}
   public void MyMethod( )
   {
      Channel.MyMethod( );
   }
}

MyContractClient proxy = new MyContractClient(CallPriority.High);
proxy.MyMethod( );
```

Callbacks and Client Safety

There are quite a few cases when a client might receive concurrent callbacks. For instance, if the client has provided a callback reference to multiple services, those services could call back to the client concurrently. Even if it has only provided a single callback reference, the service might launch multiple threads and use all of them to call on that single reference. Duplex callbacks enter the client on worker threads, and if they are processed concurrently without synchronization they might corrupt the client's state. The client must therefore synchronize access to its own in-memory state, as well as to any resources the callback thread might access. Similar to a service, a callback client can use either manual or declarative synchronization. The CallbackBehavior attribute introduced in Chapter 6 offers the ConcurrencyMode and the UseSynchronizationContext properties:

```
[AttributeUsage(AttributeTargets.Class)]
public sealed class CallbackBehaviorAttribute : Attribute,...
{
   public ConcurrencyMode ConcurrencyMode
   {get;set;}
   public bool UseSynchronizationContext
   {get;set;}
}
```

Both of these properties default to the same values as with the ServiceBehavior attribute and behave in a similar manner. For example, the default of the ConcurrencyMode property is ConcurrencyMode.Single, so these two definitions are equivalent:

```
class MyClient : IMyContractCallback
{...}

[CallbackBehavior(ConcurrencyMode = ConcurrencyMode.Single)]
class MyClient : IMyContractCallback
{...}
```

Callbacks with ConcurrencyMode.Single

When the callback class is configured with ConcurrencyMode.Single (the default), only one callback at a time is allowed to enter the callback object. The big difference, compared with a service, is that callback objects often have an existence independent of WCF. While the service instance is owned by WCF and only ever accessed by worker threads dispatched by WCF, a callback object may also interact with local client-side threads. It fact, it always interacts with at least one additional thread: the thread that called the service and provided the callback object. These client threads are unaware of the synchronization lock associated with the callback object when it is configured with ConcurrencyMode.Single. All that ConcurrencyMode.Single does for a callback object is serialize the access by WCF threads. You must therefore manually synchronize access to the callback state and any other resource accessed by the callback method, as shown in Example 8-20.

Example 8-20. Manually synchronizing the callback with ConcurrencyMode.Single

```
interface IMyContractCallback
{
   [OperationContract]
   void OnCallback( );
}
[ServiceContract(CallbackContract = typeof(IMyContractCallback))]
interface IMyContract
{
   [OperationContract]
   void MyMethod( );
}

class MyClient : IMyContractCallback,IDisposable
{
   MyContractClient m_Proxy;

   public void CallService( )
   {
      m_Proxy = new MyContractClient(new InstanceContext(this));
      m_Proxy.MyMethod( );
   }
   //This method invoked by one callback at a time, plus client threads
   public void OnCallback( )
   {
      //Access state and resources, synchronize manually
      lock(this)
      {...}
   }
   public void Dispose( )
   {
      m_Proxy.Close( );
   }
}
```

Callbacks with ConcurrencyMode.Multiple

When you configure the callback class with `ConcurrencyMode.Multiple`, WCF will allow concurrent calls on the callback instance. This means you need to synchronize access in the callback operations, as shown in Example 8-21, because they could be invoked concurrently both by WCF worker threads and by client-side threads.

Example 8-21. Manually synchronizing the callback with ConcurrencyMode.Multiple

```
[CallbackBehavior(ConcurrencyMode = ConcurrencyMode.Multiple)]
class MyClient : IMyContractCallback,IDisposable
{
   MyContractClient m_Proxy;

   public void CallService()
   {
      m_Proxy = new MyContractClient(new InstanceContext(this));
      m_Proxy.MyMethod();
   }
   //This method can be invoked concurrently by callbacks,
   //plus client threads
   public void OnCallback()
   {
      //Access state and resources, synchronize manually
      lock(this)
      {...}
   }
   public void Dispose()
   {
      m_Proxy.Close();
   }
}
```

Callbacks with ConcurrencyMode.Reentrant

The callback object can perform outgoing calls over WCF, and those calls may eventually try to reenter the callback object. To avoid the deadlock that would occur when using `ConcurrencyMode.Single`, you can configure the callback class with `ConcurrencyMode.Reentrant` as needed:

```
[CallbackBehavior(ConcurrencyMode = ConcurrencyMode.Reentrant)]
class MyClient : IMyContractCallback
{...}
```

Configuring the callback for reentrancy also enables other services to call it when the callback object itself is engaged in WCF callouts.

Callbacks and Synchronization Contexts

Like a service invocation, a callback may need to access resources that rely on some kind of thread(s) affinity. In addition, the callback instance itself may require thread affinity for its own use of the TLS, or for interacting with a UI thread. While the callback can use techniques such as those in Examples 8-4 and 8-5 to marshal the interaction to the resource synchronization context, you can also have WCF associate the callback with a particular synchronization context by setting the UseSynchronizationContext property to true. However, unlike the service, the client does not use any host to expose the endpoint. If the UseSynchronizationContext property is true, the synchronization context to use is locked in when the proxy is opened (or, more commonly, when the client makes the first call to the service using the proxy, if Open( ) is not explicitly called). If the client is using the channel factory, the synchronization context to use is locked in when the client calls CreateChannel( ). If the calling client thread has a synchronization context, this will be the synchronization context used by WCF for all callbacks to the client's endpoint associated with that proxy. Note that only the first call made on the proxy (or the call to Open( ) or CreateChannel( )) is given the opportunity to determine the synchronization context. Subsequent calls have no say in the matter. If the calling client thread has no synchronization context, even if UseSynchronizationContext is true, no synchronization context will be used for the callbacks.

Callbacks and the UI Synchronization Context

If the callback object is running in a Windows Forms synchronization context, or if it needs to update some UI, you must marshal the callbacks or the updates to the UI thread. You can use techniques such as those in Examples 8-6 or 8-8. However, the more common use for UI updates over callbacks is to have the form itself implement the callback contract and update the UI, as in Example 8-22.

Example 8-22. Relying on the UI synchronization context for callbacks

```
partial class MyForm : Form,IMyContractCallback
{
   MyContractClient m_Proxy;

   public MyForm( )
   {
      InitializeComponent( );
      m_Proxy = new MyContractClient(new InstanceContext(this));
   }
   //Called as a result of a UI event
   public void OnCallService(object sender,EventArgs args)
   {
      m_Proxy.MyMethod( ); //Affinity established here
   }
   //This method always runs on the UI thread
```

Example 8-22. Relying on the UI synchronization context for callbacks (continued)

```
   public void OnCallback( )
   {
      //No need for synchronization and marshaling
      Text = "Some Callback";
   }
   public void OnClose(object sender,EventArgs args)
   {
      m_Proxy.Close( );
   }
}
```

In Example 8-22 the proxy is first used in the CallService( ) method, which is called by the UI thread as a result of some UI event. Calling the proxy on the UI synchronization context establishes the affinity to it, so the callback can directly access and update the UI without marshaling any calls. In addition, since only one thread (and the same thread, at that) will ever execute in the synchronization context, the callback is guaranteed to be synchronized.

You can also explicitly establish the affinity to the UI synchronization context by opening the proxy in the form's constructor without invoking an operation. This is especially useful if you want to dispatch calls to the service on worker threads (or perhaps even asynchronously as discussed at the end of this chapter) and yet have the callbacks enter on the UI synchronization context, as shown in Example 8-23.

Example 8-23. Explicitly opening a proxy to establish a synchronization context

```
partial class MyForm : Form,IMyContractCallback
{
   MyContractClient m_Proxy;

   public MyForm( )
   {
      InitializeComponent( );

      m_Proxy = new MyContractClient(new InstanceContext(this));

      //Establish affinity to UI synchronization context here:
      m_Proxy.Open( );
   }
   //Called as a result of a UI event
   public void CallService(object sender,EventArgs args)
   {
      ThreadStart invoke = delegate
                           {
                              m_Proxy.MyMethod( );
                           };
      Thread thread = new Thread(invoke);
      thread.Start( );
   }
   //This method always runs on the UI thread
```

```
    public void OnCallback( )
    {
        //No need for synchronization and marshaling
        Text = "Some Callback";
    }
    public void OnClose(object sender,EventArgs args)
    {
        m_Proxy.Close( );
    }
}
```

UI thread callbacks and responsiveness

When callbacks are being processed on the UI thread, the UI itself is not responsive. Even if you perform relatively short callbacks, you must bear in mind that if the callback class is configured with `ConcurrencyMode.Multiple` there may be multiple callbacks back-to-back in the UI message queue, and processing them all at once will degrade responsiveness. You should avoid lengthy callback processing on the UI thread, and opt for configuring the callback class with `ConcurrencyMode.Single` so that the callback lock will queue up the callbacks. They can then be dispatched to the callback object one at a time, giving them the chance of being interleaved among the UI messages.

UI thread callbacks and concurrency management

Configuring the callback for affinity to the UI thread may trigger a deadlock. Suppose a Windows Forms client establishes an affinity between a callback object (or even itself) and the UI synchronization context, and then calls a service, passing the callback reference. The service is configured for reentrancy, and it calls back to the client. A deadlock now occurs because the callback to the client needs to execute on the UI thread, and that thread is blocked waiting for the service call to return. For example, Example 8-22 has the potential for this deadlock. Configuring the callback as a one-way operation will not resolve the problem here, because the one-way call still needs to be marshaled first to the UI thread. The only way to resolve the deadlock in this case is to turn off using the UI synchronization context by the callback, and to manually and asynchronously marshal the update to the form using its synchronization context. Example 8-24 demonstrates using this technique.

Example 8-24. Avoiding a callback deadlock on the UI thread

```
/////////////////////////// Client Side /////////////////////////
[CallbackBehavior(UseSynchronizationContext = false)]
partial class MyForm : Form,IMyContractCallback
{
    SynchronizationContext m_Context;
    MyContractClient m_Proxy;
```

Example 8-24. Avoiding a callback deadlock on the UI thread (continued)

```
    public MyForm( )
    {
        InitializeComponent( );
        m_Context = SynchronizationContext.Current;
        m_Proxy = new MyContractClient(new InstanceContext(this));
    }

    public void CallService(object sender,EventArgs args)
    {
        m_Proxy.MyMethod( );
    }
    //Callback runs on worker threads
    public void OnCallback( )
    {
        SendOrPostCallback setText = delegate
                                     {
                                         Text = "Manually marshaling to UI thread";
                                     };
        m_Context.Post(setText,null);
    }
    public void OnClose(object sender,EventArgs args)
    {
        m_Proxy.Close( );
    }
}
/////////////////////////// Service Side ///////////////////////
[ServiceContract(CallbackContract = typeof(IMyContractCallback))]
interface IMyContract
{
    [OperationContract]
    void MyMethod( );
}
interface IMyContractCallback
{
    [OperationContract]
    void OnCallback( );
}
[ServiceBehavior(ConcurrencyMode = ConcurrencyMode.Reentrant)]
class MyService : IMyContract
{
    public void MyMethod( )
    {
        IMyContractCallback callback = OperationContext.Current.
                                 GetCallbackChannel<IMyContractCallback>( );

        callback.OnCallback( );
    }
}
```

As shown in Example 8-24, you must use the Post( ) method of the synchronization context. Under no circumstances should you use the Send( ) method—even though the callback is executing on the worker thread, the UI thread is still blocked on the outbound call. Calling Send( ) would trigger the deadlock you are trying to avoid because Send( ) will block until the UI thread can process the request. The callback in Example 8-24 cannot use any of the safe controls (such as SafeLabel) either, because those too use the Send( ) method.

Callback Custom Synchronization Contexts

As with a service, you can install a custom synchronization context for the use of the callback. All that is required is that the thread that opens the proxy (or calls it for the first time) has the custom synchronization context attached to it. Example 8-25 shows how to attach my ThreadPoolSynchronizer to the callback object by setting it before using the proxy.

Example 8-25. Setting custom synchronization context for the callback

```
interface IMyContractCallback
{
   [OperationContract]
   void OnCallback( );
}
[ServiceContract(CallbackContract = typeof(IMyContractCallback))]
interface IMyContract
{
   [OperationContract]
   void MyMethod( );
}

class MyClient : IMyContractCallback
{
   //This method always invoked by the same thread
   public void OnCallback( )
   {....}
}

MyClient client = new MyClient( );
InstanceContext callbackContext = new InstanceContext(client);
MyContractClient proxy = new MyContractClient(callbackContext);

SynchronizationContext synchronizationContext = new ThreadPoolSynchronizer(3);
SynchronizationContext.SetSynchronizationContext(synchronizationContext);

using(synchronizationContext as IDisposable)
{
   proxy.MyMethod( );
   /* Some blocking operations until after the callback*/
   proxy.Close( );
}
```

While you could manually install a custom synchronization context (as in Example 8-25) by explicitly setting it before opening the proxy, it is better to do so declaratively, using an attribute. To affect the callback endpoint dispatcher, the attribute needs to implement the IEndpointBehavior interface presented in Chapter 6:

```
public interface IEndpointBehavior
{
    void ApplyClientBehavior(ServiceEndpoint endpoint,ClientRuntime clientRuntime);
    //More members
}
```

In the ApplyClientBehavior method, the ClientRuntime parameter contains a reference to the endpoint dispatcher with the CallbackDispatchRuntime property:

```
public sealed class ClientRuntime
{
    public DispatchRuntime CallbackDispatchRuntime
    {get;}
    //More members
}
```

The rest is identical to the service-side attribute, as demonstrated by my CallbackThreadPoolBehaviorAttribute, whose implementation is shown in Example 8-26.

Example 8-26. Implementing CallbackThreadPoolBehaviorAttribute

```
[AttributeUsage(AttributeTargets.Class)]
public class CallbackThreadPoolBehaviorAttribute : ThreadPoolBehaviorAttribute,
                                                               IEndpointBehavior
{
    public CallbackThreadPoolBehaviorAttribute(uint poolSize,Type clientType) :
                                                    this(poolSize,clientType,null)
    {}
    public CallbackThreadPoolBehaviorAttribute(uint poolSize,Type clientType,
                            string poolName) : base(poolSize,clientType,poolName)
    {
        AppDomain.CurrentDomain.ProcessExit += delegate
                                    {
                                        ThreadPoolHelper.CloseThreads(ServiceType);
                                    };
    }
    void IEndpointBehavior.ApplyClientBehavior(ServiceEndpoint serviceEndpoint,
                                        ClientRuntime clientRuntime)
    {
        IContractBehavior contractBehavior = this;
        contractBehavior.ApplyDispatchBehavior(null,serviceEndpoint,
                                        clientRuntime.CallbackDispatchRuntime);
    }
    //Rest of the implementation
}
```

In fact, I wanted to reuse as much of the service attribute as possible in the callback attribute. To that end, CallbackThreadPoolBehaviorAttribute derives from ThreadPoolBehaviorAttribute. Its constructors pass the client type as the service type to the base constructors. The CallbackThreadPoolBehavior attribute's implementation of ApplyClientBehavior( ) queries its base class for IContractBehavior (this is how a subclass uses an explicit private interface implementation of its base class) and delegates the implementation to ApplyDispatchBehavior( ).

The big difference between a client callback attribute and a service attribute is that the callback scenario has no host object to subscribe to its Closed event. To compensate, the CallbackThreadPoolBehavior attribute monitors the process exit event to close all the threads in the pool.

If the client wants to expedite closing those threads, it can use ThreadPoolBehavior. CloseThreads( ), as shown in Example 8-27.

Example 8-27. Using the CallbackThreadPoolBehavior attribute

```
interface IMyContractCallback
{
   [OperationContract]
   void OnCallback( );
}

[ServiceContract(CallbackContract = typeof(IMyContractCallback))]
interface IMyContract
{
   [OperationContract]
   void MyMethod( );
}

[CallbackThreadPoolBehavior(3,typeof(MyClient))]
class MyClient : IMyContractCallback,IDisposable
{
   MyContractClient m_Proxy;

   public MyClient( )
   {
      m_Proxy = new MyContractClient(new InstanceContext(this));
   }

   public void CallService( )
   {
      m_Proxy.MyMethod( );
   }

   //Called by threads from the custom pool
   public void OnCallback( )
   {...}

   public void Dispose( )
   {
      m_Proxy.Close( );
      ThreadPoolHelper.CloseThreads(typeof(MyClient));
   }
}
```

Callback thread affinity

Just like on the service side, if you want all the callbacks to execute on the same thread (perhaps to create some UI on the callback side), you can configure the callback class to have a pool size of 1. Or, better yet, you can define a dedicated callback attribute such as my CallbackThreadAffinityBehaviorAttribute:

```
[AttributeUsage(AttributeTargets.Class)]
public class CallbackThreadAffinityBehaviorAttribute :
                                        CallbackThreadPoolBehaviorAttribute
{
   public CallbackThreadAffinityBehaviorAttribute(Type clientType) :
                                    this(clientType,"Callback Worker Thread")
   {}
   public CallbackThreadAffinityBehaviorAttribute(Type clientType,
                          string threadName) : base(1,clientType,threadName)
   {}
}
```

The CallbackThreadAffinityBehavior attribute makes all callbacks across all callback contracts the client supports execute on the same thread, as shown in Example 8-28.

Example 8-28. Applying the CallbackThreadAffinityBehavior attribute

```
[CallbackThreadAffinityBehavior(typeof(MyClient))]
class MyClient : IMyContractCallback,IDisposable
{
   MyContractClient m_Proxy;

   public void CallService()
   {
      m_Proxy = new MyContractClient(new InstanceContext(this));
      m_Proxy.MyMethod();
   }
   //This method invoked by same callback thread, plus client threads
   public void OnCallback()
   {
      //Access state and resources, synchronize manually
   }
   public void Dispose()
   {
      m_Proxy.Close();
   }
}
```

Note that although WCF always invokes the callback on the same thread, you still may need to synchronize access to it if other client-side threads access the method as well.

Asynchronous Calls

When a client calls a service, usually the client is blocked while the service executes the call, and control returns to the client only when the operation completes its execution and returns. However, there are quite a few cases in which you will want to call operations asynchronously; that is, you'll want control to return immediately to the client while the service executes the operation in the background and then somehow let the client know that the method has completed execution and provide the client with the results of the invocation. Such an execution mode is called *asynchronous operation invocation*, and the action is known as an *asynchronous call*. Asynchronous calls allow you to improve client responsiveness and availability.

Requirements for an Asynchronous Mechanism

To make the most of the various options available with WCF asynchronous calls, you should be aware of the generic requirements set for any service-oriented asynchronous call support. These requirements include the following:

- The same service code should be used for both synchronous and asynchronous invocation. This allows service developers to focus on business logic and cater to both synchronous and asynchronous clients.

- A corollary of the first requirement is that the client should be the one to decide whether to call a service synchronously or asynchronously. That, in turn, implies that the client will have different code for each case (whether to invoke the call synchronously or asynchronously).

- The client should be able to issue multiple asynchronous calls and have multiple asynchronous calls in progress, and it should be able to distinguish between multiple methods' completions.

- Since a service operation's output parameters and return values are not available when control returns to the client, the client should have a way to harvest the results when the operation completes.

- Similarly, communication errors or errors on the service side should be communicated back to the client side. Any exception thrown during operation execution should be played back to the client later.

- The implementation of the mechanism should be independent of the binding and transfer technology used. Any binding should support asynchronous calls.

- The mechanism should not use technology-specific constructs such as .NET exceptions or delegates.

- The asynchronous calls mechanism should be straightforward and simple to use (this is less of a requirement and more of a design guideline). For example, the mechanism should, as much as possible, hide its implementation details, such as the worker threads used to dispatch the call.

The client has a variety of options for handling operation completion. After it issues an asynchronous call, it can choose to:

- Perform some work while the call is in progress and then block until completion.
- Perform some work while the call is in progress and then poll for completion.
- Receive notification when the method has completed. The notification will be in the form of a callback on a client-provided method. The callback should contain information identifying which operation has just completed and its return values.
- Perform some work while the call is in progress, wait for a predetermined amount of time, and then stop waiting, even if the operation execution has not yet completed.
- Wait simultaneously for completion of multiple operations. The client can also choose to wait for all or any of the pending calls to complete.

WCF offers all of these options to clients. The WCF support is strictly a client-side facility, and in fact the service is unaware it is being invoked asynchronously. This means that intrinsically any service supports asynchronous calls, and that you can call the same service both synchronously and asynchronously. In addition, because all of the asynchronous invocation support happens on the client side regardless of the service, you can use any binding for the asynchronous invocation.

 The WCF asynchronous calls support presented in this section is similar but not identical to the delegate-based asynchronous calls support .NET offers for regular CLR types.

Proxy-Based Asynchronous Calls

Because the client decides if the call should be synchronous or asynchronous, you need to create a different proxy for the asynchronous case. In Visual Studio 2008, when adding a service reference, you can click the Advanced button in the Add Service Reference dialog to bring up the settings dialog that lets you tweak the proxy generation. Check the "Generate asynchronous operations" checkbox to generate a proxy that contains asynchronous methods in addition to the synchronous ones. For each operation in the original contract, the asynchronous proxy and contract will contain two additional methods of this form:

```
[OperationContract(AsyncPattern = true)]
IAsyncResult Begin<Operation>(<in arguments>,
                              AsyncCallback callback,object asyncState);
<returned type> End<Operation>(<out arguments>,IAsyncResult result);
```

The `OperationContract` attribute offers the `AsyncPattern` Boolean property, defined as:

```
[AttributeUsage(AttributeTargets.Method)]
public sealed class OperationContractAttribute : Attribute
{
    public bool AsyncPattern
```

```
      {get;set;}
      //More members
   }
```

The AsyncPattern property defaults to false. AsyncPattern has meaning only on the
client side; it is merely a validation flag indicating to the proxy to verify that the
method on which this flag is set to true has a Begin<Operation>( )-compatible signature and that the defining contract has a matching method with an End<Operation>( )-
compatible signature. These requirements are verified at the proxy load time.
AsyncPattern binds the underlying synchronous method with the Begin/End pair and
correlates the synchronous execution with the asynchronous one. Briefly, when the
client invokes a method of the form Begin<Operation>( ) with AsyncPattern set to
true, this tells WCF not to try to directly invoke a method with that name on the service. Instead, WCF should use a thread from the thread pool to synchronously call
the underlying method. The synchronous call will block the thread from the thread
pool, not the calling client. The client will be blocked for only the slightest moment
it takes to dispatch the call request to the thread pool. The reply method of the synchronous invocation is correlated with the End<Operation>( ) method.

Example 8-29 shows a calculator contract and its implementing service, and the generated asynchronous proxy.

Example 8-29. Asynchronous contract and proxy

```
///////////////////////// Service Side /////////////////////////
[ServiceContract]
interface ICalculator
{
   [OperationContract]
   int Add(int number1,int number2);
   //More operations
}
class Calculator : ICalculator
{
   public int Add(int number1,int number2)
   {
      return number1 + number2;
   }
   //Rest of the implementation
}
///////////////////////// Client Side /////////////////////////
[ServiceContract]
public interface ICalculator
{
   [OperationContract]
   int Add(int number1,int number2);

   [OperationContract(AsyncPattern = true)]
   IAsyncResult BeginAdd(int number1,int number2,
                         AsyncCallback callback,object asyncState);
   int EndAdd(IAsyncResult result);
```

Example 8-29. Asynchronous contract and proxy (continued)

```
    //Rest of the methods
}
partial class CalculatorClient : ClientBase<ICalculator>,ICalculator
{
    public int Add(int number1,int number2)
    {
        return Channel.Add(number1,number2);
    }
    public IAsyncResult BeginAdd(int number1,int number2,
                                 AsyncCallback callback,object asyncState)
    {
        return Channel.BeginAdd(number1,number2,callback,asyncState);
    }
    public int EndAdd(IAsyncResult result)
    {
        return Channel.EndAdd(result);
    }
    //Rest of the methods and constructors
}
```

Asynchronous Invocation

Begin<Operation>( ) accepts the input parameters of the original synchronous operation, which may include data contracts passed by value or by reference (using the ref
modifier). The original method's return values and any explicit output parameters
(designated using the out and ref modifiers) are part of the End<Operation>( )
method. For example, for this operation definition:

```
[OperationContract]
string MyMethod(int number1,out int number2,ref int number3);
```

the corresponding Begin<Operation>( ) and End<Operation>( ) methods look like this:

```
[ServiceOperation(AsyncPattern = true)]
IAsyncResult BeginMyMethod(int number1,ref int number3,
                           AsyncCallback callback,object asyncState);
string EndMyMethod(out int number2,ref int number3,IAsyncResult result);
```

Begin<Operation>( ) accepts two additional input parameters that are not present in
the original operation signature: callback and asyncState. The callback parameter is
a delegate targeting a client-side method-completion notification event. asyncState is
an object that conveys whatever state information the party handling the method
completion requires. These two parameters are optional: the caller can choose to
pass in null instead of either one of them. For example, you could use code like the
following to asynchronously invoke the Add( ) method of the Calculator service from
Example 8-29 using the asynchronous proxy, if you have no interest in the results or
the errors:

```
CalculatorClient proxy = new CalculatorClient( );
proxy.BeginAdd(2,3,null,null); //Dispatched asynchronously
proxy.Close( );
```

As long as the client has the definition of the asynchronous contract, you can also invoke the operation asynchronously using a channel factory:

```
ChannelFactory<ICalculator> factory = new ChannelFactory<ICalculator>();
ICalculator proxy = factory.CreateChannel();
proxy.BeginAdd(2,3,null,null);
ICommunicationObject channel = proxy as ICommunicationObject;
channel.Close();
```

The problem with such an invocation is that the client has no way of getting its results.

The IAsyncResult interface

Every Begin<Operation>() method returns an object implementing the IAsyncResult interface, defined in the System.Runtime.Remoting.Messaging namespace as:

```
public interface IAsyncResult
{
    object AsyncState
    {get;}
    WaitHandle AsyncWaitHandle
    {get;}
    bool CompletedSynchronously
    {get;}
    bool IsCompleted
    {get;}
}
```

The returned IAsyncResult implementation uniquely identifies the method that was invoked using Begin<Operation>(). You can pass the IAsyncResult-implementation object to End<Operation>() to identify the specific asynchronous method execution from which you wish to retrieve the results. End<Operation>() will block its caller until the operation it's waiting for (identified by the IAsyncResult-implementation object passed in) completes and it can return the results or errors. If the method is already complete by the time End<Operation>() is called, End<Operation>() will not block the caller and will just return the results. Example 8-30 shows the entire sequence.

Example 8-30. Simple asynchronous execution sequence

```
CalculatorClient proxy = new CalculatorClient();
IAsyncResult result1 = proxy.BeginAdd(2,3,null,null);
IAsyncResult result2 = proxy.BeginAdd(4,5,null,null);

/* Do some work */

int sum;

sum = proxy.EndAdd(result1); //This may block
Debug.Assert(sum == 5);
```

Example 8-30. Simple asynchronous execution sequence (continued)

```
sum = proxy.EndAdd(result2); //This may block
Debug.Assert(sum == 9);

proxy.Close( );
```

As simple as Example 8-30 is, it does demonstrate a few key points. The first point is that the same proxy instance can invoke multiple asynchronous calls. The caller can distinguish among the different pending calls using each unique IAsyncResult-implementation object returned from Begin<Operation>( ). In fact, when the caller makes asynchronous calls, as in Example 8-30, it must save the IAsyncResult-implementation objects. In addition, the caller should make no assumptions about the order in which the pending calls will complete. It is quite possible that the second call will complete before the first one.

Although it isn't evident in Example 8-30, there are two important programming points regarding asynchronous calls:

- End<Operation>( ) can be called only once for each asynchronous operation. Trying to call it more than once results in an InvalidOperationException.

- You can pass the IAsyncResult-implementation object to End<Operation>( ) only on the same proxy object used to dispatch the call. Passing the IAsyncResult-implementation object to a different proxy instance results in an AsyncCallbackException. This is because only the original proxy keeps track of the asynchronous operations it has invoked.

Asynchronous calls and transport sessions

If the proxy is not using a transport session, the client can close the proxy immediately after the call to Begin<Operation>( ) and still be able to call End<Operation>( ) later:

```
CalculatorClient proxy = new CalculatorClient( );
IAsyncResult result = proxy.BeginAdd(2,3,null,null);
proxy.Close( );

/*Do some work */

//Sometime later:
int sum = proxy.EndAdd(result);
Debug.Assert(sum == 5);
```

Polling or Waiting for Completion

When a client calls End<Operation>( ), the client is blocked until the asynchronous method returns. This may be fine if the client has a finite amount of work to do while the call is in progress, and if after completing that work the client cannot continue its execution without the returned value or the output parameters of the operation.

However, what if the client only wants to check that the operation has completed? What if the client wants to wait for completion for a fixed timeout and then, if the operation has not completed, do some additional finite processing and wait again? WCF supports these alternative programming models to calling End<Operation>( ).

The IAsyncResult interface object returned from Begin<Operation>( ) has the AsyncWaitHandle property, of type WaitHandle:

```
public abstract class WaitHandle : ...
{
    public static bool WaitAll(WaitHandle[] waitHandles);
    public static int WaitAny(WaitHandle[] waitHandles);
    public virtual void Close( );
    public virtual bool WaitOne( );
    //More memebrs
}
```

The WaitOne( ) method of WaitHandle returns only when the handle is signaled. Example 8-31 demonstrates using WaitOne( ).

Example 8-31. Using IAsyncResult.AsyncWaitHandle to block until completion

```
CalculatorClient proxy = new CalculatorClient( );
IAsyncResult result = proxy.BeginAdd(2,3,null,null);

/* Do some work */

result.AsyncWaitHandle.WaitOne( ); //This may block
int sum = proxy.EndAdd(result); //This will not block
Debug.Assert(sum == 5);

proxy.Close( );
```

Logically, Example 8-31 is identical to Example 8-30, which called only End<Operation> ( ). If the operation is still executing when WaitOne( ) is called, WaitOne( ) will block. But if by the time WaitOne( ) is called the method execution is complete, WaitOne( ) will not block, and the client will proceed to call End<Operation>( ) for the returned value. The important difference between Examples 8-31 and 8-30 is that the call to End<Operation>( ) in Example 8-31 is guaranteed not to block its caller.

Example 8-32 demonstrates a more practical way of using WaitOne( ), by specifying a timeout (10 milliseconds in this example). When you specify a timeout, WaitOne( ) returns when the method execution is completed or when the timeout has elapsed, whichever condition is met first.

Example 8-32. Using WaitOne() to specify wait timeout

```
CalculatorClient proxy = new CalculatorClient( );
IAsyncResult result = proxy.BeginAdd(2,3,null,null);
```

Example 8-32. Using WaitOne() to specify wait timeout (continued)

```
while(result.IsCompleted == false)
{
    result.AsyncWaitHandle.WaitOne(10,false); //This may block
    /* Do some optional work */
}
int sum = proxy.EndAdd(result); //This will not block
```

Example 8-32 uses another handy property of IAsyncResult, called IsCompleted. IsCompleted lets you check the status of the call without waiting or blocking. You can even use IsCompleted in a strict polling mode:

```
CalculatorClient proxy = new CalculatorClient();
IAsyncResult result = proxy.BeginAdd(2,3,null,null);

//Sometime later:
if(result.IsCompleted)
{
    int sum = proxy.EndAdd(result); //This will not block
    Debug.Assert(sum == 5);
}
else
{
    //Do some optional work
}
proxy.Close();
```

The AsyncWaitHandle property really shines when you use it to manage multiple concurrent asynchronous methods in progress. You can use WaitHandle's static WaitAll() method to wait for completion of multiple asynchronous methods, as shown in Example 8-33.

Example 8-33. Waiting for completion of multiple methods

```
CalculatorClient proxy = new CalculatorClient();
IAsyncResult result1 = proxy.BeginAdd(2,3,null,null);
IAsyncResult result2 = proxy.BeginAdd(4,5,null,null);

WaitHandle[] handleArray = {result1.AsyncWaitHandle,result2.AsyncWaitHandle};

WaitHandle.WaitAll(handleArray);

int sum;
//These calls to EndAdd() will not block

sum = proxy.EndAdd(result1);
Debug.Assert(sum == 5);

sum = proxy.EndAdd(result2);
Debug.Assert(sum == 9);

proxy.Close();
```

To use WaitAll( ), you need to construct an array of handles. Note that you still need to call End<Operation>( ) to access the returned values. Instead of waiting for all of the methods to return, you can choose to wait for any of them to return, using the WaitAny( ) static method of the WaitHandle class. Like WaitOne( ), both WaitAll( ) and WaitAny( ) have overloaded versions that let you specify a timeout to wait instead of waiting indefinitely.

Completion Callbacks

Instead of blocking, waiting, and polling for asynchronous call completion, WCF offers another programming model altogether—completion callbacks. With this model, the client provides WCF with a method and requests that WCF call that method back when the asynchronous method completes. The client can have the same callback method handle completion of multiple asynchronous calls. When each asynchronous method's execution is complete, instead of quietly returning to the pool, the worker thread calls the completion callback. To designate a completion callback method, the client needs to provide Begin<Operation>( ) with a delegate of the type AsyncCallback, defined as:

```
public delegate void AsyncCallback(IAsyncResult result);
```

That delegate is provided as the penultimate parameter to Begin<Operation>( ).

Example 8-34 demonstrates asynchronous call management using a completion callback.

Example 8-34. Managing asynchronous call with a completion callback

```
class MyClient : IDisposable
{
   CalculatorClient m_Proxy = new CalculatorClient( );

   public void CallAsync( )
   {
      m_Proxy.BeginAdd(2,3,OnCompletion,null);
   }
   void OnCompletion(IAsyncResult result)
   {
      int sum = m_Proxy.EndAdd(result);
      Debug.Assert(sum == 5);
   }
   public void Dispose( )
   {
      m_Proxy.Close( );
   }
}
```

Unlike the programming models described so far, when you use a completion callback method, there's no need to save the IAsyncResult-implementation object returned from Begin<Operation>( ). This is because when WCF calls the completion callback, WCF provides the IAsyncResult-implementation object as a parameter. Because WCF provides a unique IAsyncResult-implementation object for each asynchronous method, you can channel multiple asynchronous method completions to the same callback method:

```
m_Proxy.BeginAdd(2,3,OnCompletion,null);
m_Proxy.BeginAdd(4,5,OnCompletion,null);
```

Instead of using a class method as a completion callback, you can just as easily use a local anonymous method or a lambda expression:

```
CalculatorClient proxy = new CalculatorClient( );
int sum;
AsyncCallback completion = (result)=>
                           {
                               sum = proxy.EndAdd(result);
                               Debug.Assert(sum == 5);
                               proxy.Close( );
                           };
proxy.BeginAdd(2,3,completion,null);
```

Note that the anonymous method assigns to an outer variable (sum) to provide the result of the Add( ) operation.

Callback completion methods are by far the preferred model in any event-driven application. An event-driven application has methods that trigger events (or requests) and methods that handle those events and fire their own events as a result. Writing an application as event-driven makes it easier to manage multiple threads, events, and callbacks and allows for scalability, responsiveness, and performance.

The last thing you want in an event-driven application is to block, since then your application does not process events. Callback completion methods allow you to treat the completion of the asynchronous operation as yet another event in your system. The other options (waiting, blocking, and polling) are available for applications that are strict, predictable, and deterministic in their execution flow. I recommend that you use completion callback methods whenever possible.

Completion callbacks and thread safety

Because the callback method is executed on a thread from the thread pool, you must provide for thread safety in the callback method and in the object that provides it. This means that you must use synchronization objects and locks to access the member variables of the client, even outer variables to anonymous completion methods. You need to provide for synchronization between client-side threads and the worker thread from the pool, and potentially synchronizing between multiple worker threads all calling concurrently into the completion callback method to handle their respective asynchronous call completion. Therefore, you need to make sure the completion callback method is reentrant and thread-safe.

Passing state information

The last parameter to Begin<Operation>() is asyncState. The asyncState object, known as a *state object*, is provided as an optional container for whatever need you deem fit. The party handling the method completion can access such a container object via the AsyncState property of IAsyncResult. Although you can certainly use state objects with any of the other asynchronous call programming models (blocking, waiting, or polling), they are most useful in conjunction with completion callbacks. The reason is simple: when you are using a completion callback, the container object offers the only way to pass in additional parameters to the callback method, whose signature is predetermined.

Example 8-35 demonstrates how you might use a state object to pass an integer value as an additional parameter to the completion callback method. Note that the callback must downcast the AsyncState property to the actual type.

Example 8-35. Passing an additional parameter using a state object

```
class MyClient : IDisposable
{
   CalculatorClient m_Proxy = new CalculatorClient();

   public void CallAsync()
   {
      int asyncState = 4; //int, for example
      m_Proxy.BeginAdd(2,3,OnCompletion,asyncState);
   }
   void OnCompletion(IAsyncResult result)
   {
      int asyncState = (int)result.AsyncState;
      Debug.Assert(asyncState == 4);

      int sum = m_Proxy.EndAdd(result);
   }
   public void Dispose()
   {
      m_Proxy.Close();
   }
}
```

A common use for the state object is to pass the proxy used for Begin<Operation>() instead of saving it as a member variable:

```
class MyClient
{
   public void CallAsync()
   {
      CalculatorClient proxy = new CalculatorClient();
      proxy.BeginAdd(2,3,OnCompletion,proxy);
   }
   void OnCompletion(IAsyncResult result)
```

```
        {
            CalculatorClient proxy = result.AsyncState as CalculatorClient;
            Debug.Assert(proxy != null);

            int sum = proxy.EndAdd(result);
            Debug.Assert(sum == 5);

            proxy.Close();
        }
    }
```

Completion callback synchronization context

The completion callback, by default, is called on a thread from the thread pool. This presents a serious problem if the callback is to access some resources that have an affinity to a particular thread or threads and are required to run in a particular synchronization context. The classic example is a Windows Forms application that dispatches a lengthy service call asynchronously (to avoid blocking the UI), and then wishes to update the UI with the result of the invocation. Using the raw Begin<Operation>() is disallowed, since only the UI thread is allowed to update the UI. You must marshal the call from the completion callback to the correct synchronization context, using any of the techniques described previously (such as safe controls). Example 8-36 demonstrates such a completion callback that interacts directly with its containing form, ensuring that the UI update will be in the UI synchronization context.

Example 8-36. Relying on completion callback synchronization context

```
partial class CalculatorForm : Form
{
    CalculatorClient m_Proxy;
    SynchronizationContext m_SynchronizationContext;

    public CalculatorForm()
    {
        InitializeComponent();
        m_Proxy = new CalculatorClient();
        m_SynchronizationContext = SynchronizationContext.Current;
    }
    public void CallAsync(object sender,EventArgs args)
    {
        m_Proxy.BeginAdd(2,3,OnCompletion,null);
    }
    void OnCompletion(IAsyncResult result)
    {
        SendOrPostCallback callback = delegate
                                      {
                                          Text = "Sum = " + m_Proxy.EndAdd(result);
                                      };
        m_SynchronizationContext.Send(callback,null);
    }
```

```
    public void OnClose(object sender,EventArgs args)
    {
        m_Proxy.Close();
    }
}
```

To better handle this situation, the ClientBase<T> base class in .NET 3.5 is extended with a protected InvokeAsync( ) method that picks up the synchronization context of the client and uses it to invoke the completion callback, as shown in Example 8-37.

Example 8-37. Async callback management in ClientBase<T>

```
public abstract class ClientBase<T> : ...
{
    protected delegate IAsyncResult BeginOperationDelegate(object[] inValues,
                                        AsyncCallback asyncCallback,object state);

    protected delegate object[] EndOperationDelegate(IAsyncResult result);

    //Picks up sync context and used for completion callback
    protected void InvokeAsync(BeginOperationDelegate beginOpDelegate,
                            object[] inValues,
                            EndOperationDelegate endOpDelegate,
                            SendOrPostCallback opCompletedCallback,
                            object userState);
    //More members
}
```

ClientBase<T> also provides an event arguments helper class and two dedicated delegates used to invoke and end the asynchronous call. The generated proxy class that derives from ClientBase<T> makes use of the base functionality. The proxy will have a public event called <Operation>Completed that uses a strongly typed event argument class specific to the results of the asynchronous method, and two methods called <Operation>Async that are used to dispatch the call asynchronously:

```
    partial class AddCompletedEventArgs : AsyncCompletedEventArgs
    {
        public int Result
        {get;}
    }

    class CalculatorClient : ClientBase<ICalculator>,ICalculator
    {
        public event EventHandler<AddCompletedEventArgs> AddCompleted;

        public void AddAsync(int number1,int number2,object userState);
        public void AddAsync(int number1,int number2);

        //Rest of the proxy
    }
```

The client can subscribe an event handler to the <Operation>Completed event to have that handler called upon completion. The big difference with using <Operation>Async as opposed to Begin<Operation> is that the <Operation>Async methods will pick up the synchronization context of the client and will fire the <Operation>Completed event on that synchronization context, as shown in Example 8-38.

Example 8-38. Synchronization-context-friendly asynchronous call invocation

```
partial class CalculatorForm : Form
{
   CalculatorClient m_Proxy;

   public CalculatorForm( )
   {
      InitializeComponent( );

      m_Proxy = new CalculatorClient( );
      m_Proxy.AddCompleted += OnAddCompleted;
   }
   void CallAsync(object sender,EventArgs args)
   {
      m_Proxy.AddAsync(2,3); //Sync context picked up here
   }
   //Called on the UI thread
   void OnAddCompleted(object sender,AddCompletedEventArgs args)
   {
      Text = "Sum = " + args.Result;
   }
}
```

One-Way Asynchronous Operations

There is little sense in trying to invoke a one-way operation asynchronously, because while one of the main features of asynchronous calls is their ability to retrieve and correlate a reply message, no such message is available with a one-way call. If you do invoke a one-way operation asynchronously, End<Operation>( ) will return as soon as the worker thread has finished dispatching the call. Aside from communication errors, End<Operation>( ) will not encounter any exceptions. If a completion callback is provided for an asynchronous invocation of a one-way operation, the callback is called immediately after the worker thread used in Begin<Operation>( ) dispatches the call. The only justification for invoking a one-way operation asynchronously is to avoid the potential blocking of the one-way call, in which case you should pass a null for the state object and the completion callback, as shown in Example 8-39.

Example 8-39. Invoking a one-way operation asynchronously

```
[ServiceContract]
interface IMyContract
{
   [OperationContract(IsOneWay = true)]
   void MyMethod(string text);

   [OperationContract(IsOneWay = true,AsyncPattern = true)]
   IAsyncResult BeginMyMethod(string text,
                              AsyncCallback callback,object asyncState);
   void EndMyMethod(IAsyncResult result);
}
MyContractClient proxy = MyContractClient();
proxy.BeginMyMethod("Async one way",null,null);

//Sometime later:
proxy.Close();
```

The problem with Example 8-39 is the potential race condition of closing the proxy. It is possible to push the asynchronous call with Begin<Operation>() and then close the proxy before the worker thread used has had a chance to invoke the call. If you want to close the proxy immediately after asynchronously invoking the one-way call, you need to provide a completion method for closing the proxy:

```
MyContractClient proxy = MyContractClient();

AsyncCallback completion = (result)=>
                           {
                               proxy.Close();
                           };
proxy.BeginMyMethod("Async one way",completion,null);
```

Asynchronous Error Handling

Output parameters and return values are not the only elements unavailable at the time an asynchronous call is dispatched: exceptions are missing as well. After calling Begin<Operation>(), control returns to the client, but it may be some time before the asynchronous method encounters an error and throws an exception, and some time after that before the client actually calls End<Operation>(). WCF must therefore provide some way for the client to know that an exception was thrown and allow the client to handle it. When the asynchronous method throws an exception, the proxy catches it, and when the client calls End<Operation>() the proxy rethrows that exception object, letting the client handle the exception. If a completion callback is provided, WCF calls that method immediately after the exception is received. The exact exception thrown is compliant with the fault contract and the exception type, as explained in Chapter 6.

 If fault contracts are defined on the service operation contract, the FaultContract attribute should be applied only on the synchronous operations.

Asynchronous calls and timeouts

Since the asynchronous invocation mechanism is nothing but a convenient programming model on top of the actual synchronous operation, the underlying synchronous call can still time out. This will result in a `TimeoutException` when the client calls `End<Operation>()`. It is therefore wrong to equate asynchronous calls with lengthy operations. By default, asynchronous calls are still relatively short (under a minute), but unlike synchronous calls, they are non-blocking. For lengthy asynchronous calls you will need to provide an adequately long send timeout.

Cleaning up after End<Operation>()

When the client calls `Begin<Operation>()`, the returned `IAsyncResult` will have a reference to a single `WaitHandle` object, accessible via the `AsyncWaitHandle` property. Calling `End<Operation>()` on that object will not close the handle. Instead, that handle will be closed when the implementing object is garbage-collected. As with any other case of using an unmanaged resource, you have to be mindful about your application-deterministic finalization needs. It is possible (in theory, at least) for the application to dispatch asynchronous calls faster than .NET can collect the handles, resulting in a resource leak. To compensate, you can explicitly close that handle after calling `End<Operation>()`. For example, using the same definitions as those in Example 8-34:

```
void OnCompletion(IAsyncResult result)
{
    int sum = m_Proxy.EndAdd(result);
    Debug.Assert(sum == 5);
    result.AsyncWaitHandle.Close();
}
```

Asynchronous Calls and Transactions

Transactions do not mix well with asynchronous calls, for a few reasons. First, well-designed transactions are of short duration, yet the main motivation for using asynchronous calls is because of the latency of the operations. Second, the client's ambient transaction will not by default flow to the service, because the asynchronous operation is invoked on a worker thread, not the client's thread. While it is possible to develop a proprietary mechanism that uses cloned transactions, this is esoteric at best and should be avoided. Finally, when a transaction completes, it should have no leftover activities to do in the background that could commit or abort independently of the transaction; however, this will be the result of spawning an asynchronous operation call from within a transaction. In short, do not mix transactions with asynchronous calls.

Synchronous Versus Asynchronous Calls

Although it is technically possible to call the same service synchronously and asynchronously, the likelihood that a service will be accessed both ways is low.

The reason is that using a service asynchronously necessitates drastic changes to the workflow of the client, and consequently the client cannot simply use the same execution sequence logic as with synchronous access. Consider, for example, an online store application. Suppose the client (a server-side object executing a customer request) accesses a Store service, where it places the customer's order details. The Store service uses three well-factored helper services to process the order: Order, Shipment, and Billing. In a synchronous scenario, the Store service first calls the Order service to place the order. Only if the Order service succeeds in processing the order (i.e., if the item is available in the inventory) does the Store service then call the Shipment service, and only if the Shipment service succeeds does the Store service access the Billing service to bill the customer. This sequence is shown in Figure 8-4.

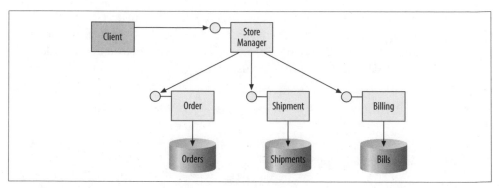

Figure 8-4. Synchronous processing of an order

The downside to the workflow shown in Figure 8-4 is that the store must process orders synchronously and serially. On the surface, it might seem that if the Store service invoked its helper objects asynchronously, it would increase throughput, because it could process incoming orders as fast as the client submitted them. The problem in doing so is that it is possible for the calls to the Order, Shipment, and Billing services to fail independently, and if they do, all hell will break loose. For example, the Order service might discover that there were no items in the inventory matching the customer request, while the Shipment service tried to ship the nonexisting item and the Billing service had already billed the customer for it.

Using asynchronous calls on a set of interacting services requires that you change your code and your workflow. As illustrated in Figure 8-5, to call the helper services asynchronously, you need to string them together. The Store service should call only the Order service, which in turn should call the Shipment service only if the order processing was successful, to avoid the potential inconsistencies just mentioned. Similarly, only in the case of successful shipment should the Shipment service asynchronously call the Billing service.

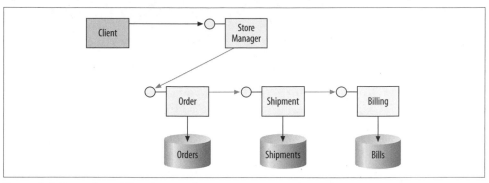

Figure 8-5. Revised workflow for asynchronous processing of an order

In general, if you have more than one service in your asynchronous workflow, you should have each service invoke the next one in the logical execution sequence. Needless to say, such a programming model introduces tight coupling between services (they have to know about each other) and changes to their interfaces (you have to pass in additional parameters, which are required for the desired invocation of services downstream).

The conclusion is that using asynchronous instead of synchronous invocation introduces major changes to the service interfaces and the client workflow. Asynchronous invocation on a service that was built for synchronous execution works only in isolated cases. When dealing with a set of interacting services, it is better to simply spin off a worker thread to call them and use the worker thread to provide asynchronous execution. This will preserve the service interfaces and the original client execution sequence.

CHAPTER 9

Queued Services

WCF enables disconnected work: the client posts messages to a queue, and the service processes them. Such interaction enables different possibilities from those presented so far, and in turn a different programming model. This chapter starts by showing you how to set up and configure simple queued services, and then focuses on aspects such as transactions, instance management, and failures, and their impact on both the business model of the service and its implementation. The chapter ends with my solution for a response service and a discussion of using the HTTP bridge for queued calls over the Internet.

Disconnected Services and Clients

The previous chapters were all predicated on a connected interaction between the client and the service, where both sides must be up and running to be able to interact with each other. However, there are quite a few cases (as well as the overall business model justification) for wanting to have disconnected interaction in a service-oriented application:

Availability
  The client may need to work against the service even when the client is disconnected; for example, when using a mobile device. The solution is to queue up requests against a local queue and send them to the service when the client is connected. Similarly, if the service is offline (perhaps because of network problems or machine crashes), you want clients to be able to continue working against the service. When the service is connected again, it can retrieve the pending calls from a queue. Even when both the client and the service are alive and running, network connectivity may be unavailable, and yet both the client and the service may want to continue with their work. Using queues at both ends will facilitate that.

Disjoint work

Whenever it is possible to decompose a business workflow into several operations that are separated in time—that is, where each operation must take place, but not necessarily immediately or in a particular order—it is usually a good idea to use queuing, because it will improve availability and throughput. You can queue up the operations and have them execute independently of each other.

Compensating work

When your business transaction may take hours or days to complete, you typically split it into at least two transactions. The first queues up the work to be completed immediately by initiating an external sequence, and the second verifies the success of the first and compensates for its failure if necessary.

Load leveling

Most systems do not have a constant level of load, as shown in Figure 9-1. If you design the system for the peak load, you will be wasting system resources through most of the load cycle, and if you design the system to handle the average load, you will not be able to handle the peak. But with queued calls, the service can simply queue up the excess load and process it at leisure. This enables you to design a system for a nominal average of the desired throughput, as opposed to the maximum load.

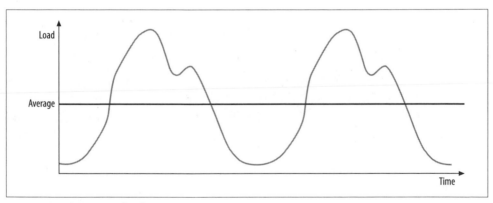

Figure 9-1. Fluctuating load

Queued Calls

WCF provides support for queued calls using the NetMsmqBinding. With this binding, instead of transporting the messages over TCP, HTTP, or IPC, WCF transports the messages over MSMQ. WCF packages each SOAP message into an MSMQ message and posts it to a designated queue. Note that there is no direct mapping of WCF messages to MSMQ messages, just like there is no direct mapping of WCF messages to TCP packets. A single MSMQ message can contain multiple WCF messages, or just a single one, according to the contract session mode (as discussed at length later). In effect, instead of sending the WCF message to a live service, the client posts the message to an MSMQ queue. All that the client sees and interacts with is the queue, not a service endpoint. As a result, the calls are inherently asynchronous (because they will execute later, when the service processes the messages) and disconnected (because the service or client may interact with local queues).

Queued Calls Architecture

As with every WCF service, in the case of a queued service the client interacts with a proxy, as shown in Figure 9-2.

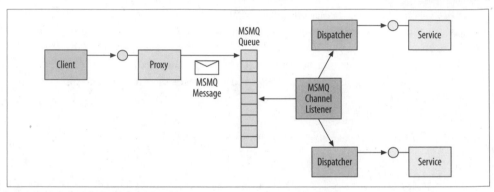

Figure 9-2. Queued calls architecture

However, since the proxy is configured to use the MSMQ binding, it does not send the WCF message to any particular service. Instead, it converts the call (or calls) to an MSMQ message (or messages) and posts it to the queue specified in the endpoint's address. On the service side, when a service host with a queued endpoint is launched, the host installs a queue listener, which is similar conceptually to the listener associated with a port when using TCP or HTTP. The queue's listener detects that there is a message in the queue, de-queues the message, and then creates the host side's chain of interceptors, ending with a dispatcher. The dispatcher calls the service instance as usual. If multiple messages are posted to the queue, the listener can create new instances as fast as the messages come off the queue, resulting in asynchronous, disconnected, and concurrent calls.

If the host is offline, messages destined for the service will simply remain pending in the queue. The next time the host is connected, the messages will be played to the service. Obviously, if both the client and the host are alive and running and are connected, the host will process the calls immediately.

Queued Contracts

A potentially disconnected call made against a queue cannot possibly return any values, because no service logic is invoked at the time the message is dispatched to the queue. Not only that, but the call may be dispatched to the service and processed after the client application has shut down, when there is no client available to process the returned values. In much the same way, the call cannot return to the client any service-side exceptions, and there may not be a client around to catch and handle the exceptions anyway. In fact, WCF disallows using fault contracts on queued operations. Since the client cannot be blocked by invoking the operation—or rather, the client is blocked, but only for the briefest moment it takes to queue up the message—the queued calls are inherently asynchronous from the client's perspective. All of these are the classic characteristics of one-way calls. Consequently, any contract exposed by an endpoint that uses the NetMsmqBinding can have only one-way operations, and WCF verifies this at service (and proxy) load time:

```
//Only one-way calls allowed on queued contracts
[ServiceContract]
interface IMyContract
{
   [OperationContract(IsOneWay = true)]
   void MyMethod( );
}
```

Because the interaction with MSMQ is encapsulated in the binding, there is nothing in the service or client invocation code pertaining to the fact that the calls are queued. The queued service and client code look like any other WCF service and client code, as shown in Example 9-1.

Example 9-1. Implementing and consuming a queued service

```
///////////////////////// Service Side /////////////////////////
[ServiceContract]
interface IMyContract
{
   [OperationContract(IsOneWay = true)]
   void MyMethod( );
}
class MyService : IMyContract
{
   public void MyMethod( )
   {...}
}
///////////////////////// Client Side /////////////////////////
MyContractClient proxy = new MyContractClient( );
proxy.MyMethod( );
proxy.Close( );
```

Configuration and Setup

When you define an endpoint for a queued service, the endpoint address must contain the queue's name and designation (that is, the type of the queue). MSMQ defines two types of queues: public and private. *Public queues* require an MSMQ domain controller installation or Active Directory integration and can be accessed across machine boundaries. Applications in production often require public queues due to the secure and disconnected nature of such queues. *Private queues* are local to the machine on which they reside and do not require a domain controller. Such a deployment of MSMQ is called a *workgroup installation*. During development, and for private queues they set up and administer, developers usually resort to a workgroup installation.

You designate the queue type (private or public) as part of the queued endpoint address:

```
<endpoint
    address = "net.msmq://localhost/private/MyServiceQueue"
    binding = "netMsmqBinding"
    ...
/>
```

In the case of a public queue, you can omit the public designator and have WCF infer the queue type. With private queues, you must include the designator. Also note that there is no $ sign in the queue's type.

Workgroup installation and security

When you're using private queues in a workgroup installation, you typically disable MSMQ security on the client and service sides. Chapter 10 discusses in detail how to secure WCF calls, including queued calls. Briefly, the default MSMQ security configuration expects users to present certificates for authentication, and MSMQ certificate-based security requires an MSMQ domain controller. Alternatively, selecting Windows security for transport security over MSMQ requires Active Directory integration, which is not possible with an MSMQ workgroup installation. For now, Example 9-2 shows how to disable MSMQ security.

Example 9-2. Disabling MSMQ security

```
<system.serviceModel>
    ...
        <endpoint name = ...
            address = "net.msmq://localhost/private/MyServiceQueue"
            binding = "netMsmqBinding"
            bindingConfiguration = "NoMSMQSecurity"
            contract = "..."
        />
    ...
```

Example 9-2. Disabling MSMQ security (continued)

```
    <bindings>
       <netMsmqBinding>
          <binding name = "NoMSMQSecurity">
             <security mode = "None"/>
          </binding>
       </netMsmqBinding>
    </bindings>
</system.serviceModel>
```

 If you must for some reason enable security for development in a workgroup installation, you can configure the service to use message security with username credentials.

Creating the queue

On both the service and the client side, the queue must exist before client calls are queued up against it. There are several options for creating the queue. The administrator (or the developer, during development) can use the MSMQ control panel applet to create the queue, but that is a manual step that should be automated. The host process can use the API of System.Messaging to verify that the queue exists before opening the host. The class MessageQueue offers the Exists( ) method for verifying that a queue is created, and the Create( ) methods for creating a queue:

```
public class MessageQueue : ...
{
    public static MessageQueue Create(string path); //Nontransactional
    public static MessageQueue Create(string path,bool transactional);
    public static bool Exists(string path);
    public void Purge( );
    //More members
}
```

If the queue is not present, the host process can first create it and then proceed to open the host. Example 9-3 demonstrates this sequence.

Example 9-3. Verifying a queue on the host

```
ServiceHost host = new ServiceHost(typeof(MyService));

if(MessageQueue.Exists(@".\private$\MyServiceQueue") == false)
{
    MessageQueue.Create(@".\private$\MyServiceQueue",true);
}
host.Open( );
```

In this example, the host verifies against the MSMQ installation on its own machine that the queue is present before opening the host. If it needs to, the hosting code creates the queue. Note the use of the true value for the transactional queue, as discussed later. Note also the use of the $ sign in the queue designation.

The obvious problem with Example 9-3 is that it hardcodes the queue name, not once, but twice. It is preferable to read the queue name from the application config file by storing it in an application setting, although there are problems even with that approach. First, you have to constantly synchronize the queue name in the application settings and in the endpoint's address. Second, you still have to repeat this code every time you host a queued service. Fortunately, it is possible to encapsulate and automate the code in Example 9-3 in my ServiceHost<T>, as shown in Example 9-4.

Example 9-4. Creating the queue in ServiceHost<T>

```
public class ServiceHost<T> : ServiceHost
{
   protected override void OnOpening( )
   {
      foreach(ServiceEndpoint endpoint in Description.Endpoints)
      {
         endpoint.VerifyQueue( );
      }
      base.OnOpening( );
   }
   //More members
}
public static class QueuedServiceHelper
{
   public static void VerifyQueue(this ServiceEndpoint endpoint)
   {
      if(endpoint.Binding is NetMsmqBinding)
      {
         string queue = GetQueueFromUri(endpoint.Address.Uri);
         if(MessageQueue.Exists(queue) == false)
         {
            MessageQueue.Create(queue,true);
         }
      }
   }
   //Parses the queue name out of the address
   static string GetQueueFromUri(Uri uri)
   {...}
}
```

In Example 9-4, ServiceHost<T> overrides the OnOpening( ) method of its base class. This method is called before opening the host, but after calling the Open( ) method. ServiceHost<T> iterates over the collection of configured endpoints. For each endpoint, if the binding used is NetMsmqBinding—that is, if queued calls are expected—ServiceHost<T> calls the extension method VerifyQueue( ) of the ServiceEndpoint type and asks it to verify the presence of the queue. The static extension VerifyQueue( ) method of QueuedServiceHelper parses the queue's name out of the endpoint's address and uses code similar to that in Example 9-3 to create the queue if needed.

Using ServiceHost<T>, Example 9-3 is reduced to:

```
ServiceHost<MyService> host = new ServiceHost<MyService>( );
host.Open( );
```

The client must also verify that the queue exists before dispatching calls to it. Example 9-5 shows the required steps on the client side.

Example 9-5. Verifying the queue by the client

```
if(MessageQueue.Exists(@".\private$\MyServiceQueue") == false)
{
   MessageQueue.Create(@".\private$\MyServiceQueue",true);
}
MyContractClient proxy = new MyContractClient( );
proxy.MyMethod( );
proxy.Close( );
```

Again, you should not hardcode the queue name and should instead read the queue name from the application config file by storing it in an application setting. And again, you will face the challenges of keeping the queue name synchronized in the application settings and in the endpoint's address, and of writing queue verification logic everywhere your clients use the queued service. You can use QueuedServiceHelper directly on the endpoint behind the proxy, but that forces you to create the proxy (or a ServiceEndpoint instance) just to verify the queue. You can, however, extend my QueuedServiceHelper to streamline and support client-side queue verification, as shown in Example 9-6.

Example 9-6. Extending QueuedServiceHelper to verify the queue on the client side

```
public static class QueuedServiceHelper
{
   public static void VerifyQueues( )
   {
      Configuration config = ConfigurationManager.OpenExeConfiguration(
                                          ConfigurationUserLevel.None);
      ServiceModelSectionGroup sectionGroup =
                         ServiceModelSectionGroup.GetSectionGroup(config);

      foreach(ChannelEndpointElement endpointElement in
                                          sectionGroup.Client.Endpoints)
      {
         if(endpointElement.Binding == "netMsmqBinding")
         {
            string queue = GetQueueFromUri(endpointElement.Address);

            if(MessageQueue.Exists(queue) == false)
            {
               MessageQueue.Create(queue,true);
            }
         }
      }
   }
```

Example 9-6. Extending QueuedServiceHelper to verify the queue on the client side (continued)

```
   }
   //More members
}
```

Example 9-6 uses the type-safe programming model offered by the ConfigurationManager class to parse a configuration file. It loads the WCF section (the ServiceModelSectionGroup) and iterates over all the endpoints defined in the client config file. For each endpoint that is configured with the MSMQ binding, VerifyQueues() creates the queue if required.

Using QueuedServiceHelper, Example 9-5 is reduced to:

```
QueuedServiceHelper.VerifyQueues();

MyContractClient proxy = new MyContractClient();
proxy.MyMethod();
proxy.Close();
```

Note that the client application needs to call QueuedServiceHelper.VerifyQueues() just once anywhere in the application, before issuing the queued calls.

If the client is not using a config file to create the proxy (or is using a channel factory), the client can still use the extrusion method VerifyQueue() of the ServiceEndpoint class:

```
EndpointAddress address = new EndpointAddress(...);
Binding binding = new NetMsmqBinding(...); //Can still read binding from config

MyContractClient proxy = new MyContractClient(binding,address);
proxy.Endpoint.VerifyQueue();

proxy.MyMethod();

proxy.Close();
```

Queue purging

When a host is launched, it may already have messages in queues, received by MSMQ while the host was offline, and the host will immediately start processing these messages. Dealing with this very scenario is one of the core features of queued services, as it enables you to have disconnected services. While this is, therefore, exactly the sort of behavior you would like when deploying a queued service, it is typically a hindrance in debugging. Imagine a debug session of a queued service. The client issues a few calls and the service begins processing the first call, but while stepping through the code you notice a defect. You stop debugging, change the service code, and relaunch the host, only to have it process the remaining messages in the queue from the previous debug session, even if those messages break the new service code. Usually, messages from one debug session should not seed the next one.

The solution is to programmatically purge the queues when the host shuts down, in debug mode only. You can streamline this with my ServiceHost<T>, as shown in Example 9-7.

Example 9-7. Purging the queues on host shutdown during debugging

```
public static class QueuedServiceHelper
{
   public static void PurgeQueue(ServiceEndpoint endpoint)
   {
      if(endpoint.Binding is NetMsmqBinding)
      {
         string queueName = GetQueueFromUri(endpoint.Address.Uri);
         if(MessageQueue.Exists(queueName) == true)
         {
            MessageQueue queue = new MessageQueue(queueName);
            queue.Purge();
         }
      }
   }
   //More members
}
public class ServiceHost<T> : ServiceHost
{
   protected override void OnClosing()
   {
      PurgeQueues();
      //More cleanup if necessary
      base.OnClosing();
   }
   [Conditional("DEBUG")]
   void PurgeQueues()
   {
      foreach(ServiceEndpoint endpoint in Description.Endpoints)
      {
         QueuedServiceHelper.PurgeQueue(endpoint);
      }
   }
   //More members
}
```

In this example, the QueuedServiceHelper class offers the static method PurgeQueue(). As its name implies, PurgeQueue() accepts a service endpoint. If the binding used by that endpoint is the NetMsmqBinding, PurgeQueue() extracts the queue name out of the endpoint's address, creates a new MessageQueue object, and purges it. ServiceHost<T> overrides the OnClosing() method, which is called when the host shuts down gracefully. It then calls the private PurgeQueues() method. PurgeQueues() is marked with the Conditional attribute, using DEBUG as a condition. This means that while the body of PurgeQueues() always compiles, its call sites are conditioned on the DEBUG symbol. In debug mode only, OnClosing() will actually call PurgeQueues().

PurgeQueues( ) iterates over all endpoints of the host, calling QueuedServiceHelper. PurgeQueue( ) on each.

 The Conditional attribute is the preferred way in .NET for using conditional compilation and avoiding the pitfalls of explicit conditional compilation with #if.

Queues, services, and endpoints

WCF requires you to always dedicate a queue per endpoint for each service. This means a service with two contracts needs two queues for the two corresponding endpoints:

```
<service name = "MyService">
   <endpoint
      address  = "net.msmq://localhost/private/MyServiceQueue1"
      binding  = "netMsmqBinding"
      contract = "IMyContract"
   />
   <endpoint
      address  = "net.msmq://localhost/private/MyServiceQueue2"
      binding  = "netMsmqBinding"
      contract = "IMyOtherContract"
   />
</service>
```

The reason is that the client actually interacts with a queue, not a service endpoint. In fact, there may not even be a service at all; there may only be a queue. Two distinct endpoints cannot share queues because they will get each other's messages. Since the WCF messages in the MSMQ messages will not match, WCF will silently discard those messages it deems invalid, and you will lose the calls. Much the same way, two polymorphic endpoints on two services cannot share a queue, because they will eat each other's messages.

Exposing metadata

WCF cannot exchange metadata over MSMQ. Consequently, it is customary for even a service that will always have only queued calls to also expose a MEX endpoint or to enable metadata exchange over HTTP-GET, because the service's clients still need a way to retrieve the service description and bind against it.

WAS hosting

When hosting a queued service in the WAS, the name of the queue must be the same as the name of the .svc file leading to the virtual directory. For example:

```
<endpoint
   address  = "net.msmq://localhost/private/WASService.svc"
   binding  = "netMsmqBinding"
   contract = "IMyQueuedContract"
/>
```

Transactions

MSMQ is a WCF transactional resource manager. When you create a queue (either programmatically or administratively), you can create the queue as a transactional queue. If the queue is transactional, it is durable, and messages always persist to disk. More importantly, posting messages to and removing messages from the queue will always be done under a transaction. If the code that tries to interact with the queue has an ambient transaction, the queue will silently join that transaction. If no ambient transaction is present, MSMQ will start a new transaction for that interaction. It is as if the queue is encased in a `TransactionScope` constructed with `TransactionScopeOption.Required`. Once in a transaction, the queue will commit or roll back along with the accessing transaction. For example, if the accessing transaction posts a message to the queue and then aborts, the queue will reject the message.

Delivery and Playback

When a nontransactional client calls a queued service, client-side failures after the call will not roll back posting the message to the queue, and the queued call will be dispatched to the service. However, a client calling a queued service may call under a transaction, as shown in Figure 9-3.

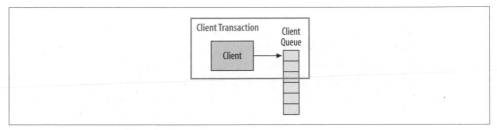

Figure 9-3. Posting to a client-side queue

The client calls are converted to WCF messages and then packaged in an MSMQ message (or messages). If the client's transaction commits, these MSMQ messages are posted to the queue and persist there. If the client's transaction aborts, the queue discards these MSMQ messages. In effect, WCF provides clients of a queued service with an auto-cancellation mechanism for their asynchronous, potentially disconnected calls. Normal connected asynchronous calls cannot be combined easily, if at all, with transactions, because once the call is dispatched there is no way to recall it in case the original transaction aborts. Unlike connected asynchronous calls, queued service calls are designed for this very transactional scenario. In addition, the client may interact with multiple queued services in the same transaction. Aborting the client transaction for whatever reason will automatically cancel all calls to those queued services.

The delivery transaction

Since the client may not be on the same machine as the service, and since the client, the service, or both could be disconnected, MSMQ maintains a client-side queue as well. The client-side queue serves as a "proxy" to the service-side queue. In the case of a remote queued call, the client first posts the message to the client-side queue. When (or if) the client is connected, MSMQ will deliver the queued messages from the client-side queue to the service-side queue, as shown in Figure 9-4.

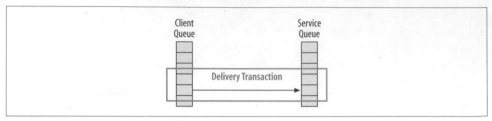

Figure 9-4. The delivery transaction

Since MSMQ is a resource manager, removing the message from the client-side queue will create a transaction (if indeed the queue is transactional). If MSMQ fails to deliver the message to the service-side queue for whatever reason (such as a network fault or service machine crash), the delivery transaction will abort, the message removal from the client-side queue will be rolled back, and the message posting to the service-side queue will also be canceled, resulting in the message being back in the client-side queue. At this point, MSMQ will try again to deliver the message. Thus, while you can configure and control failure handling (as you will see later), excluding fatal errors that can never be resolved, queued services actually enjoy a guaranteed delivery mechanism; if it is technically possible to deliver the message (within the confines of the failure-handling modes), the message will get from the client to the service. In effect, this is WCF's way of providing reliable messaging for queued services. Of course, there is no direct support for the reliable messaging protocol, as there is with connected calls; this is just the analogous mechanism.

The playback transaction

When WCF removes a message from the queue for playback to the service, this kick-starts a new transaction (assuming the queue is transactional), as shown in Figure 9-5.

The service is usually configured to participate in the playback transaction. If the playback transaction aborts (usually due to service-side exceptions), the message rolls back to the queue, where WCF detects it and dispatches it again to the service. This, in effect, yields an auto-retry mechanism. Consequently, you should keep the service's processing of the queued call relatively short, or risk aborting the playback transaction. An important observation here is that it is wrong to equate queued calls with lengthy asynchronous calls.

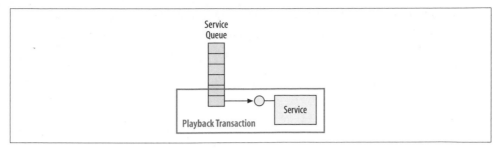

Figure 9-5. Playback transaction

Service Transaction Configuration

As just demonstrated, assuming transactional queues, there are actually three transactions involved in every queued call: client, delivery, and playback, as shown in Figure 9-6.

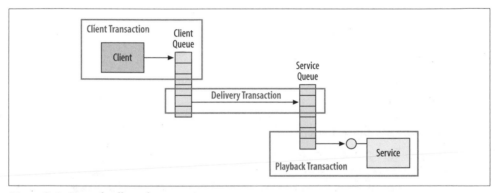

Figure 9-6. Queued calls and transactions

From a design perspective, you rarely, if ever, depict the delivery transaction in your design diagrams and you simply take it for granted. In addition, the service will never participate in the client's transaction, so in effect my four logical transactional modes from Chapter 7 (Client, Client/Service, Service, None) do not apply with queued services. Configuring the service contract operation with `TransactionFlowOption.Allowed` or `TransactionFlowOption.NotAllowed` leads to the same result—the client transaction is never provided to the service. Not only that, but `TransactionFlowOption.Mandatory` is disallowed for configuration on a queued contract, and this constraint is verified at the service load time. The real issue is the relation between the playback transaction and the service transactional configuration.

Participating in the playback transaction

From a WCF perspective, the playback transaction is treated as the incoming transaction to the service. To participate in the playback transaction, the service needs to have the operation behavior configured with TransactionScopeRequired set to true, as shown in Example 9-8 and graphically in Figure 9-5.

Example 9-8. Participating in the playback transaction

```
[ServiceContract]
interface IMyContract
{
   [OperationContract(IsOneWay = true)]
   void MyMethod( );
}
class MyService : IMyContract
{
   [OperationBehavior(TransactionScopeRequired = true)]
   public void MyMethod( )
   {
      Transaction transaction = Transaction.Current;
      Debug.Assert(transaction.TransactionInformation.
                  DistributedIdentifier != Guid.Empty);
   }
}
```

An interesting point made in Example 9-8 is that with both MSMQ 3.0 and MSMQ 4.0, every transaction always uses the DTC for transaction management, even in the case of a single service and a single playback. This might change in the next release of WCF and the .NET Framework.

Ignoring the playback transaction

If the service is configured for not having any transactions (like the service shown in Example 9-9), WCF will still use a transaction to read the message from the queue, except that transaction will always commit (barring an unforeseen failure in MSMQ itself). Exceptions and failures at the service itself will not abort the playback transaction.

Example 9-9. Ignoring the playback transaction

```
[ServiceContract]
interface IMyContract
{
   [OperationContract(IsOneWay = true)]
   void MyMethod( );
}
class MyService : IMyContract
{
   public void MyMethod( )
   {
      Transaction transaction = Transaction.Current;
      Debug.Assert(transaction == null);
   }
}
```

This scenario is depicted graphically in Figure 9-7.

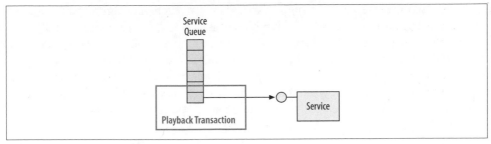

Figure 9-7. Ignoring the playback transaction

Services that do not participate in the playback transaction will not have the benefit of automated retries by WCF in the case of a playback failure, and it is possible for the played-back call to fail while the de-queued transaction commits. The main motivation for configuring queued services this way is to accommodate lengthy processing. If the service does not participate in the playback transaction, the call can take any amount of time to complete.

Using a separate transaction

You can also write a service so that it manually requires a new transaction, as shown in Example 9-10.

Example 9-10. Using a new transaction

```
class MyService : IMyContract
{
    public void MyMethod( )
    {
        using(TransactionScope scope = new TransactionScope( ))
        {
            ...
            scope.Complete( );
        }
    }
}
```

This scenario is depicted in Figure 9-8.

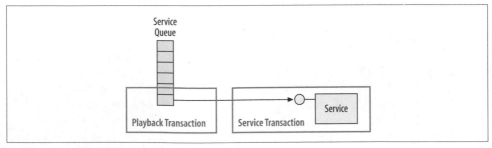

Figure 9-8. Using a new transaction

When the service uses its own new transaction for each message, it should also prevent participating in the playback transaction (by defaulting to the TransactionScopeRequired value of false) so as not to affect the playback transaction in any way. Again, this negates the benefit of the auto-retry mechanism. However, having a new transaction separate from the playback transaction gives the service the opportunity to perform its own transactional work. You would typically configure a service to use its own transaction when the queued operation being called is nice to have and should be performed under the protection of a transaction, yet does not need to be retried in case of a failure.

Nontransactional Queues

The MSMQ queues described so far were both durable and transactional. The messages persisted to the disk, and posting a message to and reading it from the queue was transactional. However, MSMQ also supports nontransactional queues. Such queues can be durable and persist on the disk or can be volatile (stored in memory). If the queue is volatile, the messages in the queue will not persist across a machine shutdown or a machine crash or just recycling of the MSMQ service.

When you create a queue (either using the MSMQ administration tool or programmatically), you can configure it to be transactional or not, and that selection is fixed for the life of the queue. Nontransactional queues do not offer any of the benefits of transactional messaging systems, such as auto-cancellation, guaranteed delivery, and auto-retries. When using a nontransactional queue, if the client transaction aborts, the message or messages will stay in the queue and be delivered to the service. If the playback transaction aborts, the messages will be lost.

As unadvisable as it is, WCF can work with nontransactional queues. MsmqBindingBase (the base class of NetMsmqBinding) offers the two Boolean properties Durable and ExactlyOnce, and these properties default to true:

```
public abstract class MsmqBindingBase : Binding,...
{
   public bool Durable
   {get;set;}
   public bool ExactlyOnce
   {get;set;}
   //More members
}
public class NetMsmqBinding : MsmqBindingBase
{...}
```

To work with a nontransactional queue, the ExactlyOnce property must be set to false. This will enable you to work both with volatile and durable queues. However, because of the lack of guaranteed delivery, when using a volatile queue WCF requires that you set the ExactlyOnce property of the binding to false otherwise,

WCF will throw an `InvalidOperationException` at the service load time. Consequently, here is a consistent configuration for a volatile nontransactional queue:

```
<netMsmqBinding>
   <binding name   = "VolatileQueue"
       durable     = "false"
       exactlyOnce = "false"
   />
</netMsmqBinding>
```

Instance Management

The contract session mode and the service instance mode have a paramount effect on the behavior of the queued calls, the way the calls are played back to the service, and the overall program workflow and allowed assumptions. The MSMQ binding cannot maintain a transport session in the connected sense, since the client is inherently disconnected. Instead, the equivalent MSMQ concept is called a *sessiongram*. If the contract is configured with `SessionMode.Allowed` (the default) or `SessionMode.NotAllowed`, there will be no sessiongram. Every call the client makes on the proxy will be converted to a single WCF message, and those WCF messages will be placed in individual MSMQ messages and posted to the queue. A client making two calls on the proxy will result in two MSMQ messages. If the contract is configured with `SessionMode.Required`, all the calls made by the client against the same proxy will be packaged in a single MSMQ message, in the order in which they were made and posted to the queue. On the service side, WCF will play the calls from the MSMQ message in the order they were made (like a recording) to the same service instance. This mode is therefore analogous to a transport session and a sessionful service.

Per-Call Queued Services

In the case of a per-call service, the client has no way of knowing whether its calls will eventually end up being played to a queued per-call service. All the client sees is the session mode of the contract. If the session mode is either `SessionMode.Allowed` or `SessionMode.NotAllowed`, there will be no sessiongram. In this case, regardless of whether the service is configured as per-call or sessionful it will amount to the same result: per-call processing and instantiation.

Nontransactional clients

When a client without an ambient transaction calls a sessiongram-less queued endpoint (as in Example 9-11), the MSMQ messages generated for each call are posted to the queue immediately after each call. If the client has an exception, the messages posted up to that point are not rejected and are delivered to the service.

Example 9-11. Nontransactional client of a sessionless queued endpoint

```
[ServiceContract]
interface IMyContract
{
   [OperationContract(IsOneWay = true)]
   void MyMethod( );
}
//Client code
using(TransactionScope scope =
                        new TransactionScope(TransactionScopeOption.Suppress))
{
   MyContractClient proxy = new MyContractClient( );

   proxy.MyMethod( ); //Message posts to queue here
   proxy.MyMethod( ); //Message posts to queue here

   proxy.Close( );
}
```

Transactional clients

With a transactional client (that is, client code with an ambient transaction) of a sessiongram-less queued endpoint (as in Example 9-12), the messages corresponding to each call are posted to the queue only when the client's transaction commits. If the client transaction aborts, all of those messages are rejected from the queue and all calls are canceled.

Example 9-12. Transactional client of a sessionless queued endpoint

```
[ServiceContract]
interface IMyContract
{
   [OperationContract(IsOneWay = true)]
   void MyMethod( );
}
//Client code
using(TransactionScope scope = new TransactionScope( ))
{
   MyContractClient proxy = new MyContractClient( );

   proxy.MyMethod( ); //Message written to queue
   proxy.MyMethod( ); //Message written to queue

   proxy.Close( );
   scope.Complete( );
} //Messages committed to queue here
```

There is no relationship between the proxy and the ambient transaction. If the client uses a transaction scope (as in Example 9-12), the client can close the proxy inside or outside the scope and may continue to use the proxy even after the transaction ends, or in a new transaction. The client may also close the proxy before or after the call to Complete( ).

Per-call processing

On the host side, the queued calls are dispatched separately to the service, and each call is played to a separate service instance. This is the case even if the service instance mode is per-session. I therefore recommend that when using a sessiongram-less queued contract, you should always explicitly configure the service as per-call and configure the contract for disallowing sessions, to increase the readability of the code and clearly convey your design decision:

```
[ServiceContract(SessionMode = SessionMode.NotAllowed)]
interface IMyContract
{...}

[ServiceBehavior(InstanceContextMode = InstanceContextMode.PerCall)]
class MyService : IMyContract
{...}
```

After each call the service instance is disposed of, just as with a connected per-call service. The per-call service may or may not be transactional. If it is transactional and the playback transaction is aborted, only that particular call is rolled back to the queue for a retry. As you will see later, due to concurrent playback and WCF's failure-handling behavior, calls to a per-call queued service can execute and complete in any order, and the client cannot make any assumptions about call ordering. Note that even calls dispatched by a transactional client may fail or succeed independently. Never assume order of calls with a sessiongram-less queued service.

Sessionful Queued Services

For sessionful queued services, the service contract must be configured with `SessionMode.Required`:

```
[ServiceContract(SessionMode = SessionMode.Required)]
interface IMyContract
{...}

class MyService : IMyContract
{...}
```

As mentioned previously, when the client queues up calls against a sessionful queued endpoint, all calls made throughout the session are grouped into a single MSMQ message. Once that single message is dispatched and played to the service, WCF creates a new dedicated service instance to handle all the calls in the message. All calls in the message are played back to that instance in their original order. After the last call, the instance is disposed of automatically.

WCF will provide both the client and the service with a unique session ID. However, the client session ID will be uncorrelated to that of the service. To approximate the session semantic, all calls on the same instance on the host side will share the same session ID.

Clients and transactions

In the case of a sessionful queued endpoint, the client must have an ambient transaction in order to call the proxy. Nontransactional clients are disallowed and will result in an InvalidOperationException:

```
[ServiceContract(SessionMode = SessionMode.Required)]
interface IMyContract
{
   [OperationContract(IsOneWay = true)]
   void MyMethod();
}

using(TransactionScope scope =
                          new TransactionScope(TransactionScopeOption.Suppress))
{
   MyContractClient proxy = new MyContractClient();

   proxy.MyMethod(); //Throws InvalidOperationException
   proxy.MyMethod();

   proxy.Close();
}
```

For a transactional client, WCF posts a single message to the queue when the transaction commits, and that single message is rejected from the queue if the transaction aborts:

```
using(TransactionScope scope = new TransactionScope())
{
   MyContractClient proxy = new MyContractClient();

   proxy.MyMethod();
   proxy.MyMethod();

   proxy.Close(); //Finish composing message, writes to queue

   scope.Complete();
} //Single message committed to queue here
```

It is important to note that the single message prepared by the proxy must be posted to the queue within the same client transaction—that is, the client must end the session inside the transaction. If the client does not close the proxy before the transaction is complete, the transaction will always abort:

```
MyContractClient proxy = new MyContractClient();
using(TransactionScope scope = new TransactionScope())
{
   proxy.MyMethod();
   proxy.MyMethod();

   scope.Complete();
} //Transaction aborts
proxy.Close();
```

This is required to enforce the atomicity of the sessiongram. All the calls in the session should either be posted to or rejected from the queue. If the client were to use the proxy in a second transaction that could commit or abort independently of the first, the results could be ambiguous or even dangerous.

An interesting side effect of this edict is that there is no point in storing a proxy to a queued sessionful endpoint in a member variable, because that proxy can only be used once in a single transaction and cannot be reused across client transactions.

Not only does the client have to close the proxy before the transaction ends, but when using a transaction scope, the client must close the proxy before completing the transaction. The reason is that closing the proxy to a queue's sessionful endpoint requires accessing the current ambient transaction, which is not possible after calling Complete(). Trying to do so results with InvalidOperationException:

```
MyContractClient proxy = new MyContractClient();
using(TransactionScope scope = new TransactionScope())
{
    proxy.MyMethod();
    proxy.MyMethod();

    scope.Complete();
    proxy.Close(); //Transaction aborts
}
```

A corollary of this requirement is that you cannot stack using statements in any order, because doing so may result in calling Dispose() in the wrong order (first on the scope, and then on the proxy):

```
using(MyContractClient proxy = new MyContractClient())
using(TransactionScope scope = new TransactionScope())
{
    proxy.MyMethod();
    proxy.MyMethod();

    scope.Complete();

} //Transaction aborts
```

Services and transactions

A sessionful queued service must be configured to use transactions in all operations by setting TransactionScopeRequired to true. Failing to do so will abort all playback transactions. The service is required to have a transaction in every operation so that all the calls in the session fail or succeed as one atomic operation (i.e., so that a failure in one of the operations causes the entire queued session to fail). In addition, the transaction must be the same transaction for all operations in the session. Partial success is impossible here, because WCF cannot return only a portion of the MSMQ message back to the queue after a failure of one of the operations but not the others.

To ensure that it is indeed the same transaction in all operations, the service must provide for transactional affinity to the instance by setting TransactionAutoComplete to false in all but the last operation in the session.

 Only a sessionful service can support a sessiongram contract, since only a service configured with InstanceContextMode.PerSession can set TransactionAutoComplete to false.

Due to a design flaw of WCF, the service cannot rely on setting TransactionAutoCompleteOnSessionClose to true to complete the transaction at the end of the session. Instead, it must have the last method call in the session complete the transaction, either automatically or manually. Failing to do so will cause all queued sessions to always abort (as all uncompleted transactions always do).

 This design flaw is scheduled to be fixed in the next release of WCF and the .NET Framework.

Example 9-13 is a template for implementing a queued sessionful service, assuming MyMethod3( ) is the last operation call in the session.

Example 9-13. Implementing a sessionful queued service

```
[ServiceContract(SessionMode = SessionMode.Required)]
interface IMyContract
{
   [OperationContract(IsOneWay = true)]
   void MyMethod1( );

   [OperationContract(IsOneWay = true)]
   void MyMethod2( );

   [OperationContract(IsOneWay = true)]
   void MyMethod3( );
}

class MyService : IMyContract
{
   [OperationBehavior(TransactionScopeRequired = true,
                      TransactionAutoComplete = false)]
   public void MyMethod1( )
   {...}

   [OperationBehavior(TransactionScopeRequired = true,
                      TransactionAutoComplete = false)]
   public void MyMethod2( )
   {...}
   [OperationBehavior(TransactionScopeRequired = true)]
   public void MyMethod3( )
```

Example 9-13. Implementing a sessionful queued service (continued)

```
   {...}
}
```

Obviously, baking into your service code the assumption that a particular method call will be the last in the session is often impractical. The best solution is to add an explicit CompleteTransaction( ) operation to the contract whose sole purpose is to complete the transaction and end the session. You should explicitly document the need to call this method at the end of the session:

```
[ServiceContract(SessionMode = SessionMode.Required)]
interface IMyContract
{
   [OperationContract(IsOneWay = true)]
   void MyMethod1( );

   [OperationContract(IsOneWay = true)]
   void MyMethod2( );

   [OperationContract(IsOneWay = true)]
   void CompleteTransaction( );
}

class MyService : IMyContract
{
   [OperationBehavior(TransactionScopeRequired = true,
                      TransactionAutoComplete = false)]
   public void MyMethod1( )
   {...}

   [OperationBehavior(TransactionScopeRequired = true,
                      TransactionAutoComplete = false)]
   public void MyMethod2( )
   {...}

   [OperationBehavior(TransactionScopeRequired = true)]
   public void CompleteTransaction( )
   {} //No code
}
```

Singleton Service

A queued singleton service can never have a session and can only implement session-less contracts. Configuring the SessionMode as either SessionMode.Allowed or SessionMode.NotAllowed has the same result: a sessiongram-less interaction. Consequently, I recommend always explicitly configuring the contracts of a queued single-ton service as sessionless:

```
[ServiceContract(SessionMode = SessionMode.NotAllowed)]
interface IMyContract
{...}
```

```
[ServiceBehavior(InstanceContextMode=InstanceContextMode.Single)]
class MyService : IMyContract
{...}
```

A nontransactional queued singleton service behaves like a regular WCF singleton as
far as instancing. Regardless of the way the clients use their proxies, individual calls
on the proxies are packaged into separate MSMQ messages and dispatched separately to the singleton, as with a per-call service. However, unlike with a per-call service, all these calls will be played back to the same single instance.

A transactional queued singleton, on the other hand, behaves by default like a per-
call service, because after every call that completes the transaction WCF will release
the singleton instance. The only difference between a true per-call service and a singleton is that WCF will allow at most a single instance of the singleton, regardless of
the number of queued messages. While you could apply the techniques described in
Chapter 7 to create a state-aware transactional singleton, you can also restore the singleton semantic by setting the ReleaseServiceInstanceOnTransactionComplete property to false and use volatile resource managers.

Example 9-14 shows a template for implementing a transactional queued singleton.

Example 9-14. Transactional queued singleton

```
[ServiceContract(SessionMode = SessionMode.NotAllowed)]
interface IMyContract
{
   [OperationContract(IsOneWay = true)]
   void MyMethod();
}

[ServiceBehavior(InstanceContextMode=InstanceContextMode.Single,
                 ReleaseServiceInstanceOnTransactionComplete = false)]
class MySingleton : IMyContract,IDisposable
{
   [OperationBehavior(TransactionScopeRequired = true)]
   public void MyMethod()
   {...}
   //More members
}
```

Calls and order

Because the calls are packaged into individual MSMQ messages, they may be played
to the singleton in any order (due to retries and transactions). In addition, calls may
complete in any order, and even calls dispatched by a transactional client may fail or
succeed independently. Never assume order of calls with a singleton.

Concurrency Management

As with a connected service, the ConcurrencyMode property governs concurrent playback of queued messages. With a per-call service, all queued messages are played at once to different instances as fast as they come off the queue, up to the limit of the configured throttle. There is no need to configure for reentrancy to support callbacks, because the operation contexts can never have callback references. There is also no need to configure for multiple concurrent access, because no two messages will ever share an instance. In short, with a queued per-call service, the concurrency mode is ignored.

When it comes to a sessionful queued service, you are required to configure the service with ConcurrencyMode.Single. The reason is that it is the only concurrency mode that allows you to turn off auto-completion, which is essential to maintain the session semantic. The calls in the message are always played to the same service instance, one at a time.

A queued singleton is really the only instancing mode that has any leeway with its concurrency mode. If the singleton is configured with ConcurrencyMode.Single, WCF will retrieve the messages all at once from the queue (up to the thread pool and throttling limits) and then queue up the calls in the internal queue the context lock maintains. Calls will be dispatched to the singleton one at a time. If the singleton is configured with ConcurrencyMode.Multiple, WCF will retrieve the messages all at once from the queue (up to the thread pool and throttling limits) and play them concurrently to the singleton. Obviously, in that case the singleton must provide for synchronized access to its state. If the singleton is also transactional, it is prone to transactional deadlocks over prolonged isolation maintained throughout each transaction.

Throttling

Queued calls have a nasty side effect of excelling in turning a low level of load into a high level of stress. Imagine an offline queued service that sustained relatively low load, such as a call per minute for one day. Once the host is launched, WCF flushes the queued calls (all 1,440 of them) to the service all at once, subjecting it to high stress. The fact that there are over 1,000 messages in the queue does not mean that your design supports 1,000 concurrent instances and calls.

Throttling a queued service is your way of controlling the stress on the service and avoiding turning load into stress. The important value to throttle is the number of concurrent playbacks. This is an effective way of throttling the number of played messages, because if the maximum number of concurrent calls is exceeded (overall stress), the excess messages will stay in the queue. With a per-call service, the throttle controls the overall number of allowed concurrent instances (and their implied resource consumption). With a per-session service, the throttle controls the number of allowed sessions. In the case of a queued singleton, you can combine a throttle value with `ConcurrencyMode.Multiple` to control just how many concurrent players are allowed (stress) and how many messages to keep in the queue (buffered load).

Delivery Failures

As discussed in Chapter 6, a connected call may fail due to either communication failures or service-side errors. Similarly, a queued call can fail due to delivery failures or service-side playback errors. WCF provides dedicated error-handling mechanisms for both types of errors, and understanding them and integrating your error-handling logic with them is an intrinsic part of using queued services.

While MSMQ can guarantee delivery of a message if it is technically possible to do so, there are multiple examples of when it is not possible to deliver the message. These include but are not limited to:

Timeouts and expiration
> As you will see shortly, each message has a timestamp, and the message has to be delivered and processed within the configured timeout. Failure to do so will cause the delivery to fail.

Security mismatches
> If the security credentials in the message (or the chosen authentication mechanism itself) do not match up with what the service expects, the service will reject the message.

Transactional mismatches
> The client cannot use a local nontransactional queue while posting a message to a transactional service-side queue.

Network problems
> If the underlying network fails or is simply unreliable, the message may never reach the service.

Machine crashes
> The service machine may crash due to software or hardware failures and will not be able to accept the message to its queue.

Purges
> Even if the message is delivered successfully, the administrator (or any application, programmatically) can purge messages out of the queue and avoid having the service process them.

Quota breaches
> Each queue has a quota controlling the maximum amount of data it can hold. If the quota is exceeded, future messages are rejected.

After every delivery failure, the message goes back to the client's queue, where MSMQ will continuously retry to deliver it. While in some cases, such as intermittent network failures or quota issues, the retries may eventually succeed, there are many cases where MSMQ will never succeed in delivering the message. In practical terms, a large enough number of retry attempts may be unacceptable and may create a dangerous amount of thrashing. Delivery-failure handling deals with how to let MSMQ know that it should not retry forever, how many attempts it should make before giving up, how much time can elapse before it gives up, and what it should do with the failed messages.

`MsmqBindingBase` offers a number of properties governing handling of delivery failures:

```
public abstract class MsmqBindingBase : Binding,...
{
   public TimeSpan TimeToLive
   {get;set;}

   //DLQ settings
   public Uri CustomDeadLetterQueue
   {get;set;}
   public DeadLetterQueue DeadLetterQueue
   {get;set;}

   //More members
}
```

The Dead-Letter Queue

In messaging systems, after an evident failure to deliver a message, that message goes to a special queue called the *dead-letter queue* (DLQ). The DLQ is somewhat analogous to a classic dead-letter mailbox at the main Post Office. In the context of this discussion, failure to deliver constitutes not only failure to reach the service-side queue, but also failure to commit the playback transaction. MSMQ on the client and on the service side constantly acknowledge to each other receipt and processing of messages. If the service-side MSMQ successfully receives and retrieves the message from the service-side queue (that is, if the playback transaction committed), it sends a positive acknowledgment (ACK) to the client-side MSMQ. The service-side MSMQ can also send a negative acknowledgment (NACK) to the client. When the client-side MSMQ receives a NACK, it posts the message to the DLQ. If the client-side MSMQ receives neither an ACK nor a NACK, the message is considered in-doubt.

With MSMQ 3.0 (that is, on Windows XP and Windows Server 2003), the dead-letter queue is a system-wide queue. All failed messages from any application go to this single repository. With MSMQ 4.0 (that is, on Windows Vista and Windows Server 2008 or later), you can configure a service-specific DLQ where only messages destined to that specific service go. Application-specific dead-letter queues grossly simplify both the administrator's and the developer's work.

When dealing with a nondurable queue, failed nontransactional messages go to a special system-wide DLQ.

Time to Live

With MSMQ, each message carries a timestamp initialized when the message is first posted to the client-side queue. In addition, every queued WCF message has a timeout, controlled by the TimeToLive property of MsmqBindingBase. After posting a message to the client-side queue, WCF mandates that the message must be delivered and processed within the configured timeout. Note that successful delivery to the service-side queue is not good enough—the call must be processed as well. The TimeToLive property is therefore somewhat analogous to the SendTimeout property of the connected bindings.

The TimeToLive property is relevant only to the posting client; it has no effect on the service side, nor can the service change it. TimeToLive defaults to one day. After continuously trying and failing to deliver (and process) a message for as long as TimeToLive allows, MSMQ stops trying and moves the message to the configured DLQ.

You can configure the time-to-live value either programmatically or administratively. For example, using a config file, here is how to configure a time to live of five minutes:

```
<bindings>
   <netMsmqBinding>
      <binding name = "ShortTimeout"
         timeToLive = "00:05:00"
      />
   </netMsmqBinding>
</bindings>
```

The main motivation for configuring a short timeout is when dealing with time-sensitive calls that must be processed in a timely manner. However, time-sensitive queued calls go against the grain of disconnected queued calls in general: the more time-sensitive the calls are, the more questionable the use of queued services is in the first place. The correct way of viewing time to live is as a last-resort heuristic used to eventually bring to the attention of the administrator the fact that the message was not delivered, not as a way to enforce business-level interpretation of the message's sensitivity.

Configuring the Dead-Letter Queue

MsmqBindingBase offers the DeadLetterQueue property, of the enum type DeadLetterQueue:

```
public enum DeadLetterQueue
{
    None,
    System,
    Custom
}
```

When `DeadLetterQueue` is set to `DeadLetterQueue.None`, WCF makes no use of a dead-letter queue. After a failure to deliver, WCF silently discards the message as if the call never happened. `DeadLetterQueue.System` is the default value of the property. As its name implies, it uses the system-wide DLQ: after a delivery failure, WCF moves the message from the client-side queue to the system-wide DLQ.

When `DeadLetterQueue` is set to `DeadLetterQueue.Custom`, the application can take advantage of a dedicated DLQ. `DeadLetterQueue.Custom` requires the use of MSMQ 4.0, and WCF verifies that at the call time. In addition, WCF requires that the application specify the custom DLQ address in the `CustomDeadLetterQueue` property of the binding. The default value of `CustomDeadLetterQueue` is null, but when `DeadLetterQueue.Custom` is employed, `CustomDeadLetterQueue` cannot be null:

```
<netMsmqBinding>
    <binding name = "CustomDLQ"
        deadLetterQueue = "Custom"
        customDeadLetterQueue = "net.msmq://localhost/private/MyCustomDLQ">
    </binding>
</netMsmqBinding>
```

Conversely, when the `DeadLetterQueue` property is set to any other value besides `DeadLetterQueue.Custom`, then `CustomDeadLetterQueue` must be null.

It is important to realize that the custom DLQ is just another MSMQ queue. It is up to the client-side developer to also deploy a DLQ service that processes its messages. All WCF does on MSMQ 4.0 is automate the act of moving the message to the DLQ once a failure is detected.

Custom DLQ verification

If a custom DLQ is required, as with any other queue, the client should verify at runtime (before issuing queued calls) that the custom DLQ exists and, if necessary, create it. Following the pattern presented previously, you can automate and encapsulate this with the `ServiceEndpoint` extension method `VerifyQueue()` of `QueuedServiceHelper`, shown in Example 9-15.

Example 9-15. Verifying a custom DLQ

```
public static class QueuedServiceHelper
{
    public static void VerifyQueue(this ServiceEndpoint endpoint)
    {
```

Example 9-15. Verifying a custom DLQ (continued)

```
    if(endpoint.Binding is NetMsmqBinding)
    {
        string queue = GetQueueFromUri(endpoint.Address.Uri);
        if(MessageQueue.Exists(queue) == false)
        {
            MessageQueue.Create(queue,true);
        }
        NetMsmqBinding binding = endpoint.Binding as NetMsmqBinding;
        if(binding.DeadLetterQueue == DeadLetterQueue.Custom)
        {
            Debug.Assert(binding.CustomDeadLetterQueue != null);
            string DLQ = GetQueueFromUri(binding.CustomDeadLetterQueue);
            if(MessageQueue.Exists(DLQ) == false)
            {
                MessageQueue.Create(DLQ,true);
            }
        }
    }
  }
  //More members
}
```

Processing the Dead-Letter Queue

The client needs to somehow process the accumulated messages in the DLQ. In the case of the system-wide DLQ, the client can provide a mega-service that supports all contracts of all queued endpoints on the system to enable it to process all failed messages. This is clearly an impractical idea, though, because that service could not possibly know about all queued contracts, let alone provide meaningful processing for all applications. The only feasible way to make this solution work would be to restrict the client side to at most a single queued service per system. Alternatively, you can write a custom application for direct administration and manipulation of the system DLQ using System. Messaging. That application will parse and extract the relevant messages and process them. The problem with that approach (besides the inordinate amount of work involved) is that if the messages are protected and encrypted (as they should be), the application will have a hard time dealing with and distinguishing between them. In practical terms, the only possible solution for a general client-side environment is the one offered by MSMQ 4.0: a custom DLQ. When using a custom DLQ, you also provide a client-side service whose queue is the application's custom DLQ. That service will process the failed messages according to the application-specific requirements.

Defining the DLQ service

Implementing the DLQ service is done like any other queued service. The only requirement is that the DLQ service be polymorphic with the original service's contract. If multiple queued endpoints are involved, you will need a DLQ per contract per endpoint. Example 9-16 shows a possible setup.

Example 9-16. DLQ service config file

```
<!-- Client side -->
<system.serviceModel>
   <client>
      <endpoint
         address  = "net.msmq://localhost/private/MyServiceQueue"
         binding  = "netMsmqBinding"
         bindingConfiguration = "MyCustomDLQ"
         contract = "IMyContract"
      />
   </client>
   <bindings>
      <netMsmqBinding>
         <binding name = "MyCustomDLQ"
            deadLetterQueue = "Custom"
            customDeadLetterQueue = "net.msmq://localhost/private/MyCustomDLQ">
         </binding>
      </netMsmqBinding>
   </bindings>
</system.serviceModel>

<!--  DLQ service side -->
<system.serviceModel>
   <services>
      <service name  = "MyDLQService">
         <endpoint
            address  = "net.msmq://localhost/private/MyCustomDLQ"
            binding  = "netMsmqBinding"
            contract = "IMyContract"
         />
      </service>
   </services>
</system.serviceModel>
```

The client config file defines a queued endpoint with the IMyContract contract. The client uses a custom binding section to define the address of the custom DLQ. A separate queued service (potentially on a separate machine) also supports the IMyContract contract. The DLQ service uses as its address the DLQ defined by the client.

Failure properties

The DLQ service typically needs to know why the queued call delivery failed. WCF therefore offers the MsmqMessageProperty class, used to find out the cause of the failure and the current status of the message. MsmqMessageProperty is defined in the System.ServiceModel.Channels namespace:

```
public sealed class MsmqMessageProperty
{
   public const string Name = "MsmqMessageProperty";
```

```
    public int AbortCount
    {get;}
    public DeliveryFailure? DeliveryFailure
    {get;}
    public DeliveryStatus? DeliveryStatus
    {get;}
    public int MoveCount
    {get;}
    //More members
}
```

The DLQ service needs to obtain the MsmqMessageProperty from the operation context's incoming message properties:

```
public sealed class OperationContext : ...
{
    public MessageProperties IncomingMessageProperties
    {get;}
    //More members
}
public sealed class MessageProperties : IDictionary<string,object>,...
{
    public object this[string name]
    {get;set;}
    //More members
}
```

When a message is passed to the DLQ, WCF will add to its properties an instance of MsmqMessageProperty detailing the failure. MessageProperties is merely a collection of message properties that you can access using a string as a key. To obtain the MsmqMessageProperty, use the constant MsmqMessageProperty.Name, as shown in Example 9-17.

Example 9-17. Obtaining the MsmqMessageProperty

```
[ServiceContract(SessionMode = SessionMode.NotAllowed)]
interface IMyContract
{
    [OperationContract(IsOneWay = true)]
    void MyMethod(string someValue);
}
[ServiceBehavior(InstanceContextMode = InstanceContextMode.PerCall)]
class MyDLQService : IMyContract
{
    [OperationBehavior(TransactionScopeRequired = true)]
    public void MyMethod()
    {
        MsmqMessageProperty msmqProperty = OperationContext.Current.
            IncomingMessageProperties[MsmqMessageProperty.Name] as MsmqMessageProperty;

        Debug.Assert(msmqProperty != null);
        //Process msmqProperty
    }
}
```

Note in Example 9-17 the use of the practices discussed so far for configuring the session mode, instance management, and transactions—the DLQ service is, after all, just another queued service.

The properties of MsmqMessageProperty detail the reasons for failure and offer some contextual information. MoveCount is the number of attempts made to play the message to the service, and AbortCount is the number of attempts made to read the message from the queue. AbortCount is less relevant to recovery attempts, because it falls under the responsibility of MSMQ and usually is of no concern. DeliveryStatus is a nullable enum of the type DeliveryStatus, defined as:

```
public enum DeliveryStatus
{
   InDoubt,
   NotDelivered
}
```

DeliveryStatus will be set to DeliveryStatus.InDoubt unless the message was positively not delivered (i.e., a NACK was received). For example, expired messages are considered in-doubt because their time to live elapsed before the service could acknowledge them one way or the other.

The DeliveryFailure property is a nullable enum of the type DeliveryFailure, defined as follows (without the specific numerical values):

```
public enum DeliveryFailure
{
   AccessDenied,
   NotTransactionalMessage,
   Purged,
   QueueExceedMaximumSize,
   ReachQueueTimeout,
   ReceiveTimeout,
   Unknown
   //More members
}
```

Implementing a DLQ service

The DLQ service cannot affect a message's properties (for example, extending its time to live). Handling of delivery failures typically involves some kind of compensating workflow: notifying the administrator; trying to resend a new message, or resending a new request with extended timeout; logging the error; or perhaps doing nothing (i.e., merely processing the failed call and returning, thus discarding the message).

Example 9-18 demonstrates a possible DLQ service implementation.

Example 9-18. Implementing a DLQ service

```
[ServiceBehavior(InstanceContextMode = InstanceContextMode.PerCall)]
class MyDLQService : IMyContract
{
   [OperationBehavior(TransactionScopeRequired = true)]
   public void MyMethod(string someValue)
   {
      MsmqMessageProperty msmqProperty = OperationContext.Current.
        IncomingMessageProperties[MsmqMessageProperty.Name] as MsmqMessageProperty;
      //If tried more than 25 times: discard message
      if(msmqProperty.MoveCount >= 25)
      {
         return;
      }
      //If timed out: try again
      if(msmqProperty.DeliveryStatus == DeliveryStatus.InDoubt)
      {
         if(msmqProperty.DeliveryFailure == DeliveryFailure.ReceiveTimeout)
         {
            MyContractClient proxy = new MyContractClient();
            proxy.MyMethod(someValue);
            proxy.Close();
         }
         return;
      }
      if(msmqProperty.DeliveryStatus == DeliveryStatus.InDoubt ||
         msmqProperty.DeliveryFailure == DeliveryFailure.Unknown)
      {
         NotifyAdmin();
      }
   }
   void NotifyAdmin()
   {...}
}
```

The DLQ service in Example 9-18 examines the cause of the failure. If WCF has tried more than 25 times to deliver the message, the DLQ service simply gives up and drops the message. If the cause for the failure was a timeout, the DLQ service tries again by creating a proxy to the queued service and calling it, passing the same arguments from the original call (the in-parameters to the DLQ service operation). If the message is in-doubt or an unknown failure took place, the service notifies the application administrator.

Playback Failures

Even after successful delivery, a message may still fail during playback to the service. Such failures typically abort the playback transaction, which causes the message to return to the service queue. WCF will then detect the message in the queue and retry.

If the next call fails too, the message will go back to the queue again, and so on. Continuously retrying this way is often unacceptable. If the initial motivation for the queued service was load leveling, WCF's auto-retry behavior will generate considerable stress on the service. You need a smart failure-handling schema that deals with the case when the call never succeeds (and, of course, defines "never" in practical terms). The failure handling will determine after how many attempts to give up, after how long to give up, and even the interval at which to try. Different systems need different retry strategies and have different sensitivity to the additional thrashing and probability of success. For example, retrying 10 times with a single retry once every hour is not the same strategy as retrying 10 times at 1-minute intervals, or the same as retrying 5 times, with each attempt consisting of a batch of 2 successive retries separated by a day. In general, it is better to hedge your bets on the causes for the failure and the probability of future success by retrying in a series of batches, to deal with sporadic and intermediate infrastructure issues as well as fluctuating application state. A series of batches, each batch comprised of a set number of retries in rapid succession, may just be able to catch the system in a state that will allow the call to succeed. If it doesn't, deferring some of the retries to a future batch allows the system some time to recuperate. Additionally, once you have given up on retries, what should you do with the failed message, and what should you acknowledge to its sender?

Poison Messages

Transactional messaging systems are inherently susceptible to repeated failure, because the retries thrashing can bring the system to its knees. Messages that continuously fail playbacks are referred to as *poison messages*, because they literally poison the system with futile retries. Transactional messaging systems must actively detect and eliminate poison messages. Since there is no telling whether just one more retry might actually succeed, you can use the following simple heuristic: all things being equal, the more the message fails, the higher the likelihood is of it failing again. For example, if the message has failed just once, retrying seems reasonable. But if the message has already failed 1,000 times, it is very likely it will fail again the 1,001st time, so it is pointless to try again. In this case, the message should be deemed a poison message. What exactly constitutes "pointless" (or just wasteful) is obviously application-specific, but it is a configurable decision. MsmqBindingBase offers a number of properties governing the handling of playback failures:

```
public abstract class MsmqBindingBase : Binding,...
{
    //Poison message handling
    public int ReceiveRetryCount
    {get;set;}

    public int MaxRetryCycles
    {get;set;}
```

```
public TimeSpan RetryCycleDelay
{get;set;}

public ReceiveErrorHandling ReceiveErrorHandling
{get;set;}

//More members
}
```

Poison Message Handling in MSMQ 4.0

With MSMQ 4.0 (available on Windows Vista and Windows Server 2008 or later), WCF retries playing back a failed message in series of batches, for the reasoning just presented. WCF provides each queued endpoint with a retry queue and an optional poison messages queue. After all the calls in the batch have failed, the message does not return to the endpoint queue. Instead, it goes to the retry queue (WCF will create that queue on the fly). Once the message is deemed poisonous, you may have WCF move that message to the poison queue.

Retry batches

In each batch, WCF will immediately retry for ReceiveRetryCount times after the first call failure. ReceiveRetryCount defaults to five retries, or a total of six attempts, including the first attempt. After a batch has failed, the message goes to the retry queue. After a delay of RetryCycleDelay minutes, the message is moved from the retry queue to the endpoint queue for another retry batch. The retry delay defaults to 30 minutes. Once that batch fails, the message goes back to the retry queue, where it will be tried again after the delay has expired. Obviously, this cannot go on indefinitely. The MaxRetryCycles property controls how many batches at the most to try. The default of MaxRetryCycles is two cycles only, resulting in three batches in total. After MaxRetryCycles number of retry batches, the message is considered a poison message.

When configuring nondefault values for MaxRetryCycles, I recommend setting its value in direct proportion to RetryCycleDelay. The reason is that the longer the delay is, the more tolerant your system will be of additional retry batches, because the overall stress will be somewhat mitigated (having been spread over a longer period of time). With a short RetryCycleDelay you should minimize the number of allowed batches, because you are trying to avoid approximating continuous thrashing.

Finally, the ReceiveErrorHandling property governs what to do after the last retry fails and the message is deemed poisonous. The property is of the enum type ReceiveErrorHandling, defined as:

```
public enum ReceiveErrorHandling
{
    Fault,
    Drop,
    Reject,
    Move
}
```

ReceiveErrorHandling.Fault

The `Fault` value considers the poison message as a catastrophic failure and actively faults the MSMQ channel and the service host. Doing so prevents the service from processing any other messages, be they from a queued client or a regular connected client. The poison message will remain in the endpoint queue and must be removed from it explicitly by the administrator or by some compensating logic, since WCF will refuse to process it again if you merely restart the host. In order to continue processing client calls of any sort, you must open a new host (after you have removed the poison message from the queue). While you could install an error-handling extension (as discussed in Chapter 6) to do some of that work, in practice there is no avoiding involving the application administrator.

`ReceiveErrorHandling.Fault` is the default value of the `ReceiveErrorHandling` property. With this setting, no acknowledgment of any sort is sent to the sender of the poison message. `ReceiveErrorHandling.Fault` is both the most conservative poison message strategy and the least useful from the system perspective, since it amounts to a stalemate.

ReceiveErrorHandling.Drop

The `Drop` value, as its name implies, silently ignores the poison message by dropping it and having the service keep processing other messages. You should configure for `ReceiveErrorHandling.Drop` if you have high tolerance for both errors and retries. If the message is not crucial, i.e., it is used to invoke a nice-to-have operation, dropping and continuing is acceptable. In addition, while `ReceiveErrorHandling.Drop` does allow for retries, conceptually you should not have too many retries—if you care that much about the message succeeding, you should not just drop it after the last failure.

Configuring for `ReceiveErrorHandling.Drop` also sends an ACK to the sender, so from the sender's perspective, the message was delivered and processed successfully. For many applications, `ReceiveErrorHandling.Drop` is an adequate choice.

ReceiveErrorHandling.Reject

The `ReceiveErrorHandling.Reject` value actively rejects the poison message and refuses to have anything to do with it. Similar to `ReceiveErrorHandling.Drop`, it drops the message, but it also sends a NACK to the sender, thus signaling ultimate delivery and processing failure. The sender responds by moving the message to the sender's dead-letter queue. `ReceiveErrorHandling.Reject` is a consistent, defensive, and adequate option for the vast majority of applications (yet it is not the default, to accommodate MSMQ 3.0 systems as well).

ReceiveErrorHandling.Move

The `ReceiveErrorHandling.Move` value is the advanced option for services that wish to defer judgment on the failed message to a dedicated third party. `ReceiveErrorHandling.Move` moves the message to the dedicated poison messages queue, and it does not send back an ACK or a NACK. Acknowledging processing of the message will be done after it is processed from the poison messages queue. While `ReceiveErrorHandling.Move` is a great choice if indeed you have some additional error recovery or compensation workflow to execute in case of a poison message, a relatively smaller set of applications will find it useful, due to its increased complexity and intimate integration with the system.

Configuration sample

Example 9-19 shows a configuration section from a host config file, configuring poison message handling on MSMQ 4.0.

Example 9-19. Poison message handling on MSMQ 4.0

```
<bindings>
   <netMsmqBinding>
      <binding name = "PoisonMessageHandling"
         receiveRetryCount    = "2"
         retryCycleDelay      = "00:05:00"
         maxRetryCycles       = "2"
         receiveErrorHandling = "Move"
      />
   </netMsmqBinding>
</bindings>
```

Figure 9-9 illustrates graphically the resulting behavior in the case of a poison message.

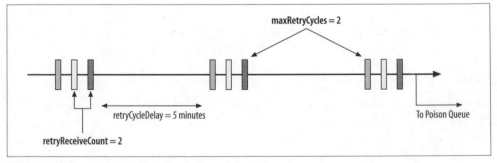

Figure 9-9. Poison message handling of Example 9-19

Poison message service

Your service can provide a dedicated poison-message-handling service to handle messages posted to its poison messages queue when the binding is configured with

`ReceiveErrorHandling.Move`. The poison message service must be polymorphic with the service's queued endpoint contract. WCF will retrieve the poison message from the poison queue and play it to the poison service. It is therefore important that the poison service does not throw unhandled exceptions or abort the playback transaction (configuring it to ignore the playback transaction, as in Example 9-9, or to use a new transaction, as in Example 9-10, is a good idea). Such a poison message service typically engages in some kind of compensating work associated with the failed message, such as refunding a customer for a missing item in the inventory. Alternatively, a poison service could do any number of things, including notifying the administrator, logging the error, or just ignoring the message altogether by simply returning.

The poison message service is developed and configured like any other queued service. The only difference is that the endpoint address must be the same as the original endpoint address, suffixed by `;poison`. Example 9-20 demonstrates the required configuration of a service and its poison message service. In Example 9-20 the service and its poison message service share the same host process, but that is certainly optional.

Example 9-20. Configuring a poison message service

```
<system.serviceModel>
   <services>
      <service name  = "MyService">
         <endpoint
            address  = "net.msmq://localhost/private/MyServiceQueue"
            binding  = "netMsmqBinding"
            bindingConfiguration = "PoisonMesssageSettings"
            contract = "IMyContract"
         />
      </service>
      <service name = "MyPoisonServiceMessageHandler">
         <endpoint
            address  = "net.msmq://localhost/private/MyServiceQueue;poison"
            binding  = "netMsmqBinding"
            contract = "IMyContract"
         />
      </service>
   </services>
   <bindings>
      <netMsmqBinding>
         <binding name = "PoisonMesssageSettings"
            receiveRetryCount    = "..."
            retryCycleDelay      = "..."
            maxRetryCycles       = "..."
            receiveErrorHandling = "Move"
         />
      </netMsmqBinding>
   </bindings>
</system.serviceModel>
```

Poison Message Handling in MSMQ 3.0

With MSMQ 3.0 (available on Windows XP and Windows Server 2003), there is no retry queue or optional poison queue. As a result, WCF supports at most a single retry batch out of the original endpoint queue. After the last failure of the first batch, the message is considered poisonous. WCF therefore behaves as if `MaxRetryCycles` is always set to 0, and the value of `RetryCycleDelay` is ignored. The only values available for the `ReceiveErrorHandling` property are `ReceiveErrorHandling.Fault` and `ReceiveErrorHandling.Drop`. Configuring other values throws an `InvalidOperationException` at the service load time.

> Neither `ReceiveErrorHandling.Fault` nor `ReceiveErrorHandling.Drop` is an attractive option. In MSMQ 3.0, the best way of dealing with a playback failure on the service side (that is, a failure that stems directly from the service business logic, as opposed to some communication issue) is to use a response service, as discussed later in this chapter.

Queued Versus Connected Calls

Although it is technically possible to use the same service code both connected and queued (with simple changes such as configuring operations as one-way, or adding another contract for the one-way operations), in reality it is unlikely that you will actually use the same service both ways. The reasons are similar to the arguments made in the context of asynchronous calls, discussed in Chapter 8. Synchronous calls and asynchronous calls addressing the same business scenario often have to use different workflows, and these differences will necessitate changes to the service code to adapt it for each case. The use of queued calls adds yet another barrier for using the same service code (both connected and disconnected): changes to the transactional semantics of the service.

Consider, for example, Figure 9-10, which depicts an online store application that uses connected calls only.

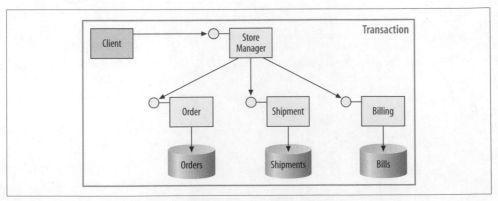

Figure 9-10. A connected application relies on a single transaction

The Store service uses three well-factored helper services to process the order: Order, Shipment, and Billing. In the connected scenario, the Store service calls the Order service to place the order. Only if the Order service succeeds in processing the order (that is, if the item is available in the inventory) does the Store service call the Shipment service, and only if the Shipment service succeeds does the Store service access the Billing service to bill the customer. The connected case involves exactly one transaction created by the client, and all operations commit or abort as one atomic operation. Now, suppose the Billing service also exposes a queued endpoint for the use of the Store service, as shown in Figure 9-11.

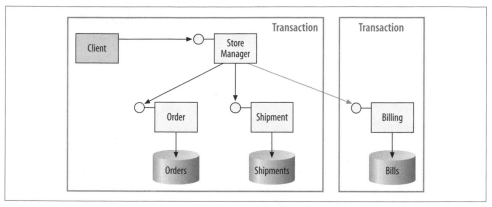

Figure 9-11. A disconnected application relies on multiple transactions

The queued call to the Billing service will be played to the service in a separate transaction from that of the rest of the store, and it could commit or abort separately from the transaction that groups Order and Shipment. This, in turn, could jeopardize the system's consistency, so you must include some logic in the Billing service to detect the failure of the other service and to initiate some compensating logic in the event that it fails to do its work. As a result, the Billing service will no longer be the same service used in the connected case.

Requiring Queuing

Since not every service can be connected and queued, and since some services may be designed for a particular option and only that option, WCF lets you constrain a service's communication pattern. The DeliveryRequirements attribute presented in Chapter 1 also lets you insist on queued or connected delivery of messages to the service:

```
public enum QueuedDeliveryRequirementsMode
{
    Allowed,
    Required,
    NotAllowed
}
```

```
[AttributeUsage(AttributeTargets.Interface|AttributeTargets.Class,
              AllowMultiple = true)]
public sealed class DeliveryRequirementsAttribute : Attribute,...
{
    public QueuedDeliveryRequirementsMode QueuedDeliveryRequirements
    {get;set;}
    public bool RequireOrderedDelivery
    {get;set;}
    public Type TargetContract
    {get;set;}
}
```

This attribute can be used to constrain a contract (and all its supporting endpoints) or a particular service type. The default value of the QueuedDeliveryRequirements property is QueuedDeliveryRequirementsMode.Allowed, so these definitions are equivalent:

```
[ServiceContract]
interface IMyContract
{...}

[ServiceContract]
[DeliveryRequirements]
interface IMyContract
{...}

[ServiceContract]
[DeliveryRequirements(QueuedDeliveryRequirements =
                      QueuedDeliveryRequirementsMode.Allowed)]
interface IMyContract
{...}
```

QueuedDeliveryRequirementsMode.Allowed grants permission for using the contract or the service with either connected or queued calls. QueuedDeliveryRequirementsMode.NotAllowed explicitly disallows the use of the MSMQ binding, so all calls on the endpoint must be connected calls. Use this value when the contract or the service is explicitly designed to be used in a connected fashion only. QueuedDeliveryRequirementsMode.Required is the opposite: it mandates the use of the MSMQ binding on the endpoint, and it should be used when the contract or the service is designed from the ground up to be queued.

Even though the DeliveryRequirements attribute offers the RequireOrderedDelivery property (discussed in Chapter 1), if QueuedDeliveryRequirementsMode.Required is used, then RequireOrderedDelivery must be false, because queued calls inherently are unordered and messages may be played back in any order.

When the DeliveryRequirements attribute is applied on an interface, it affects all services that expose endpoints with that contract:

```
[ServiceContract]
[DeliveryRequirements(QueuedDeliveryRequirements =
                      QueuedDeliveryRequirementsMode.Required)]
interface IMyQueuedContract
{...}
```

The client as well can apply the DeliveryRequirements attribute on its copy of the service contract.

When the DeliveryRequirements attribute is applied on a service class, it affects all endpoints of that service:

```
[DeliveryRequirements(QueuedDeliveryRequirements =
                      QueuedDeliveryRequirementsMode.Required)]
class MyQueuedService : IMyQueuedContract,IMyOtherContract
{...}
```

When applied on a service class while using the TargetContract property, the attribute affects all endpoints of the service that expose the specified contract:

```
[DeliveryRequirements(TargetContract = typeof(IMyQueuedContract),
                      QueuedDeliveryRequirements =
                      QueuedDeliveryRequirementsMode.Required)]
class MyService : IMyQueuedContract,IMyOtherContract
{...}
```

The Response Service

The programming model of queued calls described so far was one-sided: the client posted a one-way message to a queue, and the service processed that message. This model is sufficient when the queued operations are one-way calls by nature. However, the queued service may need to report back to its client on the result of the invocation, or return results or even errors. By default, this is not possible: WCF equates queued calls with one-way calls, which inherently forbids any such response. In addition, queued services (and their clients) are potentially disconnected. If a client posts a queued call to a disconnected service, by the time the service finally gets the message and processes it, there may no longer be a client to return the values to. The solution is to have the service report back to a client-provided queued service. I call such a service a *response service*.* Figure 9-12 shows the architecture of such a solution.

The response service is just another queued service in the system. The response service may be disconnected toward the client as well, or it may share the client's process, or be hosted in a separate process or even on a separate machine. If the response service shares the client's process, when the client is launched the response service will start processing the queued responses. Having the response service in a separate process (or even on a separate machine) from the client's helps to further decouple lifeline-wise the response service from the client or clients that use it.

---

* I first published my initial technique for a response service in the February 2007 issue of *MSDN Magazine*. In the next version of WCF and the .NET Framework, Microsoft intends to incorporate a similar solution to the one presented here.

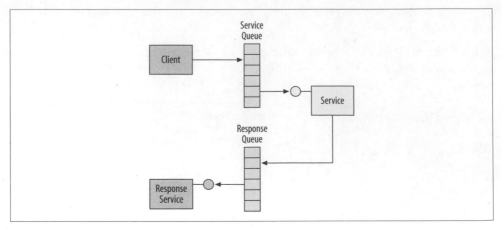

Figure 9-12. A response service

Not all queued services require a response service. Be pragmatic, and use a response service only where appropriate; that is, where it adds the most value.

Designing a Response Service Contract

As with any WCF service, the client and the service need to agree beforehand on the response contract and what it will be used for; that is, whether it will be used for returned values and error information, or just returned values. Note that you can also split the response service into two services, and have one response service for results and another for faults and errors. As an example, consider the `ICalculator` contract implemented by the queued `MyCalculator` service:

```
[ServiceContract]
interface ICalculator
{
    [OperationContract(IsOneWay = true)]
    void Add(int number1,int number2);
    //More operations
}
class MyCalculator : ICalculator
{...}
```

The `MyCalculator` service is required to respond to its client with the result of the calculation and report on any errors. The result of the calculation is an integer, and the error is in the form of the `ExceptionDetail` data contract presented in Chapter 6. The `ICalculatorResponse` contract could be defined as:

```
[ServiceContract]
interface ICalculatorResponse
{
    [OperationContract(IsOneWay = true)]
    void OnAddCompleted(int result,ExceptionDetail error);
```

```
        //More operations
    }
```

The response service supporting ICalculatorResponse needs to examine the returned error information; notify the client application, the user, or the application administrator on the method completion; and make the results available to the interested parties. Example 9-21 shows a simple response service that supports ICalculatorResponse.

Example 9-21. A simple response service

```
class MyCalculatorResponse : ICalculatorResponse
{
    public void OnAddCompleted(int result,ExceptionDetail error)
    {
        if(error != null)
        {
            //Handle error
        }
        else
        {
            MessageBox.Show("result =  " + result,"MyCalculatorResponse");
        }
    }

    //More operations
}
```

As demonstrated by Example 9-21, the response service is just that—a simple service. There is nothing special about it other than its designation as a response service.

Response address and method ID

There are two immediate problems with the implementation of both MyCalculator and MyCalculatorResponse. The first is that the same response service could be used to handle the response (or completion) of multiple calls on multiple queued services, and yet, as listed in Example 9-21, MyCalculatorResponse (and more importantly, the clients it serves) has no way of distinguishing between responses. The solution for that is to have the client that issued the original queued call tag the call by associating it with some unique ID, or at least an ID that is unique enough across that client's application. The queued service MyCalculator needs to pass that ID to the response service MyCalculatorResponse, so that it can apply its custom logic regarding that ID. Note that the service typically has no direct use for the ID; all it needs to do is pass it along.

The second problem is how to enable the queued service to discover the address of the response service. Unlike with duplex callbacks, there is no built-in support in WCF for passing the response service's reference to the queued service, so the queued service needs to manually construct a proxy to the response service and invoke the operations of the response contract. While the response contract is decided upon at design time, and the binding is always NetMsmqBinding, the queued service lacks the address of the response service to be able to respond. You could place that address in the service host config file (in a client section) but such a course of action is to be avoided. The main reason is that the same queued service could be called by multiple clients, each with its own dedicated response service and address.

One possible solution is to explicitly pass both the client-managed ID and the desired response service address as parameters to every operation on the queued service contract:

```
[ServiceContract]
interface ICalculator
{
   [OperationContract(IsOneWay = true)]
   void Add(int number1,int number2,string responseAddress,string methodId);
}
```

Much the same way, the queued service could explicitly pass the method ID to the response service as a parameter to every operation on the queued response contract:

```
[ServiceContract]
interface ICalculatorResponse
{
   [OperationContract(IsOneWay = true)]
   void OnAddCompleted(int result,ExceptionDetail error,string methodId);
}
```

The ResponseContext class

While passing the address and the ID as explicit parameters would work, it does distort the original contract, and it introduces plumbing-level parameters alongside business-level parameters in the same operation. A better solution is to have the client store the response address and operation ID in the outgoing message headers of the call. Using the message headers this way is a general-purpose technique for passing out-of-band information to the service (information that is otherwise not present in the service contract). Appendix B explains in detail the use of the incoming and outgoing headers, including the related techniques and supporting classes in *ServiceModelEx*.

Since the client needs to pass both the address and the method ID in the message headers, a single primitive type parameter will not do. Instead, use my ResponseContext class, defined in Example 9-22.

Example 9-22. The ResponseContext class

```
[DataContract]
public class ResponseContext
{
   [DataMember]
   public readonly string ResponseAddress;
```

Example 9-22. The ResponseContext class (continued)

```
    [DataMember]
    public readonly string FaultAddress;

    [DataMember]
    public readonly string MethodId;

    public ResponseContext(string responseAddress,string methodId) :
                                        this(responseAddress,methodId,null)
    {}
    public ResponseContext(string responseAddress) : this(responseAddress,
                                        Guid.NewGuid( ).ToString( ))
    {}
    public ResponseContext(string responseAddress,string methodId,
                        string faultAddress)
    {
        ResponseAddress = responseAddress;
        MethodId = methodId;
        FaultAddress = faultAddress;
    }

    public static ResponseContext Current
    {
        get
        {
            return GenericContext<ResponseContext>.Current.Value;
        }
        set
        {
            GenericContext<ResponseContext>.Current =
                                        new GenericContext<ResponseContext>(value);
        }
    }
    //More members
}
```

ResponseContext provides a place to store both the response address and the ID. In addition, if the client wants to use a separate response service for faults, ResponseContext provides a field for the fault response service address. (This chapter makes no use of that feature.) The client is responsible for constructing an instance of ResponseContext with a unique ID. While the client can supply that ID as a construction parameter, the client can also use the constructor of ResponseContext, which takes just the response address, and have that constructor generate a GUID for the ID. To streamline the act of storing a ResponseContext instance in and retrieving it from the headers, ResponseContext provides the Current property, which merely encapsulates my GenericContext<T>. The client can provide an ID for each method call (even when dealing with a sessionful queued service) by using a different instance of ResponseContext for each call.

Client-Side Programming

My HeaderClientBase<T,H> proxy base class (defined in Appendix B) is designed to automate passing information in the headers from the client to the service:

```
public abstract partial class HeaderClientBase<T,H> : ClientBase<T> where T : class
{
   protected H Header
   {get;set;}

   public HeaderClientBase(H header);
   public HeaderClientBase(H header,string endpointName);

   //More members
}
```

However, when it comes to the response context, there are differences compared with the raw headers management discussed in Appendix B: specifically, changing the context (that is, the headers) on each call as opposed to setting it only at construction time, generating method IDs and providing them to the client, and enqueuing rather than merely invoking the service call. While the client can easily use my HeaderClientBase<T,H> to do all that, all clients will have to repeat such code for every contract and proxy they have. It is better to automate and encapsulate these steps in a dedicated proxy base class such as my ResponseClientBase<T>, shown in Example 9-23.

Example 9-23. The ResponseClientBase<T> class

```
public abstract class ResponseClientBase<T> :
                          HeaderClientBase<T,ResponseContext> where T : class
{
   public readonly string ResponseAddress;

   public ResponseClientBase(string responseAddress)
   {
      ResponseAddress = responseAddress;
      Endpoint.VerifyQueue();
   }
   public ResponseClientBase(string responseAddress,string endpointName)
   {...}
   public ResponseClientBase(string responseAddress,
                          NetMsmqBinding binding,EndpointAddress address)
   {...}

   /* More constructors */

   protected string Enqueue(Action action)
   {
      string methodId = GenerateMethodId();
      Header = new ResponseContext(ResponseAddress,methodId);
      action();
      return Header.MethodId;
   }
```

Example 9-23. The ResponseClientBase<T> class (continued)

```
   protected virtual string GenerateMethodId( )
   {
      return Guid.NewGuid( ).ToString( );
   }
}
```

The constructors of ResponseClientBase<T> accept the response address and the regular proxy parameters, such as the endpoint name, address, and binding. The constructors store the response address in the read-only public field ResponseAddress. In addition, the constructors use the VerifyQueue( ) endpoint extension method to verify that the service queue (and the DLQ) exists and to create it if necessary.

ResponseClientBase<T> provides the virtual GenerateMethodId( ) method, which by default uses a GUID for the method ID. However, your subclasses of ResponseClientBase<T> can override it and provide their own unique strings, such as an incremented integer.

The heart of ResponseClientBase<T> is the Enqueue( ) method. Enqueue( ) accepts a delegate wrapping the operation to invoke. For every operation invoked by the client, Enqueue( ) generates a new method ID, provides it to a new ResponseContext object (along with the response address supplied to the constructor), and assigns the new ResponseContext object to the Header property of HeaderClientBase<T,H>. Thanks to generics, Header is of the type ResponseContext. After invoking the delegate, Enqueue( ) returns the method ID used for that call.

Using ResponseClientBase<T>

When using a ResponseClientBase<T>-derived proxy, I wanted to have all operations of the proxy return the method ID used to dispatch them (something that is very handy when managing the responses on the client side).

To that end, unlike with a normal proxy, when deriving from ResponseClientBase<T>, do not have the subclass also derive from the contract. Instead, you must provide a similar set of methods that all return a string for the method ID, not void (this is why you cannot derive from the contract—the operations on the contract are all one-way and do not return anything).

You need merely provide the contract type as a type parameter to ResponseClientBase<T> and have your proxy's implementation of the operations return the method ID returned to them by Enqueue( ). For example, for this calculator contract:

```
   [ServiceContract]
   interface ICalculator
   {
      [OperationContract(IsOneWay = true)]
      void Add(int number1,int number2);
      //More operations
   }
```

Example 9-24 shows the matching service proxy.

Example 9-24. Deriving from ResponseClientBase<T>

```
class CalculatorClient : ResponseClientBase<ICalculator>
{
   public CalculatorClient(string responseAddress) : base(responseAddress)
   {}
   public CalculatorClient(string responseAddress,string endpointName) :
                                       base(responseAddress,endpointName)
   {}
   public CalculatorClient(string responseAddress,
                     NetMsmqBinding binding,EndpointAddress address) :
                                    base(responseAddress,binding,address)
   {}
   //More constructors

   public string Add(int number1,int number2)
   {
      return Enqueue(( )=>Channel.Add(number1,number2));
   }

   //More operations
}
```

Using the proxy in Example 9-24 yields this straightforward client code:

```
string responseAddress = "net.msmq://localhost/private/MyCalculatorResponseQueue";

CalculatorClient proxy = new CalculatorClient(responseAddress);
string methodId = proxy.Add(2,3);
proxy.Close( );
```

Note how closely the client that provides the response address to the proxy corresponds to a client that provides a duplex callback object to a proxy (as demonstrated in Chapter 5). In the queued services world, the response service address is the equivalent callback reference.

> A queued response service is not limited to being used only with a queued service. You can use the same technique to pass the address and method ID to a connected service and have that service respond to a client-provided queued response service. You will need to rework ResponseClientBase<T> so that it only uses Binding, and rename Enqueue( ) to InvokeService( ).

Queued Service-Side Programming

Since duplex callback was my reference programming model in designing the support for a response service, I wanted to provide an easy way for the service to obtain a proxy for the response service (on par with the duplex case, which simply obtains the callback reference from the operation context). My solution was ResponseScope<T>, defined as:

```
    public class ResponseScope<T> : IDisposable where T : class
    {
        public readonly T Response;

        public ResponseScope( );
        public ResponseScope(string bindingConfiguration);
        public ResponseScope(NetMsmqBinding binding);

        public void Dispose( );
    }
```

ResponseScope<T> automates reading the response context from the message headers, writing the response itself to the outgoing headers, and creating (and closing) a proxy to the response service queue. All you need to do is instantiate a ResponseScope<T> object and optionally provide it with the binding or binding configuration. The Response read-only field will contain a reference to a proxy to the response service.

Example 9-25 demonstrates using ResponseScope<T>.

Example 9-25. Using ResponseScope<T>

```
class MyCalculator : ICalculator
{
    [OperationBehavior(TransactionScopeRequired = true)]
    public void Add(int number1,int number2)
    {
        int result = 0;
        ExceptionDetail error = null;

        try
        {
            result = number1 + number2;
        }
        //Don't rethrow
        catch(Exception exception)
        {
            error = new ExceptionDetail(exception);
        }
        finally
        {
            using(ResponseScope<ICalculatorResponse> scope =
                                    new ResponseScope<ICalculatorResponse>( ))
            {
                scope.Response.OnAddCompleted(result,error);
            }
        }
    }
}
```

In Example 9-25, the MyCalculator service catches any exception thrown by the business logic operation and wraps that exception with an ExceptionDetail object.

The service does not rethrow the exception. As you will see later, in the context of transactions and response services, rethrowing the exception would also cancel the response. Moreover, when using a response service, being able to respond in case of an error is a much better strategy than relying on WCF's playback error handling.

In the finally statement, regardless of exceptions, the service responds. It creates a new ResponseScope<T> object and uses the Response field to call the response service proxy, in effect enqueuing the response. The service then disposes of the response scope.

Example 9-26 shows the implementation of ResponseScope<T>.

Example 9-26. Implementing ResponseScope<T>

```
public class ResponseScope<T> : IDisposable where T : class
{
   OperationContextScope m_Scope;

   public readonly T Response;

   public ResponseScope() : this(new NetMsmqBinding())
   {}
   public ResponseScope(string bindingConfiguration) :
                                    this(new NetMsmqBinding(bindingConfiguration))
   {}
   public ResponseScope(NetMsmqBinding binding)
   {
      ResponseContext responseContext = ResponseContext.Current;

      EndpointAddress address =
                           new EndpointAddress(responseContext.ResponseAddress);

      ChannelFactory<T> factory = new ChannelFactory<T>(binding,address);
      factory.Endpoint.VerifyQueue();

      Response = factory.CreateChannel();

      //Switching context now
      m_Scope = new OperationContextScope(Response as IContextChannel);

      ResponseContext.Current = responseContext;
   }
   public void Dispose()
   {
      using(Response as IDisposable)
      using(m_Scope)
      {}
   }
}
```

This terse example contains some of the most advanced WCF code in this book. ResponseScope<T> is a disposable object—it installs a new operation context (as explained in Appendix B), and when ResponseScope<T> is disposed of, the scope restores the old operation context. The trick in implementing ResponseScope<T> is not to use an OperationContextScope instance in a using statement to scope a piece of code with a new operation context, but rather to create it in one place, store it in the m_Scope member, and dispose of m_Scope in another place. The constructor of OperationContextScope is what swaps the contexts, so merely constructing the scope swaps contexts. The Dispose( ) method of ResponseScope<T> restores the original operation context by disposing of m_Scope. To automate that behavior even in the face of exceptions, ResponseScope<T> should be used in a using statement. ResponseScope<T> takes a generic type parameter representing the response contract, and Response is of that type. Response is a proxy to the response service, and the clients of ResponseScope<T> use Response to call operations on the response service. There is no need to dispose of Response, because ResponseScope<T> does that in Dispose( ).

The constructor of ResponseScope<T> first uses ResponseContext.Current to extract the incoming response context. Since ResponseScope<T> reads the response address from the message headers of the service operation context at runtime, it must programmatically construct a proxy to the response service, using a channel factory. Note that the service can still read the exact settings to use for the NetMsmqBinding from the config file, by specifying the binding configuration name to the binding constructor. After instantiating Response, ResponseScope<T> swaps operation contexts; it then uses ResponseContext.Current to add to the new operation context's outgoing headers the response context and returns.

Note that ResponseScope<T> sends the response service the entire response context (not just the ID). This is done both for simplicity's sake and because it may be beneficial for the response service to have access to the fault and response address used.

Response Service-Side Programming

The response service accesses its response context, reads from it the method ID, and responds accordingly. Example 9-27 demonstrates a possible implementation of such a response service.

Example 9-27. Implementing a response service

```
class MyCalculatorResponse : ICalculatorResponse
{
   [OperationBehavior(TransactionScopeRequired = true)]
   public void OnAddCompleted(int result,ExceptionDetail error)
   {
      string methodId = ResponseContext.Current.MethodId;
      ...
   }
}
```

It is common for the response service to update the application's user interfaces with the queued results (or errors). Chapter 8 introduced my FormHost<F> class, which you can certainly leverage to support the queued response contract. For example:

```
class CalculatorResponse :
                        FormHost<CalculatorResponse>,
                                ICalculatorResponse
{
    [OperationBehavior(TransactionScopeRequired=true)]
    public void OnAddCompleted(int result,
                                    ExceptionDetail error)
    {
       Text = "Add returned: " + result;
       ...
    }
}
```

In fact, nothing prevents you from having the client itself be the response service as well.

Transactions

A queued service typically queues up the response as part of the incoming playback transaction. Given the queued service definition of Example 9-28, Figure 9-13 depicts the resulting transaction and the participating actions.

Example 9-28. Queuing up a response as part of the playback transaction

```
class MyCalculator : ICalculator
{
    [OperationBehavior(TransactionScopeRequired = true)]
    public void Add(int number1,int number2)
    {
        ...
        try
        {
           ...
        }
        catch //Do not rethrow
        {
           ...
        }
        finally
        {
            using(ResponseScope<ICalculatorResponse> scope =
                                    new ResponseScope<ICalculatorResponse>())
            {
                scope.Response.OnAddCompleted(...);
            }
        }
    }
}
```

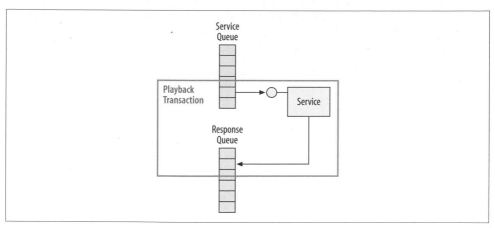

Figure 9-13. Queuing up in the playback transaction

Design-wise, the nice thing about having the queued call playback and the queued response in the same transaction is that if the playback transaction is aborted for whatever reason (including due to other services in the transaction aborting), the response is canceled automatically. This is by far the most common choice for most applications.

Note in Example 9-28 that the service catches all exceptions and does not rethrow them. This is important, because any unhandled exception (or rethrown exception) will abort the response, so there won't be any point in the service bothering to respond. Using a response service intrinsically means that the service does not rely on the automatic retry mechanism of WCF, and it handles its own business logic failures because the clients expect it to respond in a prescribed manner.

Using a new transaction

As an alternative to always having the response be part of the playback transaction, the service can respond in a new transaction by encasing the response in a new transaction scope, as shown in Example 9-29 and illustrated in Figure 9-14.

Example 9-29. Responding in a new transaction

```
class MyCalculator : ICalculator
{
   [OperationBehavior(TransactionScopeRequired = true)]
   public void Add(int number1,int number2)
   {
      ...
      finally
      {
         using(TransactionScope transactionScope =
                        new TransactionScope(TransactionScopeOption.RequiresNew))
         using(ResponseScope<ICalculatorResponse> responseScope =
                                 new ResponseScope<ICalculatorResponse>())
```

Example 9-29. Responding in a new transaction (continued)

```
        {
           responseScope.Response.OnAddCompleted(...);
        }
     }
   }
}
```

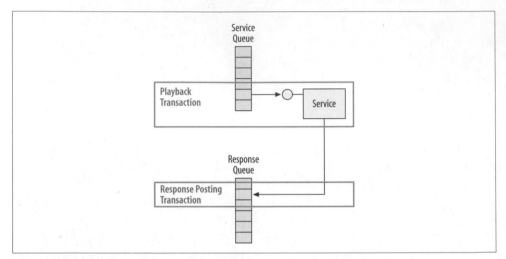

Figure 9-14. Responding in a new transaction

Responding in a new transaction is required in two cases. The first is when the service wants to respond regardless of the outcome of the playback transaction (which could be aborted by other downstream services). The second case is when the response is nice to have, and the service does not mind if the playback transaction commits but the response aborts.

Response service and transactions

Since a response service is just another queued service, the mechanics of managing and participating in a transaction are just like those of any other queued service. However, there are a few points worth mentioning in this particular context. The response service can process the response as part of the incoming response playback transaction:

```
class MyCalculatorResponse : ICalculatorResponse
{
   [OperationBehavior(TransactionScopeRequired = true)]
   public void OnAddCompleted(...)
   {...}
}
```

This is by far the most common option, because it allows for retries. That said, the response service should avoid lengthy processing of the queued response, because it may risk aborting the playback transaction. The response service can process the response in a separate transaction if the response is nice to have (as far as the provider of the response service is concerned):

```
class MyCalculatorResponse : ICalculatorResponse
{
   public void OnAddCompleted(int result,ExceptionDetail error)
   {
      using(TransactionScope scope = new TransactionScope())
      {...}
   }
}
```

When the response is processed in a new transaction, if that transaction aborts, WCF will not retry the response out of the response service's queue. Finally, for response processing of long duration, you can configure the response service not to use a transaction at all (including the playback transaction):

```
class MyCalculatorResponse : ICalculatorResponse
{
   public void OnAddCompleted(...)
   {...}
}
```

The HTTP Bridge

The MSMQ binding is designed to be employed in the intranet. It cannot go through firewalls by default, and more importantly, it uses a Microsoft-specific encoding and message format. Even if you could tunnel through the firewall, you would need the other party to use WCF as well. While requiring WCF at both ends is a reasonable assumption in the intranet, it is unrealistic to demand that from Internet-facing clients and services, and it violates the core service-oriented principles that service boundaries should be explicit and that the implementation technology used by a service should be immaterial to its clients. That said, Internet services may benefit from queued calls just like intranet clients and services, and yet the lack of an industry standard for such queued interoperability (and the lack of support in WCF) prevents such interaction. The solution to that problem is a technique I call the *HTTP bridge*. Unlike most of my other techniques shown in this book, the HTTP bridge is a configuration pattern rather than a set of helper classes. The HTTP bridge, as its name implies, is designed to provide queued calls support for clients and services connected over the Internet. The bridge requires the use of the WSHttpBinding (rather than the basic binding) because it is a transactional binding. There are two parts to the HTTP bridge. The bridge enables WCF clients to queue up calls to an Internet service that uses the WS binding, and it enables a WCF service that exposes an HTTP endpoint over the WS binding to queue up calls from its Internet clients. You can use each part of the bridge separately, or you can use them in conjunction. The bridge can only be used if the remote service contract can be queued (that is, if the contract has only one-way operations), but that is usually the case; otherwise, the client would not have been interested in the bridge in the first place.

Designing the Bridge

Since you cannot really queue up calls with the WS binding, you can facilitate that instead using an intermediary bridging client and service. When the client wishes to queue up a call against an Internet-based service, the client will in fact queue up the call against a local (that is, intranet-based) queued service called `MyClientHttpBridge`. In its processing of the queued call, the client-side queued bridge service will use the WS binding to call the remote Internet-based service. When an Internet-based service wishes to receive queued calls, it will use a queue. But because non-WCF clients cannot access that queue over the Internet, the service will use a façade: a dedicated connected service called `MyServiceHttpBridge` that exposes a WS-binding endpoint. In its processing of the Internet call, `MyServiceHttpBridge` simply makes a queued call against the local service. Figure 9-15 shows the HTTP bridge architecture.

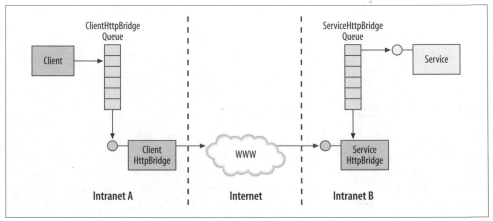

Figure 9-15. The HTTP bridge

Transaction Configuration

It is important to use transactions between `MyClientHttpBridge`, the client side of the bridge, and the remote service, and it is important to configure the service-side bridge (`MyServiceHttpBridge`) to use the Client transaction mode discussed in Chapter 7. The rationale is that by using a single transaction from the playback of the client call to the `MyClientHttpBridge` to the `MyServiceHttpBridge` (if present) you will approximate the transactional delivery semantic of a normal queued call, as shown in Figure 9-16.

Compare Figure 9-16 with Figure 9-6. If the delivery transaction in the bridge aborts for any reason, the message will roll back to the `MyClientHttpBridge` queue for another retry. To maximize the chances of successful delivery, you should also turn on reliability for the call between `MyClientHttpBridge` and the remote service.

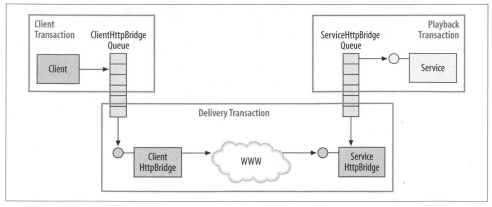

Figure 9-16. The HTTP bridge and transactions

Service-Side Configuration

MyServiceHttpBridge converts a regular connected call over the WS binding into a queued call and posts it to the service queue. MyServiceHttpBridge implements a contract that is similar, but not identical, to that of the queued service. The reason is that the service-side bridge should be able to participate in the incoming transaction, but transactions cannot flow over one-way operations. The solution is to modify the contract to support (indeed, mandate) transactions. For example, if this is the original service contract:

```
[ServiceContract]
public interface IMyContract
{
   [OperationContract(IsOneWay = true)]
   void MyMethod( );
}
```

then MyServiceHttpBridge should expose this contract instead:

```
[ServiceContract]
public interface IMyContractHttpBridge
{
   [OperationContract]
   [TransactionFlow(TransactionFlowOption.Mandatory)]
   void MyMethod( );
}
```

In essence, you need to set IsOneWay to false and use TransactionFlowOption.
Mandatory. For readability's sake, I recommend that you also rename the interface by suffixing it with HttpBridge. MyServiceHttpBridge can be hosted anywhere in the service's intranet, including in the service's own process. Example 9-30 shows the required configuration of the service and its HTTP bridge.

Example 9-30. Service-side configuration of the HTTP bridge

```
<!-- MyService Config File -->
<services>
   <service name = "MyService">
      <endpoint
         address  = "net.msmq://localhost/private/MyServiceQueue"
         binding  = "netMsmqBinding"
         contract = "IMyContract"
      />
   </service>
</services>

<!-- MyServiceHttpBridge Config File -->
<services>
   <service name  = "MyServiceHttpBridge">
      <endpoint
         address  = "http://localhost:8001/MyServiceHttpBridge"
         binding  = "wsHttpBinding"
         bindingConfiguration = "ReliableTransactedHTTP"
         contract = "IMyContractHttpBridge"
      />
   </service>
</services>

<client>
   <endpoint
      address  = "net.msmq://localhost/private/MyServiceQueue"
      binding  = "netMsmqBinding"
      contract = "IMyContract"
   />
</client>

<bindings>
   <wsHttpBinding>
      <binding name = "ReliableTransactedHTTP" transactionFlow = "true">
         <reliableSession enabled = "true"/>
      </binding>
   </wsHttpBinding>
</bindings>
```

The service MyService exposes a simple queued endpoint with IMyContract. The service MyServiceHttpBridge exposes an endpoint with WSHttpBinding and the IMyContractHttpBridge contract. MyServiceHttpBridge is also a client of the queued endpoint defined by the service. Example 9-31 shows the corresponding implementation. Note that MyServiceHttpBridge is configured for the Client transaction mode.

Example 9-31. Service-side implementation of the HTTP bridge

```
class MyService : IMyContract
{
   //This call comes in over MSMQ
   [OperationBehavior(TransactionScopeRequired = true)]
```

Example 9-31. Service-side implementation of the HTTP bridge (continued)

```
    public void MyMethod( )
    {...}
}
class MyServiceHttpBridge : IMyContractHttpBridge
{
    //This call comes in over HTTP
    [OperationBehavior(TransactionScopeRequired = true)]
    public void MyMethod( )
    {
        MyContractClient proxy = new MyContractClient( );

        //This call goes out over MSMQ
        proxy.MyMethod( );

        proxy.Close( );
    }
}
```

Client-Side Configuration

The client uses queued calls against the local `MyClientHttpBridge` service. `MyClientHttpBridge` can be hosted in the same process as the client, in a different process, or even on a separate machine on the client's intranet. The local `MyClientHttpBridge` service uses the `WSHttpBinding` to call the remote service. The client needs to retrieve the metadata of the remote Internet service (such as the definition of `IMyContractHttpBridge`) and convert it to a queued contract (such as `IMyContract`). Example 9-32 shows the required configuration of the client and its HTTP bridge.

Example 9-32. Client-side configuration of the HTTP bridge

```
<!-- Client Config File  -->
<client>
   <endpoint
      address  = "net.msmq://localhost/private/MyClientHttpBridgeQueue"
      binding  = "netMsmqBinding"
      contract = "IMyContract"
   />
</client>

<!-- MyClientHttpBridge Config File  -->
<services>
   <service name  = "MyClientHttpBridge">
      <endpoint
         address  = "net.msmq://localhost/private/MyClientHttpBridgeQueue"
         binding  = "netMsmqBinding"
         contract = "IMyContract"
      />
   </service>
</services>
```

Example 9-32. Client-side configuration of the HTTP bridge (continued)

```xml
<client>
   <endpoint
      address  = "http://localhost:8001/MyServiceHttpBridge"
      binding  = "wsHttpBinding"
      bindingConfiguration = "ReliableTransactedHTTP"
      contract = "IMyContractHttpBridge"
   />
</client>
<bindings>
   <wsHttpBinding>
      <binding name = "ReliableTransactedHTTP" transactionFlow = "true">
         <reliableSession enabled = "true"/>
      </binding>
   </wsHttpBinding>
</bindings>
```

MyClientHttpBridge exposes a simple queued endpoint with IMyContract.
MyClientHttpBridge is also a client of the connected WS-binding endpoint defined by
the service. Example 9-33 shows the corresponding implementation.

Example 9-33. Client-side implementation of the HTTP bridge

```csharp
MyContractClient proxy = new MyContractClient();

//This call goes out over MSMQ
proxy.MyMethod();

proxy.Close();

////////////////// Client-Side Bridge Implementation ////////////
class MyClientHttpBridge : IMyContract
{
   //This call comes in over MSQM
   [OperationBehavior(TransactionScopeRequired = true)]
   public void MyMethod()
   {
      MyContractHttpBridgeClient proxy = new MyContractHttpBridgeClient();

      //This call goes out over HTTP
      proxy.MyMethod();

      proxy.Close();
   }
}
```

CHAPTER 10

Security

There are several aspects pertaining to secure interaction between a client and a service. As in traditional client/server and component-oriented applications, the service needs to authenticate its callers and often also authorize the callers before executing sensitive operations. In addition, regardless of the technology, when securing a service (and its clients) as in any distributed system, you need to secure the messages while they are en route from the client to the service. Once the messages arrive securely and are authenticated and authorized, the service has a number of options regarding the identity it uses to execute the operation. This chapter will explore these classic security aspects—authentication, authorization, transfer security, and identity management—as well as something more abstract, which I call *overall security policy*: that is, your own personal and your company's (or customer's) approach to and mindset regarding security. This chapter starts by defining the various aspects of security in the context of WCF and the options available to developers when it comes to utilizing WCF and .NET security. Then, it explains how to secure the canonical and prevailing types of applications. Finally, I will present my declarative security framework, which vastly reduces the complexity of the WCF security programming model by eliminating the need to understand and tweak the many details of WCF security.

Authentication

Authentication is the act of verifying that the caller of a service is indeed who that caller claims to be. While authentication is typically referred to in the context of verification of the caller, from the client perspective there is also a need for service authentication; that is, assuring the client that the service it calls really is the service it intends to call. This is especially important with clients who call over the Internet, because if a malicious party subverts the client's DNS service, it could hijack the client's calls. WCF offers various authentication mechanisms:

No authentication

The service does not authenticate its callers, and virtually all callers are allowed.

Windows authentication

The service typically uses Kerberos when a Windows Domain Server is available, or NTLM when deployed in a workgroup configuration. The caller provides the service with its Windows credentials (such as a ticket or a token) and the service authenticates that against Windows.

Username and password

The caller provides the service with a username and a password. The service then uses these credentials against some kind of credentials store, such as Windows accounts or a custom credentials store (such as a dedicated database).

X509 certificate

The client identifies itself using a certificate. Typically, that certificate is known in advance to the service. The service looks up the certificate on the host side and validates it, thus authenticating the client. Alternatively, the service may implicitly trust the issuer of the certificate and hence the client presenting it.

Custom mechanism

WCF allows developers to replace the built-in authentication mechanisms with any protocol and credential type, such as using biometrics. These custom solutions are beyond the scope of this book.

Issued token

The caller and the service can both rely on a secure token service to issue the client a token that the service recognizes and trusts. Such a service is typically federated and encapsulates the act of authenticating and securing the call. Windows CardSpace is an example of such a secure token service. However, federated security and CardSpace are beyond the scope of this book.

Authorization

Authorization is concerned with what the caller is allowed to do: typically, which operations the client is allowed to invoke on the service. Authorizing of the caller is done under the assumption that the caller is indeed who the caller claims to be—in other words, authorization is meaningless without authentication. For authorization, the service typically relies on some kind of credentials store, where callers are mapped to logical roles. When authorizing an operation, the operation declares or explicitly demands that only certain roles can access it, and the service needs to look up the caller's role or roles from the store and verify that the caller is a member of the requested roles. Out of the box, WCF supports two credentials stores: the service can use Windows groups (and accounts) for authorization, or it can use an ASP.NET provider (such as the SQL Server provider) to store user accounts and roles. WCF also supports custom role repositories, but I have found that the easiest option by far for implementing a custom store is to implement a custom ASP.NET provider. This chapter will address the ASP.NET providers at length later.

 WCF offers an elaborate and extensible infrastructure for authenticating and authorizing the caller based on a set of claims contained in the message. However, discussion of this mechanism is beyond the scope of this book.

Transfer Security

Both authentication and authorization deal with two local aspects of security—if (and to what extent) to grant access to the caller once the service has received the message. In this respect, WCF services are not much different from traditional client/server classes. However, both authentication and authorization are predicated on secure delivery of the message itself. The *transfer* of the message from the client to the service has to be secure, or both authentication and authorization are moot. There are three essential aspects to transfer security, and all three aspects must be enforced to provide for secure services. Message *integrity* deals with how to ensure that the message itself is not tampered with en route from the client to the service. A malicious party or intermediary could, in practice, intercept the message and modify its content; for example, altering the account numbers in the case of a transfer operation in a banking service. Message *privacy* deals with ensuring the confidentiality of the message, so that no third party can even read the contents of the message. Privacy complements integrity. Without it, even if the malicious party does not tamper with the message, that party can still cause harm by gleaning sensitive information (again, such as account numbers) from the message content. Finally, transfer security must provide for *mutual authentication*, which deals with assuring the client that only the proper service is able to read the content of its message—in other words, that the client connects to the correct service. Once the credentials in the message are received, the service must authenticate those credentials locally. The mutual authentication mechanism also needs to detect and eliminate replay attacks and denial of service (DOS) attacks. In a replay attack, a malicious party records a valid message from the wire and later sends that valid message back to the service. With a DOS attack, a malicious party floods the service with messages (either valid messages or bogus invalid messages) at such a frequency as to degrade the service's availability.

Transfer Security Modes

WCF supports five different ways of accomplishing the three aspects of transfer security. Choosing the correct transfer security mode is perhaps the prime decision to be made in the context of securing a service. The five transfer security modes are None, Transport security, Message security, Mixed, and Both.

None transfer security mode

As its name implies, the *None* transfer security mode has transfer security completely turned off—in fact, all aspects of WCF security are turned off. No client credentials are provided to the service, and the message itself is wide open to any malicious party to do with it as it pleases. Obviously, setting transfer security to None is highly inadvisable.

Transport transfer security mode

When configured for *Transport* security, WCF uses a secure communication protocol. The available secure transports are HTTPS, TCP, IPC, and MSMQ. Transport security encrypts all communication on the channel and thus provides for integrity, privacy, and mutual authentication. Integrity is provided because without knowing the encryption key, any attempt to modify the message will corrupt it so that it will become useless. Privacy is provided because no party other than the recipient can see the content of the message. Mutual authentication is supported because only the intended recipient of the message can read it; the client need not be concerned with message rerouting to malicious endpoints, as those will not be able to use the message. Once the message is decrypted, the service can read the client's credentials and authenticate the client.

Transport security requires the client and the service to negotiate the details of the encryption, but that is done automatically as part of the communication protocol in the respective binding. Transport security can benefit from hardware acceleration done on the network card so as to avoid burdening the host machine's CPU with the encryption and decryption of the messages. Hardware acceleration obviously caters to high throughput, and it may even make the security overhead unnoticeable. Transport security is the simplest way of achieving transfer security, and the most performant option. Its main downside is that it can only guarantee transfer security point-to-point, meaning when the client connects directly to the service. Having multiple intermediaries between the client and the service renders Transport security questionable, as those intermediaries may not be secure. Consequently, Transport security is typically used only by intranet applications, where you can ensure a single hop between the client and the service in a controlled environment.

 When configuring any of the HTTP bindings for Transport security, WCF verifies at the service load time that the corresponding address on the endpoint uses HTTPS rather than mere HTTP.

Message transfer security mode

The *Message* transfer security mode simply encrypts the message itself. By encrypting the message, you gain integrity and privacy and enable mutual authentication, for the same reason that Transport security provides these features when the communication channel is encrypted. However, encrypting the message rather than the transport enables the service to communicate securely over nonsecure transports, such as HTTP. Because of that, Message security provides for end-to-end security, regardless of the number of intermediaries involved in transferring the message and regardless of whether or not the transport is secure. In addition, Message security is based on a set of industry standards designed both for interoperability and for thwarting common attacks such as replay and DOS attacks, and the support WCF offers for it is both rich and extensible. The downside of Message security is that it may introduce call latency due to its inherent overhead. Message security is typically used by Internet applications, where the call patterns are less chatty and the transport is not necessarily secure.

Mixed transfer security mode

The *Mixed* transfer security mode uses Transport security for message integrity and privacy as well as service authentication, and it uses Message security for securing the client's credentials. The Mixed mode tries to combine the advantages of both Transport and Message security by benefiting from the secure transport and even hardware acceleration offered by Transport security to cater to high throughput, and from the extensibility and richer types of client credentials offered by Message security. The downside of the Mixed mode is that it is only secure point-to-point, as a result of the use of Transport security. Application developers rarely need to use the Mixed mode, but it is available for advanced cases.

Both transfer security mode

As its name implies, the *Both* transfer security mode uses both Transport security and Message security. The message itself is secured using Message security, and then it is transferred to the service over a secure transport. The Both mode maximizes security, yet it may be overkill for most applications (with the exception perhaps of disconnected applications, where the additional latency it introduces will go unnoticed).

Transfer Security Mode Configuration

Configuring the transfer security mode is done in the binding, and both the client and the service must use the same transfer security mode and, of course, comply with its requirements. Like any other binding configuration, you can configure transfer security either programmatically or administratively, in a config file. All the common bindings offer a construction parameter indicating the transfer security mode, and all bindings offer a Security property with a Mode property identifying the configured mode using a dedicated enumeration. As shown in Table 10-1, not all bindings support all transfer security modes: the supported modes are driven by the target scenarios for the binding.

Table 10-1. Bindings and transfer security modes

Name	None	Transport	Message	Mixed	Both
BasicHttpBinding	Yes (default)	Yes	Yes	Yes	No
NetTcpBinding	Yes	Yes (default)	Yes	Yes	No
NetNamedPipeBinding	Yes	Yes (default)	No	No	No
WSHttpBinding	Yes	Yes	Yes (default)	Yes	No
WSDualHttpBinding	Yes	No	Yes (default)	No	No
NetMsmqBinding	Yes	Yes (default)	Yes	No	Yes

The intranet bindings (NetTcpBinding, NetNamedPipeBinding, and NetMsmqBinding) all default to Transport security. Thus, no special programming is required on behalf of the service or client developer. The reason is that on the intranet calls are typically point-to-point, and Transport security yields the best performance. However, the intranet bindings can also be configured for the None transfer mode; that is, they can be used on the same transport protocol, only without security. The NetNamedPipeBinding supports only None and Transport security—there is no sense in using Message security over IPC, since with IPC there is always exactly one hop from the client to the service. Also note that only the NetMsmqBinding supports the Both mode.

The Internet bindings all default to Message security, to enable them to be used over nonsecure transports (that is, HTTP) and to accommodate multiple hops and intermediaries. Note that while the WSHttpBinding can be configured for Transport security, the WSDualHttpBinding cannot. The reason is that this binding uses a separate HTTP channel to connect the service to the callback client, and that channel to the client-hosted callback object cannot easily be made to use HTTPS, unlike a service that is likely to be hosted in a real web server.

With one noticeable exception, all of the WCF bindings are configured with some kind of transfer security and are therefore secure by default. Only the BasicHttpBinding defaults to having no security. The reason is that the basic binding is designed to make a WCF service look like a legacy ASMX service, and ASMX is unsecured by default. That said, you can and should configure the BasicHttpBinding to use a different transfer security mode, such as Message security.

Specific binding configurations

The BasicHttpBinding uses the BasicHttpSecurityMode enum for transfer mode configuration. The enum is available via the Mode property of the Security property of the binding:

```
public enum BasicHttpSecurityMode
{
    None,
    Transport,
    Message,
```

```
        TransportWithMessageCredential,
        TransportCredentialOnly
    }
    public sealed class BasicHttpSecurity
    {
        public BasicHttpSecurityMode Mode
        {get;set;}
        //More members
    }
    public class BasicHttpBinding : Binding,...
    {
        public BasicHttpBinding();
        public BasicHttpBinding(BasicHttpSecurityMode securityMode);
        public BasicHttpSecurity Security
        {get;}
        //More members
    }
```

Security is of the type BasicHttpSecurity. One of the constructors of BasicHttpBinding takes the BasicHttpSecurityMode enum as a parameter. To secure the basic binding for Message security, you can either construct it secured or set the security mode post-construction. Consequently, in Example 10-1 binding1 and binding2 are equivalent.

Example 10-1. Programmatically securing the basic binding

```
BasicHttpBinding binding1 = new BasicHttpBinding(BasicHttpSecurityMode.Message);

BasicHttpBinding binding2 = new BasicHttpBinding();
binding2.Security.Mode = BasicHttpSecurityMode.Message;
```

Instead of programmatic settings, you can use a config file, as in Example 10-2.

Example 10-2. Administratively securing the basic binding

```
<bindings>
   <basicHttpBinding>
      <binding name = "SecuredBasic">
         <security mode = "Message"/>
      </binding>
   </basicHttpBinding>
</bindings>
```

The rest of the bindings all use their own enumerations and dedicated security classes, yet they are configured just as in Examples 10-1 and 10-2. For example, the NetTcpBinding and the WSHttpBinding use the SecurityMode enum, defined as:

```
    public enum SecurityMode
    {
        None,
        Transport,
        Message,
        TransportWithMessageCredential //Mixed
    }
```

These bindings offer a matching construction parameter and a matching Security property.

The NetNamedPipeBinding uses the NetNamedPipeSecurityMode enum, which supports only the None and Transport security modes:

```
public enum NetNamedPipeSecurityMode
{
   None,
   Transport
}
```

The WSDualHttpBinding uses the WSDualHttpSecurityMode enum, which supports only the None and Message security modes:

```
public enum WSDualHttpSecurityMode
{
   None,
   Message
}
```

The NetMsmqBinding uses the NetMsmqSecurityMode enum:

```
public enum NetMsmqSecurityMode
{
   None,
   Transport,
   Message,
   Both
}
```

NetMsmqSecurityMode is the only enum that offers the Both transfer mode.

The reason that almost every common binding has its own dedicated enum for the security mode is that the designers of WCF security opted for increased safety at the expense of overall complexity. They could have defined just a single all-inclusive enum with values corresponding to the five possible transfer security modes, but then it would have been possible at compile time to assign invalid values, such as Message security for the NetNamedPipeBinding or Transport security for the WSDualHttpBinding. Opting for specialized enums makes configuring security less error-prone, yet there are more moving parts to come to terms with.

Transport Security and Credentials

WCF lets you select from a number of possible client credential types. For example, the client can identify itself using a classic username and password, or a Windows security token. Windows credentials can then be authenticated using NTLM or Kerberos, when available. Alternatively, the client can use an X509 certificate, or choose to provide no credentials at all and be anonymous. When configuring transfer security for Transport security, however, not all bindings support all client credential types, as shown in Table 10-2.

Table 10-2. Bindings and Transport security client credentials

Name	None	Windows	Username	Certificate
BasicHttpBinding	Yes (default)	Yes	Yes	Yes
NetTcpBinding	Yes	Yes (default)	No	Yes
NetNamedPipeBinding	No	Yes (default)	No	No
WSHttpBinding	Yes	Yes (default)	Yes	Yes
WSDualHttpBinding	N/A	N/A	N/A	N/A
NetMsmqBinding	Yes	Yes (default)	No	Yes

Which types of credentials a binding supports is largely a product of the target scenario for which the binding is designed. For example, all of the intranet bindings default to Windows credentials since they are used in a Windows environment, and the BasicHttpBinding defaults to no credentials, just like a classic ASMX web service. The WSDualHttpBinding cannot use Transport security at all. The odd default is that of the WSHttpBinding, which defaults to Windows credentials to enable the binding to be used over Transport security with minimum effort out of the box.

Message Security and Credentials

When it comes to using Message transfer security, WCF lets applications use the same types of credentials as with Transport security, with the addition of the issued token credential type. Again, when configured for Message security not all bindings support all client credential types, as shown in Table 10-3.

Table 10-3. Bindings and Message security client credentials

Name	None	Windows	Username	Certificate	Issued token
BasicHttpBinding	No	No	No	Yes	No
NetTcpBinding	Yes	Yes (default)	Yes	Yes	Yes
NetNamedPipeBinding	N/A	N/A	N/A	N/A	N/A
WSHttpBinding	Yes	Yes (default)	Yes	Yes	Yes
WSDualHttpBinding	Yes	Yes (default)	Yes	Yes	Yes
NetMsmqBinding	Yes	Yes (default)	Yes	Yes	Yes

While it makes sense that all intranet bindings that support Message security default to Windows credentials, it is interesting to note that the Internet bindings (WSHttpBinding and WSDualHttpBinding) also default to Windows credentials, even though (as discussed later) Internet applications rarely use Windows credentials over HTTP. The reason for this default is to enable developers to securely use these bindings out of the box, in their correct transfer security mode, without resorting first to custom credentials stores.

The BasicHttpBinding supports username client credentials for Message security only when configured for Mixed mode. This may be a source of runtime validation errors, since the BasicHttpMessageCredentialType enum contains the BasicHttpMessageCredentialType.UserName value.

Identity Management

Identity management is the security aspect that deals with which security identity the client sends to the service and, in turn, what the service can do with the client's identity. Not only that, but when designing a service, you need to decide in advance which identity the service will execute under. The service can execute under its own identity; it can impersonate the client's identity (when applicable); or it can use a mixture of identities, alternating in a single operation between its own identity, the client's identity, or even a third identity altogether. Selecting the correct identity has drastic implications on the application's scalability and administration cost. In WCF, when enabled, the security identity flows down the call chain, and each service can find out who its caller is, regardless of the identity of the service.

Overall Policy

To the traditional commonplace security aspects of authentication, authorization, transfer security, and identity management, I would like to add one that is less technical and conventional, but to me just as important: what is your business's approach, or even your personal approach, to security? That is, what is your *security policy*? I believe that in the vast majority of cases, applications simply cannot afford not to be secured. And while security carries with it performance and throughput penalties, these should be of no concern. Simply put, it costs to live. Paying the security penalty is an unavoidable part of designing and administering modern connected applications. Gone are the days when developers could afford not to care about security and deploy applications that relied on the ambient security of the target environment, such as physical security provided by employee access cards or firewalls.

Since most developers cannot afford to become full-time security experts (nor should they), the approach I advocate for overall security policy is simple: crank security all the way up until someone complains. If the resulting application performance and throughput are still adequate with the maximum security level, leave it at that level. Only if the resulting performance is inadequate should you engage in detailed threat analysis to find out what you can trade in security in exchange for performance. In my experience, you will rarely need to actually go this route; most developers should never need to compromise security this way.

The security strategies described in this chapter follow my overall security policy. WCF's overall approach to security is very much aligned with my own, and I will explicitly point out the few places it is not (and how to rectify it). With the noticeable exception of the `BasicHttpBinding`, WCF is secured by default, and even the `BasicHttpBinding` can easily be secured. All other WCF bindings by default authenticate all callers to the service and rely on transfer security.

Scenario-Driven Approach

Security is by far the most intricate area of WCF. The following list shows the elements that govern security in every WCF operation call:

- Service contract
- Operation contract
- Fault contract
- Service behavior
- Operation behavior
- Host configuration
- Method configuration and code
- Client-side behavior
- Proxy configuration
- Binding configuration

Each of the items in the list may have a dozen or more security-related properties. Obviously, there are an overwhelming number of possible combinations and permutations. In addition, not all combinations are allowed or supported, and not all allowed combinations make sense or are consistent; for example, while technically possible, it does not make sense to use a certificate for client credentials in a homogenous Windows intranet, much as it makes little sense to use Windows accounts in an Internet application. The solution I chose for this book is to focus on a few key scenarios (and slight variations of them) that address the security needs of the majority of applications today.

The scenarios are:

- Intranet application
- Internet application
- Business-to-business application
- Anonymous application
- No security

I will demonstrate how to make each of these scenarios consistent and secure. In each scenario I will discuss how to support the security aspects of transfer security, authentication, authorization, and identity management. If you need an additional scenario, you can follow my analysis approach to derive the required security aspects and settings.

Intranet Application Scenario

The characteristics of the intranet application are that both the clients and the service use WCF, and that they are deployed in the same intranet. The clients reside behind the firewall, and you can use Windows-based security for transfer security, authentication, and authorization. You can rely on Windows accounts and groups to store the client's credentials. The intranet scenario addresses a wide range of business applications, from finance to manufacturing to in-house IT applications. The intranet scenario is also the richest scenario of all in the options it offers developers for configuring security.

This section on the intranet scenario will define the terminology, techniques, and types used in the other scenarios.

Securing the Intranet Bindings

For the intranet scenario, you should use the intranet bindings: namely, `NetTcpBinding`, `NetNamedPipeBinding`, and `NetMsmqBinding`. You can rely on Transport mode for transfer security because the calls are invariably point-to-point. Conveniently, Transport security is the default transfer mode of the intranet bindings (see Table 10-1). You can also use the default for the client credentials type, which is Windows (see Table 10-2). You need to configure this on both the client and the service.

Transport security protection level

Each of the three intranet bindings has a configurable protection level, which is the master switch for Transport protection. The three protection levels are:

None
> When configured for this protection level, WCF does not protect the message on transfer from the client to the service. Any malicious party can read the content of the message, or even alter it.

Signed
> When configured for this protection level, WCF ensures that the message could have come only from an authenticated sender and that the message integrity was not compromised during transfer. To accomplish this, WCF appends an encrypted checksum to the message. Upon receiving the message, the service calculates the checksum and compares it to the original. If the two do not match, the message is rejected. As a result, the message is impervious to tampering. However, the message content is still visible during the transfer.

Encrypted and Signed
> When configured for this protection level, WCF both signs the message and encrypts its content. The Encrypted and Signed protection level provides integrity, privacy, and authenticity.

The Signed protection level offers a clear trade-off between a measured degree of security and performance. However, I consider this to be a trade-off to avoid, and I recommend that you always opt instead for the Encrypted and Signed protection level. WCF represents the protection level with the `ProtectionLevel` enum, defined as:

```
public enum ProtectionLevel
{
    None,
    Sign,
    EncryptAndSign
}
```

Not all Internet bindings default to the same protection level. Both the `NetTcpBinding` and the `NetNamedPipeBinding` default to Encrypted and Signed, yet the `NetMsmqBinding` defaults to Signed.

NetTcpBinding configuration

`NetTcpBinding` takes a construction parameter indicating the desired transfer security mode:

```
public class NetTcpBinding : ...
{
    public NetTcpBinding(SecurityMode securityMode);
    public NetTcpSecurity Security
    {get;}
    //More members
}
```

The Security property of the type `NetTcpSecurity` contains the transfer mode (Transport or Message) and two respective properties with their specific settings:

```
public sealed class NetTcpSecurity
{
    public SecurityMode Mode
    {get;set;}
    public MessageSecurityOverTcp Message
    {get;}
    public TcpTransportSecurity Transport
    {get;}
}
```

In the intranet security scenario, you should select Transport security for the transfer security mode and set the values of the Transport property of the type `TcpTransportSecurity`:

```
public sealed class TcpTransportSecurity
{
    public TcpClientCredentialType ClientCredentialType
    {get;set;}

    public ProtectionLevel ProtectionLevel
    {get;set;}
}
```

The `Transfer` property should be initialized with the client credential type set to Windows using the `TcpClientCredentialType` enum, defined as:

```
public enum TcpClientCredentialType
{
    None,
    Windows,
    Certificate
}
```

The `Transfer` property should also have the protection level set to `ProtectionLevel.EncryptAndSign`. Since both of those settings are the defaults for this binding, these two declarations are equivalent:

```
NetTcpBinding binding1 = new NetTcpBinding( );

NetTcpBinding binding2 = new NetTcpBinding(SecurityMode.Transport);
binding2.Security.Transport.ClientCredentialType = TcpClientCredentialType.Windows;
binding2.Security.Transport.ProtectionLevel = ProtectionLevel.EncryptAndSign;
```

Alternatively, you can configure the binding using a config file:

```
<bindings>
    <netTcpBinding>
        <binding name = "TCPWindowsSecurity">
            <security mode = "Transport">
                <transport
                    clientCredentialType = "Windows"
                    protectionLevel = "EncryptAndSign"
                />
            </security>
        </binding>
    </netTcpBinding>
</bindings>
```

 The `NetTcpContextBinding` and the `WSHttpContextBinding` also offer the `ContextProtectionLevel` property of the type `ProtectionLevel`, used to indicate the desired protection level for the custom context. `ContextProtectionLevel` defaults to `ProtectionLevel.Sign`. When using Transport security, the value of `ContextProtectionLevel` is ignored (since the transport protects the whole message during transfer). In the case of Message security, due to a bug in WCF, only if the service demands higher protection than what the client uses will WCF abort the call. The same is true for the `NetNamedPipeContextBinding` defined in Appendix B (since it uses the same WCF facility).

For the sake of completeness, although it's not required by the intranet scenario, here is how to configure `NetTcpBinding` for Message security with username client credentials:

```
public enum MessageCredentialType
{
    None,
```

```
    Windows,
    UserName,
    Certificate,
    IssuedToken
}
public sealed class MessageSecurityOverTcp
{
    public MessageCredentialType ClientCredentialType
    {get;set;}
    //More members
}
NetTcpBinding binding = new NetTcpBinding(SecurityMode.Message);
binding.Security.Message.ClientCredentialType = MessageCredentialType.UserName;
```

NetTcpSecurity offers the Message property of the type MessageSecurityOverTcp. You'll need to set the credentials type using the MessageCredentialType enum. Most bindings use the MessageCredentialType enum for representing Message security client credentials.

Figure 10-1 shows the security-related elements of the NetTcpBinding.

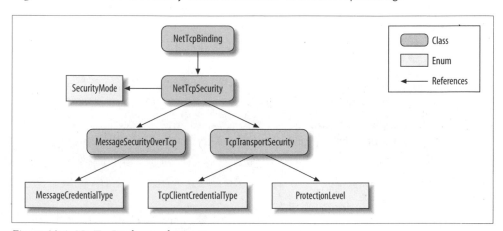

Figure 10-1. NetTcpBinding and security

NetTcpBinding has a reference to NetTcpSecurity, which uses the SecurityMode enum to indicate the transfer security mode. When Transport security is used, NetTcpSecurity will use an instance of TcpTransportSecurity containing the client credentials type via the TcpClientCredentialType enum and the configured protection level via the ProtectionLevel enum. When Message security is used, NetTcpSecurity will use an instance of MessageSecurityOverTcp containing the client credentials type via the MessageCredentialType enum.

NetNamedPipeBinding configuration

NetNamedPipeBinding takes a construction parameter indicating the desired transfer security mode:

```
public class NetNamedPipeBinding : Binding,...
{
    public NetNamedPipeBinding(NetNamedPipeSecurityMode securityMode);

    public NetNamedPipeSecurity Security
    {get;}
    //More members
}
```

The Security property of the type NetNamedPipeSecurity contains the transfer mode (Transport or None) and a single property with the specific Transport settings:

```
public sealed class NetNamedPipeSecurity
{
    public NetNamedPipeSecurityMode Mode
    {get;set;}
    public NamedPipeTransportSecurity Transport
    {get;}
}
```

For the intranet security scenario, select Transport security for the transfer security mode and set the values of the Transport property of the type NamedPipeTransportSecurity:

```
public sealed class NamedPipeTransportSecurity
{
    public ProtectionLevel ProtectionLevel
    {get;set;}
}
```

The Transfer property should be initialized with the protection level set to ProtectionLevel.EncryptAndSign. Because this is the default for the binding, these two declarations are equivalent:

```
NetNamedPipeBinding binding1 = new NetNamedPipeBinding();

NetNamedPipeBinding binding2 = new NetNamedPipeBinding(
                                    NetNamedPipeSecurityMode.Transport);
binding2.Security.Transport.ProtectionLevel = ProtectionLevel.EncryptAndSign;
```

You can also configure the binding administratively, using a config file:

```
<bindings>
   <netNamedPipeBinding>
      <binding name = "IPCWindowsSecurity">
         <security mode = "Transport">
            <transport protectionLevel = "EncryptAndSign"/>
         </security>
      </binding>
   </netNamedPipeBinding>
</bindings>
```

There is no need (or option) to set the client credentials type, since only Windows credentials are supported (see Table 10-2). Figure 10-2 shows the security-related elements of the NetNamedPipeBinding.

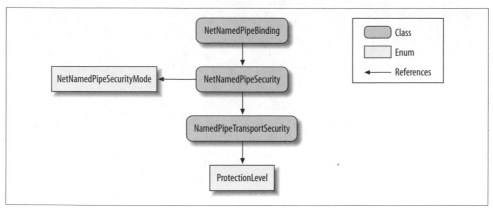

Figure 10-2. NetNamedPipeBinding and security

NetNamedPipeBinding has a reference to NetNamedPipeSecurity, which uses the NetNamedPipeSecurityMode enum to indicate the transfer security mode. When Transport security is used, NetTcpSecurity will use an instance of NamedPipeTransportSecurity containing the configured protection level via the ProtectionLevel enum.

NetMsmqBinding configuration

NetMsmqBinding offers a construction parameter for the transfer security mode and a Security property:

```
public class NetMsmqBinding : MsmqBindingBase
{
    public NetMsmqBinding(NetMsmqSecurityMode securityMode);
    public NetMsmqSecurity Security
    {get;}
    //More members
}
```

The Security property of the type NetMsmqSecurity contains the transfer mode (Transport or Message) and two respective properties with their specific settings:

```
public sealed class NetMsmqSecurity
{
    public NetMsmqSecurityMode Mode
    {get;set;}
    public MsmqTransportSecurity Transport
    {get;}
    public MessageSecurityOverMsmq Message
    {get;}
}
```

For the intranet security scenario, select Transport security for the transfer security mode and set the values of the Transport property of the type MsmqTransportSecurity:

```
public sealed class MsmqTransportSecurity
{
    public MsmqAuthenticationMode MsmqAuthenticationMode
    {get;set;}
    public ProtectionLevel MsmqProtectionLevel
    {get;set;}
    //More members
}
```

The Transfer property should be initialized with the client credential type set to Windows domain using the MsmqAuthenticationMode enum, defined as:

```
public enum MsmqAuthenticationMode
{
    None,
    WindowsDomain,
    Certificate
}
```

Windows domain is the default credentials type. In addition, you need to set the protection level to ProtectionLevel.EncryptAndSign because the MSMQ binding defaults to ProtectionLevel.Signed. The following two definitions are equivalent:

```
NetMsmqBinding binding1 = new NetMsmqBinding();
binding1.Security.Transport.MsmqProtectionLevel = ProtectionLevel.EncryptAndSign;

NetMsmqBinding binding2 = new NetMsmqBinding();
binding2.Security.Mode = NetMsmqSecurityMode.Transport;
binding2.Security.Transport.MsmqAuthenticationMode =
                                    MsmqAuthenticationMode.WindowsDomain;
binding2.Security.Transport.MsmqProtectionLevel = ProtectionLevel.EncryptAndSign;
```

Alternatively, you can configure the binding using a config file:

```
<bindings>
    <netMsmqBinding>
        <binding name = "MSMQWindowsSecurity">
            <security mode = "Transport">
                <transport
                    msmqAuthenticationMode = "WindowsDomain"
                    msmqProtectionLevel = "EncryptAndSign"
                />
            </security>
        </binding>
    </netMsmqBinding>
</bindings>
```

Figure 10-3 shows the security-related elements of the NetMsmqBinding.

NetMsmqBinding has a reference to NetMsmqSecurity, which uses the NetMsmqSecurityMode enum to indicate the transfer security mode. When Transport security is used, NetMsmqSecurity will use an instance of MsmqTransportSecurity containing the client credentials type via the MsmqAuthenticationMode enum, and the configured protection level via the ProtectionLevel enum. There are similar references to types controlling Message security.

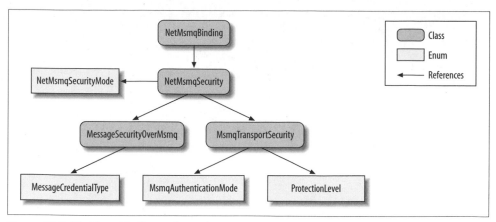

Figure 10-3. NetMsmqBinding and security

Constraining Message Protection

While a service should ideally use the highest possible level of security, it is actually at the mercy of its host, because the host is the one configuring the binding. This is especially problematic if the service is to be deployed in an unknown environment with an arbitrary host. To compensate, WCF lets service developers insist on a protection level, or rather, constrain the minimum protection level at which their service is willing to operate. Both the service and the client can constrain the protection level, independently of each other. You can constrain the protection level in three places. When constrained at the service contract, all operations on the contract are considered sensitive and protected. When constrained at the operation contract, only that operation is protected; other operations on the same contract are not. Finally, you can constrain the protection level for an individual fault contract. This can be required because sometimes the error information returned to the client is sensitive, containing parameter values, exception messages, and the call stack. The respective contract attributes offer the ProtectionLevel property of the enum type ProtectionLevel:

```
[AttributeUsage(AttributeTargets.Interface|AttributeTargets.Class,
                Inherited = false)]
public sealed class ServiceContractAttribute : Attribute
{
   public ProtectionLevel ProtectionLevel
   {get;set;}
   //More members
}
[AttributeUsage(AttributeTargets.Method)]
public sealed class OperationContractAttribute : Attribute
{
   public ProtectionLevel ProtectionLevel
   {get;set;}
   //More members
}
```

```
[AttributeUsage(AttributeTargets.Method,AllowMultiple = true,
                Inherited = false)]
public sealed class FaultContractAttribute : Attribute
{
   public ProtectionLevel ProtectionLevel
   {get;set;}
   //More members
}
```

As an example, here is how to set the protection level on a service contract:

```
[ServiceContract(ProtectionLevel = ProtectionLevel.EncryptAndSign)]
interface IMyContract
{...}
```

Setting the `ProtectionLevel` property on the contract attributes merely indicates the low-water mark; that is, the minimum protection level accepted by this contract. If the binding is configured for a lower protection level, it will result in an `InvalidOperationException` at the service load time or the time the proxy is opened. If the binding is configured for a higher level, the contract will use that level. The `ProtectionLevel` property on the contract attributes defaults to `ProtectionLevel.None`, meaning it has no effect.

The desired protection constraint is considered a local implementation detail of the service, so the required protection level is not exported with the service metadata. Consequently, the client may require a different level and enforce it separately from the service.

Even though the Internet bindings do not offer a protection level property, the protection level constraint at the service-, operation-, or fault-contract level is satisfied when using Transport or Message security. The constraint is not satisfied when security is turned off by using the None security mode.

Authentication

By default, when a client calls a proxy that targets an endpoint whose binding is configured for using Windows credentials with Transport security, there is nothing explicit the client needs to do to pass its credentials. WCF will automatically pass the Windows identity of the client's process to the service:

```
class MyContractClient : ClientBase<IMyContract>,IMyContract
{...}

MyContractClient proxy = new MyContractClient();
proxy.MyMethod(); //Client identity passed here
proxy.Close();
```

When the service receives the call, WCF will authenticate the caller on the service side. If the client's credentials represent a valid Windows account, the caller will be allowed to access the requested operation on the service.

Providing alternative Windows credentials

Instead of using the identity of the process in which it happens to be running, the client can pass alternative Windows credentials. The `ClientBase<T>` base class offers the `ClientCredentials` property of the type `ClientCredentials`:

```
public abstract class ClientBase<T> : ...
{
   public ClientCredentials ClientCredentials
   {get;}
}
public class ClientCredentials : ...,IEndpointBehavior
{
   public WindowsClientCredential Windows
   {get;}
   //More members
}
```

`ClientCredentials` contains the property `Windows` of the type `WindowsClientCredential`, defined as:

```
public sealed class WindowsClientCredential
{
   public NetworkCredential ClientCredential
   {get;set;}
   //More members
}
```

`WindowsClientCredential` has the property `ClientCredential` of the type `NetworkCredential`, which is where the client needs to set the alternative credentials:

```
public class NetworkCredential : ...
{
   public NetworkCredential();
   public NetworkCredential(string userName,string password);
   public NetworkCredential(string userName,string password,string domain);

   public string Domain
   {get;set;}
   public string UserName
   {get;set;}
   public string Password
   {get;set;}
}
```

Example 10-3 demonstrates how to use these classes and properties to provide alternative Windows credentials.

Example 10-3. Providing alternative Windows credentials

```
MyContractClient proxy = new MyContractClient();

proxy.ClientCredentials.Windows.ClientCredential.Domain   = "MyDomain";
proxy.ClientCredentials.Windows.ClientCredential.UserName = "MyUsername";
proxy.ClientCredentials.Windows.ClientCredential.Password = "MyPassword";
```

Example 10-3. Providing alternative Windows credentials (continued)

```
proxy.MyMethod( );
proxy.Close( );
```

Once you specify an alternative identity and open the proxy, the proxy cannot use any other identity later.

 If you do try specifying alternative credentials after opening the proxy, those credentials will be silently ignored.

Clients can use the technique demonstrated in Example 10-3 when the credentials provided are collected dynamically at runtime, perhaps using a login dialog box.

When working with a channel factory instead of a proxy class, the `ChannelFactory` base class offers the `Credentials` property of the type `ClientCredentials`:

```
public abstract class ChannelFactory : ...
{
   public ClientCredentials Credentials
   {get;}
   //More members
}
public class ChannelFactory<T> : ChannelFactory,...
{
   public T CreateChannel( );
   //More members
}
```

In this case, simply set the alternative credentials in the `Credentials` property, as was done in Example 10-3:

```
ChannelFactory<IMyContract> factory = new ChannelFactory<IMyContract>(...);

factory.Credentials.Windows.ClientCredential.Domain   = "MyDomain";
factory.Credentials.Windows.ClientCredential.UserName = "MyUsername";
factory.Credentials.Windows.ClientCredential.Password = "MyPassword";

IMyContract proxy = factory.CreateChannel( );
```

Note that you cannot use the static `CreateChannel( )` methods of `ChannelFactory<T>`, since you have to first instantiate a factory in order to access the `Credentials` property.

Identities

All Windows processes run with an authenticated security identity, and the process hosting a WCF service is no different. The identity is actually a Windows account whose security token is attached to the process (and to every thread in the process).

However, it is up to the application administrator to decide which identity to use. One option is to have the host run with an *interactive* user identity; that is, the identity of the user who launched the host process. An interactive identity is typically used when self-hosting and is ideal for debugging, because the debugger will automatically attach itself to the host process when launched from within Visual Studio. However, relying on an interactive identity is impractical for deployment on a server machine, where there will not necessarily be a logged-on user, and if there is a logged-on user that user may not have the necessary credentials to perform the requested work. For production deployment, you typically rely on a *designated account*, which is a preset Windows account used primarily by your service or services. To launch the service under a designated account, you can use the "Run as" shell option. However, "Run as" is useful only for simple testing. You can also have an NT service as your host and use the Control Panel Services applet to assign a designated identity to the host. If you're hosting in IIS 5/6 or the WAS, you can use those environments' configuration tools to assign a designated identity to the process from the pool.

The IIdentity interface

In .NET, the IIdentity interface (from the System.Security.Principal namespace) represents a security identity:

```
public interface IIdentity
{
    string AuthenticationType
    {get;}
    bool IsAuthenticated
    {get;}
    string Name
    {get;}
}
```

The interface lets you know whether the identity behind the interface is authenticated (and, if so, which authentication mechanism was used) and allows you to obtain the name of the identity. Out of the box, WCF takes advantage of three implementations of IIdentity offered by .NET: WindowsIdentity, GenericIdentity, and X509Identity. The WindowsIdentity class represents a Windows account. The GenericIdentity class is a general-purpose class whose main use is to wrap an identity name with an IIdentity. With both GenericIdentity and WindowsIdentity, if the identity name is an empty string, that identity is considered unauthenticated, and any other non-zero-length name is considered authenticated. Finally, X509Identity is an internal class that represents an identity that was authenticated using an X509 certificate. The identity behind an X509Identity is always authenticated.

Working with WindowsIdentity

The `WindowsIdentity` class offers a few useful methods above and beyond the mere implementation of `IIdentity`:

```
public class WindowsIdentity : IIdentity,...
{
    public WindowsIdentity(string sUserPrincipalName);
    public static WindowsIdentity GetAnonymous();
    public static WindowsIdentity GetCurrent();
    public virtual bool IsAnonymous
    {get;}
    public virtual bool IsAuthenticated
    {get;}
    public virtual string Name
    {get;}
    //More members
}
```

The `IsAnonymous` Boolean property indicates whether the underlying identity is anonymous and the `GetAnonymous()` method returns an anonymous Windows identity, typically used for impersonation to mask the real identity:

```
WindowsIdentity identity = WindowsIdentity.GetAnonymous();
Debug.Assert(identity.Name == "");
Debug.Assert(identity.IsAuthenticated == false);
Debug.Assert(identity.IsAnonymous == true);
```

The `GetCurrent()` static method returns the identity of the process where it is called. That identity is always non-anonymous and authenticated:

```
WindowsIdentity currentIdentity = WindowsIdentity.GetCurrent();
Debug.Assert(currentIdentity.Name != "");
Debug.Assert(currentIdentity.IsAuthenticated == true);
Debug.Assert(currentIdentity.IsAnonymous == false);
```

The Security Call Context

Every operation on a secured WCF service has a security call context. The security call context is represented by the class `ServiceSecurityContext`, defined as:

```
public class ServiceSecurityContext
{
    public static ServiceSecurityContext Current
    {get;}
    public bool IsAnonymous
    {get;}
    public IIdentity PrimaryIdentity
    {get;}
    public WindowsIdentity WindowsIdentity
    {get;}
    //More members
}
```

The main use for the security call context is for custom security mechanisms, as well as analysis and auditing. While it is presented here in the context of the intranet scenario, all other secured scenarios have use for the security call context as well.

Note that in spite of its name, this is the security context of the call, not the service. Two operations on the same service can definitely have different security call contexts.

The security call context is stored in the TLS, so every method on every object down the call chain from the service can access the security call context, including your service constructor. To obtain your current security call context, simply access the Current static property. Another way of accessing the security call context is via the ServiceSecurityContext property of the OperationContext:

```
public sealed class OperationContext : ...
{
    public ServiceSecurityContext ServiceSecurityContext
    {get;}
    //More members
}
```

Regardless of which mechanism you use, you will get the same object:

```
ServiceSecurityContext context1 = ServiceSecurityContext.Current;
ServiceSecurityContext context2 = OperationContext.Current.ServiceSecurityContext;
Debug.Assert(context1 == context2);
```

 Your service has a security call context only if security is enabled. When security is disabled, ServiceSecurityContext.Current returns null.

The PrimaryIdentity property of ServiceSecurityContext contains the identity of the immediate client up the call chain. If the client is unauthenticated, PrimaryIdentity will reference an implementation of IIdentity with a blank identity. When Windows authentication is used, the PrimaryIdentity property will be set to an instance of WindowsIdentity.

The WindowsIdentity property is meaningful only when using Windows authentication, and it will always be of the type WindowsIdentity. When valid Windows credentials are provided, the WindowsIdentity property will contain the corresponding client identity and will match the value of PrimaryIdentity.

 The constructor of a singleton service does not have a security call context, since it is called when the host is launched, not as a result of a client call.

Impersonation

Some resources, such as the filesystem, SQL Server, sockets, and even DCOM objects, grant access to themselves based on the caller's security token. Typically, the host process is assigned an identity with elevated permissions that are required to access such resources, so that it can function properly. Clients, however, typically have restricted credentials compared with those of the service. Legacy technologies such as unmanaged Visual Basic or C++ did not offer role-based security support, so developers used *impersonation* to address this credentials gap. Impersonation lets the service assume the client's identity, primarily in order to verify whether the client is authorized to perform the work it's asking the service to do. Impersonation has a number of key detrimental effects on your application, which will be discussed at the end of this section. Instead of impersonation, you should apply role-based security to authorize the callers, coupled with a trusted subsystem pattern across layers. That said, many developers are used to designing systems using impersonation, so both .NET and WCF support this technique.

Manual impersonation

The service can impersonate its calling client by calling the Impersonate( ) method of the WindowsIdentity class:

```
public class WindowsIdentity : IIdentity,...
{
   public virtual WindowsImpersonationContext Impersonate();
   //More members
}
public class WindowsImpersonationContext : IDisposable
{
   public void Dispose();
   public void Undo();
}
```

Impersonate( ) returns an instance of WindowsImpersonationContext containing the service's previous identity. To revert back to that identity, the service calls the Undo( ) method. To impersonate a client, the service needs to call Impersonate( ) on the identity of the caller, which is available via the WindowsIdentity property of its security call context, as shown in Example 10-4.

Example 10-4. Explicit impersonation and reversion

```
class MyService : IMyContract
{
   public void MyMethod()
   {
      WindowsImpersonationContext impersonationContext =
                  ServiceSecurityContext.Current.WindowsIdentity.Impersonate();
      try
      {
         /* Do work as client */
```

Example 10-4. Explicit impersonation and reversion (continued)

```
        }
        finally
        {
            impersonationContext.Undo( );
        }
    }
}
```

Note in Example 10-4 that the call to Undo( ) is in the finally statement, so the service will revert to its old identity even if exceptions occur. To somewhat simplify reverting, the WindowsImpersonationContext implementation of Dispose( ) also reverts, which enables you to use it in a using statement:

```
public void MyMethod( )
{
    using(ServiceSecurityContext.Current.WindowsIdentity.Impersonate( ))
    {
        /*  Do work as client */
    }
}
```

Declarative impersonation

Instead of impersonating manually, you can instruct WCF to automatically impersonate the caller of the method. The OperationBehavior attribute offers the Impersonation property of the enum type ImpersonationOption:

```
public enum ImpersonationOption
{
    NotAllowed,
    Allowed,
    Required
}
[AttributeUsage(AttributeTargets.Method)]
public sealed class OperationBehaviorAttribute : Attribute,IOperationBehavior
{
    public ImpersonationOption Impersonation
    {get;set;}
    //More members
}
```

The default value is ImpersonationOption.NotAllowed. This value indicates that WCF should not auto-impersonate, but you can write code (as in Example 10-4) that explicitly impersonates.

ImpersonationOption.Allowed instructs WCF to automatically impersonate the caller whenever Windows authentication is used, but it has no effect with other authentication mechanisms. When WCF auto-impersonates, it will also auto-revert to the previous service identity once the method returns.

The `ImpersonationOption.Required` value mandates the use of Windows authentication and will throw an exception if any other authentication mechanism is used. As its name implies, with this setting WCF will always auto-impersonate (and revert) in every call to the operation:

```
class MyService : IMyContract
{
    [OperationBehavior(Impersonation = ImpersonationOption.Required)]
    public void MyMethod()
    {
        /* Do work as client */
    }
}
```

Note that there is no way to use declarative impersonation with the service constructor because you cannot apply the `OperationBehavior` attribute on a constructor. Constructors can only use manual impersonation. If you do impersonate in the constructor, always revert as well in the constructor, to avoid side effects on the operations of the service (and even other services in the same host).

Impersonating all operations

In the event that you need to enable impersonation in all the service operations, the `ServiceHostBase` class has the `Authorization` property of the type `ServiceAuthorizationBehavior`:

```
public abstract class ServiceHostBase : ...
{
    public ServiceAuthorizationBehavior Authorization
    {get;}
    //More members
}
public sealed class ServiceAuthorizationBehavior : IServiceBehavior
{
    public bool ImpersonateCallerForAllOperations
    {get;set;}
    //More members
}
```

`ServiceAuthorizationBehavior` provides the Boolean property `ImpersonateCallerForAllOperations`, which is `false` by default. Contrary to what its name implies, when set to `true`, this property merely verifies that the service does not have any operations configured with `ImpersonationOption.NotAllowed`. This constraint is verified at service load time, yielding an `InvalidOperationException` when violated.

In effect, when Windows authentication is used, this will amount to the service automatically impersonating the client in all operations, but all the operations must be explicitly decorated with `ImpersonationOption.Allowed` or `ImpersonationOption.Required`. `ImpersonateCallerForAllOperations` has no effect on constructors.

You can set the `ImpersonateCallerForAllOperations` property programmatically or in the config file. If you set it programmatically, you can do so only before opening the host:

```
ServiceHost host = new ServiceHost(typeof(MyService));
host.Authorization.ImpersonateCallerForAllOperations = true;
host.Open();
```

If you set it using a config file, you need to reference the matching service behavior in the service declaration:

```
<services>
   <service name = "MyService" behaviorConfiguration= "ImpersonateAll">
      ...
   </service>
</services>
<behaviors>
   <serviceBehaviors>
      <behavior name = "ImpersonateAll">
         <serviceAuthorization impersonateCallerForAllOperations = "true"/>
      </behavior>
   </serviceBehaviors>
</behaviors>
```

To automate impersonating in all operations without the need to apply the `OperationBehavior` attribute on every method, I wrote the `SecurityHelper` static class, with the `ImpersonateAll()` extension methods:

```
public static class SecurityHelper
{
   public static void ImpersonateAll(this ServiceHostBase host);
   public static void ImpersonateAll(this ServiceDescription description);
   //More members
}
```

The extension methods work on both `ServiceHost` and `ServiceHost<T>`.

You can only call `ImpersonateAll()` before opening the host:

```
//Will impersonate in all operations
class MyService : IMyContract
{
   public void MyMethod()
   {...}
}
ServiceHost host = new ServiceHost(typeof(MyService));
host.ImpersonateAll();
host.Open();
```

Example 10-5 shows the implementation of `ImpersonateAll()`.

Example 10-5. Implementing SecurityHelper.ImpersonateAll()

```
public static class SecurityHelper
{
   public static void ImpersonateAll(this ServiceHostBase host)
```

Example 10-5. Implementing SecurityHelper.ImpersonateAll() (continued)

```
   {
      host.Authorization.ImpersonateCallerForAllOperations = true;
      host.Description.ImpersonateAll();
   }
   public static void ImpersonateAll(this ServiceDescription description)
   {
      foreach(ServiceEndpoint endpoint in description.Endpoints)
      {
         if(endpoint.Contract.Name == "IMetadataExchange")
         {
            continue;
         }
         foreach(OperationDescription operation in endpoint.Contract.Operations)
         {
            OperationBehaviorAttribute attribute = operation.Behaviors.
                                        Find<OperationBehaviorAttribute>();
            attribute.Impersonation = ImpersonationOption.Required;
         }
      }
   }
   //More members
}
```

In Example 10-5, ImpersonateAll( ) (for the sake of good manners) first sets the ImpersonateCallerForAllOperations property of the provided host to true, then obtains the service description from the host and calls the other overloaded extension method of ServiceDescription. This version explicitly configures all operations with ImpersonationOption.Required, by iterating over the endpoints collection of the service description. For each endpoint (except the metadata exchange endpoints), ImpersonateAll( ) accesses the operations collection of the contract. For each operation, there is always exactly one OperationBehaviorAttribute in the collection of operation behaviors, even if you did not provide one explicitly. The method then simply sets the Impersonation property to ImpersonationOption.Required.

Restricting impersonation

Authorization and authentication protect the service from being accessed by unauthorized, unauthenticated, potentially malicious clients. However, how should the client be protected from malicious services? One of the ways an adversarial service could abuse the client is by assuming the client's identity and credentials and causing harm while masquerading as the client. This tactic enables the malicious service both to leave an identity trail pointing back to the client and to elevate its own potentially demoted, less-privileged credentials to the client's level.

In some cases, the client may not want to allow the service to obtain its identity at all. WCF therefore lets the client indicate the degree to which the service can obtain the client's identity and how it can use it. Impersonation is actually a range of options indicating the level of trust between the client and the service. The `WindowsClientCredential` class provides the `AllowedImpersonationLevel` enum of the type `TokenImpersonationLevel`, found in the `System.Security.Principal` namespace:

```
public enum TokenImpersonationLevel
{
    None,
    Anonymous,
    Identification,
    Impersonation,
    Delegation
}
public sealed class WindowsClientCredential
{
    public TokenImpersonationLevel AllowedImpersonationLevel
    {get;set;}
    //More members
}
```

The client can use `AllowedImpersonationLevel` to restrict the allowed impersonation level both programmatically and administratively. For example, to programmatically restrict the impersonation level to `TokenImpersonationLevel.Identification`, before opening the proxy the client would write:

```
MyContractClient proxy = new MyContractClient();
proxy.ClientCredentials.Windows.AllowedImpersonationLevel =
                                    TokenImpersonationLevel.Identification;
proxy.MyMethod();
proxy.Close();
```

When using a config file, the administrator should define the allowed impersonation level as a custom endpoint behavior and reference it from the relevant endpoint section:

```
<client>
    <endpoint behaviorConfiguration = "ImpersonationBehavior"
        ...
    />
</client>
<behaviors>
    <endpointBehaviors>
        <behavior name = "ImpersonationBehavior">
            <clientCredentials>
                <windows allowedImpersonationLevel = "Identification"/>
            </clientCredentials>
        </behavior>
    </endpointBehaviors>
</behaviors>
```

`TokenImpersonationLevel.None` simply means that no impersonation level is assigned, so the client provides no identity information. This setting therefore amounts to the same thing as `TokenImpersonationLevel.Anonymous`, where the client provides no credentials at all. These two values are, of course, the safest from the client's perspective, but they are the least useful options from the application's perspective, since the service cannot perform any authentication or authorization. Not sharing credentials is possible only if the service is configured for anonymous access or for having no security, which is not the case with the intranet scenario. If the service is configured for Windows security, these two values yield an `ArgumentOutOfRangeException` on the client side.

With `TokenImpersonationLevel.Identification`, the service can identify the client (i.e., obtain the security identity of the calling client). The service, however, is not allowed to impersonate the client—everything the service does must be done under the service's own identity. Trying to impersonate will throw an `ArgumentOutOfRangeException` on the service side. Note, however, that if the service and the client are on the same machine, the service will still be able to impersonate the client, even when `TokenImpersonationLevel.Identification` is used. `TokenImpersonationLevel.Identification` is the default value used with Windows security and is the recommended value for the intranet scenario.

`TokenImpersonationLevel.Impersonation` grants the service permission both to obtain the client's identity and to impersonate the client. Impersonation indicates a great deal of trust between the client and the service, since the service can do anything the client can do, even if the service host is configured to use a less privileged identity. The only difference between the real client and the impersonating service is that if the service is on a separate machine from the client, it cannot access resources or objects on other machines as the client, because the service machine does not really have the client's password. In the case where the service and the client are on the same machine, the service impersonating the client can make one network hop to another machine, since the machine it resides on can still authenticate the impersonated client identity.

Finally, `TokenImpersonationLevel.Delegation` provides the service with the client's Kerberos ticket. In this case, the service can freely access resources on any machine as the client. If service is also configured for delegation, when it calls other downstream services the client's identity could be propagated further and further down the call chain. Delegation-required Kerberos authentication is not possible on Windows workgroup installations. Both the client and server user accounts must be properly configured in Active Directory to support delegation, due to the enormous trust (and hence security risk) involved. Delegation uses by default another security service called *cloaking*, which propagates the caller's identity along the call chain.

Delegation is extremely dangerous from the client's perspective, since the client has no control over who ends up using its identity, or where. When the impersonation level is set to `TokenImpersonationLevel.Impersonation`, the client takes a calculated risk: it knows which services it is accessing, and if those services are on a different machine, the client identity cannot propagate across the network. I consider delegation something that enables the service not just to impersonate the client, but to act as an imposter; security-wise, as far as the client is concerned, this is tantamount to waiving security.

Avoiding impersonation

You should design your services so that they do not rely on impersonation, and your clients should use `TokenImpersonationLevel.Identification`. Impersonation is a relic of the '90s, typically used in classic two-tier systems in the absence of role-based security support, where scalability was not a concern and managing a small number of identities across resources was doable.

As a general design guideline, the further down the call chain from the client, the less relevant the client's identity is. If you use some kind of layered approach in your system design, each layer should run under its own identity, authenticate its immediate callers, and implicitly trust its calling layer to authenticate its callers, thereby maintaining a chain of trusted, authenticated callers. This is called the *trusted subsystem* pattern. Impersonation, on the other hand, requires you to keep propagating the identity further and further down the call chain, all the way to the underlying resources. Doing so impedes scalability, because many resources (such as SQL Server connections) are allocated per identity. With impersonation, you will need as many resources as clients, and you will not be able to benefit from resource pooling (such as connection pooling). Impersonation also complicates resource administration, because you need to grant access to the resources to all of the original client identities, and there could be numerous such identities to manage. A service that always runs under its own identity poses no such problems, regardless of how many identities access that service. To control access to the resources, you should use authorization, as discussed next.

Multitier systems that do use impersonation typically gravitate toward delegation, since that is the only way to propagate the client identities across tiers and machines. In fact, the main reason developers today use impersonation has little to do with resource access authorization (which can easily be accomplished with role-based security); instead, it is used as a mechanism for auditing and identity propagation. If the application is required to provide at lower layers the identity of the topmost client or all clients up the chain, impersonation (if not full-fledged delegation) may look like a viable option. There are three good solutions for these requirements. First, if the business use cases require you to provide the top-level identity to downstream parties, there is nothing wrong with providing it as explicit method arguments since they are part of the required behavior of the system. The second solution is to use security audits (discussed later) and leave a trail across the call chain. At any point, you can reconstruct that chain of identities from the local audits. The third option is to propagate the identity of the original caller (or the entire stack of callers) in the message headers. Doing that transparently across the call chain requires passing the identities out-of-band in the headers and using the elegant generic interception technique described in Appendix E. *ServiceModelEx* contains those helper classes (look for `SecurityCallStackClientBase<T>`, `OperationSecurityCallStackAttribute`, and `SecurityCallStackBehaviorAttribute`).

Finally, relying on impersonation precludes non-Windows authentication mechanisms. If you do decide to use impersonation, use it judiciously and only as a last resort, when there is no other, better design approach.

 Impersonation is not possible with queued services.

Authorization

While authentication deals with verifying that the client is indeed who the client claims to be, most applications also need to verify that the client (or more precisely, the identity it presents) has permission to perform the operation. Since it would be impractical to program access permissions for each individual identity, it is better to grant permissions to the roles clients play in the application domain. A *role* is a symbolic category of identities that share the same security privileges. When you assign a role to an application resource, you are granting access to that resource to anyone who is a member of that role. Discovering the roles clients play in your business domain is part of your application-requirements analysis and design, just like factoring services and interfaces. By interacting with roles instead of particular identities, you isolate your application from changes made in real life, such as adding new users, moving existing users between positions, promoting users, or users leaving their jobs. .NET allows you to apply role-based security both declaratively and programmatically, if the need to verify role membership is based on a dynamic decision.

The security principal

For security purposes, it is convenient to lump together an identity and the information about its role membership. This representation is called the *security principal*.

The principal in .NET is any object that implements the IPrincipal interface, defined in the System.Security.Principal namespace:

```
public interface IPrincipal
{
   IIdentity Identity
   {get;}
   bool IsInRole(string role);
}
```

The IsInRole() method simply returns true if the identity associated with this principal is a member of the specified role, and false otherwise. The Identity read-only property provides access to read-only information about the identity, in the form of an object implementing the IIdentity interface. Out of the box, .NET offers several implementations of IPrincipal. GenericPrincipal is a general-purpose principal that has to be preconfigured with the role information. It is typically used when no authorization is required, in which case GenericPrincipal wraps a blank identity.

The WindowsPrincipal class looks up role membership information inside the Windows NT groups.

Every .NET thread has a principal object associated with it, obtained via the CurrentPrincipal static property of the Thread class:

```
public sealed class Thread
{
   public static IPrincipal CurrentPrincipal
   {get;set;}
   //More members
}
```

For example, here is how to discover the username as well as whether or not the caller was authenticated:

```
IPrincipal principal = Thread.CurrentPrincipal;
string userName = principal.Identity.Name;
bool isAuthenticated = principal.Identity.IsAuthenticated;
```

Selecting an authorization mode

As presented earlier, the ServiceHostBase class provides the Authorization property of the type ServiceAuthorizationBehavior. ServiceAuthorizationBehavior has the PrincipalPermissionMode property of the enum type PrincipalPermissionMode, defined as:

```
public enum PrincipalPermissionMode
{
   None,
   UseWindowsGroups,
   UseAspNetRoles,
   Custom
}
public sealed class ServiceAuthorizationBehavior : IServiceBehavior
{
   public PrincipalPermissionMode PrincipalPermissionMode
   {get;set;}
   //More members
}
```

Before opening the host, you can use the PrincipalPermissionMode property to select the principal mode; that is, which type of principal to install to authorize the caller.

If PrincipalPermissionMode is set to PrincipalPermissionMode.None, principal-based authorization is impossible. After authenticating the caller (if authentication is required at all), WCF installs GenericPrincipal with a blank identity and attaches it to the thread that invokes the service operation. That principal will be available via Thread.CurrentPrincipal.

When PrincipalPermissionMode is set to PrincipalPermissionMode.UseWindowsGroups, WCF installs a WindowsPrincipal with an identity matching the provided credentials.

If no Windows authentication took place (because the service did not require it), WCF will install a WindowsPrincipal with a blank identity.

PrincipalPermissionMode.UseWindowsGroups is the default value of the PrincipalPermissionMode property, so these two definitions are equivalent:

```
ServiceHost host1 = new ServiceHost(typeof(MyService));

ServiceHost host2 = new ServiceHost(typeof(MyService));
host2.Authorization.PrincipalPermissionMode =
                                    PrincipalPermissionMode.UseWindowsGroups;
```

When using a config file, you need to reference a custom behavior section assigning the principal mode:

```
<services>
    <service name = "MyService" behaviorConfiguration = "WindowsGroups">
        ...
    </service>
</services>
<behaviors>
    <serviceBehaviors>
        <behavior name = "WindowsGroups">
            <serviceAuthorization principalPermissionMode = "UseWindowsGroups"/>
        </behavior>
    </serviceBehaviors>
</behaviors>
```

Declarative role-based security

You apply service-side declarative role-based security using the attribute PrincipalPermissionAttribute, defined in the System.Security.Permissions namespace:

```
public enum SecurityAction
{
    Demand,
    //More members
}

[AttributeUsage(AttributeTargets.Class | AttributeTargets.Method)]
public sealed class PrincipalPermissionAttribute : CodeAccessSecurityAttribute
{
    public PrincipalPermissionAttribute(SecurityAction action);

    public bool Authenticated
    {get;set; }
    public string Name
    {get;set;}
    public string Role
    {get;set;}
    //More members
}
```

The `PrincipalPermission` attribute lets you declare the required role membership. For the intranet scenario, when you specify a Windows NT group as a role, you don't have to prefix the role name with your domain or machine name (if you wish to authorize against its roles). You can also explicitly specify another domain, if you have a trust relationship with it.

In Example 10-6, the declaration of the `PrincipalPermission` attribute grants access to `MyMethod( )` only to callers whose identities belong to the Managers group.

Example 10-6. Declarative role-based security on the intranet

```
[ServiceContract]
interface IMyContract
{
    [OperationContract]
    void MyMethod( );
}
class MyService : IMyContract
{
    [PrincipalPermission(SecurityAction.Demand,Role = "Manager")]
    public void MyMethod( )
    {...}
}
```

If the caller is not a member of that role, .NET throws an exception of type `SecurityException`.

 When experimenting with Windows role-based security, you often add users to or remove users from user groups. Because Windows caches user-group information at login time, the changes you make are not reflected until the next login.

If multiple roles are allowed to access the method, you can apply the attribute multiple times:

```
[PrincipalPermission(SecurityAction.Demand,Role = "Manager")]
[PrincipalPermission(SecurityAction.Demand,Role = "Customer")]
public void MyMethod( )
{...}
```

When multiple `PrincipalPermission` attributes are used, .NET verifies that the caller is a member of at least one of the demanded roles. If you want to verify that the caller is a member of both roles, you need to use programmatic role membership checks, discussed later.

While the `PrincipalPermission` attribute by its very definition can be applied on methods and classes, in a WCF service class you can apply it only on methods. The reason is that in WCF, unlike with normal classes, the service class constructor always executes under a `GenericPrincipal` with a blank identity, regardless of the authentication mechanisms used. As a result, the identity under which the constructor is running is unauthenticated and will always fail any kind of authorization attempt (even if the client is a member of the role and even when not using Windows NT groups):

```
//Will always fail
[PrincipalPermission(SecurityAction.Demand,Role = "...")]
class MyService : IMyContract
{...}
```

 Avoid sensitive work that requires authorization in the service constructor. With a per-call service, perform such work in the operations themselves, and with a sessionful service, provide a dedicated Initialize() operation where you can initialize the instance and authorize the callers.

By setting the Name property of the PrincipalPermission attribute, you can even insist on granting access only to a particular user:

```
[PrincipalPermission(SecurityAction.Demand,Name = "John")]
```

or to a particular user that is a member of a particular role:

```
[PrincipalPermission(SecurityAction.Demand,Name = "John",
                     Role = "Manager")]
```

These practices are inadvisable, however, because it is best to avoid hardcoding usernames.

 Declarative role-based security hardcodes the role name. If your application looks up role names dynamically you have to use programmatic role verification, as presented next.

Programmatic role-based security

Sometimes you need to programmatically verify role membership. Usually, you need to do that when the decision as to whether to grant access depends both on role membership and on some other values known only at call time, such as parameter values, time of day, and location. Another case in which programmatic role membership verification is needed is when you're dealing with localized user groups. To demonstrate the first category, imagine a banking service that lets clients transfer sums of money between two specified accounts. Only customers and tellers are allowed to call the TransferMoney() operation, with the following business rule: if the amount transferred is greater than 50,000, only tellers are allowed to do the transfer. Declarative role-based security can verify that the caller is either a teller or a customer, but it cannot enforce the additional business rule. For that, you need to use the IsInRole() method of IPrincipal, as shown in Example 10-7.

Example 10-7. Programmatic role-based security

```
[ServiceContract]
interface IBankAccounts
{
   [OperationContract]
   void TransferMoney(double sum,long sourceAccount,long destinationAccount);
}
static class AppRoles
{
   public const string Customer = "Customer";
   public const string Teller   = "Teller";
}
class BankService : IBankAccounts
{

   [PrincipalPermission(SecurityAction.Demand,Role = AppRoles.Customer)]
   [PrincipalPermission(SecurityAction.Demand,Role = AppRoles.Teller)]
   public void TransferMoney(double sum,long sourceAccount,long destinationAccount)
   {
      IPrincipal  principal = Thread.CurrentPrincipal;
      Debug.Assert(principal.Identity.IsAuthenticated);

      bool isCustomer = principal.IsInRole(AppRoles.Customer);
      bool isTeller   = principal.IsInRole(AppRoles.Teller);

      if(isCustomer && ! isTeller)
      {
         if(sum > 50000)
         {
            string message = "Caller does not have sufficient authority to" +
                             "transfer this sum";
            throw new SecurityException(message);
         }
      }
      DoTransfer(sum,sourceAccount,destinationAccount);
   }
   //Helper method
   void DoTransfer(double sum,long sourceAccount,long destinationAccount)
   {...}
}
```

Example 10-7 also demonstrates a number of other points. First, even though it uses
programmatic role membership verification with the value of the sum argument, it
still uses declarative role-based security as the first line of defense, allowing access
only to clients who are members of the Customer or Teller roles. Second, you can
programmatically assert that the caller is authenticated using the IsAuthenticated
property of IIdentity. Finally, note the use of the AppRoles static class to encapsulate the actual string used for the role to avoid hardcoding the roles in multiple
places.

There is a complete disconnect between role-based security and the actual principal type. When the PrincipalPermission attribute is asked to verify role membership, it simply gets hold of its thread's current principal in the form of IPrincipal, and calls its IsInRole() method. This is also true of programmatic role membership verification that uses only IPrincipal, as shown in Example 10-7. The separation of the IPrincipal interface from its implementation is the key to providing other role-based security mechanisms besides Windows NT groups, as you will see in the other scenarios.

Identity Management

In the intranet scenario, after successful authentication, WCF will attach to the operation thread a principal identity of the type WindowsIdentity, which will have the value of its Name property set to the username (or Windows account) provided by the client. Since valid credentials are provided, the security call context's two identities—the primary identity and the Windows identity—will be set to the same identity as the principal identity. All three identities will be considered authenticated. The identities and their values are shown in Table 10-4.

Windows Roles Localization

If your application is deployed in international markets and you use Windows groups as roles, it's likely the role names will not match. In the intranet scenario, the principal object attached to the thread accessing the service is of the type WindowsPrincipal:

```
public class WindowsPrincipal : IPrincipal
{
    public WindowsPrincipal(WindowsIdentity ntIdentity);

    //IPrincipal implementation
    public virtual IIdentity Identity
    {get;}
    public virtual bool IsInRole(string role);

    //Additional methods:
    public virtual bool IsInRole(int rid);
    public virtual bool IsInRole(WindowsBuiltInRole role);
}
```

WindowsPrincipal provides two additional IsInRole() methods that are intended to ease the task of localizing Windows NT groups. You can provide IsInRole() with an enum of the type WindowsBuiltInRole matching the built-in NT roles, such as WindowsBuiltInRole.Administrator or WindowsBuiltInRole.User. The other version of IsInRole() accepts an integer indexing specific roles. For example, a role index of 512 maps to the Administrators group. The MSDN Library contains a list of both the predefined indexes and ways to provide your own aliases and indexes to user groups.

Table 10-4. Identity management in the intranet scenario

Identity	Type	Value	Authenticated
Thread principal	WindowsIdentity	Username	Yes
Security context primary	WindowsIdentity	Username	Yes
Security context Windows	WindowsIdentity	Username	Yes

Note that while the host processes retain their designated identities, the principal identity will be that of the caller. I call this behavior *soft impersonation*. When it is used in conjunction with role-based security, it largely negates the need to ever perform real impersonation and replace the security token with that of the client.

Callbacks

When it comes to security on the intranet, there are several key differences between normal service operations and callbacks. First, with a callback contract you can only assign a protection level at the operation level, not the callback contract level. For example, this protection-level constraint will be ignored:

```
[ServiceContract(CallbackContract = typeof(IMyContractCallback))]
interface IMyContract
{...}

//Demand for protection level will be ignored
[ServiceContract(ProtectionLevel = ProtectionLevel.EncryptAndSign)]
interface IMyContractCallback
{...}
```

Only the service contract designating the callback contract can set a contract-level protection constraint. WCF deliberately ignores the service contract attribute on the callback contract (as explained in Chapter 5) to avoid a potential conflict between two contract attributes that apply to the same channel.

You can take advantage of operation-level demand for a protection level as follows:

```
[ServiceContract(CallbackContract = typeof(IMyContractCallback))]
interface IMyContract
{...}

interface IMyContractCallback
{
   [OperationContract(ProtectionLevel = ProtectionLevel.EncryptAndSign)]
   void OnCallback();
}
```

All calls into the callback object come in with an unauthenticated principal, even if Windows security was used across the board to invoke the service. As a result, the principal identity will be set to a Windows identity with a blank identity, which will preclude authorization and role-based security.

While the callback does have a security call context, the Windows identity will be set to a `WindowsIdentity` instance with a blank identity, which will preclude impersonation. The only meaningful information will be in the primary identity, which will be set to the service host's process identity and machine name:

```
class MyClient : IMyContractCallback
{
    public void OnCallback()
    {
        IPrincipal principal = Thread.CurrentPrincipal;
        Debug.Assert(principal.Identity.IsAuthenticated == false);

        ServiceSecurityContext context = ServiceSecurityContext.Current;
        Debug.Assert(context.PrimaryIdentity.Name == "MyHost/localhost");

        Debug.Assert(context.IsAnonymous == false);
    }
}
```

I recommend avoiding any sensitive work in the callback, since you cannot easily use role-based security.

Internet Application Scenario

In the Internet scenario, the clients or services may not be using WCF, or even Windows. If you are writing an Internet service or client, you cannot assume the use of WCF on the other end. In addition, an Internet application typically has a relatively large number of clients calling the service. These client calls originate from outside the firewall. You need to rely on HTTP for transport, and multiple intermediaries are possible. In an Internet application, you typically do not want to use Windows accounts and groups for credentials; instead, the application needs to access some custom credentials store. That said, you could still be using Windows security, as demonstrated later.

Securing the Internet Bindings

In an Internet application, you must use Message security for the transfer security mode to provide for end-to-end security across all intermediaries. The client should provide credentials in the form of a username and password, as this is a safe, low common denominator that all platforms support. For the Internet scenario, you should use the `WSHttpBinding` and the `WSDualHttpBinding`. You cannot use the basic binding because it does not provide for username credentials over Message security. In addition, if you have an intranet application that uses the `NetTcpBinding` but you do not wish to use Windows security for user accounts and groups, you should follow the same configuration as with the WS-based bindings. This is done uniformly across these bindings by selecting `MessageCredentialType.Username` for the client credentials type used with Message security. You need to configure the bindings this way both at the client and at the service.

WSHttpBinding configuration

WSHttpBinding offers the Security property of the type WSHttpSecurity:

```
public class WSHttpBinding : WSHttpBindingBase
{
    public WSHttpBinding( );
    public WSHttpBinding(SecurityMode securityMode);
    public WSHttpSecurity Security
    {get;}
    //More members
}
```

With WSHttpSecurity, you need to set the Mode property of the type SecurityMode to SecurityMode.Message. The Message property of WSHttpSecurity will then take effect:

```
public sealed class WSHttpSecurity
{
    public SecurityMode Mode
    {get;set;}
    public NonDualMessageSecurityOverHttp Message
    {get;}
    public HttpTransportSecurity Transport
    {get;}
}
```

Message is of the type NonDualMessageSecurityOverHttp, which derives from MessageSecurityOverHttp:

```
public class MessageSecurityOverHttp
{
    public MessageCredentialType ClientCredentialType
    {get;set;}
    //More members
}
public sealed class NonDualMessageSecurityOverHttp : MessageSecurityOverHttp
{...}
```

You need to set the ClientCredentialType property of MessageSecurityOverHttp to MessageCredentialType.Username. Recall that the default Message security credentials type of the WSHttpBinding is Windows (see Table 10-3).

Because Message security is the default security mode of the WSHttpBinding (see Table 10-1), these three definitions are equivalent:

```
WSHttpBinding binding1 = new WSHttpBinding( );
binding1.Security.Message.ClientCredentialType = MessageCredentialType.UserName;

WSHttpBinding binding2 = new WSHttpBinding(SecurityMode.Message);
binding2.Security.Message.ClientCredentialType = MessageCredentialType.UserName;

WSHttpBinding binding3 = new WSHttpBinding( );
binding3.Security.Mode = SecurityMode.Message;
binding3.Security.Message.ClientCredentialType = MessageCredentialType.UserName;
```

You can achieve the same configuration using a config file as follows:

```
<bindings>
    <wsHttpBinding>
        <binding name = "UserNameWS">
            <security mode = "Message">
                <message clientCredentialType = "UserName"/>
            </security>
        </binding>
    </wsHttpBinding>
</bindings>
```

Or, since Message security is the default, you can omit explicitly setting the mode in the config file:

```
<bindings>
    <wsHttpBinding>
        <binding name = "UserNameWS">
            <security>
                <message clientCredentialType = "UserName"/>
            </security>
        </binding>
    </wsHttpBinding>
</bindings>
```

Figure 10-4 shows the security-related elements of the WSHttpBinding.

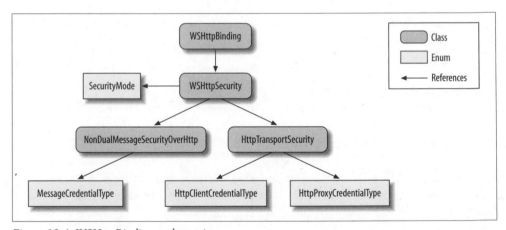

Figure 10-4. WSHttpBinding and security

WSHttpBinding has a reference to WSHttpSecurity, which uses the SecurityMode enum to indicate the transfer security mode. When Transport security is used, WSHttpSecurity will use an instance of HttpTransportSecurity. When Message security is used, WSHttpSecurity will use an instance of NonDualMessageSecurityOverHttp containing the client credentials type via the MessageCredentialType enum.

WSDualHttpBinding configuration

WSDualHttpBinding offers the Security property of the type WSDualHttpSecurity:

```
public class WSDualHttpBinding : Binding,...
{
    public WSDualHttpBinding( );
    public WSDualHttpBinding(WSDualHttpSecurityMode securityMode);
    public WSDualHttpSecurity Security
    {get;}
    //More members
}
```

With `WSDualHttpSecurity`, you need to set the `Mode` property of the type `WSDualHttpSecurityMode` to `WSDualHttpSecurityMode.Message`. The `Message` property of `WSDualHttpSecurity` will then take effect:

```
public sealed class WSDualHttpSecurity
{
    public MessageSecurityOverHttp Message
    {get;}
    public WSDualHttpSecurityMode Mode
    {get;set;}
}
```

`Message` is of the type `MessageSecurityOverHttp`, presented earlier.

You need to set the `ClientCredentialType` property of `MessageSecurityOverHttp` to `MessageCredentialType.Username`. Recall that the default Message security credentials type of `WSDualHttpBinding` is Windows (see Table 10-3).

Because Message security is the default transfer security mode of the `WSDualHttpBinding` (see Table 10-1), these definitions are equivalent:

```
WSDualHttpBinding binding1 = new WSDualHttpBinding( );
binding1.Security.Message.ClientCredentialType = MessageCredentialType.UserName;

WSDualHttpBinding binding2 = new WSDualHttpBinding(WSDualHttpSecurityMode.Message);
binding2.Security.Message.ClientCredentialType = MessageCredentialType.UserName;

WSDualHttpBinding binding3 = new WSDualHttpBinding( );
binding3.Security.Mode = WSDualHttpSecurityMode.Message;
binding3.Security.Message.ClientCredentialType = MessageCredentialType.UserName;
```

Here is the same configuration using a config file:

```
<bindings>
   <wsDualHttpBinding>
      <binding name = "WSDualWindowsSecurity">
         <security mode = "Message">
            <message  clientCredentialType = "UserName"/>
         </security>
      </binding>
   </wsDualHttpBinding>
</bindings>
```

Again, since Message security is the default, you can omit explicitly setting the mode in the config file:

```
<bindings>
   <wsDualHttpBinding>
      <binding name = "WSDualWindowsSecurity">
         <security>
            <message clientCredentialType = "UserName"/>
         </security>
      </binding>
   </wsDualHttpBinding>
</bindings>
```

Figure 10-5 shows the security-related elements of the WSDualHttpBinding.

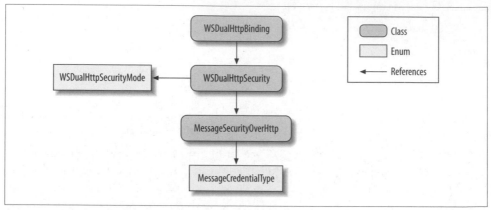

Figure 10-5. WSDualHttpBinding and security

WSDualHttpBinding has a reference to WSDualHttpSecurity, which uses the WSDualHttpSecurityMode enum to indicate the transfer security mode: Message or None. When Message security is used, WSDualHttpSecurity will use an instance of MessageSecurityOverHttp containing the client credentials type via the MessageCredentialType enum.

Message Protection

Since in the Internet scenario the client's message is transferred to the service over plain HTTP, it is vital to protect its content (both the client's credentials and the body of the message) by encrypting it. Encryption will provide for message integrity and privacy. One technical option for encryption is to use the client's password. However, WCF never uses this option, for a number of reasons. First, there are no guarantees that the password is strong enough, so anyone monitoring the communication could potentially break the encryption using a dictionary attack. Second, this approach forces the service (or more precisely, its host) to have access to the password, thus coupling the host to the credentials store. Finally, while the password may protect the message, it will not authenticate the service to the client.

Instead, to protect the message, WCF uses an X509 certificate. The certificate provides strong protection, and it authenticates the service to the client. A certificate works by using two keys, called the *public* and *private keys*, as well as a *common name* (CN) such as "MyCompanyCert." What is important about those keys is that anything encrypted with the public key can only be decrypted with the matching private one. The certificate contains the public key and the common name, and the private key is kept in some secure storage on the host machine to which the host has access. The host makes the certificate (and its public key) publicly available, so any client can access the host's endpoints and obtain the public key.

In a nutshell, what happens during a call is that WCF on the client's side uses the public key to encrypt all messages to the service. Upon receiving the encrypted message, WCF decrypts the message on the host side using the private key. Once the message is decrypted, WCF will read the client's credentials from the message, authenticate the client, and allow it to access the service. The real picture is a bit more complex, because WCF also needs to secure the reply messages and callbacks from the service to the client. One of the standards WCF supports deals with setting up such a secure conversation. In fact, several calls are made before the first request message from the client to the service, where WCF on the client's side generates a temporary shared secret it passes encrypted (using the service certificate) to the service. The client and the service will use that shared secret to protect all subsequent communication between them.

Configuring the host certificate

The `ServiceHostBase` class offers the `Credentials` property of the type `ServiceCredentials`. `ServiceCredentials` is a service behavior:

```
public abstract class ServiceHostBase : ...
{
   public ServiceCredentials Credentials
   {get;}
   //More members
}
public class ServiceCredentials : ...,IServiceBehavior
{
   public X509CertificateRecipientServiceCredential ServiceCertificate
   {get;}
   //More members
}
```

`ServiceCredentials` provides the `ServiceCertificate` property of the type `X509CertificateRecipientServiceCredential`:

```
public sealed class X509CertificateRecipientServiceCredential
{
   public void SetCertificate(StoreLocation storeLocation,
                              StoreName storeName,
                              X509FindType findType,
                              object findValue);
   //More members
}
```

You can use the `SetCertificate( )` method to instruct WCF where and how to load the service certificate. You typically provide this information in the host config file as a custom behavior under the `serviceCredentials` section, as shown in Example 10-8.

Example 10-8. Configuring the service certificate

```
<services>
   <service name = "MyService" behaviorConfiguration = "Internet">
      ...
   </service>
</services>
<behaviors>
   <serviceBehaviors>
      <behavior name = "Internet">
         <serviceCredentials>
            <serviceCertificate
               findValue     = "MyServiceCert"
               storeLocation = "LocalMachine"
               storeName     = "My"
               x509FindType  = "FindBySubjectName"
            />
         </serviceCredentials>
      </behavior>
   </serviceBehaviors>
</behaviors>
```

Using the host certificate

The client developer can obtain the service certificate using any out-of-band mechanism (such as email, or via a public web page). The client can then include in its config file in the endpoint behavior section detailed information about the service certificate, such as where it is stored on the client side and how to find it. This is by far the most secure option from the client's perspective, because any attempt to subvert the client's address resolving and redirect the call to a malicious service will fail since the other service will not have the correct certificate. This is the least flexible option as well, however, because every time the client needs to interact with a different service, the client administrator will need to rework the client's config file.

A reasonable alternative to explicitly referencing the certificates of all services the client may interact with is to store those certificates in the client's Trusted People certificate folder. The administrator can then instruct WCF to allow calls only to services whose certificates are in that folder. In that case, the client will need to obtain the service certificate at runtime as part of the initial pre-call negotiation, check to see whether it is in the Trusted People store, and, if so, proceed to use it to protect the message. This certificate negotiation behavior is the default for the WS bindings. You can disable it and use a hard-configured certificate instead, but for the Internet scenario I strongly recommend using certificate negotiation and storing the certificates in the Trusted People store.

Service certificate validation

To instruct WCF as to what degree to validate and trust the service certificate, add a custom endpoint behavior to the client's config file. The behavior should use the clientCredentials section. ClientCredentials is an endpoint behavior that offers the ServiceCertificate property of the type X509CertificateRecipientClientCredential:

```
public class ClientCredentials : ...,IEndpointBehavior
{
   public X509CertificateRecipientClientCredential ServiceCertificate
   {get;}
   //More members
}
```

X509CertificateRecipientClientCredential offers the Authentication property of the type X509CertificateRecipientClientCredential:

```
public sealed class X509CertificateRecipientClientCredential
{
   public X509ServiceCertificateAuthentication Authentication
   {get;}
   //More members
}
```

X509CertificateRecipientClientCredential provides the CertificateValidationMode property of the enum type X509CertificateValidationMode:

```
public enum X509CertificateValidationMode
{
   None,
   PeerTrust,
   ChainTrust,
   PeerOrChainTrust,
   Custom
}

public class X509ServiceCertificateAuthentication
{
   public X509CertificateValidationMode CertificateValidationMode
   {get;set;}
   //More members
}
```

Example 10-9 demonstrates setting the service certificate validation mode in the client's config file.

Example 10-9. Validating the service certificate

```
<client>
   <endpoint behaviorConfiguration = "ServiceCertificate"
      ...
   </endpoint>
</client>
<behaviors>
   <endpointBehaviors>
```

Example 10-9. Validating the service certificate (continued)

```
        <behavior name = "ServiceCertificate">
            <clientCredentials>
                <serviceCertificate>
                    <authentication certificateValidationMode = "PeerTrust"/>
                </serviceCertificate>
            </clientCredentials>
        </behavior>
    </endpointBehaviors>
</behaviors>
```

X509CertificateValidationMode.PeerTrust instructs WCF to trust the negotiated service certificate if it is present in the client's Trusted People store. X509CertificateValidationMode.ChainTrust instructs WCF to trust the certificate if it was issued by a root authority (such as VeriSign or Thwart) whose certificate is found in the client's Trusted Root Authority folder. X509CertificateValidationMode. ChainTrust is the default value used by WCF. X509CertificateValidationMode. PeerOrChainTrust allows either of those options. Since there are a number of illicit ways of obtaining a valid certificate from a public root authority, I do not recommend using this value. X509CertificateValidationMode.PeerOrChainTrust is available for tightly controlled environments that purge all public root authorities and install their own root certificates, which are used to sign other certificates.

Working with a test certificate

Developers often do not have access to their organizations' certificates, and therefore resort to using test certificates such as the ones generated by the *MakeCert.exe* command-line utility. There are two problems with test certificates. The first is that they will fail the default certificate validation on the client side, since the client uses X509CertificateValidationMode.ChainTrust by default. You can easily overcome this by installing the test certificate in the client's Trusted People store and using X509CertificateValidationMode.PeerTrust. The second problem is that WCF by default expects the service certificate name to match the service host's domain (or machine) name. This provides yet another line of defense, since typically with an Internet-facing service, the host domain name will match its certificate common name. To compensate, the client must explicitly specify the test certificate name in the endpoint identity's dns section:

```
<client>
    <endpoint
        address  = "http://localhost:8001/MyService"
        binding  = "wsHttpBinding"
        contract = "IMyContract">
        <identity>
            <dns value = "MyServiceCert"/>
        </identity>
    </endpoint>
</client>
```

Authentication

The client needs to provide its credentials to the proxy. The `ClientCredentials` property (presented earlier) of the `ClientBase<T>` base class has the `UserName` property of the type `UserNamePasswordClientCredential`:

```
public class ClientCredentials : ...,IEndpointBehavior
{
   public UserNamePasswordClientCredential UserName
   {get;}
   //More members
}

public sealed class UserNamePasswordClientCredential
{
   public string UserName
   {get;set;}
   public string Password
   {get;set;}
}
```

The client uses `UserNamePasswordClientCredential` to pass its username and password to the service, as demonstrated in Example 10-10.

Example 10-10. Providing username and password credentials

```
MyContractClient proxy = new MyContractClient();

proxy.ClientCredentials.UserName.UserName = "MyUsername";
proxy.ClientCredentials.UserName.Password = "MyPassword";

proxy.MyMethod();
proxy.Close();
```

> The client need not provide a domain name (if Windows security is used) or application name (if the ASP.NET providers are used). The host will use its service domain or a configured application name, as appropriate.

When working with a channel factory instead of a proxy class, you must set the `Credentials` property of the factory with the credentials:

```
ChannelFactory<IMyContract> factory = new ChannelFactory<IMyContract>("");

factory.Credentials.UserName.UserName = "MyUsername";
factory.Credentials.UserName.Password = "MyPassword";

IMyContract proxy = factory.CreateChannel();
using(proxy as IDisposable)
{
   proxy.MyMethod();
}
```

Note that you cannot use the static CreateChannel( ) methods of ChannelFactory<T>, since you have to instantiate a factory in order to access the Credentials property.

Once the username and password credentials are received by the WCF on the service side, the host can choose to authenticate them as Windows credentials, ASP.NET membership provider's credentials, or even custom credentials. Whichever option you choose, make sure it matches your role-based policy configuration.

The ServiceCredentials class (available via the Credentials property of ServiceHostBase) provides the UserNameAuthentication property of the type UserNamePasswordServiceCredential:

```
public class ServiceCredentials : ...,IServiceBehavior
{
   public UserNamePasswordServiceCredential UserNameAuthentication
   {get;}
   //More members
}
```

UserNamePasswordServiceCredential has the UserNamePasswordValidationMode property of a matching enum type:

```
public enum UserNamePasswordValidationMode
{
   Windows,
   MembershipProvider,
   Custom
}
public sealed class UserNamePasswordServiceCredential
{
   public MembershipProvider MembershipProvider
   {get;set;}
   public UserNamePasswordValidationMode UserNamePasswordValidationMode
   {get; set;}
   //More members
}
```

By setting the UserNamePasswordValidationMode property, the host chooses how to authenticate the incoming username and password credentials.

Using Windows Credentials

While not necessarily common, WCF lets the Internet-facing service authenticate the incoming credentials as Windows credentials. To authenticate the client's username and password as Windows credentials, you need to set UserNamePasswordValidationMode to UserNamePasswordValidationMode.Windows. Because UserNamePasswordValidationMode.Windows is the default value of the UserNamePasswordValidationMode property, these two definitions are equivalent:

```
ServiceHost host1 = new ServiceHost(typeof(MyService));

ServiceHost host2 = new ServiceHost(typeof(MyService));
host2.Credentials.UserNameAuthentication.UserNamePasswordValidationMode =
                                    UserNamePasswordValidationMode.Windows;
```

When using a config file, add a custom behavior that assigns the username and password authentication mode along with the service certificate information, as shown in Example 10-11.

Example 10-11. Internet security with Windows credentials

```
<services>
   <service name = "MyService" behaviorConfiguration = "UsernameWindows">
      ...
   </service>
</services>
<behaviors>
   <serviceBehaviors>
      <behavior name = "UsernameWindows">
         <serviceCredentials>
            <userNameAuthentication userNamePasswordValidationMode = "Windows"/>
            <serviceCertificate
               ...
            />
         </serviceCredentials>
      </behavior>
   </serviceBehaviors>
</behaviors>
```

As with the programmatic case, adding this line to the config file:

```
<userNameAuthentication userNamePasswordValidationMode = "Windows"/>
```

is optional because it is the default setting.

Authorization

If the `PrincipalPermissionMode` property of `ServiceAuthorizationBehavior` is set to its default value of `PrincipalPermissionMode.UseWindowsGroups`, once the username and password are authenticated against Windows, WCF installs a Windows principal object and attaches it to the thread. This enables the service to freely use Windows NT groups for authorization, just as with the intranet case, both declaratively and programmatically.

Identity management

As long as the principal permission mode is set to `PrincipalPermissionMode.UseWindowsGroups`, the identity management aspect of the Internet scenario is just as with the intranet scenario, including the identities of the security call context, as shown in Table 10-4. The main difference between an intranet application and an Internet application that both use Windows credentials is that with the latter the client cannot dictate the allowed impersonation level, and the host can impersonate at will. This is because WCF will assign `TokenImpersonationLevel.Impersonation` to the Windows identity of the security call context.

Using the ASP.NET Providers

By default, role-based security in WCF uses Windows user groups for roles and Windows accounts for security identities. There are several drawbacks to this default policy. First, you may not want to assign a Windows account for every client of your Internet application. Second, the security policy is only as granular as the user groups in the hosting domain. Often you do not have control over your end customers' IT departments, and if you deploy your application in an environment in which the user groups are coarse or don't map well to the actual roles users play in your application, or if the group names are slightly different, Windows role-based security will be of little use to you. Role localization presents yet another set of challenges, because role names will likely differ between customer sites in different locales. Consequently, Internet applications hardly ever use Windows accounts and groups. Out of the box, .NET 2.0 (and later) provides a custom credential management infrastructure called the ASP.NET Providers. Despite its name, non-ASP.NET applications (such as WCF applications) can easily use it to authenticate users and authorize them, without ever resorting to Windows accounts.

One of the concrete implementations of the ASP.NET providers includes a SQL Server store. SQL Server is often the repository of choice for Internet applications, so I will use it in this scenario. To use the SQL Server provider, run the setup file *aspnet_regsql.exe*, found under *%Windir%\Microsoft.NET\Framework\v2.0.50727*. The setup program will create a new database called *aspnetdb*, containing the tables and stored procedures required to manage the credentials.

The SQL Server credentials store is well designed and uses the latest best practices for credential management, such as password salting, stored procedures, normalized tables, and so on. In addition to providing a high-quality, secure solution, this infrastructure aids productivity, saving developers valuable time and effort. That said, the credential management architecture is that of a provider model, and you can easily add other storage options if required, such as an Access database.

The credentials providers

Figure 10-6 shows the architecture of the ASP.NET credentials providers.

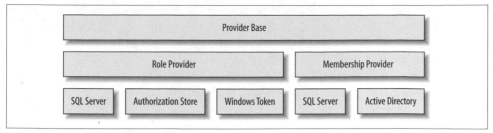

Figure 10-6. The ASP.NET provider model

Membership providers are responsible for managing users (usernames and passwords), and role providers are responsible for managing roles. Out of the box, ASP.NET offers support for membership stores in SQL Server or Active Directory, and roles can be stored in SQL Server, a file (the authorization store provider), or NT groups (the Windows token provider).

Username and password authentication is done using a class called MembershipProvider from the System.Web.Security namespace, defined as:

```
public abstract class MembershipProvider : ProviderBase
{
    public abstract string ApplicationName
    {get;set;}
    public abstract bool ValidateUser(string username,string password);
    //Additional members
}
```

MembershipProvider's goal is to encapsulate the actual provider used and the details of the actual data access, as well as to enable changing the membership provider without affecting the application itself. Depending on the configured security provider in the host config file, WCF will use a concrete data access class such as SqlMembershipProvider, targeting SQL Server or SQL Server Express:

```
public class SqlMembershipProvider : MembershipProvider
{...}
```

However, WCF interacts only with the MembershipProvider base functionality. WCF obtains the required membership provider by accessing the Provider static property of the Membership class, defined as:

```
public static class Membership
{
    public static string ApplicationName
    {get;set;}
    public static MembershipProvider Provider
    {get;}
    public static bool ValidateUser(string username,string password);
    //Additional members
}
```

Membership offers many members, which support the many aspects of user management. Membership.Provider retrieves the type of the configured provider from the System.Web section in the host config file. Unspecified, the role provider defaults to SqlMembershipProvider.

 Because all membership providers derive from the abstract class MembershipProvider, if you write your own custom credential provider it needs to derive from MembershipProvider as well.

A single credentials store can serve many applications, and those applications may define the same usernames. To allow for that, every record in the credentials store is scoped by an application name (similar to the way usernames in Windows are scoped by a domain or machine name).

The ApplicationName property of Membership is used to set and retrieve the application name, and the ValidateUser() method is used to authenticate the specified credentials against the store, returning true if they match and false otherwise. Membership.ValidateUser() is shorthand for retrieving and using the configured provider.

If you have configured your application to use the ASP.NET credentials store for authorization and if you enabled roles support, after authentication WCF will install an instance of the internal class RoleProviderPrincipal and attach it to the thread invoking the operation:

```
sealed class RoleProviderPrincipal : IPrincipal
{...}
```

RoleProviderPrincipal uses the abstract class RoleProvider for authorization:

```
public abstract class RoleProvider : ProviderBase
{
   public abstract string ApplicationName
   {get;set;}
   public abstract bool IsUserInRole(string username,string roleName);
   //Additional members
}
```

The ApplicationName property of RoleProvider binds the role provider to the particular application. The IsUserInRole() method verifies the user's role membership. Just as all membership providers must derive from MembershipProvider, all role providers (including custom role providers) must derive from RoleProvider.

RoleProvider encapsulates the actual provider used, and the role provider to use is specified in the host config file. Depending on the configured role provider, RoleProviderPrincipal uses a corresponding data access class such as SqlRoleProvider to authorize the caller:

```
public class SqlRoleProvider : RoleProvider
{...}
```

You can obtain the required role provider by accessing the `Provider` static property of the `Roles` class, defined as:

```
public static class Roles
{
    public static string ApplicationName
    {get;set;}
    public static bool IsUserInRole(string username,string roleName);
    public static RoleProvider Provider
    {get;}
    //Additional members
}
```

`Roles.IsUserInRole()` is shorthand for first accessing `Roles.Provider` and then calling `IsUserInRole()` on it. `Roles.Provider` retrieves the type of the configured provider from the host config file. If unspecified, the role provider defaults to `SqlRoleProvider`.

Credentials administration

If you use SQL Server, .NET installs website administration pages under *\Inetpub\ wwwroot\aspnet_webadmin\<version number>*. Developers can configure the application directly from within Visual Studio 2008. When you select ASP.NET Configuration from the Web Site menu, Visual Studio 2008 will launch the ASP.NET development server used for the administration pages, browse to the ASP.NET administration pages, and allow you to configure various parameters, including security. You can configure the following aspects for your application:

- Create new users and delete existing ones
- Create new roles and delete existing ones
- Allocate users to roles
- Retrieve a user's details
- Set a user's status
- Use additional features not relevant to this chapter

Shortcomings of Visual Studio 2008

There are a number of significant shortcomings to using the Visual Studio 2008-driven administration pages. First, you need Visual Studio 2008. It is unlikely that application or system administrators will have Visual Studio 2008, let alone know how to use it. The administration pages use "/" by default for the application name, and do not offer any visual way to modify that. Also, you must create a web application to activate the administration pages and there is no remote access: the application and Visual Studio 2008 must be co-located in order for Visual Studio 2008 to be able to access the application's configuration file, and the ASP.NET development server used for the administration pages cannot accept remote calls. The browser-based user interface is somewhat annoying (you need to frequently click the Back button) and rather dull. Furthermore, many features that administrators are likely to want to use are not available via the administration pages, despite the fact that the underlying provider classes support those features. Some of the things missing from the Visual Studio 2008-driven administration pages include the ability to:

- Update most if not all of the details in a user account
- Retrieve a user's password
- Change a user's password
- Reset a user's password
- Retrieve information about the number of current online users
- Remove all users from a role in one operation
- Retrieve information about the password management policy (such as length, reset policy, type of passwords, etc.)
- Test user credentials
- Verify user role membership

There are additional features that administrators are likely to want, yet they are not supported even by the provider classes. These features include the ability to retrieve a list of all of the applications in the store, the ability to remove all users from an application, the ability to remove all roles from an application, the ability to delete an application (and all its associated users and roles), and the ability to delete all applications.

 The IIS7 control panel applet also offers some administrative support for managing the roles and membership providers. However, this support is on a par with that of Visual Studio 2008.

Credentials Manager

This tools disparity motivated me to develop the Credentials Manager application, a smart client application that compensates for all of the shortcomings just listed. Figure 10-7 shows a screenshot of Credentials Manager.*

In Credentials Manager, which is available with *ServiceModelEx*, I wrapped the ASP.NET providers with a WCF service (which can be self-hosted or IIS 5/6- or WAS-hosted) and added the missing features, such as the ability to delete an application.

Credentials Manager uses the dedicated WCF service to administer the credentials store. In addition, it lets administrators select the address of the credentials service at runtime, and using the MetadataHelper class presented in Chapter 2 it verifies that the address provided does indeed support the required contracts.

---

* I first published an earlier version of Credentials Manager in my article "Manage Custom Security Credentials the Smart (Client) Way" (*CoDe Magazine*, November 2005).

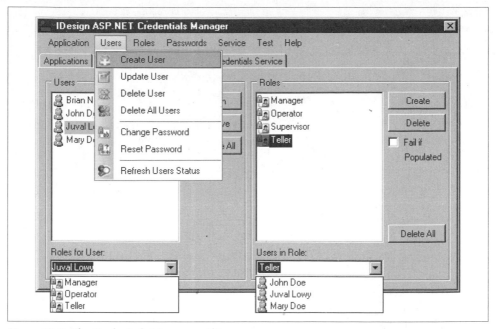

Figure 10-7. The Credentials Manager utility

Authentication

To authenticate the client's username and password using an ASP.NET provider, set the `UserNamePasswordValidationMode` property to `UserNamePasswordValidationMode.MembershipProvider`:

```
ServiceHost host = new ServiceHost(typeof(MyService));
host.Credentials.UserNameAuthentication.UserNamePasswordValidationMode =
                            UserNamePasswordValidationMode.MembershipProvider;
```

Which provider is used depends on the host config file. In addition, the host config file must contain any provider-specific settings such as a SQL Server connection string, as shown in Example 10-12.

Example 10-12. Internet security using an ASP.NET SQL Server provider

```
<connectionStrings>
   <add name= "AspNetDb" connectionString = "data source=(local);
                             Integrated Security=SSPI;Initial Catalog=aspnetdb"/>
</connectionStrings>

<system.serviceModel>
   <services>
      <service name = "MyService" behaviorConfiguration = "ASPNETProviders">
         <endpoint
            ...
         />
```

```
      </service>
   </services>
   <behaviors>
      <serviceBehaviors>
         <behavior name = "ASPNETProviders">
            <serviceCredentials>
               <userNameAuthentication
                  userNamePasswordValidationMode = "MembershipProvider"/>
               <serviceCertificate
                  ...
               />
            </serviceCredentials>
         </behavior>
      </serviceBehaviors>
   </behaviors>
</system.serviceModel>
```

The default application name will be a useless /, so you must assign your application's name. Once the ASP.NET providers are configured, WCF initializes the `MembershipProvider` property of `UserNamePasswordServiceCredential` with an instance of the configured membership provider. You can programmatically access that membership provider and set its application name:

```
ServiceHost host = new ServiceHost(typeof(MyService));
Debug.Assert(host.Credentials.UserNameAuthentication.MembershipProvider != null);
Membership.ApplicationName = "MyApplication";
host.Open( );
```

You can also configure the application name in the config file, but for that you need to define a custom ASP.NET membership provider, as shown in Example 10-13.

Example 10-13. Configuring the application name for the membership provider

```
<system.web>
   <membership defaultProvider = "MySqlMembershipProvider">
      <providers>
         <add name = "MySqlMembershipProvider"
            type = "System.Web.Security.SqlMembershipProvider"
            connectionStringName = "AspNetDb"
            applicationName = "MyApplication"
         />
      </providers>
   </membership>
</system.web>
<connectionStrings>
   <add name = "AspNetDb"
      ...
   />
</connectionStrings>
```

First, you add a system.Web section with a providers section, where you add a custom membership provider and set that to be the new default membership provider. Next, you need to list the fully qualified type name of the new provider. Nothing prevents you from referencing an existing implementation of a membership provider (such as SqlMembershipProvider, as in Example 10-13). When using the SQL provider, you must also list the connection string to use, and you cannot rely on the default connection string from *machine.config*. Most importantly, you must set the ApplicationName tag to the desired application name.

Authorization

To support authorizing the users, the host must enable role-based security by adding this to the config file:

```
<system.web>
   <roleManager enabled = "true"/>
</system.web>
```

 To enable the role manager programmatically, you have to use reflection.

Enabling roles this way will initialize the Roles class and have its Provider property set to the configured provider. To use the ASP.NET role provider, set the PrincipalPermissionMode property to PrincipalPermissionMode.UseAspNetRoles:

```
ServiceHost host = new ServiceHost(typeof(MyService));
host.Authorization.PrincipalPermissionMode =
                                  PrincipalPermissionMode.UseAspNetRoles;
host.Open( );
```

Alternatively, when using a config file, you can add a custom behavior to that effect:

```
<services>
   <service name = "MyService" behaviorConfiguration = "ASPNETProviders">
      ...
   </service>
</services>
<behaviors>
   <serviceBehaviors>
      <behavior name = "ASPNETProviders">
         <serviceAuthorization principalPermissionMode = "UseAspNetRoles"/>
         ...
      </behavior>
   </serviceBehaviors>
</behaviors>
```

After authenticating the client, the RoleProvider property of ServiceAuthorizationBehavior will be set to the configured role provider:

```
public sealed class ServiceAuthorizationBehavior : IServiceBehavior
{
   public RoleProvider RoleProvider
   {get;set;}
   //More members
}
```

The default application name will be a useless /, so you must assign your application's name using the static helper class Roles:

```
ServiceHost host = new ServiceHost(typeof(MyService));
Debug.Assert(host.Credentials.UserNameAuthentication.MembershipProvider != null);
Roles.ApplicationName = "MyApplication";
```

You can also configure the application name in the config file, but for that you need to define a custom ASP.NET role provider, as shown in Example 10-14.

Example 10-14. Configuring the application name for the role provider

```
<system.web>
   <roleManager enabled = "true" defaultProvider = "MySqlRoleManager">
      <providers>
         <add name = "MySqlRoleManager"
            type = "System.Web.Security.SqlRoleProvider"
            connectionStringName = "AspNetDb"
            applicationName = "MyApplication"
         />
      </providers>
   </roleManager>
</system.web>
<connectionStrings>
   <add name = "AspNetDb"
      ...
   />
</connectionStrings>
```

As with the membership provider, you add a system.Web section with a providers section, where you add a custom role provider and set that to be the new default role provider. Next you need to list the fully qualified type name of the new provider. As with the membership provider, you can reference any existing implementation of a role provider, such as SqlRoleProvider, in which case you must also list the connection string to use. Finally, you must set the ApplicationName tag to the desired application name.

Declarative role-based security

You can use the PrincipalPermission attribute to verify role membership just as in the intranet scenario, because all the attribute does is access the principal object attached to the thread, which WCF has already set to RoleProviderPrincipal. Example 10-15 demonstrates declarative role-based security using the ASP.NET providers.

Example 10-15. ASP.NET role provider declarative role-based security

```
class MyService : IMyContract
{
   [PrincipalPermission(SecurityAction.Demand,Role = "Manager")]
   public void MyMethod( )
   {...}
}
```

Identity Management

In the Internet scenario, when you use the ASP.NET providers, the identity associated with the principal object is a `GenericIdentity` that wraps the username provided by the client. That identity is considered authenticated. The security call context's primary identity will match the principal identity. The Windows identity, on the other hand, will be set to a Windows identity with a blank username; that is, it is unauthenticated. Table 10-5 shows the identities in this scenario.

Table 10-5. Identity management in the Internet scenario with ASP.NET providers

Identity	Type	Value	Authenticated
Thread principal	GenericIdentity	Username	Yes
Security context primary	GenericIdentity	Username	Yes
Security context Windows	WindowsIdentity	-	No

Impersonation

Since no valid Windows credentials are provided, the service cannot impersonate any of its clients.

Callbacks

When you use the ASP.NET providers, while the callback message is protected, all calls into the callback object come in with an unauthenticated principal. As a result, the principal identity will be set to a Windows identity with a blank username, which will preclude authorization and role-based security, as it is considered anonymous. Also, while the callback does have a security call context, the Windows identity will similarly be set to a `WindowsIdentity` instance with a blank identity, which will preclude impersonation. The only meaningful information will be in the primary identity, which will be set to an instance of the `X509Identity` class, with the name set to the common name of the service host certificate suffixed by a thumbprint (a hash) of the certificate:

```
class MyClient : IMyContractCallback
{
   public void OnCallback( )
   {
```

```
        IPrincipal principal = Thread.CurrentPrincipal;
        Debug.Assert(principal.Identity.IsAuthenticated == false);

        ServiceSecurityContext context = ServiceSecurityContext.Current;
        Debug.Assert(context.PrimaryIdentity.Name ==
                    "CN=MyServiceCert; D6E33B50BCF6D9609E68762F2C6A14F65679268B");
        Debug.Assert(context.IsAnonymous == false);
    }
}
```

I recommend avoiding any sensitive work in the callback, since you cannot easily use role-based security.

Business-to-Business Application Scenario

In the business-to-business scenario, the service and its clients are disparate business entities. They do not share credentials or accounts, and the communication between them is typically closed to the public. There are relatively few clients interacting with the service, and the client can only interact with the service after an elaborate business agreement has been established and other conditions have been met. Instead of Windows accounts or usernames, the clients identify themselves to the service using X509 certificates. These certificates are usually known a priori to the service. The client or service may not necessarily be using WCF, or even Windows. Therefore, if you are writing a service or a client, you cannot assume the use of WCF at the other end. The client calls originate from outside the firewall, and you need to rely on HTTP for transport. Also, multiple intermediaries are possible.

Securing the Business-to-Business Bindings

For the business-to-business scenario, you should use the Internet bindings; namely, BasicHttpBinding, WSHttpBinding, and WSDualHttpBinding. You must use Message security for the transfer security mode, to provide for end-to-end security across all intermediaries. The message will be protected using a service-side certificate, just as with the Internet scenario. However, unlike with the Internet scenario, here the clients provide credentials in the form of a certificate. This is done uniformly across these bindings by selecting MessageCredentialType.Certificate for the client credentials type to be used with the Message security mode. You need to configure this on both the client and the service. For example, to configure the WSHttpBinding programmatically, you would write:

```
WSHttpBinding binding = new WSHttpBinding();
binding.Security.Message.ClientCredentialType = MessageCredentialType.Certificate;
```

Or with a config file:

```
<bindings>
  <wsHttpBinding>
    <binding name = "WSCertificateSecurity">
```

```
        <security mode = "Message">
            <message clientCredentialType = "Certificate"/>
        </security>
    </binding>
  </wsHttpBinding>
</bindings>
```

Authentication

The service administrator has a number of options as to how to authenticate the certificates sent by the clients. If its certificate is validated, the client is considered authenticated. If no validation is done on the service side, merely sending a certificate will do. If the validation mode is set to use a chain of trust and a trusted root authority issued the certificate, the client will be considered authenticated. However, the best way of validating the client's certificate is to use *peer trust*. With this approach, the service administrator installs the certificates of all the clients allowed to interact with the service in the Trusted People store on the service's local machine. When the service receives the client's certificate, it verifies that the certificate is in the trusted store, and if so, the client is considered authenticated. I recommend using peer trust in the business-to-business scenario.

The ServiceCredentials class offers the ClientCertificate property of the type X509CertificateInitiatorServiceCredential:

```
public class ServiceCredentials : ...,IServiceBehavior
{
    public X509CertificateInitiatorServiceCredential ClientCertificate
    {get;}
    //More members
}
```

X509CertificateInitiatorServiceCredential provides the Authentication property of the type X509ClientCertificateAuthentication, which lets you configure the certificate validation mode:

```
public sealed class X509CertificateInitiatorServiceCredential
{
    public X509ClientCertificateAuthentication Authentication
    {get;}
    //More members
}
public class X509ClientCertificateAuthentication
{
    public X509CertificateValidationMode CertificateValidationMode
    {get;set;} //More members
}
```

Example 10-16 demonstrates the settings required in the host config file for the business-to-business scenario. Note in Example 10-16 that the host still needs to provide its own certificate for Message security.

Example 10-16. Configuring the host for business-to-business security

```
<services>
   <service name = "MyService" behaviorConfiguration = "BusinessToBusiness">
      ...
   </service>
</services>
<behaviors>
   <serviceBehaviors>
      <behavior name = "BusinessToBusiness">
         <serviceCredentials>
            <serviceCertificate
               ...
            />
            <clientCertificate>
               <authentication certificateValidationMode = "PeerTrust"/>
            </clientCertificate>
         </serviceCredentials>
      </behavior>
   </serviceBehaviors>
</behaviors>
```

The client needs to reference the certificate to use by including its location, name, and lookup method. This is done by accessing the ClientCredentials property of the proxy, which offers the ClientCertificate property of the type X509CertificateInitiatorClientCredential:

```
public class ClientCredentials : ...,IEndpointBehavior
{
   public X509CertificateInitiatorClientCredential ClientCertificate
   {get;}
   //More members
}
public sealed class X509CertificateInitiatorClientCredential
{
   public void SetCertificate(StoreLocation storeLocation,
                              StoreName storeName,
                              X509FindType findType,
                              object findValue);
   //More members
}
```

However, the client will typically set these values in its config file, as shown in Example 10-17.

Example 10-17. Setting the client's certificate

```
<client>
   <endpoint behaviorConfiguration = "BusinessToBusiness"
      ...
   />
</client>
   ...
<behaviors>
```

Example 10-17. Setting the client's certificate (continued)

```xml
<endpointBehaviors>
    <behavior name = "BusinessToBusiness">
        <clientCredentials>
            <clientCertificate
                findValue       = "MyClientCert"
                storeLocation = "LocalMachine"
                storeName       = "My"
                x509FindType   = "FindBySubjectName"
            />
            ...
        </clientCredentials>
    </behavior>
</endpointBehaviors>
</behaviors>
```

The config file must also indicate the service certificate validation mode. When using the BasicHttpBinding, since that binding cannot negotiate the service certificate, the client's config file needs to contain in the service certificate section of the endpoint behavior the location of the service certificate to use. Note that when using a service test certificate, as with the Internet scenario, the client's config file must still include the information regarding the endpoint's identity.

If the client is required to always provide the same certificate, the client developer can encapsulate setting the certificate in the proxy constructors:

```csharp
class MyContractClient: ClientBase<...>,...
{
    public MyContractClient( )
    {
        SetCertificate( );
    }
    /* More constructors */

    void SetCertificate( )
    {
        ClientCredentials.ClientCertificate.SetCertificate(
                                        StoreLocation.LocalMachine,
                                        StoreName.My,
                                        X509FindType.FindBySubjectName,
                                        "MyClientCert");
    }
    //Rest of the proxy
}
```

Once the client certificate is configured, there is no need to do anything special with the proxy class:

```csharp
MyContractClient proxy = new MyContractClient( );
proxy.MyMethod( );
proxy.Close( );
```

Authorization

By default, the service cannot employ principal-based, role-based security. The reason is that the credentials provided—namely, the client's certificate—do not map to either Windows or ASP.NET user accounts. Because business-to-business endpoints and services are often dedicated to a small set of clients or even a particular client, this lack of authorization support may not pose a problem. If that is indeed your case, you should set the `PrincipalPermissionMode` property to `PrincipalPermissionMode.None`, so that WCF will attach a generic principal with a blank identity as opposed to a `WindowsIdentity` instance with a blank identity.

If, on the other hand, you would still like to authorize the clients, you can actually achieve just that. In essence, all you need to do is deploy some credentials store, add each client's certificate name—that is, its common name and its thumbprint—to that repository, and then perform access checks against that store as needed.

In fact, nothing prevents you from taking advantage of the ASP.NET role provider for authorization, even if you didn't use the membership provider for authentication. This ability to use the providers separately was a core design goal for the ASP.NET provider model.

First, you need to enable the role provider in the host config file and configure the application name as in Example 10-14 (or provide the application name programmatically).

Next, add the client certificate and thumbprint to the membership store as a user, and assign roles to it. For example, when using a certificate whose common name is MyClientCert, you need to add a user by that name (such as "CN=MyClientCert; 12A06153D25E94902F50971F68D86DCDE2A00756") to the membership store, and provide a password. The password, of course, is irrelevant and will not be used. Once you have created the user, assign it to the appropriate roles in the application.

Most importantly, set the `PrincipalPermissionMode` property to `PrincipalPermissionMode.UseAspNetRoles`. Example 10-18 lists the required settings in the host config file.

Example 10-18. ASP.NET role-based security for the business-to-business scenario

```
<system.web>
   <roleManager enabled = "true" defaultProvider = "...">
      ...
   </roleManager>
</system.web>

<system.serviceModel>
   <services>
      <service name = "MyService" behaviorConfiguration = "BusinessToBusiness">
         ...
      </service>
   </services>
```

```
    <behaviors>
        <serviceBehaviors>
            <behavior name = "BusinessToBusiness">
                <serviceCredentials>
                    <serviceCertificate
                        ...
                    />
                    <clientCertificate>
                        <authentication certificateValidationMode = "PeerTrust"/>
                    </clientCertificate>
                </serviceCredentials>
                <serviceAuthorization principalPermissionMode = "UseAspNetRoles"/>
            </behavior>
        </serviceBehaviors>
    </behaviors>
    <bindings>
        ...
    </bindings>
</system.serviceModel>
```

Now you can use role-based security, just as in Example 10-15.

Identity Management

If the `PrincipalPermissionMode` property is set to `PrincipalPermissionMode.None`, then the principal identity will be a `GenericIdentity` with a blank username. The security call context's primary identity will be of the type `X509Identity` and will contain the client certificate's common name and its thumbprint. The security call context's Windows identity will have a blank username, since no valid Windows credentials were provided. If the `PrincipalPermissionMode` property is set to `PrincipalPermissionMode.UseAspNetRoles`, then both the principal identity and the security call context's primary identity will be set to an instance of `X509Identity` containing the client certificate and thumbprint. The security call context's Windows identity will have a blank username, as before. Table 10-6 details this setup.

Table 10-6. Identity management in the business-to-business scenario with ASP.NET role providers

Identity	Type	Value	Authenticated
Thread principal	`X509Identity`	Client cert name	Yes
Security context primary	`X509Identity`	Client cert name	Yes
Security context Windows	`WindowsIdentity`	-	No

Impersonation

Since no valid Windows credentials are provided, the service cannot impersonate any of its clients.

Callbacks

In the business-to-business scenario callbacks behave just as they do in the Internet scenario, since in both cases the same transfer security mechanism is used and the service identifies itself using a certificate. As with the Internet callback scenario, avoid sensitive work in the callback, since you cannot use role-based security.

Host Security Configuration

While Figure 10-8 is not specific to the business-to-business scenario, having covered this scenario, this is the first point in this chapter where I can show all the pieces of the service host pertaining to security.

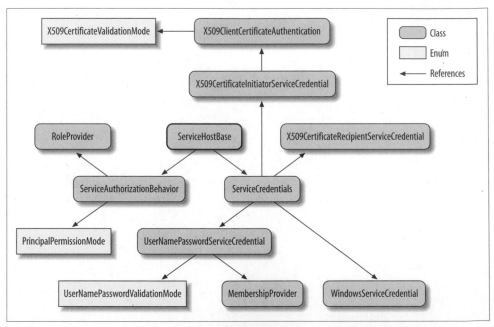

Figure 10-8. The security elements of ServiceHostBase

Anonymous Application Scenario

In the anonymous scenario, the clients access the service without presenting any credentials—they are anonymous. Nevertheless, the clients and the service do require secure message transfer, impervious to tampering and sniffing. Both Internet-facing and intranet-based applications may need to provide for anonymous yet end-to-end secure access. The anonymous scenario can have any number of clients, small or large. The clients may connect over HTTP, TCP, or MSMQ.

Securing the Anonymous Bindings

The need to secure the message and the fact that the clients may be calling over the Internet with multiple intermediaries mean that in the anonymous scenario you should use Message security. With Message security, you can easily satisfy both requirements by setting the `ClientCredentialType` property to `MessageCredentialType.None`. The service needs to be configured with a certificate to secure the message itself. For the anonymous scenario, you can use only the `WSHttpBinding`, `WSDualHttpBinding`, `NetTcpBinding`, and `NetMsmqBinding`—a mixture of both Internet and intranet bindings, as is required in this scenario. You cannot use the `NetNamedPipeBinding` or the `BasicHttpBinding`, as the former does not support Message security and the latter does not support having no credentials in the message (see Tables 10-1 and 10-3).

Configuring the allowed bindings is done similarly to the previous scenarios. The noticeable difference is in configuring for no client credentials. For example, here's how to configure the `WSHttpBinding`:

```
WSHttpBinding binding = new WSHttpBinding( );
binding.Security.Message.ClientCredentialType = MessageCredentialType.None;
```

You can also do this using a config file:

```
<bindings>
   <wsHttpBinding>
      <binding name = "WSAnonymous">
         <security>
            <message clientCredentialType = "None"/>
         </security>
      </binding>
   </wsHttpBinding>
</bindings>
```

Authentication

No client authentication is done in the anonymous scenario, of course, and the client need not provide any credentials to the proxy. For the purposes of service authentication to the client and message protection, the service needs to provide its certificate, as in Example 10-8.

Authorization

Since the clients are anonymous (and unauthenticated), authorization and role-based security are precluded. The service host should set the `PrincipalPermissionMode` property to `PrincipalPermissionMode.None` to have WCF install a generic principal with a blank identity, instead of a Windows principal with a blank identity.

Identity Management

Assuming the use of `PrincipalPermissionMode.None`, the identity associated with the principal object is a `GenericIdentity` with a blank username. That identity is considered unauthenticated. The security call context's primary identity will match the principal identity. The Windows identity, on the other hand, will be set to a Windows identity with a blank username—that is, it will be unauthenticated. Table 10-7 shows the identities in this scenario.

Table 10-7. Identity management in the anonymous scenario

Identity	Type	Value	Authenticated
Thread principal	GenericIdentity	-	No
Security context primary	GenericIdentity	-	No
Security context Windows	WindowsIdentity	-	No

Impersonation

Since the clients are anonymous, the service cannot impersonate any of its clients.

Callbacks

While the call from the client to the service is anonymous, the service does reveal its identity to the client. The primary identity of the security call context will be set to an instance of the `X509Identity` class, with the name set to the common name of the service host certificate suffixed by the certificate's thumbprint. The rest of the information is masked out. The principal identity will be set to a Windows identity with a blank username, which will preclude authorization and role-based security, as it is considered anonymous. The security call context's Windows identity will be set to a `WindowsIdentity` instance with a blank identity, which will preclude impersonation. Avoid sensitive work in the callback, since you cannot use role-based security.

No Security Scenario

In this last scenario, your application turns off security completely. The service does not rely on any transfer security, and it does not authenticate or authorize its callers. Obviously, such a service is completely exposed, and you generally need a very good business justification for relinquishing security. Both Internet and intranet services can be configured for no security, and they can accept any number of clients.

Unsecuring the Bindings

To turn off security, you need to set the transfer security mode to None. This will also avoid storing any client credentials in the message. All bindings support no transfer security (see Table 10-1).

Configuring the allowed bindings is done similarly to the previous scenarios, except the transfer security mode is set to None. For example, here's how to configure the NetTcpBinding programmatically:

```
NetTcpBinding binding = new NetTcpBinding(SecurityMode.None);
```

And here's how to do this using a config file:

```
<bindings>
   <netTcpBinding>
      <binding name = "NoSecurity">
         <security mode = "None"/>
      </binding>
   </netTcpBinding>
</bindings>
```

Authentication

No client authentication is done in this scenario, and the client does not need to provide any credentials to the proxy. Nor does the client ever authenticate the service.

Authorization

Since the clients are anonymous (and unauthenticated), authorization and role-based security are precluded. WCF will automatically set the PrincipalPermissionMode property to PrincipalPermissionMode.None to install a generic principal with a blank identity.

Identity Management

The identity associated with the principal object is a GenericIdentity with a blank username. That identity is considered unauthenticated. Unlike all the previous scenarios, in the no security scenario, the operation has no security call context, and the ServiceSecurityContext.Current returns null. Table 10-8 shows the identities in this scenario.

Table 10-8. Identity management in the no security scenario

Identity	Type	Value	Authenticated
Thread principal	GenericIdentity	-	No
Security context primary	-	-	-
Security context Windows	-	-	-

Impersonation

Because the clients are anonymous, the service cannot impersonate any of its clients.

Callbacks

Unlike in all the previous scenarios, in the absence of transfer security, callbacks come in under the client's own identity. The principal identity will be set to an instance of WindowsIdentity with the client's username. The callback will be authenticated, but there is no point in either impersonation or using role-based security since the client will only be authorizing itself. In addition, the security call context of the callback will be set to null.

Scenarios Summary

Now that you have seen the making of the five key scenarios, Tables 10-9 and 10-10 serve as a summary of their key elements. Table 10-9 lists the bindings used in each scenario. Note again that while technically you could use other bindings in almost all of the scenarios, my binding selections are aligned with the contexts in which the scenarios are used.

Table 10-9. Bindings and security scenarios

Binding	Intranet	Internet	B2B	Anonymous	None
BasicHttpBinding	No	No	Yes	No	Yes
NetTcpBinding	Yes	Yes	No	Yes	Yes
NetNamedPipeBinding	Yes	No	No	No	Yes
WSHttpBinding	No	Yes	Yes	Yes	Yes
WSDualHttpBinding	No	Yes	Yes	Yes	Yes
NetMsmqBinding	Yes	No	No	Yes	Yes

Table 10-10 shows how each of the security aspects defined at the beginning of this chapter (transfer security, service and client authentication, authorization, and impersonation) relates to each scenario.

Table 10-10. The security aspects of the various scenarios

Aspect	Intranet	Internet	B2B	Anonymous	None
Transport security	Yes	No	No	No	No
Message security	No	Yes	Yes	Yes	No
Service authentication	Windows	Certificate	Certificate	Certificate	No
Client authentication	Windows	ASP.NET	Certificate	No	No
Authorization	Windows	ASP.NET	No/ASP.NET	No	No
Impersonation	Yes	No	No	No	No

Declarative Security Framework

WCF security is truly a vast topic. The number of details to master is daunting, and intricate relationships exist between the various aspects. The programming model is very complex, and at first you're likely to have an inescapable feeling of navigating a maze. To make things even worse, getting it wrong has severe implications both at the application and the business level. To simplify things, I came up with a declarative security framework for WCF. For the service, I have provided a security attribute (with matching support for the host), and for the client I have provided a few helper classes and secure proxy classes. My declarative framework grossly simplifies WCF security configuration, placing it on a par with other aspects of WCF configuration such as transactions and synchronization. My goal was to provide a declarative model that would be simple to use and would minimize the need to understand the many details of security. As a developer, all you need to do is select the correct scenario (out of the five common scenarios discussed in this chapter), and my framework will automate the configuration. Not only that, but my framework mandates the correct options and enforces my recommendations. At the same time, my model maintains granularity and allows developers to control the underlying configuration if the need arises.

The SecurityBehaviorAttribute

Example 10-19 lists the definition of the SecurityBehaviorAttribute and the ServiceSecurity enum. ServiceSecurity defines the five scenarios supported by my framework.

Example 10-19. The SecurityBehaviorAttribute

```
public enum ServiceSecurity
{
   None,
   Anonymous,
   BusinessToBusiness,
   Internet,
   Intranet
}
[AttributeUsage(AttributeTargets.Class)]
public class SecurityBehaviorAttribute : Attribute,IServiceBehavior
{
   public SecurityBehaviorAttribute(ServiceSecurity mode);
   public SecurityBehaviorAttribute(ServiceSecurity mode,
                                    string serviceCertificateName);
   public SecurityBehaviorAttribute(ServiceSecurity mode,
                                    StoreLocation storeLocation,
                                    StoreName storeName,
                                    X509FindType findType,
                                    string serviceCertificateName);
```

Example 10-19. The SecurityBehaviorAttribute (continued)

```
    public bool ImpersonateAll
    {get;set;}
    public string ApplicationName
    {get;set;}
    public bool UseAspNetProviders
    {get;set;}
}
```

When applying the SecurityBehavior attribute, you need to provide it with the target scenario in the form of a ServiceSecurity value. You can use just the constructors of the SecurityBehavior attribute, or you can set the properties. Unset, the properties all default to reasonable values in the context of the target scenario. When selecting a scenario, the configured behavior follows to the letter my previous descriptions of the individual scenarios. The SecurityBehavior attribute yields a composable security model, allowing quite a few permutations and sub-scenarios. When using the attribute, you can even have a security-free host config file, or you can combine settings from the config file with values driven by the attribute. Similarly, your hosting code can be free of security, or you can combine programmatic host security with the attribute.

Configuring an intranet service

To configure a service for the intranet security scenario, apply SecurityBehavior with ServiceSecurity.Intranet:

```
[ServiceContract]
interface IMyContract
{
    [OperationContract]
    void MyMethod( );
}
[SecurityBehavior(ServiceSecurity.Intranet)]
class MyService : IMyContract
{
    public void MyMethod( )
    {...}
}
```

Even though the service contract used may not constrain the protection level, the attribute programmatically adds that demand to enforce message protection. You can use Windows NT groups for role-based security:

```
[SecurityBehavior(ServiceSecurity.Intranet)]
class MyService : IMyContract
{
    [PrincipalPermission(SecurityAction.Demand,Role = "Customer")]
    public void MyMethod( )
    {...}
}
```

The service can programmatically impersonate the callers, or use the operation behavior attribute for individual method impersonation. You can also configure the service to automatically impersonate all callers in all methods via the ImpersonateAll property. ImpersonateAll defaults to false, but when it's set to true the attribute will impersonate all callers in all operations without your needing to apply any operation behavior attributes or do any host configuration:

```
[SecurityBehavior(ServiceSecurity.Intranet,ImpersonateAll = true)]
class MyService : IMyContract
{...}
```

Configuring an Internet service

With the Internet scenario, you need to both configure the service for this scenario and select the service certificate to use. Note in Example 10-19 that the ServiceBehavior attribute constructor may take the service certificate name. If it's unspecified, the service certificate is loaded from the host config file as with Example 10-8:

```
[SecurityBehavior(ServiceSecurity.Internet)]
class MyService : IMyContract
{...}
```

You can also specify the service certificate name, in which case the specified certificate is loaded from the LocalMachine store from the *My* folder by name:

```
[SecurityBehavior(ServiceSecurity.Internet,"MyServiceCert")]
class MyService : IMyContract
{...}
```

If the certificate name is set to an empty string, the SecurityBehavior attribute will infer the certificate name by using the hosting machine name (or domain) for the certificate name and load such a certificate from the LocalMachine store from the *My* folder by name:

```
[SecurityBehavior(ServiceSecurity.Internet,"")]
class MyService : IMyContract
{...}
```

Finally, the attribute lets you explicitly specify the store location, the store name, and the lookup method:

```
[SecurityBehavior(ServiceSecurity.Internet,
                 StoreLocation.LocalMachine,StoreName.My,
                 X509FindType.FindBySubjectName,"MyServiceCert")]
class MyService : IMyContract
{...}
```

Note that you can combine an explicit location with an inferred certificate name:

```
[SecurityBehavior(ServiceSecurity.Internet,
                 StoreLocation.LocalMachine,StoreName.My,
                 X509FindType.FindBySubjectName,"")]
class MyService : IMyContract
{...}
```

Which credentials store to authenticate the client against is indicated by the UseAspNetProviders property. UseAspNetProviders defaults to false, meaning that the default is to authenticate the client's username and password as Windows credentials (as in Example 10-11). Because of that, when UseAspNetProviders is false you can by default use Windows NT groups for authorization and even impersonate all callers:

```
[SecurityBehavior(ServiceSecurity.Internet,"MyServiceCert",ImpersonateAll = true)]
class MyService : IMyContract
{...}
```

If UseAspNetProviders is set to true, instead of Windows credentials the SecurityBehavior attribute will use the ASP.NET membership and role providers, as prescribed for the Internet scenario:

```
[SecurityBehavior(ServiceSecurity.Internet,"MyServiceCert",
                  UseAspNetProviders = true)]
class MyService : IMyContract
{
   [PrincipalPermission(SecurityAction.Demand,Role = "Manager")]
   public void MyMethod( )
   {...}
}
```

 The attribute will programmatically enable the role manager section in the config file.

The SecurityBehavior attribute allows the use of the NetTcpBinding with ServiceSecurity.Internet along with ASP.NET providers to allow intranet applications to avoid using Windows accounts and groups, as explained previously.

Next is the issue of supplying the application name for the ASP.NET providers. That is governed by the ApplicationName property. If no value is assigned, the SecurityBehavior attribute will look up the application name from the config file, as in Examples 10-13 and 10-14. If no value is found in the host config file, the attribute will not default to using the meaningless / from *machine.config*; instead, it will by default use the host assembly name for the application name. If the ApplicationName property is assigned a value, that value will override whatever application name is present in the host config file:

```
[SecurityBehavior(ServiceSecurity.Internet,"MyServiceCert",
                  UseAspNetProviders = true,ApplicationName = "MyApplication")]
class MyService : IMyContract
{...}
```

Configuring a business-to-business service

To configure a service for the business-to-business scenario, you must set `ServiceSecurity` to `ServiceSecurity.BusinessToBusiness`. The `SecurityBehavior` attribute will use peer trust for validating the client's certificate. Configuring the service certificate is done just as with `ServiceSecurity.Internet`. For example:

```
[SecurityBehavior(ServiceSecurity.BusinessToBusiness)]
class MyService : IMyContract
{...}

[SecurityBehavior(ServiceSecurity.BusinessToBusiness,"")]
class MyService : IMyContract
{...}


[SecurityBehavior(ServiceSecurity.BusinessToBusiness,"MyServiceCert")]
class MyService : IMyContract
{...}
```

By default, with `ServiceSecurity.BusinessToBusiness`, the attribute will set the `PrincipalPermissionMode` property of the host to `PrincipalPermissionMode.None`, and the service will not be able to authorize its callers. However, setting the `UseAspNetProviders` property to true will enable use of the ASP.NET role providers, as in Example 10-18:

```
[SecurityBehavior(ServiceSecurity.BusinessToBusiness,UseAspNetProviders = true)]
class MyService : IMyContract
{...}
```

When using the ASP.NET role providers, the application name is looked up and decided upon just as with `ServiceSecurity.Internet`:

```
[SecurityBehavior(ServiceSecurity.BusinessToBusiness,"MyServiceCert",
                  UseAspNetProviders = true,ApplicationName = "MyApplication")]
class MyService : IMyContract
{...}
```

Configuring an anonymous service

To allow anonymous callers, you need to configure the attribute ›with `ServiceSecurity.Anonymous`. Configuring the service certificate is done just as with `ServiceSecurity.Internet`. For example:

```
[SecurityBehavior(ServiceSecurity.Anonymous)]
class MyService : IMyContract
{...}

[SecurityBehavior(ServiceSecurity.Anonymous,"")]
class MyService : IMyContract
{...}
```

```
[SecurityBehavior(ServiceSecurity.Anonymous,"MyServiceCert")]
class MyService : IMyContract
{...}
```

Configuring a no-security service

To turn off security completely, provide the attribute with ServiceSecurity.None:

```
[SecurityBehavior(ServiceSecurity.None)]
class MyService : IMyContract
{...}
```

Implementing the SecurityBehavior attribute

Example 10-20 is a partial listing of the implementation of SecurityBehaviorAttribute.

Example 10-20. Implementing SecurityBehaviorAttribute

```
[AttributeUsage(AttributeTargets.Class)]
class SecurityBehaviorAttribute : Attribute,IServiceBehavior
{
   SecurityBehavior m_SecurityBehavior;

   public bool ImpersonateAll
   {get;set;}
   public string ApplicationName
   {get;set;}
   public bool UseAspNetProviders
   {get;set;}

   public SecurityBehaviorAttribute(ServiceSecurity mode)
   {
      m_SecurityBehavior = new SecurityBehavior(mode);
   }
   public SecurityBehaviorAttribute(ServiceSecurity mode,
                                    string serviceCertificateName)
   {
      m_SecurityBehavior = new SecurityBehavior(mode,serviceCertificateName);
   }

   void IServiceBehavior.AddBindingParameters(ServiceDescription description,
                                       ServiceHostBase serviceHostBase,
                                       Collection<ServiceEndpoint> endpoints,
                                       BindingParameterCollection parameters)
   {
     m_SecurityBehavior.AddBindingParameters(description,serviceHostBase,
                                       endpoints,parameters);
   }
   void IServiceBehavior.Validate(ServiceDescription description,
                              ServiceHostBase serviceHostBase)
   {
      m_SecurityBehavior.UseAspNetProviders = UseAspNetProviders;
      m_SecurityBehavior.ApplicationName = ApplicationName;
      m_SecurityBehavior.ImpersonateAll = ImpersonateAll;
```

Example 10-20. Implementing SecurityBehaviorAttribute (continued)

```
      m_SecurityBehavior.Validate(description,serviceHostBase);
   }
   //Rest of the implementation
}
```

The SecurityBehavior attribute is a service behavior attribute, so you can apply it directly on the service class. When the AddBindingParameters() method of IServiceBehavior is called, the SecurityBehavior attribute enforces the binding configuration that matches the requested scenario. The Validate() method of IServiceBehavior is where the SecurityBehavior attribute configures the host. Other than that, all the attribute really does is sequence the overall order of configuration. The actual configuration is accomplished using a helper class called SecurityBehavior. Recall from other examples that it is always best to separate the attribute from its behavior, so you can reuse the behavior elsewhere. The SecurityBehavior attribute constructs an instance of SecurityBehavior, providing it with the scenario (the mode parameter) as well as the certificate name in the matching constructor. SecurityBehavior provides systematic, meticulous setting of all security scenarios using programmatic calls, encapsulating all the explicit steps described previously for each scenario. SecurityBehavior is a service behavior in its own right, and it is designed to even be used standalone, independent of the attribute. Example 10-21 contains a partial listing of SecurityBehavior, demonstrating how it operates.

Example 10-21. Implementing SecurityBehavior (partial)

```
class SecurityBehavior : IServiceBehavior
{
   ServiceSecurity m_Mode;
   StoreLocation m_StoreLocation;
   StoreName m_StoreName;
   X509FindType m_FindType;
   string m_SubjectName;

   public bool ImpersonateAll
   {get;set;}
   public bool UseAspNetProviders
   {get;set;}
   public string ApplicationName
   {get;set;}

   public SecurityBehavior(ServiceSecurity mode) :
         this(mode,StoreLocation.LocalMachine,X509FindType.FindBySubjectName,null)
   {}
   public SecurityBehavior(ServiceSecurity mode,StoreLocation storeLocation,
                        StoreName storeName,X509FindType findType,
                        string subjectName)
   {...} //Sets the corresponding members
```

Example 10-21. Implementing SecurityBehavior (partial) (continued)

```
public void Validate(ServiceDescription description,
                     ServiceHostBase serviceHostBase)
{
   if(m_SubjectName != null)
   {
      switch(m_Mode)
      {
         case ServiceSecurity.Anonymous:
         case ServiceSecurity.BusinessToBusiness:
         case ServiceSecurity.Internet:
         {
            string subjectName;
            if(m_SubjectName != String.Empty)
            {
               subjectName = m_SubjectName;
            }
            else
            {
               subjectName = description.Endpoints[0].Address.Uri.Host;
            }
            serviceHostBase.Credentials.ServiceCertificate.
             SetCertificate(m_StoreLocation,m_StoreName,m_FindType,subjectName);
            break;
         }
      }
   }
   .
   .
   .

}
public void AddBindingParameters(ServiceDescription description,
                                 ServiceHostBase serviceHostBase,
                                 Collection<ServiceEndpoint> endpoints,
                                 BindingParameterCollection parameters)
{
   .
   .
   .

   switch(m_Mode)
   {
      case ServiceSecurity.Intranet:
      {
         ConfigureIntranet(endpoints);
         break;
      }
      case ServiceSecurity.Internet:
      {
         ConfigureInternet(endpoints,UseAspNetProviders);
         break;
      }
```

Example 10-21. Implementing SecurityBehavior (partial) (continued)

```
        .
        .
        .
      }
   }
   internal static void ConfigureInternet(Collection<ServiceEndpoint> endpoints)
   {
      foreach(ServiceEndpoint endpoint in endpoints)
      {
         Binding binding = endpoint.Binding;
         if(binding is WSHttpBinding)
         {

            WSHttpBinding wsBinding = (WSHttpBinding)binding;
            wsBinding.Security.Mode = SecurityMode.Message;
            wsBinding.Security.Message.ClientCredentialType =
                                          MessageCredentialType.UserName;
            continue;
         }
         .
         .

         .
         throw new InvalidOperationException(binding.GetType( ) +
                           "is unsupported with ServiceSecurity.Internet");
      }
   }
   //Rest of the implementation
}
```

The constructors of `SecurityBehavior` store in member variables the construction parameters, such as the security mode and the details of the certificate. The `Validate( )` method is a decision tree that configures the host according to the scenario and the provided information, supporting the behavior of the `SecurityBehavior` attribute. `AddBindingParameters( )` calls a dedicated helper method for each scenario to configure the collection of endpoints the host exposes. Each helper method (such as `ConfigureInternet( )`) iterates over the collection of service endpoints. For each endpoint, it verifies whether the binding used matches the scenario and then configures the binding according to the scenario.

Host-Side Declarative Security

While configuring declarative security via the `SecurityBehavior` attribute is easy and handy, often it is up to the host to configure security, and the service just focuses on the business logic. In addition, you may be required to host services you do not develop, and those services may not happen to use my declarative security framework. The natural next step is to add declarative security support to the service host class as a set of `SetSecurityBehavior( )` extension methods:

```
public static class SecurityHelper
{
    public static void SetSecurityBehavior(this ServiceHost host,
                                    ServiceSecurity mode,
                                    bool useAspNetProviders,
                                    string applicationName,
                                    bool impersonateAll);

    public static void SetSecurityBehavior(this ServiceHost host,
                                    ServiceSecurity mode,
                                    string serviceCertificateName,
                                    bool useAspNetProviders,
                                    string applicationName,
                                    bool impersonateAll);

    public static void SetSecurityBehavior(this ServiceHost host,
                                    ServiceSecurity mode,
                                    StoreLocation storeLocation,
                                    StoreName storeName,
                                    X509FindType findType,
                                    string serviceCertificateName,
                                    bool useAspNetProviders,
                                    string applicationName,
                                    bool impersonateAll);

    //More members
}
```

Using declarative security via the host follows the same consistent guidelines as with the SecurityBehavior attribute. For example, here is how to configure the host (and the service) for Internet security with ASP.NET providers:

```
ServiceHost<MyService> host = new ServiceHost<MyService>( );
host.SetSecurityBehavior(ServiceSecurity.Internet,
                    "MyServiceCert",true,"MyApplication",false);
host.Open( );
```

Example 10-22 shows a partial listing of the declarative security support in the extension methods for the host.

Example 10-22. Adding declarative security extensions for the host

```
public static class SecurityHelper
{
    public static void SetSecurityBehavior(this ServiceHost host,
                                    ServiceSecurity mode,
                                    StoreLocation storeLocation,
                                    StoreName storeName,
                                    X509FindType findType,
                                    string serviceCertificateName,
                                    bool useAspNetProviders,
                                    string applicationName,
                                    bool impersonateAll)
    {
```

```
    if(host.State == CommunicationState.Opened)
    {
        throw new InvalidOperationException("Host is already opened");
    }
    SecurityBehavior securityBehavior = new SecurityBehavior(mode,storeLocation,
                                                    storeName,findType,
                                                serviceCertificateName);
    securityBehavior.UseAspNetProviders = useAspNetProviders;
    securityBehavior.ApplicationName = applicationName;
    securityBehavior.ImpersonateAll = impersonateAll;

    host.Description.Behaviors.Add(securityBehavior);
  }
  //More members
}
```

The implementation of SetSecurityBehavior( ) relies on the fact that the SecurityBehavior class supports IServiceBehavior. SetSecurityBehavior( ) initializes an instance of SecurityBehavior with the supplied parameters and then adds it to the collection of behaviors in the service description, as if the service were decorated with the SecurityBehavior attribute.

Client-Side Declarative Security

WCF does not allow attributes to be applied on the proxy class, and while a contract-level attribute is possible, the client may need to provide its credentials and other settings at runtime. The first step in supporting declarative security on the client side is my SecurityHelper static helper class with its set of extension methods for the proxy, defined in Example 10-23.

Example 10-23. Adding declarative security extensions for the proxy

```
public static class SecurityHelper
{
    public static void UnsecuredProxy<T>(this ClientBase<T> proxy)  where T : class;
    public static void AnonymousProxy<T>(this ClientBase<T> proxy)  where T : class;
    public static void SecureProxy<T>(this ClientBase<T> proxy,
                                 string userName,string password) where T : class;
    public static void SecureProxy<T>(this ClientBase<T> proxy,
                    string domain,string userName,string password) where T : class;
    public static void SecureProxy<T>(this ClientBase<T> proxy,string domain,
        string userName,string password,TokenImpersonationLevel impersonationLevel)
                                                                 where T : class;
    public static void SecureProxy<T>(this ClientBase<T> proxy,
                            string clientCertificateName) where T : class;
    public static void SecureProxy<T>(this ClientBase<T> proxy,
                            StoreLocation storeLocation,StoreName storeName,
              X509FindType findType,string clientCertificateName) where T : class;
    //More members
}
```

You can use SecurityHelper to configure a plain proxy according to the desired security scenario and behavior, using the dedicated static extension methods SecurityHelper offers. You can configure the proxy only before opening it. There is no need for any security settings in the client's config file or elsewhere in the client's code.

SecurityHelper is smart, and it will select the correct security behavior based on provided parameters and the method invoked. There is no need to explicitly use the ServiceSecurity enum.

For example, here is how to secure a proxy for the intranet scenario and provide it with the client's Windows credentials:

```
MyContractClient proxy = new MyContractClient();
proxy.SecureProxy("MyDomain","MyUsername","MyPassword");
proxy.MyMethod();
proxy.Close();
```

For the Internet scenario, the client only needs to provide the username and the password (remember that the decision as to whether those are Windows or ASP.NET provider credentials is a service-side decision):

```
MyContractClient proxy = new MyContractClient();
proxy.SecureProxy("MyUsername","MyPassword");
proxy.MyMethod();
proxy.Close();
```

For the business-to-business scenario, the client can specify a null or an empty string for the client certificate name if it wants to use the certificate in its config file, or it can list the certificate name explicitly:

```
MyContractClient proxy = new MyContractClient();
proxy.SecureProxy("MyClientCert");
proxy.MyMethod();
proxy.Close();
```

SecurityHelper will load the certificate from the client's LocalMachine store from the *My* folder by name. The client can also specify all the information required to find and load the certificate. To keep the design of SecurityHelper simple, when using the BasicHttpBinding in the business-to-business scenario the client must explicitly specify the service certificate location, either in the config file or programmatically.

For an anonymous client, use the AnonymousProxy() method:

```
MyContractClient proxy = new MyContractClient();
proxy.AnonymousProxy();
proxy.MyMethod();
proxy.Close();
```

and for no security at all, use the UnsecuredProxy() method:

```
MyContractClient proxy = new MyContractClient();
proxy.UnsecuredProxy();
proxy.MyMethod();
proxy.Close();
```

Implementing SecurityHelper

Internally, SecurityHelper uses SecurityBehavior to configure the proxy's endpoint and set the credentials, as shown in Example 10-24.

Example 10-24. Implementing SecurityHelper (partial)

```
public static class SecurityHelper
{
   public static void SecureProxy<T>(this ClientBase<T> proxy,
                                string userName,string password) where T : class
   {
      if(proxy.State == CommunicationState.Opened)
      {
         throw new InvalidOperationException("Proxy channel is already opened");
      }
      Collection<ServiceEndpoint> endpoints = new Collection<ServiceEndpoint>();
      endpoints.Add(proxy.Endpoint);

      SecurityBehavior.ConfigureInternet(endpoints,true);

      proxy.ClientCredentials.UserName.UserName = userName;
      proxy.ClientCredentials.UserName.Password = password;
      proxy.ClientCredentials.ServiceCertificate.Authentication.
            CertificateValidationMode = X509CertificateValidationMode.PeerTrust;
   }
   //Rest of the implementation
}
```

The SecureClientBase<T> class

The advantage of using the SecurityHelper extensions is that they can operate on any proxy—even a proxy the client developer is not responsible for creating. The disadvantage is that it is an extra step the client has to take. If you are responsible for generating the proxy, you can take advantage of my SecureClientBase<T> class, defined in Example 10-25.

Example 10-25. The SecureClientBase<T> class

```
public abstract class SecureClientBase<T> : ClientBase<T> where T : class
{
   //These constructors target the default endpoint
   protected SecureClientBase();
   protected SecureClientBase(ServiceSecurity mode);
   protected SecureClientBase(string userName,string password);
   protected SecureClientBase(string domain,string userName,string password,
                         TokenImpersonationLevel impersonationLevel);
   protected SecureClientBase(string domain,string userName,string password);
   protected SecureClientBase(string clientCertificateName);
   protected SecureClientBase(StoreLocation storeLocation,StoreName storeName,
                         X509FindType findType,string clientCertificateName);
   //More constructors for other types of endpoints
}
```

SecureClientBase<T> derives from the conventional ClientBase<T> and adds declarative security support. You need to derive your proxy from SecureClientBase<T> instead of ClientBase<T>, provide constructors that match your security scenario, and call the base constructors of SecureClientBase<T> with the supplied credentials and endpoint information:

```
class MyContractClient : SecureClientBase<IMyContract>,IMyContract
{
   public MyContractClient(ServiceSecurity mode) : base(mode)
   {}
   public MyContractClient(string userName,string password) :
                                              base(userName,password)

   {}

   /* More constructors */

   public void MyMethod( )
   {
      Channel.MyMethod( );
   }
}
```

Using the derived proxy is straightforward. For example, for the Internet scenario:

```
MyContractClient proxy = new MyContractClient("MyUsername","MyPassword");
proxy.MyMethod( );
proxy.Close( );
```

or for the Anonymous scenario:

```
MyContractClient proxy = new MyContractClient(ServiceSecurity.Anonymous);
proxy.MyMethod( );
proxy.Close( );
```

The implementation of SecureClientBase<T> simply uses the extensions of SecurityHelper (as shown in Example 10-26), so SecureClientBase<T> follows the same behaviors regarding, for example, the client certificate.

Example 10-26. Implementing SecureClientBase<T> (partial)

```
public class SecureClientBase<T> : ClientBase<T> where T : class
{
   protected SecureClientBase(ServiceSecurity mode)
   {
      switch(mode)
      {
         case ServiceSecurity.None:
         {
            this.UnsecuredProxy( );
            break;
         }
         case ServiceSecurity.Anonymous:
         {
```

Example 10-26. Implementing SecureClientBase<T> (partial) (continued)

```
            this.AnonymousProxy( );
            break;
        }
        ...
    }
}
    protected SecureClientBase(string userName,string password)
    {
        this.SecureProxy(userName,password);
    }
    //More constructors
}
```

Secure channel factory

If you are not using a proxy at all, `SecurityHelper` and `SecureClientBase<T>` will be of little use to you. For that case, I added to `SecurityHelper` a set of extension methods to the `ChannelFactory<T>` class, defined in Example 10-27.

Example 10-27. Adding declarative security extensions for ChannelFactory<T>

```
public static class SecurityHelper
{
    public static void SetSecurityMode<T>(this ChannelFactory<T> factory,
                                          ServiceSecurity mode);
    public static void SetCredentials<T>(this ChannelFactory<T> factory,
                                         string userName,string password);
    public static void SetCredentials<T>(this ChannelFactory<T> factory,
                                         string domain,string userName,string password);
    public static void SetCredentials<T>(this ChannelFactory<T> factory,
                                         string clientCertificateName);
    //More members
}
```

You need to call the `SetSecurityMode( )` method or one of the `SetCredentials( )` methods that fits your target scenario before opening the channel. For example, with a proxy to an Internet security-based service:

```
ChannelFactory<IMyContract> factory = new ChannelFactory<IMyContract>(...);
factory.SetCredentials("MyUsername","MyPassword");

IMyContract proxy = factory.CreateChannel( );

using(proxy as IDisposable)
{
    proxy.MyMethod( );
}
```

Implementing the `ChannelFactory<T>` extensions was very similar to implementing the extensions for `ClientBase<T>`, so I have omitted that code.

Duplex clients and declarative security

I also provide the SecureDuplexClientBase<T,C> class (similar to SecureClientBase<T>), which is defined in Example 10-28.

Example 10-28. The SecureDuplexClientBase<T,C> class

```
public abstract class SecureDuplexClientBase<T,C> : DuplexClientBase<T,C>
                                                        where T : class
{
   protected SecureDuplexClientBase(C callback);
   protected SecureDuplexClientBase(ServiceSecurity mode,C callback);
   protected SecureDuplexClientBase(string userName,string password,C callback);
   protected SecureDuplexClientBase(string domain,string userName,string password,
                      TokenImpersonationLevel impersonationLevel,C callback);
   protected SecureDuplexClientBase(string domain,string userName,string password,
                                                              C callback);
   protected SecureDuplexClientBase(string clientCertificateName,C callback);
   protected SecureDuplexClientBase(StoreLocation storeLocation,
                             StoreName storeName,X509FindType findType,
                             string clientCertificateName,C callback);

   /* More constructors with InstanceContext<C> and constructors that
      target the configured endpoint and a programmatic endpoint */
}
```

SecureDuplexClientBase<T,C> derives from my type-safe DuplexClientBase<T,C> class, presented in Chapter 5, and it adds declarative scenario-based security support. As when using the DuplexClientBase<T,C> class, you need to derive your proxy class from it and take advantage of either the callback parameter or the type-safe context InstanceContext<C>. For example, given this service contract and callback contract definition:

```
[ServiceContract(CallbackContract = typeof(IMyContractCallback))]
interface IMyContract
{
   [OperationContract]
   void MyMethod( );
}
interface IMyContractCallback
{
   [OperationContract]
   void OnCallback( );
}
```

your derived proxy class will look like this:

```
class MyContractClient :
              SecureDuplexClientBase<IMyContract,IMyContractCallback>,IMyContract
{
   public MyContractClient(IMyContractCallback callback) : base(callback)
   {}
   public MyContractClient(ServiceSecurity mode,IMyContractCallback callback) :
                                                     base(mode,callback)
```

```
        {}
        /* More constructors */

        public void MyMethod( )
        {
           Channel.MyMethod( );
        }
    }
```

When using SecureDuplexClientBase<T,C>, provide the security scenario or credentials, the callback object, and the endpoint information. For example, when targeting the anonymous scenario:

```
class MyClient : IMyContractCallback
{...}

IMyContractCallback callback = new MyClient( );

MyContractClient proxy = new MyContractClient(ServiceSecurity.Anonymous,callback);
proxy.MyMethod( );

proxy.Close( );
```

The implementation of SecureDuplexClientBase<T,C> is almost identical to that of SecureClientBase<T>, with the main difference being a different base class. Note that there was no point in defining declarative extensions for DuplexClientBase<T>, since you should not use it in the first place due to its lack of type safety.

Extensions for the duplex factory

When you're not using a SecureDuplexClientBase<T,C>-derived proxy to set up the bidirectional communication, you can use my declarative extensions for the DuplexChannelFactory<T,C> channel factory, defined in Example 10-29.

Example 10-29. Adding declarative security extensions for DuplexChannelFactory<T,C>

```
public static class SecurityHelper
{
   public static void SetSecurityMode<T,C>(this DuplexChannelFactory<T,C> factory,
                                 ServiceSecurity mode);
   public static void SetCredentials<T,C>(this DuplexChannelFactory<T,C> factory,
                                string userName,string password);
   public static void SetCredentials<T,C>(this DuplexChannelFactory<T,C> factory,
                            string domain,string userName,string password);
   public static void SetCredentials<T,C>(this DuplexChannelFactory<T,C> factory,
                               string clientCertificateName);
   //More members
}
```

You need to call the SetSecurityMode( ) method or one of the SetCredentials( ) methods that fits your target scenario before opening the channel. For example, when targeting the Internet scenario:

```
class MyClient : IMyContractCallback
{...}

IMyContractCallback callback = new MyClient();

DuplexChannelFactory<IMyContract,IMyContractCallback> factory =
            new DuplexChannelFactory<IMyContract,IMyContractCallback>(callback,"");
factory.SetCredentials("MyUsername","MyPassword");

IMyContract proxy = factory.CreateChannel();
using(proxy as IDisposable)
{
    proxy.MyMethod();
}
```

Implementing the extensions for DuplexChannelFactory<T,C> was very similar to implementing those for ChannelFactory<T>.

Security Auditing

I will end this chapter by presenting a useful feature WCF supports called *security audits*. As its name implies, a security audit is a logbook of the security-related events in your services. WCF can log authentication and authorization attempts, their times and locations, and the calling clients' identities. The class ServiceSecurityAuditBehavior governs auditing; it is listed in Example 10-30 along with its supporting enumerations.

Example 10-30. The ServiceSecurityAuditBehavior class

```
public enum AuditLogLocation
{
    Default, //Decided by the operating system
    Application,
    Security
}
public enum AuditLevel
{
    None,
    Success,
    Failure,
    SuccessOrFailure
}
public sealed class ServiceSecurityAuditBehavior : IServiceBehavior
{
    public AuditLogLocation AuditLogLocation
    {get;set;}
    public AuditLevel MessageAuthenticationAuditLevel
    {get;set;}
    public AuditLevel ServiceAuthorizationAuditLevel
    {get;set;}
    //More members
}
```

ServiceSecurityAuditBehavior is a service behavior. The AuditLogLocation property specifies where to store the log entries: in the application log or in the security log, both of which are in the event log on the host computer. The MessageAuthenticationAuditLevel property governs the authentication audit verbosity. Its default value is AuditLevel.None. For performance's sake, you may want to audit only failures. For diagnostic purposes, you can also audit successful authentications. Similarly, you use the ServiceAuthorizationAuditLevel property to control authorization audit verbosity. It is also disabled by default.

Configuring Security Audits

The typical way of enabling a security audit is in the host config file, by adding a custom behavior section and referencing it in the service declaration, as shown in Example 10-31.

Example 10-31. Configuring a security audit administratively

```
<system.serviceModel>
   <services>
      <service name = "MyService" behaviorConfiguration = "MySecurityAudit">
         ...
      </service>
   </services>
   <behaviors>
      <serviceBehaviors>
         <behavior name = "MySecurityAudit">
            <serviceSecurityAudit
               auditLogLocation = "Default"
               serviceAuthorizationAuditLevel  = "SuccessOrFailure"
               messageAuthenticationAuditLevel = "SuccessOrFailure"
            />
         </behavior>
      </serviceBehaviors>
   </behaviors>
</system.serviceModel>
```

You can also configure security auditing programmatically, by adding the behavior to the host at runtime before opening it. As when adding other behaviors programmatically, you can check that the host does not already have an audit behavior to avoid overriding the config file, as shown in Example 10-32.

Example 10-32. Enabling a security audit programmatically

```
ServiceHost host = new ServiceHost(typeof(MyService));

ServiceSecurityAuditBehavior securityAudit =
                  host.Description.Behaviors.Find<ServiceSecurityAuditBehavior>();
if(securityAudit == null)
{
   securityAudit = new ServiceSecurityAuditBehavior();
```

Example 10-32. Enabling a security audit programmatically (continued)

```
   securityAudit.MessageAuthenticationAuditLevel = AuditLevel.SuccessOrFailure;
   securityAudit.ServiceAuthorizationAuditLevel = AuditLevel.SuccessOrFailure;
   host.Description.Behaviors.Add(securityAudit);
}
host.Open();
```

You can streamline the code in Example 10-32 by adding the `SecurityAuditEnabled` Boolean property to `ServiceHost<T>`:

```
public class ServiceHost<T> : ServiceHost
{
   public bool SecurityAuditEnabled
   {get;set;}
   //More members
}
```

Using `ServiceHost<T>`, Example 10-32 is reduced to:

```
ServiceHost<MyService> host = new ServiceHost<MyService>();
host.SecurityAuditEnabled = true;
host.Open();
```

Example 10-33 shows the implementation of the `SecurityAuditEnabled` property.

Example 10-33. Implementing the SecurityAuditEnabled property

```
public class ServiceHost<T> : ServiceHost
{
   public bool SecurityAuditEnabled
   {
      get
      {
         ServiceSecurityAuditBehavior securityAudit =
                     Description.Behaviors.Find<ServiceSecurityAuditBehavior>();
         if(securityAudit != null)
         {
            return securityAudit.MessageAuthenticationAuditLevel ==
                                                AuditLevel.SuccessOrFailure
               &&
               securityAudit.ServiceAuthorizationAuditLevel ==
                                                AuditLevel.SuccessOrFailure;
         }
         else
         {
            return false;
         }
      }
      set
      {
         if(State == CommunicationState.Opened)
         {
            throw new InvalidOperationException("Host is already opened");
         }
         ServiceSecurityAuditBehavior securityAudit =
```

Example 10-33. Implementing the SecurityAuditEnabled property (continued)

```
                            Description.Behaviors.Find<ServiceSecurityAuditBehavior>( );
         if(securityAudit == null && value == true)
         {
             securityAudit = new ServiceSecurityAuditBehavior( );
             securityAudit.MessageAuthenticationAuditLevel =
                                                   AuditLevel.SuccessOrFailure;
             securityAudit.ServiceAuthorizationAuditLevel =
                                                   AuditLevel.SuccessOrFailure;
             Description.Behaviors.Add(securityAudit);
         }
      }
   }
}
   //More members
}
```

In the get accessor, the SecurityAuditEnabled property accesses the description of the service and looks for an instance of ServiceSecurityAuditBehavior. If one is found, and if both the authentication and the authorization audits are set to AuditLevel.SuccessOrFailure, SecurityAuditEnabled returns true; otherwise, it returns false. In the set accessor, the property enables the security audit only if the description does not contain a previous value (because the config file does not contain the audit behavior). If no prior behavior is found, SecurityAuditEnabled sets both the authentication and authorization audits to AuditLevel.SuccessOrFailure.

Declarative Security Auditing

You can also write an attribute that surfaces the security audit options at the service level. I chose to add that support in the form of a single Boolean property of the SecurityBehavior attribute called SecurityAuditEnabled:

```
[AttributeUsage(AttributeTargets.Class)]
public class SecurityBehaviorAttribute : Attribute,IServiceBehavior
{
    public bool SecurityAuditEnabled
    {get;set;}
    //More members
}
```

The default of SecurityAuditEnabled is false (i.e., no security audit). Using this property complements the rest of the declarative security model. For example:

```
[SecurityBehavior(ServiceSecurity.Internet,UseAspNetProviders = true,
              SecurityAuditEnabled = true)]
class MyService : IMyContract
{...}
```

Example 10-34 shows how that support was added to the SecurityBehavior attribute.

Example 10-34. Implementing a declarative security audit

```
[AttributeUsage(AttributeTargets.Class)]
public class SecurityBehaviorAttribute : Attribute,IServiceBehavior
{
   public bool SecurityAuditEnabled
   {get;set;}

   void IServiceBehavior.Validate(ServiceDescription description,
                                  ServiceHostBase serviceHostBase)
   {
     if(SecurityAuditEnabled)
     {
       ServiceSecurityAuditBehavior securityAudit = serviceHostBase.Description.
                              Behaviors.Find<ServiceSecurityAuditBehavior>();
       if(securityAudit == null)
       {
          securityAudit = new ServiceSecurityAuditBehavior();
          securityAudit.MessageAuthenticationAuditLevel =
                                              AuditLevel.SuccessOrFailure;
          securityAudit.ServiceAuthorizationAuditLevel =
                                              AuditLevel.SuccessOrFailure;
          serviceHostBase.Description.Behaviors.Add(securityAudit);
       }
       //Rest same as Example 10-20
     }
   }
   //Rest of the implementation
}
```

The Validate( ) method of IServiceBehavior enables auditing using the same verbosity level as ServiceHost<T>, again avoiding overriding the config file.

Introduction to Service-Orientation

This book is all about designing and developing service-oriented applications using WCF—yet there is considerable confusion and hype concerning what service-orientation is and what it means. To make matters worse, most of the vendors in this space equate their definition of service-orientation with their products and services. The vendors (Microsoft included) add to the confusion by equating service-orientation with high-end Enterprise applications, where handling high scalability and throughput is a must (mostly because they all contend for that market, where the business margins are made).

This appendix presents my understanding of what service-orientation is all about and attempts to put it in a concrete context. My take is different from that of the large vendors, but I believe it is more down-to-earth, rooted as it is in trends and the natural evolution of our industry. As you will see, I believe that service-orientation is not a breakthrough or a quantum leap of thought, but rather the next gradual step (and probably not the last step) in a long journey that spans decades.

To understand where the software industry is heading with service-orientation, you should first appreciate where it came from. After a brief discussion of the history of software engineering and its overarching trend, this appendix defines service-oriented applications (as opposed to mere architecture), explains what services themselves are, and examines the benefits of the methodology. It then presents the main principles of service-orientation and augments the abstract tenets with a few more practical and concrete points to which most applications should adhere. Finally, the appendix concludes with a look to the future.

A Brief History of Software Engineering

The first modern computer was an electromechanical, typewriter-sized device developed in Poland in the late 1920s for enciphering messages. The device was later sold to the German Commerce Ministry, and in the 1930s the German military adopted it for enciphering all wireless communication. Today we know it as the Enigma.

Enigma used mechanical rotors to change the route of electrical current flow to a light board in response to a letter key being pressed, resulting in a different letter being output (the ciphered letter). Enigma was not a general-purpose computer: it could only do enciphering and deciphering (which today we call encryption and decryption). If the operator wanted to change the encryption algorithm, he had to physically alter the mechanical structure of the machine by changing the rotors, their order, their initial positions, and the wired plugs that connected the keyboard to the light board. The "program" was therefore coupled in the extreme to the problem it was designed to solve (encryption), and to the mechanical design of the computer.

The late 1940s and the 1950s saw the introduction of the first general-purpose electronic computers for defense purposes. These machines could run code that addressed any problem, not just a single predetermined task. The downside was that the code executed on these computers was in a machine-specific "language" with the program coupled to the hardware itself. Code developed for one machine could not run on another. In fact, at the time there was no distinction between the software and the hardware (indeed, the word "software" was coined only in 1958). Initially this was not a cause for concern, since there were only a handful of computers in the world anyway. As machines became more prolific, this did turn into a problem. In the early 1960s the emergence of assembly language decoupled the code from specific machines, enabling it to run on multiple computers. That code, however, was now coupled to the machine architecture: code written for an 8-bit machine could not run on a 16-bit machine, let alone withstand differences in the registers or available memory and memory layout. As a result, the cost of owning and maintaining a program began to escalate. This coincided more or less with the widespread adoption of computers in the civilian and government sectors, where the more limited resources and budgets necessitated a better solution.

In the 1960s, higher-level languages such as COBOL and FORTRAN introduced the notion of a *compiler*: the developer would write in an abstraction of machine programming (the language), and the compiler would translate that into actual assembly code. Compilers for the first time decoupled the code from the hardware and its architecture. The problem with those first-generation languages was that the code resulted in nonstructured programming, where the code was internally coupled to its own structure via the use of jump or go-to statements. Minute changes to the code structure often had devastating effects in multiple places in the program.

The 1970s saw the emergence of structured programming via languages such as C and Pascal, which decoupled the code from its internal layout and structure using functions and structures. The 1970s was also the first time developers and researchers started to examine software as an engineered entity. To drive down the cost of ownership, companies had to start thinking about reuse—that is, what would make a piece of code able to be reused in other contexts. With languages like C, the basic unit of reuse is the *function*. But the problem with function-based reuse is that the function is coupled to the data it manipulates, and if the data is global, a change to benefit one function in one reuse context is likely to damage another function used somewhere else.

Object-Orientation

The solution to these problems that emerged in the 1980s, with languages such as Smalltalk and later C++, was object-orientation. With object-orientation, the functions and the data they manipulated were packaged together in an object. The functions (now called *methods*) encapsulated the logic, and the object encapsulated the data. Object-orientation enabled domain modeling in the form of a class hierarchy. The mechanism of reuse was class-based, enabling both direct reuse and specialization via inheritance. But object-orientation was not without its own acute problems. First, the generated application (or code artifact) was a single, monolithic application. Languages like C++ have nothing to say about the binary representation of the generated code. Developers had to deploy huge code bases every time they needed to make a change, however minute, and this had a detrimental effect on the development process and on application quality, time to market, and cost. While the basic unit of reuse was a class, it was a class in source format. Consequently, the application was coupled to the language used—you could not have a Smalltalk client consuming a C++ class or deriving from it. Language-based reuse implied uniformity of skill (all developers in the organization had to be skilled enough to use C++), which led to staffing problems. Language-based reuse also inhibited economy of scale, because if the organization was using multiple languages it necessitated duplication of investments in framework and common utilities. Finally, having to access the source files in order to reuse an object coupled developers to each other, complicated source control, and coupled teams together, since it made independent builds difficult. Moreover, inheritance turned out to be a poor mechanism for reuse, often harboring more harm than good because the developer of the derived class needed to be intimately aware of the implementation of the base class (which introduced vertical coupling across the class hierarchy).

Object-orientation was oblivious to real-life challenges, such as deployment and versioning issues. Serialization and persistence posed yet another set of problems. Most applications did not start by plucking objects out of thin air; they had some persistent state that needed to be hydrated into objects. However, there was no way of enforcing compatibility between the persisted state and the potentially new object code. Object-orientation assumed the entire application was always in one big process. This prevented fault isolation between the client and the object, and if the object blew up, it took the client (and all other objects in the process) with it. Having a single process implies a single uniform identity for the clients and the objects, without any security isolation. This makes it impossible to authenticate and authorize clients, since they have the same identity as the object. A single process also impedes scalability, availability, responsiveness, throughput, and robustness. Developers could manually place objects in separate processes, yet if the objects were distributed across multiple processes or machines there was no way of using raw C++ for the invocations, since C++ required direct memory references and did not support distribution. Developers had to write host processes and use some remote call technology (such as TCP sockets) to remote the calls, but such invocations looked nothing like native C++ calls and did not benefit from object-orientation.

Component-Orientation

The solution for the problems of object-orientation evolved over time, involving technologies such as the static library (*.lib*) and the dynamic library (*.dll*), culminating in 1994 with the first component-oriented technology, called COM (Component Object Model). Component-orientation provided interchangeable, interoperable binary components. With this approach, instead of sharing source files, the client and the server agree on a binary type system (such as IDL) and a way of representing the metadata inside the opaque binary components. The components are discovered and loaded at runtime, enabling scenarios such as dropping a control on a form and having that control be automatically loaded at runtime on the client's machine. The client only programs against an abstraction of the service: a contract called the *interface*. As long as the interface is immutable, the service is free to evolve at will. A proxy can implement the same interface and thus enable seamless remote calls by encapsulating the low-level mechanics of the remote call. The availability of a common binary type system enables cross-language interoperability, so a Visual Basic client can consume a C++ COM component. The basic unit of reuse is the interface, not the component, and polymorphic implementations are interchangeable. Versioning is controlled by assigning a unique identifier for every interface, COM object, and type library.

While COM was a fundamental breakthrough in modern software engineering, most developers found it unpalatable. COM was unnecessarily ugly because it was bolted on top of an operating system that was unaware of it, and the languages used for writing COM components (such as C++ and Visual Basic) were at best object-oriented but not component-oriented. This greatly complicated the programming model, requiring frameworks such as ATL to partially bridge the two worlds. Recognizing these issues, Microsoft released .NET 1.0 in 2002. .NET is (in the abstract) nothing more than cleaned-up COM, MFC, C++, and Windows, all working seamlessly together under a single new component-oriented runtime. .NET supports all the advantages of COM and mandates and standardizes many of its ingredients, such as type metadata sharing, dynamic component loading, serialization, and versioning.

While .NET is at least an order of magnitude easier to work with than COM, both COM and .NET suffer from a similar set of problems:

Technology and platform

The application and the code are coupled to the technology and the platform. Both COM and .NET are available only on Windows. Both also expect the client and the service to be either COM or .NET and cannot interoperate natively with other technologies, be they Windows or not. While bridging technologies such as web services make interoperability possible, they force the developers to let go of almost all of the benefits of working with the native framework, and they introduce their own complexities and coupling with regard to the nature of the interoperability mechanism. This, in turn, breaks economy of scale.

Concurrency management

When a vendor ships a component, it cannot assume that its clients will not access it with multiple threads concurrently. In fact, the only safe assumption the vendor can make is that the component will be accessed by multiple threads. As a result, the components must be thread-safe and must be equipped with synchronization locks. However, if an application developer is building an application by aggregating multiple components from multiple vendors, the introduction of multiple locks renders the application deadlock-prone. Avoiding the deadlocks couples the application and the components.

Transactions

If multiple components are to participate in a single transaction, the application that hosts them must coordinate the transaction and flow the transaction from one component to the next, which is a serious programming endeavor. This also introduces coupling between the application and the components regarding the nature of the transaction coordination.

Communication protocols

If components are deployed across process or machine boundaries, they are coupled to the details of the remote calls, the transport protocol used, and its implications for the programming model (e.g., in terms of reliability and security).

Communication patterns

The components may be invoked synchronously or asynchronously, and they may be connected or disconnected. A component may or may not be able to be invoked in either one of these modes, and the application must be aware of its exact preference. With COM and .NET, developing asynchronous or even queued solutions was still the responsibility of the developer, and any such custom solutions were not only difficult to implement but also introduced coupling between the solution and the components.

Versioning

Applications may be written against one version of a component and yet encounter another in production. Both COM and .NET bear the scars of DLL Hell (which occurs when the client at runtime is trying to use a different, incompatible version of the component than the one against which it was compiled), so both provide a guarantee to the client: that the client would get at runtime exactly the same component versions it was compiled against. This conservative approach stifled innovation and the introduction of new components. Both COM and .NET provided for custom version-resolution policies, but doing so risked DLL Hell-like symptoms. There was no built-in versioning tolerance, and dealing robustly with versioning issues coupled the application to the components it used.

Security

Components may need to authenticate and authorize their callers, but how does a component know which security authority it should use, or which user is a member of which role? Not only that, but a component may want to ensure that the communication from its clients is secure. That, of course, imposes certain restrictions on the clients and in turn couples them to the security needs of the component.

Off-the-shelf plumbing

In the abstract, interoperability, concurrency, transactions, protocols, versioning, and security are the glue—the plumbing—that holds any application together.

In a decent-sized application, the bulk of the development effort and debugging time is spent on addressing such plumbing issues, as opposed to focusing on business logic and features. To make things even worse, since the end customer (or the development manager) rarely cares about plumbing (as opposed to features), the developers typically are not given adequate time to develop robust plumbing. Instead, most handcrafted plumbing solutions are proprietary (which hinders reuse, migration, and hiring) and are of low quality, because most developers are not security or synchronization experts and because they were not given the time and resources to develop the plumbing properly.

The solution was to use ready-made plumbing that offered such services to components. The first attempt at providing decent off-the-shelf plumbing was MTS (Microsoft Transactions Server), released in 1996. MTS offered support for much more than transactions, including security, hosting, activation, instance management, and synchronization. MTS was followed by J2EE (1998), COM+ (2000), and .NET Enterprise Services (2002). All of these application platforms provided adequate, decent plumbing (albeit with varying degrees of ease of use), and applications that used them had a far better ratio of business logic to plumbing. However, by and large these technologies were not adopted on a large scale, due to what I term the *boundary problem*. Few systems are an island; most have to interact and interoperate with other systems. If the other system doesn't use the same plumbing, you cannot interoperate smoothly. For example, there is no way of propagating a COM+ transaction to a J2EE component. As a result, when crossing the system boundary, a component (say, component A) had to dumb down its interaction to the (not so large) common denominator between the two platforms. But what about component B, next to component A? As far as B was concerned, the component it interacted with (A) did not speak its flavor of the plumbing, so B also had to be dumbed down. As a result, system boundaries tended to creep from the outside inward, preventing the ubiquitous use of off-the-shelf plumbing. Technologies like Enterprise Services and J2EE were useful, but they were useful in isolation.

Service-Orientation

If you examine the brief history of software engineering just outlined, you'll notice a pattern: every new methodology and technology incorporates the benefits of its preceding technology and improves on the deficiencies of the preceding technology. However, every new generation also introduces new challenges. Therefore, I say that *modern software engineering is the ongoing refinement of the ever-increasing degrees of decoupling.*

Put differently, coupling is bad, but coupling is unavoidable. An absolutely decoupled application would be useless, because it would add no value. Developers can only add value by coupling things together. Indeed, the very act of writing code is coupling one thing to another. The real question is how to wisely choose what to be coupled to. I believe there are two types of coupling, good and bad. Good coupling is business-level coupling. Developers add value by implementing a system use case or a feature, by coupling software functionality together. Bad coupling is anything to do with writing plumbing. What was wrong with .NET and COM was not the concept; it was the fact that developers could not rely on off-the-shelf plumbing and still had to write so much of it themselves. The real solution is not just off-the-shelf plumbing, but rather *standard* off-the-shelf plumbing. If the plumbing is standard, the boundary problem goes away, and applications can utilize ready-made plumbing. However, all technologies (.NET, Java, etc.) use the client thread to jump into the object. How can you possibly take a .NET thread and give it to a Java object? The solution is to avoid call-stack invocation and instead to use message exchange. The technology vendors can standardize the format of the message and agree on ways to represent transactions, security credentials, and so on. When the message is received by the other side, the implementation of the plumbing there will convert the message to a native call (on a .NET or a Java thread) and proceed to call the object. Consequently, any attempt to standardize the plumbing has to be message-based.

And so, recognizing the problems of the past, in the late 2000s the service-oriented methodology has emerged as the answer to the shortcomings of component-orientation. In a service-oriented application, developers focus on writing business logic and expose that logic via interchangeable, interoperable service endpoints. Clients consume those endpoints (not the service code, or its packaging). The interaction between the clients and the service endpoint is based on a standard message exchange, and the service publishes some standard metadata describing what exactly it can do and how clients should invoke operations on it. The metadata is the service equivalent of the C++ header file, the COM type library, or the .NET assembly metadata, yet it contains not just operation metadata (such as methods and parameters) but also plumbing metadata. Incompatible clients—that is, clients that are incompatible with the plumbing expectations of the object—cannot call it, since the call will be denied by the platform. This is an extension of the object- and component-oriented compile-time notion that a client that is incompatible with an object's metadata cannot call it. Demanding compatibility with the plumbing (on top of the operations) is paramount. Otherwise, the object must always check on every call that the client meets its expectations in terms of security, transactions, reliability and so on, and thus the object invariably ends up infused with plumbing. Not only that, but the service's endpoint is reusable by any client compatible with its interaction constraints (such as synchronous, transacted, and secure communication), regardless of the client's implementation technology.

In many respects, a service is the natural evolution of the component, just as the component was the natural evolution of the object, which was the natural evolution of the function. Service-orientation is, to the best of our knowledge as an industry, the correct way to build maintainable, robust, and secure applications.

The result of improving on the deficiencies of component-orientation (i.e., classic .NET) is that when developing a service-oriented application, you decouple the service code from the technology and platform used by the client from many of the concurrency management issues, from transaction propagation and management, and from communication reliability, protocols, and patterns. By and large, securing the transfer of the message itself from the client to the service is also outside the scope of the service, and so is authenticating the caller. The service may still do its own local authorization, however, if the requirements so dictate. Similarly, as long as the endpoint supports the contract the client expects, the client does not care about the version of the service. There are also tolerances built into the standards to deal with versioning tolerance of the data passed between the client and the service.

Benefits of Service-Orientation

Service-orientation yields maintainable applications because the applications are decoupled on the correct aspects. As the plumbing evolves, the application remains unaffected. A service-oriented application is robust because the developers can use available, proven, and tested plumbing, and the developers are more productive because they get to spend more of the cycle time on the features rather than the plumbing. This is the true value proposition of service-orientation: enabling developers to extract the plumbing from their code and invest more in the business logic and the required features.

The many other hailed benefits, such as cross-technology interoperability, are merely a manifestation of the core benefit. You can certainly interoperate without resorting to services, as was the practice until service-orientation. The difference is that with ready-made plumbing you rely on the plumbing to provide the interoperability for you.

When you write a service, you usually do not care which platform the client executes on—that is immaterial, which is the whole point of seamless interoperability. However, a service-oriented application caters to much more than interoperability. It enables developers to cross boundaries. One type of boundary is the technology and platform, and crossing that boundary is what interoperability is all about. But other boundaries may exist between the client and the service, such as security and trust boundaries, geographical boundaries, organizational boundaries, timeline boundaries, transaction boundaries, and even business model boundaries. Seamlessly crossing each of these boundaries is possible because of the standard message-based interaction. For example, there are standards for how to secure messages and establish a secure interaction between the client and the service, even though both may reside in domains (or sites) that have no direct trust relationship. There is also a standard that enables the transaction manager on the client side to flow the transaction to the transaction manager on the service side, and have the service participate in that transaction, even though the two transaction managers never enlist in each other's transactions directly.

I believe that every application should be service-oriented, not just Enterprise applications that require interoperability and scalability. Writing plumbing in any type of application is wrong, constituting a waste of your time, effort, and budget, resulting in degradation of quality. Just as with .NET every application was component-oriented (which was not so easy to do with COM alone) and with C++ every application was object-oriented (which was not so easy to do with C alone), when using WCF, every application should be service-oriented.

Service-Oriented Applications

A *service* is a unit of functionality exposed to the world over standard plumbing. A *service-oriented application* is simply the aggregation of services into a single logical, cohesive application (see Figure A-1), much as an object-oriented application is the aggregation of objects.

The application itself may expose the aggregate as a new service, just as an object can be composed of smaller objects.

Inside services, developers still use concepts such as specific programming languages, versions, technologies and frameworks, operating systems, APIs, and so on. However, between services you have the standard messages and protocols, contracts, and metadata exchange.

The various services in an application can be all in the same location or be distributed across an intranet or the Internet, and they may come from multiple vendors and be developed across a range of platforms and technologies, versioned independently, and even execute on different timelines. All of those plumbing aspects are hidden from the clients in the application interacting with the services. The clients

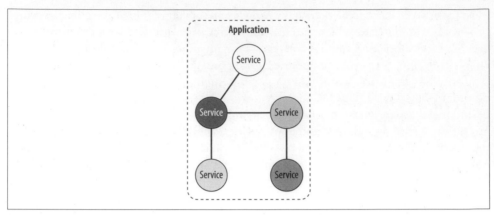

Figure A-1. A service-oriented application

send the standard messages to the services, and the plumbing at both ends marshals away the differences between the clients and the services by converting the messages to and from the neutral wire representation.

Tenets and Principles

The service-oriented methodology governs what happens in the space between services (see Figure A-1). There is a small set of principles and best practices for building service-oriented applications, referred to as the *tenets of service-oriented architecture*:

Service boundaries are explicit
> Any service is always confined behind boundaries, such as technology and location. The service should not make the nature of these boundaries known to its clients by exposing contracts and data types that betray such details. Adhering to this tenet will make aspects such as location and technology irrelevant. A different way of thinking about this tenet is that the more the client knows about the implementation of the service, the more the client is coupled to the service. To minimize the potential for coupling, the service has to explicitly expose functionality, and only operations (or data contracts) that are explicitly exposed will be shared with the client. Everything else is encapsulated. Service-oriented technologies should adopt an "opt-out by default" programming model, and expose only those things explicitly opted-in. This tenet is the modern incarnation of the old object-oriented adage that the application should maximize encapsulation and information hiding.

Services are autonomous
> A service should need nothing from its clients or other services. The service should be operated and versioned independently from the clients, enabling it to evolve separately from them. The service should also be secured independently,

so it can protect itself and the messages sent to it regardless of the degree to which the client uses security. Doing this (besides being common sense) further decouples the client and the service.

Services share operational contracts and data schema, not type-specific metadata

What the service decides to expose across its boundary should be type-neutral. The service must be able to convert its native data types to and from some neutral representation and should not share indigenous, technology-specific things such as its assembly version number or its type. In addition, the service should not let its client know about local implementation details such as its instance management mode or its concurrency management mode. The service should only expose logical operations. How the service goes about implementing those operations and how it behaves should not be disclosed to the client.

Services are compatible based on policy

The service should publish a policy indicating what it can do and how clients can interact with it. Any access constraints expressed in the policy (such as the need for reliable communication) should be separate from the service implementation details. Put differently, the service must be able to express, in a standard representation of policy, what it does and how clients should communicate with it. Being unable to express such a policy indicates poor service design. Note that a non-public service may not actually publish any such policy. This tenet simply implies that the service should be able to publish a policy if necessary.

Practical Principles

Well-designed applications should try to maximize adherence to the tenets just listed. However, those tenets are very abstract, and how they are supported is largely a product of the technology used to develop and consume the services, and of the design of the services. Consequently, just as not all code written in C++ is fully object-oriented, not all WCF applications may fully comply with the basic tenets just described. I therefore supplement those tenets with a set of more down-to-earth practical principles:

Services are secure

A service and its clients must use secure communication. At the very least, the transfer of messages from the clients to the service must be secured, and the clients must have a way of authenticating the service. The clients may also provide their credentials in the message so that the service can authenticate and authorize them.

Services leave the system in a consistent state

Conditions such as partially succeeding in executing the client's request are forbidden. All resources the service accesses must be in a consistent state after the client's call. If an error occurs the system state should not be only partially affected, and the service should not require the help of its clients to recover the system back to a consistent state after an error.

Services are thread-safe

The service must be designed so that it can sustain concurrent access from multiple clients. The service should also be able to handle causality and logical thread reentrancy.

Services are reliable

If the client calls a service, the client will always know in a deterministic manner whether the service received the message. In-order processing of messages is optional.

Services are robust

The service should isolate its faults, preventing them from taking it down (or taking down any other services). The service should not require clients to alter their behavior according to the type of error the service has encountered. This helps to decouple the clients from the service on the error-handling dimension.

Optional Principles

While I view the practical principles as mandatory, there is also a set of optional principles that may not be required by all applications (although adhering to them as well is usually a good idea):

Services are interoperable

The service should be designed so that any client, regardless of its technology, can call it.

Services are scale-invariant

It should be possible to use the same service code regardless of the number of clients and the load on the service. This will grossly simplify the cost of ownership of the service as the system grows and allow different deployment scenarios.

Services are available

The service should always be able to accept clients' requests and should have no downtime. Otherwise, if the service has periods of unavailability the client needs to accommodate them, which in turn introduces coupling.

Services are responsive

The client should not have to wait long for the service to start processing its request. If the service is unresponsive the client needs to plan for that, which in turn introduces coupling.

Services are disciplined

The service should not block the client for long. The service may perform lengthy processing, but only as long as it does not block the client. Otherwise, the client will need to accommodate that, which in turn introduces coupling.

What's Next?

Since service-oriented frameworks provide off-the-shelf plumbing for connecting services together, the more granular those services are, the more use the application can make of this infrastructure, and the less plumbing the developers have to write. Taken to the ultimate conclusion, every class and primitive should be a service, to maximize the use of the ready-made plumbing and to avoid handcrafting plumbing. This, in theory, will enable effortlessly transactional integers, secure strings, and reliable classes. But in practice, is that viable? Can .NET support it? Will future platforms offer this option?

I believe that as time goes by and service-oriented technologies evolve, the industry will see the service boundary pushed further and further inward, making services more and more granular, until the most primitive building blocks will be services. This would be in line with the historical trend of trading performance for productivity via methodology and abstraction. As an industry, we have always traded performance for productivity. .NET, where every class is treated as a binary component, is slower than COM, but the productivity benefit justifies this. COM itself is orders of magnitude slower than C++, yet developers opted for COM to address the problems of object-orientation. C++ is likewise slower than C, but it did offer the crucial abstractions of objects over functions. C in turn is a lot slower than raw assembly language, but the productivity gains it offered more than made up for that.

My benchmarks show that WCF can easily sustain hundreds of calls per second per class, making it adequate for the vast majority of business applications. While of course there is a performance hit for doing so, the productivity gains more than compensate, and historically, it is evident that this is a trade-off you should make. WCF does have detrimental overhead, but it's to do with ownership, not performance (which is adequate). Imagine a decent-sized application with a few hundred classes, each of which you wish to treat as a service. What would the Main( ) method of such an application look like, with hundreds of service host instances to be instantiated, opened, and closed? Such a Main( ) method would be unmaintainable. Similarly, would a config file with many hundreds of service and client endpoint declarations be workable?

The truth is that in practical terms, WCF cannot support (out of the box) such large-scale granular use. It is designed to be used between applications and across layers in the same application, not in every class. Just as COM had to use C++ and Windows, WCF is bolted on top of .NET. The language used (C# or Visual Basic) is merely component-oriented, not service-oriented, and the platform (.NET) is component-oriented, not service-oriented. What is required is a service-oriented platform, where the basic constructs are not classes but services. The syntax may still define a class, but it will be a service, just as every class in .NET is a binary component, very different from a C++ class. The service-oriented platform will support a config-less metadata repository, much like .NET generalized the type library and IDL concepts of COM. In this regard, WCF is merely a stopgap, a bridging technology between the world of components and the world of service (much like ATL once bridged the world of objects and C++ with the world of components, until .NET stepped in to provide native support for components at the class and primitive level).

A Service-Oriented Platform

If you take a wider view, every new idea in software engineering is implemented in three waves: first there is the methodology, then the technology, then the platform.

For example, object-orientation as a methodology originated in the late '70s. The top C developers at the time did develop object-oriented applications, but this required manually passing state handles between functions and managing tables of function pointers for inheritance. Clearly, such practices required a level of conviction and skills that only very few had. With the advent of C++ in the early '80s came the technology, allowing every developer to write object-oriented applications. But C++ on its own was sterile, and required class libraries. Many developers wrote their own, which of course was not productive or scalable. The development of frameworks such as MFC as an object-oriented platform, with types ranging from strings to windows, is what liberated C++ and enabled it to take off.

Similarly, take component-orientation: in the first half of the '90s, developers who wanted to use COM had to write class factories and implement IUnknown, and concoct registry scripts and DLL entries. As a methodology, COM was just inaccessible. Then ATL came along, and this technology enabled developers to expose mere C++ classes as binary components. But the programming model was still too complex, since Windows knew nothing about COM, and the language was still object-oriented, lacking support for basic constructs such as interfaces. .NET as a component-oriented runtime provided the missing platform support for components at the class, primitive, language, and class library level.

Service-orientation emerged as a methodology in the early 2000s, but at the time it was practically impossible to execute. With WCF, developers can expose mere classes as services, but the ownership overhead prevents widespread and granular use. I do not have a crystal ball, but I see no reason why the waves of methodology/technology/platform should stop now. Extrapolating from the last 30–40 years of software engineering, we are clearly missing a service-oriented platform. I believe the next generation of technologies from Microsoft will provide just that.

Every class as a service

Until we have a service-oriented platform, must we suffer the consequences of either unacceptable ownership overhead (granular use of WCF) or productivity and quality penalties (handcrafted custom plumbing)?

Chapter 1 introduces my InProcFactory class, which lets you instantiate a service class over WCF:

```
public static class InProcFactory
{
    public static I CreateInstance<S,I>() where I : class
                                          where S : I;
    public static void CloseProxy<I>(I instance) where I : class;
    //More members
}
```

When using InProcFactory, you utilize WCF at the class level without ever resorting to explicitly managing the host or having client or service config files:

```
[ServiceContract]
interface IMyContract
{...}

class MyService : IMyContract
{...}

IMyContract proxy = InProcFactory.CreateInstance<MyService,IMyContract>();
proxy.MyMethod();
InProcFactory.CloseProxy(proxy);
```

This line:

```
IMyContract proxy = InProcFactory.CreateInstance<MyService,IMyContract>();
```

is syntactically equivalent to the C# way of instantiating a class type:

```
IMyContract proxy = new MyService();
```

The difference syntax-wise is that with C#, there is no need to specify the queried interfaces since the compiler will examine the class, see if it supports the interface, and implicitly cast the class to the assigned interface variable. As it lacks compiler support for services, InProcFactory requires you to specify the required contract.

However, the big difference between instantiating the class over WCF rather than C# is that when you do this all the powerful WCF features described in the rest of this book kick in: call timeout, encrypted calls, authentication, identity propagation, transaction propagation, transaction voting, instance management, error masking, channel faulting, fault isolation, buffering and throttling, data versioning tolerance, synchronization, synchronization context affinity, and more. With very little effort, you can also add tracing and logging, authorization, security audits, profiling and instrumentation, and durability, or intercept the calls and add many degrees of extensibility and customization.

InProcFactory lets you enjoy the benefits of WCF without suffering the ownership overhead. To me, InProcFactory is more than a useful utility—it is a glimpse of the future.

APPENDIX B

Headers and Contexts

In every method for every call on a .NET object, there are explicit arguments passed in as method parameters and implicit parameters available for the method body. Such implicit parameters include the thread the call executes on (available via `Thread.Current`); the call's app domain (available via `AppDomain.Current`); the call's transactions, if any (available via `Transaction.Current`); the call synchronization context (available via `SynchronizationContext.Current`); the security principal of the call (available via `Thread.CurrentPrincipal`); and even the little-known execution context of the call itself (available via `Thread.CurrentContext`). These *out-of-band* parameters provide in effect the logical execution context of the call, essential for the functioning of the object and .NET itself. But how can you pass additional contextual parameters to your WCF service, forming your own custom context? Such a need is surprisingly common and useful: for example, Chapter 4 uses a custom context to manage the instance IDs of durable services, Chapter 8 uses a custom context to provide the call priority, and Chapter 9 uses a custom context to pass the address of a queued response service. This appendix presents and contrasts two distinct techniques for passing and managing custom contexts, using the message headers or the dedicated context binding. For both options, I will share dedicated helper classes designed to streamline and automate the interaction. You will also see some advanced WCF programming techniques.

Message Headers

Every WCF message contains a collection of outgoing and incoming message headers. When the client wishes to send out-of-band parameters to the service, it does so by adding those parameters to the outgoing headers. The service then reads those parameters from the incoming headers.

The operation context offers collections of incoming and outgoing headers, available via the `IncomingMessageHeaders` and `OutgoingMessageHeaders` properties:

```
public sealed class OperationContext : ...
{
    public MessageHeaders IncomingMessageHeaders
    {get;}

    public MessageHeaders OutgoingMessageHeaders
    {get;}

    //More members
}
```

Each collection is of the type MessageHeaders (that is, a collection of MessageHeader objects):

```
public sealed class MessageHeaders : ...
{
    public void Add(MessageHeader header);
    public T GetHeader<T>(int index);
    public T GetHeader<T>(string name,string ns);
    //More members
}
```

The class MessageHeader is not intended for application developers to interact with directly. Instead, use the MessageHeader<T> class, which provides for type-safe and easy conversion from a CLR type parameter to a message header:

```
public abstract class MessageHeader : ...
{...}

public class MessageHeader<T>
{
    public MessageHeader();
    public MessageHeader(T content);
    public T Content
    {get;set;}
    public MessageHeader GetUntypedHeader(string name,string ns);
    //More members
}
```

You can use any serializable or data contract type as the type parameter for MessageHeader<T>. You construct a MessageHeader<T> around a CLR type, and then use the GetUntypedHeader( ) method to convert it to a MessageHeader and store it in the outgoing headers. GetUntypedHeader( ) requires you to provide it with the generic type parameter name and namespace, which will be used later to look up the header from the headers collection. (Actually, using the name and namespace is just a suggestion; any unique value will do for this purpose. Since the type name and namespace combination tends to be unique, it is commonly used.) You perform the lookup via the GetHeader<T>( ) method of MessageHeaders. Calling GetHeader<T>( ) obtains the value of the type parameter of the MessageHeader<T> used.

Client-Side Header Interaction

As mentioned previously, the client needs to add the parameter to the outgoing headers collection. However, what if the client is not a WCF service, so it does not have an operation context? As it turns out, this doesn't matter if the client is a service, since once the call enters a service, the operation context becomes immutable, so the client cannot write to its outgoing headers even if it has an operation context. The solution for all clients (services and non-services alike) is to create a new operation context and write to its outgoing headers. WCF enables a client to adopt a new operation context via the `OperationContextScope` class, defined as:

```
public sealed class OperationContextScope : IDisposable
{
    public OperationContextScope(IContextChannel channel);
    public OperationContextScope(OperationContext context);
    public void Dispose();
}
```

Using `OperationContextScope` is a general technique for spinning a new context when the one you have is inadequate. The constructor of `OperationContextScope` replaces the current thread's operation context with the new operation context. Calling `Dispose()` on the `OperationContextScope` instance restores the old context (even if it was null). If you do not call `Dispose()`, that may damage other objects on the same thread that expect the previous context. As a result, `OperationContextScope` is designed to be used inside a using statement and provide only a scope of code with a new operation context, even in the face of exceptions (hence its name):

```
using(OperationContextScope scope = new OperationContextScope(...))
{
    //Do work with new context
    ...
}//Restores previous context here
```

When constructing a new `OperationContextScope` instance, you provide its constructor with the inner channel of the proxy used for the call (and thus affect the message). Example B-1 shows the steps required to send an integer to a service in the message headers.

Example B-1. Passing integer in headers by the client

```
[ServiceContract]
interface IMyContract
{
    [OperationContract]
    void MyMethod();
}
class MyContractClient : ClientBase<IMyContract>,IMyContract
{...}

//Client code:
MessageHeader<int> numberHeader = new MessageHeader<int>(123);
```

```
MyContractClient proxy = new MyContractClient( );
using(OperationContextScope contextScope =
                              new OperationContextScope(proxy.InnerChannel))
{
   OperationContext.Current.OutgoingMessageHeaders.Add(
                          numberHeader.GetUntypedHeader("Int32","System"));

   proxy.MyMethod( );
}
proxy.Close( );
```

The client first constructs an instance of `MessageHeader<int>`, initializing it with the value 123. The client then uses the `GetUntypedHeader( )` method to convert the type-safe integer header to a non-type-safe representation, using the integer name and namespace as keys, and add that to the outgoing headers inside a new operation context scope. The call to the service is also inside the scope. After exiting the operation context scope, the client closes the proxy in the original operation context scope (if any).

Service-Side Header Interaction

Example B-2 shows the matching service code required to read the integer from the incoming message headers. Note that the service must know in advance the keys required to look up the number from the headers.

Example B-2. Reading integer from headers by the service

```
class MyService : IMyContract
{
   public void MyMethod( )
   {
      int number = OperationContext.Current.IncomingMessageHeaders.
                                    GetHeader<int>("Int32","System");
      Debug.Assert(number == 123);
   }
}
```

Logically, the service treats the out-of-band integer passed to it as a number context. Any party down the call chain from the service can also read the number context from the operation context.

Encapsulating the Headers

Both the client and the service will benefit greatly from encapsulating the interaction with the message headers by defining a `NumberContext` helper class, as shown in Example B-3.

Example B-3. The NumberContext helper class

```
class NumberContext
{
   public static int Current
   {
      get
      {
         OperationContext context = OperationContext.Current;
         if(context == null)
         {
            return 0;
         }
         return context.IncomingMessageHeaders.GetHeader<int>("Int32","System");
      }
      set
      {
         OperationContext context = OperationContext.Current;
         MessageHeader<int> numberHeader = new MessageHeader<int>(value);
         context.OutgoingMessageHeaders.Add(
                               numberHeader.GetUntypedHeader("Int32","System"));
      }
   }
}
```

Using `NumberContext` mimics the use of any built-in .NET context, since it offers the
Current static property, which gets and sets the appropriate headers collection. Using
NumberContext, Example B-1 is reduced to the code shown in Example B-4.

Example B-4. Using NumberContext by the client

```
MyContractClient proxy = new MyContractClient();
using(OperationContextScope contextScope =
                               new OperationContextScope(proxy.InnerChannel))
{
   NumberContext.Current = 123;

   proxy.MyMethod();
}
proxy.Close();
```

Likewise, Example B-2 is reduced to Example B-5.

Example B-5. Using NumberContext by the service

```
class MyService : IMyContract
{
   public void MyMethod()
   {
      int number = NumberContext.Current;
      Debug.Assert(number == 123);
   }
}
```

The GenericContext<T> helper class

While both Example B-4 and Example B-5 are a marked improvement over direct interaction with the headers, such use of the headers is still problematic, since it involves defining helper classes with repeated, complicated code for every use of message headers as a logical context. The solution is to generalize the technique shown in Example B-3 using a generic type parameter. This is exactly what my GenericContext<T> class, shown in Example B-6, does. GenericContext<T> and the rest of the helper classes in this chapter are available with *ServiceModelEx*.

Example B-6. The GenericContext<T> class

```
[DataContract]
public class GenericContext<T>
{
   [DataMember]
   public readonly T Value;

   internal static string TypeName;
   internal static string TypeNamespace;

   static GenericContext()
   {
      //Verify [DataContract] or [Serializable] on T
      Debug.Assert(IsDataContract(typeof(T)) || typeof(T).IsSerializable);

      TypeNamespace = "net.clr:" + typeof(T).FullName;
      TypeName = "GenericContext";
   }
   static bool IsDataContract(Type type)
   {
      object[] attributes =
                  type.GetCustomAttributes(typeof(DataContractAttribute),false);
      return attributes.Length == 1;
   }

   public GenericContext(T value)
   {
      Value = value;
   }

   public GenericContext() : this(default(T))
   {}
   public static GenericContext<T> Current
   {
      get
      {
         OperationContext context = OperationContext.Current;
         if(context == null)
         {
            return null;
         }
         try
```

Example B-6. The GenericContext<T> class (continued)

```
        {
            return context.IncomingMessageHeaders.
                            GetHeader<GenericContext<T>>(TypeName,TypeNamespace);
        }
        catch
        {
            return null;
        }
    }
    set
    {
        OperationContext context = OperationContext.Current;
        Debug.Assert(context != null);

        //Having multiple GenericContext<T> headers is an error
        bool headerExists = false;
        try
        {
            context.OutgoingMessageHeaders.
                            GetHeader<GenericContext<T>>(TypeName,TypeNamespace);
            headerExists = true;
        }
        catch(MessageHeaderException exception)
        {
            Debug.Assert(exception.Message == "There is not a header with name " +
                                    TypeName + " and namespace " +
                                    TypeNamespace + " in the message.");
        }
        if(headerExists)
        {
            throw new InvalidOperationException("A header with name " + TypeName +
                                        " and namespace " + TypeNamespace +
                                        " already exists in the message.");
        }
        MessageHeader<GenericContext<T>> genericHeader =
                                new MessageHeader<GenericContext<T>>(value);
        context.OutgoingMessageHeaders.Add(
                        genericHeader.GetUntypedHeader(TypeName,TypeNamespace));
    }
  }
}
```

GenericContext<T> lets you treat any serializable or data contract type parameter as a logical context, and its static constructor validates that. The type parameter used is a generic yet type-safe and application-specific custom context. GenericContext<T> uses "GenericContext" for the type name and the full name of T for the namespace to reduce the chance of a conflict. GenericContext<T> also validates that the outgoing headers do not already contain such a type parameter. Both the client and the service can use GenericContext<T> as-is. All a client has to do to pass some custom context to the service is set the static Current property inside a new OperationContextScope:

```
GenericContext<int>.Current = new GenericContext<int>(123);
```

On the service side, to read the value out of the headers, any downstream party can write:

```
int number = GenericContext<int>.Current.Value;
```

Alternatively, you can wrap GenericContext<T> with a dedicated context. Using GenericContext<T>, the NumberContext of Example B-3 is reduced to the code shown in Example B-7.

Example B-7. NumberContext using GenericContext<T>

```
class NumberContext
{
   public static int Current
   {
      get
      {
         return GenericContext<int>.Current.Value;
      }
      set
      {
         GenericContext<int>.Current = new GenericContext<int>(value);
      }
   }
}
```

Streamlining the Client

Even when using GenericContext<T>, the client code (as in Example B-4) is far too raw and exposed, requiring every invocation of the proxy to use an operation context scope. It is better to encapsulate these steps in the proxy itself. The constructors of the proxy should all take additional parameters for the value to pass in the headers. Inside every method, the proxy will create a new operation context and add the value to the outgoing headers collection. This will avoid on every invocation polluting the client code with the interaction with the logical context and the operation context.

Using the same contract definition as in Example B-1, Example B-8 shows such a proxy used to pass an out-of-band number in the message headers.

Example B-8. Encapsulating the headers and the operation context scope

```
class MyContractClient : ClientBase<IMyContract>,IMyContract
{
   readonly int Number;

   public MyContractClient(int number)
   {
      Number = number;
   }
```

```
public MyContractClient(int number,string endpointName) : base(endpointName)
{
   Number = number;
}

//More constructors

public void MyMethod()
{
   using(OperationContextScope contextScope =
                                   new OperationContextScope(InnerChannel))
   {
      NumberContext.Current = Number;

      Channel.MyMethod();
   }
}
}
```

All the constructors of the proxy in Example B-8 accept the number to pass to the service and save it in a read-only variable. The proxy uses the `NumberContext` class of Example B-7 to encapsulate the interaction with the headers.

Using the proxy from Example B-8, the client code from Example B-4 is reduced to:

```
MyContractClient proxy = new MyContractClient(123);
proxy.MyMethod();
proxy.Close();
```

The HeaderClientBase<T,H> proxy class

The problem with the technique demonstrated in Example B-8 is that you would have to repeat such code in every method in the proxy, and for every other proxy that wishes to pass out-of-band parameters. It is therefore preferable to encapsulate these steps further in a dedicated proxy class, and even avoid the interaction with the operation context altogether using message interception. To that end, I wrote `HeaderClientBase<T,H>`, defined in Example B-9.

Example B-9. The HeaderClientBase<T,H> proxy base class

```
public abstract partial class HeaderClientBase<T,H> : InterceptorClientBase<T>
                                                          where T : class
{
   protected H Header
   {get;set;}

   public HeaderClientBase() : this(default(H))
   {}
   public HeaderClientBase(string endpointName) : this(default(H),endpointName)
   {}
```

```
    public HeaderClientBase(H header)
    {
        Header = header;
    }
    public HeaderClientBase(H header,string endpointName) : base(endpointName)
    {
        Header = header;
    }

    //More constructors

    protected override void PreInvoke(ref Message request)
    {
        GenericContext<H> context = new GenericContext<H>(Header);
        MessageHeader<GenericContext<H>> genericHeader =
                                new MessageHeader<GenericContext<H>>(context);
        request.Headers.Add(genericHeader.GetUntypedHeader(
                    GenericContext<H>.TypeName,GenericContext<H>.TypeNamespace));
    }
}
```

The type parameter H can be any serializable or data contract type. In order for you to use it with or without header information, HeaderClientBase<T,H> offers two sets of constructors—one set that accepts a header and one set that does not. The constructors that accept the header store it in the protected Header property. HeaderClientBase<T,H> derives from the InterceptorClientBase<T> class defined in Appendix E as part of a generic interception framework. InterceptorClientBase<T> provides the PreInvoke( ) virtual method where its subclasses can hook the outgoing message and interact with it. The overridden version of PreInvoke( ) creates a new instance of GenericContext<H>, and manually adds it to the request message headers. Note that the value of the header is read every time by accessing the Header property.

Context Bindings

With .NET 3.5, WCF gained three additional bindings dedicated to managing custom contexts. These bindings, found in the *System.WorkflowServices.dll* assembly, are the BasicHttpContextBinding, the NetTcpContextBinding, and the WSHttpContextBinding. The context bindings all derive from their respective regular bindings:

```
    public class BasicHttpContextBinding : BasicHttpBinding
    {
        /* Same constructors as BasicHttpBinding */
    }

    public class NetTcpContextBinding : NetTcpBinding
    {
        /* Same constructors as NetTcpBinding */
    }
```

```
    public ProtectionLevel ContextProtectionLevel
    {get;set;}
}
public class WSHttpContextBinding : WSHttpBinding
{
    /* Same constructors as WSHttpBinding */

    public ProtectionLevel ContextProtectionLevel
    {get;set;}
}
```

In the case of the `NetTcpContextBinding` and the `WSHttpContextBinding`, the `ContextProtectionLevel` indicates how to protect the context while in transfer, as discussed in Chapter 10.

The context bindings are used exactly the same way as their base bindings, yet they add support for a dedicated context management protocol. These bindings can be used with or without a context. The context protocol lets you pass as a custom context a collection of strings in the form of pairs of keys and values, stored implicitly in the message headers. There are several important differences between using a context binding and using the direct message headers for passing out-of-band parameters to a custom context:

- With a context binding, you can only set the information to pass to the service once, before opening the proxy (or using it for the first time). After that, the custom context is cached, and any attempt to modify it results in an error. With the message headers, every call to the services on the same proxy may contain different headers.

- With the context binding, you can only pass as parameters simple strings in the form of a keys/values dictionary. This is a liability when trying to pass composite types that go beyond simple values. With message headers, any serializable or data contract type will do.

- The use of strings means there is inherently no type safety with the context parameters. While this is also true with message headers, my `GenericContext<T>` does restore the missing type safety.

- Out of the box, only a limited set of bindings support the context protocol. Glaringly missing are the IPC and MSMQ bindings. The message headers technique works over any binding.

Client-Side Context Binding Interaction

The client sets the context to send to the service using the `IContextManager` interface:

```
public interface IContextManager
{
    IDictionary<string,string> GetContext();
    void SetContext(IDictionary<string,string> context);
```

```
    bool Enabled
    {get;set;}
}
```

The client obtains the reference to the IContextManager interface by accessing the proxy's inner channel properties:

```
public abstract class ClientBase<T> : ICommunicationObject where T : class
{
    public IClientChannel InnerChannel
    {get;}
    //More members
}
public interface IClientChannel : IContextChannel,...
{...}
public interface IContextChannel : IChannel,...
{...}
public interface IChannel : ICommunicationObject
{
    T GetProperty<T>() where T : class;
}
```

The InnerChannel property supports the IChannel interface, which offers the GetProperty<T>() method:

```
MyContractClient proxy = new MyContractClient();
IContextManager contextManager = proxy.InnerChannel.GetProperty<IContextManager>();
```

Once the client obtains IContextManager, it can copy the current context by calling the GetContext() method. The context is merely a dictionary of strings as keys and values. Since the dictionary returned from GetContext() is a copy of the actual context, the client cannot use it to change the context. Instead, the client needs to call the SetContext() method, providing the new context. The client can override the old context or just add values to the old context and then set it back in, as shown in Example B-10.

Example B-10. Setting the context on the proxy

```
MyContractClient proxy = new MyContractClient();
IContextManager contextManager = proxy.InnerChannel.GetProperty<IContextManager>();

//Just add in, not overwriting dictionary
IDictionary<string,string> context = contextManager.GetContext();
context["NumberContext"] = "123";
contextManager.SetContext(context);

proxy.MyMethod();

proxy.Close();
```

Service-Side Context Binding Interaction

The service reads the context values from the incoming message properties, accessed via the operation context:

```
public sealed class OperationContext : ...
{
   public MessageProperties IncomingMessageProperties
   {
      get;
   }
   //More members
}
```

MessageProperties is a non-type-safe dictionary that accepts a string key and returns the matching object value:

```
public sealed class MessageProperties : IDictionary<string,object>
{...}
```

To obtain the context property, the service uses the static string ContextMessageProperty.Name. This returns an object of the type ContextMessageProperty, defined as:

```
[Serializable]
public class ContextMessageProperty : IMessageProperty
{
   public IDictionary<string,string> Context
   {get;}
   public static string Name
   {get;}

   //More members
}
```

The Context property of ContextMessageProperty is the same dictionary of parameters passed by the client. Example B-11 shows the required service-side steps to read the number context passed in Example B-10.

Example B-11. Reading the context by the service

```
class MyService : IMyContract
{
   public void MyMethod( )
   {
      ContextMessageProperty contextProperty = OperationContext.Current.
                        IncomingMessageProperties[ContextMessageProperty.Name]
                                                  as ContextMessageProperty;

      Debug.Assert(contextProperty.Context.ContainsKey("NumberContext"));

      string number = contextProperty.Context["NumberContext"];

      Debug.Assert(number == "123");
```

Example B-11. Reading the context by the service (continued)
```
   }
}
```

Streamlining the Client

You can streamline the steps required of the client to read or write to the context using my ContextManager static helper class, shown in Example B-12.

Example B-12. Client-side methods of ContextManager
```
public static class ContextManager
{
   public static void SetContext(IClientChannel innerChannel,
                                 string key,string value)
   {
      SetContext(innerChannel,CreateContext(key,value));
   }

   public static void SetContext(IClientChannel innerChannel,
                                 IDictionary<string,string> context)
   {
      IContextManager contextManager = innerChannel.GetProperty<IContextManager>();
      contextManager.SetContext(context);
   }

   public static IDictionary<string,string> CreateContext(string key,string value)
   {
      IDictionary<string,string> context = new Dictionary<string,string>();
      context[key] = value;
      return context;
   }

   public static IDictionary<string,string> UpdateContext(
                                                IClientChannel innerChannel,
                                                string key,string value)
   {
      IContextManager contextManager = innerChannel.GetProperty<IContextManager>();

      IDictionary<string,string> context =
                      new Dictionary<string,string>(contextManager.GetContext());
      context[key] = value;
      return context;
   }

   //Proxy extensions
   public static void SetContext<T>(this ClientBase<T> proxy,
                                    string key,string value) where T : class
   {
      SetContext(proxy.InnerChannel,key,value);
   }
```

```
    public static void SetContext<T>(this ClientBase<T> proxy,
                        IDictionary<string,string> context) where T : class
    {
        SetContext(proxy.InnerChannel,context);
    }
    public static IDictionary<string,string> UpdateContext<T>(
            this ClientBase<T> proxy,string key,string value) where T : class
    {
        return UpdateContext(proxy.InnerChannel,key,value);
    }
}
```

ContextManager offers overloaded versions of the SetContext( ) method that allow the client to set a new context on a proxy's inner channel, using a single key/value pair or a collection of such pairs in a dictionary. These methods are useful both with a proxy class and with a channel factory. ContextManager also exposes setting the context as an extension method on the proxy class. You can use the CreateContext( ) method to create a new dictionary or the UpdateContext( ) method to add a key/value pair to an existing context. Using ContextManager, Example B-10 is reduced to:

```
MyContractClient proxy = new MyContractClient( );
proxy.SetContext("NumberContext","123");
proxy.MyMethod( );
proxy.Close( );
```

However, relying on SetContext( ) this way requires you to explicitly use it upon every instantiation of the proxy. It is better to encapsulate ContextManager in a dedicated proxy class, such as my ContextClientBase<T>:

```
public abstract class ContextClientBase<T> : ClientBase<T> where T : class
{
    public ContextClientBase( );
    public ContextClientBase(string endpointName);
    public ContextClientBase(string key,string value);
    public ContextClientBase(IDictionary<string,string> context);
    public ContextClientBase(string key,string value,string endpointName);
    public ContextClientBase(IDictionary<string,string> context,
                                string endpointName);
    //More constructors
}
```

The constructors of ContextClientBase<T> accept the usual proxy parameters, such as the endpoint name or binding and address, as well as the contextual parameters to send the service (either a single key/value pair, or a collection of keys and values using a dictionary). Your proxy can derive directly from ContextClientBase<T>:

```
class MyContractClient : ContextClientBase<IMyContract>,IMyContract
{
    public MyContractClient(string key,string value) : base(key,value)
    {}
    /* More constructors */
    public void MyMethod( )
```

```
    {
        Channel.MyMethod( );
    }
}
```

Using `ContextClientBase<T>`, Example B-10 is reduced to:

```
MyContractClient proxy = new MyContractClient("NumberContext","123");
proxy.MyMethod( );
proxy.Close( );
```

Example B-13 shows the implementation of `ContextClientBase<T>`.

Example B-13. Implementing ContextClientBase<T>

```
public abstract class ContextClientBase<T> : ClientBase<T> where T : class
{
    public ContextClientBase(string key,string value,string endpointName)
                          : this(ContextManager.CreateContext(key,value),endpointName)
    {}
    public ContextClientBase(IDictionary<string,string> context,string endpointName)
                                                        : base(endpointName)
    {
        SetContext(context);
    }

    /* More constructors */

    void SetContext(IDictionary<string,string> context)
    {
        VerifyContextBinding( );
        ContextManager.SetContext(InnerChannel,context);
    }
    void VerifyContextBinding( )
    {
        BindingElementCollection elements = Endpoint.Binding.CreateBindingElements( );

        if(elements.Contains(typeof(ContextBindingElement)))
        {
            return;
        }

        throw new InvalidOperationException("Can only use context binding");
    }
}
```

A few of the constructors of `ContextClientBase<T>` use `ContextManager` to create a new context and pass it to another constructor, which calls the `SetContext( )` helper method. `SetContext( )` first verifies that the binding used is indeed a context binding and then uses `ContextManager` to set the context. Verifying that the binding indeed supports the context protocol is done by searching for the `ContextBindingElement` in the collection of binding elements. This way of verifying is better than looking at the binding type, since it also works automatically with a custom context binding.

Streamlining the Service

For the service, the `ContextManager` helper class encapsulates the interaction with operation context and message properties. `ContextManager` provides the `GetContext()` method:

```
public static class ContextManager
{
   public static string GetContext(string key);

   //More members
}
```

Using `GetContext()`, the service code in Example B-11 is reduced to:

```
class MyService : IMyContract
{
   public void MyMethod()
   {
      string number = ContextManager.GetContext("NumberContext");

      Debug.Assert(number == "123");
   }
}
```

Example B-14 shows the implementation of `GetContext()`.

Example B-14. Implementing GetContext()

```
public static class ContextManager
{
   public static string GetContext(string key)
   {
      if(OperationContext.Current == null)
      {
         return null;
      }
      if(OperationContext.Current.IncomingMessageProperties.
                                  ContainsKey(ContextMessageProperty.Name))
      {
         ContextMessageProperty contextProperty =
      OperationContext.Current.IncomingMessageProperties[ContextMessageProperty.Name]
                                              as ContextMessageProperty;
         if(contextProperty.Context.ContainsKey(key) == false)
         {
            return null;
         }
         return contextProperty.Context[key];
      }
      else
      {
         return null;
      }
   }
}
```

GetContext( ) is similar to the explicit steps taken in Example B-11, except it adds state and error management. If the context does not contain the request key (or if no context was found), GetContext( ) returns null.

Creating a Custom Context Binding

WCF provides context support for the basic, WS, and TCP bindings. Missing from that list is the IPC binding. It would be valuable to have that support for the IPC binding for custom context support on the same machine. Creating such a custom binding is a worthy exercise, and it serves as a good demonstration of how to write a custom binding.

ServiceModelEx contains the NetNamedPipeContextBinding class, defined as:

```
public class NetNamedPipeContextBinding : NetNamedPipeBinding
{
   /* Same constructors as NetNamedPipeBinding */

   public ProtectionLevel ContextProtectionLevel
   {get;set;}
}
```

NetNamedPipeContextBinding is used exactly like its base class, and you can use it with or without a context. Both the client and the host can use this binding programmatically as-is, by instantiating it like any other built-in binding. However, when using a custom binding in conjunction with a config file, you need to inform WCF where the custom binding is defined.

To that end, *ServiceModelEx* also defines the NetNamedPipeContextBindingElement and NetNamedPipeContextBindingCollectionElement helper classes:

```
public class NetNamedPipeContextBindingElement : NetNamedPipeBindingElement
{
   public NetNamedPipeContextBindingElement();
   public NetNamedPipeContextBindingElement(string name);
   public ProtectionLevel ContextProtectionLevel
   {get;set;}
}
public class NetNamedPipeContextBindingCollectionElement :
                  StandardBindingCollectionElement<NetNamedPipeContextBinding,
                                          NetNamedPipeContextBindingElement>
{}
```

You need to add the type of NetNamedPipeContextBindingCollectionElement and its assembly to the list of binding extensions, naming NetNamedPipeContextBinding as a custom binding. You can do this on a per-application basis by adding it to the application config file. Due to a deficiency in the WCF configuration system, when doing this you must also add a dummy binding configuration section for NetNamedPipeContextBinding, even if no endpoint (client or service) makes use of it.

Example B-15 shows such an application-specific config file for the host side, but you have to enter the same directives in the client's config file as well.

Example B-15. Adding per-application administrative custom binding support

```
<system.serviceModel>
   <extensions>
      <bindingExtensions>
         <add name = "netNamedPipeContextBinding"
            type = "ServiceModelEx.NetNamedPipeContextBindingCollectionElement,
                  ServiceModelEx"
         />
      </bindingExtensions>
   </extensions>

   <services>
      <service name = "...">
         <endpoint
            address = "net.pipe://..."
            binding = "netNamedPipeContextBinding"
            contract = "..."
         />
      </service>
   </services>
   <bindings>
      <netNamedPipeContextBinding>
         <binding name = "ContextIPC"/>
      </netNamedPipeContextBinding>
   </bindings>
</system.serviceModel>
```

Alternatively, you can add NetNamedPipeContextBindingCollectionElement to *machine.config* to affect every application on the machine. In that case, there is no need to list the binding extensions in the client or service config file, and there is no need to add a dummy binding configuration section. Example B-16 shows such a configuration.

Example B-16. Adding machine-wide administrative custom binding support

```
<!--In machine.config-->
<bindingExtensions>
   <add name = "wsHttpContextBinding" type = "..."/>
   <add name = "netTcpContextBinding" type = "..."/>

   <add name = "netNamedPipeContextBinding"
      type = "ServiceModelEx.NetNamedPipeContextBindingCollectionElement,
            ServiceModelEx"
   />
   <!--Additional bindings-->
</bindingExtensions>

<!--In app.config-->
<system.serviceModel>
```

```
    <services>
      <service name = "...">
        <endpoint
           address = "net.pipe://..."
           binding = "netNamedPipeContextBinding"
           contract = "..."
        />
      </service>
    </services>
</system.serviceModel>
```

Of course, you can configure a binding section to customize any property of NetNamedPipeContextBinding, whether it comes from NetNamedPipeBinding or from NetNamedPipeContextBinding:

```
    <bindings>
      <netNamedPipeContextBinding>
         <binding name = "TransactionalContextIPC"
            contextProtectionLevel = "EncryptAndSign"
            transactionFlow = "True"
         />
      </netNamedPipeContextBinding>
    </bindings>
```

Implementing NetNamedPipeContextBinding

Example B-17 lists the implementation of NetNamedPipeContextBinding and its supporting classes.

Example B-17. Implementing NetNamedPipeContextBinding

```
public class NetNamedPipeContextBinding : NetNamedPipeBinding
{
   internal const string SectionName = "netNamedPipeContextBinding";

   public ProtectionLevel ContextProtectionLevel
   {get;set;}

   public NetNamedPipeContextBinding()
   {
      ContextProtectionLevel = ProtectionLevel.EncryptAndSign;
   }
   public NetNamedPipeContextBinding(NetNamedPipeSecurityMode securityMode) :
                                                    base(securityMode)
   {
      ContextProtectionLevel = ProtectionLevel.EncryptAndSign;
   }
   public NetNamedPipeContextBinding(string configurationName)
   {
      ContextProtectionLevel = ProtectionLevel.EncryptAndSign;
      ApplyConfiguration(configurationName);
   }
```

```csharp
public override BindingElementCollection CreateBindingElements()
{
    BindingElement element = new ContextBindingElement(ContextProtectionLevel,
                                   ContextExchangeMechanism.ContextSoapHeader);

    BindingElementCollection elements = base.CreateBindingElements();
    elements.Insert(0,element);

    return elements;
}

void ApplyConfiguration(string configurationName)
{
    Configuration config =
          ConfigurationManager.OpenExeConfiguration(ConfigurationUserLevel.None);
    ServiceModelSectionGroup sectionGroup =
                          ServiceModelSectionGroup.GetSectionGroup(config);

    BindingsSection bindings = sectionGroup.Bindings;

    NetNamedPipeContextBindingCollectionElement section =
            (NetNamedPipeContextBindingCollectionElement)bindings[SectionName];

    NetNamedPipeContextBindingElement element =
                                    section.Bindings[configurationName];
    if(element == null)
    {
        throw new ConfigurationErrorsException();
    }
    else
    {
        element.ApplyConfiguration(this);
    }
}
}
public class NetNamedPipeContextBindingElement : NetNamedPipeBindingElement
{
    const string ContextProtectionLevelName = "contextProtectionLevel";

    public NetNamedPipeContextBindingElement()
    {
        Initialize();
    }
    public NetNamedPipeContextBindingElement(string name) : base(name)
    {
        Initialize();
    }
```

```
    void Initialize( )
    {
        ConfigurationProperty property =
                               new ConfigurationProperty(ContextProtectionLevelName,
                                                     typeof(ProtectionLevel),
                                             ProtectionLevel.EncryptAndSign);
        Properties.Add(property);

        ContextProtectionLevel = ProtectionLevel.EncryptAndSign;
    }
    protected override void OnApplyConfiguration(Binding binding)
    {
        base.OnApplyConfiguration(binding);

        NetNamedPipeContextBinding netNamedPipeContextBinding =
                                       binding as NetNamedPipeContextBinding;
        Debug.Assert(netNamedPipeContextBinding != null);

        netNamedPipeContextBinding.ContextProtectionLevel = ContextProtectionLevel;
    }
    protected override Type BindingElementType
    {
        get
        {
            return typeof(NetNamedPipeContextBinding);
        }
    }

    public ProtectionLevel ContextProtectionLevel
    {
        get
        {
            return (ProtectionLevel)base[ContextProtectionLevelName];
        }
        set
        {
            base[ContextProtectionLevelName] = value;
        }
    }
}

public class NetNamedPipeContextBindingCollectionElement :
                                   StandardBindingCollectionElement
              <NetNamedPipeContextBinding,NetNamedPipeContextBindingElement>
{}
```

The constructors of `NetNamedPipeContextBinding` all delegate the actual construction to the base constructors of `NetNamedPipeBinding`, and the only initialization they do is setting the context protection level to default to `ProtectionLevel.EncryptAndSign`.

The heart of any binding class is the CreateBindingElements( ) method. NetNamedPipeContextBinding accesses its base binding collection of binding elements and adds to it the ContextBindingElement. Inserting this element into the collection adds support for the context protocol. The rest of Example B-17 is mere bookkeeping to enable administrative configuration. The ApplyConfiguration( ) method is called by the constructor, which takes the binding section configuration name. ApplyConfiguration( ) uses the ConfigurationManager class (discussed in Chapter 9) to parse out of the config file the netNamedPipeContextBinding section, and from it an instance of NetNamedPipeContextBindingElement. That binding element is then used to configure the binding instance by calling its ApplyConfiguration( ) method. The constructors of NetNamedPipeContextBindingElement add to its base class Properties collection of configuration properties a single property for the context protection level. In OnApplyConfiguration( ) (which is called as a result of calling ApplyConfiguration( ) on NetNamedPipeBindingElement by NetNamedPipeContextBinding. ApplyConfiguration( )), the method first configures its base element and then sets the context protection level according to the configured level.

The NetNamedPipeContextBindingCollectionElement type is used to bind NetNamedPipeContextBinding with the NetNamedPipeContextBindingElement. This way, when adding NetNamedPipeContextBindingCollectionElement as a binding extension, the configuration manager knows which type to instantiate and provide with the binding parameters.

 Since you can use NetNamedPipeContextBinding with or without a context, the InProcFactory class presented in Chapter 1 actually uses the NetNamedPipeContextBinding to enable transparent support for custom contexts if required.

Publish-Subscribe Service

Using raw duplex callbacks for events has numerous drawbacks. The primary concern is that it often introduces too much coupling between the publisher and the subscribers. The subscriber has to know where all the publishing services are in the application and connect to them. Any publisher that the subscriber is unaware of will not be able to notify the subscriber of events. This in turn makes adding new subscribers (or removing existing ones) difficult in an already deployed application. There is no way for a subscriber to ask to be notified whenever anyone in the application raises a particular type of event. In addition, the subscriber must make multiple, potentially expensive calls to each publisher, both to subscribe and to unsubscribe. Different publishers may fire the same event but offer slightly different ways to subscribe and unsubscribe, which of course couples the subscribers to those methods.

Much the same way, the publisher can only send notifications to subscribers it knows about. There is no way for the publisher to deliver an event to whomever wishes to receive it, or to broadcast an event. In addition, all publishers must have the necessary code to manage the list of subscribers and the publishing act itself. This code has almost nothing to do with the business problem the service is designed to solve, and it can get fairly complex if advanced features such as concurrent publishing are employed. Since the publishers cannot assume the subscribers are all disciplined (i.e., do not take long to process the event), they must publish concurrently on multiple threads. To avoid maxing out the system when there are many subscribers, the publisher needs to multiplex the events on threads from a thread pool. Such publishing logic is not trivial, yet all publishers will have to have it.

Furthermore, duplex-based callbacks introduce coupling between the lifetime of the publisher and the subscribers. The subscribers have to be up and running in order to subscribe to and receive events.

There is no way for a subscriber to ask that if an event is fired, the application should create an instance of the subscriber and let it handle the event. Since proxy references are nonserializable, they must reside in memory in some form of list. If the publisher's process (or host machine) crashes, the subscriptions will be lost, yet none of the subscribers will be aware of that.

Security represents yet another dimension of coupling: the subscribers need to be able to authenticate themselves against all publishers, across all security modes and credentials used. The publisher must also have enough security credentials be allowed to fire the event, and different subscribers may have different role membership mechanisms.

Finally, setting up subscriptions has to be done programmatically. There is no easy administrative way to configure subscriptions in the application or administratively change the subscriber's preferences when the system is running.

These problems are not actually specific to WCF duplex calls. They also characterize past technologies, such as COM connection points and .NET delegates—all are tightly coupled event-management mechanisms that rely on object references.

The Publish-Subscribe Design Pattern

The solution to the problems just described is to design around them using what is known as the *publish-subscribe* design pattern. The idea behind the pattern is a simple one: decouple the publishers from the subscribers by introducing a dedicated subscription service and a dedicated publishing service in between, as shown in Figure C-1.

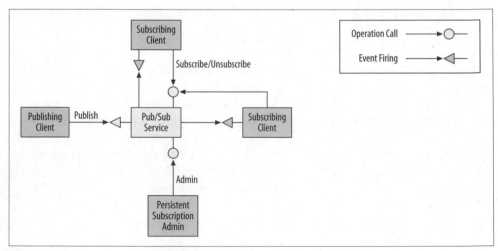

Figure C-1. A publish-subscribe system

Subscribers that want to subscribe to events register with the subscription service, which manages the lists of subscribers (and provides a similar ability to unsubscribe). Similarly, all publishers use the publisher service to fire their events, and avoid delivering the events directly to the subscribers. The subscription and publishing services provide a layer of indirection that decouples your system. No longer do the subscribers have any knowledge about the identity of the publishers—they can subscribe to a type of event and will receive that event from any publisher. The subscription mechanism is uniform across all publishers. In fact, no publisher has to manage any subscription list, and the publishers have no idea who the subscribers are. They simply deliver the events to the publishing service, to be delivered to any interested subscriber.

Subscriber Types

You can even define two types of subscribers: *transient subscribers* are in-memory running subscribers, and *persistent subscribers* are subscribers that persist on the disk, representing services to invoke when the event takes place. For transient subscribers, you can use the duplex callback mechanism as a handy way of passing the callback reference to the running service. For the persistent subscribers, all you really need to record is the subscriber address as a reference. When the event is raised, the publishing service will call to the persistent subscriber address and deliver the event to it. Another important distinction between the two types of subscriptions is that you can store a persistent subscription on the disk or in a database. Doing so will persist the subscription across application shutdowns or machine crashes and reboots, thus enabling administrative configuration: the subscriber is persistent and the subscription is persistent. Obviously, you cannot save transient subscriptions across an application shutdown, and you will need to set them up explicitly every time the application starts: the subscriber is transient, and so is the subscription.

The Publish-Subscribe Framework

ServiceModelEx contains a simple-to-use, industrial-strength publish-subscribe framework. I wanted to provide not just a publish-subscribe service, but also a general-purpose framework that automates implementing such services and adding the support for any application in just one line of code (if that). The first step in building the framework was to factor the publish-subscribe management interfaces and provide separate contracts for transient and persistent subscriptions and for publishing.*

Managing Transient Subscriptions

For managing transient subscriptions, I defined the ISubscriptionService interface shown in Example C-1.

---

* I first published my publish-subscribe framework in my article "WCF Essentials: What You Need to Know About One-Way Calls, Callbacks, and Events" (*MSDN Magazine*, October 2006).

Example C-1. The ISubscriptionService interface manages transient subscribers

```
[ServiceContract]
public interface ISubscriptionService
{
   [OperationContract]
   void Subscribe(string eventOperation);

   [OperationContract]
   void Unsubscribe(string eventOperation);
}
```

Note that ISubscriptionService does not identify the callback contract its implementing endpoint expects. Being a general-purpose interface, it is unaware of particular callback contracts. It is up to the using application to define those callback contracts. The callback interface is provided in the using application by deriving from ISubscriptionService and specifying the desired callback contract:

```
public interface IMyEvents
{
   [OperationContract(IsOneWay = true)]
   void OnEvent1();

   [OperationContract(IsOneWay = true)]
   void OnEvent2(int number);

   [OperationContract(IsOneWay = true)]
   void OnEvent3(int number,string text);
}

[ServiceContract(CallbackContract = typeof(IMyEvents))]
public interface IMySubscriptionService : ISubscriptionService
{}
```

Typically, every operation on the callback contract corresponds to a specific event. The subinterface of ISubscriptionService (IMySubscriptionService, in this example) does not need to add operations. The transient subscription management functionality is provided by ISubscriptionService. In each call to Subscribe() or Unsubscribe(), the subscriber needs to provide the name of the operation (and therefore the event) it wants to subscribe to or unsubscribe from. If the caller wishes to subscribe to all events, it can pass an empty or null string.

My framework offers an implementation for the methods of ISubscriptionService in the form of the generic abstract class SubscriptionManager<T>:

```
public abstract class SubscriptionManager<T> where T : class
{
   public void Subscribe(string eventOperation);
   public void Unsubscribe(string eventOperation);
   //More members
}
```

The generic type parameter for SubscriptionManager<T> is the events contract. Note that SubscriptionManager<T> does not implement ISubscriptionService.

The using application needs to expose its own transient subscription service in the form of an endpoint that supports its specific subinterface of ISubscriptionService. To do so, the application needs to provide a service class that derives from SubscriptionManager<T>, specify the callback contract as a type parameter, and derive from that specific subinterface of ISubscriptionService. For example, to implement a transient subscription service using the IMyEvents callback interface:

```
[ServiceBehavior(InstanceContextMode = InstanceContextMode.PerCall)]
class MySubscriptionService : SubscriptionManager<IMyEvents>,IMySubscriptionService
{}
```

MySubscriptionService doesn't need any code because IMySubscriptionService does not add any new operations, and SubscriptionManager<T> already implements the methods of ISubscriptionService.

Note that just deriving from SubscriptionManager<IMyEvents> is insufficient because it does not derive from a contract interface—you must add the derivation from IMySubscriptionService to support transient subscriptions.

Finally, the using application needs to define an endpoint for IMySubscriptionService:

```
<services>
   <service name = "MySubscriptionService">
      <endpoint
         address  = "..."
         binding  = "..."
         contract = "IMySubscriptionService"
      />
   </service>
</services>
```

Example C-2 shows how SubscriptionManager<T> manages transient subscriptions.

Example C-2. The transient subscribers management in SubscriptionManager<T>

```
public abstract class SubscriptionManager<T> where T : class
{
   static Dictionary<string,List<T>> m_TransientStore;

   static SubscriptionManager()
   {
      m_TransientStore = new Dictionary<string,List<T>>();
      string[] methods = GetOperations();
      Action<string> insert = (methodName)=>
                              {
                                 m_TransientStore.Add(methodName,new List<T>());
                              };
      methods.ForEach(insert);
   }
```

```
static string[] GetOperations()
{
   MethodInfo[] methods = typeof(T).GetMethods(BindingFlags.Public|
                                               BindingFlags.FlattenHierarchy|
                                               BindingFlags.Instance);
   List<string> operations = new List<string>(methods.Length);

   Action<MethodInfo> add = (method)=>
                            {
                                Debug.Assert(!operations.Contains(method.Name));
                                operations.Add(method.Name);
                            };
   methods.ForEach(add);
   return operations.ToArray();
}
static void AddTransient(T subscriber,string eventOperation)
{
   lock(typeof(SubscriptionManager<T>))
   {
      List<T> list = m_TransientStore[eventOperation];
      if(list.Contains(subscriber))
      {
         return;
      }
      list.Add(subscriber);
   }
}
static void RemoveTransient(T subscriber,string eventOperation)
{
   lock(typeof(SubscriptionManager<T>))
   {
      List<T> list = m_TransientStore[eventOperation];
      list.Remove(subscriber);
   }
}

public void Subscribe(string eventOperation)
{
   lock(typeof(SubscriptionManager<T>))
   {
      T subscriber = OperationContext.Current.GetCallbackChannel<T>();
      if(String.IsNullOrEmpty(eventOperation) == false)
      {
         AddTransient(subscriber,eventOperation);
      }
      else
      {
         string[] methods = GetOperations();
         Action<string> addTransient = (methodName)=>
                                       {
                                           AddTransient(subscriber,methodName);
                                       };
```

```
            methods.ForEach(addTransient);
        }
    }
}

public void Unsubscribe(string eventOperation)
{
    lock(typeof(SubscriptionManager<T>))
    {
        T subscriber = OperationContext.Current.GetCallbackChannel<T>( );
        if(String.IsNullOrEmpty(eventOperation) == false)
        {
            RemoveTransient(subscriber,eventOperation);
        }
        else
        {
            string[] methods = GetOperations( );
            Action<string> removeTransient = (methodName)=>
                                            {
                                            RemoveTransient(subscriber,methodName);
                                            };
            methods.ForEach(removeTransient);
        }
    }
}
//More members
}
```

SubscriptionManager<T> stores the transient subscribers in a generic static dictionary called m_TransientStore:

```
    static Dictionary<string,List<T>> m_TransientStore;
```

Each entry in the dictionary contains the name of the event operation and all its subscribers in the form of a linked list. The static constructor of SubscriptionManager<T> uses reflection to get all the operations of the callback interfaces (the type parameter for SubscriptionManager<T>) and initializes the dictionary to have all the operations with empty lists. The Subscribe( ) method extracts the callback reference from the operation call context. If the caller specifies an operation name, Subscribe( ) calls the helper method AddTransient( ). AddTransient( ) retrieves the list of subscribers for the event from the store, and if the list does not contain the subscriber, it adds it in.

If the caller specifies an empty string or null for the operation name, Subscribe( ) calls AddTransient( ) for each operation in the callback contract.

Unsubscribe( ) operates in a similar manner. Note that the caller can subscribe to all events and then unsubscribe from a particular one.

Managing Persistent Subscribers

For managing persistent subscribers, I defined the IPersistentSubscriptionService interface shown in Example C-3.

Example C-3. The IPersistentSubscriptionService interface manages persistent subscribers

```
[ServiceContract]
public interface IPersistentSubscriptionService
{
   [OperationContract]
   [TransactionFlow(TransactionFlowOption.Allowed)]
   void Subscribe(string address,string eventsContract,string eventOperation);

   [OperationContract]
   [TransactionFlow(TransactionFlowOption.Allowed)]
   void Unsubscribe(string address,string eventsContract,string eventOperation);
   //More members
}
```

To add a persistent subscriber, the caller needs to call Subscribe( ), providing the address of the subscriber, the event's contract name, and the specific event operation itself. To unsubscribe, the caller calls Unsubscribe( ) with the same information. Note that IPersistentSubscriptionService does not imply in any way where the subscribers persist on the service side—that is an implementation detail.

The class SubscriptionManager<T>, presented previously, also implements the methods of IPersistentSubscriptionService:

```
[BindingRequirement(TransactionFlowEnabled = true)]
public abstract class SubscriptionManager<T> where T : class
{
   public void Unsubscribe(string address,string eventsContract,
                           string eventOperation);
   public void Subscribe(string address,string eventsContract,
                         string eventOperation);
   //More members
}
```

SubscriptionManager<T> stores the persistent subscribers in SQL Server. It is configured to use the Client/Service transaction mode (presented in Chapter 7), and it enforces that mode using my BindingRequirement attribute.

The generic type parameter for SubscriptionManager<T> is the events contract. Note that SubscriptionManager<T> does not derive from IPersistentSubscriptionService. The using application needs to expose its own persistent subscription service, but there is no need to derive a new contract from IPersistentSubscriptionService because no callback references are required. The application simply derives from SubscriptionManager<T>, specifying the events contract as a type parameter and adding a derivation from IPersistentSubscriptionService. For example:

```
[ServiceBehavior(InstanceContextMode = InstanceContextMode.PerCall)]
class MySubscriptionService : SubscriptionManager<IMyEvents>,
                                          IPersistentSubscriptionService
{}
```

There's no need for any code in MySubscriptionService because SubscriptionManager<T> already implements the methods of IPersistentSubscriptionService.

Note that just deriving from SubscriptionManager<IMyEvents> is insufficient, because SubscriptionManager<IMyEvents> does not derive from a contract interface—you must add the derivation from IPersistentSubscriptionService to support persistent subscriptions.

Finally, the application needs to define an endpoint for IPersistentSubscriptionService:

```
<services>
   <service name = "MySubscriptionService">
      <endpoint
         address  = "..."
         binding  = "..."
         contract = "IPersistentSubscriptionService"
      />
   </service>
</services>
```

The implementation of the methods of IPersistentSubscriptionService by SubscriptionManager<T> is shown in Example C-4. Example C-4 is very similar to Example C-2, except the subscribers are stored in SQL Server, not in memory in a dictionary.

Example C-4. Persistent subscriber management in SubscriptionManager<T>

```
public abstract class SubscriptionManager<T> where T : class
{
   static void AddPersistent(string address,string eventsContract,
                             string eventOperation)
   {
      //Store the subscription in SQL Server
   }

   static void RemovePersistent(string address,string eventsContract,
                                string eventOperation)
   {
      //Remove the subscription from SQL Server
   }

   [OperationBehavior(TransactionScopeRequired = true)]
   public void Subscribe(string address,string eventsContract,
                         string eventOperation)
   {
```

```
        if(String.IsNullOrEmpty(eventOperation) == false)
        {
            AddPersistent(address,eventsContract,eventOperation);
        }
        else
        {
            string[] methods = GetOperations();
            Action<string> addPersistent = (methodName)=>
                                    {
                                    AddPersistent(address,eventsContract,methodName);
                                    };
            methods.ForEach(addPersistent);
        }
    }

    [OperationBehavior(TransactionScopeRequired = true)]
    public void Unsubscribe(string address,string eventsContract,
                            string eventOperation)
    {
        if(String.IsNullOrEmpty(eventOperation) == false)
        {
            RemovePersistent(address,eventsContract,eventOperation);
        }
        else
        {
            string[] methods = GetOperations();
            Action<string> removePersistent = (methodName)=>
                                    {
                                    RemovePersistent(address,eventsContract,methodName);
                                    };
            methods.ForEach(removePersistent);
        }
    }
    //More members
}
```

If the application wants to support both transient and persistent subscribers for the same events contract, simply derive the subscription service class from both the specialized subinterface of ISubscriptionService and IPersistentSubscriptionService:

```
[ServiceBehavior(InstanceContextMode = InstanceContextMode.PerCall)]
class MySubscriptionService : SubscriptionManager<IMyEvents>,
                          IMySubscriptionService,IPersistentSubscriptionService
{}
```

and expose the two matching endpoints:

```
<services>
   <service name = "MySubscriptionService">
      <endpoint
         address  = "..."
         binding  = "..."
         contract = "IMySubscriptionService"
      />
```

```
            <endpoint
                address  = "..."
                binding  = "..."
                contract = "IPersistentSubscriptionService"
            />
        </service>
    </services>
```

Event Publishing

The parts of the publish-subscribe framework shown so far have dealt only with the aspects of subscription management. The framework also enables easy implementation of the publishing service. The publishing service should support the same events contract as the subscribers, and it should be the only point of contact known to the publishers in the application. Because the publishing service exposes the events contract in an endpoint, you need to mark the events contract as a service contract, even if you only use it for duplex callbacks with transient subscribers:

```
[ServiceContract]
public interface IMyEvents
{
    [OperationContract(IsOneWay = true)]
    void OnEvent1( );

    [OperationContract(IsOneWay = true)]
    void OnEvent2(int number);

    [OperationContract(IsOneWay = true)]
    void OnEvent3(int number,string text);
}
```

The publish-subscribe framework contains the helper class PublishService<T>, defined as:

```
public abstract class PublishService<T> where T : class
{
    protected static void FireEvent(params object[] args);
}
```

PublishService<T> requires as a type parameter the type of the events contract. To provide your own publishing service, derive from PublishService<T> and use the FireEvent( ) method to deliver the event to all subscribers, be they transient or persistent, as shown in Example C-5.

Example C-5. Implementing an event-publishing service

```
[ServiceBehavior(InstanceContextMode = InstanceContextMode.PerCall)]
class MyPublishService : PublishService<IMyEvents>,IMyEvents
{
    public void OnEvent1( )
    {
        FireEvent( );
    }
}
```

Example C-5. Implementing an event-publishing service (continued)

```
    public void OnEvent2(int number)
    {
        FireEvent(number);
    }
    public void OnEvent3(int number,string text)
    {
        FireEvent(number,text);
    }
}
```

Note that you can use FireEvent( ) to fire any type of event, regardless of the parameters, because of the use of the params object array.

Finally, the application needs to expose an endpoint for the publishing service with the events contract:

```
<services>
    <service name = "MyPublishService">
        <endpoint
            address  = "..."
            binding  = "..."
            contract = "IMyEvents"
        />
    </service>
</services>
```

Example C-6 shows the implementation of PublishService<T>.

Example C-6. Implementing PublishService<T>

```
public abstract class PublishService<T> where T : class
{
    protected static void FireEvent(params object[] args)
    {
        string action = OperationContext.Current.IncomingMessageHeaders.Action;
        string[] slashes = action.Split('/');
        string methodName = slashes[slashes.Length-1];

        FireEvent(methodName,args);
    }
    static void FireEvent(string methodName,params object[] args)
    {
        PublishPersistent(methodName,args);
        PublishTransient(methodName,args);
    }
    static void PublishPersistent(string methodName,params object[] args)
    {
        T[] subscribers = SubscriptionManager<T>.GetPersistentList(methodName);
        Publish(subscribers,true,methodName,args);
    }
```

Example C-6. Implementing PublishService<T> (continued)

```
   static void PublishTransient(string methodName,params object[] args)
   {
      T[] subscribers = SubscriptionManager<T>.GetTransientList(methodName);
      Publish(subscribers,false,methodName,args);
   }
   static void Publish(T[] subscribers,bool closeSubscribers,string methodName,
                                                     params object[] args)
   {
      WaitCallback fire = (subscriber)=>
                          {
                             Invoke(subscriber as T,methodName,args);
                             if(closeSubscribers)
                             {
                                using(subscriber as IDisposable)
                                {}
                             }
                          };
      Action<T> queueUp = (subscriber)=>
                          {
                             ThreadPool.QueueUserWorkItem(fire,subscriber);
                          };
      subscribers.ForEach(queueUp);
   }
   static void Invoke(T subscriber,string methodName,object[] args)
   {
      Debug.Assert(subscriber != null);
      Type type = typeof(T);
      MethodInfo methodInfo = type.GetMethod(methodName);
      try
      {
         methodInfo.Invoke(subscriber,args);
      }
      catch
      {}
   }
}
```

To simplify firing the event, the FireEvent( ) method accepts the parameters to pass to the subscribers—yet its caller does not provide it with the name of the operation to invoke on the subscribers. Instead, FireEvent( ) extracts the method name from the incoming message headers. It then uses an overloaded FireEvent( ) that accepts the method name. That method in turn uses the helper method PublishPersistent( ) to publish to all persistent subscribers, and the PublishTransient( ) helper method to publish to all transient subscribers. The publishing methods operate in an almost identical way: they access SubscriptionManager<T> to retrieve their respective subscribers list, and then use the Publish( ) method to fire the event. The subscribers are returned in the form of an array of proxies to the subscribers, which is passed to the Publish( ) method.

Publish( ) could have simply invoked the subscribers at this point. However, I wanted to support concurrent publishing of events, so that if any subscriber is undisciplined and takes a long time to process the event, this will not preclude the other subscribers from receiving the event in a timely manner. Having the event operations marked as one-way is no guarantee of asynchronous invocation, and besides, I wanted to support concurrent publishing even when the event operation is not marked as a one-way operation. Publish( ) defines two anonymous methods. The first calls the Invoke( ) helper method, which fires the event to the individual subscriber provided and then closes the proxy if so specified. Because Invoke( ) was never compiled against the specific subscriber type, it uses reflection and late binding for the invocation. Invoke( ) also suppresses any exceptions raised by the invocation, because these are of no interest to the publishing party. The second anonymous method queues up the first anonymous method to be executed by a thread from the thread pool. Finally, Publish( ) invokes the second anonymous method on every subscriber in the provided array.

Note how uniformly PublishService<T> treats the subscribers—it almost does not matter if they are transient or persistent. The only difference is that after publishing to a persistent subscriber, you need to close the proxy. This uniformity is achieved by the helper methods GetTransientList( ) and GetPersistentList( ) of SubscriptionManager<T>. Of these two, GetTransientList( ) is the simpler one:

```
public abstract class SubscriptionManager<T> where T : class
{
    internal static T[] GetTransientList(string eventOperation)
    {
        lock(typeof(SubscriptionManager<T>))
        {
            if(m_TransientStore.ContainsKey(eventOperation))
            {
                List<T> list = m_TransientStore[eventOperation];
                return list.ToArray();
            }
            return new T[]{};
        }
    }
    //More members
}
```

GetTransientList( ) looks up in the transient store all the subscribers to the specified operation and returns them as an array. GetPersistentList( ) faces a bigger challenge: there is no ready-made list of proxies to persistent subscribers; the only thing known about them is their addresses. GetPersistentList( ) therefore needs to instantiate the persistent subscribers' proxies, as shown in Example C-7.

Example C-7. Creating the persistent subscribers proxy list

```
public abstract class SubscriptionManager<T> where T : class
{
   internal static T[] GetPersistentList(string eventOperation)
   {
      string[] addresses =  GetSubscribersToContractEventOperation(
                                          typeof(T).ToString( ),eventOperation);

      List<T> subscribers = new List<T>(addresses.Length);

      foreach(string address in addresses)
      {
         Binding binding = GetBindingFromAddress(address);
         T proxy = ChannelFactory<T>.CreateChannel(binding,
                                          new EndpointAddress(address));
         subscribers.Add(proxy);
      }
      return subscribers.ToArray( );
   }
   static string[] GetSubscribersToContractEventOperation(string eventsContract,
                                                string eventOperation)
   {
      //Query SQL Server for the subscribers to the event
   }
   static Binding GetBindingFromAddress(string address)
   {
      if(address.StartsWith("http:") || address.StartsWith("https:"))
      {
         WSHttpBinding binding = new WSHttpBinding( );
         binding.ReliableSession.Enabled = true;
         binding.TransactionFlow = true;
         return binding;
      }
      if(address.StartsWith("net.tcp:"))
      {
         NetTcpBinding binding = new NetTcpBinding( );
         binding.ReliableSession.Enabled = true;
         binding.TransactionFlow = true;
         return binding;
      }
      /* Similar code for the IPC and MSMQ bindings */
      Debug.Assert(false,"Unsupported binding specified");
      return null;
   }
   //More members
}
```

To create a proxy for each subscriber, `GetPersistentList( )` needs the subscriber's address, binding, and contract. The contract is, of course, the type parameter for `SubscriptionManager<T>`. To obtain the addresses `GetPersistentList( )` calls

GetSubscribersToContractEventOperation( ), which queries the subscribers store and returns as an array the addresses of all of the persistent subscribers who have subscribed to the specified event. All GetPersistentList( ) needs now is the binding used by each subscriber. For that GetPersistentList( ) calls the helper method GetBindingFromAddress( ), which infers the binding to use from the address schema. GetBindingFromAddress( ) treats all HTTP addresses as indicating use of the WSHttpBinding. In addition, GetBindingFromAddress( ) turns on reliability and transaction propagation for each binding, to enable including the event in the publisher's transaction when one-way operations are not used, such as with this events contract:

```
[ServiceContract]
interface IMyEvents
{
   [OperationContract]
   [TransactionFlow(TransactionFlowOption.Allowed)]
   void OnEvent1( );

   [OperationContract]
   [TransactionFlow(TransactionFlowOption.Allowed)]
   void OnEvent2(int number);

   [OperationContract]
   [TransactionFlow(TransactionFlowOption.Allowed)]
   void OnEvent3(int number,string text);
}
```

Administering Persistent Subscribers

While you can add and remove persistent subscriptions at runtime by using the methods of the IPersistentSubscriptionService interface shown in Example C-3, because of their persistent nature, managing the subscriptions is best done via some kind of administration tool. To that end, IPersistentSubscriptionService defines additional operations that answer various queries against the subscribers store, as shown in Example C-8.

Example C-8. The IPersistentSubscriptionService interface

```
[DataContract]
public struct PersistentSubscription
{
   [DataMember]
   public string Address
   {get;set;}

   [DataMember]
   public string EventsContract
   {get;set;}
```

Example C-8. The IPersistentSubscriptionService interface (continued)

```
    [DataMember]
    public string EventOperation
    {get;set;}
}

[ServiceContract]
public interface IPersistentSubscriptionService
{
    //Administration operations
    [OperationContract]
    [TransactionFlow(TransactionFlowOption.Allowed)]
    PersistentSubscription[] GetAllSubscribers();

    [OperationContract]
    [TransactionFlow(TransactionFlowOption.Allowed)]
    PersistentSubscription[] GetSubscribersToContract(string eventsContract);

    [OperationContract]
    [TransactionFlow(TransactionFlowOption.Allowed)]
    string[] GetSubscribersToContractEventType(string eventsContract,
                                               string eventOperation);
    [OperationContract]
    [TransactionFlow(TransactionFlowOption.Allowed)]
    PersistentSubscription[] GetAllSubscribersFromAddress(string address);
    //More members
}
```

All of these administration operations utilize a simple data contract called `PersistentSubscription`, which contains the address of the subscriber, the subscribed contract, and the event. `GetAllSubscribers()` simply returns the list of all subscribers. `GetSubscribersToContract()` returns all subscribers to a specific contract, and `GetSubscribersToContractEventType()` returns all subscribers to a particular event operation on a specified contract. Finally, for the sake of completeness, `GetAllSubscribersFromAddress()` returns all subscribers that provided a specified address.

My publish-subscribe framework includes a sample persistent subscription administration tool called Persistent Subscription Manager, shown in Figure C-2.

The administration tool uses `IPersistentSubscriptionService` to add and remove subscriptions. To add a new subscription, you need to provide it with the metadata exchange address of the events contract definition. You can use the metadata exchange address of the persistent subscriber itself or the metadata exchange address of the publishing service (such as the one shown in Example C-5), because they are polymorphic. Enter the metadata exchange base address in the MEX Address text box and click the Lookup button. The tool will programmatically retrieve the metadata of the event service and populate the Contract and Event combo boxes. Retrieving the metadata and parsing its content is done using my `MetadataHelper` class, presented in Chapter 2.

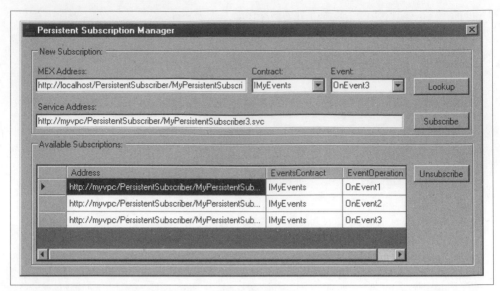

Figure C-2. The Persistent Subscription Manager application

Once you've provided the address of the persistent subscriber, click the Subscribe button. Persistent Subscription Manager then adds the subscription by calling to the subscription service (`MySubscriptionService` in the examples so far). The address for the subscription service is maintained in the Persistent Subscription Manager config file.

Singleton subscriber

While duplex operations are, in general, the only way to subscribe a live object, there is one exception to that rule: a singleton subscriber. You can treat a singleton service as just another persistent subscriber and add its address to the subscription store. This technique is particularly useful for user-interface applications that need to monitor some events. You can use my `FormHost<F>` (presented in Chapter 8) to expose the form as a singleton, and then add the form as a persistent subscriber. You can add the form using the Persistent Subscription Manager tool, or the form can subscribe itself upon startup.

 The publish-subscribe pattern also decouples the system security-wise. Publishers only need to authenticate themselves against a single publishing service, as opposed to multiple subscribers and potentially multiple security mechanisms. The subscribers in turn only need to allow the publishing service, rather than all publishers in the system, to deliver events; they trust the publishing service to properly authenticate and authorize the publishers. Applying role-based security on the publishing service enables you to easily enforce in one place various rules regarding who is allowed to publish an event across the system.

Queued Publishers and Subscribers

Instead of using the synchronous bindings to either publish or subscribe to the events, you can use the `NetMsmqBinding`. A queued publish-subscribe service combines the benefits of a loosely coupled system and the flexibility of disconnected execution. When using queued events, all events on the contract must, of course, be marked as one-way operations. As shown in Figure C-3, you can use queuing at either end independently.

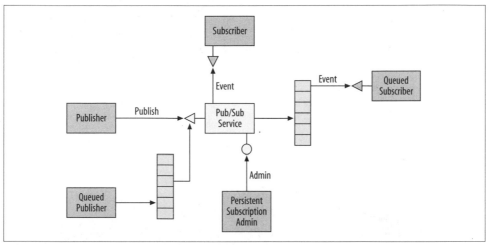

Figure C-3. Queued publish-subscribe deployment

You can have a queued publisher and connected synchronous subscribers, you can have a connected publisher publishing to queued subscribers, or you can have both queued publishers and queued subscribers. Note, however, that you cannot have queued transient subscriptions—there is no support within the MSMQ binding for duplex callbacks, since that would render the disconnected aspect of the communication useless. As before, you can use the administration tool to manage the subscribers, and the administration operations are still connected and synchronous.

Queued publisher

To utilize a queued publisher, the publishing service needs to expose a queued endpoint using the MSMQ binding. When firing events at a queued publisher, the publishing service can be offline, or the publishing client itself can be disconnected. Note that when publishing two events to a queued publishing service, there are no guarantees as to the order in which these events will be delivered to and processed by the end subscribers. Due to the asynchronous concurrent publishing, there is no order even when the events contract is configured for a session.

Queued subscriber

To deploy a queued subscriber, the persistent subscribing service needs to expose a queued endpoint. This will enable the subscriber to be offline even when the publisher is online. When the subscriber connects again, it will receive all of its queued-up events. In addition, queued subscribers can handle the case when the publishing service itself is disconnected, because no events are lost. Of course, having both a queued publisher and subscriber allows both to work offline at the same time.

When multiple events are fired at a single queued subscriber, there are no guarantees as to the order of delivery of the events, even when the events contract is configured for a session.

Code-Access Security

Code-access security, introduced in .NET 1.0, is probably the single differentiating capability-wise aspect of .NET compared with unmanaged code. The core advantage of .NET compared with the unmanaged world of C++ and COM is one of productivity, not capability. With the exception of code-access security, virtually anything that can be done by .NET can be done with unmanaged code. *Code-access security* is built into the very fabric of .NET, affecting every operation in managed code—something that unmanaged code can never achieve. The first release of WCF offered no support for code-access security. The *System.ServiceModel* assembly did not allow any partially trusted callers, and by demanding full trust of all its callers, WCF disabled code-access security support. This meant that developers wanting to take advantage of code-access security were very limited in their endeavor. Developers could use permission attributes to restrict the permissions granted to their services, but as discussed next, this came at a nontrivial cost and liability. Developers could manipulate the proxy to enable partially trusted clients to call WCF services (by granting it and asserting full trust, as discussed next), but in so doing, they waived all benefits of code-access security toward the clients. Furthermore, developers had no way of hosting a WCF service in a partial-trust environment.

The second release of WCF introduced rudimentary support for code-access security for some of the HTTP bindings, and only for a limited set of scenarios. For this limited support, WCF had to allow for partially trusted callers to the *System.ServiceModel* assembly. This change enabled me to write a small framework that provides for comprehensive support for code-access security, enabling partially trusted clients, partially trusted services, and partially trusted hosts, all without compromising the WCF programming model or code-access security. That framework and the approach leading to it are the subjects of this appendix. You will also get to see some advanced WCF and .NET programming techniques along the way.*

---

* I first published my technique for supporting CAS in WCF in the articles "Code Access Security in WCF, Part 1" and "Code Access Security in WCF, Part 2" (*MSDN Magazine*, April and July 2008).

Code-Access Security at a Glance

.NET defines 24 different *security permissions*, governing almost any type of operation. There are file I/O permissions, UI permissions, reflection permissions, security permissions, network permissions, data access permissions, and so on. Each permission type can be instantiated for a particular permission instance, such as permission to read from a specific file in the case of the file I/O permission or permission to display specific types of windows with the UI permission. Each permission type may also be completely denied (such as no file I/O operations at all) or completely granted (such as unrestricted file I/O access).

Permissions are grouped into *permission sets*, and every assembly is always assigned a set of permissions. .NET defines five standard permission sets, such as FullTrust (implies all permissions) and Execution (permission to access only the CPU). Administrators can use the .NET configuration tool to define custom permission sets, and developers can either define custom permission sets programmatically, use a permission set file, or define a ClickOnce application manifest with the permission set required by their application. Upon loading an assembly, the CLR assigns that assembly its permissions. Assemblies are granted these permissions based on some form of *evidence* substantiating their identities. The evidence may be origin-based, requiring an examination of where the assembly is loaded from (for example, all code coming from the global assembly cache [GAC] is granted full trust), or the permissions may be granted on the basis of some form of content-based evidence, such as the strong name of the assembly.

Each app domain is always assigned a permission set called the *app domain security policy*, and any assembly loaded in that app domain can only perform operations allowed by that permission set. Attempts to perform other operations will result in a security exception. By default, new app domains are launched with the FullTrust permission set, and since all code originating from the local machine also gets FullTrust by default, most .NET applications just work out of the box, while in effect not utilizing code-access security at all. This renders the code (and the user, the data, the machine, or even the network) susceptible to a variety of problems, from security attacks such as viruses or worms to plain user mistakes—just like unmanaged code.

—continued—

Code that is executing in less than full trust is called *partially trusted* code. Whenever any piece of managed code tries to access any resource or perform any operation against the .NET Framework (including interoperating with unmanaged code), .NET verifies that the assembly containing that code has the required permissions to perform the operation. If that assembly lacks a demanded permission, .NET throws a security exception, thus aborting the operation. However, since a trusted assembly can be lured by a malicious less-trusted assembly into performing operations the latter does not itself have permission to execute, it is insufficient to demand the permissions of only the assembly performing the operations. .NET therefore walks the entire stack of callers, verifying that every caller up the stack has the required permissions. This stack walk is called a *security demand*, and it is performed regardless of the assembly's permissions. Your code can also *assert* a permission—that is, stop a stack walk by asserting that every caller up the stack has the demanded permissions. You can only assert permissions you already have, and only if you have the special security assertion permission. It is always a good idea when asserting one permission to demand another in its place.

Developers can demand or assert permissions programmatically using dedicated permission classes, or use a matching set of attributes. Developers can also actively refuse permissions at the assembly, class, or method level. Refusing permissions or permitting only the limited set of permissions the code requires to execute reduces the cross section for a luring attack. For more on code-access security, see Chapter 12 of my book *Programming .NET Components*, Second Edition (O'Reilly), where I devote more than 100 pages to this fundamental technology and its application.

Code-Access Support in .NET 3.5

In .NET 3.5, WCF allows only a limited set of scenarios to execute in partial trust. It allows only the BasicHttpBinding, the WSHttpBinding, and the WebHttpBinding (with the notable exclusion of the WSDualHttpBinding) to be called under partial trust, and only with either no transfer security at all or Transport security. Furthermore, in the case of the WSHttpBinding, aspects such as Message security, reliable messaging, and transactions are disallowed. All partial-trust-enabled bindings must use text encoding. A WCF service (or client) running under partial trust cannot use additional WCF facilities, such as diagnostics and performance counters. To enable usage in a partially trusted environment, the System.ServiceModel assembly allows for partial trust callers by including the AllowPartiallyTrustedCallers attribute as part of the assembly definition:

```
[assembly: AllowPartiallyTrustedCallers]
```

In the first release of WCF, omitting this attribute precluded all partial trust use. In .NET 3.5, enforcing the limited set of supported features is now the responsibility of the bindings. Each non-HTTP binding actively demands full trust of its caller, be it the client proxy or the service host. The allowed HTTP bindings themselves do not demand full trust, but instead demand permissions according to the context of use. On the client side, the allowed HTTP bindings demand permission to execute (security permission with execution flag) and permission to connect to the service (web permission with connect flag to the target URI). On the host side, the allowed HTTP bindings demand the permissions listed in Table D-1.

Table D-1. Allowed HTTP bindings' demands on the host

Scenario	Security	Web	Reflection
WS with no security or Transport security	Execution, Infrastructure	Accept calls to URI	
Basic with no security or Transport security	Execution, Infrastructure	Accept calls to URI	
Web with no security or Transport security	Execution, Infrastructure	Accept calls to URI	
Above bindings with internal service type in separate assembly			Unrestricted
Above bindings with authenticated calls	Control principal		

The allowed HTTP bindings all demand permission to execute and permission to modify the infrastructure (security permission with infrastructure flag), and permission to accept calls on the URI configured for their endpoint (web permission with accept flag to the URI). When the calls are authenticated, the allowed HTTP bindings also demand permission to control the thread principal (security permission with principal control flag) because after authentication, for the duration of the call and regardless of the binding, WCF will install a new principal with an identity matching the provided client's credentials. If the service type provided to the host constructor is defined as an internal type of another assembly, the host also demands unrestricted reflection permission to be able to load that type using reflection.

Beyond these demands on the client or the host, there are additional limitations on configuration. For example, the config file cannot contain any reference to any certificate store (for service-side or client-side certificate credentials), since touching the certificate store will cause WCF to demand full trust. Administrators have to configure these certificates separately, using tools such as *HttpConfig.exe*.

A problem with basing the host-side permissions demand solely on the binding is that the hosted service instance is implicitly given these permissions, even if it does not require them to function. For example, the service instance could control the principal or reflect the internal types of other assemblies on the host machine. It would have been better to design the bindings to demand their permissions and yet somehow provide the host with a way of granting different permissions to the service, while ensuring that the service permissions were a subset of the hosting code's permissions.

Clearly, .NET 3.5's support falls short of comprehensive code-access security support for WCF. Ideally, you would like to be able to tap into the full power of WCF, from distributed transactions, to reliable calls, to various security credential types, to intranet (or even same-machine) applications with the TCP and IPC bindings, not to mention duplex callbacks, asynchronous calls, diagnostics and tracing, instrumentation, and of course queued calls over MSMQ, and do all that without compromising on code-access security (that is, resorting to full trust). There are three distinct areas where such support is required: partially trusted clients, partially trusted services, and partially trusted hosts.

Partially Trusted Clients

To enable clients at any partial-trust level to use any WCF feature and binding, you need to block the bindings' demand for full trust. The only way to do that is to have the proxy itself assert full trust. Asserting full trust can easily be done via the `PermissionSetAttribute`, using the `Assert` flag of the `SecurityAction` enum and specifying the string "FullTrust" for the permission name:

```
[PermissionSet(SecurityAction.Assert,Name = "FullTrust")]
```

In addition, you must prevent the client from directly accessing any method of the base class of `ClientBase<T>` (which still demands full trust), so the proxy needs to hide the commonly used methods `Close( )` and `Dispose( )`. Having the proxy class itself access methods or properties of `ClientBase<T>` (such as `Channel` or constructors) is fine, since the proxy asserts full trust. The problem is that in order to assert full trust, the proxy itself must be granted full trust, which is something the partially trusted client is not able to provide in the first place. Consequently, you need to factor out the proxy class to its own assembly, mark it as `public`, and grant that assembly full trust. In .NET 2.0 and later, you can grant the proxy's assembly full trust using the Configuration control panel applet by identifying the assembly using some content-based evidence, such as its strong name. You can also install the proxy assembly in the client's GAC. Since all assemblies coming from the GAC are granted full trust, the proxy will also thereby gain full trust. You also need to allow partially trusted callers to the assembly using the `AllowPartiallyTrustedCallers` attribute. Finally, you need to add to the proxy's assembly the definition of the contract used by the proxy (and mark the contract as `public` as well). This is required because WCF demands full trust of all assemblies up the call chain, and if the contract comes from a partially trusted assembly the demand will fail. Example D-1 shows such a contract and such proxy definitions.

Example D-1. Asserting full trust by the proxy

```
[assembly: AllowPartiallyTrustedCallers]

[ServiceContract]
public interface IMyContract
{
   [OperationContract]
   void MyMethod();
}

[PermissionSet(SecurityAction.Assert,Name = "FullTrust")]
public class MyContractClient : ClientBase<IMyContract>,IMyContract,IDisposable
{
   public MyContractClient()
   {}

   public MyContractClient(string endpointName) : base(endpointName)
   {}

   /* More constructors */

   public void MyMethod()
   {
      Channel.MyMethod();
   }
   public new void Close()
   {
      base.Close();
   }
   void IDisposable.Dispose()
   {
      Close();
   }
}
```

Client-Side Demands

The problem with the technique shown in Example D-1 is that it is a potential security breach. Suppressing the security demands of WCF means that any partially trusted client can now call any WCF service. Consider a client that was not granted permissions to connect to a TCP socket or a website. While that client will not be able to use sockets or HTTP programming directly, it will be able to bypass that limitation by calling out from the restricted client environment over WCF. The solution for that is to use a dedicated subclass of ClientBase<T> that on the one hand will assert the blank WCF demand for full trust, and on the other will demand the appropriate specific security permissions according to what the client is trying to do. My PartialTrustClientBase<T> class, shown in Example D-2, is such a proxy class.

Example D-2. The PartialTrustClientBase<T> class

```
public abstract class PartialTrustClientBase<T> : ClientBase<T>,IDisposable
                                                       where T : class
{
   [PermissionSet(SecurityAction.Assert,Name = "FullTrust")]
   public PartialTrustClientBase()
   {}
   [PermissionSet(SecurityAction.Assert,Name = "FullTrust")]
   public PartialTrustClientBase(string endpointName) : base(endpointName)
   {}
   [PermissionSet(SecurityAction.Assert,Name = "FullTrust")]
   public PartialTrustClientBase(Binding binding,EndpointAddress remoteAddress) :
                                               base(binding,remoteAddress)

   {}

   //Useful only for clients that want full-brunt raw demands from WCF
   protected new T Channel
   {
      [PermissionSet(SecurityAction.Assert,Name = "FullTrust")]
      get
      {
         return base.Channel;
      }
   }

   [PermissionSet(SecurityAction.Assert,Name = "FullTrust")]
   new public void Close()
   {
      base.Close();
   }
   void IDisposable.Dispose()
   {
      Close();
   }

   protected virtual void Invoke(Action action)
   {
      if(IsAsyncCall(action.Method.Name))
      {
         DemandAsyncPermissions();
      }
      DemandSyncPermissions(action.Method.Name);
      CodeAccessSecurityHelper.PermissionSetFromStandardSet(
                                  StandardPermissionSet.FullTrust).Assert();

      action();
   }
   protected virtual R Invoke<R>(Func<R> func)
   {
      if(IsAsyncCall(func.Method.Name))
      {
         DemandAsyncPermissions();
      }
```

Example D-2. The PartialTrustClientBase<T> class (continued)

```
      DemandSyncPermissions(func.Method.Name);
      CodeAccessSecurityHelper.PermissionSetFromStandardSet(
                                 StandardPermissionSet.FullTrust).Assert();

      return func();
   }

   protected virtual void DemandAsyncPermissions()
   {
      CodeAccessSecurityHelper.DemandAsyncPermissions();
   }
   protected virtual void DemandSyncPermissions(string operationName)
   {
      this.DemandClientPermissions(operationName);
   }
   bool IsAsyncCall(string operation)
   {
      if(operation.StartsWith("Begin"))
      {
         MethodInfo info = typeof(T).GetMethod(operation);
         object[] attributes = info.GetCustomAttributes(
                                 typeof(OperationContractAttribute),false);
         Debug.Assert(attributes.Length == 1);
         return (attributes[0] as OperationContractAttribute).AsyncPattern;
      }
      return false;
   }
}
```

PartialTrustClientBase<T> is used just like the regular proxy base class. You still need to grant full trust to the proxy class derived from it and allow partially trusted callers. However, unlike the code in Example D-1, PartialTrustClientBase<T> does not assert full trust at the class level. Instead, it asserts full trust locally, just when required. In addition, PartialTrustClientBase<T> may be used to demand code-access security permissions.

Suppressing demands with PartialTrustClientBase<T>

If you derive your proxy class from PartialTrustClientBase<T> and have the proxy assert full trust as in Example D-3, no demands will be placed on the calling client.

Example D-3. No demands from PartialTrustClientBase<T>

```
[PermissionSet(SecurityAction.Assert,Name = "FullTrust")]
public class MyContractClient : PartialTrustClientBase<IMyContract>,IMyContract
{
   public MyContractClient()
   {}

   public MyContractClient(string endpointName) : base(endpointName)
   {}
```

Example D-3. No demands from PartialTrustClientBase<T> (continued)

```
    public void MyMethod()
    {
        Channel.MyMethod();
    }
}
```

The only difference between Example D-3 and Example D-1 is that Example D-3 is cleaner, since the hiding of Close() and Dispose() is now done by PartialTrustClientBase<T>. The proxy in Example D-3 still suppresses all security demands by WCF, potentially enabling partially trusted clients to do more than intended and exposing them to luring attacks.

Raw WCF demands with PartialTrustClientBase<T>

The more security-conscious use of PartialTrustClientBase<T> is not to assert full trust by the proxy, as shown in Example D-4.

Example D-4. Allowing raw WCF security demands

```
public class MyContractClient : PartialTrustClientBase<IMyContract>,IMyContract
{
    public MyContractClient()
    {}
    public MyContractClient(string endpointName) : base(endpointName)
    {}
    public void MyMethod()
    {
        Channel.MyMethod();
    }
}
```

To support such use, PartialTrustClientBase<T> surgically asserts full trust on its constructors and its Close() method. In addition, PartialTrustClientBase<T> hides the Channel property of ClientBase<T> and asserts full trust on the get accessor. This is sufficient to suppress the WCF binding's demand for full trust, since that demand is made when constructing, opening, and closing the proxy, not when actually using it. The interesting effect of structuring the proxy this way is that now the client code will be subjected to the raw WCF security demands—that is, all the security demands required to marshal the call to the service!

For example, if the proxy is using the TCP binding, the proxy will first demand of the client permission to execute (all managed code requires that permission). Second, the proxy will demand of the client permission to connect to the port on the service machine, and unrestricted DNS permissions (required to resolve the host's address). Third, there are some collateral permission demands unrelated to the use of TCP, pertaining to the context of the call. If the client wishes to use Windows security and send the user's interactive identity, the proxy will demand environment permission access to the USERNAME variable. If the client wishes to send alternative

Windows credentials, the proxy will demand security permission to control the principal. If the client wants to dispatch calls asynchronously or receive duplex callbacks, the proxy will demand permissions to control the policy and the evidence (both are flags of the security permission, required when bouncing calls between threads). If the client wishes to use reliable messaging, the proxy will demand policy control as well. If the client uses Message security with username credentials, with service certificate negotiation and without validating the negotiated service certificate, the proxy will additionally demand permission to control the policy and the evidence. If the client utilizes the WCF diagnostics and tracing facility, the proxy will demand access to the COMPUTERNAME environment variable (to be able to trace it) and unmanaged code access (presumably to access the log files, so this should actually have been a file I/O permission instead). Finally, the proxy will demand of the client permission to execute unmanaged code.

Unmanaged code access is a highly privileged security permission, granted only to the most trustworthy code. Granting this permission may amount to disabling code-access security, since unmanaged code is exempted from code-access security. Classes and frameworks designed to work in a partial-trust environment never demand unmanaged code access (even if they use interop); instead, they demand a more narrow permission describing the nature of the unmanaged operation to be performed. The TCP channel (or the pieces of WCF it uses) demands unmanaged code access simply because its designer never thought it would be used by a partially trusted client as in Example D-4. There are also certain WCF capabilities that bluntly resort to full-trust demands, even though there are perfectly matching permissions types. For example, any attempt to propagate a transaction requires full trust (instead of the use of the distributed transaction permission), and any access of a certificate store requires full trust (instead of the use of the certificate store permission). Table D-2 shows the raw WCF security demands invoked by code such as that in Example D-4 when the bindings are set to their default settings, and the permissions demanded by a few key scenarios, such as transactions, reliability, diagnostics, asynchronous calls, certificate store access, and Message security.

Table D-2. Raw WCF client-side demands

Scenario	Permissions
TCP	Security permission with execution and unmanaged code, unrestricted DNS permission, Socket permission to connect to port on target host
IPC	Security permission with execution, unmanaged code, control policy, and control evidence
WS and WS-Dual	Security permission with execution and unmanaged code, Web permission to connect to URI
Basic and web	Security permission with execution, web permission to connect to URI

Scenario	Permissions
MSMQ	Security permission with execution and unmanaged code
Asynchronous calls, duplex over TCP	Security permission to control policy and evidence
RM over TCP	Security permission to control policy
Windows security with interactive user credentials	Environment permission to read USERNAME
Windows security with alternative credentials	Security permission to control principal, Environment permission to read USERNAME
Diagnostic tracing	Security permission with unmanaged code, Environment permission to read COMPUTERNAME
Username creds, Message security with service cert negotiation and without service cert validation	Security permission to control policy and evidence, Store permission to enumerate certificates
Username creds, TCP Message security with service cert negotiation and without service cert validation	Security permission to control policy and evidence
Any certificate store access,	Full trust
Transaction propagation	
Username creds, Message security without service cert negotiation or with service cert validation, Certificate creds	Full trust

The only bindings that do not demand unmanaged code access are the basic and web bindings. The WS binding defaults to Message security, resulting in an unmanaged code-access permission demand.

Structured demands with PartialTrustClientBase<T>

As you can see from Table D-2, key valuable aspects of WCF (such as transactions, reliable messaging, unlimited Message security interaction, and certificate store access) all require full trust, thus rendering code such as that in Example D-4 pointless in a partial-trust environment. Furthermore, the demand made for unmanaged code access by virtually all of the non-HTTP bindings (and the WS binding with Message security) is unacceptable, negating the very idea of code-access security and partially trusted clients.

To enable appropriate, secure, and correct use of WCF by partially trusted clients, PartialTrustClientBase<T> offers two Invoke( ) methods, defined as:

```
protected virtual void Invoke(Action action);
protected virtual R Invoke<R>(Func<R> func)
```

The Invoke( ) methods accept a delegate to invoke. That delegate wraps the operation call, and the difference between the two methods is in the need to return a value. Example D-5 shows a proxy deriving from PartialTrustClientBase<T> using the Invoke( ) methods.

Example D-5. Generating structured demands with PartialTrustClientBase<T>

```
public class MyContractClient : PartialTrustClientBase<IMyContract>,IMyContract
{
   public MyContractClient()
   {}

   public MyContractClient(string endpointName) : base(endpointName)
   {}

   public void MyMethod1(int number)
   {
      Invoke(( )=>Channel.MyMethod1(number));
   }
   public bool MyMethod2(int number)
   {
      return Invoke(( )=>Channel.MyMethod2(number));
   }
}
```

The Invoke( ) methods will first demand the appropriate code-access security permissions according to the scenario of the calling client and the target service endpoint. If the client is granted those permissions—that is, no security exception is raised by the demands—the Invoke( ) methods will programmatically assert full trust and proceed to invoke the requested operation, satisfied that the client has the right permissions to call the service. I call such behavior *structured permission demands*.

The Invoke( ) methods cannot use an attribute to declaratively assert full trust, since that would mask out any permissions they demand. Instead, the implementation of the Invoke( ) methods in Example D-2 first checks whether the call was invoked asynchronously (using the AsyncPattern flag of the operation contract) and then, if so, demands the appropriate permissions using the DemandAsyncPermissions( ) helper method. The Invoke( ) methods then demand the synchronous permissions using the DemandSyncPermissions( ) helper method. For the call itself, the Invoke( ) methods programmatically assert full trust using my CodeAccessSecurityHelper class:

```
public enum StandardPermissionSet
{
   Internet,
   LocalIntranet,
   FullTrust,
   Execution,
   SkipVerification
}
public static class CodeAccessSecurityHelper
{
   public static PermissionSet PermissionSetFromStandardSet(
                                       StandardPermissionSet standardSet);

   public static void DemandClientPermissions<T>(this ClientBase<T> proxy,
                                       string operationName)
                                                     where T : class;
```

```
    public static void DemandAsyncPermissions();

    //More members
}
```

The `PermissionSetFromStandardSet()` method takes an enum value representing one of the standard .NET permission sets and returns the matching instance of `PermissionSet`:

```
public interface IStackWalk
{
    void Assert();
    void Demand();
    void Deny();
    void PermitOnly();
}
public enum PermissionState
{
    None,
    Unrestricted
}
public class PermissionSet : IStackWalk,... //More interfaces
{
    public PermissionSet(PermissionState state);
    public IPermission AddPermission(IPermission permission);
    public void Assert();
    public void Demand();

    public static void RevertAssert();

    //More members
}
```

`PermissionSet`, as its name implies, is a collection of permissions, but it can also represent the super-permission set FullTrust (which is not really a set of individual permissions; it is more like a single permission). The `PermissionSet` class supports the `IStackWalk` interface, which lets you install a stack-walk modifier, such as a modifier that stops the demand for the permissions in the permission set by asserting that all callers up the stack have those permissions. The stack-walk modifier is removed automatically when the method that installed it returns. You can also explicitly remove it with the static `RevertAssert()` method of `PermissionSet`.

Both the `DemandAsyncPermissions()` and `DemandSyncPermissions()` helper methods of `PartialTrustClientBase<T>` use corresponding methods on `CodeAccessSecurityHelper` to make their demands.

Table D-3 shows the structured demands raised by the `PartialTrustClientBase<T>`. `Invoke()` methods as a function of the binding used and other aspects of the scenario, such as the use of transactions, reliability, certificate store access, diagnostics, callbacks, and asynchronous calls.

Table D-3. Structured security demands of PartialTrustClientBase<T> with default binding values

Scenario	Permissions
TCP	Security permission with execution, unrestricted DNS permission, Socket permission to connect to port on target host
IPC	Security permission with execution, control policy, and control evidence
WS, Basic	Security permission with execution, Web permission to connect to URI
WS-Dual	Security permission with execution, Web permission to connect to URI and accept callbacks to callback address, minimal ASP.NET hosting permission
MSMQ	Security permission with execution, MSMQ permission to send to queue
RM over TCP	Security permission to control policy
Duplex over TCP, Asynchronous calls (AsyncPattern), Username credentials, Message security with service cert negotiation and without service cert validation	Security permission to control policy and evidence
Windows security with interactive user credentials	Environment permission to read USERNAME
Windows security with alternative credentials	Security permission to control principal
Transaction propagation	Unrestricted distributed transaction permission
Username credentials, Message security without service cert negotiation or with service cert validation, Certificate credentials	Store permission to enumerate stores, open stores, and enumerate certificates
Diagnostic tracing	Environment permission to read COMPUTERNAME, File I/O permission to path discovery, append, and write to log files

Analyzing the demands of PartialTrustClientBase<T>.Invoke( )

I based the structured demands of PartialTrustClientBase<T>.Invoke( ) on a few elements. First, whenever possible, I tried to approximate the raw demands on the client raised by WCF, as shown in Table D-2. That said, I did smooth WCF's rough edges (since it was not designed for comprehensive partial-trust use). None of the bindings and scenarios in Table D-3 demand full trust or unmanaged code access. Second, there are plenty of places in .NET that were designed for use in partial-trust environments in similar contexts, so where appropriate I relied on the same demands as those. Finally, in the other cases, to compensate for suppressing the full-trust demands, I used experience, familiarity with code-access security, and common sense to map WCF activities to demands for dedicated permission types.

When the WS-Dual binding is used, the Invoke( ) methods demand web permission to connect to the target endpoint, as with any other HTTP binding. However, to allow for hosting the callback object, they also demand minimal ASP.NET hosting permission and web permission to accept the calls to the callback address.

When the MSMQ binding is used, the Invoke( ) methods demand MSMQ permission to send messages to the target queue.

With any attempt to propagate the client's transaction to the service, the Invoke( ) methods demand unrestricted distributed transaction permission. This is the case when a transaction-aware binding is used, when transaction flow is enabled in the binding, when transaction flow at the operation level is allowed, and when the client has an ambient transaction.

Any attempt by the proxy to access the certificate store triggers demands for permissions to enumerate the certificate stores, to open a store, and to enumerate the certificates in a store. This will happen when the client uses certificate credentials, when Message security is used and the client needs to validate the negotiated service certificate, or when the client does not negotiate a certificate and instead just loads a certificate to use for securing the message.

When the client uses WCF diagnostics, the Invoke( ) methods demand environment permission to read the computer name and file I/O permissions against the log and trace files used.

Implementing client-side structured demands

As mentioned already, the demands are carried out by CodeAccessSecurityHelper, whose partial implementation is shown in Example D-6.

Example D-6. Implementing CodeAccessSecurityHelper (partial)

```
public static class CodeAccessSecurityHelper
{
   public static PermissionSet PermissionSetFromStandardSet(
                                    StandardPermissionSet standardSet)
   {
      PermissionSetAttribute attribute =
                         new PermissionSetAttribute(SecurityAction.Demand);
      attribute.Name = standardSet.ToString( );
      return attribute.CreatePermissionSet( );
   }
   internal static void DemandAsyncPermissions( )
   {
      IPermission permission = new SecurityPermission(
      SecurityPermissionFlag.ControlEvidence|SecurityPermissionFlag.ControlPolicy);
      permission.Demand( );
   }

   public static void DemandClientPermissions<T>(this ClientBase<T> proxy,
                                    string operationName)
                                    where T : class
   {
      DemandClientConnectionPermissions(proxy.Endpoint);
      DemandTransactionPermissions(proxy.Endpoint,operationName);
      DemandTracingPermissions( );
      DemandClientSecurityPermissions(proxy);
      DemandEnvironmentPermissions(proxy);
      DemandClientStorePermissions(proxy.Endpoint);
   }
```

Example D-6. Implementing CodeAccessSecurityHelper (partial) (continued)

```
internal static void DemandClientConnectionPermissions(ServiceEndpoint endpoint)
{
   PermissionSet connectionSet = new PermissionSet(PermissionState.None);

   if(endpoint.Binding is NetTcpBinding)
   {
       connectionSet.AddPermission(new SocketPermission(
                                      NetworkAccess.Connect,TransportType.Tcp,
                          endpoint.Address.Uri.Host,endpoint.Address.Uri.Port));

       connectionSet.AddPermission(new DnsPermission(
                                          PermissionState.Unrestricted));
   }

   /* Rest of the bindings */

   connectionSet.Demand( );
}

internal static void DemandTransactionPermissions(ServiceEndpoint endpoint)
{
   DemandTransactionPermissions(endpoint,null);
}
internal static void DemandTransactionPermissions(ServiceEndpoint endpoint,
                                                  string operationName)
{
   bool transactionFlow = false;
   bool flowOptionAllowed = false;

   if(endpoint.Binding is NetTcpBinding)
   {
      NetTcpBinding tcpBinding = endpoint.Binding as NetTcpBinding;
      transactionFlow = tcpBinding.TransactionFlow;
   }

   /* Checking other bindings */

   if(transactionFlow)
   {
      if(Transaction.Current != null)
      {
         //If operationName is null, then at least one operation
         //needs to allow flow to trigger demand
         foreach(OperationDescription operation in endpoint.Contract.Operations)
         {
            string name = operationName ?? operation.Name;
            if(name != operation.Name)
            {
               continue;
            }
```

```
            TransactionFlowAttribute attribute =
                        operation.Behaviors.Find<TransactionFlowAttribute>();
            if(attribute == null)
            {
                continue;
            }
            if(attribute.Transactions != TransactionFlowOption.NotAllowed)
            {
                flowOptionAllowed = true;
                break;
            }
        }
        if(flowOptionAllowed)
        {
            IPermission distributedTransactionPermission =
                                    new DistributedTransactionPermission(
                                        PermissionState.Unrestricted);
            distributedTransactionPermission.Demand();
        }
      }
    }
  }
  //Rest of the implementation
}
```

All permission types in .NET support the IPermission interface:

```
public interface IPermission : ...
{
    void Demand();
    //More members
}
```

Demanding any permission is done by instantiating the permission object and call-ing its implementation of the Demand() method. This is exactly what the DemandAsyncPermissions() method does to demand the permission to control the policy and the evidence when invoking a call asynchronously. When constructing a permission set, you can add individual permissions to it and then call Demand() on the permission set to demand all permissions in the set. The extension method DemandClientPermissions() of CodeAccessSecurityHelper does the bulk of the demands on behalf of PartialTrustClientBase<T> (using an extension enables using it with any proxy class). It has a series of helper methods, all demanding permissions for their respective aspects. Example D-6 shows the code for DemandClientConnectionPermissions(), used to demand connectivity permissions according to the binding. It examines the binding type used by the proxy and adds the appropriate permissions (according to Table D-3) to a permission set object. It then calls Demand() on the permission set. The DemandTransactionPermissions() method first verifies that the proxy is using a binding capable of transaction flow.

If so, it verifies that the calling client actually has an ambient transaction to propagate (i.e., that Transaction.Current is not null). If so, it scans the collection of operations for the endpoint's contract, looking for the operation currently invoked. When it finds it, DemandTransactionPermissions( ) retrieves that operation's collection of operation behaviors and looks for the TransactionFlowAttribute. If the attribute is configured to allow transaction propagation, DemandTransactionPermissions( ) demands the distributed transaction permission.

In a similar manner, DemandClientPermissions( ) uses other helper methods to demand the appropriate permissions.

 To enable partially trusted clients and callbacks, I defined the class PartialTrustDuplexClientBase<T,C>. This class is used and implemented very much like PartialTrustClientBase<T>, except it adds duplex support:

```
public abstract class PartialTrustDuplexClientBase<T,C> :
                        DuplexClientBase<T,C>
                                        where T : class
{...}
```

Partially Trusted Services

In .NET 3.0, the only way for a service to execute in partial trust was to explicitly permit only the permissions required for it to operate, and implicitly deny all other permissions. One way of achieving that is to apply the matching permission attributes with the SecurityAction.PermitOnly flag. Consider the service in Example D-7.

Example D-7. Using permission attributes for a partially trusted service

```
[SecurityPermission(SecurityAction.PermitOnly,Execution = true)]
[UIPermission(SecurityAction.PermitOnly,
            Window = UIPermissionWindow.SafeTopLevelWindows)]
class MyService : IMyContract
{
   public void MyMethod( )
   {
      Form form = new TestForm( );
      form.ShowDialog( );
   }
}
```

The service requires permission to execute (as does all managed code) and permission to display safe windows. Stacking multiple permit-only permission attributes on a class yields at runtime a single permission set that .NET uses to allow only those permissions and actively deny all others, by installing a dedicated stack-walk modifier. Even if the assembly the service resides in (as well as the app domain) grants the service full trust, all other permissions will be denied. For instance, if the service tries to perform an operation such as opening a file, that will trigger a security exception because the demand for file I/O will encounter the stack-walk modifier, which will actively deny having that permission. All the service can do is execute in its virtual sandbox and display safe windows. Not only that, but .NET will change the window caption and display a warning tag on the displayed form to inform the user that the application is partially trusted, as seen in Figure D-1.

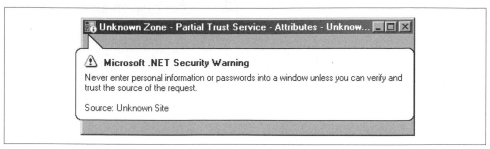

Figure D-1. A window displayed from partially trusted code

Instead of specifying the permissions as attributes, you can list them in a permission set XML file and provide that file's name to the `PermissionSetAttribute`, as shown in Example D-8.

Example D-8. Using a permission set file for a partially trusted service

```
<!-- MyServicePermissions.xml -->
<PermissionSet class = "System.Security.PermissionSet">
   <IPermission class = "System.Security.Permissions.SecurityPermission"
                         Flags = "Execution"
   />
   <IPermission class = "System.Security.Permissions.UIPermission"
                         Window = "SafeTopLevelWindows"
   />
</PermissionSet>

[PermissionSet(SecurityAction.PermitOnly,File = "MyServicePermissions.xml")]
class MyService : IMyContract
{
   public void MyMethod( )
   {
      Form form = new TestForm( );
      form.ShowDialog( );
   }
}
```

Note that the permission set file is used only at compile time, not during deployment. The compiler will fuse the permitted permissions into the class metadata, as with individual attributes. If the file is not present, the build will fail.

AppDomainHost

There are several problems with the attribute-based approach to partially trusted services. First, every time there is a change in what the service does—or, for that matter, in any of the downstream classes it uses—you will need to modify the stack of attributes or the permission set file. The service is therefore coupled to those downstream classes, and the maintenance cost is increased.

Second, because the permissions are part of the service definition, there is no way to use the service with different permissions as a product of the hosting environment. That is, you cannot dynamically give it more or fewer permissions.

Third, and most important, it is unlikely that most services will actually go to the trouble of analyzing the security permissions required for them to operate and meticulously reducing their granted permissions in order to run with the least possible privileges and permissions. If anything, it is the host that should be concerned about what exactly the service it loads is up to, and yet the host by default has no ability to affect the service's permissions. WCF's ServiceHost hosts all services in full trust. It would be better for the host, as well as for the service's own protection, to allow the host to grant the service whichever permissions it deems appropriate.

To that end, I wrote the class AppDomainHost, defined in Example D-9.

Example D-9. The class AppDomainHost

```
public class AppDomainHost : IDisposable
{
   //Create new app domain in full trust
   public AppDomainHost(Type serviceType,params Uri[] baseAddresses);
   public AppDomainHost(Type serviceType,string appDomainName,
                        params Uri[] baseAddresses);

   //Create new app domain with specified permission set
   public AppDomainHost(Type serviceType,PermissionSet permissions,
                        params Uri[] baseAddresses);
   public AppDomainHost(Type serviceType,PermissionSet permissions,
                        string appDomainName,params Uri[] baseAddresses);

   public AppDomainHost(Type serviceType,StandardPermissionSet standardSet,
                        string appDomainName,params Uri[] baseAddresses);

   //Additional constructors that take standard permission set,
   //permission set filename, and an existing app domain

   public void Open();
   public void Close();
   public void Abort();

   //More members
}
```

AppDomainHost can be used just like the WCF-provided ServiceHost:

```
AppDomainHost host = new AppDomainHost(typeof(MyService));
host.Open();
```

The difference is that AppDomainHost will host the provided service type in a new app domain, not in the app domain of its caller. The new app domain name will default to "AppDomain Host for", suffixed with the service type and a new GUID. You can also specify a name for the new app domain:

```
AppDomainHost host = new AppDomainHost(typeof(MyService),"MyService App Domain");
host.Open();
```

The new app domain is created with full trust by default. However, placing the service in a separate app domain is the key to managing partially trusted services. AppDomainHost allows you to provide the permissions for the new app domain. For example, to host this service:

```
class MyService : IMyContract
{
   public void MyMethod()
   {
      Form form = new TestForm();
      form.ShowDialog();
   }
}
```

with the same permissions as in Example D-7, you would write:

```
PermissionSet permissions = new PermissionSet(PermissionState.None);
permissions.AddPermission(new SecurityPermission(
                                        SecurityPermissionFlag.Execution));
permissions.AddPermission(new UIPermission(
                                     UIPermissionWindow.SafeTopLevelWindows));

AppDomainHost host = new AppDomainHost(typeof(MyService),permissions);
host.Open();
```

You can also use a permission set file, but unlike with Example D-8, the file is needed only at runtime and can be modified post-deployment. You can also specify one of the standard named permission sets.

A single host process can have as many instances of AppDomainHost as required, each hosting the same or a different service type and each with any arbitrary set of permissions, as shown in Example D-10.

Example D-10. Hosting the same service type with different permissions

```
//Default is service with full trust
AppDomainHost host0 = new AppDomainHost(typeof(MyService),
                  "Full Trust App Domain",new Uri("net.tcp://localhost:6000"));
host0.Open();
```

Example D-10. Hosting the same service type with different permissions (continued)

```
//With just enough permissions to do work
PermissionSet permissions1 = new PermissionSet(PermissionState.None);
permissions1.AddPermission(new SecurityPermission(
                           SecurityPermissionFlag.Execution));
permissions1.AddPermission(new UIPermission(
                           UIPermissionWindow.SafeTopLevelWindows));

AppDomainHost host1 = new AppDomainHost(typeof(MyService),permissions1,
                "My Partial Trust App Domain",new Uri("net.tcp://localhost:6001"));
host1.Open();


//With not enough permissions to do work
PermissionSet permissions2 = new PermissionSet(PermissionState.None);
permissions2.AddPermission(new SecurityPermission(
                           SecurityPermissionFlag.Execution));

AppDomainHost host2 = new AppDomainHost(typeof(MyService),permissions2,
                     "Not enough permissions",new Uri("net.tcp://localhost:6002"));
host2.Open();


//Using one of the named permission sets
AppDomainHost host3 = new AppDomainHost(typeof(MyService),StandardPermissionSet.Internet,
                     "Named permission set",new Uri("net.tcp://localhost:6003"));
host3.Open();
```

Implementing AppDomainHost

There are two parts to implementing AppDomainHost: creating a new app domain and injecting a service host instance into it, and then having the service host (and the service instance) execute in partial trust. To create a service host instance and to activate it in a separate app domain, I wrote the class ServiceHostActivator, shown in Example D-11.

Example D-11. The ServiceHostActivator class (partial)

```
class ServiceHostActivator : MarshalByRefObject
{
   ServiceHost m_Host;

   public void CreateHost(Type serviceType,Uri[] baseAddresses)
   {
      m_Host = new ServiceHost(serviceType,baseAddresses);
   }
   public void Open()
   {
      m_Host.Open();
   }
   public void Close()
   {
```

```
      m_Host.Close( );
   }
   public void Abort( )
   {
      m_Host.Abort( );
   }

   //Rest of the implementation
}
```

ServiceHostActivator is a simple wrapper around a standard WCF-provided ServiceHost instance. ServiceHostActivator derives from MarshalByRefObject, so AppDomainHost can call it across the app domain boundary. The CreateHost( ) method encapsulates constructing a new ServiceHost instance. The rest of the methods of ServiceHostActivator just forward the remote calls to the underlying host instance. AppDomainHost offers several overloaded constructors. These constructors all call each other (see Example D-12), even creating a new app domain along the way. Eventually, the public constructors end up using a protected constructor that takes the service type, the new app domain instance, the permission set for the new domain, and the base addresses.

Example D-12. Implementing AppDomainHost (partial)

```
public class AppDomainHost : IDisposable
{
   ServiceHostActivator m_ServiceHostActivator;

   public AppDomainHost(Type serviceType,params Uri[] baseAddresses) :
                     this(serviceType,"AppDomain Host for "+serviceType+"
                     "+Guid.NewGuid( ),baseAddresses)
   {}

   public AppDomainHost(Type serviceType,string appDomainName,
                     params Uri[] baseAddresses) : this(serviceType,
                     new PermissionSet(PermissionState.Unrestricted),
                     appDomainName,baseAddresses)
   {}

   public AppDomainHost(Type serviceType,PermissionSet permissions,
                     string appDomainName,params Uri[] baseAddresses) :
                     this(serviceType,AppDomain.CreateDomain(appDomainName),
                     permissions,baseAddresses)
   {}

   //More constructors

   protected AppDomainHost(Type serviceType,AppDomain appDomain,
                     PermissionSet permissions,Uri[] baseAddresses)
   {
      string assemblyName = Assembly.GetAssembly(
                                 typeof(ServiceHostActivator)).FullName;
```

```
      m_ServiceHostActivator = appDomain.CreateInstanceAndUnwrap(
                            assemblyName,typeof(ServiceHostActivator).ToString())
                                                  as ServiceHostActivator;

      appDomain.SetPermissionsSet(permissions);

      m_ServiceHostActivator.CreateHost(serviceType,baseAddresses);
   }
   public void Open()
   {
      m_ServiceHostActivator.Open();
   }
   public void Close()
   {
      m_ServiceHostActivator.Close();
   }
   public void Abort()
   {
      m_ServiceHostActivator.Abort();
   }
   void IDisposable.Dispose()
   {
      Close();
   }
}
```

The protected constructor of AppDomainHost uses .NET Remoting to inject into the new app domain an instance of ServiceHostActivator, ending up with a Remoting proxy to it stored in the m_ServiceHostActivator member.

The new app domain is created with full trust by default. AppDomainHost uses the SetPermissionsSet() AppDomain extension method of CodeAccessSecurityHelper to install in the new app domain a new code-access security policy, permitting only the supplied permissions and denying the rest. Example D-13 shows the implementation of SetPermissionsSet().

Example D-13. Implementing SetPermissionsSet()

```
public static class CodeAccessSecurityHelper
{
   public static void SetPermissionsSet(this AppDomain appDomain,
                                    PermissionSet permissions)
   {
      PolicyLevel policy = PolicyLevel.CreateAppDomainLevel();
      policy.RootCodeGroup.PolicyStatement = new PolicyStatement(permissions);
      appDomain.SetAppDomainPolicy(policy);
   }
   //More members
}
```

Assigning the permissions to the new app domain is as simple as creating a new security policy at the app domain level and calling the SetAppDomainPolicy() method of the AppDomain class:

```
public sealed class AppDomain : MarshalByRefObject,...
{
   public void SetAppDomainPolicy(PolicyLevel domainPolicy);
   //More members
}
```

 A similar technique to Example D-13 is what ClickOnce uses to enforce the partial-trust execution of ClickOnce-deployed applications.

When you call the other methods of AppDomainHost, such as Open() or Close(), the proxy to ServiceHostActivator calls to the other app domain and has it there open or close its host instance. Since the service instance will execute in the app domain that happened to open its host, the service will also execute under that app domain's security policy.

Partially Trusted Hosts

The approach presented thus far for partially trusted services was predicated on having the code that uses AppDomainHost be running under full trust. This is because ServiceHost and the bindings will demand full trust in any hosting scenario not listed in Table D-1.

But what if the code launching the host is only partially trusted? You could use a similar solution to that employed by the clients, placing AppDomainHost and ServiceHostActivator in a fully trusted assembly, allowing partially trusted callers, and having them both assert full trust:

```
[PermissionSet(SecurityAction.Assert,Unrestricted = true)]
public class AppDomainHost : IDisposable
{...}

[PermissionSet(SecurityAction.Assert,Unrestricted = true)]
class ServiceHostActivator : MarshalByRefObject
{...}
```

While this approach works, it suffers from the same problems listed previously when the client blindly granted full trust to the proxy: it circumvents code-access security and disables a crucial security mechanism, introducing two security problems. First, it is incorrect to assume that the code opening the host has permissions to accept calls on the transport channels and to participate in WCF activities such as distributed transactions. Second, by asserting full trust and suppressing the stack walk, you leave open the possibility for the partially trusted code that launched the host to create a service with higher privileges to do its dirty deeds for it. For example, the hosting code may not have file I/O permissions, but it can use AppDomainHost to accept calls to a service with file I/O permissions.

The solution is simple: AppDomainHost and ServiceHostActivator should not employ a blank assertion of full trust. Instead, they should only assert locally, when needed, and then revert back to the existing permissions. In addition, AppDomainHost should challenge the code using it and demand of it appropriate hosting permissions (such as accepting calls), and it should verify that the hosting code is granted at least the permissions under which it wishes to run the service. This will prevent restricted and partially trusted code from using a service hosted in a separate app domain with more permissions. The net result is structured host-side security demands.

Structured Host-Side Security Demands

The reworked ServiceHostActivator, suitable for partially trusted callers, is shown in Example D-14.

Example D-14. Asserting and demanding permissions with ServiceHostActivator (partial)

```
class ServiceHostActivator : MarshalByRefObject
{
   public void CreateHost(Type serviceType,Uri[] baseAddresses)
   {
      CodeAccessSecurityHelper.PermissionSetFromStandardSet(
                                   StandardPermissionSet.FullTrust).Assert();

      m_Host = new ServiceHost(serviceType,baseAddresses);

      PermissionSet.RevertAssert();

      m_Host.DemandHostPermissions();
   }
   //Behavior demands happen here, must assert
   [PermissionSet(SecurityAction.Assert,Unrestricted = true)]
   public void Open()
   {
      m_Host.Open();
   }
    //Rest same as Example D-11
}
```

The CreateHost() method of ServiceHostActivator cannot declaratively assert full trust, since this would prevent it from demanding the appropriate host permissions of the calling code. Instead, it programmatically uses CodeAccessSecurityHelper to create a full-trust permission set, asserts it, and then proceeds to create the host. When WCF demands full trust, the assertion prevents that demand from going up the call stack. After creating the host, CreateHost() explicitly reverts the assertion.

CreateHost() then calls on the just-created host instance the extension helper method DemandHostPermissions() of CodeAccessSecurityHelper, to demand the hosting permissions. DemandHostPermissions() examines the host object and demands the appropriate permissions. For example, if the host supports a TCP endpoint, DemandHostPermissions() will demand permission to execute and permission to accept TCP calls on the endpoint URI. If reliable messaging is used over TCP, DemandHostPermissions() will demand permission to control the policy. There are quite a few additional possible demands, as shown in Table D-4.

Table D-4. Structured host-side demands with AppDomainHost

Scenario	Permissions
TCP	Security permission with execution, Socket permission to accept TCP calls on URI
IPC	Security permission with execution, control policy, and control evidence
MSMQ	Security permission with execution, MSMQ permission to read from queue
WS, WS-Dual, Basic, Web	Security permission with execution, Web permission to accept calls on URI
RM over TCP	Security permission to control policy
Authenticated calls	Security permission to control principal
Transaction propagation	Unrestricted distributed transaction permission
Username creds with Message security, Certificate creds with validation, Service cert	Store permission to enumerate stores, open stores, and enumerate certificates
Diagnostic tracing	Environment permission to read COMPUTERNAME, File I/O permission to path discovery, append, and write to log files
WCF service performance counters	Performance counter permissions to write to service counter, write to endpoint counter, and write to operation counter
WCF all performance counters	Performance counter permissions to write to service counter, write to endpoint counter, write to operation counter, and write to host counter
ASP.NET providers	Minimal ASP.NET hosting permission

As on the client side, use of the IPC binding demands permission to control the policy and evidence. Use of the MSMQ binding triggers a demand for permission to read from the endpoint queue. Use of any of the HTTP bindings triggers a demand to accept calls on the endpoint address. If the binding uses authenticated calls, DemandHostPermissions() will demand permission to control the principal. Use of a transaction-aware binding with transaction flow enabled will cause a demand for unrestricted distributed transaction permission if there is at least one operation on the endpoint's contract with transaction flow allowed (or mandatory). Any access to the certificate store, such as with Message security, client certificate validation, or use of a service certificate to protect the message, will cause a demand for permission to enumerate the store, open a store, and enumerate the certificates. If the service performs diagnostics, DemandHostPermissions( ) will demand access to the COMPUTERNAME environment variable and file I/O permission to that file. If the host uses WCF performance counters, DemandHostPermissions( ) will demand permission to write to the counters at the reported level. If the host relies on the ASP.NET providers for caller authentication or role membership, DemandHostPermissions( ) will demand minimal ASP.NET hosting permission (all providers require that permission). When calling back over the WS-Dual binding, the binding itself will demand web permission to connect to the callback endpoint, so there is no need for AppDomainHost to explicitly demand that permission when launching the host.

Implementing structured host demands

Example D-15 shows the partial implementation of DemandHostPermissions( ).

Example D-15. Implementing DemandHostPermissions( ) (partial)

```
public static class CodeAccessSecurityHelper
{
   internal static void DemandHostPermissions(this ServiceHost host)
   {
      foreach(ServiceEndpoint endpoint in host.Description.Endpoints)
      {
         DemandHostConnectionPermissions(endpoint);
         DemandHostSecurityPermissions(endpoint);
         using(TransactionScope scope = new TransactionScope())
         {
            DemandTransactionPermissions(endpoint);
         }
      }
      DemandHostStorePermissions(host);
      DemandPerformanceCounterPermissions();
      DemandTracingPermissions();
      DemanAspNetProvidersPermissions(host);
   }
   internal static void DemandHostConnectionPermissions(ServiceEndpoint endpoint)
   {
      PermissionSet connectionSet = new PermissionSet(PermissionState.None);
      if(endpoint.Binding is NetTcpBinding)
      {
         connectionSet.AddPermission(new SocketPermission(NetworkAccess.Accept,
                                 TransportType.Tcp,endpoint.Address.Uri.Host,
                                 endpoint.Address.Uri.Port));
      }

      /* Checking the other bindings */

      connectionSet.Demand();
   }
```

```
static void DemanAspNetProvidersPermissions(ServiceHost host)
{
   bool demand = false;

   foreach(IServiceBehavior behavior in host.Description.Behaviors)
   {
      if(behavior is ServiceCredentials)
      {
         ServiceCredentials credentialsBehavior =
                                       behavior as ServiceCredentials;

         if(credentialsBehavior.UserNameAuthentication.
                         UserNamePasswordValidationMode ==
                         UserNamePasswordValidationMode.MembershipProvider)
         {
            demand = true;
            break;
         }
      }
      if(behavior is ServiceAuthorizationBehavior)
      {
         ServiceAuthorizationBehavior serviceAuthorization =
                               behavior as ServiceAuthorizationBehavior;
         if(serviceAuthorization.PrincipalPermissionMode ==
            PrincipalPermissionMode.UseAspNetRoles && Roles.Enabled)
         {
            demand = true;
            break;
         }
      }
   }
   if(demand)
   {
      IPermission permission =
            new AspNetHostingPermission(AspNetHostingPermissionLevel.Minimal);
      permission.Demand();
   }
}
//Rest of the implementation
}
```

DemandHostPermissions() first performs endpoint-specific demands. It iterates over the collection of the service's endpoints, and for each endpoint it demands its respective connectivity, security, and transaction permissions. For the transactions demand it creates a temporary ambient transaction using a transaction scope, in order to use the same method as on the client side. After the endpoint demands, DemandHostPermissions() demands permissions determined by the service host configuration; specifically, certificates store access permissions, performance counter permissions, tracing permissions, and ASP.NET providers permissions.

For example, to demand the ASP.NET providers permission, it obtains the collection of service behaviors and checks whether the host's service credentials behavior uses the membership provider or the host's service authorization behavior uses the roles providers; if so, it demands the ASP.NET hosting permission.

AppDomainHost also needs some reworking to support structured demands in a partial-trust environment, as shown in Example D-16.

Example D-16. Asserting with AppDomainHost

```
[SecurityPermission(SecurityAction.Assert,ControlAppDomain = true)]
[ReflectionPermission(SecurityAction.Assert,Unrestricted = true)]
public class AppDomainHost : IDisposable
{
   protected AppDomainHost(Type serviceType,AppDomain appDomain,
                           PermissionSet permissions,Uri[] baseAddresses)
   {
      //Cannot grant service permissions the host does not have
      permissions.Demand( );

      //Rest of constructor same as in Example D-12
   }
   //Rest same as in Example D-12
}
```

Since AppDomainHost creates a new app domain, it asserts the permission to control the app domain. Since it uses reflection to inject the host in the other app domain, it asserts unrestricted reflection permission. Most importantly, before creating the service host in the new app domain, AppDomainHost demands the requested permissions for the service of the code that calls it. This ensures that partially trusted code can only launch and host a service that is permitted to do at most as the calling code.

Additional aspects of AppDomainHost

While AppDomainHost does not support ICommunicationObject, it does offer its events model and state machine management. AppDomainHost also copies a few static variables from the calling app domain to the new app domain it creates (specifically, it uses ServiceHostActivator to copy over the ASP.NET providers application name). To that end, AppDomainHost temporarily asserts the ASP.NET hosting permission, accesses the providers and copies the values of the membership and roles application names, and then reverts the assertion.

Generic Interceptor

At its core, WCF is nothing more than an extensibility model. All the built-in attributes, behaviors, and infrastructure are implemented using this open and public extensibility model. In theory, every developer has as much access and power as any member of the WCF team. As demonstrated throughout this book (with the exception of my security extensions), as long as you are familiar with the extensibility model, with a mere few lines of code you can inject powerful behavior and customization into your application. In practice, however, dealing with the interception mechanism requires intimate knowledge of the WCF architecture. To simplify matters, I wanted to provide an easy-to-use abstraction on top of the WCF extensibility model that would, in a way, extend the extensibility model itself, allowing for intercepting all calls to the service, both on the client and the service side, in a general manner and adding custom behavior, without having to deal with the inner workings of WCF. This appendix presents a small framework I call the *generic interceptor*, available with *ServiceModelEx*. It also demonstrates some advanced WCF programming techniques, as well as the thought process behind designing such extensions.

Intercepting Service Operations

Recall from Chapter 1 that in the abstract, all WCF does when intercepting calls is perform pre- and post-call operations. Adding custom steps to this interception mechanism is probably the most common way of extending WCF.

Every endpoint dispatcher has a reference to an interface called IOperationInvoker, defined as:

```
public interface IOperationInvoker
{
   object[] AllocateInputs();
   object Invoke(object instance,object[] inputs,out object[] outputs);

   //Asynchronous invocation methods
}
```

The dispatcher uses the Invoke( ) method to invoke the calls on the service instance. In providing for the invocation, IOperationInvoker is the right place to plug in your code. Specifically, assigning the dispatcher your implementation of IOperationInvoker will enable you to hook it in.

The Generic Invoker

The first step in implementing my generic interceptor framework was to provide an abstract implementation of IOperationInvoker that enables custom pre- and post-call steps, as shown in Example E-1.

Example E-1. The GenericInvoker class

```
public abstract class GenericInvoker : IOperationInvoker
{
   readonly IOperationInvoker m_OldInvoker;

   public GenericInvoker(IOperationInvoker oldInvoker)
   {
      m_OldInvoker = oldInvoker;
   }
   public virtual object[] AllocateInputs()
   {
      return m_OldInvoker.AllocateInputs();
   }
   protected virtual void PreInvoke(object instance,object[] inputs)
   {}

   //Always called, even if operation had an exception
   protected virtual void PostInvoke(object instance,object returnedValue,
                                     object[] outputs,Exception exception)
   {}

   public object Invoke(object instance,object[] inputs,out object[] outputs)
   {
      PreInvoke(instance,inputs);
      object returnedValue = null;
      object[] outputParams = new object[]{};
      Exception exception = null;
      try
      {
         returnedValue = m_OldInvoker.Invoke(instance,inputs,out outputParams);
         outputs = outputParams;
         return returnedValue;
      }
      catch(Exception operationException)
      {
         exception = operationException;
         throw;
      }
```

```
    finally
    {
        PostInvoke(instance,returnedValue,outputParams,exception);
    }
  }
  // Additional asynchronous methods
}
```

GenericInvoker defines two virtual methods, PreInvoke( ) and PostInvoke( ). PreInvoke( ) accepts the input parmeters as well as the target instance, and PostInvoke( ) accepts the output parameters and the returned value as well as the instance and the exception (if one took place). GenericInvoker has an empty implementation for both methods. It is up to subclasses of GenericInvoker to override one or both of these methods and add the custom steps.

GenericInvoker accepts as a construction parameter the old implementation of IOperationInvoker that was associated with the service. This old implementation does the heavy lifting of allocating the input parameters for the operations, as well as actually invoking the service. GenericInvoker aims at being as nonintrusive as possible, so it cannot interfere with that implementation; at any rate, it would not be wise to do so, as that would entail a large amount of work. GenericInvoker therefore saves the old invoker in a member variable, and delegates to it its implementation of AllocateInputs( ). The heart of GenericInvoker is the Invoke( ) method. In it, GenericInvoker first calls the PreInvoke( ) method (allowing its subclass to perform some pre-call processing) and then proceeds to invoke the operation using the old invoker. GenericInvoker encases the invocation in a try/catch/finally block. Regardless of how the operation ends (with or without an exception), GenericInvoker calls the PostInvoke( ) method, providing it with the retuned results and the exception, and allowing the subclass to perform custom post-call processing.

Installing the Interceptor

I wanted to provide for a declarative way of installing the operation, both at the operation level and at the service level. The trick in doing that is implementing the work once at the operation level, and then having the service level install all the operation-level attributes. The IOperationBehavior interface is the operation-level extension that lets you customize the dispatcher for an operation, in the ApplyDispatchBehavior( ) method:

```
public interface IOperationBehavior
{
    void ApplyDispatchBehavior(OperationDescription operationDescription,
                               DispatchOperation dispatchOperation);
    //More methods
}
```

Any method-level attribute that implements IOperationBehavior will be given a chance to affect the dispatcher (in this case, setting its operation invoker) in the ApplyDispatchBehavior() method. ApplyDispatchBehavior() provides the dispatchOperation parameter of the type DispatchOperation:

```
public sealed class DispatchOperation
{
   public IOperationInvoker Invoker
   {get;set;}

   //More members
}
```

Setting the Invoker property replaces the implementation of IOperationInvoker used. It's as simple as that.

Example E-2 shows the implementation of my OperationInterceptorBehaviorAttribute.

Example E-2. The OperationInterceptorBehavior attribute

```
[AttributeUsage(AttributeTargets.Method)]
public abstract class OperationInterceptorBehaviorAttribute :
                                             Attribute,IOperationBehavior
{
   protected abstract GenericInvoker CreateInvoker(IOperationInvoker oldInvoker);

   public void ApplyDispatchBehavior(OperationDescription operationDescription,
                          DispatchOperation dispatchOperation)
   {
      IOperationInvoker oldInvoker = dispatchOperation.Invoker;
      dispatchOperation.Invoker = CreateInvoker(oldInvoker);
   }
   //More methods
}
```

The OperationInterceptorBehaviorAttribute is an abstract class with an abstract protected method called CreateInvoker(). CreateInvoker() takes the old invoker and returns some implementation of GenericInvoker. The implementation of ApplyDispatchBehavior() first saves the old invoker in a local variable and then calls CreateInvoker() to provide a new invoker while wrapping the old invoker. The newly created invoker is duly set on the dispatcher as the invoker to use from now on. Having a concrete subclass of the OperationInterceptorBehavior attribute will enable you to apply the custom invoker discreetly on some, but perhaps not all, of the methods of the service. If you wish to apply the attribute on all operations, it is better to enforce this design decision at the service level using my ServiceInterceptorBehaviorAttribute, defined in Example E-3.

Example E-3. The ServiceInterceptorBehavior attribute

```
[AttributeUsage(AttributeTargets.Class)]
public abstract class ServiceInterceptorBehaviorAttribute :
                                              Attribute,IServiceBehavior
{
   protected abstract OperationInterceptorBehaviorAttribute
                                          CreateOperationInterceptor( );

   public void ApplyDispatchBehavior(ServiceDescription serviceDescription,...)
   {
      foreach(ServiceEndpoint endpoint in serviceDescription.Endpoints)
      {
         foreach(OperationDescription operation in endpoint.Contract.Operations)
         {
            if(operation.Behaviors.
                          Find<OperationInterceptorBehaviorAttribute>( ) != null)
            {
               continue;
            }
            operation.Behaviors.Add(CreateOperationInterceptor( ));
         }
      }
   }
   //More members
}
```

ServiceInterceptorBehavior too is an abstract attribute. It provides the abstract protected method CreateOperationInterceptor( ), which returns some implementation of the OperationInterceptorBehavior attribute. ServiceInterceptorBehavior supports the IServiceBehavior interface, whose ApplyDispatchBehavior( ) method provides the description of the service:

```
public interface IServiceBehavior
{
   void ApplyDispatchBehavior(ServiceDescription serviceDescription,...);
   //More methods
}
```

The ServiceDescription class contains a collection of service endpoints:

```
public class ServiceDescription
{
   public ServiceEndpointCollection Endpoints
   {get;}

   //More members
}

public class ServiceEndpointCollection : Collection<ServiceEndpoint>
{...}
```

Every endpoint has a `Contract` property containing the contract description:

```
public class ServiceEndpoint
{
   public ContractDescription Contract
   {get;}

   //More members
}
```

The contract description has a collection of operation descriptions:

```
public class ContractDescription
{
   public OperationDescriptionCollection Operations
   {get;}

   //More members
}

public class OperationDescriptionCollection : Collection<OperationDescription>
{...}
```

Each operation description has a collection of operation behaviors:

```
public class OperationDescription
{
   public KeyedByTypeCollection<IOperationBehavior> Behaviors
   {get;}

   //More members
}
```

The service-level attribute needs to add to this collection of behaviors an `OperationInterceptorBehavior` attribute.

In its implementation of `ApplyDispatchBehavior( )`, `ServiceInterceptorBehavior` iterates over the collection of service endpoints. For each endpoint, it iterates over its operation collection. For each operation, it checks to see whether its behavior collection already contains an implementation of the `OperationInterceptorBehavior` attribute. This check is required in case the developer applied (by mistake) both an operation- and a service-level attribute. If the behavior collection does not contain the `OperationInterceptorBehavior` attribute, `ApplyDispatchBehavior( )` adds it.

Intercepting Client Calls

To intercept client-side calls WCF provides the interface `IClientMessageInspector`, defined as:

```
public interface IClientMessageInspector
{
   object BeforeSendRequest(ref Message request,IClientChannel channel);
   void AfterReceiveReply(ref Message reply,object correlationState);
}
```

The `BeforeSendRequest()` method is called just before the message is sent down the wire, allowing you to affect the request message. Similarly, the `AfterReceiveReply()` method is your chance to interact with the reply message for post-call processing.

The client runtime represented by the `ClientRuntime` class contains a collection of message inspectors:

```
public sealed class ClientRuntime
{
   public SynchronizedCollection<IClientMessageInspector> MessageInspectors
   {get;}

   //More members
}
```

You can add your message inspector to the collection by associating the proxy with an endpoint behavior. That behavior needs to add the inspector in the `ApplyClientBehavior()` method:

```
public interface IEndpointBehavior
{
   void ApplyClientBehavior(ServiceEndpoint endpoint,ClientRuntime clientRuntime);
   //More members
}
```

To encapsulate these steps I wrote the class `InterceptorClientBase<T>` defined in Example E-4.

Example E-4. The InterceptorClientBase<T> class

```
public abstract class InterceptorClientBase<T> : ClientBase<T> where T : class
{
   public InterceptorClientBase()
   {
      Endpoint.Behaviors.Add(new ClientInterceptor(this));
   }
   public InterceptorClientBase(string endpointName) : base(endpointName)
   {
      Endpoint.Behaviors.Add(new ClientInterceptor(this));
   }

   //More constructors

   protected virtual void PreInvoke(ref Message request)
   {}

   protected virtual void PostInvoke(ref Message reply)
   {}

   class ClientInterceptor : IEndpointBehavior,IClientMessageInspector
   {
      InterceptorClientBase<T> Proxy
      {get;set;}
```

Example E-4. The InterceptorClientBase<T> class (continued)

```
    internal ClientInterceptor(InterceptorClientBase<T> proxy)
    {
        Proxy = proxy;
    }
    object IClientMessageInspector.BeforeSendRequest(ref Message request,
                                                IClientChannel channel)
    {
        Proxy.PreInvoke(ref request);
        return null;
    }
    void IClientMessageInspector.AfterReceiveReply(ref Message reply,
                                                object correlationState)
    {
        Proxy.PostInvoke(ref reply);
    }

    void IEndpointBehavior.ApplyClientBehavior(ServiceEndpoint endpoint,
                                        ClientRuntime clientRuntime)
    {
        clientRuntime.MessageInspectors.Add(this);
    }
    //Rest of the implementation
    }
}
```

InterceptorClientBase<T> defines a nested private class called ClientInterceptor
that implements both IEndpointBehavior and IClientMessageInspector. The constructors of InterceptorClientBase<T> add an instance of ClientInterceptor to the
proxy's collection of endpoint behaviors. Inside ClientInterceptor, the implementation of ApplyClientBehavior() adds itself to the collection of client runtime interceptors. InterceptorClientBase<T> provides two virtual methods, PreInvoke() and
PostInvoke() for the use of derived classes. The constructor of ClientInterceptor
takes a back reference to the calling InterceptorClientBase<T>, and it uses that reference to call back to the PreInvoke() and PostInvoke() methods during the calls to
BeforeSendRequest() and AfterReceiveReply() respectively.

The Trace Interceptors

The first example I'll show of using the generic interceptors framework is for tracing
and logging. Example E-5 shows a simple example of implementing a generic service-
side interceptor called ParameterTracerInvoker.

Example E-5. The ParameterTracerInvoker

```
class ParameterTracerInvoker : GenericInvoker
{
   public ParameterTracerInvoker(IOperationInvoker oldInvoker) : base(oldInvoker)
   {}

   protected override void PreInvoke(object instance,object[] inputs)
   {
      Trace.WriteLine("Input Parameters: ");

      foreach(object argument in inputs)
      {
         Trace.WriteLine(argument.ToString( ));
      }
   }
   protected override void PostInvoke(object instance,object returnedValue,
                                      object[] outputs,Exception exception)
   {

      foreach(object output in outputs)
      {
         Trace.WriteLine("Output Parameters: ");
         Trace.WriteLine(output.ToString( ));
      }

      Trace.WriteLine("Returned: " + returnedValue ?? String.Empty);
   }
}
```

ParameterTracerInvoker derives from GenericInvoker. Its constructor accepts the old invoker and passes it to the constructor of GenericInvoker. The implementations of PreInvoke( ) and PostInvoke( ) trace to the Output window in Visual Studio the values of the input and output parameters, respectively. You can install the ParameterTracerInvoker on service operations by defining the OperationParameterTracerAttribute:

```
   public class OperationParameterTracerAttribute :
                                          OperationInterceptorBehaviorAttribute
   {
      protected override GenericInvoker CreateInvoker(IOperationInvoker oldInvoker)
      {
         return new ParameterTracerInvoker(oldInvoker);
      }
   }
```

All the method-level attribute needs to do is derive from OperationInterceptorBehaviorAttribute and override the CreateInvoker( ) method, returning an instance of ParameterTracerInvoker wrapping the old invoker.

Example E-6 demonstrates using the OperationParameterTracer attribute.

Example E-6. Using OperationParameterTracerAttribute

```
[ServiceContract]
interface IMyContract
{
    [OperationContract]
    string MyMethod1(int number,string text);

    [OperationContract]
    string MyMethod2(int number);
}

class MyService : IMyContract
{
    [OperationParameterTracer]
    public string MyMethod1(int number,string text)
    {
        return "Some Result 1";
    }

    public string MyMethod2(int number)
    {
        return "Some Result 2";
    }

}
```

Using the definitions from Example E-6, the following client code:

```
MyContractClient proxy = new MyContractClient();
proxy.MyMethod1(287,"Hello");
proxy.MyMethod2(42);
proxy.Close();
```

would trace:

```
Input Parameters:
287
Hello
Output Parameters:
Returned: Some Result 1
```

To apply the `ParameterTracerInvoker` at the service level, define the `ServiceParameterTracerAttribute` as:

```
public class ServiceParameterTracerAttribute : ServiceInterceptorBehaviorAttribute
{
    protected override OperationInterceptorBehaviorAttribute
                                            CreateOperationInterceptor()
    {
        return new OperationParameterTracerAttribute();
    }
}
```

All the service-level attribute needs to do is derive from ServiceInterceptorBehaviorAttribute and override the CreateOperationInterceptor() method, returning an instance of OperationParameterTracerAttribute.

Example E-7 demonstrates using the ServiceParameterTracer attribute.

Example E-7. Using ServiceParameterTracerAttribute

```
[ServiceParameterTracer]
class MyService : IMyContract
{
   public string MyMethod1(int number,string text)
   {
      return "Some Result 1";
   }

   public string MyMethod2(int number)
   {
      return "Some Result 2";
   }
}
```

Using the definitions of Example E-7, the following client code:

```
MyContractClient proxy = new MyContractClient();
proxy.MyMethod1(287,"Hello");
proxy.MyMethod2(42);
proxy.Close();
```

would trace:

```
Input Parameters:
287
Hello
Returned: Some Result 1
Input Parameters:
42
Returned: Some Result 2
```

You can use the service-side interceptor independently from the client, or you can intercept and trace on the client using the TracerClientBase<T> class shown in Example E-8.

Example E-8. The TracerClientBase<T> class

```
public class TracerClientBase<T> : InterceptorClientBase<T> where T : class
{
   protected override void PreInvoke(ref Message request)
   {
      string action = request.Headers.Action;
      string[] slashes = action.Split('/');
      string methodName = slashes[slashes.Length-1];
```

```
    Trace.WriteLine("***** Calling : " + methodName + "() *****");
}

protected override void PostInvoke(ref Message reply)
{
    string action = reply.Headers.Action;
    string[] slashes = action.Split('/');
    string methodName = slashes[slashes.Length-1];

    methodName = methodName.Replace("Response","");

    Trace.WriteLine("**** Returning from : " + methodName + "() ****");
    }
}
```

The class `TracerClientBase<T>` derives from `InterceptorClientBase<T>`, and it overrides the `PreInvoke()` and `PostInvoke()` methods. The overridden methods trace the invoked operation name. You use `TracerClientBase<T>` just as a regular proxy base class, as shown in Example E-9.

Example E-9. Deriving from TracerClientBase<T>

```
class MyContractClient : TracerClientBase<IMyContract>,IMyContract
{
    public string MyMethod1(int number,string text)
    {
        return Channel.MyMethod1(number,text);
    }

    public string MyMethod2(int number)
    {
        return Channel.MyMethod2(number);
    }
}
```

Using the proxy from Example E-9 with the service from Example E-7, the following code:

```
MyContractClient proxy = new MyContractClient();
proxy.MyMethod1(287,"Hello");
proxy.Close();
```

would trace:

```
**** Calling operation: MyMethod1() ****
Input Parameters:
287
Hello
Returned: Some Result 1
**** Returning from operation: MyMethod1() ****
```

Identity Stack Propagation

The second example of using the generic interceptor is about security identity propagation. As explained in Chapter 10, impersonation as a mechanism for identity propagation has many liabilities. Still, sometimes your service is required to pass the identity of the original caller (or all callers) down to the resources or other services with which it interacts. Instead of impersonating the callers or passing their identities as explicit parameters, you can pass the identities out-of-band, in the message headers, and use the generic interceptor to automate processing of those identities.

The first step is to define the stack of callers. To that end, I defined the SecurityCallFrame, which represents a single caller identity as well as some additional information about the caller, such as its address and the operation it invoked:

```
[DataContract]
public class SecurityCallFrame
{
    [DataMember(IsRequired = true)]
    public string Authentication
    {get;}

    [DataMember(IsRequired = true)]
    public string IdentityName
    {get;}

    [DataMember(IsRequired = true)]
    public string Address
    {get;}

    [DataMember(IsRequired = true)]
    public string Operation
    {get;}

    //More members
}
```

Next, I defined the security call stack:

```
[DataContract]
public class SecurityCallStack
{
    internal void AppendCall();

    public SecurityCallFrame OriginalCall
    {get;}

    public int Count
    {get;}

    public SecurityCallFrame[] Calls
    {get;}

    //More members
}
```

The implementation details of these types are irrelevant for this appendix.

Using the GenericContext<T> from Appendix B, I defined the security call stack context:

```
[DataContract]
public class SecurityCallStackContext
{
   public static SecurityCallStack Current
   {
      get
      {
         if(GenericContext<SecurityCallStack>.Current == null)
         {
            return null;
         }
         return GenericContext<SecurityCallStack>.Current.Value;
      }
      set
      {
         GenericContext<SecurityCallStack>.Current =
                                  new GenericContext<SecurityCallStack>(value);
      }
   }
}
```

To automate passing the call stack, I then defined the class SecurityCallStackClientBase<T> shown in Example E-10.

Example E-10. The SecurityCallStackClientBase<T> class

```
public abstract partial class HeaderClientBase<T,H> : InterceptorClientBase<T>
{
   protected H Header
   {get;set;}

   protected override void PreInvoke(ref Message reply);

   //Rest of the implementation
}
public abstract class SecurityCallStackClientBase<T> :
                                     HeaderClientBase<T,SecurityCallStack>
{
   protected SecurityCallStackClientBase()
   {
      InitializeCallStack();
   }

   //More constructors

   void InitializeCallStack()
   {
      if(OperationContext.Current == null || Header == null)
      {
         Header = new SecurityCallStack();
      }
```

```
      else
      {
         Header = SecurityCallStackContext.Current;
      }
   }
   protected override void PreInvoke(ref Message request)
   {
      Header.AppendCall( );
      base.PreInvoke(ref request);
   }
}
```

SecurityCallStackClientBase<T> derives from HeaderClientBase<T,H> (also defined in Appendix B), and HeaderClientBase<T,H> in turn derives from InterceptorClientBase<T>.

Every time the client invokes calls on the SecurityCallStackClientBase<T> proxy, the proxy will automatically append the current identity to the call stack and pass it in the headers. If all services down the call chain use SecurityCallStackClientBase<T> (or manually use SecurityCallStackContext), on every call the call stack will contain the new frame.

Security Call Stack Interceptor

To process and manage the identities stack, define a subclass of the generic interceptor. The processing could be as simple as logging the identities, or as complex as digitally signing the call stack to prevent spoofing by malicious intermediaries along the call chain and validating the current call stack, as shown in Example E-11.

Example E-11. Validating and logging the call stack with an interceptor

```
class SecurityCallStackInterceptor : GenericInvoker
{
   public SecurityCallStackInterceptor(IOperationInvoker oldInvoker) :
                                                       base(oldInvoker)
   {}

   protected override void PreInvoke(object instance,object[] inputs)
   {
      SecurityCallStack callStack = SecurityCallStackContext.Current;

      if(callStack != null)
      {
         LogCallChain(callStack);
         ValidateCallChain(callStack);
         SignCallChain(callStack);
      }
   }
```

```
    void LogCallChain(SecurityCallStack callStack)
    {...}

    void ValidateCallChain(SecurityCallStack callStack)
    {
        //Perform custom validation steps here
    }

    void SignCallChain(SecurityCallStack callStack)
    {
        //Digitally sign call stack here
    }
}
```

You can apply the SecurityCallStackInterceptor at the operation or service level using dedicated one-liner attributes:

```
    public class OperationSecurityCallStackAttribute :
                                            OperationInterceptorBehaviorAttribute
    {
        protected override GenericInvoker CreateInvoker(IOperationInvoker oldInvoker)
        {
            return new SecurityCallStackInterceptor(oldInvoker);
        }
    }
    public class SecurityCallStackBehaviorAttribute :
                                            ServiceInterceptorBehaviorAttribute
    {
        protected override OperationInterceptorBehaviorAttribute
                                            CreateOperationInterceptor()
        {
            return new OperationSecurityCallStackAttribute();
        }
    }
```

WCF Coding Standard

A comprehensive coding standard is essential for successful product delivery: it helps in enforcing best practices and avoiding pitfalls, and it makes knowledge dissemination across the team easier. Traditionally, coding standards are thick, laborious documents, spanning hundreds of pages and detailing the rationale behind every directive. While these are better than no standard at all, such efforts are usually indigestible by the average developer. In contrast, the WCF coding standard presented here is very thin on the "why" and very detailed on the "what." I believe that while fully understanding every insight that goes into a particular programming decision may require reading books and even years of experience, applying a standard should not. When absorbing a new developer into your team, you should be able to simply point the newcomer at the standard and say: "Read this first." Being able to comply with a good standard should come before fully understanding and appreciating it— that should come over time, with experience. The WCF coding standard presented in this appendix captures dos and don'ts, pitfalls, guidelines, and recommendations, drawing on the best practices and helper classes discussed throughout this book.

General Design Guidelines

1. All services must adhere to these principles:
   a. Services are secure.
   b. Service operations leave the system in a consistent state.
   c. Services are thread-safe and can be accessed by concurrent clients.
   d. Services are reliable.
   e. Services are robust.

2. Services can optionally adhere to these principles:
   a. Services are interoperable.
   b. Services are scale-invariant.

c. Services are available.

d. Services are responsive.

e. Services are disciplined and do not block their clients for long.

Essentials

1. Place service code in a class library, not in any hosting EXE.

2. Do not provide parameterized constructors to a service class, unless it is a singleton that is hosted explicitly.

3. Enable reliability in the relevant bindings.

4. Provide a meaningful namespace for contracts. For outward-facing services, use your company's URL or equivalent URN with a year and month to support versioning. For example:

   ```
   [ServiceContract(Namespace = "http://www.idesign.net/2009/06")]
   interface IMyContract
   {...}
   ```

   For intranet services, use any meaningful unique name, such as MyApplication. For example:

   ```
   [ServiceContract(Namespace = "MyApplication")]
   interface IMyContract
   {...}
   ```

5. With intranet applications on Windows XP and Windows Server 2003, prefer self-hosting to IIS hosting.

6. On Windows Vista and Windows Server 2008 or later, prefer WAS hosting to self-hosting.

7. Enable metadata exchange.

8. Always name all endpoints in the client config file.

9. Do not use SvcUtil or Visual Studio 2008 to generate a config file.

10. When using a tool such as Visual Studio 2008 to generate the proxy, do clean up the proxy.

11. Do not duplicate proxy code. If two or more clients use the same contract, factor the proxy to a separate class library.

12. Always close or dispose of the proxy.

Service Contracts

1. Always apply the ServiceContract attribute on an interface, not a class:

```
//Avoid:
[ServiceContract]
class MyService
{
    [OperationContract]
    public void MyMethod()
    {...}
}
//Correct:
[ServiceContract]
interface IMyContract
{
    [OperationContract]
    void MyMethod();
}
class MyService : IMyContract
{
    public void MyMethod()
    {...}
}
```

2. Prefix the service contract name with an I:

```
[ServiceContract]
interface IMyContract
{...}
```

3. Avoid property-like operations:

```
//Avoid:
[ServiceContract]
interface IMyContract
{
    [OperationContract]
    string GetName();

    [OperationContract]
    void SetName(string name);
}
```

4. Avoid contracts with one member.

5. Strive to have three to five members per service contract.

6. Do not have more than 20 members per service contract. Twelve is probably the practical limit.

Data Contracts

1. Avoid inferred data contracts (POCO). Always be explicit and apply the `DataContract` attribute.

2. Use the `DataMember` attribute only on properties or read-only public members.

3. Avoid explicit XML serialization on your own types.

4. Avoid message contracts.

5. When using the `Order` property, assign the same value to all members coming from the same level in the class hierarchy.

6. Support `IExtensibleDataObject` on your data contracts. Use explicit interface implementation.

7. Avoid setting `IgnoreExtensionDataObject` to `true` in the `ServiceBehavior` and `CallbackBehavior` attributes. Keep the default of `false`.

8. Do not mark delegates and events as data members.

9. Do not pass .NET-specific types, such as `Type`, as operation parameters.

10. Do not accept or return ADO.NET `DataSets` and `DataTables` (or their type-safe subclasses) from operations. Return a neutral representation such as an array.

11. Suppress the generation of a generic type parameter hash code and provide a legible type name instead.

Instance Management

1. Prefer the per-call instance mode when scalability is a concern.

2. If setting `SessionMode.NotAllowed` on the contract, always configure the service instancing mode as `InstanceContextMode.PerCall`.

3. Do not mix sessionful contracts and sessionless contracts in the same service.

4. Avoid a singleton unless you have a natural singleton.

5. Use ordered delivery with a sessionful service.

6. Avoid instance deactivation with a sessionful service.

7. Avoid demarcating operations.

8. With durable services, always designate a completing operation.

Operations and Calls

1. Do not treat one-way calls as asynchronous calls.

2. Do not treat one-way calls as concurrent calls.

3. Expect exceptions from a one-way operation.

4. Enable reliability even on one-way calls. Use of ordered delivery is optional for one-way calls.

5. Avoid one-way operations on a sessionful service. If used, make it the terminating operation:

```
[ServiceContract(SessionMode = SessionMode.Required)]
interface IMyContract
{
    [OperationContract]
    void MyMethod1( );

    [OperationContract(IsOneWay = true,IsInitiating = false,IsTerminating = true)]
    void MyMethod2( );
}
```

6. Name the callback contract on the service side after the service contract name, suffixed by Callback:

```
interface IMyContractCallback
{...}
[ServiceContract(CallbackContract = typeof(IMyContractCallback))]
interface IMyContract
{...}
```

7. Strive to mark callback operations as one-way.

8. Use callback contracts for callbacks only.

9. Avoid mixing regular callbacks and events on the same callback contract.

10. Event operations should be well designed:

    a. void return type

    b. No out-parameters

    c. Marked as one-way operations

11. Avoid using raw callback contracts for event management, and prefer using the publish-subscribe framework.

12. Always provide explicit methods for callback setup and teardown:

```
[ServiceContract(CallbackContract = typeof(IMyContractCallback))]
interface IMyContract
{
    [OperationContract]
    void DoSomething( );

    [OperationContract]
    void Connect( );

    [OperationContract]
    void Disconnect( );
}
interface IMyContractCallback
{...}
```

13. Use the type-safe DuplexClientBase<T,C> instead of DuplexClientBase<T>.

14. Use the type-safe DuplexChannelFactory<T,C> instead of DuplexChannelFactory<T>.

15. When debugging or in intranet deployment of callbacks over the WSDualHttpBinding, use the CallbackBaseAddressBehavior attribute with CallbackPort set to 0:

```
[CallbackBaseAddressBehavior(CallbackPort = 0)]
class MyClient : IMyContractCallback
{...}
```

Faults

1. Never use a proxy instance after an exception, even if you catch that exception.

2. Avoid fault contracts and allow WCF to mask the error.

3. Do not reuse the callback channel after an exception even if you catch that exception, as the channel may be faulted.

4. Use the FaultContract attribute with exception classes, as opposed to mere serializable types:

```
//Avoid:
[OperationContract]
[FaultContract(typeof(double))]
double Divide(double number1,double number2);


//Correct:
[OperationContract]
[FaultContract(typeof(DivideByZeroException))]
double Divide(double number1,double number2);
```

5. Avoid lengthy processing such as logging in IErrorHandler.ProvideFault().

6. With both service classes and callback classes, set IncludeExceptionDetailInFaults to true in debug sessions, either in the config file or programmatically:

```
public class DebugHelper
{
    public const bool IncludeExceptionDetailInFaults =
#if DEBUG
        true;
#else
        false;
#endif
}
[ServiceBehavior(IncludeExceptionDetailInFaults =
                DebugHelper.IncludeExceptionDetailInFaults)]
class MyService : IMyContract
{...}
```

7. In release builds, do not return unknown exceptions as faults except in diagnostic scenarios.

8. Consider using the `ErrorHandlerBehavior` attribute on the service, both for promoting exceptions to fault contracts and for automatic error logging:

```
[ErrorHandlerBehavior]
class MyService : IMyContract
{...}
```

9. Consider using the `CallbackErrorHandlerBehaviorAttribute` on the callback client, both for promoting exceptions to fault contracts and for automatic error logging:

```
[CallbackErrorHandlerBehavior(typeof(MyClient))]
class MyClient : IMyContractCallback
{
    public void OnCallabck()
    {...}
}
```

Transactions

1. Never manage transactions directly.

2. Apply the `TransactionFlow` attribute on the contract, not the service class.

3. Do not perform transactional work in the service constructor.

4. Using this book's terminology, configure services for either Client or Client/Service transactions. Avoid None or Service transactions.

5. Using this book's terminology, configure callbacks for either Service or Service/Callback transactions. Avoid None or Callback transactions.

6. When using the Client/Service or Service/Callback mode, constrain the binding to flow transactions using the `BindingRequirement` attribute.

7. On the client, always catch all exceptions thrown by a service configured for None or Service transactions.

8. Enable reliability and ordered delivery even when using transactions.

9. In a service operation, never catch an exception and manually abort the transaction:

```
//Avoid:
[OperationBehavior(TransactionScopeRequired = true)]
public void MyMethod()
{
    try
    {
        ...
    }
    catch
    {
        Transaction.Current.Rollback();
    }
}
```

10. If you catch an exception in a transactional operation, always rethrow it or another exception.

11. Keep transactions short.

12. Always use the default isolation level of `IsolationLevel.Serializable`.

13. Do not call one-way operations from within a transaction.

14. Do not call nontransactional services from within a transaction.

15. Do not access nontransactional resources (such as the filesystem) from within a transaction.

16. With a sessionful service, avoid equating the session boundary with the transaction boundary by relying on auto-complete on session close.

17. Strive to use the `TransactionalBehavior` attribute to manage transactions on sessionful services:

```
[Serializable]
[TransactionalBehavior]
class MyService : IMyContract
{
    public void MyMethod()
    {...}
}
```

18. When using a sessionful or transactional singleton, use volatile resource managers to manage state and avoid explicitly state-aware programming or relying on WCF's instance deactivation on completion.

19. With transactional durable services, always propagate the transaction to the store by setting SaveStateInOperationTransaction to true.

Concurrency Management

1. Always provide thread-safe access to:

    a. Service in-memory state with sessionful or singleton services

    b. Client in-memory state during callbacks

    c. Shared resources

    d. Static variables

2. Prefer `ConcurrencyMode.Single` (the default). It enables transactional access and provides thread safety without any effort.

3. Keep operations on single-mode sessionful and singleton services short in order to avoid blocking other clients for long.

4. When using `ConcurrencyMode.Multiple`, you must use transaction auto-completion.

5. Consider using `ConcurrencyMode.Multiple` on per-call services to allow concurrent calls.

6. Transactional singleton service with `ConcurrencyMode.Multiple` must have `ReleaseServiceInstanceOnTransactionComplete` set to false:

```
[ServiceBehavior(InstanceContextMode = InstanceContextMode.Single,
                 ConcurrencyMode = ConcurrencyMode.Multiple,
                 ReleaseServiceInstanceOnTransactionComplete = false)]
class MySingleton : IMyContract
{...}
```

7. Never self-host on a UI thread, and have the UI application call the service.

8. Never allow callbacks to the UI application that called the service unless the callback posts the call using `SynchronizationContext.Post( )`.

9. When supplying the proxy with both synchronous and asynchronous methods, apply the `FaultContract` attribute only to synchronous methods.

10. Keep asynchronous operations short. Do not equate asynchronous calls with lengthy operations.

11. Do not mix transactions with asynchronous calls.

Queued Services

1. On the client, always verify that the queue (and a dead-letter queue, when applicable) is available before calling the queued service. Use `QueuedServiceHelper.VerifyQueues( )` for this purpose.

2. Always verify that the queue is available when hosting a queued service (this is done automatically by `ServiceHost<T>`).

3. Except in isolated scenarios, avoid designing the same service to work both queued and non-queued.

4. The service should participate in the playback transaction.

5. When participating in the playback transaction, avoid lengthy processing in the queued service.

6. Avoid sessionful queued services.

7. When using a singleton queued service, use a volatile resource manager to manage the singleton state.

8. When using a per-call queued service, explicitly configure the contract and the service to be per-call and sessionless:

```
[ServiceContract(SessionMode = SessionMode.NotAllowed)]
interface IMyContract
{...}

[ServiceBehavior(InstanceContextMode = InstanceContextMode.PerCall)]
class MyService : IMyContract
{...}
```

9. Always explicitly set contracts on a queued singleton to disallow sessions:

```
[ServiceContract(SessionMode = SessionMode.NotAllowed)]
interface IMyContract
{...}

[ServiceBehavior(InstanceContextMode = InstanceContextMode.Single)]
class MyService : IMyContract
{...}
```

10. The client should call a queued service inside a transaction.

11. On the client side, do not store a queued service proxy in a member variable.

12. Avoid relatively short values of TimeToLive, as they negate the justification for a queued service.

13. Avoid nontransactional queues.

14. When using a response queue, have the service participate in the playback transaction and queue the response in that transaction.

15. Have the response service participate in the response playback transaction.

16. Avoid lengthy processing in a queued response operation.

17. With MSMQ 3.0, prefer a response service to a poison queue service dealing with failures of the service itself.

18. With MSMQ 4.0, use ReceiveErrorHandling.Reject for poison messages unless you have advanced processing with ReceiveErrorHandling.Move. Avoid ReceiveErrorHandling.Fault and ReceiveErrorHandling.Drop.

19. With MSMQ 4.0, consider the use of a response service to handle service playback failures.

20. Unless dealing with a sessionful contract and service, never assume the order of queued calls.

Security

1. Always protect the message and provide for message confidentiality and integrity.

2. In an intranet, you can use Transport security as long as the protection level is set to EncryptAndSign.

3. In an intranet, avoid impersonation. Set the impersonation level to TokenImpersonationLevel.Identification.

4. When using impersonation, have the client use TokenImpersonationLevel.Impersonation.

5. Use the declarative security framework and avoid manual configuration.

6. Never apply the `PrincipalPermission` attribute directly on the service class:

```
//Will always fail:
[PrincipalPermission(SecurityAction.Demand,Role = "...")]
public class MyService : IMyContract
{...}
```

7. Avoid sensitive work that requires authorization at the service constructor.

8. Avoid demanding a particular user, with or without demanding a role:

```
//Avoid:
[PrincipalPermission(SecurityAction.Demand,Name = "John")]
public void MyMethod()
{...}
```

9. Do not rely on role-based security in the client's callback operations.

10. With Internet clients, always use Message security.

11. Allow clients to negotiate the service certificate (the default).

12. Use the ASP.NET providers for custom credentials.

13. When developing a custom credentials store, develop it as a custom ASP.NET provider.

14. Validate certificates using peer trust.

15. Strive to run the client under partial trust. Grant the client permission only to:

   a. Execute

   b. Display the user interface (if required)

   c. Connect to the service

   d. Obtain local credentials

16. When you own the service host environment, run the service and the host under full trust. Grant Microsoft and ECMA full trust, but remove all other code groups and grant them no permissions.

17. When hosting in partial trust, grant the host and the service permission only to:

   a. Execute

   b. Accept client calls

   c. Obtain local credentials

   d. Authenticate and authorize the client

   e. Access local resources if required

ServiceModelEx Catalog

CollectionExtensions

Category: C# 3.0

Description: Augments the LINQ collection extensions with additional methods.

See Also: ArrayExtensions

ArrayExtensions

Category: C# 3.0

Description: Provides all the LINQ extensions that return a collection except when operating on an array, in which case they return an array. Augments the LINQ collection extensions with additional methods for arrays.

See Also: CollectionExtensions

AppDomainHost

Category: Hosting

Description: Hosts the service in a separate app domain. Can apply permission sets on the new app domain.

See Also: CodeAccessSecurityHelper

InProcFactory

Category: Hosting

Description: Instantiates a .NET class over WCF. No config file or host is required.

See Also: DuplexClientBase<T,C>
ServiceThrottleHelper
NetNamedPipeContextBinding

ServiceHost<T>

Category: Hosting

Description: Adds type safety to ServiceHost, adds support for string-based base addresses, streamlining and automation of metadata publishing, adding any error handler extensions, adding the ErrorHandlerBehavior to the service, including exception details in faults, verifying all queues, purging queues on shutdown in debug mode, enabling security audits, and reading throttle values.

See Also: LogbookManager
LogbookManagerClient
LogbookManager
ErrorHandlerHelper
DebugHelper
QueuedServiceHelper

MetadataHelper

Category: Contracts

Description: Performs type-safe contract queries of service metadata.

DataContractSerializer<T>

Category: Data Contracts

Description: Generic type-safe wrapper of DataContractSerializer.

DataTableHelper

Category: Data Contracts

Description: Automates converting a table to an array of items.

ServiceThrottleHelper

Category: Instance Management

Description: Sets throttle extensions for `ServiceHost`.

IInstanceStore<ID,T>

Category: Durable Services

Description: Defines an interface for any instance store.

See Also: `FileInstanceStore<ID,T>`
                    `TransactionalMemoryStore<ID,T>`

FileInstanceStore<ID,T>, FilePersistenceProvider, FilePersistenceProviderFactory

Category: Durable Services

Description: File-based store; corresponding provider and provider factory.

See Also: `IInstanceStore<ID,T>`
                    `TransactionalMemoryProviderFactory`
                    `TransactionalInstanceProviderFactory`

MemoryProvider, MemoryProviderFactory

Category: Durable Services

Description: Abstract provider and provider factory for in-memory store.

See Also: `TransactionalMemoryProviderFactor`
                    `TransactionalInstanceProviderFactory`
                    `TransactionalMemoryProvider`
                    `TransactionalInstanceProvider`

TransactionalMemoryStore<ID,T>, TransactionalMemoryProvider, TransactionalMemoryProviderFactory

Category: Durable Services

Description: In-memory transactional store shared across clients; corresponding provider and provider factory.

See Also:
```
IInstanceStore<ID,T>
TransactionalInstanceProviderFactory
FilePersistenceProviderFactory
```

TransactionalInstanceStore<ID,T>, TransactionalInstanceProvider, TransactionalInstanceProviderFactory

Category: Durable Services

Description: Per client session in-memory transactional store; corresponding provider and provider factory.

See Also:
```
IInstanceStore<ID,T>
TransactionalMemoryProviderFactory
FilePersistenceProviderFactory
```

InstanceContext<T>, DuplexClientBase<T,C>, DuplexChannelFactory<T,C>

Category: Operations

Description: Provide type safety for the client with callback contracts, via either a proxy class or a channel factory.

See Also:
```
SecureDuplexClientBase<T,C>
PartialTrustDuplexClientBase<T,C>
```

WsDualProxyHelperCallbackBaseAddressBehaviorAttribute

Category: Operations

Description: Open an available port for the duplex WS proxy.

DebugHelper

Category: Faults

Description: Constant to include exception details in faults in debug mode only, extension for FaultException<ExceptionDetail> to extract the CLR exception.

ErrorHandlerHelper

Category: Faults

Description: Used for promoting exceptions and logging errors to LogbookManager.

See Also: ErrorHandlerBehaviorAttribute
CallbackErrorHandlerBehaviorAttribute

ErrorHandlerBehaviorAttribute, CallbackErrorHandlerBehaviorAttribute

Category: Faults

Description: Used for declaratively promoting exceptions and logging errors to LogbookManager; attributes for service and callback.

See Also ServiceHost<T>
ErrorHandlerHelper

ILogbookManager, LogbookManagerClient, LogbookManager

Category: Faults

Description: Service contract for logging errors; proxy for the contract; the logbook service itself.

See Also: ErrorHandlerHelper

BindingRequirementAttribute

Category: Transactions, General

Description: Used for declaratively enforcing the Client/Service propagation mode on the service or the callback object, declaratively insisting on an intranet-only binding, and declaratively requiring reliability.

ResourceManager, TransactionalLock

Category: Transactions

Description: Helper classes useful when implementing a transactional resource manager.

See Also: Transactional<T>

Transactional<T>

Category: Transactions

Description: A generic volatile resource manager. Performs transactions on any serializable type without compromising on the type programming model.

See Also: ResourceManager
TransactionalLock

TransactionalCollection<C,T>

Category: Transactions

Description: A generic abstract volatile resource manager collection, useful when implementing a custom transactional collection.

See Also: Transactional<T>

TransactionalArray<T>, TransactionalDictionary<K,T>, TransactionalLinkedList<T>, TransactionalList<T>, TransactionalQueue<T>, TransactionalSortedDictionary<K,T>, TransactionalSortedList<K,T>, TransactionalStack<T>

Category: Transactions

Description: The array and all the collections in .NET as transactional volatile resource managers. The collections and the array are polymorphic with the nontransactional built-in collections and are completely interchangeable.

See Also: TransactionalCollection<C,T>

TransactionalBehaviorAttribute

Category: Transactions

Description: Enables transparent transactional programming on a per-session service. Negates the need to use a per-call service just for transactions.

See Also:
```
TransactionalMemoryStore<ID,T>
TransactionalMemoryProvider
TransactionalMemoryProviderFactory
Transactional<T>
TransactionalDictionary<K,T>
NetNamedPipeContextBinding
```

FormHost<F>

Category: Concurrency and Windows Forms

Description: Turns a Windows Forms form into a service, without affecting the form's implementation. Service calls simply update the UI.

SafeButton, SafeLabel, SafeListBox, SafeProgressBar, SafeStatusBar, SafeTextBox, SafeTrackBar

Category: Concurrency and Windows Forms

Description: Controls that can be accessed by any service or callback call, on any thread, to update the UI.

See Also:
```
FormHost<F>
```

ThreadPoolSynchronizer, ThreadPoolBehaviorAttribute, CallbackThreadPoolBehaviorAttribute, ThreadPoolHelper

Category: Custom Synchronization Context

Description: Custom thread pool synchronization context; attributes to apply it declaratively on the service or a callback object; helper class to close the threads in the pool.

See Also:
```
AffinitySynchronizer
PrioritySynchronizer
ThreadAffinityBehaviorAttribute
PriorityCallsBehaviorAttribute
```

AffinitySynchronizer, ThreadAffinityBehaviorAttribute, CallbackThreadAffinityBehaviorAttribute, HostThreadAffinity

Category: Custom Synchronization Context

Description: Custom synchronization context providing thread affinity; attributes to apply it on the service and the callback; extension methods to apply at the host level.

See Also: ThreadPoolSynchronizer
ThreadPoolBehaviorAttribute
CallbackThreadPoolBehaviorAttribute

PrioritySynchronizer, PriorityClientBase<T>, PriorityContext, PriorityCallsBehaviorAttribute

Category: Custom Synchronization Context

Description: Custom synchronization context executing calls by priority; proxy class to pass priority in headers; helper class to extract priority from headers; attribute to apply priority processing on service.

See Also: ThreadPoolSynchronizer
ThreadPoolBehaviorAttribute
GenericContext<T>
HeaderClientBase<T,H>

QueuedServiceHelper

Category: Queued Services

Description: Used for verifying all queues on the client, verifying a queue for an endpoint as an extension, and purging a queue.

See Also: ServiceHost<T>

ResponseClientBase<T>, ResponseScope<T>, ResponseContext

Category: Queued Services

Description: Framework for supporting a response service. Proxy class for the client to pass a response address and method IDs; scope to automate the service interacting with the response service proxy; response context for direct manipulation.

See Also: GenericContext<T>
HeaderClientBase<T,H>

CredentialsManager, AspNetSqlProviderService

Category: Security and ASP.NET Providers

Description: Smart client application for managing the ASP.NET credentials store; WCF service wrapping the ASP.NET providers.

See Also: `MetadataHelper`

SecureClientBase<T>, SecureDuplexClientBase<T,C>, SecurityBehaviorAttribute, SecurityHelper, ServiceSecurity

Category: Declarative Security

Description: Declarative security framework. Declarative security proxy class for regular and duplex calls; attribute for declarative support for the service; declarative security extension methods for regular and duplex type-safe channel factories; declarative security extension methods for the host; extension methods for automatic impersonation; enumeration for declarative security scenarios.

See Also: `DuplexClientBase<T,C>`
                `DuplexChannelFactory<T,C>`

HeaderClientBase<T,H>, GenericContext<T>

Category: Message Headers

Description: Streamlines passing custom out-of-band parameters to the proxy; helper class for extracting and setting the information in the headers.

See Also: `InterceptorClientBase<T>`

ContextClientBase<T>, ContextManager

Category: Context Bindings

Description: Streamlines passing custom out-of-band parameters to the proxy over the context bindings; helper class for extracting and setting the information in the context and managing standard IDs.

See Also: `GenericContext<T>`
                `HeaderClientBase<T,H>`

NetNamedPipeContextBinding, NetNamedPipeContextBindingElement, NetNamedPipeContextBindingCollectionElement

Category: Context Bindings

Description: Adds the context protocol to the IPC binding; helper classes (not required for direct use) for enabling administrative configuration.

See Also: `ContextClientBase<T>`
`ContextManager`
`InProcFactory`

PersistentSubscriptionServiceClient, IPersistentSubscriptionService, ISubscriptionService, PersistentSubscription, PublishService<T>, SubscriptionManager<T>, PersistentSubscriptionManager

Category: Publish-Subscribe

Description: Framework for implementing publish-subscribe solution. Proxy class for adding persistent subscribers; service contracts for the publishing and subscription services; base classes for the implementation of the publishing and subscription services; demo application for managing persistent subscriptions.

See Also: `MetadataHelper`
`DuplexClientBase<T,C>`
`DuplexChannelFactory<T,C>`

PartialTrustClientBase<T>, PartialTrustDuplexClientBase<T,C>, CodeAccessSecurityHelper

Category: Code-Access Security

Description: Framework for restoring code-access security support to WCF, which can be used in conjunction with `AppDomainHost` for partially trusted hosts and services. Proxy classes for partially trusted clients (both regular and type-safe duplex proxies); helper class offering extensions for direct manipulation of the `PermissionSet` class and strongly typed standard permission set management.

See Also: `DuplexClientBase<T,C>`
`AppDomainHost`

GenericInvoker, OperationInterceptorBehaviorAttribute, ServiceInterceptorBehaviorAttribute

Category: Generic Interceptor

Description: Framework for easy injection of an interceptor to do pre- or post-call processing; attributes for operation- and service-level declarative use.

See Also: SecurityCallStackInterceptor
OperationSecurityCallStackAttribute
SecurityCallStackBehaviorAttribute

InterceptorClientBase<T>

Category: Generic Interceptor

Description: Proxy base class for easy interception of client calls.

See Also: HeaderClientBase<T,H>

SecurityCallFrame, SecurityCallStack, SecurityCallStackContext, SecurityCallStackClientBase<T>, SecurityCallStackInterceptor, OperationSecurityCallStackAttribute, SecurityCallStackBehaviorAttribute

Category: Security Identities

Description: Framework for propagating the stack of callers' identities in the message headers; definitions of the call stack and supporting types; proxy class enabling the client to push its identity; interceptor for managing the call stack; attributes to inject the interceptor at the operation or service level.

See Also: GenericInvoker
OperationInterceptorBehaviorAttribute
ServiceInterceptorBehaviorAttribute
GenericContext<T>
HeaderClientBase<T,H>

Index

A

aborted transactions, 282, 312
absolute addresses, 35
ACID properties, 283–285
Address structure, 107
addresses
    callback, 232–235
    elements of, 4
    endpoints and, 25, 26
    examples, 5
    format, 5
    HTTP addresses, 6
    IPC addresses, 6
    MSMQ addresses, 6
    peer network addresses, 7
    TCP addresses, 5
    transport schemas, 5
ADO.NET data sets and tables, 132–134
AffinitySynchronizer class, 411, 727
aliasing
    EnumMember attribute, 131
    operation overloading, 71
    Serializable attribute and, 97
ambient transactions
    defined, 300
    setting, 302–303
App.Config file, 13
AppDomainHost class, 720

Application class
    DoEvents() method, 404
    OpenForms collections, 390, 396
array extensions, 19
ArrayExtensions class, 19, 720
arrays, converting tables, 135–137
ASMX web services, 21, 66
AspNetSqlProviderService class, 728
AsyncCallbackException, 433
asynchronous calls
    completion callbacks, 436–441
    concurrency management, 428–445
    defined, 428
    error handling, 442, 443
    invoking, 431–433
    one-way operations, 441, 442
    polling, 433–436
    proxy-based, 429–430
    requirements, 428, 429
    synchronous calls and, 444–445
    transactions and, 443
    waiting for completion, 433–436
asynchronous operation invocation, 428
auditing, security, 600–604
authentication
    mutual, 511
    security and, 509, 510
authorization, security and, 510
automatic synchronization, 371

We'd like to hear your suggestions for improving our indexes. Send email to *index@oreilly.com*.

denial of service (DOS) attacks, 511
deserialization
    data contract events, 107–108
    messages, 90
    .NET, 91
dictionaries, 149–151
DispatchRuntime class
    ChannelDispatcher property, 278
    SynchronizationContext property, 411
distributed ID (distributed transaction
        identifier), 301
Distributed Transaction Coordinator
        (DTC), 296–299, 301
distributed transactions, 287
DLQ (dead-letter queue), 473–480
DOS (denial of service) attacks, 511
DTC (Distributed Transaction
        Coordinator), 296–299, 301
duplex operations (see callback operations)
duplex proxies
    callback operations, 216–219
    DuplexChannelFactory<T,C>
        class, 228–229
    type safety and, 225–228
DuplexChannelFactory<T,C>
        class, 228–229, 723
DuplexClientBase<T,C> class, 226–228
DuplexClientBase<T> class
    callback addresses, 233
    duplex proxies, 216, 217, 219
    type safety, 225–228
    VerifyCallback() method, 227
durable services
    automatic behavior, 194–200
    context bindings for instance
        IDs, 188–193
    explicit instance IDs, 184–186
    FileInstanceStore<ID,T> class, 183
    functionality, 181
    initiating, 182
    instance IDs and, 182–184
    instance IDs in headers, 186
    instance management, 352–353
    instance management modes, 182
    terminating, 182
    transactional behavior, 354–359
DurableOperation attribute, 353, 355
DurableOperation behavior attribute
    CanCreateInstance property, 195
    CompletesInstance property, 195, 196
    functionality, 195

DurableOperationContext class
    AbortInstance() method, 197
    CompleteInstance() method, 197
    InstanceId property, 197
DurableService attribute
    functionality, 194
    instance ID management, 352
    persistence providers, 197, 354
    SaveStateInOperationTransaction
        property, 352, 356
    UnknownExceptionAction property, 249

E

EndpointAddress class, 52
EndpointNotFoundException, 245
endpoints
    "lollipop" notation, 26
    administrative configuration, 26–29
    defined, 25
    MEX, 35–39
    programmatic configuration, 29–31
    proxies and, 50
    queues and, 456
    RSS feeds, 56
enumerations
    data contracts, 130–131
    serialization, 130
EnumMember attribute
    aliasing, 131
    functionality, 130
    Value property, 131
equivalence, data contracts, 119–122
ErrorHandlerBehavior class, 277
ErrorHandlerBehaviorAttribute class, 274,
        276, 724
ErrorHandlerHelper class
    exception promotion, 268
    functionality, 724
    LogError() method, 270, 271
    PromoteException() method, 268, 269,
        274, 280
errors (see faults)
events
    data contracts and, 107–109
    deserialization, 107–108
    functionality, 236
    operations and, 236–239
    serialization, 107–108
exception promotion, 267–269
ExceptionDetail class, 255–265
exceptions (see faults)

About the Author

Juval Löwy is a software architect and the principal of IDesign, specializing in .NET architecture consulting and advanced .NET training. Juval is Microsoft's regional director for the Silicon Valley, working with Microsoft on helping the industry adopt WCF. He participates in the Microsoft internal design reviews for future versions of .NET and related technologies. He has published numerous articles regarding almost every aspect of .NET development, and is a frequent presenter at development conferences. Microsoft has recognized Juval as a Software Legend, one of the world's top .NET experts and industry leaders. Contact him at *www.idesign.net*.

Colophon

The animal on the cover of *Programming WCF Services*, Second Edition, is an angelfish. Angelfish are found in tropical and subtropical reefs around the world; there are at least 86 different species. The average size of an angelfish is about 7 to 12 inches (20 to 30 cm) long, but their size varies greatly, as does their coloring, which changes with maturity. Their diet consists of algae, worms, and various shellfish and small sea creatures. A spine on the gill cover differentiates the angelfish from the also colorful butterfly fish. Depending on the species, angelfish have different mating habits. Some mate for life in territorial pairs, while others create harems of female fish with one dominant male. All angelfish are protogynous hermaphrodites, which means that if the dominant male were to die or leave the group, a female would morph into a male for mating purposes.

In some countries angelfish are used for food, but mostly they are caught for aquariums. Rare species of angelfish can range in price from hundreds to thousands of dollars. In addition to collectors, reef destruction and continual environmental degradation threaten angelfish.

The cover image is from Wood's *Reptiles, Fishes, Insects, &c.* The cover font is Adobe ITC Garamond. The text font is Linotype Birka; the heading font is Adobe Myriad Condensed; and the code font is LucasFont's TheSansMonoCondensed.

Try the online edition
free for 45 days

Get the information you need when you need it, with Safari Books Online. Safari Books Online contains the complete version of the print book in your hands plus thousands of titles from the best technical publishers, with sample code ready to cut and paste into your applications.

Safari is designed for people in a hurry to get the answers they need so they can get the job done. You can find what you need in the morning, and put it to work in the afternoon. As simple as cut, paste, and program.

To try out Safari and the online edition of the above title FREE for 45 days, go to www.oreilly.com/go/safarienabled and enter the coupon code BIOVHXA.

To see the complete Safari Library visit:
safari.oreilly.com